MARITIMERS
Ashore & Afloat
VOLUME 2

Interesting People, Places and Events
Related to the Bay of Fundy and its Rivers

MARITIMERS

Ashore
& Afloat

VOLUME 2

Interesting People, Places and Events
Related to the Bay of Fundy and its Rivers

Stanley T. Spicer

LANCELOT PRESS
Hantsport, Nova Scotia

ISBN 0-88999-541-9
Published 1994

LANCELOT PRESS LIMITED, Hantsport, Nova Scotia.
Office and production facilities situated on Highway No. 1, 1/2 mile east of Hantsport.

MAILING ADDRESS:
P.O. Box 425, Hantsport, N.S. B0P 1P0

ACKNOWLEDGEMENT: This book has been published with the assistance of the Nova Scotia Department of Tourism and Culture and the Canada Council.

Contents — Volume Two

Contents — Volume One

Chapter 1. The Bay of Fundy

Tides and currents — its coastline — early explorations — privateers — some of the bay's mysteries.

Chapter 2. In The Days of the Pioneers

The Acadians — those who came after: New England Planters, Pre-Loyalists, Loyalists.

Chapter 3. Profiles of People

Two early business tycoons: Alexander 'Boss' Gibson of Marysville, N.B. and Amos 'King' Seaman of Minudie, N.S.

Chapter 4. In Times of Conflict

For Valour: William Hall, V.C., John Chipman Kerr, V.C., Cyrus Wesley Peck, V.C., Milton Fowler Gregg, V.C. — Dalhousie University Stationary Hospital — the tragic end of the hospital ship *Llandovery Castle*.

Chapter 5. Ashore and Afloat

Vessels under sail, an introduction — launchings, two ships — some notable Fundy vessels — when their end came — vessels that disappeared — an early shipbuilder, John Owens of Saint John — a captain under sail, Robert Dewis — the captain who was first, Joshua Slocum — the Chignecto Ship Railway, one man's dream.

Dedication

To Gwen
For So Many Good Reasons

History is the witness that testifies to the passing of time; it illumines reality, vitalizes memory, provides guidance in daily life, and brings us tidings of antiquity.

Cicero

Acknowledgments

To present as accurately as possible stories on a variety of people, places and events in Nova Scotia and New Brunswick requires a strong dependence on individuals and institutions with the appropriate resources. I am deeply grateful to: John Bigelow, Halifax; Reg. Bowser, Moncton; Mac Campbell, C.B.C., Charlottetown; the late Donald Ells, Tidnish Cross Roads, N.S.; Mrs. Ella Fraser, Advocate, N.S.; Lowell Huntley, Scott's Bay, N.S. and Stanley Richardson, Fredericton.

Numerous institutions and government agencies provided inestimable assistance which I acknowledge with gratitude. They include:

Harriet Irving Library, University of New Brunswick, Fredericton.

Moncton Museum and Brenda Orr.

Mount Allison University Library and Archives, Sackville, John Pinson, Cherryl Ennals and Donna Beals.

New Brunswick Museum, Saint John and Robert S. Elliot.

Provincial Archives of New Brunswick, Fredericton and Janet Toole.

Public Archives of Nova Scotia, Halifax.

Saint John Free Public Library.

Permission to reprint is noted with thanks to:

Halifax Chronicle-Herald — "A Childhood Spent on Isle Haute" by Ella Fraser.

Nova Scotia Historical Review, Halifax — "Canning In The Seventies" by Margaret E. Ells.

Foreword

When Canada entered the twentieth century the country was still clinging to the last vestiges of the Victorian era. The horse and carriage, a strict morality code and male dominance were very much the order of the day while electric lights, the telephone and indoor plumbing were rather new novelties still treated with suspicion by many. The railway had pushed through to the west coast and people were moving to settle the vast lands east and west of the Rockies. Manufacturing had largely settled in Central Canada while on the Atlantic coast the once prosperous Maritimes were witnessing the end of the Age of Sail and the beginning of long economic doldrums.

Now in these closing years of the same century we look back on two world conflicts which forever changed not only a way of life but brought tremendous social, political and economic changes to the world stage. Today we live in an age of space exploration; we can travel faster than the speed of sound; inventions like computers, fax machines, television, organ transplants and instruments capable of destroying our world are taken for granted.

But we pay a price. The small farm or business owned by the same family for generations is giving way to large, impersonal operations. Necessity has made us a more mobile people and fewer of us can remain in the same community as that of our ancestors. Indeed many of the old stable vocations like fishing and lumbering no longer offer a dependable living for all who would pursue them. We find ourselves in a technological age more and more dependent on machines operated by a few highly skilled persons. It becomes an impersonal life and people are increasingly beginning to search for their roots, to find values they can understand and to which they can cling.

It was just at the beginning of this century that a Scottish educator, Dr. Blaikie, said:

> The greatest misfortune that can happen to any people is to have no noble deeds and no heroic personalities to look back to: for as a wise Present is the seed of a fruitful Future, so a great Past is a seed of a hopeful Present.

In this complex age to have roots, to know ourselves we need to know how we arrived in our own Present. Those who came before in their own way paved the way for our Present. Some achieved prominence in their time, most did not but the way they lived, their accomplishments great or small, all contributed to a Past which helped found our Present. To portray something of such people, their communities, institutions and way of life is the essence of the two volumes in this work.

Stanley T. Spicer
Spencers Island, N.S.

Illustrations

Rev. Silas T. Rand with two Indian boys. (Courtesy Acadia University Archives)

Lighthouse on Ile Haute. (Courtesy Mrs. Ella Fraser, Advocate, N.S.)

Abraham Gesner, Inventor of Kerosene. (Courtesy Public Archives of Nova Scotia)

Prescott House, Starr's Point, N.S. (Courtesy Public Archives of Nova Scotia)

Sir Frederick Borden Estate, Canning, N.S. (Courtesy Old King's Courthouse Heritage Museum, Kentville, N.S.)

Launching of the Schooner *Fieldwood*, 1920. Last Vessel launched from the Bigelow shipyard. (Original photo by A.L. Hardy. Reproduction by Lark Photographic Services, Canning, N.S.)

Canning, N.S. Fire, June 23, 1912. (Courtesy Leon Barron, New Minas, N.S.)

Gideon Palmer, Shipbuilder, Dorchester, N.B. (Courtesy Westmorland Historical Society)

Barque *Maggie Chapman*, 780 tons. Built by William Hickman, Dorchester Island, 1868. (Courtesy New Brunswick Museum)

Dorchester, N.B. Streetscape Circa 1890. (Courtesy Mount Allison University Archives, Westmorland Historical Society)

Acacia Villa School, Early Years of Twentieth Century. (Courtesy Acadia University Archives)

Truro Bearcats Hockey Team 1930-31. (Courtesy Nova Scotia Sport Heritage Centre)

Moncton Hawks Hockey Team 1932-33. (Courtesy Moncton Museum)

Boxer Sam Langford. (Courtesy Nova Scotia Sport Heritage Centre)

Charles Gorman, Saint John's World Speedskating Champion. (Courtesy New Brunswick Museum)

1.
Profiles of People

These are the stories of six disparate people: a missionary among native peoples; a childhood life on an isolated island; a Nova Scotia strong man; a teacher's life of yesteryear; an inventor; and a pioneer horticulturist. Together they present men and women and the differing lives they led in another time.

Micmac Missionary of the Maritimes
In the middle decades of the nineteenth century shipyards ringed the harbours, rivers and coastlines of the Maritime provinces and the products of these yards and the men who sailed them were known around the world. It was a time of hardy seafarers, wealthy merchants and shipowners and politicians who were forging this new country called Canada.

Yet among these giants of their time, one of the most remarkable men of them all sat quietly at a desk in Halifax on a February day in 1869 and wrote, "I have only six cents. I wish to obtain some things for my wife. I thought of going home today. I think now I will wait for tomorrow."

This was the Reverend Silas Tertius Rand, already a missionary among the Micmacs for twenty-three years. Now, on this day in 1869, he was without money and half a hundred miles from his home in Hantsport. Undoubtedly he could have

Rev. Silas T. Rand with two Indian boys. Courtesy Acadia University Archives.

obtained funds simply by asking a few friends. But that was not Rand's way. Instead he prayed. The next day a man who had once heard him preach on his work with the Indians stopped him on the street and gave him a half sovereign. Another gave him two dollars and a half. This enabled him to return home where four dollars had arrived in the mail. Within a week various donations totalled over fifty-two dollars.

16

For the man who devoted forty years of his life to missionary work among the Micmacs this was the usual pattern. Often he was completely without funds but never did he ask for a penny. Always he would pray and somehow money became available when it was most needed.

The career of the Reverend Silas Rand is a unique story of devotion and perseverance. He had little formal schooling but largely by self-instruction he was able to qualify for the Baptist ministry. Later he would give up the relative comforts and certainties of a pastorate to seek out the Micmacs, teach them, work with them and for long periods of time live with them. In addition to his missionary work, Rand's literary output was prodigious. He translated most of the Bible into Micmac and published both English-Micmac and Micmac-English dictionaries. At his death he left over 12,000 pages of manuscript on his various works with the Indians and a daily journal which he kept for half a century written day to day in many of the languages which he had mastered.

In most of his work Rand was alone. The Baptist Church was interested but could contribute little in the way of finances and no additional missionaries to help him. The Micmac Missionary Society was organized in 1849 for the purpose of furthering missionary work among the Micmacs. It was supposed to pay Rand a salary of £200 a year but it was never quite able to live up to its aims and after 1864 Rand depended solely upon voluntary gifts from Christians of various faiths.

The life of a missionary was far from Silas Rand's thoughts during his boyhood years. Born in May 1810 in Cornwallis, Nova Scotia, a few miles from Kentville, he was the son of Silas and his second wife, Deborah (Tupper) Rand. His mother was a sister of

Dr. Charles Tupper, father of the future Prime Minister, Sir Charles. Education was rare for a youngster in Rand's time. His father taught him the rudiments of reading and the skills of working the family farm. His mother, herself possessed of little formal education, was a beautiful reader and fond of writing verse. Rand once said of her, "It is my mother to whom I owe all of my interest and talent in the art of versifyng. She created more beauty in reading poetry than anyone I ever knew." His passion for verse stayed with him all his life and with it was a hobby of translating hymns into Latin. Among some one hundred hymns which he translated were 'Abide With Me'; 'Guide Me, O Thou Great Jehovah'; and 'Rock of Ages.'

Rand's formal schooling was scanty and irregular at best in its early stages, depending mostly on a succession of itinerant female teachers who appeared to have little to qualify themselves. One, apparently, did not even know how to spell her name.

When he was eighteen, Rand began a seven-year apprenticeship in stone masonry, the principal calling of his father and grandfather. At the same time he undertook the study of Latin under a gruelling schedule he set for himself. Each day, six days a week, he rose before dawn and studied for an hour or so. From dawn until noon he worked at his trade and then studied again during the noon break. After his work was done at sunset, he continued his studies by candlelight. After a few years, during which he also undertook to teach other boys in the district, Rand attended Horton Academy, an affiliate of Acadia College in Wolfville, Nova Scotia, for a period of four weeks.

By 1834 Rand had compiled sufficient academic qualifications to be ordained a Baptist minister. This had been a gradual evolution throughout his youth. Stone masonry and farming held no interest but helping people and his deep religious convictions made the choice of vocation easy. In addition his passion for languages was growing rapidly.

The young pastor took charge of his first church in Parrsboro, Nova Scotia. There he ministered to his people and undertook the study of Greek and Hebrew. After two years he went back to Horton Academy for a few months to further his language study.

Rand's interest in and ability to assimilate languages were phenomenal. In his prime he could speak and write English, German, French, Latin, Greek, Hebrew, Spanish, Italian and modern Greek as well as the Micmac and Maliseet tongues. Nearly all of these he taught himself through rigid periods of study. The language which Rand preferred above all others was Micmac for, as he once said, "It is marvellous in its construction, regularity and fullness and the one in which I do the most good."

After his term in Parrsboro, Rand held a succession of pastorates in Horton, Liverpool and Windsor in Nova Scotia, as well as in Charlottetown, Prince Edward Island. While in Liverpool, in 1838, he married Jane McNutt who would become a constant source of strength in the difficult years ahead. During these peaceful years of ministry and study little or no thought was given to the real work to which he would soon dedicate his life. It happened in a rather round-about manner.

In the 1840s a strong missionary zeal was sweeping over Nova Scotia. Missionaries were being sent by many churches to the far reaches of the world, including the Baptists who were particularly interested in Burma and the South Sea Islands. This disturbed Professor Isaac Chipman of Acadia College who, while fully in agreement with sending missionaries to far-off places, felt that something should also be done to help those at home, namely the Indian population.

During these years, around the middle of the nineteenth century, there was a popular misconception that the Indians in the three Maritime provinces were slowly dying out. Except for the Roman Catholics whose priests had worked among the Indians for two centuries, there had been practically nothing done by the white people to help or even accept these original inhabitants of the land. In fact the Indians were suppressed as much as possible and denied the use of schools and other amenities of the white man's civilization.

Despite their problems, however, census figures showed that instead of a decrease in population, the number of Indians was gradually increasing. Whereas in 1851 there was a total of just over 2,100 in the Maritimes, the figure rose to 3,800 in the next three decades.

Professor Chipman felt that much missionary work should be done among the Indian people. He mentioned his concern to Silas Rand and suggested that the pastor was the ideal man for such a challenge. Rand accepted almost immediately and resigned his ministry. This took courage for Rand was now a family man accustomed to the routines of the pastoral life. But, in 1846, he chose a missionary career which promised no organizational assistance, no funds and almost certain resistance from many of the Indians themselves. It was a career destined to span forty eventful years.

Rand's first obstacle was language. He did not understand Micmac and, in turn, the Indians had

20

never received any encouragement to learn English. Fortunately he became acquainted with a Frenchman by the name of Joe Brooks who had lived with the Indians most of his life and was thoroughly familiar with their language and customs. An intelligent man, Brooks was of immeasurable help to Rand in the learning of Micmac and of the Indian way of life.

In beginning his work, Rand travelled a great deal visiting the Indian settlements and living with them from time to time. He attempted to establish himself as a friend and teacher rather than any type of authoritative preacher. His interest in the Indians was genuine and he became widely accepted among them. He never considered himself a Baptist missionary in the sense that he preached his own faith to the exclusion of others. Nor was it his belief that the Indians should be divided into separate churches. Rather he believed that his duty was to lead them to the point where they were Christians and could choose their own church.

Silas Rand's interests were broader than the purely religious side of his mission. He was sincerely interested in their general welfare and determined to help them. Just as he had mastered the Micmac and Maliseet languages, he now encouraged the Indians to learn English. To this end he wrote a grammar which, over the years, helped many in learning to read and write. This was no easy task. For over two hundred years practically the only literature available to the Indians was a prayer book prepared by Roman Catholic missionaries. These missionaries had learned the language and reduced it to a system of characters for purposes of the prayer book. The book itself, written in these characters, had not been published but was copied laboriously by hand and then committed to memory.

Rand did not confine his efforts to the Indian environment alone. Constantly he preached on their behalf from pulpits all over the Maritimes. Possibly more than anyone else he rejoiced when schools were opened to the Indians and by 1888 he was able to record that many were taking advantage of this privilege.

In his years of travel from Indian settlement to settlement Rand did more than preach, lead prayers and sing the old hymns. He was instrumental in resurrecting and preserving the legends of the Micmacs. Everywhere he went Rand sought out the old people and patiently wrote down the tales of their gods, their beliefs and hopes. His records include more than 900 pages of these stories, many of them about the great Indian god-man Glooscap.

And how did this lone missionary survive his years of travel, living among the Indians and never sure where his next dollar was coming from?

One day, a few years before his death, Rand was asked about his health. His reply was:

When you are seventy-six years old, can walk ten miles without being noticeably fatigued; eat as heartily and chew as well as ever you could; sleep sound and wake up in the morning without a single trouble of mind or pain of body; with your eye as keen as it was twenty years previously, and can pick up a poem of five hundred lines, read it through before breakfast, and then after reading it through on five subsequent occasions, repeat it from end to end without a break — you need have no immediate fears for your health.

But age and failing health began to take their toll

and in October 1889 the Reverend Silas Tertius Rand passed away in his eightieth year. He was buried in the Riverbank cemetery at Hantsport, Nova Scotia among many of the master mariners and shipbuilders which gave the little town such prominence in the 1800s.

Rand received a full measure of honors before his death including honorary doctorates from Acadia, Queen's and King's College. He built well and much of the work he began is now carried on by government agencies established for this purpose. Quietly and in his own way Rand left for succeeding generations a rich heritage culminating in a better understanding of the Indian and more concern for his problems.

Of the many tributes addressed to the Micmac missionary, perhaps the most unique and descriptive appeared in a little paper in 1883, shortly before his retirement:

S tanding today still in the way,
I n health and strength almost beyond compeers,
L ife's beaten road, I too have trod,
A nd borne the load by the grace of God
S afely thus for three and seventy years.

T he way has not been wholly through a vale of
tears;
R ich floods of light have cheered my sight
A nd visions bright have banished doubts and
fears,
N or will I cease God's name to bless,
D ependent still through coming days and years.

Lighthouses and Life on Isle Haute
Although considerable shipping sailed in and out of

the Bay of Fundy in the eighteenth century and early decades of the nineteenth century, there were few lighthouses along its dangerous coast and many vessels were lost.

The first lighthouse to be built on Fundy waters was on Partridge Island at the mouth of Saint John harbour in 1791. It was followed by lighthouses at Brier Island in 1809, Point Prim at the entrance to Digby Gut in 1817, Head Harbour on Campobello Island in 1829 and those on Gannet Rock and at Lepreau, New Brunswick, both built in 1831. Over the years to follow some sixty lighthouses would be constructed on both sides of the bay with additional structures stationed along its major tributaries.

As lighting technology improved, each light was given its own signal. For instance, the light on Isle Haute showed a two second flash followed by a five second eclipse while the Partridge Island light at Saint John showed eight flashes per minute. By day mariners could identify lighthouses by their individual shape and color combination such as:

Cape Fourchu	Hexagonal tower with red and white vertical stripes
Brier Island	White octagonal tower with three red horizontal bands
Cape Spencer, N.B.	Red tower with a white band

In the early years lighthouses were financed by a duty imposed on the tonnage of vessels using the waters but after Confederation they were placed under the control of the Canadian government. Now

24

nearly all lighthouses are automated but for many years they were manned by one or more lightkeepers who maintained the structure and equipment and kept the light burning from sunset to sunrise.

Among the more isolated lighthouses was the one on Isle Haute. A rocky prominence rising more than 300 feet from sea level, the island stands as a sentinel at the entrance to Minas Channel in the upper reaches of the Bay of Fundy. It is automated now but for many years the light was manned and lightkeepers and their families lived on the island. A few years ago Mrs. Ella Morris Fraser described for the *Halifax Chronicle-Herald* her childhood life on Isle Haute. This is her story.

Isle Haute is a small island in the Bay of Fundy, about ten miles from Advocate, Nova Scotia. The island is one and a half miles long and one-half mile wide at the widest point. High bluffs surround much of the island.

At one place on the south side of the island we used to go down to the beach to pick dulse. At another spot on the north side, my brother and I would go to pick gooseberries. Both of these places were covered with trees and shrubs which offered safety to the children.

At the extreme west end one could go down a grassy slope which provided no entrance to the beach. This slope was a great nesting place for gulls. Each nest contained one to three large speckled eggs. Young gulls of all ages could be seen there during the summer.

The lighthouse was built in 1878. The light consisted of six large, cone-shaped reflectors with an oil-filled lamp set in each one. Each day, the lamps were filled, the chimneys cleaned and

Lighthouse on Ile Haute. Courtesy Mrs. Ella Fraser, Advocate, N.S.

the reflectors polished.

It was a revolving type light with a weight attached to a wire cable that slowly descended from the light to the basement inside a casing. It was brought up again by means of a hand crank. During the day the light rested on a wedge inserted at top floor level.

This light was later replaced by small three-panel reflectors and a small tank which held fuel and air pumped into it.

The first lightkeeper was Captain Card who lived on the island with his wife. Unfortunately, nothing is known about their family or where they went after leaving Isle Haute.

The next to take charge of the light were Mr.

26

and Mrs. Judson Reid. He was from Advocate and after several years he left the island and worked in a shipyard in his home town.

Percy Morris, my father, took charge of the light in 1904. My mother, my brother, Wilson, and I moved to the island. A second daughter, Viola, was born in 1908 and a son, Everett, was born in 1914.

During the first few years, we crossed the bay in a sailboat. Later my father had a motor put in the boat. It was the first motorboat to cross the bay.

While installing the motor at the West Advocate beach he had many onlookers. Once the motor was in place, the boat was in the water and he was ready to start the engine, everyone left in a hurry.

The landing place was on the north side of the island. Father built a wharf on each side of the landing and the boat was hauled up above high water. There was a woods road from the landing to the lighthouse, all up hill. The first part of the road was quite steep, while the rest sloped gradually.

There is a lake at the beach. On one side of the lake there is a spot called Indian Flat. Indians were supposed to have camped there at one time. Arrowheads have been found there.

There is also a stream of water coming out of the side of the hill at the beach. The stream was lovely and cold and many times during the summer Wilson and I would run down the hill to get a kettle of good, cold water for the noon meal.

Father cleared a lot of land so we always wintered 60 or more sheep. We had lots of lambs in the spring. We usually had two or more pets who were lovingly brought up on a bottle.

Rabbits were the only wild animals on the island. They were numerous. We would pick up the baby ones in the field, getting badly scratched for our efforts.

A New Brunswick company put some foxes on the island, hoping they would increase in number and value. But the foxes failed to do so. We fed them cooked fish meal with lard added to make their pelts shine. Their arrival ended the rabbit population.

Wild strawberries, raspberries and gooseberries grew in abundance. They were nearly as large as cultivated ones and had a delicious flavour.

The only means of communication with the mainland was by making fires. One fire meant that all was well. Two meant illness, while three meant a doctor was needed. Four fires meant that somebody had died. During our stay on the island all were put to use.

In the summer of 1913, the signals were reversed from Advocate to the island. The doctors — Dr. Hill, Dr. Fillmore and others — were all on the island. People in Advocate made three fires. Those on the island knew that a doctor was needed and responded with one fire.

Mrs. Smith's horse ran away while she was driving at Cape d'Or. She was thrown out of the wagon and suffered a broken leg. The doctors returned to Advocate to care for the patient.

Four fires needed to be lit only once on the island. The helper passed away. Mother and her niece, Bertha, were there alone with two small children. Father had gone ashore and was storm-stayed there.

Bertha carried a lantern and a can of oil to the beach, gathered enough wood and built the fires.

Father had a small open boat which was not suitable for rough weather. When he saw the four fires, he hired a large boat from C.T. White and Company. The captain was Charles Cole. J.H. Morris went along as well.

The heavy seas broke the cabin windows. The men had to land at the east end of the island. They carried the helper's body back to the boat and returned to Advocate.

A few years later, a young man, Fred Harding, was killed on his 20th birthday when he climbed down a bluff to look for gulls' eggs. He lost his footing and fell about 50 feet down a steep bank.

Father and a Mr. Weir searched all night but could not find him. At daybreak they launched a small boat and rowed around the island until they found his body. They transported the body to Advocate and returned on the same tide.

Captain Kidd's treasure was said to have been buried on the island. Over the years, many people came to dig for it. They were superstitious and would only dig at night. They always moved a few feet away from the spot before they spoke.

One day, Father and a Mr. McGrath knew where the searchers would be digging that night. During the day, the two men buried an old iron kettle at the spot and returned that night to see the fun.

When the searchers' shovels struck iron, they dropped everything and rushed down the hill, shouting: "We struck it! We struck it!"

One can imagine their disappointment when they went back and dug up nothing but an old iron pot.

Lobster fishermen came to the island every spring from the South Shore. Line fishing was plentiful. Men would see pollock jumping near the east bar and, launching a small boat, they would catch as many as they needed. There is no line fishing there now.

Before cars were plentiful, seldom a week went by during the summer without a boatload of people coming to the island sightseeing, fishing or picking berries.

Sometimes the weather would be too rough for a return trip and the sightseers would have to spend the night. We always enjoyed having them.

One July 12, 300 people arrived at the island, coming by steamer and boats from all of the South Shore and Advocate.

A merchant from Advocate, a Mr. Goldstein, took candy and fruit to sell. When he arrived at the island, he loaded a wagon to take things to the lighthouse. The wheel came off the wagon and all the goodies spilled over the road. There was a mad scramble to gather them up again.

On the same day, as the children were playing ball, one of the boys, Cecil, stooped to pick up the ball. As he did so, our watchdog grabbed him by the seat of the pants. Mr. Goldstein was also a tailor. He put young Cecil over two chairs and sewed up the tear. The rest of the day, the dog was in the doghouse.

A boatload of people never seemed to be too many. Once, as we said goodbye to one group which had been with us a week, another arrived.

Mother made herself busy in the kitchen preparing a meal for the new arrivals. She sent one of the older children to wash the napkins and iron them dry with the flat iron which had to be heated on the wood stove. The younger children were sent to the fields to pick berries for the supper meal.

We felt the Halifax Explosion in 1917 but we didn't know what had happened until we came over to the mainland in the spring. In those days, the bay was full of ice and impossible to get over during the winter months.

Cousin Bertha was living in Halifax at the time and we were unaware of her harrowing experience until much later. As she was carrying a baby downstairs, the stairway gave way from the explosion. She received cuts from flying glass but neither she nor the baby in her arms was injured seriously.

In the summer there were lots of ships, both large and small, sailing up and down the bay. One or two of the smaller ones went ashore on the bar during thick fog. They floated off at high tide with no damage done. We had a small hand foghorn but the sound didn't carry far.

Mother taught us the three Rs before we were old enough to start school. Later we four children went to school in Advocate.

Some years, Mother stayed on the mainland with us. Other times, we boarded with different families but we were always eager to go back to the island the day school closed.

I recall one trip, on the last day of school, when the weather was so rough we couldn't land and had to go back to Advocate, arriving there about 2 o'clock in the morning. We stayed the night with Capt. and Mrs. William Collins.

In those days there were no radios, televisions or stereos. We had to provide our own amusement. We would hitch a young calf to a sled and have wild rides. We also entertained ourselves by sliding down the long roof of the barn. This was great fun but rather hard on our clothes.

The older children helped in the hay field, in the garden and with other chores. We also tapped maple trees and boiled down the sap to make syrup.

I learned to crochet, knit, quilt and hook mats at an early age.

Father retired in 1941. Don and Viola Morris were the next lightkeepers. They stayed on Isle Haute until 1946. John Fullerton was the next to take over.

The lighthouse and all the buildings burned on September 30, 1956. There is a tower erected there now on the same location as the former building. The tower is serviced by a helicopter.

The road is grown up now and there are no buildings on the beach to welcome visitors stranded in bad weather. A few years ago, my brother and some young people were camping on Isle Haute. The weather became too rough for a boat to return for them. His wife called Search and Rescue and my brother and his friends were brought back to the mainland by helicopter.

There is little now to indicate that families once lived on the island but the childhood memories live on for those who were reared on Isle Haute.

There is a postscript to Ella Fraser's story. When her father, Percy Morris, retired from the island in 1941 it was Ella's sister Viola and her husband, Don Morris, who took over the light for the next five years.

The brother Wilson began his seafaring career on the three-masted schooner *Nova Queen* and went on to command American oil tankers for many years. Everett, the youngest brother, would lose his life later in a mishap aboard a tugboat in Saint John. Ella, the author of this story, is now in her early nineties. Still vigorous, she knits, crochets, quilts and is active in her church in Advocate Harbour. Every so often her thoughts go back to her childhood years on Isle Haute.

John Orpin — The Gentle Giant

It is a matter of record that two of Nova Scotia's strong men of their time were identified with the little village on the south coast of the Bay of Fundy now known as Morden. The first was Pierre Melanson, the hunter and trapper known far and wide for his strength and endurance, the one who led 300 of his people away from Belleisle when the Acadians were being expelled. He and most of his followers perished after a winter of hardship and starvation at Morden.

Just over a half century later, in 1808, a boy was born in Morden and named John Orpin. The boy grew into a giant of a man, over six feet in height and weighing more than two hundred pounds, all bone and muscle. For all his size Orpin was remarkably quick and agile and it is said that he was double-jointed in both hands and wrists and was equipped with double rows of teeth in both his upper and lower jaws. Though he knew and respected his own strength, John Orpin was of a quiet and friendly nature and never used his power for his own advantage.

In Orpin's younger years the mail was carried through the Annapolis Valley along the post road and it was up to the villages along the Bay of Fundy coast to have someone pick up the mail at the post road and deliver it to the inhabitants. These mail carriers were frequently attacked, beaten and robbed. After several such attacks on Morden mail carriers, Orpin was asked to carry the mail.

One day in 1838 he was transporting the mail on horseback when a fallen tree blocked his way. He dismounted to move the tree and was suddenly fired upon by four men waiting in ambush. Wounded slightly in the shoulder, Orpin raised his musket and shot one of the men in the leg. The other three charged him with clubs but Orpin moved fast. He wrenched the club from one man, disarmed a second and knocked their heads together. When they fell to the ground senseless, the remaining attacker fled for his life.

Orpin reloaded his musket, tied the wounded man on his horse and, marching his two prisoners in front, continued on to Morden. When the men of the village heard of the incident they were outraged and the next morning at daybreak a party of eight men set out after the fleeing outlaw. They caught the man and brought him back to Morden. When the wounded one was sufficiently recovered, the four were sent to Windsor under heavy guard for trial.

It would be a two-day journey on foot and late in the afternoon of the first day about half the distance had been covered and the men made camp for the night. Sometime in the darkness two of the prisoners freed their bonds, set upon the lone sentry guarding them, beat him viciously and escaped into the woods. The men of Morden were furious. Leaving the two remaining prisoners well-bound and guarded, the men went after the two escapees, caught them and returned to camp. Then and there they hanged all four and returned home. Word of the hangings eventually worked its way to the seat of justice in Windsor and an official promptly visited Morden. When he learned the facts of the case it was decided that justice had been duly rendered and nothing more was said of the matter.

There were other tales of John Orpin's strength. Once a team of oxen was unable to pull a heavy load. Orpin unhitched the team and pulled the load to its destination. Then in 1858 he made a trip to Saint John. His reputation preceded him and a group of sea captains in the port city decided to arrange a weightlifting competition. To oppose Orpin they selected a huge Irish dockworker known for his prodigious strength and a sailor on a visiting Swedish vessel who stood four inches over six feet and weighed some 250 pounds. A large anchor was chosen for the test. At the time Orpin was past fifty, his opponents young men in their prime.

The Irishman was the first to test his strength. With all his might he was able to lift the anchor about two inches off the ground. The Swede came next and he raised the anchor to his knees. Then John Orpin stepped forward. He lifted the anchor with ease then turned it so it was vertical and invited each opponent to stand on a fluke. He lifted the anchor and both men well off the ground. The contest was over.

Some years later Orpin was appointed Collector of Customs for the port of Morden. One day in 1870, a vessel arrived with a cargo from a foreign port. Orpin stepped on board and advised the captain of the duty that must be paid. The captain refused and sailed away down the bay. Orpin was suspicious of the captain's motives so he followed the vessel on land. As he suspected, the vessel put into another port and when she came to the wharf the Customs Collector was there. What Orpin did not know was that the vessel had an enormous cook on board and the captain had bribed him to keep Orpin off the vessel.

When John Orpin, now in his early sixties, boarded the vessel, he was met with a blow to the face by the cook. Orpin shook it off and tried to reason with the man for fist fighting was not part of his nature. The cook struck him twice more and still Orpin tried to talk to his antagonist. But the cook, perhaps feeling that the Customs man was a coward, spat full in his face. No one, ever, had done that to John Orpin. His fist flashed out once, the cook went over backward and was dead when he hit the deck. The captain, knowing that witnesses had heard of his deal with the cook and fearing the consequences, reported the man had fallen from aloft and died from his injuries. There was no inquiry.

John Orpin was familiar with the story of the hardships suffered by the Acadians when they wintered at Morden in 1755-56. In his youth he had seen the oaken cross erected on the grave of Pierre Melanson and his wife. But by the 1880s time and weather had taken their toll and the cross was gone. It was Orpin who fashioned another cross, one which stood until the government erected a more permanent cross of beach stones.

The strong man lived a long life. Towards the end of that life someone wrote of him:

> With ninety years now sitting gracefully on his venerable brow, he is spending the summer evening of his long life in a cozy cottage, nestling among the shrubbery just out of reach of the waves of the Bay of Fundy, and on the spot where the Acadians spent their black winter. The ninety winters which have gone over his head

have not wrought great havoc on his manly form ... His body in mould and grace was like a Greek statue — his brow high and intellectual, his nose prominent and of the Roman type, his mouth finely formed, indicating mildness and solidity of character; arms and legs symmetrical and firmly knit together with heavy muscles and nerves magnetic, mercurial and ready at the call of his will, to flash into his muscular system almost superhuman power.

When John Orpin died in 1899 at the age of ninety-one, another link was forged with the Acadians of the Morden winter. He was buried in the cemetery by St. Mary's Church in Auburn, the church that was plastered with the ground mussel shells left behind by the fugitive Acadians. On his tombstone were carved the words:

I am as a wonder unto many but the Lord
is my strong helper.

A Rural School Teacher — Georgia Crowe Dunbar
It was late in the evening of August 26, 1916 when the crowded bus pulled into Spencers Island from Parrsboro. The bus was only a car but it provided a daily service six days a week between Parrsboro and Advocate carrying passengers, light freight and the mail. This evening it had a trunk strapped to one running board and a box of piglets on the other. At the back, on a platform covered with canvas, were the mailbags and some suitcases. It had been a dark twenty-five mile journey for there were no electric lights in the houses along the way and the bus was the lone occupant of the unpaved road. Thus did twenty-one-year-old Miss Georgia Crowe arrive to

take charge of the one-room rural school at Spencers Island.

Georgia Crowe's story began on her parent's farm at Old Barns, near Truro. One of nine children, eight girls and a boy, Georgia grew up on a mixed farm. They grew strawberries, cherries, plums, pears, several varieties of apples as well as vegetables and the livestock included hens, turkeys, sheep, pigs, cattle and horses.

In these early years of the century, children were expected to do their share of the chores. Georgia carried wood, helped around the house and weeded the garden. In summer she drove the horses, especially during the haying season. Sometimes it was the mower, sometimes the rake and often she drove the hay wagon to the barn where the hay was off-loaded to the mow above.

> "One time," she recalled, "I was driving the mower when the blade became clogged with hay. I stopped the horse, got down and was pulling the hay out when I heard my father calling furiously for me to get out of there. I didn't realize I could have lost an arm if the horse started."

Georgia's first years of education were in the local one-room school about a mile from the farm. When she was ready for high school it meant a walk of over two miles to the railway station to go to Colchester Academy in Truro. In the beginning it was not a particularly pleasant experience. On her first day at the academy she was directed to a classroom, entered and seated herself in the first vacant seat. Some giggles and snickers caused her to look around and find she was surrounded by boys. In those days boys sat on one side of the room and girls on the other. It took a little while to get used to the ways of the town school.

Georgia Crowe graduated from Colchester Academy with her Grade eleven. She had decided on a teaching career so in her final year she took several additional courses taught by the principal which gave her Minimum Professional Qualifications. These allowed her to teach for one year before entering Normal School. That summer she enrolled in another course which included spending considerable time in Victoria Park in Truro where the students studied birds and collected butterflies, moths, bees and insects. "I had ammunition for years to come," she said.

Thus equipped she ventured into teaching. Her first school was at Green's Creek near Truro. There were only six or seven pupils so it was a good situation for a beginning teacher but the salary was not magnificent. "I received $145 for the year, payable when someone paid their school tax." However, a government grant did look after her room and board.

September 1915 found Georgia Crowe enrolled in Normal School. Four girls roomed together in town and the meals served were not lavish. Each weekend Georgia headed for home to stock up on food for the coming week. In the spring, after graduation, she accepted the school at Spencers Island for the year 1916-17. Her mother thought Georgia was going to the ends of the earth but as she said, "I managed to get to the ends of the earth in one day."

In Spencers Island she boarded with a retired sea captain and his wife. On the day before school opened she heard some dire tales of what older boys had done to some previous teachers to make their lives miserable. If there was trepidation there was also resolve. When school opened on Monday morning the pupils learned from the first who was in charge. In time these same older boys became her friends and never once during the year did she have to resort to corporal punishment. Misdemeanors, usually the possession of cigarettes, were handled by assigning extra work.

There were over fifty pupils in the school ranging from Grade one through Grade nine. It was a one-room school but upstairs there was a second room used for concerts, school meetings and closing exercises. In winter a large stove at the back of the classroom kept nearby children too warm while those at the front remained too cold. The school hours were from mine to four with an hour for lunch and fifteen-minute recesses at 10:30 a.m. and 3:00 p.m.

At the time, the most important subjects were the three R's: reading, writing and arithmetic but Miss Crowe also taught health, history, geography and social studies. Always the day began with a Bible story and a song and on most Friday afternoons the week would end with a spelling bee. Many of the older pupils would stay until nearly five for extra help after the younger ones had gone home. Slates were used for arithmetic but scribblers were the main work books and when the shipyard whistle blew at 5:00 p.m., it was a rare day that the teacher did not carry home an armload of scribblers to correct and mark.

When the Christmas season arrived, a concert was staged in the upstairs room and twenty dollars was raised for the Belgian Relief Fund for the country was in the midst of war. The program consisted of carols, recitations, a play and a drill. The teacher took part in the drill and months later one of the older boys took her out in a field with his gun to teach her how to aim and shoot. He was sure she had closed the wrong eye when she aimed at something, back in the Christmas drill. But the teacher was not unfamiliar with guns and she outshot her young opponent. The subject was not mentioned again. The young man went on to become a sea captain.

Georgia Crowe found friends in the little community. She was often invited out for meals by parents and frequently went for wagon rides or, in winter, sleigh rides. During the year a three-masted schooner was being built in the shipyard and she was a regular visitor. It turned out that her interest was not so much in the vessel as in one of the workmen, a man she would marry years later.

When the school year ended, Miss Crowe went in an open motor boat up the Bay of Fundy to Parrsboro where she boarded the train for Truro and home. For her year at Spencers Island she received just over $200 although the government again covered her room and board.

Always possessed of an inquiring mind, Georgia Crowe liked to see new places and meet new challenges. The next year she went to the north shore of Nova Scotia to teach in Wallace before coming back to the Parrsboro shore to be principal of the Advocate school.

Then wanderlust struck again. A number of teachers she knew were going west so she went with them, travelling on a homesteaders train where you got your own meals, made your own berth and where there was a small compartment equipped to make hot tea or coffee.

On arrival in Saskatchewan, Georgia went to the appropriate government office and was immediately assigned Grades four to eight in the school at

Rosthern, near Prince Albert. New immigrants were arriving regularly, especially Russians and often the train would drop a carload of people who spoke no English and had precious few belongings. The clerk in the general store needed to be proficient in seven languages to get along.

Most of the students in Georgia Crowe's classes were well into their teens because of language difficulties and their previous school experience. During the year it was common to find many of these young people outside the school crying their eyes out, homesick for the land they had left. "It was an interesting but difficult year," she remembered.

In the next two years Rosthern was followed by teaching assignments in the Saskatchewan communities of Summerberry and Dunheld. The latter village covered a lot of territory. Her boarding house was eleven miles from the one store and she walked two miles to the school. It turned out to be a short year. In November she was invited to a school board meeting to be advised that there were no funds left to pay the teacher and the school would be closed. Georgia returned home to Nova Scotia and for the next few years taught in and around the Truro area.

By 1927 she decided on a complete but temporary break from teaching and went to Boston. Job opportunities were scarce but she was selected to undertake training in selling children's encyclopedias door-to-door. Everything went well while she was with a more experienced saleslady but once she started on her own she said, "I knew I was on the fast track to poverty."

It was by chance she landed a position on the staff of a home for children. Sponsored by a group of wealthy Boston ladies, the large, three-story home was situated in the Beacon Hill section of the city. The matron was from Ontario, the cook from Nova Scotia and the matron wanted another Nova Scotian to work with the children. There were from ten to fifteen children at any one time ranging in age from two to eighteen. Some had been abused at home, some had been thrown out of their homes and some had run away. The sponsors had agents in various parts of Massachusetts looking out for such children and Miss Crowe remarked, "When the doorbell rang, we never knew what to expect."

When girls were brought to the home their heads were thoroughly examined for most had head lice. The treatment was to saturate the hair with essence of larkspur and wrap it for the night. One two-year-old brought to the home was so badly abused that she would crouch in a corner and refuse to move. One day the mother arrived to visit the child. Georgia dressed her in pretty clothes and took her downstairs to the visitor's room. The mother's only comment, "You always was a bad rat." Georgia's summation of her time at the home was, "What a year!"

Georgia Crowe returned to Nova Scotia and taught in Truro until 1934 when she took a twenty-year hiatus from teaching. She married and became Mrs. Clifford Dunbar. However, there came a time when her husband was no longer able to work because of ill health. Georgia agreed to take the Spencers Island school for the 1954-55 year and ended up staying until the school closed for good in the spring of 1960. She closed out her teaching career at the new consolidated school in Advocate, retiring in 1963, shortly after the death of her husband.

The desire to see new places remained. In her years of retirement Georgia Dunbar toured Europe, she took a bus tour to Florida, and across the southern United States to California. She visited Expo in Montreal in 1967 and two years later, at the age of seventy-four, sailed to Australia.

Georgia Crowe Dunbar died in February 1990 at the age of ninety-four just after setting down on paper some of her memories. If her name is not likely to appear in future history books, it is long remembered by hundreds whose lives she touched.

Abraham Gesner — Man of Many Talents

A stone in the Camp Hill cemetery in Halifax, erected by Imperial Oil in 1933, bears the inscription:

> Abraham Gesner, M.D., F.G.S., Geologist, born at Cornwallis, N.S., May 2nd, 1797. Died at Halifax April 29th, 1864. His treatise on the Gcology and Minerology of Nova Scotia, 1836, was one of the earliest works dealing with these subjects in the Province, and about 1852 he was the American inventor of the process of kerosene oil.

These few words pay tribute to a man who in his time was a farmer, trader, surgeon, geologist, author, invcntor, manufacturer and professor.

The Gesners, originally of German stock, at some point moved to Holland and from there immigrated to America, settling near New York. Abraham's father, Henry, and his twin brother were both ardent Loyalists and at the close of the American Revolutionary War Henry obtained a land grant of 400 acres at Cornwallis. There he married a local Pineo girl and the couple produced twelve children, the sixth being Abraham.

Young Abraham received the meagre education

44

Abraham Gesner, Inventor of Kerosene. Courtesy Public Archives of Nova Scotia

then available to youngsters and performed his share of work around the family farm. But even as a young man he was spending much of his time collecting insects, wildflowers and rock specimens. Sometimes described as a dreamer and a showman, Gesner early on became involved in the business of transporting horses to the West Indies. It was a venture that was not only financially unsuccessful, it almost cost him his life. Once he was shipwrecked in the West Indies and another time his vessel was wrecked on Brier Island, Nova Scotia. He and the crew were washed ashore but barely survived their ordeal in the freezing waters.

In 1822 Gesner married Harriett, the daughter of a prominent Kentville physician, Dr. Isaac Webster. Whether this connection with the medical profession was a factor is not known but Gesner soon embarked on his own medical career. He studied medicine at St. Bartholomew's Hospital and surgery at Guy's Hospital in London. Reputed to be a brilliant scholar, he studied chemistry and geology on the side. When his studies were completed, Gesner returned to Nova Scotia and began his medical practice in Parrsboro.

The practice of medicine at this time was at best a rudimentary science. There was no anaesthesia, with the possible exception of rum, nor were there clinical thermometers. The best practice that could be offered consisted of simple diagnosis, minor surgery including the setting of broken bones and extraction of teeth as well as management of labor when it was too difficult for the local midwife. To visit his patients the doctor either walked or rode on horseback. Carriages were not yet used in most rural areas as the roads were little more than footpaths.

It was soon apparent that geology held more interest for Gesner than medicine. In Parrsboro he was not only in a rich coal-producing area but also in one of the world's great fossil regions. During his early years here, when making his rounds visiting patients, seldom did he return without a collection of rock specimens. Later the role was reversed. When he went out looking for specimens, he took along his black medical bag in case he came upon a person in pain.

In 1836 Gesner published his first work, *Remarks On The Geology And Minerology Of Nova Scotia*. In the following year he closed his medical practice in Parrsboro to undertake a geological survey of the Grand Lake region in New Brunswick. His work was apparently impressive as he was engaged by the provincial government to do a geological survey of the whole province of New Brunswick. He began in 1838 and by 1842 the project was nearing completion when, for some reason, the government withdrew further funding. Gesner pressed on, however, by using his own funds and, by borrowing, managed to finish the survey.

Throughout his years in Parrsboro and while working on the New Brunswick survey, Gesner had continued to add to his collection of birds, animals, fauna and rocks. These were mounted and displayed but, according to contemporary estimates, there were now some 4,000 items, far too many for his home in Saint John. In 1842 the collection was moved to the new Mechanics' Institute building in Saint John. At this point Gesner had completed his geological survey of the province but he was in debt. His creditors took over the collection in payment and most turned their shares over to the Mechanics' Institute. The collection thus became the forerunner of the New Brunswick Museum.

Gesner had reached a low point in his life. In

1843 he returned to Cornwallis and resumed the practice of medicine, all the while continuing to write papers on his geological surveys. His career took a new turn when the government of Nova Scotia appointed him Commissioner of Indians for the province. This required him to travel about Nova Scotia visiting Indian settlements and reporting annually to the government. In 1850 he moved to Sackville, N.S. and two years later to Halifax in order to be closer to the seat of government. During these years Gesner's restless mind had turned to electricity. He devised an electric motor driven by a voltaic battery, but his most important invention was a retort which enabled him to distill an oil from coal. Events were now directing Gesner toward his greatest accomplishments.

In 1850 he met Lord Dundonald who had come to Halifax as Admiral of the British North America Squadron. This remarkable sailor-scientist had been credited as being the original discoverer of illuminating gas. Now he had been commissioned by the British government to investigate the possibility of producing fertilizer for the coffee and sugar plantations in the West Indies from the asphalt deposits in Trinidad. These Trinidadian deposits were visited by a Nova Scotian sea captain in 1907 who wrote of them:

> The Pitch Lake is quite a wonder in itself. Rather lower than the surrounding country. The tubs of pitch are filled in the lake, brought on a trolley car, put on a wire and taken to the ship over a mile away. We were told the lake settles six inches for every 100,000 tons taken out.

Lord Dundonald appointed Gesner as his

assistant and while they were not able to develop a fertilizer, Gesner did develop a process of distilling a clean oil from the asphalt. In this process a waxy substance in equal proportion to the oil was also produced so Gesner first named the oil keroselaine from the two Greek words for oil and wax. The name gradually changed to keroselene and finally to kerosene.

With his discovery Abraham Gesner moved from the role of scientist-inventor to that of manufacturer. He formed a company in Halifax to produce kerosene but the project failed. In 1853 he moved to New York, patented his process and assigned the patents to the Asphalt Mining And Kerosene Gas Company of Williamsburg, New York. He remained for ten years and took an active part in the company's operations and in the construction of the production plant at Hunter's Point, N.Y. While there he wrote his last known publication, *A Practical Treatise On Coal, Petroleum And Other Distilled Oils.*

The outbreak of the American Civil War began to interfere with the plant's operations and in 1863 Gesner sold his interests in the company and moved back to Halifax where he was appointed Professor of Natural History at Dalhousie University. He held this position for only a year before passing away. During his lifetime Abraham Gesner had been recognized for his geological efforts. Among his honors he had been made a Fellow of the Royal Geological Society of London and a member of the Geological Society of Canada, the Academy of Natural Sciences in Philadelphia and the Geological Society of New York.

It was this man, born of humble beginnings near the shores of Minas Basin, who took homes and businesses from the tallow candle to the kerosene lamp, and who gave lighthouses brighter lights than ever before, that Imperial Oil recognized in 1933.

A Pioneer Horticulturist — Charles Ramage Prescott

Some of the more distinguished sons and daughters of Nova Scotia and New Brunswick once lived along the shores of the Bay of Fundy. Among them must rank Charles Ramage Prescott, the Nova Scotian who contributed so much to the fruit growing industry in his native province.

If, however, Charles rose to prominence in his own right, his father was also worthy of note. Jonathan Prescott was a soldier and physician who had served as a captain of engineers at Louisbourg in 1745. After the capture of the fort he received lands in Halifax, at Louisburg and in Chester. It was in the latter place that an incident occurred which gave evidence of the senior Prescott's resourcefulness.

During the years of the American Revolution and the Napoleonic Wars many privateers from Nova Scotia sailed forth to prey upon enemy shipping, but it was not a one-way traffic. American privateers also raided Nova Scotian shipping and pillaged coastal communities.

One day in 1782 three American privateers sailed into Chester harbour and began firing at the town. Captain Jonathan Prescott, commanding the local militia, ordered the guns in the blockhouse loaded. But the powder was damp and the guns failed to fire. Fresh ammunition was brought up and this time the guns worked and one of the privateers was hit. It beat a hasty retreat behind an island in the harbour.

Late in the day crews of the privateers landed to attack the town by land. They were on one side of the harbour and Prescott and his small band of militia men were on the other. In the courtly way of another

50

time during battle, Captain Prescott called out an invitation for the leaders of the privateers to have tea with him. While the sailors were enjoying the hospitality of the Prescott home there was a loud knocking on the door and the voice of a Prescott boy called out, "Are you there father? Where shall I billet the hundred men sent from Lunenburg by Colonel Creighton?" Captain Prescott replied, "Billet them in Houghton's barn, that's the only place big enough." The Americans smiled at the ruse. One said, "Sir I've been fooled by a trick like that before and once is enough." "When hostilities are resumed in the morning you will find out if it is a trick," answered Captain Prescott.

After the visit Prescott and his son escorted the privateersmen back to their vessels. In the gathering dusk the Americans were surprised to see many red-coated figures marching in the distance. One of the American captains turned to his host, "I see some British soldiers did arrive. Forgive me for doubting the word of a gentleman. It would be useless to attack you. And now, sir, I bid you good-bye. We sail with the tide."

When Jonathan Prescott saw the enemy vessels outward bound he was very much relieved. The red-coated soldiers the Americans had seen were the women of Chester. In those days the women wore long heavy cloaks lined with scarlet cloth. That evening they had turned their cloaks inside out. By staying close enough to be seen but not close enough to be identified, they had fooled the men of the privateers.

Through two marriages Jonathan Prescott fathered twelve children. The ninth was Charles Ramage, born on January 6, 1772 in Halifax. Young Charles began his working life as a merchant in that city and he was soon in the forefront of the capital city's business establishment. In February 1811 his name was among those on the Halifax Committee of Trade which was interested in the establishment of a Provincial Joint Stock Bank. But his success in commerce was tempered by ill-health and he was advised to move away from the frequently foggy Atlantic coast. Perhaps Prescott had envisioned this possibility for some years earlier he had purchased one hundred acres of good farm land at Starr's Point, near Port Williams and on the shores of Minas Basin. Here he began construction of a large Georgian house, built of brick and containing seven fireplaces. In 1812, at the age of forty and financially secure, Prescott moved to Starr's Point. He soon erected large greenhouses and set about bringing in new fruits to the valley and grafting new varieties of apples. He would contribute much to the apple industry soon to burgeon throughout the Annapolis Valley.

The growing of apples in Nova Scotia had begun with the first French settlers in the early 1600s but it was two and a half centuries before apples began to come into their own as an export commodity. The reasons were numerous. The middle decades of the nineteenth century were years of great economic prosperity in the Maritime provinces. The mining, fishing and shipbuilding industries were thriving, helped along by the Reciprocity Treaty with the United States. Under the terms of this Treaty, between the years 1854 to 1866, various products including those of the farm, sea, mine and forest were allowed to flow between the two countries free of duty. Thus the large American market was open to farm produce, fish, lumber and coal from Canada's Maritime provinces. It was at this time that many farmers in Nova Scotia turned to specializing more in

52

Prescott House, Starr's Point, N.S. Courtesy Public Archives of Nova Scotia

specific products such as potatoes, foxes and apples. After Confederation serious efforts began to develop the apple for export. In his *History of Kings County*, Dr. A.W.H. Eaton wrote:

By 1870 every farm in the fruit-growing sections of Annapolis, Kings and Hants Counties had on it many fruit-bearing trees. The complete apple yield of the Annapolis Valley for that year was a hundred thousand barrels, of which twelve thousand were exported, chiefly to England. The market for Annapolis Valley apples, at first was

53

chiefly in the United States, but about 1870-75 exportation to the British markets began. In 1892 the orchards of the valley are said to have covered 25,000 acres, and to have produced 300,000 barrels, about half of which were sent abroad.

This rapid export growth would continue. The annual average of apples shipped from the province in the period 1896-1900 was 261,879 barrels and by 1921-26 the annual average rose to 1,286,172 barrels. There were several reasons for this expansion; the apple trees were young and the control of disease and pests was relatively simple; production costs were low and most of the apples for export were shipped from Port Williams in the heart of the apple growing country. And, most important, the Nova Scotia apple was well received in the United Kingdom, the primary market.

All of this development took place after Charles Prescott's time but it was he who played a major role in making it all possible. On his estate at Starr's Point, which he called Acacia Grove, Prescott introduced new varieties of apples and proved they could thrive in the Annapolis Valley climate. Here he grafted Gravensteins, Ribston Pippins, Blenheim, Alexandra and Golden Pippins which he imported from England. From the United States he brought in the Baldwin, Rhode Island Greening, Esopus Spitz, Sweet Bough, Early Harvest and the Spy. And from Montreal he introduced the Fameuse, Pomme Gris and Canada Reinette. Not all of these varieties gained popular favor but several, including the Gravenstein, Spy, Baldwin and Pippin did exceedingly well.

Prescott's interests ranged beyond apples. He introduced varieties of peaches, pears, plums and grapes and again proved that they could be successfully grown in the Annapolis Valley. Over the years he was recognized for his horticultural achievements at home and abroad. In 1825 he was named president of the infant King's County Horticultural Society and in his lifetime was an honorary member of the horticultural societies in Boston, New York and London, England. Once he was well established at Starr's Point, Prescott became active in politics and represented Cornwallis Township in the Nova Scotia Legislature from 1818 to 1820. Five years later, in August 1825, he was appointed to the powerful Legislative Council in Halifax.

Charles Ramage Prescott died on June 11, 1859 in his eighty-eighth-year. In an obituary the *Nova Scotian* newspaper stated:

> The press of Nova Scotia has never recorded the death of a worthier man; that there are many in all ranks of life who will bear willing testimony to his worth in private and in public life. His hospitable dwelling, it is further said, was the favorite resort of many successive governors. And to his numerous friends a visit to Mr. Prescott's was considered one of the greatest treats.

The Prescott estate remained in the family for a number of years but eventually was sold. There were years of neglect and a period when the great house was used as a rooming house for migrant farm workers.

In 1942 a great-granddaughter of Prescott, Mary Allison Prescott, was able to purchase the property. She spent the rest of her life restoring it to its former grandeur and was successful in reacquiring much of the original furniture. On her death in 1969, as was her wish, the province took over Acacia Grove and it is now part of the Nova Scotia Museum complex. It stands now as a memorial to this great pioneer horticulturist.

2.
Portraits of Two Communities and an Institution

They are situated on opposite sides of the Bay of Fundy but the stories of Canning, Nova Scotia and Dorchester, New Brunswick have much in common. Adjacent tidal rivers played a strong role in their individual economies. Each area was settled first by Acadians and later by pre-Loyalists and both have impressive shipbuilding histories. In their time Canning and Dorchester each dwarfed surrounding communities in population and later each was vastly outnumbered by the same surrounding communities. After years of prosperous growth the two went into decline and here the similarities end. Canning rebounded to become a vibrant, modern centre while Dorchester never regained its former place in the economic sun. Together the two villages played important roles in the developing story of their respective provinces.

Private schools like King's Collegiate and Edgehill in Windsor and Netherwood and Rothesay Collegiate in Rothesay have long histories as part of the educational systems in Nova Scotia and New Brunswick. But there was one school that was unique. Acacia Villa School lasted less than seventy years and for much of that time it was noted for its harsh discipline and spartan living conditions. Yet from the ranks of its students and teachers came some of the country's outstanding leaders and its founder became the first president of the University of New Brunswick.

Canning, Nova Scotia — Its Storied Past

The village nestles close to the North Mountain, not far from majestic Cape Blomidon and the waters of Minas Basin. Its main street runs east and west along a river, now merely a trickle, but one which once floated vessels that sailed the oceans of the world. More than a century has passed since its population far exceeded the neighboring towns of Kentville and Wolfville. This is Canning, a village with a storied past.

The Acadians first settled the area in the late 1600s. They located east of Canning and called their village Habitant and the nearby river the Habitant River. The Acadians cleared the land, dyked the rich meadows and built solid, prosperous farms on the fertile soil. Then came the expulsion in 1755 and they were driven out. The farms were abandoned, the dykes gradually fell into disrepair and salt water swept through to ruin the lowlands.

It was the New England Planters who next arrived on the scene. Between July 1761 and December 1764 some 145 families came to the area. Most were awarded grants of 500 acres in a combination of upland, woodland and marshland. Their settlement struggles were aided considerably when, two decades later, the Loyalists came to settle much of present-day Canning, but then known as Apple Tree Landing. The name was due to an old apple tree that stood near the centre of the village. When the tree was no longer visible the name was changed to Habitant Corner and remained so until about 1830 when the village was named Canning in honor of either George Canning, the former British Prime Minister or his nephew, Viscount Charles John Canning.

Despite its old name of Apple Tree Landing and a later long association with the apple industry, it was the potato which first brought prosperity to Canning. In 1844 a disease struck the New England crop and a great demand quickly arose for Nova Scotia potatoes. The price for the vegetable rose from forty cents a bushel to $1.25 and most were shipped from Canning. One contemporary wrote of "wagons and carts from all parts of the township, loaded with potatoes, filled the streets from morning till night, the vessels for their reception lying at the wharves as many as eleven deep." One can picture the potatoes being dug in the fields, loaded into carts and taken to the waiting vessels where they were dumped into the vessels' holds. Clearly it was long before the days of produce inspection.

Legend has it that the first vessel built at Apple Tree Landing was launched by Dr. William Baxter in 1800. Be that as it may, it was almost another forty years before shipbuilding began in earnest. Four men, Ebenezer Bigelow, Edward Pineo, Joseph Northrup and Edward Lockwood banded together and built a 143-ton vessel, the *Sam Slick*, for Halifax owners and followed her with a second vessel, the 98-ton brigantine *Isabella*. From then until after the turn of the century shipbuilding would be an integral part of the local industry and the leaders would be several generations of Bigelows.

The early vessels were small, generally in the seventy to 150-ton range, and most were rigged as schooners. They were important to the local farming community as the transportation of their produce depended on vessels. And it was the potato during these times which brought the most money and which was the source of prosperity in the area. The

1840s and 1850s were years of growth. More houses and stores were erected and a hotel was built. In the late 1840s a factory opened for the manufacture of cutlery and its machinery was driven by something new — steam. In 1847 another shipyard was opened on the riverbank, behind the present business district, by Elias and Arnold Burbidge and Charles R. Northrup. Their first vessel was a brigantine named the *Elizabeth Hastings* for a Captain Gault of Saint John. Captain Gault was long remembered locally as he paid for his vessel with Mexican silver dollars which he carried around with him in a bag. A further contributing factor in these years was the Reciprocity Treaty of 1854. It created a new potato boom with New England markets, especially Boston, and farmers around responded happily.

Meanwhile the Bigelow shipyard at the east end of the village was also busy. It was the Bigelows who encouraged James Blenkhorn to come to Canning from the Parrsboro shore where he had been a blacksmith and had done the iron work for new vessels in Advocate and Spencers Island. Blenkhorn set up his blacksmith shop adjacent to the Bigelow shipyard and established what would later be known as the firm Blenkhorn and Sons Edge Tool Manufacturers and Coal Dealers. Under James, his son Sidney and grandson Scott, the business would last for 120 years, closing in 1962 with the advent of power tools and a diminishing local demand for coal. In the beginning years Blenkhorn not only did the iron work on the new vessels, he manufactured by hand the adzes, broadaxes and other tools used in the Bigelow yard. As the years went by steam power was introduced and gradually a new tempering system, several small blast furnaces and heavy trip hammers were added. In its heyday the firm employed a dozen or more men and its axes were shipped across the country from Newfoundland to British Columbia.

Canning was in the midst of its greatest period of prosperity when, a little before midnight on July 15, 1866, fire broke out. It would be the most catastrophic fire in the county's history to that time. The morning of the fire two vessels were on the stocks in the Bigelow shipyard. One was a barque, framed up and her hull partially planked. The other was a small schooner, not yet sparred but ready for launching. That day the noon tide was unusually high and Ebenezer Bigelow made a snap decision to launch the little vessel. Thus the schooner was in the river when church bells warned of the fire. The conflagration began in a store at the west end of the village and spread rapidly along the main street. The weather had been hot and dry, wells were low and many of the wooden buildings were close together. There was no equipment to fight the fire and men and boys used buckets, dishpans, anything that would hold water in their futile efforts to stop the spread of the flames.

One saving factor was that high water arrived a little after 1:00 a.m. The newly launched schooner crammed to the rails with women, children, furniture and goods from the stores floated safely in the river. Later the vessel would be named the *Escape*. As the fire continued to move east, householders and storeowners in the path worked frantically to save what they could and piles of furniture and goods littered the streets and nearby fields.

As the fire came relentlessly towards the Bigelow shipyard, a group of boys decided to do what they could to save the barque. They took all the utensils they could find, filled them in the river and kept pouring water on the sides of the vessel. Soon a huge pile of lumber in the shipyard went up in flames. The heat was intense and the fire was perilously close to the barque but the boys kept doggedly at their work and in the end the vessel was saved except for slightly scorched sides.

Just over a year later, on August 30, 1867, when the shipyard had been rebuilt and the barque completed, she was launched and given the name *Providence*. In the following year the *Providence* would again live up to her name. Her story begins in December 1868 when a small schooner, the *Industry*, left the LaHave River for Halifax only fifty-four miles distant. On board were the captain, Lewis Sponagle; the vessel's owner, Ronald Currie; three seamen and two passengers, one being young Angeline Publicover, who was going to Halifax to buy her wedding dress.

All day in a light breeze the schooner sailed towards her destination and shortly after midnight Sambro Light, guardian of Halifax Harbour, was in sight. Suddenly a storm beat down, entrance into the harbour was impossible and the *Industry* was put about to return to LaHave. In the process the foresail split and the one can of kerosene on board upset. There would be no more light for passengers or crew. As the vessel neared LaHave the gale shifted and drove her out in the Atlantic. For three days and nights the schooner ran under bare poles. Somehow the crew managed to jettison the deck load of cord wood from the rolling, pitching schooner but the water tank was struck and smashed. Only two gallons of fresh water remained. Then salt water ruined the provisions and for two weeks the seven on board sustained life on ten hard tack biscuits. To make matters worse, the pounding of the seas opened up the vessel's seams and constant pumping was necessary to keep her afloat.

Christmas dinner consisted of one soggy raw potato found in the bilge and cut into seven pieces. Then, on December 29, when the exhausted men could no longer man the pumps and hope was gone, the schooner was sighted by a passing vessel. The complement of the *Industry* was taken off, less than an hour before the schooner went to the bottom. The survivors were taken to London and then returned to Halifax where they arrived on February 12, 1869, sixty-three days after leaving the LaHave River for the short sail to Halifax. The rescuing vessel was the *Providence*.

The Canning fire of 1866 utterly destroyed the main street except for one store which remained intact. In four hours some forty buildings were demolished including stores, the hotel and houses. The damage was estimated to be $250,000 and hundreds were left homeless. Yet the ashes had barely cooled before the residents began to rebuild. By 1868 every store and house had been reconstructed and a new and freshly painted Canning was ready to face the world.

But fire struck again and it was just as catastrophic. All the new buildings were lost except, curiously, the one that had escaped the fire two years before. This time reconstruction was much slower. Houses and stores were rebuilt and once again vessels were launched from the Bigelow shipyard but the village had lost much of its spirit. And, as time went on, other forces came into play. In the waning years of the century the day of the wooden square-rigger was ending and when the railway connection to Kentville was opened it lessened the demand for shipping out of Canning. Householders began to see

Canning, N.S. Fire, June 23, 1912. Courtesy Leon Barron, New Minas, N.S.

their offspring leaving home in greater numbers to seek opportunities elsewhere, particularly in Boston and the New England States. In the years ahead some new industry would come to the village but its greatest days had passcd. Canning's population which exceeded 3,200 in 1881 dropped to 639 by 1901.

In an essay written in 1929 and republished in the *Nova Scotia Historical Review* in 1988, the late Margaret Ells Russell eloquently portrayed the social and religious life in Canning during the 1870s:

> In the seventies there were four chief classes of people in Canning: shipbuilders, sea captains, merchants and farmers. Of these the

64

shipbuilders were fewest and wealthiest. The sea captains and their wives formed an interesting part of society, for in the good old days, the wife sailed with the captain and they both had the advantages of much travel. The merchants and their clerks were a goodly number of prosperous, peace-loving citizens; but all these classes together did not equal the number of farmers. The farmers were well-to-do; they had large houses and larger barns, and they had the freedom and health that their vigorous out-of-door life gave them.

The religious welfare of the community was guarded by three churches. Some of the wealthy inhabitants had pews in all three. The Methodist Church was at one end of the village, the Free Baptist Church at the other end and the Baptist Church in the middle. Everybody went to church Sunday morning. It was a kind of rite. In the morning the family stayed in bed an hour later than on the other days of the week. They had breakfast at half-past eight. Then they scattered to wash the dishes, sweep the kitchen floor, and get ready their 'go-to-meeting clothes.'

The ministers belonged to the 'good' old-fashioned school that considered dancing an amusement for frivolous and light-headed persons, and playing cards an invention of the devil. Sermon after sermon they preached on the punishment that awaits the dancer and the whist player. 'Lost Heir' and 'Nations,' however, could be played with ecclesiastical sanction. Conscientious, church-going parents forbade their children to dance but the children learned anyway at school during recess. Parents were horrified at the thought of touching a 'spot' card;

but the children went up in the haymow and taught themselves to play 'Forty-Five' and 'Casino.'

There were families, however, who did not obey to the letter the instructions of their spiritual advisors and the parties were many and delightful on winter nights. The invitations would be sent out a week before, and during the time between acceptance and 'the' night, the preparations were extensive. The family that entertained was kept constantly busy. They dusted everything in and out of sight; they scrubbed the whole house till it shone; they decorated the drawing room till it took on a festive air in keeping with the odors that emanated from the kitchen. All kinds of dainties were being prepared by the hospitable housewife and her daughters, while the men of the family polished the floors and andirons, hung decorations and brought the biggest logs from the woodshed to fill the fireplaces.

In the breathing spaces between cooking the ordinary meals and preparing the party feast, Madam examined the bustled, hoop-skirted gowns and the sombre evening suits, and found flaws where no one else would have done. The girls were given the garments with full instructions for making them immaculate. Then, with the use of soap and water, followed by much starch and prolonged application of the flat-iron, the work of rejuvenation began. Every frill must be white as snow and stiff as a ramrod, every infinitesimal crease must be ironed out, every suggestion of a wrinkle pressed to smoothness ...

The guests had also been through much

preparation and when they arrived around eight o'clock, they made a colourful and pleasing picture. Dancing began immediately, to the music of violin and piano, and lasted till midnight. The waltz, the lancers, the polka and quadrille followed each other in graceful succession. The great logs burned cheerily in the fireplaces and cast a ruddy glow over the room and the quickly moving figures. ... At midnight the guests went into the dining-room and supper was served. After four hours of exercise they might be expected to eat heartily, and the repast before them was sumptuous. From the sliced turkey that began the meal, through the innumerable courses, to the Washington and mince pies and rich coffee that ended it, everything was delicious. Nobody attempted to dance after such a feast. They sat around the table and talked until it was time to leave. Then the horses were put into the shafts, the guests bade farewell and sleigh-bells tinkled musically as the horses trotted homeward.

There were amusements in which the young people took part. In the summer there was bathing on the grass-covered marsh, but few enjoyed it enough to learn to swim. There were family picnics, school picnics and church picnics, where everyone had a 'wonderful' time — and suffered for days afterwards from sunburn, mosquito bites and indigestion. There were quilting parties, husking bees and house-warmings at different seasons; there were Hallowe'en, Christmas and St. Valentine's parties, birthday feasts, pie socials and concerts. The chief sports in winter were skating and coasting. Since skating depended on there being no wind when the pond froze, it was not to be enjoyed every day but, when the ice was good, all the younger members of the community went out on the pond. ... It was particularly enjoyable at night when the children were in bed; the ice less crowded, and all the light that was necessary was shed by the moon.

Coasting lasted most of the winter. There are five good hills in Canning, all excellent for sliding. ... The coasters had long sleds, stout boards with runners at each end. The pilot lay prone on the steering end, his hands grasping the wooden tops of the runners; four or five girls and boys sat behind him, each holding to the one in front of him for dear life; the 'starter' gave the sled a push, ran beside it while it gathered speed, and then scrambled on as best he could; and they all went sailing down the hill, shouting like Indians, till they were spilled off at the end of the slide. On a bright, frosty night, what fun to work up a tremendous appetite by coasting two hours or more, and then go indoors and stuff oneself with sandwiches, crullers, cookies, hot chocolate and pulled molasses candy.

They enjoyed life in Canning in the seventies. They were not idle people, but they had learned how to mix work and play to get the most from life. ... Most of the men and women had been brought up on the principle of 'work before play,' and they knew that play is a hundred times sweeter when it is well-earned.

Still dominating the centre of Canning's business district is a monument erected to the memory of Lieutenant Harold Borden killed in the Boer War in 1900. Lieutenant Borden's father, Sir Frederick, was

Sir Frederick Borden Estate, Canning, N.S. Courtesy Old King's
Courthouse Heritage Museum, Kentville, N.S.

a Canning physician and businessman appointed
Minister of Militia and Defense in Sir Wilfred
Laurier's Liberal government in 1896. During his
decade and a half in office Sir Frederick made
significant contributions towards removing Canada's
military from under British control and making it a
truly Canadian entity. He opened several larger
militia training centres, one being nearby Camp
Aldershot and it was he who was largely
instrumental in initiating Canada's navy. Sir
Frederick was the prime mover in involving Canadian
troops in South Africa's Boer War, the war that cost
his own son's life.

In 1913 a postal inspector wrote a description of
Canning in a letter to the Postmaster General in
Ottawa:

Canning is a thriving and progressive village with a population of 1000. The village is well and substantially built. It lies in the midst of a rich and extensive farming district, one of the best in Nova Scotia. It is growing steadily with the development of the country which it serves. It includes 260 families, it has 25 places of business. Its public school has four departments, with 200 pupils enrolled. The Bank of Nova Scotia has an agency there. The Western Union Telegraph Company and the Dominion Express have offices. There are three churches; two hotels; a public library and an Armouries Building. It is provided with an excellent Water System and has an efficient Fire Department. Considerable shipping is owned in the village, which is a regular port of call for steamers on Minas Basin and St. John routes. It has six factories in operation. It is situated on, and is a station of, the Dominion Atlantic Railway Company's branch line from Kentville to Kingsport, over which from four to eight trains pass daily.

The intervening years have brought changes. Horses and carts no longer travel the main street, the last vessel was launched in 1920 and an aboiteau has reduced the once-busy river to a tiny stream. Even the railway has passed into history.

But the Canning of the 1990s is moving into the twenty-first century. There is industry in the area and prosperous farms produce apples, potatoes, hogs and poultry. The village boasts a modern and efficient fire department, water and sewer systems, schools, service clubs, a newspaper and four churches. There are grocery stores, a bank, drug store, restaurants and other local businesses along with medical personnel to serve the area. Its residents have cars, computers, televisions and they can travel by air. They have a way of life undreamed of by those who came before and who lived in the halcyon days of this historic village.

The Bigelows — Shipbuilders and Wharfbuilders
The story of the Bigelows is intertwined with the history of Canning. For over a century they were the leading shipbuilders in the village; they were landowners and farmers and when shipbuilding declined they turned to building wharves around the Bay of Fundy.

The first of the family to arrive in the area came with the New England Planters about 1761 or 1762 to occupy lands once cleared and settled by the departed Acadians. Isaac Bigelow, his wife Abigail and their thirteen children only stayed a few years before returning to New England. Many decades later a great, great grandson, Dr. Wilfred A. Bigelow, would describe Isaac as the "founder of Kingsport and the first man to build a vessel on the Minas Basin."

One son did remain in Nova Scotia to firmly establish the family fortunes. Amasa Bigelow pursued lumbering and farming interests and it is believed that he and Jehiel DeWolf Jr. entered into a partnership pioneering shipbuilding in Mud Creek, now Wolfville. The enterprise had a short life as did Amasa. He died as the result of an accident in 1796 at the age of fifty-one and thus passed from the scene.

The first child of Amasa and Roxanna Cone was Ebenezer and it was he who began the shipbuilding dynasty in Canning and area. Through Isaac's original grant the Bigelows had acquired several hundred acres of land in Kingsport and here, in Canning and on the nearby Bay of Fundy coast, the Bigelows would build vessels. While Ebenezer's first recorded vessel was the schooner *John Gilpin* launched in 1826, there are strong indications that he had built some small vessels prior to that date. Later, as previously noted, he entered into the partnership with Pineo, Northrup and Lockwood but after building two vessels the partners had a falling out and each went his own way. For Bigelow that way was shipbuilding.

Ebenezer had married Nancy Rand and of their six children the fifth was a son, Ebenezer Jr. Young Ebenezer was born to shipbuilding and by his early teens was turning out small boats. In 1839 when Ebenezer the younger was twenty-five his father bought him a tract of land at the eastern end of Canning. This became the Bigelow shipyard in the village and Ebenezer Jr. and his brothers Abraham and David would all be involved in the enterprise. The shipyard continued to produce vessels until the tern schooner *Fieldwood* was launched in 1920.

Ebenezer Jr. married Waity Sanford and among their ten children were two sons, John Emmerson and Gideon. Both became ship designers and master builders. A daughter, Carrie, in the years to come married Captain Hiram Coalfleet, master of the Bigelow-built barque *Providence*, when the complement of the schooner *Industry* was rescued.

John Emmerson married Hannah Blenkhorn, daughter of James the blacksmith, and one of their children was a son, Halle, born in 1876. Halle worked in the Bigelow shipyard in Kingsport and later turned to building wharves. His death in 1947 brought to an end the generations of Bigelows involved in shipbuilding and wharfbuilding.

Just before his death, when he was in his late eighties, John E. Bigelow compiled from memory a list of vessels built by the family over the years. A search of vessel registries has added further names to the list but still it should not be considered as absolute.

In perusing this list of vessels several factors should be kept in mind:

1. The master builder superintended the building of a vessel and frequently was also the designer. Herein the master builder is designated by the initials M.B. The term builder can be confusing. Sometimes it refers to the person putting up most or all of the money to build a vessel and sometimes to the one who actually supervised construction.

2. Vessels of the period were owned on the basis of sixty-four equal shares. Often when several persons owned shares in a vessel, one shareholder would be appointed by the others as the managing owner and took responsibility for managing the affairs of the vessel.

3. When shares owned are listed, this was at the time of launching. Shares were often sold and resold during the vessel's life.

4. Vessels are measured in tons, one hundred cubic feet equalling one ton. In general the measurement applied to the space allocated for cargo.

5. Until the later years of the wooden shipbuilding industry, Cornwallis was listed as the building site. This could have referred to Canning,

Kingsport or other centres in the vicinity.

6. It will be noted that shipbuilding followed an irregular schedule. Some years two or more vessels might be built, other years none. This was usually the result of immediate economic conditions and the consequent demand for vessels.

7. The registries tended to make no distinction between Ebenezer Sr. and Jr. when both were active as builders. At this point in time it is impossible to make the distinction.

These then are the known vessels designed and/or built by the Bigelows or built by others in the Bigelow shipyard:

Rig	Name	Year Built	Tonnage	Place Built/ Comments
Schooner	*John Gilpin*	1826	55	Cornwallis. Ebenezer Bigelow M.B.
Schooner	*Amythest*	1830	98	Parrsboro. Ebenezer Bigelow M.B.
Brig	*Emerald*	1833	136	Cornwallis. Ebenezer Bigelow M.B.
Schooner	*Rachel*	1834	67	Advocate, N.S. Samuel Bigelow M.B. for Captain David Loomer
Brig	*Sam Slick*	1840	143	Canning. Ebenezer Bigelow M.B. with E. Pineo, J. Northrup

Rig	Name	Year Built	Tonnage	Place Built/ Comments
				and E. Lockwood
Brigantine	*Isabella*	1841	98	Canning. Ebenezer Bigelow M.B. with E. Pineo, J. Northrup and E. Lockwood
Schooner	*Troubadour*	1841	59	Cornwallis. Ebenezer Bigelow M.B.
Schooner	*Velocity*	1843	111	Cornwallis. Ebenezer Bigelow M.B.
Schooner	*Boston*	1845	62	Cornwallis. Ebenezer Bigelow M.B.
Brig	*Nancy*	1845	109	Cornwallis. Ebenezer Bigelow M.B.
Brigantine	*Mary*	1846	80	Cornwallis. Ebenezer Bigelow M.B.
Schooner	*Return*	1846	75	Cornwallis. Ebenezer Bigelow M.B.
Brigantine	*Halifax*	1847	92	Cornwallis. Ebenezer Bigelow M.B.
Brig	*Nancy*	1847	111	Cornwallis. Ebenezer Bigelow M.B.
Schooner	*Pilgrim*	1848	40	Cornwallis. Ebenezer Bigelow M.B.

Rig	Name	Year Built	Tonnage	Place Built/ Comments
Schooner	*Minerva*	1849	71	Cornwallis. Ebenezer Bigelow M.B.
Brig	*Chebucto*	1850	98	Cornwallis. Ebenezer Bigelow M.B.
Barque	*Margaret Dewar*	1850	189	Cornwallis. Ebenezer Bigelow M.B.
Brigantine	*Vivid*	1850	132	Cornwallis. Ebenezer Bigelow M.B.
Schooner	*Adonis*	1851	65	Ebenezer Bigelow M.B. Believed built in Westport, N.S.
Brig	*Florida*	1851	115	Cornwallis. Ebenezer Bigelow M.B.
Schooner	*Ransom*	1852	87	Canning. Ebenezer Bigelow Jr. M.B. and half-owner.
Brigantine	*Cordelia*	1853	143	Cornwallis. Ebenezer Bigelow M.B.
Brig	*America*	1854	165	Cornwallis. Ebenezer Bigelow M.B.
Sloop	*John*	1854	12	Cornwallis. Ebenezer Bigelow M.B. and sole owner.

Rig	Name	Year Built	Tonnage	Place Built/ Comments
Brigantine	*Forward*	1856	131	Cornwallis. Builder not listed. Ebenezer Bigelow Jr. half-owner.
Schooner	*Volunteer*	1861	120	Cornwallis. Ebenezer Bigelow Jr. M.B. and half-owner.
Brigantine	*W.H. Harris*	1862	191	Cornwallis. Ebenezer Bigelow Jr. M.B. and half owner.
Ship	*Armstrong*	1863	817	Cornwallis. Ebenezer Bigelow M.B. Bigelows' largest vessel to date.
Brigantine	*E. Bigelow*	1863	134	Cornwallis. Ebenezer Bigelow Jr. M.B. and half-owner.
Brig	*Aura*	1864	257	Cornwallis. Ebenezer Bigelow M.B.
Brigantine	*Branch*	1864	196	Cornwallis. Ebenezer Jr. and John E. Bigelow M.B. Owned 40 shares.
Brigantine	*Canning*	1864	230	Cornwallis. Ebenezer Bigelow probable builder.

Rig	Name	Year Built	Tonnage	Place Built/ Comments
Brigantine	*Fred Clark*	1865	146	Canning. Ebenezer Bigelow Jr. M.B. Owned 21 shares.
Brig	*Grace Darling*	1865	245	Cornwallis. Built by the Bigelows; they were half-owners.
Brig	*Oak Point*	1865	257	Ebenezer Bigelow M.B. Possibly built in Kingsport. Bigelows owned 44 shares.
Schooner	*Wellington*	1865	94	Canning. Ebenezer Bigelow M.B.
Schooner	*Escape*	1866	58	Canning. Ebenezer Bigelow M.B. Escaped Canning fire 1866. Lost with all hands near Digby Gut in 1874.
Schooner	*Lily* or *Lilly*	1866	54	Cornwallis. E. Bigelow probable builder. Owned 24 shares.
Barque	*Providence*	1867	478	Canning. Ebenezer Jr.

Rig	Name	Year Built	Tonnage	Place Built/ Comments
				and John E. Bigelow M.B. Owned 26 shares.
Brigantine	*Wolfville*	1867	244	Cornwallis. Isaac Bigelow probable builder; also a shareholder.
Brigantine	*Spring Bird*	1868	177	Cornwallis. Ebenezer Jr. and John E. Bigelow M.B. Bigelows owned 48 shares.
Brigantine	*Sea Bird*	1869	202	Cornwallis. Ebenezer Bigelow Jr. M.B. Bigelows were sole owners.
Schooner	*Recruit*	1870	131	Canning. Built and owned outright by the Bigelows.
Schooner	*Gerent*	1871	162	Cornwallis. Built and owned outright by the Bigelows.
Schooner	*Advance*	1872	76	Parrsboro for David Merriam. Probably built by Ebenezer Jr. or John E. Bigelow
Schooner	*Northern Home*	1872	162	Cornwallis. Ebenezer

Rig	Name	Year Built	Tonnage	Place Built/ Comments
				Bigelow Jr. M.B. Bigelows were half-owners.
Schooner	*Southern Home*	1873	201	Cornwallis. Ebenezer Bigelow Jr. and John E. Bigelow M.B. Bigelows owned 16 shares.
Barque	*Advocate*	1874	635	Advocate. Gideon Bigelow designer. Ebenezer Bigelow Jr. part owner.
Schooner	*Boxwood*	1874	40	Cornwallis. Ebenezer Bigelow Jr. M.B. and managing owner.
Barquentine	*Canning*	1874	657	Canning. E. Bigelow and Sons M.B.
Barque	*Calcutta*	1876	1283	Spencers Island. Gideon Bigelow designer.
Brigantine	*Ransom*	1876	245	Cornwallis. E. Bigelow and Sons M.B. Bigelows owned 56 shares.
Brig	*Atlantic*	1877	116	Falmouth. Gideon Bigelow M.B.

Rig	Name	Year Built	Tonnage	Place Built/ Comments
Sloop	*Pilot*	1878	14	Cornwallis. Built by the Bigelows. May have been a pilot boat.
Barque	*Recovery*	1878	1027	Cornwallis. Gideon Bigelow M.B.Bigelows owned 20 shares.
Barque	*Conductor*	1880	1063	Canning. Gideon Bigelow M.B.
Ship*	*E.J. Spicer*	1880	1318	Spencers Island. (See note at end of list.)
Brigantine	*Survivor*	1880	194	Cornwallis. Gideon Bigelow M.B. David Bigelow owned 20 shares.
Ship	*Arbela*	1881	1117	Canning. Gideon Bigelow M.B.
Schooner	*Novelty*	1881	97	Cornwallis. Gideon Bigelow M.B.
Barque	*Wenona*	1882	511	Canning. John E. Bigelow M.B.
Schooner	*Canning Packet*	1883	105	Canning. John E. Bigelow M.B. Bigelows owned 56 shares.
Schooner	*Unexpected*	1883	117	Canning. John E. Bigelow M.B.

Rig	Name	Year Built	Tonnage	Place Built/ Comments
Sloop	*Pilot*	1886	14	Cornwallis. Samuel Bigelow sole owner. May have been a pilot boat.
Schooner	*Resolution*	1886	144	Canning. John E. Bigelow M.B.
Brigantine*	*G.B. Lockhart*	1887	296	(See note at end of list.)
Schooner	*Boniform*	1888	148	Cornwallis. John E. Bigelow M.B.
Schooner	*Frances Z.*	1888	146	Clementsport. John E. Bigelow M.B.
Brig	*Osceola*	1889	124	Advocate. Built by the Bigelows for Sidney Smith and Son.
Barque	*Argenta*	1890	629	Eatonville. Believe Bigelows built vessel. F.R. Eaton owner.
Tern Schooner	*Blomidon*	1891	271	Canning. John E. Bigelow M.B. for Alfred Potter.
Barquentine	*Winnifred*	1891	432	Canning. W.H. Baxter builder. Built in the Bigelow yard.
Tern Schooner	*Bahama*	1892	321	Canning. John E. Bigelow M.B. for Alfred Potter. Wrecked 1913, salvaged and renamed *Rescue*.

Rig	Name	Year Built	Tonnage	Place Built/ Comments
Tern Schooner	*Preference*	1893	243	Canning. John E. Bigelow M.B.
Steamer	*Brunswick*	1901	184	Canning. John E. Bigelow M.B. Carried freight and passengers between Bay of Fundy ports.
Tern Schooner	*Advance*	1902	294	Canning. John E. Bigelow M.B. Wrecked, West Indies, 1914.
Tern Schooner	*General George H. Hogg*	1918	407	Canning. Harvey MacAloney builder. Built in the Bigelow yard.
Tern Schooner	*Cape Blomidon*	1919	408	Canning. John E. Bigelow M.B. Last Bigelow-built vessel.
Tern Schooner	*Fieldwood*	1920	435	Canning. Lockwood and Fielding builders. Built in the Bigelow yard. Last vessel built there.

In addition to the above, there is some indication that the Bigelows may have been involved in the building of the schooners *Evelyn Leckie*, *Homeward* (no dates), *Eagle* (1861), and the barque *Medford* (1877). However, no definite documentation has been located although the Bigelows did own some shares in the *Medford*.

Launching of the Schooner *Fieldwood*, 1920. Last vessel launched from the Bigelow shipyard. Original photo by A.L. Hardy. Reproduction by Lark Photographic Services, Canning, N.S.

Notes*

Ship *E.J. Spicer* (1880). Family records list the *E.J. Spicer* as a Bigelow-built ship. The registries list Amasa Loomer as the master builder. However, the Bigelows owned twelve shares so it may have been a cooperative venture.

Brigantine *G.B. Lockhart* (1887). In 1885 the Bigelows began construction of a vessel, designed by Gideon Bigelow, for an unnamed owner. The keel was laid and the frames in place when the owner backed out. J.B. North, whose shipyard was near Hantsport, bought the partly completed hull. The Bigelows disassembled it and towed the pieces to the

North yard where the brigantine was completed in 1887.

The Kingsport Shipbuilding Facility. It is impossible to verify in many cases which vessels were built in Canning and which in Kingsport. Records do indicate that some thirty-five vessels were reclassified and/or repaired at the Kingsport facility.

Wharfbuilding

As shipbuilding declined, John E. Bigelow turned to wharfbuilding. In this he was joined by his son Halle who had previously worked in the Kingsport shipyard. According to family records the Bigelows built the following wharves around the Bay of Fundy. The dates are in some instances approximate.

Apple River	1906
Carr's Brook	1913
Digby	1908
East Ferry, Digby Neck	1932
Harbourville	1929
New Edinburgh	1910
Mill Creek Extension	1923
Port Greville Extension	1905
Port Williams	1930
Scott's Bay Breakwater	1928
Tennycape	1911
West Advocate	1912
Windsor	1926
Wolfville	1927

Other wharves built, repaired or extended by Halle Bigelow included:

Baxter's Harbour
Deep Brook Gypsum Pier

Hall's Harbour
Kingsport
Little Cove, Scott's Bay
Spencers Island

Dorchester, New Brunswick — Its Sons and Ships
The village lies between Moncton and Sackville, by-passed by the Trans Canada highway and showing little in the way of commercial activity. True, there is a highly-acclaimed restaurant in the old Bell Inn, a museum in the Keillor House and an historic collection in St. James Presbyterian Church. And, of course, the Penitentiary. Across the marsh is Dorchester Island, deserted now except for the summer home of its current owner, Reg. Bowser of Moncton. Yet there was a time when many ocean-going vessels were built on the island, where the county court held sway, and where more than 200 people lived.

In the village there are a number of large old residences that hint of a time when Dorchester was the economic and cultural centre of southeastern New Brunswick and its population far outnumbered that of nearby Moncton. Perhaps most interesting of all is the number of the village's sons who weave in and out of its history, men who made their names in the political and business arenas at home and away. Shipbuilders of note, federal and provincial cabinet ministers and premiers were among those who called Dorchester home.

The first European settlers in the area were Acadian French. The first Acadian appears to have been Pierre Thibeaudeau who, with his large family of twelve children, moved to the area from near Port Royal in 1691. Later some thirty-five Acadian families settled along the Petitcodiac and

86

Memramcook Rivers preferring, as always, to settle near marshlands and marshlands there were in abundance.

At the time of the expulsion the Acadians saw their farms burned and their livestock confiscated but, unlike Grand Pré and elsewhere, not many were rounded up and deported. The British and New Englanders seemed to hope they would simply go away. Instead, after the expulsion, many Acadians returned and picked up their lives once again. One was young René Landry who followed a tortuous path to return to the valley of the Memramcook. At the time of the expulsion he fled to what is now Prince Edward Island to avoid deportation but luck was not his ally. On the island he and others were rounded up and shipped off to France. A few years later he returned, first to St. Pierre-Miquelon, then Windsor, Nova Scotia and finally in 1767 to his old home area. Years later, a direct descendant, Armand Landry, would be the first Acadian elected to the New Brunswick Legislature where he worked, often with Albert Smith, on behalf of the Acadians. His son, Pierre, would have an even more distinguished career. Pierre became Westmorland County's first warden, served as provincial secretary and was the province's first Acadian Chief Justice. A strong defender of Acadian culture and identity, Pierre Landry was the first Acadian to be knighted by a British monarch. He died during the first World War while two of his sons were serving overseas with the allied forces.

The long arm of the land-hungry surveyor, J.F.W. Des Barres, also reached into the Dorchester region. Through various grants and purchases he obtained 40,000 acres between the Memramcook and Petitcodiac Rivers. In 1775 he settled some fifty

Acadian families on his lands as tenants and others came as squatters. By 1803 the Acadians outnumbered the English around the two rivers. Eventually Des Barres and his descendents lost much of their land when it was not registered with the newly formed New Brunswick government. Then the Des Barres were careless in looking after their affairs and by 1841 all of their lands had been turned over to other hands, either by purchase or court action.

The first English settlers in Dorchester, called Memramcook until 1789, were Yorkshire people who arrived between 1772 and 1775. Among them were John Chapman, Andrew Weldon and John Keillor. Chapman was the grandfather of Robert Andrew, one of Dorchester's foremost shipbuilders in the years to come. Andrew Weldon was granted the land on which the penitentiary was later placed and then there was John Keillor.

Keillor became one of Dorchester's best known citizens. Like his father who had come to the Isthmus of Chignecto in 1774, John was a stone mason and his grant included much of what is the present village. It is said that during the American Revolution he captured the rebel from Sackville, Richard Uniacke, bound him up and carted him to the garrison at Fort Cumberland in a cart load of pigs. A few short years later Uniacke would be the Speaker in the Nova Scotia Legislature. In any event John Keillor came to Dorchester in the early 1780s and built a log cabin at the foot of the village hill. He was a farmer and trader and he prospered. By 1813, perhaps following his own trade, he built his stone mansion just up the hill from his log cabin.

A big, bluff man with a voice to match, Keillor would stand in front of his house and shout orders to his farm helpers across the marsh some two miles distant. He became a Judge of the Inferior Court for the County of Westmorland and sometimes dealt in land. Keillor donated four acres of land for a county court house which substantially aided Dorchester in becoming the shiretown of Westmorland County in 1803. The court house was a curious mix. Its first floor housed the jail and a tavern while the courtroom and two jury rooms occupied the second floor. When John Keillor died in 1839 at the age of eighty, Moncton consisted of less than a dozen wooden houses.

The early history of the village of Dorchester is intertwined with that of Dorchester Island. The island, about fifty-five acres in total, is located on the Memramcook River, a little to the north of Shepody Bay. Its story began in 1784 when Amos Botsford acquired the island along with tracts of marshland and upland in the Dorchester area.

Botsford was born in Newton, Connecticut in 1744 and graduated from Yale College in 1763. He entered law and in the next few years acquired properties in New Haven. However, he was a Loyalist and in 1779 was forced to abandon his properties and look to Canada. Commissioned by Sir Guy Carleton to help arrange the settlement of Loyalists in Nova Scotia, Botsford came to Annapolis Royal in 1782. Two years later, when New Brunswick became a separate province, he moved to Dorchester and the island. He built a large stone mansion on the island and quickly became involved in local and provincial affairs. Among other offices he was a county magistrate and registrar of deeds. When the first New Brunswick Legislature went into session Botsford was elected Speaker, a position he held continuously for the next twenty-six years until his death in 1812.

During those years he was almost always referred to as Speaker Botsford. His stay on the island was relatively short-lived. In 1790 he moved to Westcock and built another mansion which he sold along with the island to Elijah Ayer Jr. in 1797.

Ayer was a rather fascinating figure in the early history of Dorchester. He is sometimes referred to as captain and other times as commander or commodore. His father had received a 2,000 acre grant on the Isthmus of Chignecto and both father and son ran into difficulties in 1776. A band of New Englanders led by Colonel Jonathan Eddy were determined to capture Fort Cumberland in this the first year of the American Revolution. They were joined by the two Ayers possibly because Jonathan Eddy Jr. was Elijah Ayer Jr.'s brother-in-law. The assault on the fort was a pathetic failure and as a result Ayer Senior was deprived of his lands on the Isthmus and forced to flee. The younger Ayer later became an Indian agent for the American government and followed other pursuits before purchasing Dorchester Island.

Once settled on the island Elijah Ayer Jr. encouraged further settlement and he was probably Dorchester's first shipbuilder. Local records suggest he built at least one small schooner, the *Hope*, on the island sometime prior to 1807. When the Westmorland County courthouse burned in 1801 near Fort Cumberland, Ayer offered his mansion, and court was held there until a new courthouse was built in Dorchester village two years later. When the War of 1812 broke out, Ayer apparently switched his allegiance and went privateering. He died in Buctouche, New Brunswick in 1837 at the age of eighty-four.

In the early years of the century the population in

and around Dorchester was steadily increasing. Census figures for the year 1803 list 938 men, women and children in Dorchester Parish with the majority being Acadians. The early English settlers were largely dependent on the Acadians along the Memramcook River for meat, eggs and other provisions until their own farms became established. Some supplies began arriving early by water from Saint John but ice in the river during the winter months precluded any landings and necessitated some carefully planned stockpiling. Prices for goods landed in Dorchester from Saint John in 1785 included:

1 gallon of rum	10 shillings
1 pound of tea	4 shillings
6 pounds of tobacco	6 shillings
4 pounds of sugar	5 shillings, 4 pence
2 yards of linen	5 shillings
1 pound 10 penny nails	1 shilling

Money was extremely scarce and most goods were obtained by barter. In these first years the vast majority of settlers began with log cabins, Amos Botsford being one of the very few who could immediately build a permanent home. And from the beginning rum played an important role in the life of the community. It was plentiful and cheap, and by 1798 four licenses to sell liquor had been granted to Dorchester residents. It was a commodity used at funerals, weddings, barn raisings and country frolics, and even the leading families, the Keillors and Weldons were among those selling it. The only dissidents were found among the Wesleyan faith.

These settlers were an industrious people and in a relatively short time they had built their homes, schools, stores, chapels and a wharf on the southern end of the island. Once the settlement had taken root the travelling shoemaker, schoolmaster and tailor arrived on the scene. But travel in these early years was difficult. It was the second decade of the nineteenth century before blazed trails began giving way to any form of roads. The first farm wagons were introduced into Dorchester in 1818 by Andrew Weldon and Ira Hicks, both purchased from a Yankee trader. About this time the first stage coach made its way into the village and from 1820 on Dorchester was the transfer point for mail stages from Saint John, Chatham and Halifax.

These years signalled the dawn of Dorchester's time of prosperity, a time that would last until nearly the end of the century. There were several contributing factors besides the arrival of the stage coaches. The location of the new courthouse in the village, which became the county shiretown, the gradual increase in shipbuilding and the expanded marine traffic to and from the island all helped to bring an influx of politicians, lawyers, shipwrights, sailors and farmers to the village. The number of taverns grew apace. Curiously, until the Westmorland Bank was established in Moncton in 1854, Dorchester residents had no place to deposit their money. By necessity cash was hidden in the home, and the bank's failure in 1867 did nothing to instill confidence in the citizens for this new way of handling money. It was 1882 before the Royal Bank ventured into the village and opened a branch.

In this early time of growth another man arrived in Dorchester destined to influence affairs locally, provincially and nationally. Edward Barron Chandler was the grandson of a Loyalist, Joshua Chandler of New Haven, who was imprisoned for his sympathies

92

to the British Crown. Escaping, he and his family came to Fort Cumberland in 1783 but four years later Joshua and three of his children died when their little vessel ran aground at Mispec, near Saint John, in wintry weather.

Edward Barron Chandler was born in 1800, the son of Cumberland County sheriff Charles H. Chandler. He was called to the bar in 1821 and the following year married Phoebe Millidge in Westcock. Chandler brought his bride to Dorchester behind him on horseback and the couple moved into John Keillor's old log cabin. Ten years later he was able to build his own large stone house which he called Rocklyn and in time it sheltered the Chandler family of six children as well as seven servants. In 1827 Chandler was elected to the New Brunswick Legislature where he remained until 1884 when he moved to the Legislative Council. There were two main passions in his political life, the development of railways and the federation of the Canadian provinces.

In 1850 Chandler accompanied Joseph Howe to England to promote the Intercolonial Railway and he became deeply involved in the railway from its beginnings until it was completed. As a pro-Confederate he took part in the Confederation meetings in Charlottetown, Quebec, and later in London. It was these leanings which brought him into conflict with his former law student, friend and neighbor, Albert Smith. As an ardent supporter of provincial rights and responsibilities, he frequently crossed swords with the nationalist Sir John A. MacDonald even though both were conservatives. In 1878 Chandler was appointed New Brunswick's Lieutenant-Governor and two years later he died in office. In his time Edward Barron Chandler was recognized as one of the most influential and able political figures on the Canadian scene.

Not all of Dorchester's leading citizens were politicians or men of the sea. As the community developed there appeared traders, men who traded household goods for the produce of farmers and fishermen. Usually addressed as Squire, the traders were generally looked upon with a suspicious eye as men who were greedy and selfish, even if they provided a necessary service. And it was true that they made a profit trading with the local people and profited again when they sold the produce elsewhere.

One trader who was the most successful of them all and who had another side to his character was William Crane. The son of a Loyalist, Colonel Jonathan Crane, a prominent resident of Horton, Nova Scotia, William moved to the Sackville area by way of Parrsboro and in 1813 married Susan Dixon Roach. About this time he opened a store in Dorchester and following the old barter system he offered needed goods for the home and farm in return for the usual produce. He became enormously successful, to the extent of owning his own vessels to carry the produce to market. Crane financed his own ventures and financially backed others, even those who called him greedy.

In 1837 he accompanied Joseph Howe, Thomas Chandler Haliburton and Samuel Cunard on a voyage to England. It was a time when the steamship was beginning to take on practical overtones. Indeed the next year the British steamships *Sirius* and *Great Western* would cross the Atlantic to New York in eighteen and fifteen days respectively. This was much better time than most sailing vessels could achieve against the prevailing westerly winds. Howe and Crane were able to work on the visionary

Cunard's behalf with the British government and the wealthy Crane is credited with providing the financial backing for the beginning of the Cunard Line.

The other side of Crane's character came to light in 1846 when local crops failed. Crane ordered a cargo of flour from Boston and its free distribution was governed by one order — "that those most in need come first." He made his profits, but it is also said that he carried the farmers until they could harvest their crops. When William Crane died in 1853 at the age of sixty-nine he reportedly held 650 mortgages and owned forty-nine properties.

By the middle of the nineteenth century Dorchester was beginning to come into full bloom. A government wharf had been constructed on the northwest end of the island and in Dorchester Parish there were twenty-seven sawmills employing 280 men, four tanneries, eight gristmills, seven churches, seventeen schools and a population of 3,681. A decade later, in 1861, when Moncton's population stood at 1,396, the Parish of Dorchester could boast:

448	farmers	7	gristmills
612	houses	21	schools
10	stores	2	weaving establishments
8	churches	2	doctors
25	shipbuilders	29	sawmills — one steam-operated
52	servants	11	lawyers

The disproportionate number of lawyers in the village were drawn there because of the courthouse and Dorchester being the shiretown of Westmorland County. All had their offices in the village centre, the 'Corner' as it was called by some and 'The Devil's Half

Acre' by many more. Lawyers' offices and taverns sat side by side and as W.C. Milner wrote of the Corner:

> It was the meeting place of all classes, representing 'rich man, poor man, beggar man, thief' — politicians ambitious to save the country; litigants visited there to woo the goddess Justice; lawyers whose ideal of justice was a fat bill of costs; debtors placed under restraint, with the idea they could pay in confinement what they failed in when free; jurymen, witnesses and other attendants at the various courts; jailors, farmers, shipmasters, ship carpenters — all forming a small but democratic world; — all on the dead level before the Bar of John Barleycorn, where perfect equality was maintained at six cents a glass.

One of the lawyers practicing there at the time was Dorchester-born Acalus L. Palmer. A graduate of King's College in Fredericton, he studied law with the eminent Edward Barron Chandler and a fellow student was Albert Smith. Called to the bar in 1845 at the age of twenty-five he practiced law in Dorchester for two decades. Palmer was not only a practicing lawyer, he was also a millowner and a shipowner. Among his vessels were the *Fanny Palmer, Kate Upham, Martha Ann Palmer* and the *Charley Palmer*. In the mid 1860s he moved to Saint John where he was elected Member of Parliament for Saint John County. By now a man of wealth, he lost his home and possessions in the great Saint John fire of 1877, a loss said to exceed $100,000.

In 1879 Palmer became a Judge in the Supreme Court of New Brunswick and he remained on the bench until 1894. When he died five years later he owned the Mispec Woolen Mill and was a director of the Maritime Bank.

If the coming of the railroad was a boon to Dorchester for a few years, in the end it would be a contributing factor to its decline. In 1857 the European and North American Railroad opened between Saint John and Shediac and Dorchester was connected by a stagecoach service. Where the mails once arrived weekly at the village, now there was daily mail service. Eleven years later a branch of the European and North American began operations between Moncton and Dorchester and in 1869 the line was continued on to Sackville. By 1872 rail traffic was possible between Saint John and Halifax on the Intercolonial Railway which had taken over the European and North American in 1870. When the railway shops burned in Shediac in 1871, Moncton was selected as the new site. It was the real beginning for the town and people were drawn from various parts of Westmorland and Albert counties to work in the new shops. As part of the continuing rail development, about 1876 a spur line was built from the main Intercolonial line at Dorchester to the government wharf on the island.

In the third decade of the century, just when Dorchester was beginning to blossom, a boy was born in Shediac Cape who in time would share with Edward Barron Chandler the distinction of being Dorchester's outstanding citizen.

Albert Smith was born in 1822 at Shediac Cape, a direct descendent of a Pilgrim Father who landed at Plymouth Rock, Massachusetts in 1620. A great grandson of that first Smith on these shores came to Shediac Cape in 1787 and his grandson, Albert Smith's father was a prosperous merchant, lumberman and Shediac's first postmaster. Young

Albert was born into relative wealth, unlike his future mentor Chandler who came from very poor surroundings. It became something of a paradox in later years.

At the age of twenty-one Smith went to Dorchester where he was accepted as a law student with Chandler and in 1847 he opened his own law practice. But the legal profession took second place among Smith's main ambitions in life and the first was politics. In 1852 he won a seat in the provincial legislature and he would hold the seat as a provincial and federal member for the next thirty years, nearly all of them in opposition to Chandler, and the paradox soon came to light. Chandler rose from his penurious childhood to become a member of the small, influential ruling class in Fredericton, a friend of governors and their defender. Smith, from his position of relative wealth was a lifelong champion of the common people. Throughout his political career he was a friend and ally of the Acadians and he never neglected his constituents. He and Chandler were on opposite sides on another issue. Chandler believed a unified Maritimes would have greater strength in the new, federated Canada. Smith saw Confederation driving a prosperous New Brunswick into the position of a have-not province while the country's wealth settled in central Canada.

One issue on which the two agreed was the development of railways. They joined forces in a successful effort to get the European and North American Railway looped through Dorchester and Sackville even though the planners wanted it to follow a more direct route through Shediac and Baie Verte. The loop added an extra half hour to the journey between Moncton and Halifax.

Smith was only in the Legislature two years when

he began a campaign against the Anglican King's College in Fredericton. To him the college was using government funds better used elsewhere and it was another symbol of the privileged few in the capital. One of his favorite arguments was that in its twenty-five years of existence the college had graduated just eighty-two young men at an enormous cost. It was largely due to his efforts that King's College was transformed into a provincial institution in 1859, the University of New Brunswick.

An able parliamentarian and a ferocious debater, Smith was for all intents and purposes leader of the Smashers by 1856. The Smashers, later the Reform Party and still later the Liberals, were sworn enemies of the privileged class and Smith was the most vocal of all. The mantle of 'Smasher of Privilege' and 'Bully-Boy' Smith rested easily on his shoulders just as did his other sobriquet, 'The Lion of Westmorland.'

As the confederation debate moved even closer to its inevitable conclusion Smith waged his bitter battle in opposition and he had on his side the majority of Acadians in the province. His main arguments at the time centred on the premises that confederation would bring direct taxation and higher tariffs as well as taking on the burden of the immense public debt for railways. When an election was called in the spring of 1865 Smith won a decisive victory and as premier his government was successful in stalling confederation for over a year. But dark clouds were appearing on Smith's horizon. The Americans refused to renew the Reciprocity Treaty thus denying any further free access of Canadian natural products to American markets. Then the Fenians were threatening the Maine-New Brunswick border and while little damage was done there was a growing feeling that protection was needed against the Americans and this fuelled the pro-Confederate cause. Perhaps most difficult of all, Smith's party was no longer unified on the anti-confederation issue. In April 1866 Smith was forced to resign and in the ensuing election Sir Leonard Tilley swept to power. Smith's party salvaged but eight seats including his own.

In 1867 Confederation became fact and Albert Smith forsook provincial politics for the federal scene. He was elected Member of Parliament for Westmorland County and he took to Ottawa all of his formidable skills as a debater and parliamentarian. It was not long before he was recognized as the main upholder of Maritime rights. Although they were on opposite sides of the House, Prime Minister John A. MacDonald soon gained great respect for the battler from New Brunswick. He offered Smith the Lieutenant-Governorship of his native province but Smith declined. He still had fish to fry in the new nation's capital.

When MacDonald's Conservatives were defeated by Liberal Alexander MacKenzie in 1873 Smith was immediately brought into the cabinet as Minister of Marine and Fisheries and it was he who frequently acted as House leader for the government when Prime Minister MacKenzie was absent. It was during his tenure in the cabinet that Smith arranged for the Maritime penitentiary to be built in Dorchester. The reason is not clear, perhaps he saw the coming decline in wooden shipbuilding and its consequences for Dorchester and certainly being close to the geographic centre of the Maritimes the village was in a strategic location.

In 1877 Smith represented the Canadian government in Washington in an effort to seek compensation for fish taken by Americans in

Canadian waters. Nothing much was expected from his efforts but Smith managed a $5 million settlement. He was immediately recommended for knighthood and on May 25, 1878 he was created a Knight Commander of St. Michael and St. George. The 'Bully-Boy' was now Sir Albert Smith, the first native-born New Brunswicker to be knighted by a British monarch.

Two years later the MacKenzie government lost the election although Smith retained his seat. But over the next four years the man who had helped bring the railway and penitentiary to Dorchester, who had represented his country so well for three decades had no more gifts left in his bag. In 1882 he was defeated by Josiah Wood and, curiously, one who helped bring him down was Pierre Landry, the staunch advocate of Acadian culture.

Sir Albert never got over his defeat. He became a brooding and listless man and on June 30, 1883 the 'old man' as some had come to call him passed away. He was sixty-one. He and his teacher, friend and adversary, Edward Barron Chandler lie near each other in the Dorchester Rural Cemetery.

While Chandler and Smith were waging their battles in distant political arenas Dorchester was prospering. As the village became a destination point for marine traffic and a way station for stage coaches, hotels began to appear. Probably the first was on the island and operated by a Wilbur. In his letter to a friend in 1858 William Cochrane wrote of "getting nice quarters with Mr. Wilbur" on the island. The Dorchester Hotel was built in the centre of the village on the site later occupied by the Windsor Hotel. It was owned by John Hickman until 1850 when his son, William, bought it and managed it for three years. William then bought the Bell Inn which he operated for ten years as a hotel, stagecoach station and tavern before converting it into his private residence. When he owned the Bell Inn it was described as "filled with the finest mahogany, silver and other furnishings." The building goes back at least to 1811 and some place its origin as early as 1786. It is the oldest stone building in New Brunswick. The name was derived from a huge iron bell which once hung near its front door, very likely to the discomfort of sleeping guests.

As the century wound down the palatial Windsor Hotel was erected in 1895. Five stories in height and boasting 200 rooms, a dining room and ladies' parlor, the hotel had a solid mahogany bar in the basement said to be the longest east of Montreal. The basement was a popular gathering place through the years and even during prohibition it was a place where the thirsty could find relief.

The early settlers, Acadian and English, held strong religious beliefs. An Acadian chapel was built in Upper Dorchester prior to the expulsion. The British settlers had barely settled themselves in Dorchester when Bishop William Black organized a Methodist Church in 1780. It was a period of great religious fervor and two years later the Bishop was complaining that he had lost seventy of his flock to Preacher Henry Alline of the New Light Sect, an offshoot of Calvanism. This fervor led to the village's first hanging. One of Preacher Alline's converts, Amos Babcock, was hanged in 1804 for murdering his sister-in-law after attending a New Light rally in Shediac.

Trinity Anglican Church was consecrated on August 21, 1843 by Bishop John Inglis, Lord Bishop of Nova Scotia near the end of a 3,000-mile journey of visitation in Nova Scotia and along the eastern coast of New Brunswick. Earlier St. Ann's Episcopal Church had been built in Westcock in 1817 largely due to the leadership of the Botsford family.

The English Roman Catholics erected their church in 1880 on land donated by Sir Albert Smith and the Baptist Church was built about the same time.

An industry which prospered in the Dorchester area for many years was the quarrying of rocks, particularly in Rockland and Beaumont. Large quantities of brown freestone were sent to the rapidly expanding cities along the American east coast. In 1861 some 125 men were employed in the production of 5,000 tons of stone. Some of the local stone was used in building Saint John's first courthouse and, later, in the building of the penitentiary. Grindstones were also produced and sent to American markets until the end of Reciprocity when the United States placed a high tariff on building stone and grindstones which practically wiped out the market. A further adjunct to the industry was the manufacture of pulpstones. These stones were finished round, about four feet in width and several feet in thickness and were used in paper mills for grinding up pulpwood. This aspect of the quarrying business lasted until the early years of World War II.

It was shipbuilding that made the name of Dorchester known around the world. When the first vessel was launched is uncertain. Persistent local records credit Elijah Ayer Jr. as the first shipbuilder and this may well be the case. Certainly the earliest Dorchester vessel found in the registries was the schooner *Good Intent* of 92 tons launched in 1816 by an unknown builder. The momentum gradually increased through the next few decades but in terms of larger vessels, the first builders of consequence were McMorran and Dunn. John McMorran and James L. Dunn established their shipyard on the southern end of the island and between 1854 and 1857 launched five ships, all but one in excess of 1,000 tons. One of their vessels, the ship *Welsford* had a tragic end. Launched in 1856 the *Welsford* was lost on her maiden voyage when she went ashore on Cape Race, Newfoundland on Christmas Day, 1856. Her master and twenty-three of the crew perished. Perhaps because of the loss of the *Welsford* McMorran and Dunn only stayed on the island to finish the ship *James Smith* in 1857 before they moved to Saint John where they built several more vessels.

As the pace of shipbuilding increased, Dorchester came to know the loss of more vessels. For instance on January 11, 1866 the *Saint John Freeman* reported:

> The brigantine *Alice Grey* which sailed from Dorchester (Rockland) about five months ago with a load of stone for Baltimore has not been heard from since. It is supposed she foundered with all on board. She was about 260 tons burthen and had a crew of six and the captain. The vessel was built at Dorchester in 1861.

Over the years numerous men built vessels in Dorchester but three were by far the most prolific:

Gideon Palmer: Lieutenant Gideon Palmer came to Dorchester from Fort Cumberland to take up a land grant of 195 acres along the creek that bears his name. A Loyalist, he became a mill owner, farmer and magistrate. His son Gideon was born in 1808

Gideon Palmer,
Shipbuilder,
Dorchester, N.B.
Courtesy Westmorland
Historical Society

and in the course of time he inherited his father's mills. In 1854 the younger Gideon turned to shipbuilding with the launch of the brigantine *Bloomer*. Over the next twenty-one years he turned out a total of thirteen barques, six brigantines, one brig and two schooners. When Gideon passed away in 1880 his sons Philip, Barlow and Hiram took over the Palmer yard and launched several more vessels. One, the brigantine *Jak-a-Vuka* was built for the Fiji Island trade and bore the name of a Fiji chief. Their last recorded vessel was the schooner *Greta* launched in 1899.

Robert Andrew Chapman: Robert Chapman's father was a prominent farmer in Dorchester who sold his farm and moved to Rockland with his son. Robert Andrew served as High Sheriff for Westmorland County and was Fishery Commissioner of the province for a time. However, it was as a shipbuilder that he was best known. His first vessels were the brig *Edward Barron* and the small schooner *Swan*, both launched in 1861, and his last was the schooner *Sarah Godfrey* built in 1883. In all Chapman built seven brigantines, one brig, one barquentine, twelve barques, six schooners and one ship. The ship, the *S.B. Weldon*, at 1531 tons, was his largest vessel.

William Hickman: Hickman had various business interests. Born in 1823 he was a hotel owner, tavern keeper and involved in stage coaches. When Joseph Salter's shipyard in Moncton went bankrupt in 1859, Salter's financial backer, Oliver Jones, took over the yard and operated it for another three years before closing it for good. William Hickman began building vessels in Hillsborough in 1863 and he employed many of the men from the Salter yard. Hickman built three vessels in Hillsborough, the last and largest being the barque *Fanny Atkinson* launched in 1865. He then moved back to Dorchester and established his shipyard on the southern end of the island on the bank of the Memramcook River. His first vessel there was the barque *Thomas Cochran* launched in 1867 and his last was the schooner *Ethel Emmerson* built in 1882. The registries list Hickman's output as fourteen barques, one brigantine, two ships and one schooner.

Barque *Maggie Chapman*, 780 tons. Built by William Hickman, Dorchester Island, 1868. Courtesy New Brunswick Museum

The list of vessels to follow all appear in the registries. A few others are added solely on the basis of local evidence. However, at least 109 documented vessels were turned out in Dorchester and Rockland and sixty-eight of these were produced by Gideon Palmer, Robert A. Chapman and William Hickman. In all it was a truly significant contribution to the province's output in the age of sail.

In presenting this list every attempt was made to name the master builder rather than the person who placed the order. For instance in the registries lawyer Acalus L. Palmer was sometimes listed as the builder but the master builder was in all probability Gideon Palmer.

Rig	Name	Year Built	Tonnage	Builder	Place
Brigantine	A.L. Palmer	1876	490	R.A. Chapman	Rockland
Barque	Alabama	1877	999	R.A. Chapman	Rockland
Brigantine	Alaska	1874	529	R.A. Chapman	Rockland
Brigantine	Alfaretta	1863	227	R.A. Chapman	Rockland
Barque	Algeria	1871	620	R.A. Chapman	Rockland
Brigantine	Alice Grey	1861	182	Wm. Wilkie	Dorchester
Barque	Annetta	1864	408	Gideon Palmer	Dorchester
Schooner	Annie G.	1886	116	Thos. Wilbur	Dorchester
Barque	Arabia	1875	957	R.A. Chapman	Rockland
Barque	Arcadia	1873	788	R.A. Chapman	Rockland
Brigantine	Augusta	1872	355	George Buck	Dorchester
Barque	Australia	1878	999	R.A. Chapman	Rockland
Barque	Barlow	1862	360	Gideon Palmer	Dorchester
Brigantine	Beaver	1871	208	McKelvie and Smith	Rockland
Barque	Bel Stewart	1871	603	Gideon Palmer	Dorchester
Barque	Bertha Anderson	1877	544	Wm. Hickman	Dorchester
Brigantine	Bessie May	1875	342	Edward Chambers	Dorchester
Schooner	Blanche	1836	65	Edward Dowling	Dorchester
Brigantine	Bloomer	1854	116	Gideon Palmer	Dorchester
Barque	Brothers and Sisters	1872	656	Gideon Palmer	Dorchester

Rig	Name	Year Built	Tonnage	Builder	Place
Barquentine	*C.V. Chandler*	1881	415	R.A. Chapman	Rockland
Schooner	*Cappella*	1866	191	R.A. Chapman	Rockland
Ship	*Castilion*	1856	1064	McMorran and Dunn	Dorchester
Brigantine	*Catharine*	1858	215	Gideon Palmer	Dorchester
Brigantine	*Cavour*	1864	230	R.A. Chapman	Rockland
Ship	*Charley Hickman*	1871	904	Wm. Hickman	Dorchester
Barque	*Charley Palmer*	1863	585	Gideon Palmer (Probable)	Dorchester
Schooner	*Clara J. Wilbur*	1883	195	T.B. Wilbur	Dorchester
Barque	*Cynthia Palmer*	1864	335	Gideon Palmer	Dorchester
Barque	*David Taylor*	1869	599	R.A. Chapman	Rockland
Schooner	*Dorchester*	1835	47	J. McElmen	Dorchester
Ship	*Dorchester*	1854	1336	McMorran and Dunn	Dorchester
Brig	*Edward Barron*	1861	218	R.A. Chapman	Rockland
Schooner	*Edwin Botsford*	1831	48	Mansfield Cornwell?	Dorchester
Schooner	*Emma C.*	1883	100	James Chambers	Dorchester

Rig	Name	Year Built	Tonnage	Builder	Place
Schooner	*Ethel Emmerson*	1882	176	Wm. Hickman	Dorchester
Brigantine	*Fanny Palmer*	1859	194	Gideon Palmer (Probable)	Dorchester
Brigantine	*Flying Scud*	1875	344	George Buck	Dorchester
Barque	*G. Palmer*	1863	306	Gideon Palmer	Dorchester
Brigantine	*G.P. Sherwood*	1870	400	R.A. Chapman	Rockland
Ship	*General Windham*	1856	795	McMorran and Dunn	Dorchester
Schooner	*Good Intent*	1816	92	Not Known	Dorchester
Schooner	*Greta*	1899	146	Hiram Palmer	Dorchester
Barquentine	*H.W. Palmer*	1882	471	Philip Palmer	Dorchester
Barque	*Harriet Hickman*	1873	851	Wm. Hickman	Dorchester
Schooner	*Ida May*	1862	99	Gideon Palmer	Dorchester
Barque	*J.B. Newcomb*	1875	890	R.A. Chapman	Rockland
Barque	*J.C. Lamb*	1872	482	Wm. Hickman	Dorchester
Ship	*J.I. Smith*	1881	1277	Wm. Hickman	Dorchester
Brigantine	*Jak-a-Vuka*	1883	149	Philip Palmer	Dorchester
Ship	*James Smith*	1857	1108	McMorran and Dunn	Dorchester
Schooner	*Jennie Palmer*	1889	77	Philip Palmer	Dorchester

Rig	Name	Year Built	Tonnage	Builder	Place
Barque	*John Hickman*	1880	1240	Wm. Hickman	Dorchester
Barque	*John Rutherford*	1872	984	Wm. Hickman	Dorchester
Brigantine	*Johnny Smith*	1875	490	Wm. Hickman	Dorchester
Barque	*Joseph Hickman*	1877	954	Wm. Hickman	Dorchester
Brig	*Joshua King*	1869	290	Gideon Palmer	Dorchester
Brigantine	*Kate Upham*	1864	298	Gideon Palmer (Probable)	Dorchester
Schooner	*Kate Wilson*	1878	85	Edward Bowser	Rockland
Barque	*Larch*	1845	704	Stephen Binney	Dorchester
Schooner	*Lena*	1877	93	R.A. Chapman	Rockland
Brigantine	*Leona*	1866	300	R.A. Chapman	Rockland
Barque	*Lewis Smith*	1876	1093	R.A. Chapman	Rockland
Barque	*Lizzie Wright*	1872	933	R.A. Chapman	Rockland
Barque	*Maggie Chapman*	1868	780	Wm. Hickman	Dorchester
Barque	*Maggie L. Carvill*	1870	867	Wm. Hickman	Dorchester
Barque	*Maggie Reynolds*	1867	495	Gideon Palmer	Dorchester
Brigantine	*Mansfield*	1833	155	G.D. Robinson	Dorchester
Schooner	*Margaret*	1840	19	Thos. Ayer	Dorchester
Brigantine	*Martha Ann Palmer*	1864	299	Gideon Palmer (Probable)	Dorchester

Rig	Name	Year Built	Tonnage	Builder	Place
Barque	*Mary E. Chapman*	1873	696	R.A. Chapman	Rockland
Brigantine	*Mary Jane Wilbur*	1866	350	Wm. Wilbur	Dorchester
Barque	*Mary Lowerison*	1868	573	Gideon Palmer	Dorchester
Brigantine	*Matilda Buck*	1877	271	R.A. Chapman	Rockland
Barque	*Matilda C. Smith*	1873	684	Gideon Palmer	Dorchester
Schooner	*Memramcook*	1863	57	Harrison Lewis (Owner)	Dorchester
Barque	*Orontes*	1878	699	James Harris	Dorchester
Brigantine	*Otter*	1873	358	McKelvie and Smith	Rockland
Schooner	*P.J. Palmer*	1881	415	Philip Palmer	Dorchester
Brigantine	*Prince of Wales*	1860	193	Gideon Palmer	Dorchester
Barque	*Queen of the Fleet*	1876	941	Gideon Palmer	Dorchester
Barque	*R.B. Chapman*	1872	555	R.A. Chapman	Rockland
Schooner	*Robbie Godfrey*	1882	164	R.A. Chapman	Rockland
Barque	*Robert A. Chapman*	1874	982	R.A. Chapman	Rockland

Rig	Name	Year Built	Tonnage	Builder	Place
Schooner	*Rosebud*	1863	46	Gideon Palmer	Dorchester
Barque	*Ruth Palmer*	1875	934	Gideon Palmer	Dorchester
Ship	*S.B. Weldon*	1878	1531	R.A. Chapman	Rockland
Not Specified	*Sarah Ann*	1826	283	Wm. Turner	Dorchester
Barque	*Sarah Chambers*	1874	1000	Wm. Hickman	Dorchester
Schooner	*Sarah Godfrey*	1883	186	R.A. Chapman	Rockland
Barque	*Sarah King*	1864	342	Wm. Wilbur	Dorchester
Barque	*Sarah M. Smith*	1869	774	Wm. Hickman	Dorchester
Not Specified	*Sea Flower*	1825	67	John Faulkner	Dorchester
Schooner	*Sprightly*	1834	20	A. Wallet	Dorchester
Brigantine	*Star Of The Sea*	1864	196	G. Bourke	Dorchester
Ship	*Sunny South*	1854	1196	David Forbes	Dorchester
Schooner	*Swan*	1861	53	R.A. Chapman	Rockland
Barque	*Thomas Cochran*	1867	627	Wm. Hickman	Dorchester
Barque	*Thos. Keillor*	1875	1096	Wm. Hickman	Dorchester
Schooner	*Union*	1836	82	Joseph Atkinson	Dorchester
Schooner	*Vernon*	1857	97	Thos. Ayer	Dorchester
Brigantine	*Victoria*	1865	228	Not Specified	Dorchester
Brigantine	*Village Belle*	1860	177	George Buck	Dorchester

Rig	Name	Year Built	Tonnage	Builder	Place
Schooner	*Vista*	1872	132	R.A. Chapman	Rockland
Schooner	*W.K. Chapman*	1864	131	James Chambers	Dorchester
Ship	*Welsford*	1856	1292	McMorran and Dunn	Dorchester
Barque	*William Cochran*	1879	1157	Wm. Hickman	Dorchester
Barque	*Wm. K. Chapman*	1878	1077	Wm. Hickman	Dorchester
Brigantine	*Young Dorchester*	1856	211	Gideon Palmer (Probable)	Dorchester

Some records have listed several additional vessels all built in Dorchester. These have not been found in the registries but since most were launched in the early shipbuilding years they are included:

Rig	Name	Year Built	Tonnage	Builder
Schooner	*Dorchester*	1824	?	A. Weldon and Wm. Sayre
Schooner	*Emperor*	1857	19	Frank Coleman
Schooner	*Hope*	Before 1808	Approx. 70	Elijah Ayer Jr.
Schooner	*Jane*	About 1820	?	Crane and Turner
Schooner	*Margaret*	1848	19	J. Kinnear
Schooner	*Mary*	1836	68	Roderick McNeil

Dorchester, N.B. Streetscape Circa 1890. Courtesy Mount Allison University Archives, Westmorland Historical Society

In the last two decades of the nineteenth century, Dorchester's bright years of prosperity began to dim. By the mid-1880s the shipbuilding industry was nearing its end and nothing appeared to take its place. The economic inpetus had shifted to Moncton with its railway shops and other industry. Incorporated as a city in 1890 with a population of 8,740, Moncton was now the industrial and commercial centre for southeastern New Brunswick.

At the turn of the century only three lawyers were practicing in Dorchester and most of the lawyers working at the courthouse commuted from Moncton or Saint John. And, like Canning, many of the younger people were drifting away to find work — to the 'Boston States,' out west or elsewhere in the Maritimes.

Activity on the island was centred around the government wharf and coastal shipping remained for several more years. In 1906 thirty-three vessels cleared the island and among their cargoes were nearly six million feet of deals. However, during the first World War when steel was in short supply, the railway to the wharf was taken up and by 1918 no one lived on the island.

Politically two more of Dorchester's sons would follow in the footsteps of Chandler and Smith. Daniel Hanington was New Brunswick's premier in 1882-83 and had as his provincial Secretary Pierre Landry. Henry R. Emmerson was premier from 1897 to 1900 before moving to the federal cabinet. His son, also H.R., was a member of the House of Commons and was later appointed to the Senate. He served on the committee with the daunting task of selecting a new Canadian flag.

Unlike Canning, Dorchester's population did not suffer a major decline. But it moved. When the penitentiary, schools and a few businesses were the only sources of employment left, local residents travelled to Moncton or other nearby centres to work and to shop.

Dorchester's great years are remembered today by its few large houses, its historical collection and by its fading memories. But it was a village that carved an important niche in the history of these Maritime provinces.

Acacia Villa School

In July 1852 one of the more remarkable educational institutions ever founded in Maritime Canada opened its doors. Situated at Hortonville on the shores of Nova Scotia's Minas Basin, this residential school would list among its students and teachers a number

Acacia Villa School, early years of twentieth century. Courtesy Acadia University Archives

destined to become outstanding Canadians in their chosen fields of endeavor.

Acacia Villa School, first called the Lower Horton Seminary, began when the era of square-rigged vessels was nearing its peak, when sea captains often took their wives to sea with them and enrolled their sons in private schools. It was a time when much of the province's population lived in rural areas and if farmers' sons were needed at home during the planting, growing and harvesting seasons, they could be sent off to school during the winter months. And, it was a time when the responsibility for the education of children rested more with the parents than with government.

The school was founded during the so-called Age of Enlightenment in Nova Scotia by Dr. Joseph R.

117

Hea. Free schools were instituted, at least to some degree. Public libraries were being established and debating societies were popular. A provincial superintendent of education, Sir William Dawson, was appointed and a Normal School for the training of teachers began operations. Acacia Villa was in the vanguard of the awakening and it was a superior school for the times.

In its first years the school offered residential accommodation for up to twenty boys. It advertised, "A thorough training in the Greek, Latin and French languages with elementary courses in German, Spanish and Hebrew, if desired." Special attention was placed on English and exercises in composition and declamation were required each week in addition to sessions in miscellaneous reading under the direction of Dr. Hea.

After the school's first year of operation, in the spring of 1853, Dr. Hea published a circular which included the following items of information:

1. The Seminary is conducted by Joseph R. Hea, a graduate of King's College, Fredericton, and late Professor of the French, Latin and Greek languages in Sackville Academy, with which he has been connected from its first opening until 1852.

2. Appreciating the great anxieties of parents in reference to their children at school, the social and moral habits of the pupils have the utmost care and watchfulness of the heads of the establishment, while moral and religious instruction forms an important part of the educational training to which each individual is subjected.

3. There are two terms in the year commencing

15th January and 15th July. The intermediate quarters commence 1st April and 1st October. It is desirable that pupils should enter on the first day of the term or quarter, if possible.

4. There are two vacations of a month each, commencing 15th June and 15th December.
5. Books, stationery, etc. can be obtained at the Seminary.
6. <u>Terms</u>

   For board and tuition in the ordinary branches of an English education, £7-10-0 per quarter. Extra charges for higher branches, not to exceed, in all, £1-5-0 per quarter. French, on the Ollendorf method £1-0-0 per quarter.
7. The aim of the plan of instruction marked out is to give a thorough scholastic training to a limited number, who are instructed in every branch by the proprietor himself. A collegiate education is not aimed at; but it is designed to give a thorough preparation for the active business and social position of the country we live in, while the pupil is still surrounded by the guards and comforts of the domestic circle.

In these early years life at the school was spartan. Four or more boys slept to a room. One hot air furnace more or less heated the whole building and the only hot water available was in the basement where four bath tubs were located. On Saturday nights the study period was regularly interrupted by a teacher calling out the names of the next four boys who were to proceed to the basement for their weekly bath. On the second floor, where the dormitory rooms were situated, one pump which brought up water from a tank in the basement, served the student body. Each boy would fill the big pitcher from the commode in his room with cold water, wash in the basin in his room and throw the slops out of the window.

In 1860 Dr. Hea was appointed President of the University of New Brunswick. The school was purchased by Arthur McNutt Patterson who so dominated the school and its personnel over the next forty-seven years that it was commonly known as 'The Patterson School.'

Arthur McN. Patterson, a native of Aylesford, N.S., had graduated from Mount Allison University and later, in 1872, would be granted a Master of Arts degree from the same institution. He had taught at Horton Academy and later at Sackville Academy, an affiliate of Mount Allison. Patterson's first wife was Margaret Ann Allison and when she died in 1867 he married her sister Nancy. Both were nieces of Charles Frederick Allison, the founder of Mount Allison University.

Under Patterson discipline was all-pervading at the school. If there is evidence that unmanageable boys were sent to Acacia Villa, there is also evidence that they learned to behave while there. They had little choice. One story handed down concerned two boys who ran away from the school and were picked up by police in Windsor, some fourteen miles away. Upon being notified, Patterson went for the two in a horse and carriage, tied ropes around their necks and made them walk home behind the carriage. If the story lacks definite verification there is no doubt that Patterson was a strict, even harsh, disciplinarian.

Yet his administration formed a curious dichotomy. If a boy felt pain from a brass-edged ruler during the day, that evening he might be listening with close attention to Mrs. Patterson as she read adventure stories to the boys. If a young man caught

120

chewing tobacco received a blow to the side of the head in the afternoon, that same young man would be quietly attending prayers in the evening. Parents were advised not to send their boys pastries, cakes or other treats and to send little pocket money. They were also instructed not to visit the school. There were to be no outside influences present.

Dr. Frank Parker Day in his book, *The Autobiography Of A Fisherman*, recalled something of his experiences as a young teacher at Acacia Villa:

> I was seventeen and ready to enter my sophomore year in the university, but as I could not go on until I had some money, I got a position as under master in the dreariest of boarding schools at a salary of one hundred and fifty dollars a year with board and lodging. At this school, which was well run by a heavy-handed, old-fashioned schoolmaster, were gathered boys who were backward or unmanageable at home; some were feebleminded and obscene, others downright rowdies. Corporal punishment was the order of the day. I used to teach all day and have charge of study hours and a dormitory every other night. The boys in my dormitory, many of whom were older and stronger than I, had to be in bed and quiet by nine o'clock. Of course, there was a scuffle nearly every night, and it was hell, simply hell for me. To console myself I used to reason thus: "Well, I've stood it for five weeks, therefore I can endure it for thirty more." In my narrow room that was miserably heated, I kept up hope and courage by thinking of trout streams and still-waters and by recalling every detail of some happy fishing excursion. I used to

121

say to myself: "This will make me tough anyway. I need never be afraid of anything in the future, for I shall never endure anything more unpleasant or irksome than this." That was a sound conjecture; the war was not half so soul-degrading.

This was the same Frank Parker Day who would later become a champion heavyweight boxer at Oxford, command the famed 185th Battalion during World War I, author several books and be a college president.

In contrast to Day's recollections, many of the boys took with them more pleasant memories of their stay at Acacia Villa. They remembered playing hockey on the frozen swamp, stealing apples from nearby orchards, saving Asepto soap wrappers to get box cameras as premiums, marching in a body to the Methodist Church in Grand Pré every Sunday and sitting in the front pews on either side, having rugby games and knowing in advance every item of food that would be served at the table three times a day year in and year out. They remembered too frequent fist fights behind the barn when a teacher invariably got wind of it and made sure the combatants shook hands after the battle.

The daily schedule accounted for every minute and in 1908-09 it was:

7:00	Rising Bell
7:30	Breakfast. Morning Prayers
8:15	Physical Drill
8:45	Preparatory Bell
9:00	Morning School
12:00	Dinner
1:00	Afternoon School

3:30   Recreation, Games, etc.
5:30   Evening Meal
6:00   Study
8:00   Close Junior Study. Evening Prayers
8:45   Close Senior Study
9:00   Junior Lights Out
9:45   Senior Lights Out

The study period was supervised by a teacher and each Friday evening was devoted to letter writing. It is not known if there was any form of censorship.

Prior to 1905 there is no mention of girls attending the school but from that year on they were admitted and took an active part in the life of the institution.

During the earlier part of the twentieth century the school year at Acacia Villa was divided into four quarters, the first two of seven weeks' duration each and the last two of ten weeks' each. Classes began in late August and concluded with closing exercises near the end of May.

In 1897 every pupil was requested to bring a Bible, three suits of clothes, four day shirts and two night shirts, two pairs of boots and one pair of slippers, an umbrella, rubbers, waterproof coat, hair brush and comb, shoe brush and blacking. In 1908 the following additions were listed: overcoat, warm gloves or mittens, tooth brush, two bath towels, one laundry bag, napkin ring, one sweater and a pair of gymnasium shoes.

By 1907-08 three different curricula were offered: matriculation, general education and business. Reading, penmanship, spelling and letter writing were compulsory in all courses and for every student. In addition two other courses were offered: shorthand and typing, and music.

Despite his academic demands, Patterson saw to it that extra-curricular activities were provided. The Acacia Villa Literary Society met every second week with debates, readings and music programs. Sports were emphasized and skating, hockey, basketball, soccer, cricket and baseball were the popular activities. Then students were taken on rides to nearby Evangeline Beach, to Wolfville and other surrounding centres. Concerts were staged from time to time and parties involving games, music and refreshments were regularly mentioned for the school prided itself on being a 'Family School.'

When Patterson bought the school in 1860, it consisted of two buildings, the Old Cottage and the Commercial Building. The upper floor of the Old Cottage contained dormitory rooms, five or six beds to a room, for the younger boys. On the ground floor were more bedrooms, the parlors and the dining room. The Commercial Building had two large classrooms.

In 1891 a larger building was constructed. Its third floor was an assembly hall accommodating up to 300 people. The second floor consisted of dormitory rooms with single and double beds while the first floor contained two large classrooms connected by folding doors. These doors were opened for the evening study periods. The whole structure was heated by hot air from a furnace in the basement and students later recalled that there were many cold and drafty areas in the dead of winter. Also in the basement was the bathroom with its four tubs.

Two years later, in 1893, another building was purchased to provide dormitory facilities for twelve to fifteen boys and a teacher. In 1900 a building was erected to house the library, reading, music and typewriting rooms and the school hospital. Then, too, the school could boast of a science laboratory, a sports field and a gymnasium measuring sixty feet by thirty feet.

Living and tuition costs gradually increased over the years. If it cost parents $144 to send their son to the school for the year in 1865, the fee had increased to $166 by 1897-98 and to $255 for the 1917-18 academic year. In each instance there were small additional costs for such courses as music, typewriting and special language training.

Arthur McNutt Patterson was a burly figure with a flowing beard and the physical strength to meet all demands. He could be tough, at least once throwing an unruly young man through a window, sash and all to a twelve foot drop to the ground. Yet those who remembered him agreed that he was fair and just

Acacia Villa was a school which would accept the social misfits of the times. Slow learners were encouraged and stimulated. Good students proceeded at their own pace and sometimes became teachers at the school. The boys who were uncontrollable at home came to the school and learned proper behavior. Boys suffering from epilepsy or who possessed various physical infirmities were welcomed. Patterson offered individual attention and, in some ways, he was perhaps years ahead of his time.

When Arthur McNutt Patterson took over the school in 1860 there were twenty students and one teacher. By 1897-98, the enrollment had reached eighty-one, its peak year. After that the number began to slowly dwindle until only thirty-eight were registered in 1917-18. The once proud school had become obsolete. The population was becoming more urbanized, the old windships were fading from the seas and sea captains were no longer enrolling their sons. The public school system was becoming vastly improved and Acacia Villa with its kerosene lamps, drafty buildings and lack of running water had failed to move with the times. In 1920 it closed its doors for good. Today the buildings are all gone and only a cairn marks its place.

But if the name of Acacia Villa is fading from memory, the accomplishments of many of its students, graduates and teachers would contribute significantly to education, business and the professions, in Canada and beyond. A very few of these men include:

Ralph Bell —	Businessman, Philanthropist, Chancellor of Mount Allison University
Harold Bigclow —	For many years Professor of Chemistry at Mount Allison
Frederick Borden —	Minister of Militia in the Laurier Government
Robert Laird Borden —	Prime Minister of Canada in World War I
David Grey Davis —	First Professor of Education at Acadia; Principal, Nova Scotia Normal College
Frank Parker Day —	Rhodes Scholar, Soldier, Author, President of Union College, New York
Allister Fraser —	Lieutenant-Governor of Nova Scotia

Izaak Walton Killam — Businessman and Philanthropist

Frank Patterson — Historian and Judge in the Supreme Court of Nova Scotia

Lloyd Shaw — Prominent in Business

3.
Great Teams and Great Athletes

Far off I hear the rolling, roaring cheers.
They come to me from many yesterdays,
From record deeds that cross the fading years,
And light the landscape with their brilliant plays,
Great stars that knew their days in fame's
  bright sun.
I hear them tramping to oblivion.

Grantland Rice

While the history of the Fundy area and its rivers tells of pioneers clearing their lands, of shipmasters sailing vessels to far-off ports, of men and women marching off to wars and an emerging society taking form, there was another ingredient in the social fabric — sport.

Teams like the Yarmouth Gateways, St. Stephen-St. Croix, Saint John Beavers, Kentville Wildcats, Moncton Hawks, Windsor Maple Leafs, Amherst Ramblers and Truro Bearcats have, in their time, filled many a headline. The Acadia and Mount Allison university teams and athletes have earned their share of championships in both men's and women's intercollegiate competitions.

Perhaps the first time that world attention was directed to these provinces in a sport's sense was in 1867, the year of Canada's birth as a nation. Four Saint John oarsmen, George Price, Robert Fulton,

Elijah Ross and Samuel Hutton travelled to Paris where they won the world title in the four-oared race. Although they won major international races before and after this event, it was the 1867 championship which gave them their enduring name, 'The Paris Crew.' Nearly a century later, in 1951, a Nova Scotia curling rink led by skip Don Oyler of Kentville won the MacDonald Brier emblematic of Canadian men's curling supremacy when, for the first time, a rink went through the entire Brier without a loss.

While sport in its various forms goes back to the days of early settlement, it was the period between the two world wars when, arguably, sport had its greatest impact at the community level. Through the boom years of the 1920s and the depression-ridden '30s sport thrived. Television had not come into being, cars and roads did not attract a great amount of travel and that young instrument radio enhanced rather than competed with sports events. It was a time when grandstands were filled and rinks were crowded for regular games let alone play-offs. It was also a time when the Allan Cup, the symbol of Canadian championship in senior amateur hockey, ranked, at worst, a close second to the Stanley Cup.

Among the innumerable teams competing in various sports in these years, three are deserving of special mention: one for its indomitable spirit, one for its longevity at the top of its sport and one for establishing two noteworthy records.

The Truro Bearcats have had a long and brilliant record in both hockey and baseball. One of the more remarkable chapters in the team's history was written by the 1930-31 hockey edition as it embarked in pursuit of the Allan Cup. Before the campaign was over the team would be indelibly dubbed 'The Seven Survivors.'

Truro Bearcats hockey team, 1931. Left to right: Leo Sargent, Goalie; Frank Lavigne, "Flying Frenchman"; Pete Mill, Captain; Sammy Murdock, "Foxy"; Charles Jemmett, "Chuck"; Carson Ryan, "Tubby"; Ollie Proulx; Reg Shields; Avard Mann, Manager; Owen Lennon; Jack Seaman, Trainer.
Courtesy Nova Scotia Sport Heritage Centre

The Bearcats had earned an enviable record in the late 1920s winning the Maritime senior hockey title in 1925-26, 1927-28, 1929-30 and 1930-31. Their reign was interrupted in 1926-27 by the Kentville Wildcats, led by the durable Waldon Kennedy who played senior hockey for some twenty-five years, and in 1928-29 by the Bathurst Papermakers.

Even in the stark depression years not all players on senior teams were local products. The 1930-31 Bearcats line-up was: Goal — Leo Sargent, Ontario; Defence — Frankie Lavigne, Ontario, Pete Mill, Truro and Avard Mann, Port Elgin, N.B.; Forwards — Reg Shields, Ontario, Ollie Proulx, Ontario, Tubby Ryan,

130

Truro, Chuck Jemmett, New York and Owen Lennon and Sammy Murdock of New Glasgow.

The team played in the old Eastern League with New Glasgow, Kentville and Halifax. Truro won the league title in the spring of 1931, then calamity struck. The Canadian Amateur Hockey Association decreed that Sargent, Shields and Jemmett had violated the Association's residence rule and were ineligible for further play-off competition. Undaunted the remnants of the team decided to continue anyway. An intermediate goalie, Earl Wright, was picked up and the Bearcats went on the play-off trail. Lunenburg and Amherst fell before the undermanned team but the Amherst series marked the end of the play-offs for Avard Mann. When the Truro squad met a strong McGill University team in a two-game, total goal series it had one substitute on the bench.

The first game was played in the Halifax Forum before a lively crowd of 6,000. McGill won 2-1 despite being outshot by the Truro squad 43-20. The second game was played in Moncton and led by the magnificent work of goalie Wright the Bearcats stormed back to win 4-2 and take the series in total goals 5-4. It was then that the team was given the sobriquet 'The Seven Survivors.'

Truro moved on to Toronto to meet the Hamilton Tiger Cats in the Eastern Canadian finals and a young broadcaster named Foster Hewitt would broadcast the series. It was anti-climactic. Hamilton won both games handily 6-2 and 5-1. The Bearcats had simply run out of steam but the plucky Seven Survivors had earned a lasting niche in the annals of Maritime sport.

At the other end of the Bay of Fundy another team in another sport was beginning its own dynasty, the St. Stephen baseball team. Playing under the names Mohawks, Kiwanis, and St. Croix, the team dominated New Brunswick and Maritime senior baseball throughout the 1930s. Beginning in 1931 St. Stephen won nine consecutive New Brunswick championships and seven Maritime titles. The team's maritime domination through the decade was interrupted in 1935 by the smooth fielding Yarmouth Gateways and ended in 1939, first by a great team of Liverpool Larrupers led by the Seaman brothers — Dan, Kal, Garnet and Ike and then by the second World War.

The St. Stephen teams in those years were coached by Arthur Middlemiss, Aubrey (Baldy) Moffatt and Orville Mitchell. The players included Lefty Brownell, Ken Kallenburg, Jim Morrell, Charlie Godfrey, Artie Lowe, Phil McCarroll, Rainnie Moffatt and Gordon Coffey. It was with good reason that the St. Stephen senior baseball teams of the 1931-39 period were inducted into the New Brunswick Sports Hall of Fame in 1971. Seldom, if ever, has a Maritime team in any sport compiled a comparable record.

Early in the reign of the St. Stephen baseball teams, a hockey team was assembled some 160 miles to the east, the Moncton Hawks. The Hawks could be the first team to bring the coveted Allan Cup to the Maritimes and the only Canadian team to win the cup in two successive years.

In 1932-33 the team roster was: Goal — Jimmy Foster; Defence — Bill Gill, Len Burridge and Bill Walker; Forwards — Duke McDonald, Dud James, Bill Miller, Frankie LeBlanc, Sammy McManus, Aubrey Webster, Bert Connolly, Knucker Irvine and Monty Muckle. In reserve was Ed Kervin.

The following year the team was virtually unchanged except Daddy Bubar was signed as the

132

back-up goalie. Bubar went on to star for the Halifax Wolverines when that team won the Allan Cup in 1935, the last Maritime team to capture the trophy. The Moncton team was composed of players from across the country, a country by now immersed in the worst depression the world had known, but it brought cheer to the thousands of fans who avidly followed its exploits.

In 1932-33 the Hawks played in the strong Big Three league along with the Charlottetown Abegweits and the Halifax Wolverines. The Hawks won the league championship then defeated the Saint John Beavers for the right to represent the Maritimes in the Allan Cup playdowns. The Montreal Royals came to Moncton only to fall easily to the Hawks in a two-game, total goal series. The Hawks then travelled to Maple Leaf Gardens in Toronto where they eliminated the Niagara Falls Cataracts in two straight games. Finally the team made the long train trip to Vancouver. There they blanked the Saskatoon Quakers in straight games 3-0 and 2-0 to gain possession of the Canadian amateur senior hockey championship and the Allan Cup.

The scene which greeted the team's arrival back in Moncton on April 21, 1933 can only be imagined. Thousands of fans were at the C.N. station and thousands more lined the parade route as the players were borne by a ladder truck through the business district and on to the Moncton Stadium where 4,000 attended a civic reception. The times were hard but Moncton was in its glory.

The following year the Hawks were again to make history. This time they played the Halifax Wolverines for the Maritime title and won in three straight games before sell-out crowds at the Moncton Stadium. The Wolverines were a powerful team featuring players

Moncton Hawks hockey team 1932-33. From top centre,
clockwise: Jimmy Foster, Bill Gill, Bill Walker, Aubrey Webster,
Knucker Irvine, Bert Connolly, Frankie LeBlanc, Jigger Smith —
Trainer, Monty Muckle, Sammy McManus, Duke McDonald,
Dud James, Bill Miller, Len Burrage. Inset: left, Percy Nicklin —
Coach; right, Ambrose Wheeler, Manager.
Courtesy Moncton Museum

like Bill Cowley, a future Boston Bruins star, Frankie
Graham, Vince Ferguson, Ernie Mosher, Chummy
Lawlor and Owen Lennon who would form the team's
nucleus in 1935 when it won the Allan Cup.

The Hawks were then required to take on the
Mount Allison University team, a team that was given
absolutely no chance. The first game followed the
script as Moncton rolled over the university team 10-

1. However, in the second game, the Hawks undoubtedly carrying the burden of supreme over-confidence, were held to a 2-2 tie although easily winning the two-game, total goal series. Moncton went on to eliminate the McGill University Red Raiders and the Hamilton Tiger Cats before meeting Fort William in the Allan Cup final. Fort William shut out the Hawks 2-0 in the first game but Moncton came back to win the next two 4-2 and 5-1. The team had won the Canadian championship for the second straight year.

Before returning home the Moncton Hawks made a side trip to play the Detroit White Stars for something called the North American Amateur Championship. The New Brunswick team dropped the first game 2-1 but captured the next two 4-1 and 13-3. Thus the players came home with both the Canadian and North American titles in their possession.

The scene which greeted the Hawks when they arrived in Moncton on April 13, 1934 was one of jubilant bedlam. An estimated 15,000 braved heavy rain and crowded around the station and stood along the parade route to the Stadium. Inside another 4,000 watched and listened as Mayor C.H. Blakeny delivered an address of welcome and the Allan Cup was presented to Captain Dud James. The players were presented medals by the Canadian Amateur Hockey Association, signet rings from the City of Moncton and suede windbreakers from the city's citizens. Thus ended the two-year championship campaign by a great senior hockey team.

Over the years the region has produced some great individual athletes. One of the earlier stars was Fred Cameron of Advocate, N.S. who won the Boston Marathon in 1910 and who was greeted by 5,000 admirers when he stepped off the train at Amherst after his victory. Moncton's Gordon Drillon, who remains the last Toronto Maple Leaf to win the National Hockey League scoring championship, was also a top-notch softball pitcher. Amherst produced Jimmy Gray who starred in university sports as well as in amateur baseball and hockey. Mary Ellen Driscoll of Rothesay has been among the top-ranked lady golfers in Canada for many years. These are just a few of the many top athletes who have come from the Fundy region.

But two athletes are worthy of special mention. They came from opposite sides of the Bay of Fundy. One achieved greatness in the shadowy, brutal world of professional boxing in the early years of this century. The other was a world champion in a vastly different sport, speedskating. These are their stories.

Sam Langford — Nova Scotia's Uncrowned World Champion

There were many superlatives written about Sam Langford, the boxer. The Canadian Press once named him the "fighter of the half century." Nat Fleischer, long-time editor of *Ring Magazine* and perhaps the foremost authority on boxing, ranked Langford the seventh best heavyweight in boxing history although he never fought for the world heavyweight championship. Grantland Rice, long the dean of American sports writers, called him the best fighting man he had ever seen and Joe Williams, a veteran boxing reporter described Langford as the best fighter the ring ever saw. Hype Igoe, possibly the most respected boxing writer of them all, wrote in the old *New York Journal*, "Langford is the greatest fighter, pound for pound, who ever lived."

Sam Langford was born in Weymouth, Nova

Scotia, the great-grandson of William Langford, a slave who escaped from the southern United States during the Revolutionary War. Sam's father, also William, worked in sawmills and while short and stocky was known for his strength and endurance. There is some uncertainty about the date of Sam's birth. Some place it as March 4, 1886 while others claim he was born in 1883. It is known, however, that he left home at an early age. One account says that at the age of eleven he was an ox driver for a Digby log hauler. For this work he received free room and board and one dollar a week in cash. A few years later he rode the rails to Boston where he soon found work washing glasses and cleaning up in a saloon. One day a customer came in and ordered three glasses of beer. Sam happened to be behind the bar and the customer, perhaps trying to take advantage of the youth, attempted to leave without paying the fifteen cent bill. A fight ensued, young Sam thrashed his man and retrieved the fifteen cents. The marvelling saloon owner who had come on the scene promptly steered Sam into boxing.

The early years of the twentieth century were difficult times for a black boxer. Racism was rampant and Langford was often forced to go easy with white opponents who were not good enough to carry his gloves, just to get fights. When the black Jack Johnson reigned as heavyweight champion from 1908 until 1915 there was a constant search for a white hope. One reason Langford could never meet Johnson in a title match was the expressed opinion that two blacks fighting for the title would never attract a paying gate. Then during much of Langford's career boxing remained illegal in many places and matches often took the form of undercover operations with small crowds and

Boxer Sam Langford. Courtesy Nova Scotia Sport Heritage Centre

smaller purses for the combatants. It was 1920 before New York set up a state boxing commission and began to bring some order into the sport.

Just how many professional fights Langford had in a career spanning more than twenty years is not known. Some estimates place it between 250 and 642. Sam said he fought "between 500 and 600 times." He was known to fight two and three times a night in various rings around Boston early in his career but, at best, records were not carefully maintained in those days.

Sam Langford stood just 5'6" in height and ring observers of the time agreed that his best fighting weight was about 172 pounds. Until he reached full growth and campaigned as a heavyweight, he fought in all classes from featherweight through light-heavyweight and as a heavyweight he frequently took on opponents up to ten inches taller and sixty pounds heavier.

Langford made his recorded debut in professional boxing in a fight for which he received a watch, and promptly pawned it for thirty dollars. During his first two years it is said he had forty-five fights. At the age of seventeen he defeated the great Joe Gans, the lightweight champion of the world, only to be refused the title because ring officials ruled he was eight ounces over the weight limit. It was just the first of many disappointments and roadblocks Langford would come to know in his long career.

In 1903 Langford fought a twelve-round draw with Jack Blackburn, rated one of the most scientific boxers in the world. The two would fight four times in the next two years with one being a no-decision bout and Langford winning the rest. Blackburn went on to be the teacher of Joe Louis who many rank among the greatest heavyweight champions of all time.

The former Nova Scotian's one encounter with Jack Johnson came in 1906, two years before Johnson won the heavyweight title. At the time Sam weighed 146 pounds and Johnson came in at 185. While Langford officially lost the fifteen round decision, most ring authorities present said that he was the clear winner. Suffice to say that never again would Johnson accept his challenges. Once the two met in the sports department of the *Boston Globe* and

Johnson agreed to a fight if Langford would put up $10,000. The next morning Sam and his manager returned to close the deal but Johnson never showed up.

The following year Langford knocked out Tiger Smith, the Welsh-born middleweight champion of the world, in the fourth round. It was a non-title fight for a purse of $2,000, just one of the several times he fought world champions but never when the title was at stake.

In 1910 Sam Langford had another bout with a world champion. He fought a six-round, no-decision battle with Stanley Ketchell, the reigning middleweight king, for a purse of $300. Sam was told by his manager to go easy in the hope that the scrap would lead to a title fight. According to contemporary records Langford won the first three rounds and was content to simply block punches for the rest of the fight. Six months later Ketchell was shot and killed.

The story of Langford's ring career is filled with multiple fights against the same opponent. This was the only way the Boston Tarbaby, as he was often called, could get fights and make some money. Many of his most brutal and memorable battles were against three other blacks — Harry Wills who outweighed him by fifty pounds and was seven inches taller, Joe Jeanette who fought at 205 pounds and the smaller Sam McVey who weighed in around 195 pounds. Just how many times he fought each is somewhat uncertain but he probably fought Jeanette fourteen times and McVey fifteen times, losing only twice to each man. Most of these fights took place between 1905 and 1920.

The battles between Langford and Wills were particularly ferocious. In all the two met between fifteen and eighteen times in the years 1914 through

1922 although some insist they fought twenty-three times. In one fight Langford was knocked down four times in the first round but came back and knocked Wills out in the eighth round. In another bout Langford K.O.'d Wills in the nineteenth round but only after he had been floored nine times in the first two rounds. The rules were much more lenient in those days regarding the stoppage of fights. Most records indicate that the much larger Wills won eight of their battles, Langford two and the rest were no-decisions.

Against some of his lesser opponents Langford would often name the moment of the knockout. Then there was a match with a fighter named Jim Flynn. A journalist by the name of H.M. Walker had written something which Sam did not appreciate and that night Walker was seated at ringside. During the course of the fight Langford maneuvered Flynn into position and as he knocked Flynn out of the ring and on to the lap of the astonished Walker, Langford called out, "Mr. Walker, here comes your champion."

Sam Langford travelled the world in search of fights and curiously most of the fighters he met were Americans. He defeated Jim Barry of Chicago twice in Australia and in England he knocked out Patrick Curran, another American. Langford only fought once in his native Canada. In 1921 he knocked out the Australian Peter Jackson in Toronto.

Another giant with whom Langford tangled on two occasions was Freddie Fulton who stood 6'5" and weighed 227 pounds. In 1917 the two met and Langford suffered an injury which resulted in the loss of sight in his left eye. His longtime manager, Joe Woodman, begged him to quit and when Sam refused, Woodman left him. Langford then developed a cataract in his right eye and still he continued to fight under a succession of managers. When he fought for the Mexican Championship he was nearly blind and it is reported that he talked to his opponent and when the opponent answered, Langford struck. If talking did not work he struck at the sound of his opponent's feet. Langford won the fight but his great days were over. Later two operations brought back partial sight until 1942, but then he was blind for the rest of his life.

Sam Langford's official career was between 1902 and 1924 and Nat Fleischer always maintained his best years were between 1912 and 1915. He was forty or more when he finally retired and if he is only credited officially with 252 professional fights, it is certain he had many more, probably hundreds more. If he was never given the chance to fight for the world heavyweight championship, he did hold the English, Spanish and Mexican titles. In his whole career Langford probably earned about $300,000, an immense sum when, for instance, in 1914 tailored suits cost twenty-two dollars, eggs were about twenty cents a dozen and newspapers cost a penny. But Sam, like many boxers who came before and after him enjoyed the good life. He sported a gold tooth, smoked quality cigars and lived well. He loved making money and spending money and shortly after his career was over he was penniless.

In the 1930s he returned to Nova Scotia and toured with the Bill Lynch Shows. It was simply an act to put a former great boxer on display, an act where he would take on all comers for a few dollars. During the Second World War Langford was on relief. A sports writer for a New York newspaper found him living in a Harlem tenement and initiated a financial drive on his behalf. Among the contributors were Jack Dempsay and Fritzie Zivic, both former world champions, and band leader Count Basie. The resulting fund of over $10,000 gave Langford a monthly income of just under fifty dollars a month. In 1952 Gene Tunney, another former champion, and others added enough to give Langford a monthly pension of slightly more than one hundred dollars.

Sam Langford's last two years were spent in a rest home in Boston. Totally blind but wearing cheap, plastic spectacles, his favorite diversion was listening to the Wednesday night fights on the little radio he kept in his room. Always he was gentle, soft-spoken and completely without bitterness. The times he lived and fought in deprived him of a chance at what he wanted most, the heavyweight championship. His own doings brought him poverty at the end. Yet he was content. Sam Langford died on January 12, 1956 just weeks after being admitted to Boxing's Hall of Fame. He is also an honored member of the Canadian Sports Hall of Fame and the Hall of Fame in his native province, Nova Scotia.

This great-grandson of a slave who began fighting when barely into his teens and who continued to fight for well over two decades was indeed Nova Scotia's great uncrowned king of the ring.

Charles I. Gorman — Saint John's World Champion

In February 1940 when Charles Ingraham Gorman passed away at the relatively young age of forty-two, sportswriter H.J. Osborne penned this brief tribute to the speedskater in the *Saint John Telegraph-Journal:*

> When he quit competitive speedskating for good Charlie was looked on as a champion of champions.

The man who was often called 'the man with the million dollar legs' and 'the human dynamo' was born on July 6, 1897 in Saint John, the son of William J. and Mary Ann (Ingraham) Gorman. If the family had previously shown no particular athletic ability, young Charley was about to break the mold. He was on skates as soon as he could walk and he thought he took part in his first race at the age of ten. It is certain that he never forgot the sound of his first starter's gun.

Gorman's early start in speedskating was undoubtedly influenced by the popularity of the sport in Saint John. It began in the 1850s and climaxed with Gorman's triumphs in the 1920s. The centres for North American speedskating at the time revolved around Saint John, Newburgh, Pennsylvania and Minneapolis. By the time young Gorman came along the sport clearly had a rich heritage in the city, particularly in its north end. In the 1870s and early 1880s prominent Saint John skaters included G. Wilford Campbell, Reginald Bayard, Walter and J. Twining Hartt, George B. Hogan, Arthur Magee and Charles and Arthur Coster. Then there were Charles and William Whelpley who learned to skate near their home on the St. John River's Long Reach.

By the early 1880s William Whelpley was the local champion but around 1884 an unknown country boy came along, Hugh McCormick, who upset Whelpley. In 1890 McCormick travelled to Minneapolis and defeated Alex Paulson, an outstanding Norwegian skater who had held the world professional title for eight years. McCormick went on to win fifty-five of sixty major races in his career and was Saint John's first world champion in the sport.

In the early years of the twentieth century other young Saint John skaters made their mark. Fred

144

Charles Gorman, Saint John's World Speedskating Champion.
Courtesy New Brunswick Museum

Logan began competitive skating in 1896 and reigned as Maritime champion from 1907 to 1911. In 1907, his peak year, Logan won the North American Championship at Saranac Wood, New York. Another fine skater was Hilton Belyea, an outstanding oarsman, who once defeated the United States skating champion, Bobby MacLean, in a match race in Saint John.

It was into this kind of setting that Charles Gorman began his speedskating career and he began with a total dedication of purpose that stayed with him throughout his competitive years. Gorman cycled constantly to build up his legs and in his prime was described as "a muscular young man of about 185 to 190 pounds with powerful legs and possessed of extraordinary coordination and lightning reflexes." He had something else too, a competitive fire that burns in the heart of champions. Second place was never good enough.

While he was still in his teens young Charley won the Maritime Senior Speedskating Championship. Seemingly he was on his way but dark clouds gathered on the horizon. The first World War began and soon the skater enlisted in the 104th Battalion. It was while in the army that Gorman displayed his superlative abilities as an all-round athlete. He boxed, competed in track and field, the 100-yard dash being his favorite event, and played baseball, sometimes as an infielder and sometimes as a pitcher. Indeed after the war he received offers to play professional ball but turned them down in favor of his first love, speedskating.

In October 1915 Gorman was posted to the 140th Battalion and in September 1916 he went overseas. Trained as a machine gunner, Gorman went to France in April 1917 as a corporal with the Sixth

Brigade Machine Gun Company. He went through the bloody battles at Vimy Ridge and Hill 70, then on September 9, 1918, just two months before the Armistice, he was wounded twice in the right leg and foot. He received treatment in hospitals in France and England before returning to Canada for discharge in May 1919. But a piece of shrapnel remained undiscovered in his foot.

Charles Gorman returned to competitive skating in 1920 but for sometime his progress was slow, no doubt hampered in part by his war wound. However, in 1921 he tied for third place in the Canadian Outdoor Championships in Montreal and later that winter tied the world record for the 440 yards at Lake Placid, New York. The Lake Placid newspaper called it "the most spectacular finish ever witnessed in an ice skating contest on this continent."

The years 1922 and 1923 were not vintage Gorman years. Yet in preparation for the 1923 season Gorman and a friend and fellow skater, Ray Lawson, had retreated to a lake deep in the New Brunswick woods where they spent a month skating day in and day out. It did him little good. In a meet at Newburgh a skate cut eliminated him from further action in the meet and later, at a Lake Placid meet, his wounded foot began to swell and fester. A doctor found and removed the undiscovered piece of shrapnel. To end his rather undistinguished season Gorman returned to Saint John where he was defeated by three Americans in a meet on Lily Lake.

The 1924 Winter Olympics were scheduled for Chamonix, France, and Gorman was selected for the Canadian team. The government, however, refused to allow him to go to the Games' site early so he did not don skates until the day of his first event. He failed to win a medal in the 500 metres and was equally unsuccessful in the 5,000 metre event. At this point in his career Gorman was still inexperienced in the tactics used by European speedskaters and because of his combative style, he had to deal with more than the usual amount of blocking and interference by his opponents. It was a problem the aggressive Gorman continually faced. But Chamonix marked a turning point in his career. Since returning to competition following the war his competitive story was one of numerous disappointments interrupted by occasional flashes of success. Now his star began to rise in earnest.

Returning home from the Olympics Charley Gorman proceeded to the United States National Outdoor Championship at Lake Saranac, New York where he set a world record for the 440 yards. Later he won a meet at Lake Placid and that spring tied a world indoor record at the U.S. Nationals in Pittsburgh. Then the following year he set a new world indoor time for the 440 yards at the Victoria Rink in Saint John, a rink built in 1863 and described as a "great domed edifice with attractive lighting and a raised platform on which a band played waltzes during regular skating sessions."

In 1926 Gorman won general acknowledgement as the world's top speedskater when he won the world championship over five miles at Lily Lake, Saint John by defeating Clas Thunberg of Finland in a blinding snowstorm before a crowd of almost 20,000.

That victory set the stage for 1927, Gorman's greatest year. In January and February he skated in five major competitions, two of them international, and won sixteen of the twenty-three races in which he competed. During the course of his epic year he set six world records: 200 yards indoors and outdoors, 1/6 mile indoors and outdoors, 440 yards indoors and outdoors and he tied the record for the outdoor 220 yards.

Gorman would skate competitively only one more year. In 1928 he was considered a solid choice for a gold medal at the Winter Olympics at St. Moritz but as in 1924 the medals eluded him and later that year he retired from competition.

Overall Charley Gorman's record in his chosen sport was spectacular. He set seven world records and accumulated 153 medals and trophies. Several of his records stood the test of time. When he died in 1940 four world records still bore his name and all were set between 1925 and 1927.

After retirement and making the difficult adjustment to life after competition, Gorman opened a service station at the corner of Portland and Main. The station was owned by a rising young businessman in Saint John, K.C. Irving, and later Gorman took a second Irving station. He managed both successfully and the two became fast friends.

By the late 1930s Gorman's health began to fail and he was diagnosed as having Hodgkin's Disease. He entered a private nursing home in St. Martins but was moved to St. Joseph's Hospital where he died on February 11, 1940, some five months short of his forty-third birthday. In time he would become a member of the Canadian Amateur Athletic Union Hall of Fame, the Canadian Sports Hall of Fame and the New Brunswick Sports Hall of Fame.

If Charles Ingraham Gorman was always known as an aggressive, combative skater by his opponents, there was another side to the man which was illustrated by an incident after his skating career was over. One day a young boy rushed into Gorman's service station and excitedly announced, "I've just got a job as a messenger with C.N." Gorman glanced at the boy's dilapidated bike, promptly went to the phone and ordered him a new one. The lad never forgot. For years on the anniversary of Charlie Gorman's death a memoriam appeared in a Saint John newspaper signed by the boy, Gregory Pierce. Mr. Pierce went on to work for Canadian National Telecommunications for nearly half a century.

As one contemporary sports writer once wrote, "Charley Gorman had no peer. He was the nonpareil."

4.
When Catastrophe Strikes

> The truly noble and resolved spirit raises itself and becomes more conspicuous in times of disaster and ill fortune.
>
> Plutarch

Catastrophe in its various forms is not unfamiliar with those who live near the sea. Vessels, fishing boats and men have been lost. In Yarmouth alone they numbered in the hundreds of vessels and hundreds of men. Gales and hurricanes along with resultant flooding have ravaged land and property and taken lives. There was the strange year of 1816, the year of no summer when frost and cold weather visited in every month and crops refused to grow.

Then there was fire, the scourge of towns and cities crowded with wooden buildings. In 1897 Windsor was devastated by a fire which levelled much of the town and caused an estimated $2 million in damage. Moncton was the scene of a fire in 1906 which burned over six acres of ground and destroyed the Intercolonial Railway Shops. It is unlikely, however, that any community during the last century suffered more from fire than Saint John. In all there were eight major conflagrations during the 1800s alone.

Two events illustrate this darker side of life. One, the Saxby Gale, is unique because it was predicted

151

so far in advance. The other, the Great Saint John Fire in 1877, portrays the havoc created by the start of a small blaze in a store.

Saxby's Great Gale

Countless storms and hurricanes have lashed the Bay of Fundy and its coastlines over the years but none has achieved the lasting notoriety of the Saxby Gale.

One of its more remarkable aspects was that the gale was forecast nearly a year in advance. Lieutenant James Saxby of the British Navy wrote the London press in November 1868:

> I now bet to state with regard to 1869 at 7:00 a.m., October 5, the Moon will be at the part of her orbit which is nearest the Earth. Her attraction, therefore, will be at its maximum force. At noon on the same day the Moon will be on the Earth's equator, a circumstance which never occurs without a marked atmospheric disturbance and at 2 p.m. of the same day lines drawn from the Earth's centre would cut the Sun and the Moon in the same arc of right ascension (the Moon's attraction and the Sun's attraction will therefore be acting in the same direction); in other words, the new Moon will be on the Earth's equator when in perigee, and nothing more threatening can, I say, occur without miracle. With your permission, I will, during September next (1869) for the safety of mariners, briefly remind your readers of this warning. In the meantime, there will be time for the repair of unsafe sea walls, and for the circulation of this notice throughout the world.

For several days before Saxby's predicted date, a warm southerly wind blew along the Bay of Fundy. Then a storm began to move up the eastern seaboard of the United States. It struck hard in Washington, D.C. with wind and rain, graveyards were washed away and coffins were seen floating down the city's Tiber Canal. In Philadelphia there was flooding and wind damage and in parts of New England roads and railways were washed out.

The storm reached the Bay of Fundy on October 4, one day early. The morning had dawned fine and warm but by afternoon the heat had become oppressive, the wind had turned squally and high water arrived unusually early. By evening the wind had reached hurricane force and was battering the length and breadth of Fundy Bay. All around the head of the bay the wind-driven rain fell in torrents, roads were flooded and bridges carried away. Coach travel was impossible, vessels were blown ashore and wrecked and wharves suffered extensive damage. One barn housing livestock was lifted up and deposited some 300 feet away. Haystacks and haybarns were swept out to sea and telegraph poles were blown down. At Great Village the residents claimed the tide reached the height of one hundred feet, more than twice its normal level. In some places homes had several feet of water over their second-story floors. It was two weeks before the lowlands drained and then the fields were left with a muddy brown mass from which arose an indescribable stench.

In Windsor, Water Street became a canal and there was seven feet of water in the Baptist Church. Homes and stores were flooded and stacks of lumber disappeared from wrecked wharves. The *Halifax Chronicle* of October 8, 1869 described some of the damage in the Windsor area:

> Windsor: About 11 o'clock Monday night four dykes at Poverty Point, near Smith Island, gave way, and ten minutes afterwards the lowlands for miles around were flooded, and their contents much damaged. ... Many cattle and sheep were drowned. Mr. P. Miles lost 34 sheep. The tide rose four feet higher than it was ever known before. ... At Falmouth and Newport the dykes were carried away and the land flooded. ...

One local resident described the Great Horton Dyke at Grand Pré:

> Our dyke is a monument of the skill, industry, enterprise and thoroughness of Acadian farmers. But once, in two centuries since they built it, has the 'turbulent tide' made a breach in the work and flooded the land. The 'Saxby Tide' in the autumn of 1869, made a clean sweep of it, carrying masses of it out bodily. The whole 3000 acres were flooded, cattle were drowned and 'Long Island' became an island in reality. The salt left on the land destroyed the crop of grass for three years.

The Tantramar Marsh between Amherst N.S. and Sackville N.B. received the full force of the storm. A mail carrier named Chesley and his passenger, Miss Huldah Bray, were crossing the marsh when the seas washed over the dykes. The wagon and passengers were carried a half-mile along the marsh. Chesley was seriously injured and Miss Bray was drowned. The *Amherst Gazette* portrayed the damage:

154

At half past 10 o'clock on Monday night the dykes overflowed. The water having gradually accumulated on the marshes to a depth of from one to two feet, a wave similar to a tidal bore swept up with a roaring noise and great velocity, carrying almost everything before it; stacks of hay, fences and in many cases well-filled barns succumbing to its power. Four men who went to Fort Lawrence creek to secure a schooner sought shelter from the wind in a barn. The tide rising, they abandoned the barn and took to a fence which extended from it to the upland, and by passing along which they hoped to be safe. The waves swept away the fence. Two of the men managed to reach some poles and save themselves. The others were drowned. An old man named Stewerd, belonging to Minudie, engaged in cutting grass at Minudie Point, was in the habit of spending his nights in a barn there. On the Terrific night, finding the barn afloat and breaking up, he succeeded in clinging to a passing haystack. After being for some time at the mercy of wind and tide, hope almost failed as he was being fast borne seaward, when his lifebuoy grounded on the top of the dyke, seemingly at the very brink of destruction. He was rescued by means of a boat on the following day. A horse which was in the barn was drowned.

A resident of Hopewell Hill in Albert County, New Brunswick, Mrs. Ann Eliza Rogers wrote in her diary:

October 5, 1869 — One of the worst storms that ever was known here was last night. The wind has been blowing for several days from the southeast. The tides very high, a regular tidal wave. It came up to the Upland, six feet higher than ever known before. Nearly all the barns and haystacks on the marsh were floated to the upland or taken out to sea. A great deal of damage done to the dykes. Several cattle drowned. It was just as bad at Hillsborough. The schooner 'Bessie' laying at the wharf was brought over the dyke some distance up the marsh. The bridges have been taken out over the River, Saw Mill Creek, Sodom Creek and Calkin's Creek.

Then in entries a few days later as more news came in:

October 11 — The people are drying their hay. There will be one-half lost.
October 13 — Hillsborough fared very bad. The railroads for both plaster and coal have been torn out.

Down the Bay of Fundy at Saint John there was devastation along the waterfront. Shingles and roofing were flying and seas swept over the wharves in the harbour. Vessels broke loose from their moorings and drove ashore. The lower floors in waterfront buildings were flooded and several warehouses were demolished. Shipyards suffered damage and fish weirs simply disappeared.

Thomas Earle, the lightkeeper of Beacon Light at the mouth of the harbour, attempted to leave when the storm first struck but he was driven back by the high seas. When the bottom floor of the lighthouse flooded and waves were washing over the top of the light, breaking windows and the protective globe

156

around the gas flame, Earle took refuge on the middle floor. But the now unprotected flame started a fire which threatened to engulf the lighthouse. Somehow Earle managed to locate a spare globe and set it in place before extinguishing the fire. The light continued to function and the lightkeeper saved himself and the structure.

The battery guarding the harbour mouth was flooded, its stockade wrecked and the earthenworks surrounding it were torn apart. One man living near the harbour was forced to leave his home at the height of the storm. When he returned he found his house sitting in the middle of the street.

And there was loss of life. Near Point Lepreaux the barque *Genii* was wrecked and eleven persons drowned. On Campobello Island over eighty buildings were destroyed while in St. George and St. Andrews the roofs of houses were blown off and the streets were strewn with rubble. The spire of the Episcopal Church in St. Stephen fell before the wind and the railway bridge in Milltown toppled into the falls below.

While the destruction went on all around Fundy, Halifax waited. Preparations were made for the storm's onslaught; anything moveable on the waterfront had been chained down or removed to safer places and mooring lines on vessels were doubled. But little of the storm reached the city and there was almost a plaintive note in the *Halifax Morning Chronicle* on the following day:

> The storm of Monday night was not a success in the city — did not come up to the expectations of the public.

The writer was not able to comment on the

damage suffered elsewhere as all the telegraph lines were down. But for many years all succeeding storms were measured by the force of the Saxby Gale, the storm that had been forecast a year in advance.

A City In Flames, Saint John, 1877

Wednesday, June 20, 1877 began as another hot, early summer day in Saint John. Stores, shipyards and businesses opened as usual and women went about their daily work in the homes. There was nothing to suggest that before the day was over many lives would be changed, some forever.

At 2:30 in the afternoon fire broke out in Joseph Fairweather's store at York Point in Portland. There was a strong wind blowing and, like all cities of the time, Saint John was filled with wooden buildings, close together and all dry as tinder. Within half an hour the city was burning in a dozen locations and before it was over nine hours later, about two-fifths of the city was laid waste. In all 1,612 houses were levelled leaving some 2,700 families and 16,000 people homeless. The fire ravaged the city's main downtown area and 600 businesses were burned out.

It was not a fire that spread in any kind of orderly fashion. The wind blew burning bits of wood in all directions and set new fires blocks away from the main conflagration. Sections of the city considered safe burned while others appearing to be in the path of the flames escaped. The heat was so intense that stone, marble and brick buildings crumpled before the flames.

Once the fire had gained a foothold in the area of Smythe Street and Drury Lane it raced along the lower part of Union Street and branched out on Mill and George Streets. The wharves at Market Slip

158

burned along with eleven small schooners berthed there. Then fire broke out in Lower Cove near the Barrack Square and began to move in an easterly direction. The men manning the city's four steam fire engines, along with those from Portland and Carleton were now confronted with two major fires. They did all they could but their efforts were futile, either to subdue the fires or to contain them in any manageable locality.

Then the flames swept down Germain Street consuming everything in their path including the Anglican Trinity Church erected in 1791. George Stewart in his book, *The Story of the Great Fire In Saint John*, published in the year of the fire, wrote a brief tribute to the church: "Old Trinity, the most historic edifice in the city, the first church, the quaintest structure — the last link which bound the old and the new together." But Old Trinity was only one of the edifices which burned. Other churches, the Wiggins Orphanage in Lower Cove and the Victoria Hotel were among the landmarks wiped out. All of the city's newspapers, the *Globe, News, Freeman, Telegraph, Watchman* and *Religious Intelligence* were lost although the *Globe* somehow managed to bring out a small edition the next day using borrowed presses. In that edition the *Globe* had this to say:

> Words cannot describe the condition of Saint John today. With the larger part of the city in ruins, her principal business places destroyed, her public buildings in ashes, her manufacturers and workshops wrecked, her finest private residences burned to the ground, thousands of homeless men and women and children wandering aimlessly about the streets

or stretched despondently on the wharves and in the fields, the sight is a sad and deplorable one.

During the nine-hour conflagration the fire had destroyed most of the buildings surrounded on the north by Union Street and on the other three sides by the harbour. It was the very heart of Saint John and the loss was estimated to be about twenty-seven million dollars of which no more than one quarter would be covered by insurance. Curiously one of the streets burned out bore the name of Fire Proof Alley.

As in any catastrophe the fire revealed the best and worst in people. While hundreds of men valiantly fought the flames others looted and drunken men and boys robbed children struggling to save a few meagre possessions from their burning homes. One cunning woman carefully helped a widow gather together some possessions while her children stole the widow's jewelry and silver.

And people tended to save what they saw first. Ordinary kitchenware was carried to safety while expensive furniture burned. A man saved an old tub and dipper while his valuable books and private papers were lost. A wife asked her husband to remove a bag containing the family's silver plate. He carried out a rag bag instead. Costly pianos were dropped out of third floor windows and smashed. There was the young bride who loaded a wagon with her best silver, furniture and bedding and sent it on to her mother. The mother's house burned while her own was saved.

The disaster affected people in different ways. Men who had fought the fire for hours elsewhere returned exhausted only to find their own homes gone. There were those who had invested their life savings in multi-family homes or tenements and rented them out as their sole source of income who lost everything. Skilled workers, shipwrights, riggers and millwrights lost their tools and were out of work until they could raise funds to replace them.

When the Digby ferry steamed into the harbour many of the passengers saw their own homes on fire. Some had left children at home but the captain did not dare to dock the vessel for some hours while the passengers were fraught with anxiety.

The ashes had barely cooled when the city fathers took action. Two hundred special constables were sworn in to help maintain law and order. Relief stations were established to aid the homeless. Within three days following the fire a military unit was engaged in bringing down damaged walls and buildings.

Offers of assistance soon poured in. Within two months over 300 cash donations were received ranging from a few dollars to thousands. They came from individuals, organizations, towns and cities from across Canada and the United States. There were over 150 donations of clothing, food, furniture and fuel and Lieutenant-Governor Tilley placed $25,000 at the disposal of the city.

By Monday, June 25, five days after the fire, the *Globe* was able to report:

> Already on every hand there are signs of preparation for a general resumption of business. In every direction new buildings are being commenced, some to be temporary, some to be permanent. Those able are resuming work on ships; hundreds of previously unemployed are working on the ruins.

Throughout the city, in the shops, on the streets and in the reports of the city administrators there was an air of optimism. The city was down but it was not finished. Out of the ashes would rise a new city better than before. And it happened.

5.
Ashore and Afloat

As the world moved into the twentieth century dramatic changes were taking place on the seas. The centuries-old dependence on windpower was giving way to steam, gasoline and, later, diesel power. The square-rigged vessels were slipping into oblivion and for a few decades only the fore and aft rigged schooners were left to use sail. And, increasingly, these vessels were being fitted with auxiliary power. These changes not only affected propulsion, they had a profound impact on the design of vessels.

When the era of the wooden, cargo-carrying sailing vessel was ending most of the shipyards in these provinces closed. One yard which operated through much of the age of sail and lasted until the age of fibreglass belonged to —

The Boatbuilding Richardsons of Deer Island, N.B.
Deer Island, Grand Manan and Campobello form a trio of picturesque islands in the western end of the Bay of Fundy. Fishing is the main occupation of their residents and has been since the time of first settlement.

It was on the rocky east coast of Deer Island that Thomas Richardson laid the foundation for a family boatbuilding business, a business that would remain in the family for more than a century. In the years to come men from New York, the southern United

States, Maine, Massachusetts and several Canadian provinces would seek out the Richardsons. All had one objective, the construction of a quality boat.

Born in 1824, Thomas Richardson began to build boats for the fishermen while still a young man. Many of his boats were the high-stern pinkie, a type then widely used by fishermen. Generally under thirty feet in length, these boats were all built of natural growth materials. Crooked trees were sought out and roots were cut and sided with a broad axe and shaped with an adze. Most were lapstrake and all were propelled by sail. He was a careful builder, a craftsman and his name soon spread among the fishing community.

Thomas had a son George Everett, born in 1859, who from a very early age displayed an aptitude for the boatbuilding business. One day when young George was twelve, a fisherman visited the Richardsons to order a fishing boat. The elder Richardson was booked to capacity but he suggested to the fisherman that he contract with young George. Such was the faith of the fisherman in the Richardsons that he did so and the twelve-year-old boy did indeed build the boat.

If Thomas had planted the seed for the boatbuilding business, it was George who brought it to full flower. George was only twenty when his father turned the operation over to him. By the 1880s the sardine business was underway and larger boats were required to carry the small fish. He began to build pinkies, schooners and sloops in the forty to fifty foot range and when gas engines began to come into use about the turn of the century, some of these vessels were cut in two and lengthened to provide room for an engine and additional cargo.

In the 1890s George set up a sawmill to

manufacture his own lumber. He got some of his logs on Deer Island but most were brought by scow or in rafts from the mainland, then they were sawn and piled to dry. Pine was most often used for planking and for decks, yellow birch for keels and sternposts, cedar for shelves and clamps, spruce for the ceilings, floors, bulkheads, masts, booms and gaffs. When steam-bent frames came into use, American white oak and later ash were brought in. In the last two decades of the nineteenth century, wages were usually fifteen cents an hour and the men worked a ten-hour day, six days a week.

It was in the early years of this century that George Richardson contracted to build two boats, each sixty-five feet in length. Since they were to be used to carry fish to American markets, the regulations of the time specified that the boats had to be built in the United States. He arranged to build them in Lubec, Maine and took his own crew. When the first was finished she was brought to Deer Island and rigged. Then George sailed the *Hazel Leah* to Eastport. Forty years later he made his last run to Eastport in the same vessel.

George's family consisted of six girls and five boys. The boys, Horace, Percy, Hazen, Heber and Albion were all involved in the business and each could build a boat from the design stage to launching. Between 1910 and 1912 the output of the Richardson yard included three vessels in the sixty-five foot range. One, the schooner *Cora Gertie* later gained a measure of fame when she went ashore on the New Brunswick coast during prohibition with a full cargo of rum. The second, the *Prince* was built for the Biological Station in St. Andrews and the third, the *Page* was launched for Connors Brothers in Black's Harbour. The *Page* continued as a working boat until she was lost on the Wolves in 1969. It is worthy of note that the *Cora Gertie* and the *Page* each cost $2,500, complete with hull, rigging and spars.

In the immediate years to follow the Richardsons were building boats large and small and some had remarkably long lives. The schooner-rigged *Alma*, built in 1916 was still working in the 1970s and another sardine carrier, the *Brunswick Maid*, launched in 1920, was also working in the '70s.

By 1926 Albion had finished school and he went into partnership with his father under the firm name of George E. Richardson and Son. Through the '20s the firm continued to turn out boats and at this time a generator was purchased so that power tools and electric lights could be brought into use. The generator was the source of power until hydro came to Deer Island in 1938.

During the depression years of the 1930s the Richardsons remained busy with one notable addition. Yachting became increasingly popular and the firm began to include yachts in its output. The first of the decade was a fifty-foot yacht, the schooner *Grey Dawn*, launched for Frank Whelpley of Saint John in 1930. From then on the Richardsons combined both power and sailing yachts with their usual fishing craft. Among their more notable vessels in this decade was the first ferry scow built to connect Deer Island with L'Etete on the mainland. And, in 1937, they built the last pinkie to be launched in the area. In all nearly thirty craft were built in these economically difficult years in addition to small boats and repair work. Through all these years George Richardson figured that a boat forty-five to fifty feet in length should not take longer than ten weeks in the shop.

In 1941 Albion Richardson left Deer Island and

moved to Black's Harbour to build and repair boats for Connors Brothers. His brother Heber took over the business and Heber's sons and nephews formed the nucleus of the work force. Heber had first started working with his father at the age of sixteen. Seven years later he left to go fishing and pursued that occupation until he returned to the boatbuilding business in the early 1940s. From then until 1960 the Richardson firm launched thirty-eight wooden boats of various designs ranging from thirty to sixty feet in length, in addition to repair work and the building of many small boats and tenders.

It was first and always a family business. If, on occasion, additional men were taken on for specific jobs, there were never any plans for a significant expansion. Quality rather than quantity remained the watchword, and three new boats a year was a good average in addition to repair work and small boat construction.

The plant always remained at the site chosen by Thomas Richardson. A large shed was the centre of building activity while smaller buildings housed equipment and materials. There were two outside slips for repair work and additional repairs were carried out on boats moored to the Richardson wharves. A typical day in these post-war years might see two yachts under construction, two fishing vessels on the slips undergoing repairs, and another boat being rebuilt alongside a wharf.

The fate of the Richardson-built boats was not always known to the builders. One afternoon Heber decided to take in a movie at a Maine theatre. During a newsreel he saw a number of vessels seized by the United States Coast Guard for rum-running. Among them he was astonished to see the eighty-seven foot *Ethel Cora*, one of the largest vessels built in the family yard.

Occasionally Richardson boats travelled afar. In 1934 George had built the forty-seven foot yawl *Zetes* from the design of W.J. Roué of *Bluenose* fame. In the early 1960s an explosion and fire badly damaged the yacht at Saint John. Heber purchased the wreck, brought her back to Deer Island and rebuilt her from the waterline up. Sold to Douglas Kirby of Saint John and renamed the *Lady K II*, she was the first boat from New Brunswick to enter the Marblehead to Halifax race. In 1977 Kirby sold the *Lady K II* in Florida to an Australian and she was taken to the Mediterranean and then to Australia.

During the early 1960s boatbuilding continued at the Richardson plant. Two motor sailers, two ketches, four cabin cruisers, a sailboat and a diving tender were among the boats launched. But the end of the business was in sight. In 1965 Heber Richardson turned sixty-five and he was facing the great swing toward fibreglass boats. It was not his wish to move from wood and in that year he closed the shop.

In more than a century hundreds of fishing boats and yachts had come out of the Richardson yard. It was a business that knew good times and bad but always the firm's aim for quality survived. The Richardsons began in the era of the square-rigged windship and they were still going in the age of the jet.

The yard is silent now. Family members use it for storage and for repairs to their own boats. No more will shining new yachts or solid fishing vessels come out of the big shed. But it was an enterprise that during its heyday contributed much to marine activity along the eastern seaboard.

168

The Captain Was A Lady — Molly Kool

If the story of Robert Dewis in Volume I portrays something of the career of a sea captain who took his lofty, square-rigged vessels across the oceans of the world, the story of Captain Molly Kool has little in common except that both were master mariners. The unique factor in her story is that in her time she was the first woman in North America and only the second in the world to hold a master's ticket and the first was a Russian.

The Molly Kool story begins with her father, Paul, born on a little Dutch vessel that sailed the canals of Holland. Orphaned early in life, Paul lived in an orphanage until the age of twelve when he joined the Royal Dutch Navy. At eighteen he and a few others deserted their ship in Australia and young Kool signed on a merchant vessel. The ship was later wrecked in Shediac Bay, New Brunswick. Paul eventually made his way to Alma, N.B. where he obtained work on scows owned by C.T. White and Son.

In 1914 Paul married Myrtle Anderson, an Alma girl. During the first World War he worked on various scows and helped build some of the large schooners launched by the C.T. White firm in Alma. But he wanted to get back to sea again and after the war was able to take command of the motor scow *Riverside* freighting gravel for Blakeny and Sons in Moncton. Later he took charge of two other Blakeny scows, the *Alice B.* and the *Dorothy B.* Then, in 1930, as the Great Depression worsened, Paul made a bold decision. He decided to build his own scow and he put everything he owned into her.

The scow was seventy feet long on deck and thirty-nine feet on the bottom. Her beam was twenty-two feet amidships, then narrowed in to eighteen feet at the bow and stern. This was a feature of Paul's own design as most scows were simple rectangles carrying the same width from end to end. She had no hold and all cargoes were carried on deck. The scow had two gas engines and on her fifty-four foot mast was rigged a gaff-headed mainsail. On the after end was a wheelhouse, accommodations for the captain and crew and the engine room. The scow was named the *Jean K.* after one of Kool's daughters.

Paul and Myrtle Kool had eight children, three of whom died young. The second child, Myrtle or Molly, was born in 1916. Home was an old Loyalist house in Alma, still with the original fireplace and cooking utensils. If the family was comfortable it was far from wealthy. There was no indoor plumbing and for a long time no electricity. The Kools always had a garden and they kept a few chickens, a cow and a couple of pigs. Molly went to the local school, completed Grade ten and particularly liked math and geography. As she grew older she had notions of being a nurse, but there was no money and anyway the sea was in her blood.

While still a school student Molly began going with her father on the *Jean K.* during summer vacations. By this time Captain Paul Kool was a recognized figure on both sides of the Bay of Fundy and was the best-known of the numerous skippers of scows on the Petitcodiac River. It was he who helped pioneer winter scowing on the Bay where previously these vessels had only operated from early spring to late fall.

When Molly finished school she went to sea full-time with her father. He taught her seamanship, how to steer, run the winch, splice rope, sew canvas and repair engines. In those times there were no radars, lorans or depth finders. Coastal navigation was by chart, compass and judgment and the girl was an adept student. The one skill she acquired but never enjoyed was cooking, even in her later married life.

Living conditions on the scow were primitive at best. With an all-male crew there were no problems in sharing the small cabin. However, when Molly came aboard she and her father partitioned off the cabin so that the crew slept on the port side and the Kools had tiny cubicles on the starboard side. The toilet was a seat in a corner of the engine room with a bucket under but if the engines were not running every sound could be heard in the cabin. It was a problem which always confronted Molly's modesty.

When in larger ports like Saint John, there were always sights to see and people to visit. But many times their port was a rough dock near a mill. There they spent their evenings playing cards, reading or yarning. A radio provided some entertainment — when it worked. In the 1930s an experienced deckhand on the *Jean K.* was paid about thirty dollars a month. Molly received the going rate, no more, no less as she served as cabin boy, cook, deckhand and mate. As an adult Molly was self-described as being five feet seven inches in height and 'around 140 to 150 pounds.' And she was strong. There are those still living around the Bay of Fundy where the *Jean K.* used to load lumber that say, "Molly could pick up a nine inch by three inch deal, put it on her shoulder and walk off with it as easily as most men." She was also a good swimmer, something that would stand her in good stead at least once in her seafaring life.

As time went on Molly began to think of qualifying for her mate's papers. The fact that she would be the first on this continent never entered her head. But when she applied for admission into the navigation school in Saint John, conducted by Captain Richard Pollock, she was rebuffed. The school had never had a woman apply, but Molly was nothing if not persistent and eventually she was accepted. After four months of intensive study she passed the examination and Captain Pollock would say with some pride that she was the brightest student ever enrolled in the school.

Now Molly was not only a certified officer and a proven sailor, she could talk the sailor's language and she knew her rights. A Norwegian captain learned this the hard way. In the summer of 1938 the *Jean K.* was tied to a wharf in Moncton with a cargo of lumber on board. The tug *Wasson* lay directly ahead with a scow also loaded with lumber. Captain Paul Kool had gone ashore and left his twenty-two-year-old mate, Molly, in charge.

It was about high water when the Norwegian freighter *Salamis* came steaming up the river and imperiously blew her whistle for the scows to leave so she could berth. The *Wasson* left with her tow but the *Jean K.* stayed defiantly in her berth. When an exchange of pleasantries between the captain and the lady mate failed to resolve the impasse, the freighter edged alongside the *Jean K.* and two seamen climbed down to cast off the scow's lines. It was a mistake. They were met by a furious Molly brandishing a belaying pin. The seamen fled back to the safety of the freighter. However, Captain Gunderson of the *Salamis* was as stubborn as Molly. He reversed engines, placed the bow of the freighter against the *Jean K.*'s stern and eased ahead until the scow's lines snapped and she drifted out into the river. Molly lost no time in contacting a lawyer and instituting a suit against the *Salamis*. The matter was settled out of court but the mate had shown she

172

was not one to be taken lightly.

In 1939 Molly decided to sit for her master's ticket. Once again she was pioneering but now she had established a solid reputation and was readily accepted into the navigation school in Yarmouth, Nova Scotia. When the time came for her examination she found not one but two experienced captains facing her. The authorities were making certain that no favoritism would be shown because of her sex. However, she passed the examination with ease and her ticket entitled her to take a commercial vessel anywhere on the coast of North America. By way of celebration, on April 19, 1939, she wired her sister Jean, "Call me captain from now on."

It was not long after Molly became captain that her father, suffering from ulcers, turned command of the *Jean K.* over to her. In those years the scow carried a variety of cargoes. Frequently lumber was loaded at Albert County ports in New Brunswick for Saint John or carried to waiting vessels anchored in West Bay near Parrsboro. One whole summer the scow freighted gravel up a small creek on the Tantramar Marsh for use on the site of the Canadian Broadcasting Corporation's station between Sackville and Aulac, New Brunswick. Sometimes there were large veneer logs to carry from Alma or from Digby to Saint John, and in the spring there were weir poles to go from St. Stephen to Grand Manan. On occasion lumber was freighted between Victoria Mills near Fredericton to Saint John. During the war the scow carried pulpwood to the paper mills in Bucksport, Maine. In short the *Jean K.* loaded lumber, gravel. logs or any other cargo that would bring in a dollar during the Depression years.

As master of the scow, Molly Kool entered a new world, one of assuming full responsibility for a vessel, its complement and cargo through fog, gales, drifting ice and the tides and currents of Fundy. If she wore her blue seaman's jacket with its brass buttons and four gold rings on the sleeve with pride, she knew another side of seafaring. Navigation, standing watch for twenty-four hours at a time when the weather was bad, taking her trick at the wheel and checking the engines every half hour for oil and grease — these were all part of her daily life at sea. And she had her share of narrow escapes. A few years ago she recalled one incident when her father was still in command:

> We were running down the Bay in a southeaster which is bad in the Bay of Fundy and you have a riptide so it is very rough. We began taking on water and finally lost one engine. We put the sail on but we lost part of that so we only had about half a sail. Then we lost the wheel ropes so we had nothing to steer with but my father was a good sailor. He wore the scow around on that little piece of sail. It was very, very rough but he got the wheel ropes repaired and we worked her into a little cove just beyond the cape (Spencer). By this time we were full of water so we anchored. The lightkeeper and his son had come down to the beach so we got in our boat and went ashore. They met us, pulled us through the surf high and dry, and took us up to the lighthouse. He had a horse and sleigh and took us to the nearest telephone where we could call someone to come and get us. The next day the wind had died down. We got the tugboat, picked up the scow, took her in and drained her then got ready to go to sea again. We lost the deckload of course.

All of this happened shortly after Molly had been a guest on Robert Ripley's program, "Believe It Or Not."

Another much closer call occurred when the *Jean K.* was entering Saint John harbour in dense fog with a full cargo of lumber. Suddenly out of the mist loomed the Eastern Steamship vessel S.S. *Yarmouth.* Captain Paul and two deckhands barely had time to leap on top of their lumber cargo before the steamer rammed the *Jean K.* Molly was at the wheel and the impact knocked her overboard. She was drawn completely under the scow and came up the other side. Why she was not cut to pieces by the thrashing propellers always remained a mystery. A passing fisherman picked up the swimming Molly and took her ashore where she got a tug to bring the damaged scow into port.

During her career Molly had other opportunities. Once she was offered the third mate's berth on a Norwegian vessel. She declined and on the next voyage the vessel was lost with all hands. Then, after her marriage, she had a chance to take command of a tug out of Parrsboro. Again she declined with the words, "I don't know anything about tugboating."

In the summer of 1944 one of the *Jean K.*'s engines caught fire near Bucksport, Maine and the scow was badly damaged. While repairs were being made Molly lived ashore where she met Ray Blaisdell, a shipping clerk in a local business. When the scow was towed back to Alma to complete repairs, Molly and Ray were on board. They were married in Alma and soon after Molly turned the scow over to her brother John.

December 1945 found the *Jean K.* once again in trouble off Cape Spencer. Loaded with lumber and bound for Saint John, she lost one engine and began drifting towards the rocks. Captain John Kool set off flares which were seen by a nearby pilot boat. The pilot boat attempted to tow the scow clear but the leaking vessel was too unwieldy. The *Jean K.* was abandoned but she was not quite through. Full of water the hulk drifted across the Bay of Fundy and went ashore near Digby Gut. Her registry was closed on January 11, 1946.

Ray Blaisdell died in 1962 and five years later Molly married John Carney. The couple settled in Orrington, Maine where Molly found work on shore. She had finished with the sea.

If her career as captain only lasted five years, Molly Kool had served many more years on the *Jean K.* Those who knew her in those years in ports on the Bay of Fundy and along its rivers remember her as competent, courageous and 'one tough lady.' She was a legend in her own time.

The Lobster Fishery and A Fundy Fisherman
If provincial tourism publications persist in spelling it Scots Bay, the local inhabitants are adamant that the proper spelling is Scott's Bay and so it appears on local signs. The hamlet is tucked behind Cape Split near the entrance to Minas Basin and stretches around the shore of the little bay. Unlike one-industry fishing communities elsewhere, the residents of Scott's Bay are involved in a number of vocations. Nearly a dozen are employed in the fishery, others raise poultry while still others are in the lumbering industry. And there is something of a paradox. Some who live in Scott's Bay work in the nearby Annapolis Valley while several residents of the valley own summer cottages in or near Scott's Bay.

Some years ago the local school fell victim to

regional consolidation and the children are now bussed about eighteen kilometers to Canning. The one church is union and is shared by the Baptist and United denominations. A single store serves the immediate needs of the community. At the far end of Scott's Bay, towards Cape Split, is the wharf, the centre of the local fishery. It is new and sturdy and was built through a cooperative arrangement between the federal government and the fishermen. The government provided the ballast rock and timbers and the men built the wharf. Responsibility for maintenance of the wharf, the harbour and the lighted channel marker rests with a local organization, the Little Cove Harbour Authority.

Scott's Bay is home to Lowell Huntley, an inshore fisherman. A stocky, affable man in his late forties with close-cut greying hair, Huntley responds to questions with thoughtful, articulate answers. It is probable that these qualities helped place him on various advisory committees serving the fishery. The father of two boys, Huntley lives with his wife and family in a comfortable century-old house built by his grandfather.

Although his father and an uncle fished before him, Lowell Huntley did not immediately follow in their steps. He worked for a number of years on gypsum boats running to the south from Hantsport, Nova Scotia, was employed in construction work for a time and, for a change of pace, served with Dominion Stores. But the call of the sea was there and in 1977 he went into a partnership and began fishing for groundfish, especially flounders. However, the partnership did not last, in part because Huntley is an independent man and preferred to go his own way.

His present boat, his fourth, is a diesel-powered

thirty-five foot fibreglass craft. During the winter of 1992-93 Huntley essentially moved to a bed and breakfast establishment on Cape Sable Island. Using Stanley Greenwood's boatship Huntley built his own boat with occasional help from Greenwood and a local team of ladies who specialized in laying up fibreglass. With one hired hand he fishes for lobster and flounder along the southern shore of Minas Channel and in part of the Minas Basin. The season for his area runs from the first of May until the end of July and again in October and November.

The actual process of fishing is only part of the life of a lobster fisherman. Lowell Huntley sets 300 traps in both the summer and fall seasons. These he builds himself which includes knitting the heads and collecting the flat stones to weight the traps. The traps must be kept in repair and each year a number are lost in storms. In the 1990 fall season Huntley lost twenty-seven traps which had to be replaced. Then there is bait. He catches his own herring for the summer season but in the fall he procures herring and mackerel from the province's south shore. And always the boat and engine must be kept in good working order.

As it is with all who pursue fish for a living Huntley has had his share of adventures fighting bone-chilling gales, blinding snow and rough seas. But he has also known warm summer days when Fundy's waters are tranquil and the gulls wheel overhead looking for their next meal. It is his chosen way of life, he wants nothing else but he has serious concerns about the fishery and its future.

Lowell Huntley sums up the basic problem as simply too many boats chasing too few fish and the problem is not confined to his area. In 1957 Maine lobstermen caught twenty-four million lobsters with

250,000 traps. In 1989 the Maine fishermen again caught twenty-four million lobsters but this time they used over two million traps. And Huntley thinks about fishermen who invest heavily in new boats and gear but with the various quota restrictions having ever-lessening chances of paying off their investment let alone making a living. Then in years when lobsters are relatively plentiful, prices invariably drop, sometimes below the cost of catching them. "Fishing," he says, "is a chancy business."

As for himself Huntley has so far been unsuccessful in obtaining a scallop license for those periods outside the lobster season. In the meantime he takes tour parties to Cape Split, Cape Blomidon, across to Parrsboro and, in past years, researchers from Acadia University to Ile Haute where they have been studying mice of a variety not found elsewhere. In spite of it all Huntley remains optimistic that the industry will right itself and the history of the lobster fishery suggests he may well be right.

Lobsters were known along Canada's east coast long before they were fished commercially. A Captain Leigh wrote in 1597, "Called at the harbour named by the natives Cibou" (Sydney). "In this place are the greatest multitude of lobsters that ever was heard of, for we caught in one hawle with a little draw-net above 140."

Samuel Butler, the English satirical poet, may have been the first to mention lobster in literature when he wrote in 1662:

> The sun had long since in the lap
> Of Thetis taken out his nap,
> And, like a lobster boil'd the morn
> From black to red began to turn.

The commercial lobster fishery on the east coast is about as old as Canada itself. The first landings date back to the mid 1860s and by 1885 the catch in the Atlantic provinces approached one million pounds. In 1900 the value of Nova Scotia's annual catch was $7,809,152 and New Brunswick's was $3,769,742. Since the lobsters brought about ten dollars per hundredweight or ten cents a pound shipped live to Boston, the total values indicate that the crustaceans were indeed plentiful.

It was around the turn of the century that improvements began to be made in both boats and gear. A contemporary writer described the boats of the period as "models of beauty and marvels of seaworthiness." They cost about $200 each and most were open and fine-lined. Gasoline engines were being introduced and by 1915 few sailing craft were employed in lobstering. Over time traps were improved and power haulers added to reduce the strenuous work of hauling hundreds of traps from the depths day after day.

The business of shipping live lobsters to the American market began in the 1870s when a half-dozen barrels of lobsters packed in wet moss were shipped to the New England states. By 1900 some 2,000 crates, each containing 140 pounds, were being transported weekly to Boston with most coming from the south shore of Nova Scotia. In these years a good fisherman might bring in about 4,000 pounds in a year for which he would receive approximately eighty dollars. By the late 1920s a fisherman who landed 1,600 pounds might receive about $110. Fishing in those times was not the road to wealth.

In 1918 a familiar story began to unfold. The Atlantic lobster catch dropped to twenty-seven

180

million pounds and there were fears for the future of the industry. New government regulations appeared and attempts to establish hatcheries proved largely unsuccessful. But the industry rebounded as it would again and again in the future. During the Depression Years of the 1930s, if lobsters were plentiful, prices hit rock bottom. While some fishermen along the Bay of Fundy might get ten cents a pound, others were selling the crustaceans for ten cents apiece regardless of size. It was a time when children from the more comfortable homes in seaside communities took meat, cheese or peanut butter sandwiches to school. The poorer children brought lobster.

Even by the late 1940s there were no restrictions on the number of traps a fisherman could set and some were putting close to 600 on the bottom. At this point lobsters over nine inches in length were generally classed as markets, those between seven and nine inches canners and smaller lobsters were returned to the sea by regulation.

From about the turn of the century until the second World War much of the catch was canned, and in these years over 900 small canneries functioned along Canada's east coast. The lobsters were taken from the boats to the canneries and immediately boiled in large kettles. The arms, claws and tails were removed, the meat separated and bodies discarded all in a kind of assembly-line operation. The meat was packed in cans with some salted fresh water and sealed. Then the cans were boiled for three to four hours. A small hole was made to let any air escape from the cans, then they were resealed, labelled and packed for shipment. By the 1960s storage and shipping techniques had improved to the point where less than ten per cent of the catch was canned while most were marketed live or as frozen lobster meat.

In 1965 some 35,000 licensed fishermen were setting over two and a half million traps and the landings exceeded forty million pounds with a value of more than $24 million. Even then, with good catches, there were concerns for the future and the now familiar cry was heard, "Too many boats chasing too few fish."

For years now stringent regulations have been in effect governing fishing districts, seasons, licenses, minimum size limits and gear. Inspectors regularly visit processing plants to ensure proper sanitation standards and quality control, and research programs in New Brunswick and Nova Scotia work to improve the future of the industry.

The object of all this, the lobster, would not win any beauty contests. Those unfamiliar with the crustacean find it decidedly unattractive but its meat is considered a delicacy in many parts of the world. It prefers a rocky bottom and spends much of its time burrowed under rocks. When it comes upon a trap the round opening in the knitted head or end of the trap allows the lobster access to the 'parlor' and bait. But the trap design is such that rarely can the lobster escape. They are somewhat cannibalistic in nature and given the opportunity will maim other lobsters — to say nothing of fishermen. For this reason the claws are pegged or restrained by heavy rubber bands as soon as they are removed from the trap.

The story of the lobster fishery resembles a roller coaster. Good years are followed by bad years and high prices in tandem with low prices. But fishermen like Lowell Huntley are optimistic and Huntley has every intention of staying in the game.

Bibliography

Books and Other Bound Publications

Belliveau, John E. *The Splendid Life of Albert Smith.* Windsor: Lancelot Press, 1976.

Bigelow, Dr. W.A. *Forceps, Fin and Feather.* Altona, Manitoba: D.W. Frieson and Sons, 1969.

Bowser, Reg. B. *Dorchester Island and Related Areas.* Dorchester: Privately Printed, 1985.

Davidson, James D. (Ed.). *Mud Creek, The Story of Wolfville, N.S.* Wolfville: Wolfville Historical Society, 1985.

Day, Frank Parker. *The Autobiography of A Fisherman.* New York: Doubleday, Page and Company, 1927.

————. *The Good Citizen — Josiah Wood Lectures.* Sackville: Mount Allison University, 1947.

Foley, Ace. *The First Fifty Years, Life and Times of A Sportswriter.* Windsor: Lancelot Press, 1970.

Larracey, Edward. *Chocolate River, A Story of The Petitcodiac River.* Hantsport: Lancelot Press, 1985.

Lawrence, J.W. *Footprints Or Incidents In Early History of N.B.* Saint John: J. and A. MacMillan, 1893.

Machum, Lloyd. *A History of Moncton.* Moncton: City of Moncton, 1965.

MacNutt, W.S. *New Brunswick — A History: 1784-1867.* Toronto: MacMillan of Canada, 1963.

Marshall, M.V. *A Short History of Acacia Villa School.* Wolfville: Acadia University Institute, 1963.

Milner, W.C. *Early History of Dorchester and Surrounding Area.* Sackville: Tribune Press, 1932.

Monro, Alexander. *New Brunswick With A Brief Outline of N.S. and P.E.I.* Halifax: John Nugent, 1855.

Murray, Frances. *Memoir of LeBaron Botsford, M.D.* Saint John: J. & A. MacMillan, 1892.

Petchey, Helen M. *The Palmer Brothers In The Chignecto.* Privately Printed, 1990.

__________. *The Parish Church At Dorchester Corner.* Saint John: Lingley Printing Company, 1982.

Quinpool, John. *First Things In Acadia.* Halifax: First Things Publishers, Ltd., 1936.

Stewart, George. *The Story of The Great Fire In Saint John.* Toronto: Belford Bros., 1877.

Women's Institute. *History of Great Village, N.S.* Great Village: Women's Institute, 1963.

Women's Institute. *The Story of Five Islands, N.S.* Sackville: Tribune Press, 1969.

Young, Dr. Alexander. *Beyond Heroes — A Sports History of Nova Scotia.* Hantsport: Lancelot Press, 1988.

List of Lights and Fog Signals, Atlantic Coast. Ottawa:

Queen's Printer, 1965.

Articles, Typescripts, Diaries and Letters

Berton, Margaret. *Economic History of Dorchester.* Typescript, Undated.

Bickerton, A. Marie. *Old Times, Canning, N.S.* Canning: Typescript, Undated.

Bowker, Francis E. *Address on Molly Kool.* Mystic: May, 1979.

Brooks, Alan A. "The Golden Age and The Exodus — Canning." Halifax: *Acadiensus*, Vol. XI, No. 1, 1981.

Cushing, Eileen C. "The Great Fire of Saint John." Saint John: *N.B. Historical Society Collection*, No. 17, 1961.

Doyle, Arthur T. "Heroes of New Brunswick." Fredericton: *Daily Gleaner*, May 5, September 15, 1984.

Dunbar, Georgia Crowe. *Letters To The Author.* Truro: 1989 and 1990.

Ells, Margaret E. "Canning In The Seventies." Halifax: *N.S. Historical Review*, Vol. 8, No. 2, 1988.

Frayne, Trent. "The Greatest Fighter Who Ever Lived." Toronto: *Maclean's Magazine*, February 15, 1955.

Hatchard, Keith A. "The Nova Scotia Apple Industry." Halifax: *N.S. Historical Quarterly*, Vol. 7, 1977.

How, H.R. *The Story of Dorchester.* Oakville: Typescript, 1967.

Humphrey, John. "The Richardson Yard of Deer Island." Fredericton: *The Binnacle*, Fall 1990.

MacLean, Peter. "The Saxby Gale." Fredericton: *Atlantic Advocate*, Vol. 69, No. 5, 1979.

MacRae, G.E. "Sam Langford, Nova Scotia's Greatest Fighter." Fredericton: *Atlantic Advocate*, August, 1981.

Richardson, Albion. *Boatbuilding In Charlotte County — A Bit of Family History.* Typescript, Undated.

Rogers, Ann Eliza. *Personal Diaries, 1852-1896.* Moncton Museum, Unpublished.

Scotney, D. "Samson of The Valley." Fredericton: *Atlantic Advocate*, August, 1966.

Smith, W.D.F. "Charles Ingraham Gorman." Saint John: *N.B. Historical Society Collection*, No. 17, 1961.

Squires, W. Austin. "Abraham Gesner." Fredericton: *Atlantic Advocate*, January, 1963.

Tibbitts, D.C. "The Saxby Gale." Fredericton: *Atlantic Advocate*, October, 1967.

Toole, Janet. *Taped Interview With Capt. Molly Kool.* November, 1987.

Wilder, D.G. "Lobster Outlook Bright." Fredericton: *Atlantic Advocate*, October, 1965.

Williams, Trevor. "The Williams Lobster Factory 1901-1935." Halifax: *N.S. Historical Review*, Vol. 8, No. 1, 1988.

Young, Dr. Alexander. "The Boston Tarbaby." Halifax: *N.S. Historical Quarterly*, Vol. 4, No. 3, 1974.

Sou'Wester. Yarmouth: Various Issues, 1990.

National Fishermen. Rockland, Maine: Various Issues.

Index

MicroRNA Protocols

METHODS IN MOLECULAR BIOLOGY™

John M. Walker, SERIES EDITOR

METHODS IN MOLECULAR BIOLOGY™

MicroRNA Protocols

Edited by

Shao-Yao Ying

*Department of Cell and Neurobiology, Keck School of Medicine,
University of Southern California, Los Angeles, CA*

HUMANA PRESS ✳ TOTOWA, NEW JERSEY

Preface

Native small regulatory RNAs of about 22 nt in eukaryotes have emerged as evolutionarily conserved molecules that can repress translation or degrade the RNA transcripts of target genes, depending on the degree of complementarity. They are called microRNAs (miRNAs). Consequently, miRNAs fine-tune protein synthesis, manifesting numerous biological characteristics as a result of the control and coordination of large sets of genes. miRNAs are noncoding regulatory RNAs important for development and cell homeostasis, including exonic and intronic miRNAs. Exonic miRNAs, such as *lin-4* and *let-7*, are transcribed by RNA polymerases II (Pol-II) or III (Pol-III) as a large oligo-nucleotide precursor, and further processed by Drosha and Dicer RNases to form mature miRNAs.

Unlike the express processes of exonic miRNAs, intron-derived miRNAs (Id-miRNAs) are generated during intron processing of messenger RNAs (mRNAs). In mammals, both kinds of miRNAs are endogeneous single-stranded molecules that mediate their activities through partial complementarity with the target genes, whereas short interfering RNAs (siRNAs) are mostly exogeneous double-stranded molecules acted upon with complete complementarity against the target genes. Conceivably, siRNAs are synthetic molecules consisting of two perfectly matched miRNAs; one sense and one antisense, exerting miRNA-like activity.

miRNAs, small single-stranded hairpin RNAs capable of interfering with intracellular mRNAs that contain partial complementarity, are useful for the design of new therapies against cancer polymorphism and viral mutation. This characteristic is different from siRNA because a rigid complete complementarity is required for siRNA-induced RNAi gene silencing. miRNA was originally discovered in *Caenorhabditis elegans* as native RNA fragments that modulate a wide range of genetic regulatory pathways during animal development. Recently, findings of intron-derived miRNA in *C. elegans*, mouse, and human have led to a novel therapeutic strategy, using the miRNA generated by polymerase II (Pol-II) RNA transcription and splicing. The advantages of using miRNA over siRNA are that they are (1) long-acting, (2) stable in vivo, (3) highly RNA promoter-compatible, (4) multiple targeting, and (5) of no overt toxicity. This type of gene therapy is highly target-selective and suppresses sequence-specific genes, including mutants and polymorphisms. After comparing miRNA with numerous small regulatory RNAs involving sequence-specific gene silencing, it is clear that most are miRNA-like molecules.

Even though siRNA is not native in mammalian and human cells, their native counterparts in lower animals are processed by similar mechanisms, such as Dicer and RISC (Science 2002; 297:2056–2060). miRNA represents a broad spectrum of cellular self-defense tools against transgenes and viral genes that provide a unique vehicle for gene therapy.

The ability to efficiently, stably produce and deliver sufficient amounts of miRNA into the proper target cell without overt toxicity requires fine tuning of the technology before it can be tried clinically. The pharmacokinetics, cellular safety, and functional stability of miRNA expression in animals needs to be examined to ascertain that the artificial miRNAs are stable, effective, and non-toxic in vivo. In eukaryotic cells, the Pol-II-based transcription process is highly regulated and can be adjusted through diverse RNA promoters and transcription factors, thus, the Pol-II-mediated miRNA generation system provides efficient and safe application in gene therapy.

Until the early 1990s, the dogma was that DNA, the blueprint, was transcribed to mRNA, which was then translated into polypeptide or protein, resulting in a specific function reflecting a specific trait. On the other hand, the Human Genome Project completed the process of determining, sequencing, and mapping about 30,000 protein-coding genes among the 3 billion nucleotide base pairs of the human genome; however, the conventional genes only contribute about 3% of the human genome. For many years, the small noncoding RNAs were considered unwanted debris and discarded. These molecules probably were removed during molecular sizing procedures of RNAs; however, increasing lines of evidence suggest that the noncoding portions (i.e., intron) of gene transcripts play an important role in the regulatory pathways of global function in cells and organisms. With the advent of various miRNA genes, it became possible to interpret physiological variations that reflect individual differences, including weights, heights, and responses to various drugs. The functional role of miRNAs meant that suddenly one DNA may consist of multiple genes with pluripotent functions; some for translation, and others for regulation of the quantity of timely protein synthesis. This new discovery of miRNA genes, which has been facilitated by the rapid accumulation of computerized sequence data for human miRNAs, means that biomedical researchers can now manipulate specific mRNA expression using miRNAs in their research plans.

In view of the high conservation of the miRNAs in modulation of gene expression, the main objective of *MicroRNA Protocols* is to provide diverse, novel, and useful descriptions of miRNAs in several species, including plants, worms, flies, fish, chicks, mice, and humans. These include some useful adaptations and applications that could be relevant to the wider research community who are already familiar with the identification of miRNAs. For example, a variety of different adaptations are described that have been employed to develop miRNAs as a potential drug design.

miRNA has opened a new avenue for our understanding of gene expression and will become one of the most widely applied techniques in biomedical research, playing a major role in the molecular investigation of disease pathogenesis. Determination of the applicable miRNAs at the molecular level is already beginning to inform the design of new therapeutic strategies. It is our hope that *MicroRNA Protocols* will stimulate the reader to explore diverse ways to understand the mechanisms by which miRNAs facilitate the molecular aspects of biomedical research.

Shao-Yao Ying

Contents

Contributors

DMITRY A. BELOSTOTSKY • *Department of Biological Sciences, State University of New York, Albany, NY*

YAMINA BENNASSER • *Molecular Virology Section, Laboratory of Molecular Microbiology, National Institute of Allergy and Infectious Diseases, National Institute of Health, Bethesda, MD*

DONALD C. CHANG • *Department of Cell and Neurobiology, Keck School of Medicine, University of Southern California, Los Angeles, CA*

SHIN-JU E. CHANG • *Department of Cell and Neurobiology, Keck School of Medicine, University of Southern California, Los Angeles, CA*

JULIA A. CHEKANOVA • *Department of Biological Sciences, State University of New York, Albany, NY*

CHANG-ZHENG CHEN • *Department of Microbiology and Immunology, Baxter Laboratory of Genetic Pharmacology, Institute for Stem Cell, Cancer and Medicine, Stanford University School of Medicine, Stanford, CA*

CHUN-HONG CHEN • *Division of Biology, California Institute of Technology, Pasadena, CA*

THIMMAIAH P. CHENDRIMADA • *Gene Expression and Regulation Program, and Molecular and Cellular Oncogenesis Program, The Wistar Institute, Philadelphia, PA*

BRYAN R. CULLEN • *Center for Virology and Department of Molecular Genetics and Microbiology, Duke University Medical Center, Durham, NC*

RANHUI DUAN • *Department of Human Genetics, Emory University School of Medicine, Atlanta, Georgia*

PAZ EINAT • *Paz Einat Consulting and Inventions, Nes Ziona, Israel*

YOICHI R. FUJII • *Molecular Biology and Retroviral Genetics Group, Nagoya City University, Nagoya, Japan*

RICHARD I. GREGORY • *Gene Expression and Regulation Program, and Molecular and Cellular Oncogenesis Program, The Wistar Institute, Philadelphia, PA*

SAM GRIFFITHS-JONES • *Wellcome Trust Sanger Institute, Wellcome Trust Genome Campus, Hinxton, UK*

MING GUO • *Department of Neurology, Brain Research Institute, The David Geffen School of Medicine at UCLA, Los Angeles, CA*

BRUCE A. HAY • *Division of Biology, California Institute of Technology, Pasadena, CA*

SHENG-HE HUANG • *Division of Infectious Diseases, Department of Pediatrics, University of Southern California, Children's Hospital Los Angeles, Los Angeles, CA*

AKIRA ISHIZUKA • *Institute for Genome Research, University of Tokushima, Tokushima, Japan*

KUAN-TEH JEANG • *Molecular Virology Section, Laboratory of Molecular Microbiology, National Institute of Allergy and Infectious Diseases, National Institute of Health, Bethesda, MD*

PENG JIN • *Department of Human Genetics, Emory University School of Medicine, Atlanta, Georgia*

BINO JOHN • *Computational Biology Center, Memorial Sloan-Kettering Cancer Center, New York, NY*

AMBROSE Y. JONG • *Division of Hematology-Oncology, Department of Pediatrics, University of Southern California, Children's Hospital Los Angeles, Los Angeles, CA*

CHRYSSA KANELLOPOULOU • *The Dana-Farber Cancer Institute, Department of Cancer Biology, Harvard Medical School, Boston, MA*

CATHERINE KIDNER • *Institute of Molecular Plant Sciences, Edinburgh University and Royal Botanic Gardens, Edinburgh, Scotland*

JACEK KROL • *Laboratory of Cancer Genetics, Institute of Bioorganic Chemistry, Polish Academy of Sciences, Noskowskiego, Poznan, Poland*

WLODZIMIERZ J. KRZYZOSIAK • *Laboratory of Cancer Genetics, Institute of Bioorganic Chemistry, Polish Academy of Sciences, Noskowskiego, Poznan, Poland*

SHU-YUN LE • *Laboratory of Experimental and Computational Biology, NCI Center for Cancer Research, National Cancer Institute, Frederick, MD*

SHI-LUNG LIN • *Department of Cell and Neurobiology, Keck School of Medicine, University of Southern California, Los Angeles, CA*

YI-HSIN LIU • *Center for Craniofacial Molecular Biology and Graduate Program in Craniofacial Biology, School of Dentistry, University of Southern California, Los Angeles, CA*

FENG LUO • *Division of Hematology-Oncology, University of Southern California and Children's Hospital Los Angeles, Los Angeles, CA*

DEBORA S. MARKS • *Department of Systems Biology, Harvard Medical School, Boston, MA*

MICHAEL Z. MICHAEL • *Department of Gastroenterology and Hepatology, Flinders Medical Center, Flinders University School of Medicine, Bedford Park, Australia*

JOSEPH D. MILLER • *Department of Cell and Neurobiology, Keck School of Medicine, University of Southern California, Los Angeles, CA*

HYEYOUNG MIN • *Department of Microbiology and Immunology, Baxter Laboratory of Genetic Pharmacology, Institute for Stem Cell, Cancer and Medicine, Stanford University School of Medicine, Stanford, CA*

STEFAN A. MULJO • *The CBR Institute for Biomedical Research and Department of Pathology, Harvard Medical School, Boston, MA*

SHINYA OMOTO • *Molecular Biology and Retroviral Genetics Group, Nagoya City University, Nagoya, Japan*

MARC REHMSMEIER • *Bielefeld University, CeBiTec, Junior Research Group Bioinformatics of Regulation, Bielefeld, Germany*

KUNIAKI SAITO • *Institute for Genome Research, University of Tokushima, Tokushima, Japan*

CHRIS SANDER • *Computational Biology Center, Memorial Sloan-Kettering Cancer Center, New York, NY*

RAMIN SHIEKHATTER • *Gene Expression and Regulation Program, and Molecular and Cellular Oncogenesis Program, The Wistar Institute, Philadelphia, PA*

HARUHIKO SIOMI • *Institute for Genome Research, University of Tokushima, Tokushima, Japan*

MIKIKO C. SIOMI • *Institute for Genome Research, University of Tokushima, Tokushima, Japan*

NEIL R. SMALHEISER • *Department of Psychiatry and UIC Psychiatric Institute, University of Illinois-Chicago, Chicago, IL*

PETER F. STADLER • *Institute for Theoretical Chemistry, University of Vienna, Vienna, Austria*

ANDREA TANZER • *Institute for Theoretical Chemistry, University of Vienna, Vienna, Austria*

MARJA TIMMERMANS • *Cold Spring Harbor Laboratory, Cold Spring Harbor, NY*

VETLE I. TORVIK • *Department of Psychiatry and UIC Psychiatric Institute, University of Illinois-Chicago, Chicago, IL*

LING-TAO WU • *Department of Pathology, University of Southern California, Children's Hospital Los Angeles, Los Angeles, CA*

JIING-KUAN YEE • *Department of Pathology, City of Hope, Duarte, CA*

MAN LUNG YEUNG • *Molecular Virology Section, Laboratory of Molecular Microbiology, National Institute of Allergy and Infectious Diseases, National Institute of Health, Bethesda, MD*

SHAO-YAO YING • *Department of Cell and Neurobiology, Keck School of Medicine, University of Southern California, Los Angeles, CA*

YAN ZENG • *Department of Pharmacology, University of Minnesota, Minneapolis, MN*

FENGFENG ZHUANG • *Center for Craniofacial Molecular Biology and Graduate Program in Craniofacial Biology, School of Dentistry, University of Southern California, Los Angeles, CA*

The MicroRNA

Overview of the RNA Gene That Modulates Gene Functions

Shao-Yao Ying, Donald C. Chang, Joseph D. Miller, and Shi-Lung Lin

Summary

MicroRNAs (miRNAs), widely distributed, small regulatory RNA genes, target both messenger RNA (mRNA) degradation and suppression of protein translation based on sequence complementarity between the miRNA and its targeted mRNA. Different names have been used to describe various types of miRNA. During evolution, RNA retroviruses or transgenes invaded the eukaryotic genome and inserted itself in the noncoding regions of DNA, conceivably acting as transposon-like jumping genes, providing defense from viral invasion and fine-tuning of gene expression as a secondary level of gene modulation in eukaryotes. When a transposon is inserted in the intron, it becomes an intronic miRNA, taking advantage of the protein synthesis machinery, i.e., mRNA transcription and splicing, as a means for processing and maturation. Recently, miRNAs have been found to play an important, but not life-threatening, role in embryonic development. They might play a pivotal role in diverse biological systems in various organisms, facilitating a quick response and accurate plotting of body physiology and structures. Based on these unique properties, manufactured intronic miRNAs have been developed for in vitro evaluation of gene function, in vivo gene therapy, and generation of transgenic animal models. The biogenesis and identification of miRNAs, potential applications, and future directions for research are presented in this chapter, hopefully providing a guideline for further miRNA and gene function studies.

Key Words: Small RNA; noncoding RNAs; siRNA; miRNA; intronic miRNA; transposons; biogenesis; mechanism; identification; targeting; fine-tuning; gene function; gene therapy; antiviral vaccine; drug development; future directions.

1. Introduction

The miRNA is a form of small, single-stranded RNA, 18- to 25-nucleotides (nt) long. It is transcribed from DNA, and instead of being translated into protein, it regulates the functions of other genes in protein synthesis. Therefore, miRNAs are genes that modulate other protein-coding genes.

From: *Methods in Molecular Biology, vol. 342: MicroRNA Protocols*
Edited by: S. Ying © Humana Press Inc., Totowa, NJ

Even after considering the thousands of new putative genes identified from sequencing of the human genome, as well as the genes encoding transfer RNAs (tRNAs), ribosomal RNA (rRNAs), and small nucleolar RNA (snoRNAs), nearly 95% of the genome is noncoding DNA, a percentage that varies from species to species. Changes in these sequences are frequently associated with clinical and circumstantial malfunction. Some of these noncoding sequences are responsible for RNA-mediated gene silencing through an RNA interference (RNAi)-like mechanism. One potentially important class of genes corresponding to RNAs that lack significant open reading frames, and seem to encode RNA as their final product, is the miRNAs. These miRNAs can play critical roles in development, protein secretion, and gene regulation. Some of them are naturally occurring antisense RNAs, whereas others have structures that are more complex. To understand the diseases caused by dysregulation of these miRNAs, a tissue-specific expression system is needed to recreate the function and mechanism of individual miRNAs in vitro and in vivo.

This chapter provides a simple and general view of the concept that RNAs can directly regulate gene functions, with particular attention to a step-by-step approach to the study of miRNA. Hopefully, this information will help researchers who are new to this field to overcome problems encountered in the functional analysis of miRNA.

1.1. Small RNAs or Noncoding RNAs

A noncoding RNA (ncRNA) is any RNA molecule that functions without being translated into a protein. A ncRNA is also called a small RNA (sRNA). Less frequently, it is called nonmessenger RNA, small nonmessenger RNA, tiny noncoding RNA, small modulatory RNA, or small regulatory RNA. Broadly speaking, the DNA sequence from which an ncRNA is transcribed can be considered a RNA gene.

In this chapter, we will confine our discussion to sRNAs; that is, transcripts of fewer than 300 nt that participate directly in RNA processing and degradation, but indirectly in protein synthesis and gene regulation. Because type II RNA polymerases (Pol-II) are inefficient in generating sRNAs of this size, the sRNAs are either directly transcribed by type III RNA polymerases or indirectly processed from a large transcript of Pol-II.

1.1.1. Transfer RNA

The most prominent example of ncRNA is tRNA, which is involved in the process of translation and is the first type of sRNA that was identified and characterized *(1)*. tRNA is RNA that transfers a specific amino acid to a growing polypeptide chain at the ribosomal site of protein synthesis during translation. The tRNA is a sRNA, 74- to 93-nt long, consisting of amino acid attachment and codon recognition sites, allowing translation of specific amino acids into a polypeptide. The secondary and tertiary structure of tRNAs are cloverleafs with four to five domains and an L-shaped three-dimensional structure, respectively.

1.1.2. Nucleolar RNA

Another example of ncRNA is rRNA. rRNA is the primary constituent of ribosomes. rRNA is transcribed from DNA and, in eukaryotes, it is processed in the nucleolus before being transported through the nuclear membrane. rRNA may produce snoRNAs, the second type of sRNA. Many of the newly discovered snoRNAs are synthesized in an intron-processing pathway. Several snoRNAs and sno-ribonucleoproteins (RNPs) are known to be needed for processing of rRNA, but precise functions remain to be defined. In principle, snoRNAs could have several roles in ribosome synthesis including: folding of pre-rRNA, formation of rRNP substrates, catalyzing RNA cleavages, base modification, assembly of pre-ribosomal subunits, and export of product rRNP particles from the nucleus to the cytoplasm.

The snoRNA acts as a guide to direct pseudouridylation and 2'-*O*-ribose methylation of rRNA in the nucleolus. Consequently, the snoRNA guides the snoRNP complex to the modification site of the target rRNA via sequence hybridization. The proteins then catalyze the modification of bases in the rRNA. Therefore, this type of RNA is also called guided RNA.

The snoRNA is also associated with proteins forming part of the mammalian telomerase, as well as with proteins involved in imprinting on the paternal chromosomes. It is encoded in introns of genes transcribed by Pol-II, even when some of the host genes do not code for proteins. As a result, the intron, but not the exon, of these genes is evolutionarily conserved in vertebrates. In this way, some of the introns of the genes employed in plants or invertebrates are still functioning in vertebrates.

The structure of snoRNAs consists of conserved sequences base-paired to their target RNAs. Nearly all vertebrate guide snoRNAs originate from introns of either protein-coding or ncRNAs transcribed by Pol-II, whereas only a few yeast guide snoRNAs derive from introns, suggesting that introns accumulated during evolution reflect the conservation of transgenes incorporated into the introns, as mentioned above *(2–4)*. These introns are processed through pathways involving endonucleolytic cleavage by ribonuclease (RNase) III-related enzymes, exonucleolytic trimming, and possibly RNA-mediated cleavage, which occur in large complexes called exosomes *(5,6)*.

1.1.3. Nuclear RNA

Small nuclear RNA (snRNA) is a class of sRNA molecules that are found within the nuclei of eukaryotic cells. They are involved in a variety of important processes, such as RNA splicing (removal of introns from heteronuclear RNA) and maintaining the telomeres. snRNA are always associated with specific proteins, and the complexes are referred to as snRNP. Some examples of snRNA are U2 snRNAs, pre-5S rRNAs, and U6 snRNAs. U2 snRNAs in embryonic stem cells and pre-5S rRNAs in *Xenopus* oocytes facilitate cell survival after ultraviolet irradiation by binding to the conserved protein, R_0. Eukaryotic U6 snRNAs are the five types of spliceosomal RNA involved in messenger RNA (mRNA) splicing (U1–U6). These snRNAs have a secondary structure consisting of a stem-loop, an internal loop, a stem-closing internal loop, and the conserved protein-binding site *(7)*.

1.1.4. Phage and Viral RNA

Another form of small RNAs is 30 ribonucleotides in length and functions as a priming initiator for bacteriophage F1 DNA replication *(8,9)*. This function is solely to initiate a given site on the phage DNA, suggesting a primitive defense against foreign pathogen invasion. The phage T4-derived intron is involved in a RNA–RNA interaction in the inhibition of protein synthesis *(10)*.

1.1.5. Small Interfering RNA

The small interfering RNAs (siRNAs) are small double-stranded RNA (dsRNA) molecules, 20- to 25-nt in length, that interfere with the expression of genes via a part of RNAi involving the enzyme Dicer. The siRNA story began with the observation of pigment expression in the *Petunia* plant. van der Krol et al. *(11)* tried to intensify flower pigmentation by introducing additional genes, but unexpectedly observed reduced floral pigmentation in some plants, suggesting that gene silencing may be involved in naturally occurring regulation of gene function. This introduction of multiple transgenic copies of a gene into the *Petunia* plant resulted in gene silencing of not only the transgenic, but also the endogenous gene copy, as has been observed by others *(12)*. This suggests that cosuppression of homologous genes (the transfer gene and the endogenous gene) and possibly methylation, are involved *(12,13)*. This phenomenon is termed RNAi. Note that the transgene introduced to the *Petunia* plant is a dsRNA, which is perfectly complementary to the target gene.

When dsRNA was injected into *Caenorhabditis elegans*, Fire and his coworkers noticed gene silencing and RNAi *(14)*. RNAi is a mechanism by which small regulatory RNAs possessing a sequence complementary to that of a portion of a target gene interfere with the expression of that gene. It is thought that the dsRNA, once it enters the cells, is cut up by an RNase-III familial endonuclease, known as Dicer. Dicer consists of an amino-terminal helicase domain, a PAZ domain, two RNase III motifs, and a dsRNA-binding motif. Therefore, Dicer binds to the dsRNA and excises the dsRNA into siRNAs. These siRNAs locate other single-stranded RNA molecules that are completely complementary to either strand of the siRNA duplex. Then, the RNA-degrading enzymes (RNases) destroy the RNAs complementary to the siRNAs. This phenomenon is also called post-transcriptional gene silencing (PTGS) or transgene quelling. In other words, gene silencing can be activated by introducing transgenes, RNA viruses, or dsRNA sequences that are completely complementary to the targeted gene transcripts.

In mammals, dsRNAs longer than 30 nt will activate an antiviral response, which will lead to the nonspecific degradation of RNA transcripts, the production of interferon, and the overall shutdown of host cell protein synthesis *(15)*. As a result, long dsRNA will not produce gene-specific RNAi activity in mammalian cells *(16)*.

Several terms have been used to describe the same or similar phenomenon in different biological systems of different species, including siRNAs *(17)*, small temporal RNAs *(18)*, heterochromatic siRNAs *(19)*, and small modulatory dsRNAs *(20)*.

1.1.6. MicroRNA

miRNAs are small, single-stranded RNA genes possessing the reverse complement of the mRNA transcript of another protein-coding gene. These miRNAs can inhibit the expression of the target protein-coding gene. miRNA was first observed in *C. elegans* as RNA molecules of 18- to 23-nt that are complementary to the 3' untranslated regions

(UTR) of the target transcripts, including the *lin-4 (21)* and *let-7 (22)* genes. As a result, the development of the worm was regulated by these RNA genes. Subsequently, miRNAs were found to occur in diverse organisms, ranging from worms, to flies, to humans *(23)*, suggesting that these molecules represent a gene family that has evolved from an ancient ancestral sRNA gene.

The miRNA is thought to be transcribed from DNA that is not translated, but regulates the expression of other genes. Primary transcripts of the miRNA genes (pri-miRNAs) are long RNA transcripts consisting of at least a hairpin-like miRNA precursor. Pri-miRNAs are processed in the nucleus to precursor (pre)-miRNAs by the ribonuclease Drosha, with the help of microprocessor *(24)* and exported from the nucleus by Exportin-5 *(25)*. The 60- to 90-nt miRNA precursors form the stem and loop structures, and the cytoplasmic RNase III enzyme, Dicer, excises the miRNA from the pre-miRNA hairpin stem region. miRNAs and siRNAs seem to be closely related, especially taking the dsRNA and hairpin structures into account. The siRNA can be considered a duplex form of miRNA in which the RNA molecule contains both miRNA and its reverse complement. Therefore, one can consider siRNAs a type of miRNA precursor.

miRNAs suppress gene expression based on their complementarity to a part of one or more mRNAs, usually at a site in the 3'-UTR. The annealing of the miRNA to the target mRNA inhibits protein translation. In some cases, the formation of dsRNA through the binding of miRNA triggers the degradation of the mRNA transcript through a process similar to RNAi, although, in other cases, it is thought that the miRNA complex blocks the protein translation machinery or otherwise prevents protein translation without causing the mRNA to be degraded.

Because most of the miRNA suppresses gene function based on partial complementarity, conceivably, one miRNA may target more than one mRNA, and many miRNAs may act on one mRNA, coordinately modulating the intensity of gene expression in various tissues and cells. Therefore, miRNAs may have a broad function in fine-tuning the protein-coding genes. Indeed, the discovery of miRNAs has revolutionized our understanding of gene regulation in the postgenome era.

1.1.7. Intronic miRNA

Some small regulatory RNAs are produced from intronic RNA fragments. For example, snoRNAs are produced from intronic segments from genes encoding ribosomal proteins and nucleolar proteins. In addition, some sRNAs are produced from genes in which exons no longer have the capacity to encode proteins. This type of intron processing involves RNase III-related enzymes, exonucleolytical trimming, and, possibly, RNA-mediated cleavage. Therefore, intronic miRNA is a new class of miRNA derived from the processing of introns of a protein-coding gene.

The major difference between the intronic miRNAs and the previously described intergenic miRNAs, such as *lin-4* and *let-7*, is the requirement of Pol-II and spliceosomal components for the biogenesis of intronic miRNAs *(26)*. Both intronic and intergenic miRNAs may share the same assembly process, namely the RNA-induced silencing complex (RISC), the effector of RNAi-related gene silencing. Although siRNA-associated RISC assembly has been used to predict miRISC assembly, the link between final miRNA maturation and RISC assembly remains to be determined. The characteristics of Dicer and RISC in siRNA vs miRNA mechanisms are distinctly different *(27,28)*.

The intronic miRNAs need to fulfill the following requirements. First, they share the same promoter with their encoding gene transcripts. Second, they are located in the non-protein-coding region of a primary gene transcript (the pre-mRNA). Third, they are co-expressed with the gene transcripts. Last, they are removed from the transcript of their coding genes by nuclear RNA splicing and excision processes to form mature miRNAs.

Certain of the currently identified miRNAs are encoded in the genomic intron region of a gene, but they are of an orientation opposite to that of the protein-coding gene transcript. Therefore, these miRNAs are not considered to be intronic miRNAs because they do not share the same promoter with the gene and they are not released from the protein-coding gene transcript by RNA splicing. The promoters of these miRNAs are located in the antisense direction to the gene, probably using the gene transcript as a potential target for the antisense miRNAs. A good example of this type of miRNA is *let-7c*, which is an intergenic miRNA located in the antisense region of the intron of a gene.

1.1.7.1. Transposon and Intronic miRNA

The intronic and other ncRNAs may have evolved to provide a second level of gene expression in eukaryotes, enabling fine-tuning of the complex network of gene activity. In bacterial and organellar genomes, group II introns contain both catalytic RNAs and retrotransposable elements. The retrotransposable elements make this type of intron mobile. Therefore, these introns are reversely spliced directly into a DNA target site and subsequently reverse transcribed by the intron-encoded gene. After insertion into the DNA, the introns are spliced out of the gene transcript to minimize the damage to the host.

There is a potential evolutionary relationship between group II introns and both eukaryotic spliceosomal introns and non-LTR-retrotransposons. Taking advantage of this feature, it is feasible to design mobile group II introns to be incorporated into gene-targeting vectors as "targetrons," to specifically target various genes *(29)*. There is evidence that introns in *Caenorhabditis* genes are recently gained and some of them are actually derived from "donor" introns present in the same genome. Further, a few of these new introns apparently derive from other introns in the same gene *(30)*. Perhaps the splicing machinery determines where introns are added to genes. On the other hand, some newly discovered brain-specific snoRNAs of unknown function are encoded in introns of tandem repeats, and the expression of these introns is paternally imprinted.

From an evolutionary vantage, transposons are probably very old and may exist in the common ancestor genome. They may enter the host multiple times for selfish parasitical reasons. This feature of transposons is similar to that of retroviruses. Too much transposon activity can destroy a genome. To counterattack the activity of transposons and viruses, some organisms developed a mechanism to remove and/or silence the activity of transposons and viruses. For example, bacteria frequently delete their genes so that transposons and retroviruses incorporated in the genome are removed. In eukaryotes, miRNA is a way of reducing transposon activity. Conceivably, miRNA may be involved in resistance against viruses, similar to the diversity of antibody production in an immune system, or in a to-be-identified mechanism for fighting disease.

Identical twins derived from the same zygote have the same genetic information in their nuclear DNA. Any differences between monozygotic twins later in life are mostly the result of environmental influences rather than genetic inheritance. However, monozygotic twins may not share all of their DNA sequences. Female monozygotic twins can differ because of differences in X-chromosome inactivation. Consequently, one female twin can have an X-linked condition, such as muscular dystrophy, and the other twin can be free of the condition. Monozygotic twins frequently demonstrate slightly different (but definitely distinguishing) disease susceptibility and, more generally, different physiology. For example, myotonic dystrophy is a dominantly inherited, multisystemic disease with a consistent constellation of seemingly unrelated and rare clinical features, including myotonia, muscular dystrophy, cardiac conduction defects, posterior iridescent cataracts, and endocrine disorders *(31)*. Type 2 myotonic dystrophy is caused by a CCTG expansion (mean, ~5000 repeats) located in intron 1 of the zinc finger protein 9 gene *(32)*. It is possible that monozygotic twins with this disorder display symptom heterogeneity because of miRNAs or different levels of insertion of intronic genes.

Class II transposons can cut and paste. The enzyme transposase binds to the ends of the transposon, which are repeats, and the target site on the genome, which is cut to leave sticky ends. These two components are joined together by ligases. In this way, transposons increase the size of the genome because they leave multiple copies of themselves in the genome. It is highly possible that transposons are selectively advantageous for the genome to modulate gene regulation via miRNAs. It is not be too far-fetched to suggest that when transposons are inserted in the introns of the protein-coding gene, under appropriate conditions, they, a part of them, or their secondary structures, may become intronic miRNAs.

2. Biogenesis and Mechanism of miRNAs

The investigation of the biogenesis and mechanism of miRNAs still is in its infancy. siRNA seems to be a form of miRNA duplex predominantly occurring in plants and lower animals. The biogenesis and mechanism of siRNAs are very similar to those of miRNA. However, there are some differences between these two pathways.

Five steps are involved in miRNA biogenesis in vertebrates. First, miRNA is generated as a long pri-miRNA, most likely mediated by Pol-II *(33,34)*. The pri-miRNA is transcribed from the genome. Second, the long pri-miRNA is excised by Drosha-like RNase III endonucleases and/or spliceosomal components to form the approx 60- to 70-nt pre-miRNA. The pre-miRNA exhibits considerable secondary structure, including regions of imperfectly paired dsRNA, which are sequentially cleaved to one or more miRNAs. This step depends on the origin of the pri-miRNA, whether located in an exon or an intron, respectively *(24,33)*. Third, the pre-miRNA is exported out of the nucleus by Ran-GTP and a receptor, Exportin-5 *(25,35)*. Fourth, in the cytoplasm, Dicer-like endonucleases cleave the pre-miRNA to form mature 18- to 25-nt-long miRNA. Last, the mature miRNA is incorporated into a RNP to form the RISC, which executes

RNAi-related gene silencing *(36,37)*. Only one of the two strands is the miRNA; the other counterpart is named miRNA*. The mature miRNA can block mRNA translation based on partial complementarity between the miRNA and the targeted mRNA, particularly via base pairing with the 3' UTR of the mRNA. If there is a perfect complementarity between the miRNA and the targeted mRNA, mRNA degradation occurs similarly to that mediated by siRNA. Autoregulatory negative feedback via miRNAs regulates some genes, including those involved in the RNA silencing mechanism itself.

Although the assembly of RISC for siRNA has been reported in an in vitro system, and a similar assembly probably also occurs for miRNA, the link between final miRNA maturation and RISC assembly remains unknown. However, there is evidence that the actions of Dicer and RISC in siRNA and miRNA processing are distinct *(27)*. In recent studies using zebrafish, it was demonstrated that the stem-loop structure of the pre-miRNAs is involved in strand selection for mature miRNA during RISC assembly. These findings further suggest that the duplex structure of siRNA may not be strictly required for the assembly of miRNA-associated RISC in vivo. Proposed pathways for the biogenesis of miRNA are based on the in vitro model developed for siRNA. For these reasons, future work needs to focus on distinguishing the individual properties and differences in action of Dicer and RISC in siRNA and miRNA processing. Conceivably, siRNA is a defense mechanism against immediate insertion of viral genes or transposons in plants and lower animals. In contrast, over evolutionary time, miRNA selects segments of transposons for incorporation into the genome for fine-tuning of gene regulation in vertebrates, including human beings. This hypothesis for the differences between siRNA and miRNA gene silencing may provide a clue toward explaining the prevalence of native siRNAs in invertebrates and their relative scarcity in mammals.

In plants, siRNAs and their dsRNA precursors trigger DNA methylation, as well as RNAi *(38–40)*. Another functional type of siRNAs is a specialized ncRNA molecule that is X-chromosome encoded, Xist. Xist is preferentially expressed from only one of the two female X chromosomes and builds up in *cis* along the chromosome from which it was transcribed. That X chromosome is tightly packaged in transcriptionally inactive heterochromatin; therefore, only one female X chromosome is active. This phenomenon is associated with DNA methylation. Similarly, the viruses, transgenes, and transposons that have been incorporated into the introns of the mammalian genome during evolution may take advantage of these characteristics by splicing the pri-miRNAs, and incorporating them into Dicer-like proteins for gene silencing and mRNA degradation.

Argonaute (AGO) I is a key protein that is required for both the siRNA and miRNA pathways, and it is likely to be the endonuclease that cleaves the mRNA targeted by the RISC *(41,42)*. Elucidating the roles of the full complement of the AGO protein family will reveal further modulation of the RISC, and, more generally, of sRNA regulation. Additional proteins involved in the RISC at the convergence of the PTGS and miRNA pathways have been reported *(43,44)*.

Introns account for the largest proportion of noncoding sequences in the protein-coding DNA of the genome. The transcription of the genomic protein-coding DNA generates pre-mRNA, which contains four major parts, including the 5' UTR, the pro-

tein-coding exon, the noncoding intron, and the 3' UTR. In broad terms, both the 5' UTR
and the 3' UTR can be seen as a kind of intron extension; however, their processing during mRNA translation is different from that of the intron located between two protein-
coding exons, termed the in-frame intron. The in-frame intron was originally thought
to be a huge genetic wasteland in gene transcripts, but this stereotypical misconception was abandoned because of the finding of intronic miRNAs. To this day, the biogenesis of intronic miRNAs remains to be determined (**Fig. 1**).

3. Identification

Currently, there are four major ways to identify miRNAs. They are:

1. Direct cloning.
2. Computer search of the genome.
3. miRNA microarray search in different species.
4. Artificial preparation of intronic miRNA for targeting known gene sequences.

The conventional direct cloning of short RNA molecules, as in the cloning of *let-7*
and *lin-4*, is still the method of choice to identify new miRNAs. Conceivably, one can
isolate the sRNAs and sequence them individually. Thus far, results have been dominated by a few highly expressed miRNAs. However, once the miRNA is identified, its
role in other organisms, including human beings, can be explored. For example, *let-7*
was originally identified in *C. elegans*. Subsequently, reduced expression of the *let-7*
miRNA *(45)* and Dicer *(46)* in human lung cancers suggested that the alteration of *let-7*
expression is associated with clinical and biological effects.

There are numerous new computational methods that provide ways to estimate the
total number of miRNA genes in different animals *(47–50)*. Fundamentally, each program identifies highly conserved genomic noncoding regions that possess stem-loop
structures with specific "seed" sequences, and complementarity of the first 8- to 10-nt.
Then, the secondary structure is examined in terms of both the forward and reverse com-
plements of the sequence. In addition, the following criteria help to identify miRNAs:
the longest helical arm, the free energy of the arm, short internal loops, and asymmetric
and bulged loops. The identified miRNAs are usually more heterogeneous than those
that are discovered experimentally, suggesting that traditional cloning has a high false–
negative rate or miss rate. However, computational techniques may suffer from a high
false-alarm rate. Therefore, validation of the identified miRNAs by Northern blot analysis and functional study is critical. These methods are still evolving and there is a possibility of one-to-many and many-to-one relationships between the miRNAs and their
targets. Potentially thousands of mammalian targets may be identified with this approach.

To facilitate such investigations, an oligonucleotide microchip for genome-wide
miRNA profiling in diverse tissues of various species was developed *(51–53)*. Some
of these chips use locked nucleic acid-modified oligonucleotides to allow both miRNA
in situ hybridization and miRNA expression profiling *(53)*. Again, this approach can
identify regulation via a large class of miRNAs. A good example is the studies of
miRNAs regulating brain morphogenesis in zebrafish *(54)*.

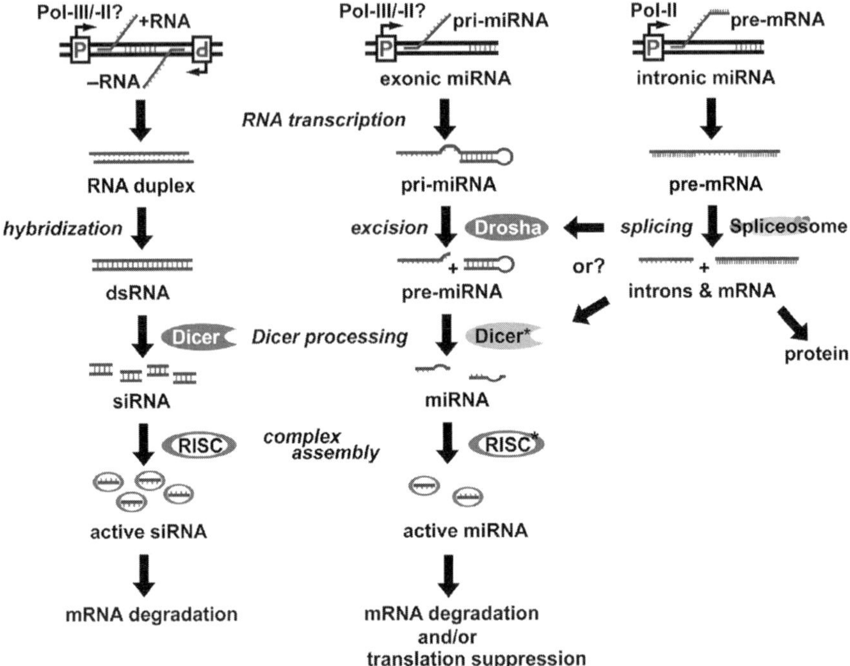

Fig. 1. Comparison of biogenesis and RNA interference mechanisms among small interfering RNA (siRNA), intergenic (exonic) micro RNA (miRNA), and intronic miRNA. siRNA is likely formed by two perfectly complementary RNAs transcribed from two different promoters (although this remains to be determined) and further processing into 19- to 22-bp duplexes by the ribonuclease (RNase) III familial endonuclease, Dicer. The biogenesis of intergenic miRNAs, e.g., *lin-4* and *let-7*, involves a long transcript precursor (pre)-miRNA, which is probably generated by type II RNA polymerase (Pol-II) promoters or type III RNA polymerase promoters, whereas intronic miRNAs are transcribed by the Pol-II promoters of its encoded genes and coexpressed in the intron regions of the gene transcripts (pre-mRNA). After RNA splicing and further processing, the spliced intron may function as a primary transcript (pri)-miRNA for intronic miRNA generation. In the nucleus, the pri-miRNA is excised by Drosha RNase to form a hairpin-like pre-miRNA template, and is then exported to the cytoplasm for further processing by Dicer* to form mature miRNAs. The Dicers for siRNA and miRNA pathways are different. All three small regulatory RNAs are finally incorporated into a RNA-induced silencing complex, which contains either strand of siRNA or the single strand of miRNA. The effect of miRNA is considered more specific and less adverse than that of siRNA because only one strand is involved. However, siRNAs primarily trigger messenger RNA (mRNA) degradation, whereas miRNAs can induce either mRNA degradation or suppression of protein synthesis, depending on the sequence complementarity to the target gene transcripts.

4. Applications

Application of miRNA is common in plants. The first experimentally observed RNAi was demonstrated by the discoloration of flowers after introduction of dsRNAs. miRNAs do not solely mediate gene regulation in flowering plants; the regulation of a similar type of plant gene can be used to silence a fruit-ripening gene. The latter approach has been applied to create hardier tomatoes by engineered repression of the tomato-ripening gene through homology-based silencing.

The following areas are potential applications of miRNAs in vertebrates:

a. Analysis of gene function.
b. Evaluation of function and effectiveness of miRNA.
c. Design and development of novel gene therapy.
d. Design and development of anti-viral vaccines.
e. Development of loss-of-function transgenic animals.

4.1. Analysis of Gene Function

The human genome contains more than 22 billion bases. Analyzing and understanding these sequences is a challenge to all natural science. Numerous high-throughput screening programs have been developed in the postgenome era. Good examples of the usefulness of such programs are the discoveries that *lin-4* and *let-7* miRNAs, originally identified in *C. elegans*, control the timing of fate specification of neuronal and hypodermal cells during larval development. Subsequently, these miRNAs were found to be conserved in mammals, with potential functions in development and disease *(55,56)*. Although most programs are focused on global computational screens, others aim at screening or isolating all miRNAs with a specific function in the genome. For instance, retroviral insertional mutagenesis in mouse hematopoietic tumors provides a potent cancer gene-discovery tool in the postgenome sequence era. The multiple high-throughput insertional mutagenesis screening projects were, thus, designed for identifying new cancer genes. Using a short hairpin RNAi expression library against the entire human transcriptome, attempts were made to screen for sRNAs in the genome *(57,58)*.

With the completion of genome-sequencing projects, a major challenge will be to understand gene function and regulation. Achieving this goal will require determining how miRNAs modulate gene expression. The various gene-silencing mechanisms based on complete or partial complementarity and their intertwined actions are beginning to reveal the sensitive control mechanisms that modify gene expression at the post-transcriptional and RNA turnover levels.

Intronic miRNA also represents a new frontier in genetics research. The evidence of intronic miRNA-induced silencing of gene expression in cell lines, zebrafish, chicken embryos, and mouse skin demonstrates that this ancient intron-mediated gene regulation system is highly conserved in eukaryotes. Intronic regulation of gene expression is mediated through the activation of miRNA-mediated RNAi effects. From an evolutionary vantage point, the genome exhibits a remarkable increase in the complexity and variety of introns in higher plants and animals; therefore, the influence of intronic gene regulation to facilitate genome stability and gene coordination progressively increases phylogenetically. Conceivably, dysregulation of intronic miRNAs is highly likely to reveal the intertwined actions between intronic miRNA and gene expression, leading to a better understanding of the genetic etiology of human diseases. The success of intronic miRNA generation by artificial means in vivo may provide a powerful tool to study the mechanism by which miRNAs induce diseases and will, hopefully, provide novel gene therapies.

4.2. Evaluation of miRNA Function and Effectiveness

Prediction of miRNA candidates using analytical software has identified thousands of genomic hairpin sequences. For instance, the human DiGeorge syndrome critical region gene 8 (*DGCR8*), and its *Drosophila melanogaster* homolog, were identified in this fashion. The biochemical and whole cell-based data demonstrating the requirement of *DGCR8* for the maturation of miRNA primary transcripts has been acquired. Further, RNAi knockdown experiments with fly and human *DGCR8* showed both accumulation and reduction of pri-miRNAs, as well as mature miRNAs. In this manner, the function of, effectiveness of, and interaction between miRNAs and enzyme processing complexes can be demonstrated *(59)*.

To date, the function of the vast majority of miRNAs so identified remains to be determined. Because direct transfection of hairpin-like pre-miRNAs in mammalian cells is not always sufficient to trigger effective RISC assembly, a key step for RNAi-related gene silencing, our intronic miRNA-expressing system was developed to overcome this problem and, indeed, successfully increased the efficiency and effectiveness of miRNA-associated RNAi induction in vitro and in vivo. Nevertheless, there are still problems in the efficient use of miRNA. Indeed, evaluating the function and effectiveness of the miRNAs identified thus far may contribute greatly to our understanding of gene regulation and the control of the differentiation and development of cells.

Based on the strand complementarity between the designed miRNA and its target gene sequence, we have also developed a miRNA isolation protocol to purify and identify the mature miRNAs generated by the intronic miRNA-expressing system. Several intronic miRNAs have been confirmed active in vitro and in vivo. As shown by this proof-of-principle method, we now have the necessary knowledge to design more efficient and effective pre-miRNA inserts for the intronic miRNA-expressing system.

4.3. Design and Development of Novel Gene Therapy

We are undergoing an epoch-marking transition into the postgenome era, which opens up data sources of unprecedented scale. This information can be used for designing and developing potential drugs as novel gene therapies. Furthermore, the elucidation of genomic control of gene activities mediated via miRNA may play a crucial role in the characterization and treatment of disease at the molecular level. At the same time, our still very limited knowledge of the biological functions of genes and proteins at different levels of cellular organization is preventing full exploitation of the available data. We believe that the recent discovery of miRNAs will fill the gap and lead to unlimited functional prediction based on the DNA–miRNA and RNA–miRNA paradigm. In theory, oncogene and transgene expression could be inhibited by synthetic miRNAs, a simple, effective gene therapy. Thus, miRNAs or their machineries are now known to be involved in several human diseases, including cancer and neurological disorders. Specific removal of the target genes by miRNAs or their associate mediators can be developed as a simple gene therapy *(60)*.

4.4. Design and Development of Antiviral Vaccine

By the same token, antiviral vaccines can be developed. The problems in preventing viral infections, such as HIV, are as follows: first, the global prevalence of epidemic proportions is mainly caused by the high mutation rate of the HIV genome that gradually generates strains that are more resistant to highly active antiretroviral therapies. Second, the HIV provirus is capable of integrating into a host cellular genome to escape from the inhibitory effects of the treatment, thus, inactivating the viral replication cycle rather than destroying the latent viral genome, resulting in an increased number of HIV carriers. Such an increase of drug-resistant HIV strains and their carriers has posed great challenges and financial burdens for the AIDS prevention programs. To alleviate such problems, miRNAs can trigger either translation repression or RNA degradation depending on their degree of complementarity with the target genes. Our approach, using vector-based miRNA to overcome the complications of HIV mutation is a breakthrough in the field. We think that the knowledge obtained from this research will facilitate the development of antiviral drugs and vaccines against HIV infections *(61, 62)*. Similar approaches for the treatment of viral diseases will target avian flu, severe acute respiratory syndrome, hepatitis B, herpes, and poliomyelitis.

4.5. Development of Loss-of-Function Transgenic Animals

The ability to use miRNA and its machinery for silencing target-gene expression has created much excitement as a novel and simple means to develop loss-of-function transgenic animals. To define the function of a critical molecule in miRNA processing, zebrafish models have been developed that carry loss-of-function mutations.

This type of animal model has provided an unprecedented resource for miRNA research because this approach can be used to create miRNAs for use in loss-of-function studies. It is clear that miRNAs also hold great promise as therapeutic tools because of their sequence-specific targeting, particularly against infectious diseases with frequent mutations. Another potential use of transgenic animal models using miRNAs is the testing of gene functions and drug mechanisms in vivo.

Using man-made miRNA, one can establish loss of function in zebrafish, chicken, and mice. The loss-of-function transgenic zebrafish could not have been achieved with siRNAs because of promoter incompatibility, but have been developed with intronic miRNAs. The zebrafish, possessing numerous features similar to human biological systems, is most suitable for etiological and pathological studies of human diseases, particularly mechanisms by which the loss of a specific signal molecule causes a disease or disorder. All pharmaceutically developed drugs can be screened with this approach in loss-of-function transgenic zebrafish. In addition, this approach may shed light on the effects of miRNAs on embryonic development, environmental impacts, and micromodulation of gene functions, particularly brain and heart functions. Indeed, insight regarding structure–function features of a candidate gene involved in pathobiology and the mechanisms in which the candidate gene operates, can be illuminated with the help of miRNA transgenic animal models carrying a loss-of-function mutation within the candidate gene.

Appendix

Argonaute (AGO): A large protein family that constitutes key components of RISCs. AGO proteins are characterized by two unique domains, PAZ and PIWI, whose functions are not fully understood. Current evidence suggests that the PAZ domain binds the 2-nt overhang of the 3' end of the siRNA duplex, whereas the PIWI domain of some AGO proteins confers slicer activity. PAZ and PIWI domains are both essential to guide the interaction between the siRNA and the target mRNA for cleavage or translational repression. Distinct AGO members have distinct functions. For example, human AGO2 programs siRNA-associated RISCs to cleave the mRNA target, whereas other AGO members do not.

Cosuppression: A phenomenon similar to PTGS, but silencing multiple homologous genes via a transgene or dsRNA.

Dicer (DCR): An enzyme of the RNase III endonuclease family consisting of multiple domains, which cleaves dsRNA or stem-loop structured RNA precursors into sRNAs, and forms siRNAs and miRNAs, respectively. Dicer possesses a potential helicase activity and an additional domain of undetermined function, and is essential for RNAi in *Drosophila* and *C. elegans.*

Drosha: A nuclear RNase III endonuclease that is implicated in the cleavage of pri-miRNA into pre-miRNA before the nuclear export of miRNA precursors.

Epigenetics: Changes in gene expression not caused by the DNA code and that occur across at least one generation.

Exportin-5: A nuclear transmembrane protein that transports pre-miRNA from the nucleus to the cytosol.

Microprocessor: A nuclear complex composed of Drosha and Pasha that functions in miRNA biogenesis from the pri-miRNA to the pre-miRNA.

MicroRNA (miRNA): A type of noncoding small RNA (~21–23 nt) produced by DCR from a stem-loop structured RNA precursor. miRNAs are widely expressed in animal and plant cells as RNA–protein complexes (RNPs), termed miRISCs, and have been implicated in the control of development because they target specific gene transcripts for destruction or translational suppression.

Post-transcriptional gene silencing (PTGS): An intracellular gene regulation mechanism in which a transgene or dsRNA triggers the degradation or the translational suppression of a gene transcript containing high complementarity to the transgene or dsRNA.

Pseudogene: A defective segment of DNA that resembles a gene but cannot be transcribed into RNA.

RNA-induced silencing complex (RISC): An RNA–protein complex that targets its perfectly or partially complementary mRNA for cleavage or translational repression. siRNA programs a siRISC and miRNA programs a miRISC. RISCs (both siRISC and miRISC) can be divided into two types: cleaving and noncleaving. Current evidence suggests that the type of AGO protein, an essential RISC component, determines whether a RISC is cleaving or noncleaving.

RNA interference (RNAi): A PTGS phenomenon induced by either single-stranded miRNA or double-stranded siRNA.

Short hairpin RNA: A single-stranded oligonucleotide containing two complementary regions that form a duplex structure with a short hairpin loop.

Small interfering RNA (siRNA): A type of sRNA (~21–25 nt) produced by Dicer, a dsRNA-specific enzyme of the RNase III family. siRNA is the key component of siRISCs and triggers the silencing of its complementary mRNA.

Transgene: dsDNA or DNA–RNA hybrid duplex capable of being transcribed by RNA polymerases and affecting the expression of an intracellular gene.

Acknowledgment

The work was supported by a grant from the National Institutes of Health, CA 85722.

References

1. Holley, R. W. (1965) Structure of an alanine transfer ribonucleic acid. *JAMA* **194,** 868–871.
2. Maxwell, E. S. and Fournier, M. J. (1995) The small nucleolar RNAs. *Annu. Rev. Biochem.* **64,** 897–934.
3. Tycowski, K. T., Shu, M. D., and Steitz, J. A. (1996) A mammalian gene with introns instead of exons generating stable RNA products. *Nature* **379,** 464–466.
4. Filipowicz, W. (2000) Imprinted expression of small nucleolar RNAs in brain: time for RNomics. *Proc. Natl. Acad. Sci. USA* **97,** 14,035–14,037.
5. Allmang, C., Kufel, J., Chanfreau, G., Mitchell, P., Petfalski, E., and Tollervey, D. (1999) Functions of the exosome in rRNA, snoRNA and snRNA synthesis. *EMBO J.* **18,** 5399–5410.
6. van Hoof, A. and Parker, R. (1999) The exosome: a proteasome for RNA? *Cell* **99,** 347–350.
7. Frank, D. N., Roiha, H., and Guthrie, C. (1994) Architecture of the U5 small nuclear RNA. *Mol. Cell. Biol.* **14,** 2180–2190.
8. Stavianopoulos, J. G., Karkus, J. D., and Charguff, E. (1971). Nucleic acid polymerase of the developing chicken embryos: a DNA Polymerase preferring a hybrid template. *Proc. Natl. Acad. Sci. USA* **68,** 2207–2211.
9. Stavianopoulos, J. G., Karkus, J. D., and Charguff, E. (1972) Mechanism of DNA replication by highly purified DNA polymerase of chicken embryos. *Proc. Natl. Acad. Sci. USA* **69,** 2609–2613.
10. Wank, H. and Schroeder, R. (1996) Antibiotic-induced oligomerisation of group I intron RNA. *J. Mol. Biol.* **258,** 53–61.
11. van der Krol, A. R., Mur, L. A., Beld, M., Mol, J. N., and Stuitje, A. R. (1990) Flavonoid genes in petunia: addition of a limited number of gene copies may lead to a suppression of gene expression. *Plant Cell* **2,** 291–299.
12. Napoli, C., Lemieux, C., and Jorgensen, R. A. (1990) Introduction of a chimeric chalcone synthase gene into *Petunia* results in reversible co-suppression of homologous genes in trans. *Plant Cell* **2,** 279–289.
13. Matzke, M. A., Primig, M. J., Trnovsky, J., and Matzke, A. J. M. (1989) Reversible methylation and inactivation of marker genes in sequentially transformed tobacco plants. *EMBO J.* **8,** 643–649.
14. Fire, A., Xu, S., Montgomery, M. K., et al. (1998) Potent and specific genetic interference by double-stranded RNA in *Caenorhabditis elegans*. *Nature* **391,** 806–811.
15. Shi, Y. (2003) Mammalian RNAi for the masses. *Trends Genet.* **19,** 9–12.

16. Sui, G., Soohoo, C., el Affar, B., et al. (2002) A DNA vector-based RNAi technology to suppress gene expression in mammalian cells. *Proc. Natl. Acad. Sci. USA* **99,** 5515–5520.

17. Elbashir, S. M., Lendeckel, W., and Tuschl, T. (2001) RNA interference is mediated by 21- and 22-nucleotide RNAs. *Genes Dev.* **15,** 188–200.

18. Pasquinelli, A. E., Reinhart, B. J., Slack, F., et al. (2000) Conservation of the sequence and temporal expression of let-7 heterochronic regulatory RNA. *Nature* **408,** 86–89.

19. Reinhart, B. J. and Bartel, D. P. (2002) Small RNAs correspond to centromere heterochromatic repeats. *Science* **297,** 1831.

20. Kuwabara, T., Hsieh, J., Nakashima, K., Taira, K., and Gage, F. H. (2004) A small modulatory dsRNA specifies the fate of adult neural stem cells. *Cell* **116,** 779–793.

21. Lee, R. C., Feinbaum, R. L., and Ambros, V. (1993) The C. elegans heterochronic gene lin-4 encodes small RNAs with antisense complementarity to lin-14. *Cell* **75,** 843–854.

22. Lau, N. C., Lim, L. P., Weinstein, E. G., and Bartel, D. P. (2001) An abundant class of tiny RNAs with probable regulatory roles in Caenorhabditis elegans. *Science* **294,** 858–862.

23. Lagos-Quintana, M., Rauhut, R., Meyer, J., Borkhardt, A., and Tuschl, T. (2003) New microRNAs from mouse and human. *RNA* **9,** 175–179.

24. Lee, Y., Ahn, C., Han, J., et al. (2003) The nuclear RNase III Drosha initiates microRNA processing. *Nature* **425,** 415–419.

25. Lund, E., Guttinger, S., Calado, A., Dahlberg, J. E., and Kutay, U. (2003) Nuclear export of microRNA precursors. *Science* **303,** 95–98.

26. Ying, S. Y. and Lin, S. L. (2005) Intronic microRNAs (miRNAs). *Biochem. Biophys. Res. Commun.* **326,** 515–520.

27. Lee, Y. S., Nakahara, K., Pham, J. W., et al. (2004) Distinct roles for Drosophila Dicer-1 and Dicer-2 in the siRNA/miRNA silencing pathways. *Cell* **117,** 69–81.

28. Tang, G. (2005) siRNA and miRNA: an insight into RISCs. *Trends Biochem. Sci.* **30,** 106–114.

29. Lambowitz, A. M. and Zimmerly, S. (2004) Mobile group II introns. *Annu. Rev. Genet.* **38,** 1–35.

30. Coghlan, A. and Wolfe, K. H. (2004) Origins of recently gained introns in Caenorhabditis. *Proc. Natl. Acad. Sci. USA* **101,** 11,362–11,367.

31. Harper, P. S. (1989) *Myotonic Dystrophy* (Saunders, London, ed. 2).

32. Liquori, C. L., Ricker, K., Moseley, M. L., et al. (2001) Myotonic dystrophy type 2 caused by a CCTG expansion in intron 1 of ZNF9. *Science* **293,** 864–867.

33. Lin, S. L., Chang, D., Wu, D. Y., and Ying, S. Y. (2003) A novel RNA splicing-mediated gene silencing mechanism potential for genome evolution. *Biochem. Biophys. Res. Commun.* **310,** 754–760.

34. Lee, Y., Kim, M., Han, J., et al. (2004) MicroRNA genes are transcribed by RNA polymerase II. *EMBO J.* **23,** 4051–4060.

35. Yi, R., Qin, Y., Macara, I. G., and Cullen, B. R. (2003) Exportin-5 mediates the nuclear export of pre-microRNAs and short hairpin RNAs. *Genes Dev.* **17,** 3011–3016.

36. Schwarz, D. S., Hutvagner, G., Du, T., Xu, Z., Aronin, N., and Zamore, P. D. (2003) Asymmetry in the assembly of the RNAi enzyme complex. *Cell* **115,** 199–208.

37. Khvorova, A., Reynolds, A., and Jayasena, S. D. (2003) Functional siRNAs and miRNAs exhibit strand bias. *Cell* **115,** 209–216.

38. Jones, L., Hamilton, A. J., Voinnet, O., Thomas, C. L., Maule, A. J., and Baulcombe, D. C. (1999). RNA-DNA interactions and DNA methylation in post-transcriptional gene silencing. *Plant Cell* **11,** 2291–2301.

39. Vaistij, F. E., Jones, L., and Baulcombe, D. C. (2002). Spreading of RNA targeting and DNA methylation in RNA silencing requires transcription of the target gene and a putative RNA-dependent RNA polymerase. *Plant Cell* **14,** 857–867.

40. Béclin, C., Boutet, S., Waterhouse, P., and Vaucheret, H. (2002). A branched pathway for transgene-induced RNA silencing in plants. *Curr. Biol.* **12,** 684–688.

41. Okamura, K., Ishizuka, A., Siomi, H., and Siomi, M.C. (2004) Distinct roles for Argonaute proteins in small RNA-directed RNA cleavage pathways. *Genes Dev.* **18,** 1655–1666.

42. Kidner, C. A. and Martienssen, R. A. (2005) The role of ARGONAUTE1 (AGO1) in meristem formation and identity. *Dev. Biol.* **280,** 504–517.

43. Liu, J., Valencia-Sanchez, M. A., Hannon, G. J., and Parker, R. (2005) MicroRNA-dependent localization of targeted mRNAs to mammalian P-bodies. *Nat. Cell. Biol.* **7,** 719–723.

44. Meister, G., Landthaler, M., Patkaniowska, A., Dorsett, Y., Teng, G., and Tuschl, T. (2004) Human Argonaute2 mediates RNA cleavage targeted by miRNAs and siRNAs. *Mol. Cell.* **15,** 185–197.

45. Takamizawa, J., Konishi, H., Yanagisawa, K., et al. (2004) Reduced expression of the let-7 microRNAs in human lung cancers in association with shortened postoperative survival. *Cancer Res.* **64,** 3753–2756.

46. Karube, Y., Tanaka, H., Osada, H., et al. (2005) Reduced expression of Dicer associated with poor prognosis in lung cancer patients. *Cancer Sci.* **96,** 111–115.

47. Xu, P., Guo, M., and Hay, B. A. (2004) MicroRNAs and the regulation of cell death. *Trends Genet.* **20,** 617–624.

48. Jin, P., Alisch, R. S., and Warren, S. T. (2004) RNA and microRNAs in fragile X mental retardation. *Nat. Cell Biol.* **6,** 1048–1053.

49. Gesellchen, V. and Boutros, M. (2004) Managing the genome: microRNAs in Drosophila. *Differentiation* **72,** 74–80.

50. McManus, M. T. (2003) MicroRNAs and cancer. *Semin. Cancer Biol.* **13,** 253–258.

51. Liu, C. G., Calin, G. A., Meloon, B., et al. (2004) An oligonucleotide microchip for genome-wide microRNA profiling in human and mouse tissues. *Proc. Natl. Acad. Sci. USA* **101,** 9740–8744.

52. Miska, E. A., Alvarez-Saavedra, E., Townsend, M., et al. (2004) Microarray analysis of microRNA expression in the developing mammalian brain. *Genome Biol.* **5,** R68.

53. Valoczi, A., Hornyik, C., Varga, N., Burgyan, J., Kauppinen, S., and Havelda, Z. (2004) Sensitive and specific detection of microRNAs by northern blot analysis using LNA-modified oligonucleotide probes. *Nucleic Acids Res.* **32,** e175

54. Giraldez, A. J., Cinalli, R. M., Glasner, M. E., et al. (2005) MicroRNAs regulate brain morphogenesis in zebrafish. *Science* **308,** 833–838.

55. Lai, E. C., Tomancak, P., Williams, R. W., and Rubin, G. M. (2003) Computational identification of Drosophila microRNA genes. *Genome Biol.* **4,** R42.

56. Brown, J. R. and Sanseau, P. (2005) A computational view of microRNAs and their targets. *Drug Discov. Today* **10,** 595–601.

57. Miyagishi, M., Matsumoto, S., and Taira, K. (2004) Generation of and shRNAi expression library against the whole human transcripts. *Virus Res.* **102,** 117–124.

58. Nagl, S. B. (2002) Computational function assignment for potential drug targets: from single genes to cellular systems. *Curr. Drug Targets* **3,** 387–399.

59. Landthaler, M., Yalcin, A., and Tuschl, T. (2004) The human DiGeorge syndrome critical region gene 8 and Its D. melanogaster homolog are required for miRNA biogenesis. *Curr. Biol.* **14,** 2162–2167.

60. Pardridge, W. M. (2004) Intravenous, non-viral RNAi gene therapy of brain cancer. *Expert Opin. Biol. Ther.* **4,** 1103–1113.
61. Zamore, P. D. (2004) Plant RNAi: How a viral silencing suppressor inactivates siRNA. *Curr. Biol.* **9,** R198–200.
62. Lecellier, C. H., Dunoyer, P., Arar, K., et al. (2005) A cellular microRNA mediates anti-viral defense in human cells. *Science* **308,** 557–561.

2

Structure Analysis of MicroRNA Precursors

Jacek Krol and Wlodzimierz J. Krzyzosiak

Summary

MicroRNA biogenesis occurs in several steps from their precursors having irregular hairpin structures. The highly variable architecture of these stem-and-loop structures, which have terminal loops of various sizes and diverse structure destabilizing motifs present in their stem sections, may strongly influence the process of microRNA liberation. In order to better understand this process, more details regarding its structural basis are required. A substantial part of this information may be derived from the structure analysis of microRNA precursor using biochemical methods. Here we show how the analysis with the use of various nucleases and metal ions is performed. The presented protocols include the design of DNA template-phage promoter fusions to generate natural precursor ends, and the tests performed to check the sequence and structure homogeneity of the in vitro transcripts prior to probing their structures.

Key Words: miRNA; miRNA precursor; structure analysis.

1. Introduction

MicroRNAs (miRNAs) are a large family of short 20- to 25-nucleotide (nt) long single-stranded noncoding RNAs identified in many eukaryotes, from nematodes to humans *(1,2)*. They trigger the translational inhibition of target messenger RNAs by binding to their 3'-untranslated region *(3,4)*. Genes encoding miRNA contribute more than 1% to the total gene content of the investigated organisms *(2,5)*, making this regulatory mechanism more common than previously thought. Specific miRNAs were shown to be engaged in the regulation of apoptosis and cell proliferation in *Drosophila*, neuronal asymmetry in *Caenorhabditis elegans*, leaf and flower development in plants, hematopoietic differentiation in humans, and the control of human cell development *(6,7)*. The biological function of a great majority of miRNAs remains unknown.

The primary transcripts of the miRNA genes (pri-miRNAs) are generated by RNA polymerase II *(8)* as unclustered monocistronic or clustered polycistronic RNAs, which may be several hundred nucleotides long. The pri-miRNAs, which typically form a

From: *Methods in Molecular Biology, vol. 342: MicroRNA Protocols*
Edited by: S. Ying © Humana Press Inc., Totowa, NJ

stem and loop structure, are processed in the nucleus to shorter, approx 60-nt, hairpin precursor (pre)-miRNAs by the ribonuclease, Drosha *(9)*, which acts together with the double-stranded (dsRNA)-binding protein, DiGeorge syndrome critical region gene 8, in a complex termed Microprocessor (**Fig. 1A**) *(10)*. Drosha leaves a 2-nt overhang at the 3' end of pre-miRNA and defines one end of the mature miRNA strand. After the overhang recognition, pre-miRNAs are exported from the nucleus by Exportin-5 *(11)* and further processed to miRNAs by a cytoplasmic ribonuclease, Dicer *(12,13)*.

Dicer is composed of several functional domains: the Piwi-Argonaute-Zwille (PAZ) domain, which is used for high-affinity binding to the 3' overhanging nucleotides of pre-miRNA, the helicase domain, the DUF283 subunit, the dsRNA binding domain, and two ribonuclease (RNase) III catalytic domains (**Fig. 1B**) that form the intramolecular dimer during pre-miRNA cleavage *(14)*. The pre-miRNA is processed by Dicer symmetrically, as proposed for the siRNA *(15,16)*. Usually, only the miRNA strand of the excised duplex intermediate is stabilized by the successful entering of the RNA-induced silencing complex (RISC) *(17,18)*. The miRNA* strand and the remainder of the precursor is degraded (**Fig. 1A**).

The process of excision of the miRNA–miRNA* duplex is controlled by various structure-destabilizing elements present in the precursor hairpin *(19)*, and the existence of sequence determinants or antideterminants of the Dicer cleavage has also been proposed *(20)*. The pre-miRNAs are predicted to form irregular hairpin structures containing various base mismatches, internal loops, and bulges *(21)*. However, these predicted structures need to be experimentally verified to serve as a reliable basis for the analysis of structural aspects of miRNA biogenesis. The necessity of the experimental structure analysis was documented in a recent study, in which differences were shown to exist between the majority of predicted and experimentally established precursor structures *(22)*.

The steps of experimental procedure used for the structure probing of miRNA precursors are shown in the diagram in **Fig. 2**. In brief, they include RNA synthesis by in

Fig. 1. *(Opposite page)* (**A**) The mechanism of microRNA (miRNA) biogenesis *(13)*; after miRNA is produced by the activity of two class III ribonucleases, Drosha and Dicer, and selected by the RNA-induced silencing complex (RISC). After the transcription by RNA polymerase II, the primary transcript of the miRNA gene (pri-miRNA) is cleaved in the nucleus by Drosha, forming a heterodimeric complex (named Microprocessor), with the double-stranded RNA (dsRNA)-binding protein, DiGeorge syndrome critical region 8 (DGCR8). Drosha generates the miRNA precursor (pre-miRNA), which binds Exportin-5 and is exported to the cytoplasm. In the cytoplasm, Dicer binds to the pre-miRNA and generates a duplex intermediate comprising the active miRNA (indicated in gray color) and inactive miRNA* strands. The cleavage sites of the nucleases Drosha and Dicer are indicated by black triangles. After the preferential duplex unwinding at the miRNA 5' end, the active strand is selectively incorporated into RISC by the miRNA-specific RISC assembly. The activated miRNA–RISC complex directs either translational repression or degradation of the targeted messenger RNA, depending on the degree of sequence complementarily. (**B**) A schematic illustration of the domain structure of human Drosha and Dicer proteins. RIII, ribonuclease III catalytic domain; dsRBD, dsRNA-binding domain. The "x" symbol indicates the inactive ribonuclease center in one of the RIII Dicer domains.

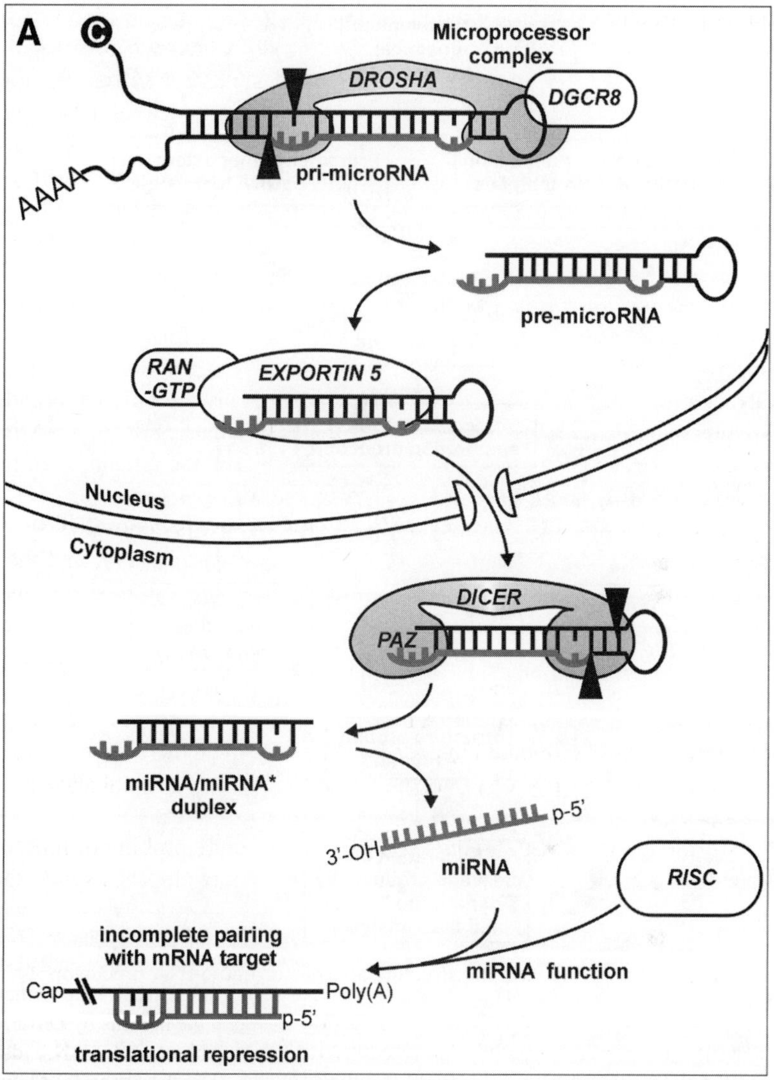

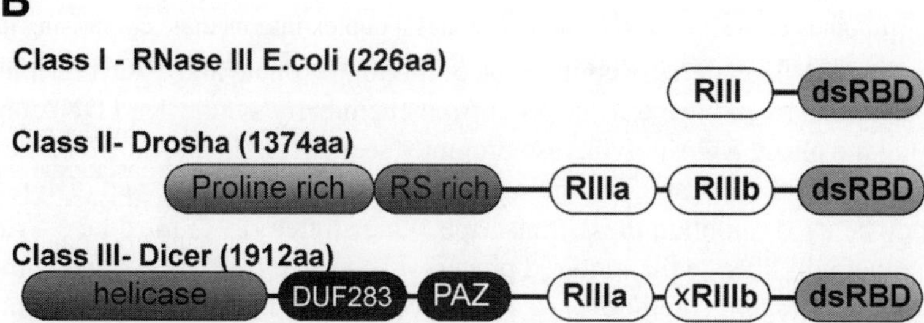
A
Microprocessor complex
DROSHA
DGCR8
pri-microRNA
AAAA
pre-microRNA
RAN -GTP
EXPORTIN 5
Nucleus
Cytoplasm
DICER
PAZ
miRNA/miRNA* duplex
3'-OH
p-5'
miRNA
RISC
incomplete pairing with mRNA target
Cap
Poly(A)
p-5'
miRNA function
translational repression
B
Class I - RNase III E.coli (226aa)
RIII
dsRBD
Class II- Drosha (1374aa)
Proline rich
RS rich
RIIIa
RIIIb
dsRBD
Class III- Dicer (1912aa)
helicase
DUF283
PAZ
RIIIa
xRIIIb
dsRBD

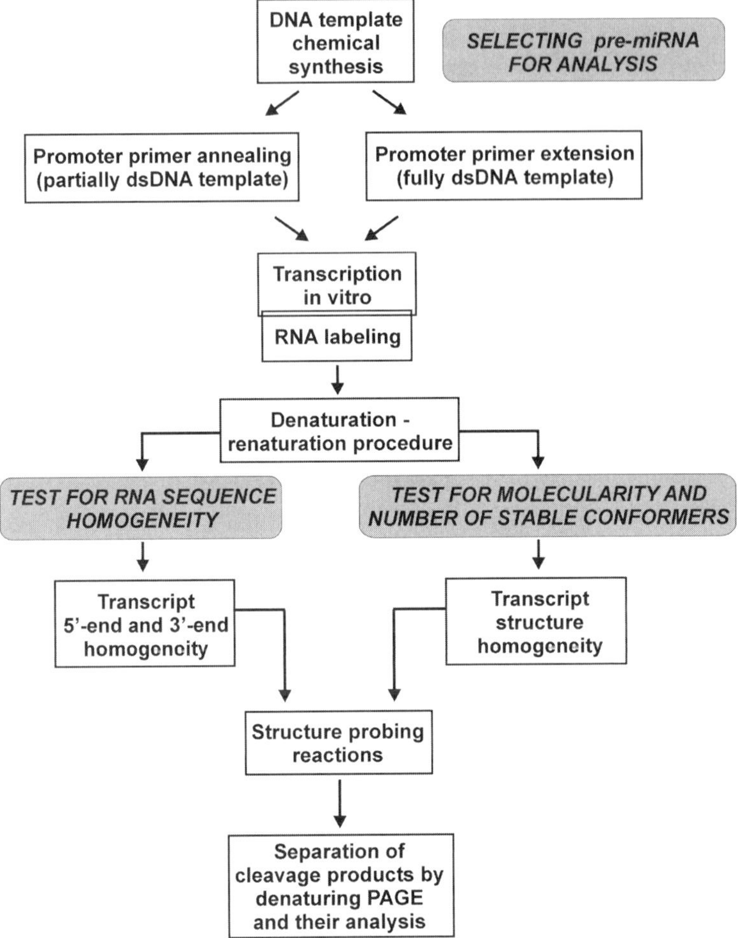

Fig. 2. Steps involved in the structure analysis of microRNA precursors.

vitro transcription, necessary to ensure the required RNA sequence devoid of 5' end *(23)* and 3' end *(24)* heterogeneities. After RNA labeling, the tests for transcript sequence and structure homogeneity are performed, and the RNA is subjected to structure-probing reactions.

Human miRNA precursors contain the 5'-monophosphate and 3'-OH termini. They may be obtained by in vitro transcription from chemically synthesized DNA templates containing the phage RNA polymerase promoter sequence. The pre-miRNAs have various sequences at their 5' end, beginning either with G, C, A, or U, and different strategies may be used to obtain these transcripts. One strategy is to introduce a ribozyme structure that will liberate the required precursor sequence from the extended transcript *(14)*. Another possible method is to introduce a short initiator oligoribonucleotide homologous to the precursor 5' end to the in vitro transcription mixture *(25)*. The most

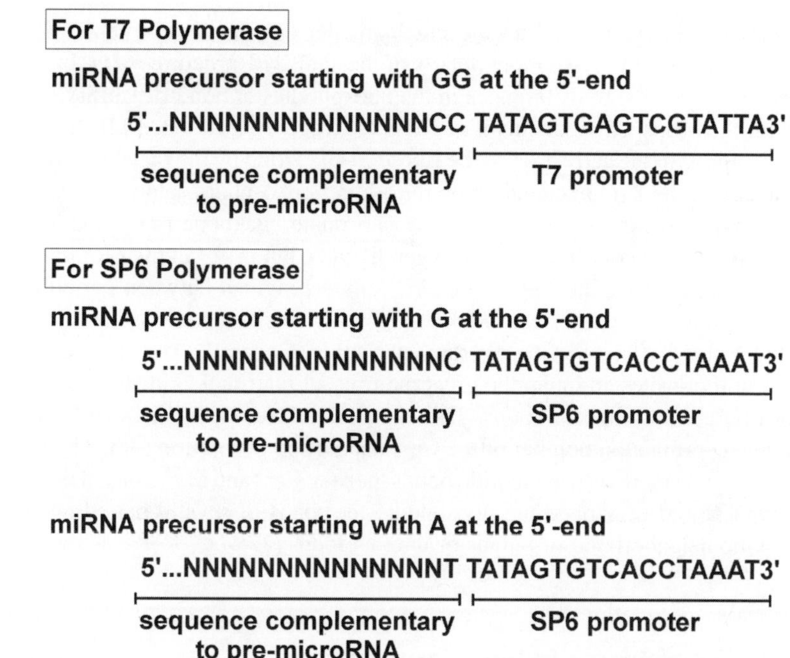

Fig. 3. Phage RNA polymerase promoter sequences enabling the generation of the required transcript ends by in vitro transcription.

simple approach, which is described in this chapter, takes advantage of the alternative T7 and SP6 RNA polymerase promoters *(26,27)*. They provide correct 5' end sequences for a number of miRNA precursors, whose sequences start, for example, with a single G or A residue (**Fig. 3**).

The chemical and enzymatic probing of nucleotide accessibility *(28,29)* can be used to rapidly obtain reliable structure information, taking advantage of the distinct specificity of different chemical reagents and nucleases. Ribonucleases T1 and T2 and nuclease S1 recognize the single-stranded regions of RNA *(30,31)*, and they map the terminal loops of the precursor hairpins as well *(22)*. The double-stranded helical regions are cleaved by ribonuclease V1. This small, 15-kDa protein from cobra venom *(32)*, which accommodates only one strand of a helix at its recognition site, requires a helical sugar phosphate backbone conformation for its activity *(33)*. The minimum V1 recognition site is usually six nucleotides, three at each side of the cleavage site, and their conformation may strongly influence the cleavage efficiency *(33)*. Ribonuclease V1, showing some preference for recognizing simple sequence repeats, reveals the distribution of a specific, more regular helical conformation along the miRNA precursor hairpin *(22)*.

The nucleases map small internal loops, bulges, and mismatches poorly. On the contrary, nearly all of these stem-structure irregularities are well-recognized by metal ions: Mg^{2+} *(34,35)*, Mn^{2+} *(36)*, Ca^{2+} *(37)*, and Pb^{2+} ions *(38–40)*. The advantageous feature of metal ions is that their hydrates are much smaller than nucleases, penetrate folded RNAs more easily, and reveal more details of the analyzed structures *(41)*. In addition, metal ions are sensitive to differences in the phosphodiester bond flexibility, in accordance with the proposed mechanism of RNA cleavage by lead ions *(42)*. In brief, the reaction begins with the activation of the ribose 2'-OH group by the metal ion hydroxide, and the attack of the 2'-*O*-nucleophile on the adjacent phosphorus atom, which requires the conformational flexibility of the sugar phosphate backbone *(43)*. The Mg^{2+} and Ca^{2+} ions both prefer coordination to oxygen ligands, but differ in their ionic radii and coordination geometry. The Mg^{2+} and Ca^{2+} ions distinguish between paired and unpaired nucleotides most precisely *(44,45)*. The reactive phosphodiester bonds mapped by the Mg^{2+} and Ca^{2+} ions often overlap each other. Generally, the Ca^{2+} ions induce cleavages at more sites and map the great majority of internucleotide bonds present in numerous bulges and internal loops. This is in accordance with the flexible geometry and variable coordination number of the Ca^{2+} aquacation in solution *(45)*. The Pb^{2+} and Mn^{2+} ions cleaved more internucleotide bonds than the Ca^{2+} and Mg^{2+} ions in the miRNA precursors. They also mapped the phosphodiester bonds of several paired nucleotides located in the neighborhood of bulges or internal loops *(22)*.

2. Materials

2.1. DNA Templates for In Vitro Transcription

1. DNA oligomers obtained by chemical synthesis were purchased from commercial sources.
2. T7 promoter primer, 5'TAATACGACTCACTATAGG.
3. SP6 promoter primer, 5'ATTTAGGTGACACTATA.
4. 10% polyacrylamide gel (acrylamide:*bis* acrylamide ratio, 19:1) buffered with 1X TBE (89 m*M* Tris, 89 m*M* boric acid, and 20 m*M* ethylenediaminetetraacetic acid [EDTA], pH 8.0).
5. *Taq* DNA polymerase 5 U/μL in storage buffer A (Promega, Madison, WI).
6. Set of 2.5 m*M* deoxyribonucleoside triphosphates (dNTPs) (Promega).
7. 2X TE buffer: 20 m*M* Tris-HCl, 2 m*M* EDTA.
8. 10X TBE buffer: 890 m*M* Tris-HCl, 890 m*M* boric acid, and 20 m*M* EDTA.
9. Stains-All dye reagent (Serva, Heidelberg, Germany).
10. Microcon YM30 microcentrifuge tubes (Millipore, Billerica, MA).

2.2. In Vitro Transcription

1. 200 U/μL T7 RNA polymerase (Epicentre, Madison, WI) and 200 U/μL SP6 RNA polymerase (Fermentas, Burlington).
2. Set of 5 m*M* NTPs (Roche, Mannheim), 10 m*M* guanosine, and 10 m*M* adenosine.
3. 40 U/μL RNaseOUT recombinant ribonuclease inhibitor (Invitrogen, Carlsbad, CA).
4. Urea, EDTA, and dyes (UED) buffer: 7.5 *M* urea and 20 m*M* EDTA with dyes (bromophenol blue and xylenecyanol FF; Fluka, Buchs, Switzerland).
5. Elution buffer: 0.3 *M* sodium acetate, pH 5.2, 0.5 m*M* EDTA, and 0.1% sodium dodecylsulfate.

2.3. RNA-Labeling Reagents

1. 4500 Ci/mmol [γ-^{32}P] adenosine triphosphate (ATP) (MP Biomedicals, Irvine, CA).
2. 3000 Ci/mmol [5'-^{32}P] cytidine-3', 5'-biphosphate (pCp) (Perkin Elmer, Wellesley, MA).

3. 3000 Ci/mmol [α-^{32}P] cytidine triphosphate (CTP) (MP Biomedicals).
4. 10 U/μL T4 polynucleotide kinase (Epicenter).
5. 20 U/μL T4 RNA ligase (Fermentas).
6. 2 U/μL alkaline phosphatase, calf intestinal (Pharmacia, Rockville, MD).

2.4. Testing RNA Sequence and Structure Homogeneity

1. Formamide buffer: 99% formamide, 0.5 mM MgCl$_2$.
2. 2X T2 buffer: 20 mM sodium citrate, pH 5.0, and 7 M urea.
3. 0.2 U/μL T1 ribonuclease (USB, Cleveland, OH).
4. Structure-probing buffer A: 12 mM Tris-HCl, pH 7.2, 48 mM NaCl, and 1.2 mM MgCl$_2$.
5. Structure-probing buffer B: 12 mM Tris-HCl, pH 8.5 or 9.0, and 48 mM NaCl.
6. 140 U/μL nuclease S1 (Amersham Biosciences, Piscataway, NJ), 100 U/μL ribonuclease T1 (USB), 20 U/μL T2 (Invitrogen), 0.1 U/μL V1 (Ambion, Austin, TX).
7. Ion solutions: 30 mM MgCl$_2$, 30 mM CaCl$_2$, 30 mM Pb(CH$_3$COO)$_2$.

3. Methods

3.1. RNA Structure Prediction Procedure and Setting Variables

RNA secondary structure prediction was performed using the mfold program, version 3.1. This program is designed to determine the optimal and suboptimal secondary structures of RNA calculated for a 1 M NaCl solution at 37°C, and to count free energy contributions for various secondary structure motifs. The structure prediction is usually performed with the suboptimality parameter set at 10%. At this setting, the program shows all of the structures that have a free energy of formation of up to 10% higher than the optimal structure.

3.2. DNA Template/Promoter Purification

1. Dilute the DNA oligomer, which has a sequence of the antisense strand of the miRNA precursor, with the attached phage promoter sequence (*see* **Note 1**) to a concentration of 100 pmol/μL with RNase- and deoxyribonuclease-free water.
2. Add 20 μL of UED buffer to 20 μL of the DNA oligomer solution in **Subheading 3.2.**, incubate the sample at 95°C for 1 min, and immediately load the sample on the pre-electrophoresed 10% (acrylamide:*bis* acrylamide ratio, 19:1) polyacrylamide gel (420 × 340 × 1 mm), buffered with 1X TBE. Perform the electrophoresis at 600 V/40 mA for 10 min and then at 1200 V/90 mA for 3 h.
3. Stain the gel with 0.1% Stains-All dye (Serva) at room temperature for 30 min.
4. Cut the band corresponding to the desired DNA template and elute the DNA to 500 μL of elution buffer at 4°C overnight.
5. Precipitate the DNA with three volumes of EtOH and resuspend the pellet in 20 μL of water. Store at –20°C.

3.3. Preparation of DNA Templates for In Vitro Transcription (see Note 2)

3.3.1. Annealing Procedure

1. Mix 8 μL (600 pmol) of the purified template oligomer and 8 μL (600 pmol) of T7 or SP6 promoter primer with 16 μL of 2X TE buffer.
2. Incubate the sample at 90°C for 5 min and cool the sample slowly to 37°C for 10 min.

3.3.2. Primer Extension Procedure

1. Mix 2 µL (final concentration, 200 pmol) of purified template oligomer, 5 µL (1 mmol) of T7 or SP6 promoter primer, and 8 µL of dNTPs (200 µM each) with 10 µL of standard 1X polymerase chain reaction (PCR) buffer and 0.5 µL (0.5 U) of *Taq* DNA polymerase in a 100-µL reaction.
2. Perform the primer extension: 50 cycles at 94°C for 15 s and 45°C for 15 s.
3. Purify the dsDNA product using Microcon YM30 centrifugal filter devices, according to the manufacturer's (Millipore) instructions, and dilute the DNA template to 60 µL with water.

3.4. In Vitro Transcription With Phage Polymerases

The pre-miRNA transcripts can be prepared by in vitro transcription with T7 or SP6 RNA polymerases.

1. In a 50-µL volume at room temperature, mix the 40 pmol of DNA template (12 µL of DNA after the primer extension procedure or 2 µL of DNA after phage promoter primer annealing), 50 µM of rNTPs, 30 µL of 10 m*M* guanosine (preheated to 65°C for 3 min) or adenosine solution (*see* **Note 3**), 10 µL of 1X standard transcription buffer, 40 U of ribonuclease inhibitor, RNase Out, and 400 U of T7 or SP6 RNA polymerase.
2. Incubate the reaction mixture at 37°C for 1.5 h.
3. After EtOH precipitation at –20°C overnight, resuspend the transcript in 20 µL of water and add 20 µL of UED buffer.
4. Purify the in vitro transcription product in a denaturing 10% polyacrylamide gel, excise the product band, elute the RNA from the gel with RNA elution buffer, and precipitate with EtOH as described in **Subheading 3.2.** Resuspend the pellet in a 10 µL of RNase-free water. Store at –80°C.

3.5. RNA-Labeling Procedures

3.5.1. 5' End Labeling

1. Mix 10 µL of purified pre-miRNA transcript (~1 nmol) with 3 µL of 4500 Ci/mmol [γ-^{32}P] ATP, 1.5 µL of 10X T4 polynucleotide kinase buffer, and 1 µL of T4 polynucleotide kinase.
2. Incubate the mixture at 37°C for 10 min.
3. Stop the labeling reaction by adding an equal volume of UED buffer.
4. Purify the labeled RNA in 10% polyacrylamide gel, as described for DNA template purification in **Subheading 3.2.** After electrophoresis, attach the labeling markers to the gel and place the gel in the autoradiography cassette with the X-ray film for approx 3 min. After autoradiography, correctly orient the film with respect to the markers and cut out the single gel band corresponding to the desired RNA.
5. Elute the RNA with approx 500 µL of the elution buffer at 4°C overnight. Precipitate the RNA with EtOH, and resuspend the pellet in approx 20 µL of RNase-free water.

3.5.2. 3' End Labeling

1. Mix 10 µL of purified pre-miRNA transcript with 5 µL of 3000 Ci/mmol [5'-^{32}P] pCp, 2 µL of reaction buffer, 2 µL of 10 m*M* ATP, and 2 µL of T4 RNA ligase in a volume of 20 µL.
2. Incubate the reaction mixture at 4°C for 16 h.
3. Optionally (*see* **Note 4**): add 2 µL of 10X alkaline phosphatase buffer and 1 µL of alkaline phosphatase and incubate at 37°C for 20 min.
4. Purify the labeled RNA as described in **Subheading 3.4.**

3.5.3. Internal Labeling

1. For internal labeling, the pre-miRNA RNA is synthesized by in vitro transcription, as described in **Subheading 3.4.**, with the exception that the set of NTPs (5 m*M* ATP, 5 m*M* GTP, 5 m*M* UTP, and 0.5 m*M* CTP) is supplemented with 5 µL of 3000 Ci/mmol [α-^{32}P] CTP.
2. Incubate the reaction mixture at 37°C for 1.5 h.
3. Purify the labeled RNA as described in **Subheading 3.4.**

3.6. 5′ End and 3′ End Sequence Homogeneity Testing *(see Note 5)*

1. The limited T1 ribonuclease ladder generated from the 5′ end-labeled transcript of a discrete length is visually inspected for the presence of extra fragments not predicted from the correct nucleotide sequence. These extra fragments are usually one nucleotide longer than the expected T1 fragments. The presence of such extra bands in addition to those expected from the correct sequence indicates the 5′ end heterogeneity. It indicates that some of the transcripts are longer by one nucleotide at the 5′ end and shorter by one nucleotide at the 3′ end (**Fig. 3**).

3.7. Structure Homogeneity and Molecularity Testing *(see Note 6)*

1. Incubate approx 5 pmol (30.000 cpm) of the 5′ end-labeled transcript in a structure-probing solution (buffer A: 10 m*M* Tris-HCl, pH 7.2, 40 m*M* NaCl, and 1 m*M* MgCl$_2$) at 90°C for 1 min, followed by slow cooling to 37°C.
2. Mix with an equal volume of the same buffer containing 7% sucrose and dyes.
3. Load the samples onto a 10% nondenaturing polyacrylamide gel (dimensions, 150 × 140 × 1 mm; acrylamide:*bis* acrylamide ratio, 29:1) buffered with the structure-probing buffer. Perform electrophoresis at 100 V at a controlled temperature of 37°C, with a buffer circulation at 2 L/h.
4. Dry the gel and visualize the RNA by autoradiography.

3.8. Structure Probing With Nucleases *(see Note 7)*

1. Subject the ^{32}P-end-labeled transcript to a denaturation and renaturation procedure before structure probing. For a single reaction, in an 8-µL volume, mix the ^{32}P-end-labeled RNA (~10 pmol; 60.000 cpm) and structure-probing buffer A to obtain a final concentration of 12 m*M* Tris-HCl, pH 7.2, 48 m*M* NaCl, and 1.2 m*M* MgCl$_2$. Heat the sample at 90°C for 1 min and leave the reaction mixture in a thermal block for slow (~5 min) cooling to 37°C.
2. Add 2 µL of nuclease water solution at one of three different concentrations. Typically used concentrations are: T1 (0.5, 1.0, and 1.5 U/µL), T2 (0.15, 0.2, and 0.25 U/µL), V1 (0.15, 0.2, and 0.25 U/mL), and nuclease S1 (1.5, 3.0, and 6.0 U/µL) (*see* **Note 8**). Incubate at 37°C for 10 min.
3. Stop the reaction by adding 10 µL of 7.5 *M* urea and 20 m*M* EDTA with dyes.

3.9. Structure Probing With Metal Ions

1. Before structure probing, subject the ^{32}P-end-labeled transcript to a denaturation and renaturation procedure. For single reaction with Pb^{2+} ions, in an 8-µL volume, mix the ^{32}P-end-labeled RNA solution (~10 pmol; 60.000 cpm) and structure-probing buffer A to obtain a final concentration of 12 m*M* Tris-HCl, pH 7.2, 48 m*M* NaCl, and 1.2 m*M* MgCl$_2$. For a single reaction with Mn^{2+}, Mg^{2+}, or Ca^{2+} ions, in an 8-µL volume, mix the ^{32}P-end-labeled RNA (~10 pmol; 60.000 cpm) and structure-probing buffer B to obtain a concentration of 12 m*M* Tris-HCl, pH 8.5 or 9.0, and 48 m*M* NaCl.

2. Heat the sample at 90°C for 1 min followed by slow cooling to 37°C.
3. Add 2 µL of the metal ions solution at the appropriate concentrations. Use the $Pb(CH_3COO)_2$ solution at 0.5, 1.0, and 2.0 mM; the $MgCl_2$ solution at 3, 10, and 15 mM; the $CaCl_2$ solution at 3, 15, and 30 mM; or the $MnCl_2$ solution at 3, 10, and 15 mM.
4. At 37°C, incubate the RNA with Pb^{2+} ions for 10 min, with Mn^{2+} ions for 2 h, and with Mg^{2+} or Ca^{2+} ions for 16 h.
5. Stop the reaction by adding 10 µL of solution containing 7.5 M urea and 20 mM EDTA with dyes.

3.10. Gel Electrophoresis and Autoradiography

1. Denature the sample briefly by a 30-s incubation at 90°C before loading the gel.
2. Analyze the cleavage products by electrophoresis in a 15% polyacrylamide gel (dimensions 420 × 340 × 0.4 mm) (acrylamide:*bis* acrylamide ratio, 19:1) buffered with 1X TBE under denaturing conditions.
3. Generate the alkaline hydrolysis ladder by incubating 2 µL of the end-labeled RNA (~10 pmol) with 9 µL of formamide containing 0.5 mM $MgCl_2$ at 100°C for 10 min. Stop the reaction by adding 9 µL of UED buffer.
4. Generate the T1 ladder by incubating 2 µL of the end-labeled RNA (~10 pmol) with 3 µL of semidenaturing buffer (10 mM sodium citrate, pH 5.0, and 3.5 M urea) for 20 s at 100°C. Place the tube with the reaction mixture on ice immediately and keep it on ice for 5 min. Add 1 µL of T1 ribonuclease (1 U/µL), and incubate at 55°C for 12 min. Stop the reaction by adding 14 µL of UED buffer.
5. Typical structure analysis with a single probe requires six gel lanes: the incubation control line (without a probe), three lanes of reactions with a probe used at different concentrations, a lane of alkaline hydrolysis ladder, and a lane of T1 ladder. Typically, 3 µL of each sample is loaded into each gel well.
6. Run the electrophoresis at 40 mA/1500 V for approx 2 h.
7. Transfer the gel onto Whatman 3MM paper, cover with plastic wrap, and subject to autoradiography at –80°C with an intensifying screen.

3.11. Phosphor Imaging and Quantitative Analysis of Cleavages

1. Place the dried gel into the PhosphorImager cassette for 16 h.
2. Scan the screen on a Typhoon (Molecular Dynamics) laser densitometer operating at 633 nm.
3. Analyze the peak heights obtained from gel bands representing the relative cleavage efficiency at the corresponding sites, as shown in *(46–48)*.

4. Notes

1. The in vitro transcription of the desired pre-miRNA is performed from the DNA template obtained by chemical synthesis, which offers the DNA template designed to contain the antisense miRNA precursor sequence extended by the phage promoter sequence, so that the end of the latter defines the 5' end of the former (**Fig. 3**).
2. If using synthetic DNA templates for in vitro transcription, at least the promoter portion of the template has to be double-stranded. For such templates, the promoter primer annealing procedure is performed to obtain a double-stranded promoter region. For GC-rich templates with high propensities to form secondary structures, we recommend performing primer extension to obtain a fully double-stranded template. The disadvantage of using the primer-extension procedure is the increased risk of introducing 3' end heterogeneity into the DNA template.

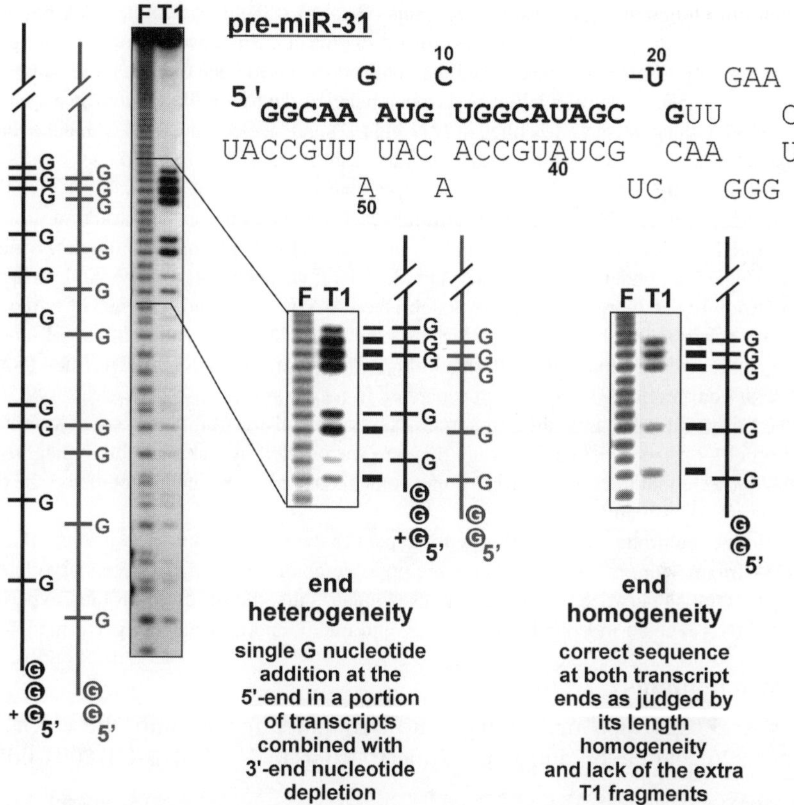

Fig. 4. Examples of end sequence heterogeneity in the 5' end-labeled microRNA (miRNA) precursor transcript. The predicted secondary structure of miR-31 precursor (pre-miR-31) with a boldface miRNA sequence is shown. RNA cleavages by T1 ribonuclease (T1) are performed in semidenaturing conditions for mapping all G residues. The vertical lines with positions of G residues indicated represent various compositions of T1 fragments that are observed in the presented autoradiograms, derived from precursors with a 5' end heterogeneity (left) and a homogenous sequence (right). F, formamide ladder.

3. Guanosine or adenosine is added to the reaction mixture at the appropriate concentrations to introduce them at the 5' end in a high proportion of transcripts. This makes the 5' end dephosphorylation step unnecessary before its labeling. The guanosine concentration in the water solution used is the highest possible concentration and is determined by the nucleoside solubility in water. Adenosine may be used at the same or higher concentration for SP6 transcription beginning with A.

4. If using the labeled pre-miRNA transcript in the reaction with Dicer, it is necessary to produce the pre-miRNA that contains the specific ends: 5'-monophosphate and 3'-OH.

5. Because of the tendency of different RNA polymerases to add extra nucleotides to the ends of transcripts (usually n +1) that are not encoded by the template, some pre-miRNAs may contain extra nucleotides at their 5' (**Fig. 4**) and/or 3' ends. This sequence heterogeneity, which is highly undesired in detailed structural studies, can be suppressed by reducing the

length of consecutive mononucleotide tracts (G or A) at the 3' end of the RNA polymerase promoter. With relatively short pre-miRNAs (~60 nt), it is easy to cut out single bands representing discrete sequences from the gel. The strongest band usually corresponds to the correct sequence. Alternatively, transcripts labeled at their 5' or 3' end may be exhaustively digested with nuclease as described in *(23)* and *(37)* and labeled fragments with either homogeneous or heterogeneous lengths are visualized in a 20% polyacrylamide gel, as described in **Subheading 3.10.**

6. A test for structure homogeneity is strongly recommended before the structure probing of pre-miRNA. Some RNAs may form two or more stable conformers or dimers, which can be detected in nondenaturing polyacrylamide gels. If such a gel shows one stable conformer, its structure can be relatively easily established. In case of the coexistence of two or more stable conformers, the single conformers may be isolated from the native gel, and their structures probed separately. Alternatively, structure probing may be performed on a mixture of conformers, which are then separated in native gel, as described earlier *(49,50)*.

7. The failure of nucleases, and, in some cases, of metal ions, to detect small symmetrical internal loops and mismatches when they are surrounded by stable double-helical regions, may indicate that these motifs form noncanonical base pairs, which do not distort the duplex structure significantly.

8. Optimize the probe concentration with respect to every transcript to assure less than 10% RNA fragmentation and to minimize the possible contributions from secondary cleavages. To distinguish between the primary and secondary cuts, the structure-probing experiments with RNA labeled independently at the 5' end and 3' end may also be performed.

Acknowledgments

This work was supported by the State Committee for Scientific Research, grant 2P05A08826, and the EC Integrated Project "RIGHT" No. LSHB-CT-2004-005276.

References

1. Lee, R. and Ambros, V. (2001) An extensive class of small RNAs in Caenorhabditis elegans. *Science* **294,** 862–864.
2. Lagos-Quintana, M., Rauhut, R., Lendlecker, W., and Tuschl, T. (2001) Identification of novel genes coding for small expressed RNAs. *Science* **294,** 853–858.
3. Lee, R. C., Feinbaum, R. L., and Ambros, V. (1993) The C. elegans heterochronic gene lin-4 encode small RNAs with antisense complementarity to lin-14. *Cell* **75,** 843–854.
4. Slack, F. J., Basson, M., Liu, Z., Ambros, V., Horvitz, H. R., and Ruvkun, G. (2000) The lin-41 RBCC gene acts in the C. elegans heterochronic pathway between the let-7 regulatory RNA and the LIN-29 transcription factor. *Mol. Cell* **5,** 659–669.
5. Largos-Quintana, M., Rauhut, R., Meyer, J., Borkhardt, A., and Tuschl, T. (2003) New microRNAs from mouse and human. *RNA* **9,** 175–179.
6. Bartel, D. P. (2004) MicroRNAs: genomics, biogenesis, mechanism, and function. *Cell* **116,** 281–297.
7. Tomari, Y. and Zamore, P. D. (2005) Perspective: machines for RNAi. *Genes Dev.* **19,** 517–529.
8. Lee, Y., Kim, M., Han, J., et al. (2004) MicroRNA genes are transcribed by RNA polymerase II. *EMBO J.* **23,** 4051–4060.
9. Lee, Y., Ahn, C., Han, J., et al. (2003) The nuclear RNase III Drosha initiates microRNA processing. *Nature* **425,** 415–419.
10. Gregory, R. I., Yan, K., Amuthan, G., et al. (2004) The microprocessor complex mediates the genesis of microRNAs. *Nature* **432,** 235–240.

11. Lund, E., Guttinger, S., Calado, A., Dahlberg, J. E., and Kutay, U. (2003) Nuclear export of microRNA precursors. *Science* **303,** 95–98.
12. Hutvágner, G., McLachlan, J., Pasquinelli, A. E., Balint, E., Tuschl, T., and Zamore, P. D. (2001) A cellular function for the RNA-interference enzyme Dicer in the maturation of the let-7 small temporal RNA. *Science* **293,** 834–838.
13. Cullen, B. R. (2004) Transcription and processing of human microRNA precursors. *Mol. Cell* **16,** 861–865.
14. Zhang, H., Kolb, F., Jaskiewicz, L., Westhof, E., and Filipowicz, W. (2004) Single processing center models for human Dicer and bacterial RNase III. *Cell* **118,** 57–68.
15. Hutvágner, G. and Zamore, P. D. (2002) A microRNA in a multiple-turnover RNAi enzyme complex. *Science* **297,** 2056–2060.
16. Ketting, R. F., Fischer, S. E., Bernstein, E., Sijen, T., Hannon, G. J., and Plasterk, R. H. (2001) Dicer functions in RNA interference and in synthesis of small RNA involved in developmental timing in C. elegans. *Genes Dev.* **15,** 2654–2659.
17. Khvorova, A., Reynolds, A., and Jayasena, S. D. (2003) Functional siRNAs and miRNAs exhibit strand bias. *Cell* **115,** 209–216.
18. Schwarz, D. S., Hutvágner, G., Du, T., Xu, Z., Aronin, N., and Zamore, P. D. (2003) Asymmetry in the assembly of the RNAi enzyme complex. *Cell* **115,** 199–208.
19. Krol, J. and Krzyzosiak, W. J. (2004) Structural aspects of microRNA biogenesis. *IUBMB Life* **56,** 95–100.
20. Zeng, Y. and Cullen, B. R. (2003) Sequence requirements for microRNA processing and function in human cells. *RNA* **9,** 112–123.
21. Zuker, M. (2003) Mfold web server for nucleic acid folding and hybridization prediction. *Nucleic Acids Res.* **31,** 3406–3415.
22. Krol, J., Sobczak, K., Wilczynska, U., et al. (2004) Structural features of microRNA precursors and their relevance to miRNA biogenesis and siRNA/shRNA design. *J. Biol. Chem.* **279,** 42,230–42,239.
23. Krzyzosiak, W. J., Napierala, M., and Drozdz, M. (1999) RNA structure modules with trinucleotide repeat motifs. In: *RNA Biochemistry and Biotechnology* (Barciszewski, J. and Clark, B. F. C., eds.), Kluwer Academic Publishers, Dordrecht, pp. 303–314.
24. Krzyzosiak, W. J., Denman, R., Nurse, K., et al. (1987) In vitro synthesis of 16S ribosomal RNA containing single base changes and assembly into a functional 30S ribosome. *Biochemistry* **26,** 2353–2364.
25. Gaur, R. K., Hanne, A., and Krupp, G. (2004) Combination of chemical and enzymatic RNA synthesis. *Methods Mol. Biol.* **252,** 9–17.
26. Lee, S. S. and Kang, C. (1993) Two base pairs at –9 and –8 distinguish between the bacteriophage T7 and SP6 promoters. *J. Biol. Chem.* **268,** 19,299–19,304.
27. Shin, I., Kim, J., Cantor, C., and Kang, C. (2000) Effect of saturation mutagenesis of the phage SP6 promoter on transcription activity, presented by activity logos. *Proc. Natl. Acad. Sci. USA.* **97,** 3890–3895.
28. Ehresmann, C., Baudin, F., Mougel, M., Romby, P., Ebel, J. P., and Ehresmann, B. (1987) Probing the structure of RNAs in solution. *Nucleic Acids Res.* **15,** 9109–9128.
29. Giege, R., Helm, M., and Florentz, C. (2001) Classical and novel chemical tools for RNA structure probing. In: *RNA* (Soll, D., Nishimura S., and Moore, P. B., eds.), Elsevier Sciences, Oxford, pp. 71–89.
30. Knapp, G. (1989) Enzymatic approaches to probing of RNA secondary and tertiary structure. *Methods Enzymol.* **180,** 192–212.
31. Napierala, M. and Krzyzosiak, W. J. (1997) CUG repeats present in myotonin kinase RNA form metastable "slippery" hairpins. *J. Biol. Chem.* **272,** 31,079–31,085.

32. Favorova, O. O., Fasiolo, F., Keith, G., Vassilenko, S. K., and Ebel, J. P. (1981) Partial digestion of tRNA—aminoacyl-tRNA synthetase complexes with cobra venom ribonuclease. *Biochemistry* **20,** 1006–1011.

33. Lowman, H. B. and Draper, D. E. (1986) On the recognition of helical RNA by cobra venom V1 nuclease. *J. Biol. Chem.* **261,** 5396–5403.

34. Marciniec, T., Ciesiolka, J., Wrzesinski, J., and Krzyzosiak, W. J. (1989) Identification of the magnesium, europium and lead binding sites in E. coli and lupine tRNAPhe by specific metal ion-induced cleavages. *FEBS Lett.* **243,** 293–298.

35. Ciesiolka, J., Wrzesinski, J., Gornicki, P., Podkowinski, J., and Krzyzosiak, W. J. (1989) Analysis of magnesium, europium and lead binding sites in methionine initiator and elongator tRNAs by specific metal-ion-induced cleavages. *Eur. J. Biochem.* **186,** 71–77.

36. Wrzesinski, J., Michalowski, D., Ciesiolka, J., and Krzyzosiak, W. J. (1995) Specific RNA cleavages induced by manganese ions. *FEBS Lett.* **374,** 62–68.

37. Streicher, B., Westhof, E., and Schroeder, R. (1996) The environment of two metal ions surrounding the splice site of a group I intron. *EMBO J.* **15,** 2556–2564.

38. Krzyzosiak, W. J., Marciniec, T., Wiewiorowski, M., Romby, P., Ebel, J. P., and Giege, R. (1988) Characterization of the lead(II)-induced cleavages in tRNAs in solution and effect of the Y-base removal in yeast tRNAPhe. *Biochemistry* **27,** 5771–5777.

39. Ciesiolka, J., Michalowski, D., Wrzesinski, J., Krajewski, J., and Krzyzosiak, W. J. (1998) Patterns of cleavages induced by lead ions in defined RNA secondary structure motifs. *J. Mol. Biol.* **275,** 211–220.

40. Gornicki, P., Baudin, F., Romby, P., et al. (1989) Use of lead(II) to probe the structure of large RNA's. Conformation of the 3' terminal domain of E. coli 16S rRNA and its involvement in building the tRNA binding sites. *J. Biomol. Struct. Dyn.* **6,** 971–984.

41. Michalowski, D., Wrzesinski, J., and Krzyzosiak, W. J. (1996) Cleavages induced by different metal ions in yeast tRNA(Phe) U59C60 mutants. *Biochemistry* **35,** 10,727–10,734.

42. Brown, R. S., Hingerty, B. E., Dewan, J. C., and Klug, A. (1983) Pb(II)-catalysed cleavage of the sugar-phosphate backbone of yeast tRNAPhe-implications for lead toxicity and self-splicing RNA. *Nature* **303,** 543–546.

43. Brown, R. S., Dewan, J. C., and Klug, A. (1985) Crystallographic and biochemical investigation of the lead (II)-catalyzed hydrolysis of yeast phenylalanine tRNA. *Biochemistry* **24,** 4785–4801.

44. Pan, T., Long, G. M., and Uhlenbeck, O. C. (1993) Divalent metal ions in RNA folding and catalysis. In: *The RNA World* (Gesteland, R. F. and Atkins, J. F., eds.), Cold Spring Harbor Laboratory Press, New York, pp. 271–302.

45. Pyle, A. M. (1996) Role of metal ions in ribozymes. In: *Metal Ions in Biological Systems* (Sigel, A. and Sigel, H., eds.), Marcel Dekker, Basel, pp. 479–520.

46. Sobczak, K., de Mezer, M., Michlewski, G., Krol, J., and Krzyzosiak, W. J. (2003) RNA structure of trinucleotide repeats associated with human neurological diseases. *Nucleic Acids Res.* **31,** 5469–5482.

47. Michlewski, G. and Krzyzosiak, W. J. (2004) Molecular architecture of CAG repeats in human disease related transcripts. *J. Mol. Biol.* **340,** 665–679.

48. Sobczak, K. and Krzyzosiak, W. J. (2005) CAG repeats containing CAA interruptions form branched hairpin structures in spinocerebellar ataxia type 2 transcripts. *J. Biol. Chem.* **280,** 3898–3910.

49. Napierala, M., Michalowski, D., de Mezer, M., and Krzyzosiak, W. J. (2005) Facile FMR1 mRNA structure regulation by interruptions in CGG repeats. *Nucleic Acids Res.* **33,** 451–463.

50. Sobczak, K. and Krzyzosiak, W. J. (2002) Structural determinants of BRCA1 translational regulation. *J. Biol. Chem.* **277,** 17,349–17,358.

3

MicroRNA Biogenesis

Isolation and Characterization of the Microprocessor Complex

Richard I. Gregory, Thimmaiah P. Chendrimada, and Ramin Shiekhattar

Summary

The recently discovered microRNAs (miRNAs) are a large family of small regulatory RNAs that have been implicated in controlling diverse pathways in a variety of organisms *(1,2)*. For posttranscriptional gene silencing, one strand of the miRNA is used to guide components of the RNA interference machinery, including Argonaute 2, to messenger RNAs (mRNAs) with complementary sequences *(3,4)*. Thus, targeted mRNAs are either cleaved by the endonuclease Argonaute 2 *(5,6)*, or protein synthesis is blocked by an as yet uncharacterized mechanism *(7,8)*. Genes encoding miRNAs are transcribed as long primary miRNAs (pri-miRNAs) that are sequentially processed by components of the nucleus and cytoplasm to yield a mature, approx 22-nucleotide (nt)-long miRNA *(9)*. Two members of the ribonuclease (RNase) III endonuclease protein family, Drosha and Dicer, have been implicated in this two-step processing *(10–13)*. To further our understanding of miRNA biogenesis and function it will be essential to identify the protein complexes involved. We were interested in defining the proteins required for the initial nuclear processing of pri-miRNAs to the approx 60- to 70-nt stem-loop intermediates known as precursor miRNAs (pre-miRNAs) *(9,10)*. This led to our identification of a protein complex we termed Microprocessor, which is necessary and sufficient for processing pri-miRNA to pre-miRNAs *(14)*. The Microprocessor complex comprises Drosha and the double-stranded RNA-binding protein DiGeorge syndrome critical region 8 gene (*DGCR8*), which is deleted in DiGeorge syndrome *(15,16)*.

In this chapter, we detail the methods used for the biochemical isolation and identification of the Microprocessor complex from human cells. We include a protocol for the in vitro analysis of pri-miRNA processing activity of the purified Microprocessor complex.

Key Words: MicroRNA; miRNA; RNAi; Drosha; DGCR8; Microprocessor.

From: *Methods in Molecular Biology, vol. 342: MicroRNA Protocols*
Edited by: S. Ying © Humana Press Inc., Totowa, NJ

1. Introduction

This chapter presents a biochemical approach for the purification and characterization of multi-subunit protein complexes from human cells. Although we present the isolation of the Drosha protein and its associated polypeptides, the strategy can be adapted to accommodate the investigator's particular focus; indeed, we have previously applied this approach to purify numerous different protein complexes *(17,18)*. The example we provide describes the approach leading to our isolation of the Microprocessor complex. The discovery of Microprocessor and our demonstration that the Microprocessor complex constitutes the cellular machinery responsible for the processing of long pri-miRNAs to pre-miRNA intermediates, identified Microprocessor as a critical component of the miRNA biogenesis pathway *(14)*.

1.1. Generating a FLAG™–Drosha Stable Cell Line

This purification technique requires the generation of a stable cell line expressing a FLAG-tagged version of the protein of interest. The FLAG epitope comprises a unique sequence of eight amino acids that is specifically recognized by the anti-FLAG M2 monoclonal antibody and, therefore, amenable to affinity purification. We cloned the complementary DNA (cDNA) of human Drosha to a mammalian expression vector containing the FLAG sequence. The plasmid construct we used contains the cytomegalovirus promoter to drive high levels of FLAG–Drosha fusion protein expression in transfected cells. This approach of using a FLAG tag for affinity purification avoids the rigors of conventional chromatography and provides a reliable method for the recovery of protein complexes. Because of its small size, the addition of the FLAG tag usually does not interfere with the activity/function of the tagged protein, or disrupt interactions with protein-binding partners. In addition, commercially available, monoclonal, anti-FLAG antibodies are highly specific to the epitope tag and, therefore, generate very little nonspecific background during the protein purification. Another advantage of this approach is that the immunopurified complexes can be recovered from the anti-FLAG agarose beads under nondenaturing conditions (by elution using FLAG peptide) and, therefore, this approach maintains the integrity of the protein eluate.

For Microprocessor isolation, we generated a stable HEK293 cell line expressing FLAG–Drosha. We chose HEK293 cells because they express endogenous Drosha, have a rapid doubling time, and are easily transfected. We used a cotransfection protocol whereby one plasmid encodes FLAG–Drosha, whereas the other contains a drug-selection marker. We recommend puromycin selection more than the commonly used neomycin selection because of its more potent toxicity to naïve cells, as well as the lower cost of the reagent. Stable cell lines should be generated from a monoclonal population, necessitating cell colony isolation. In our experience, polyclonal populations of cell lines stably expressing transgenes tend to lose expression of the transgenic cDNA. After transfection and cell selection, we screened for positive clones by small-scale immunoprecipitation from whole cell lysates using anti-FLAG antibodies conjugated to agarose beads. The immunopurified material was checked for FLAG–Drosha expression by Western blot analysis. We selected a cell line that expressed high levels of FLAG–Drosha and expanded these cells.

1.2. Preparation of Nuclear Extract and Immunoprecipitation

The stable HEK293-derived cell line expressing FLAG–Drosha was expanded to approx 100 to 200 15-cm culture plates. Once the cells reached confluence, they were harvested by trypsinization, collected by centrifugation, and rinsed with phosphate-buffered saline (PBS). For immunoprecipitation, we prepared nuclear extract from the cells using a simple protocol based on that originally described by Dignam et al. *(19)*. Although it is possible to perform immunoprecipitation on whole cell lysate, to minimize contaminating peptides and to maximize protein complex recovery, we routinely separate nuclear extract from contaminating cytoplasmic components. Nuclear enrichment involves an initial homogenization step to disrupt cell membranes. A low-speed centrifugation step separates most of the cytosol from the intact nuclei. A second homogenization in a high-salt buffer disrupts the nuclear membrane, and, after a high-speed centrifugation, enables the soluble nuclear extract to be isolated from the pelleted debris. We determine the protein concentration of the nuclear extract by standard Bradford assays. After dialysis of the crude nuclear extract against 50 m*M* KCl (BC50), we typically retrieve 100 to 200 mg of nuclear extract from 100 to 200 15-cm plates. This dialyzed nuclear extract, after addition of phenylmethyl sulfonyl fluoride (PMSF) (to 0.2 m*M*), is used directly for immunoprecipitation. After extensive washes, the affinity-purified FLAG–Drosha and interacting proteins were eluted from the beads. This affinity eluate was analyzed by silver staining and Western blotting (*see* **Fig. 1A**). As with any affinity chromatography, an important control is immunoprecipitation of naïve cells for comparison; we typically observe two contaminating polypeptides that are also present in mock immunoprecipitations of naïve HEK293 extract.

We next determined the identity of Drosha-associated polypeptides. Individual polypeptides were excised from the gel and subjected to mass spectrometric sequencing. Nineteen specific Drosha-associated polypeptides were identified in two independent sequencing analyses. The Drosha-associated proteins were comprised of specific classes of RNA-associated proteins displaying common structural domains. These included the DEAD- and DEAH-box family of RNA helicases, proteins with double-stranded RNA binding domains, heterogeneous nuclear ribonucleoproteins, and the Ewing sarcoma family of proteins containing a RNA recognition motif and a zinc-finger domain *(14)*.

1.3. Isolation of Drosha-Containing Complexes by Gel Filtration Chromatography

To examine the elution profile of Drosha and to demonstrate that the Drosha-associated polypeptides constitute a multiprotein complex, the FLAG-affinity eluate was fractionated on a Superose 6 gel filtration column. Fractions of the Superose 6 chromatography were concentrated by trichloroacetic acid (TCA) precipitation and analyzed by sodium dodecylsulfate (SDS) polyacrylamide gel electrophoresis (PAGE) followed by silver staining (**Fig. 1B**). This analysis revealed the presence of Drosha in two distinct complexes, a high-molecular-weight complex composed of most Drosha-associated polypeptides (fractions 16–18) and a smaller, migrating (fractions 24–26; ~600 kDa) Drosha-containing complex (**Fig. 1B**).

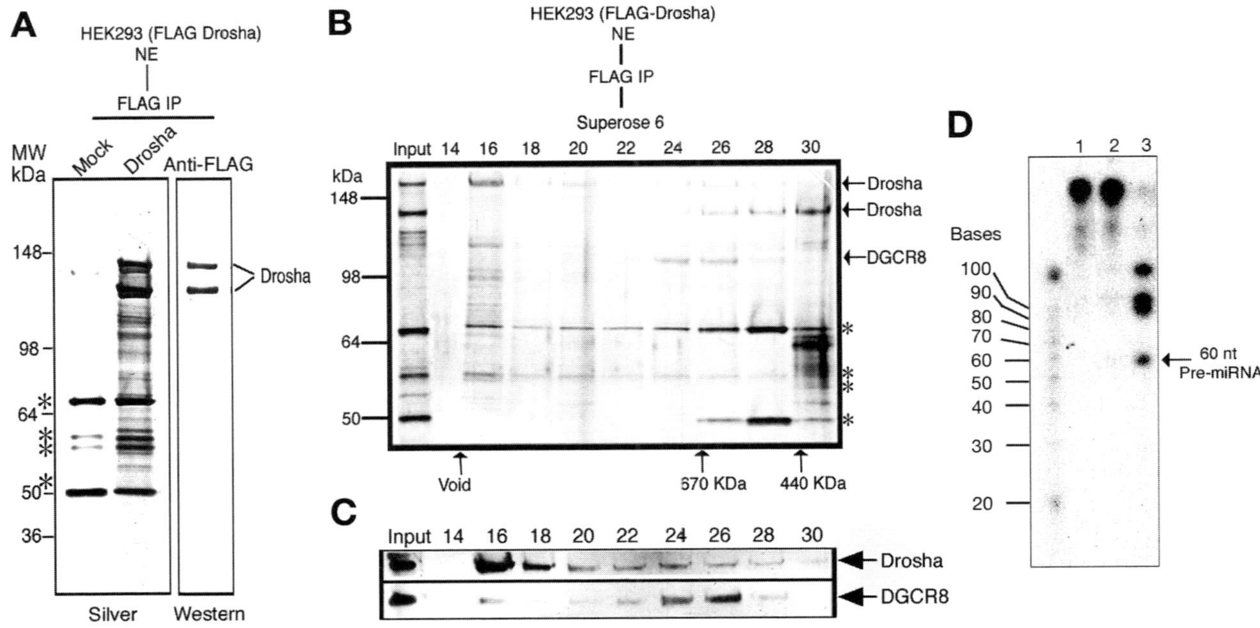

36

1.4. Preparation of Pri-miRNA Substrates for In Vitro Processing Assays

Previously, an assay was established to monitor pri-miRNA processing using in vitro transcribed RNAs corresponding to particular pri-miRNAs *(10)*. We cloned a PCR product of the miRNA gene cluster corresponding to miRNAs 23a~27a~24-2 to a pGEM®-T Easy Vector (Promega) by TA cloning®. The orientation of the insert was determined by DNA sequencing. The plasmid was linearized by restriction endonuclease digestion using a suitable enzyme (SpeI) that cuts at the 3' end of the miRNA gene cluster. To generate the pri-miRNA substrate of approx 450 nts containing three miRNAs, we performed run-off transcription using the Riboprobe® (Promega) in vitro transcription system. The in vitro transcription was performed according to the manufacturer's instructions with T7 polymerase, and supplemented with α^{32}P-cytidine triphosphate (CTP), which, after deoxyribonuclease digestion, phenol:chloroform purification, and RNA precipitation,

---

Fig. 1. *(Opposite page)* (**A**) Isolation of Drosha-containing complexes. FLAG–Drosha was isolated from a HEK293-derived nuclear extract prepared from a cell line stably expressing FLAG–Drosha. An untagged HEK293 cell line was used as the mock control (Mock). After elution of the immunoaffinity eluate from the M2 anti-FLAG beads, 10 µL of each fraction was resolved on an sodium dodecylsulfate (SDS)–polyacrylamide (4 to 12%) gel, and proteins were visualized by silver staining and Western blot analysis using anti-FLAG antibodies. Molecular masses (MW) of the marker proteins (left) and the bands representing FLAG–Drosha (right) are indicated. We observed two bands corresponding to Drosha, the smaller of which corresponds to an amino-terminally truncated protein, most likely arising from proteolytic cleavage during the complex purification. Asterisks denote contaminating polypeptides that we also detect in the mock immunoprecipitation (IP). (**B**) FLAG affinity eluate was fractionated on a Superose 6 gel filtration column, and the even fractions of the column were subjected to trichloroacetic acid precipitation followed by SDS-polyacrylamide gel electrophoresis (PAGE) and silver staining. Fractions of the column are denoted at the top, whereas molecular weight markers are indicated at the bottom. Asterisks denote contaminating polypeptides. Multiple sequencing analyses have determined SHK1 kinase binding protein 1 (SKB1), methylosome protein 50 (MEP50), and α-tubulin as common contaminants of FLAG affinity purification. (**C**) Western blot of the Superose 6 column fractions using anti-Drosha and anti-DGCR8 antibodies shows a peak in fractions 24 to 26. (**D**) Pri-miRNA processing activity of Superose 6 gel filtration column fractions. We compared processing activity of the large Drosha-containing complex (fraction 17 of the Superose 6 gel filtration column) with that of the small Drosha-containing complex (fraction 25) by normalizing for the amount of Drosha. After dialysis of the column fractions, 2 µL of fraction 17 (lane 2) or 10 µL of fraction 25 (lane 3), corresponding to 50 ng of Drosha protein (determined by comparison with known amounts of bovine serum albumin co-migrated on SDS-PAGE), were assayed for miRNA processing using a pri-miRNA 23a~27a~24-2 fragment. Column fractions were incubated with approx 0.2 pmoles of ^{32}P-labeled pri-miRNA at 37°C for 90 min in reaction-buffer conditions. Lane 1 represents a control reaction without Drosha protein. After gel migration (15% denaturing PAGE) and autoradiography, miRNA processing was monitored by detection of the 60-nt specific cleavage product. Accumulation of pre-miRNA in lane 3 demonstrates that the bulk of the miRNA processing activity resides in the small Drosha-containing complex. Mass spectrometric protein sequencing and Western blot of the small complex identified two proteins, Drosha and the double-stranded RNA-binding protein, DiGeorge syndrome critical region (DGCR)-8, as components of the approx 600 kDa complex, termed Microprocessor, that processes pri-miRNA to pre-miRNA.

generally yielded approx 10 µg RNA in 50 µL H$_2$O. This pri-miRNA can be used directly as a substrate for in vitro processing assays, however, we sometimes chose to gel purify the pri-miRNA to remove unincorporated nucleotides and to ensure a homogeneous population of full-length RNA molecules.

1.5. In Vitro Processing of Pri-miRNA by the Microprocessor Complex

We analyzed fractions of the Superose 6 gel filtration column for miRNA-processing activity. Because the Superose 6 gel filtration column is operated under high-salt conditions (500 m*M* KCl), it was necessary to dialyze the column fractions against reaction buffer (50 m*M* KCl) before performing functional analysis. Dialysis also served to eliminate ethylenediaminetetraacetic acid (EDTA) from the samples, an important consideration given the MgCl$_2$ dependence of the processing reaction. Although we have not rigorously tested the energy requirements of Drosha-mediated pri-miRNA cleavage, by convention, we supplement the reaction buffer with adenosine triphosphate (ATP) and creatine phosphate. After incubation of Superose 6 column fractions with the pri-miRNA substrate, RNA purification, and gel migration, followed by exposure of the gel to X-ray film, the processing activity was monitored by the specific accumulation of a band migrating at 60-nt that corresponds to the predicted size of the pre-miRNA hairpin. The analysis of the Superose 6 gel filtration column fractions revealed the presence of miRNA-processing activity in two distinct peaks corresponding to the two Drosha-containing complexes *(14)*. Although the larger complex (fractions 16–18) displayed some miRNA-processing activity, the bulk of the miRNA-processing activity co-eluted with the smaller (~600 kDa) Drosha complex *(14)*. To determine the polypeptide composition of the smaller Drosha-containing complex, we pooled fractions 25 to 27 of the Superose 6 column and TCA precipitated the proteins. Subsequent mass spectrometric sequencing of bands excised from a SDS-PAGE gel identified Drosha and the double-stranded RNA binding protein, DGCR8, as the sole components of this (~600 kDa) complex (**Fig. 1B**). Western blot analysis of the Superose 6 column fractions using anti-Drosha and anti-DGCR8 polyclonal antibodies confirmed the association of these two proteins, which peaks in fraction 26 (**Fig. 1C**). To more precisely compare the pri-miRNA processing of the two Drosha-containing complexes, we performed processing assays using equal amounts of each complex, by normalizing for the amount of Drosha protein via quantitative Western blots (**Fig. 1D**). This analysis revealed that pri-miRNA processing activity co-eluted with the Drosha–DGCR8 complex (fraction 25), therefore, we named this complex Microprocessor *(14)*.

2. Materials

2.1. Generating a FLAG–Drosha Stable Cell Line

2.1.1. Transfection and Colony Selection

1. HEK293 cells from the American Type Culture Collection (Rockville, MD).
2. Fetal bovine serum and Dulbecco's Modified Eagle Medium media (GibcoBRL, Gaithersburg, MD).
3. PBS, pH 7.3 (GibcoBRL).

4. 0.05% (w/v) trypsin solution (Sigma, St. Louis, MO).
5. pFLAG–cytomegalovirus-2 (Sigma) containing Drosha cDNA.
6. Fugene-6□ transfection reagent (or similar transfection reagent).
7. Puromycin (2.5 mg/mL stock) (Sigma).
8. Pyrex cloning cylinders (Corning, Corning, NY).
9. Silicone grease (Corning).

2.1.2. Screening Cell Lines by Immunoprecipitation and Western Blot

1. PBS, pH 7.3.
2. Lysis Buffer: 20 mM Tris-HCl (pH 8.0), 137 mM NaCl, 1 mM EDTA, 1% Triton X-100, 10% glycerol, 1.5 mM MgCl$_2$, 0.2 mM PMSF, and 0.5 mM dithiothreitol (DTT).
3. FLAG agarose beads (Sigma).
4. BC500 buffer: 20 mM Tris-HCl (pH 7.8), 500 mM KCl, 0.2 mM EDTA, 10% glycerol, 10 mM β-mercaptoethanol (pH 7.8), 0.2% Nonidet P-40 (NP40), 0.2 mM PMSF, and 1 μg/ mL of aprotinin, leupeptin, and pepstatin (protease inhibitors, from Roche).
5. FLAG peptide (5 μg/μL stock in ddH$_2$O) (Sigma).
6. 2X SDS gel-loading buffer: 100 mM Tris-HCl (pH 6.8), 200 mM DTT, 4% SDS, 20% glycerol, and 0.2% bromophenol blue.
7. Precast (4–12% or 4–20%) Tris-glycine SDS-PAGE gel (Invitrogen, Carlsbad, CA).
8. 1X gel-running buffer: 25 mM Tris, 190 mM glycine, and 0.1% SDS, pH 8.3.
9. Polyvinylidene fluoride membrane (e.g., Immobilon-P; Millipore, Billerica, MA).
10. 1X transfer buffer: 25 mM Tris, 190 mM glycine, and 40% methanol.
11. Nonfat dry milk.
12. Anti-FLAG M2 antibody (Sigma).
13. 1X TTBS: 10 mM Tris-HCl (pH 7.5), 50 mM NaCl, and 0.05% Tween-20.
14. Alkaline phosphatase (AP)-conjugated (calf intestinal alkaline phosphatase) anti-mouse IgG secondary antibody (Promega).
15. 50 mg/mL 5-bromo-4-chloro-3-indolyl phosphate *p*-toluidine salt in *N,N*-dimethyl formamide (Fisher Biotech).
16. 50 mg/mL *p*-nitro blue tetrazolium chloride in 70% *N,N*-dimethyl formamide (USB Corp.).
17. AP buffer: 100 mM Tris-HCl (pH 9.5), 100 mM NaCl, and 5 mM MgCl$_2$.

2.2. Purification of Drosha-Associated Complexes

2.2.1. Preparing Nuclear Extract

1. 100 15-cm plates of HEK293-derived stable cells expressing FLAG–Drosha.
2. PBS, pH 7.3.
3. Buffer A: 10 mM Tris-HCl (pH 8.0), 10 mM KCl, 1.5 mM MgCl$_2$, 0.5 mM DTT, and 0.2 mM PMSF.
4. Buffer C: 20 mM Tris-HCl (pH 8.0), 420 mM NaCl, 1.5 mM MgCl$_2$, 25% glycerol, 0.2 mM EDTA, 0.5 mM DTT, and 0.5 mM PMSF.
5. Glass dounce (with pestle type B) (Wheaton, Millville, NJ).
6. SpectraPor dialysis tubing (10,000 molecular weight cutoff) from Spectrum (Houston, TX).
7. Immunoprecipitation buffer: 20 mM Tris-HCl (pH 8.0), 50 mM KCl, 0.2 mM EDTA, 10% glycerol, 10 mM β-mercaptoethanol (pH 7.8), 0.2 mM PMSF, and 1μg/mL of aprotinin, leupeptin, and pepstatin.

2.2.2. Immunoprecipitation

1. Anti-FLAG agarose beads (Sigma).

2. PBS, pH 7.3.
3. BC500 buffer: 20 mM Tris-HCl (pH 7.8), 500 mM KCl, 0.2 mM EDTA, 10% glycerol, 10 mM β-mercaptoethanol (pH 7.8), 0.2% NP40, 0.2 mM PMSF, and 1 µg/mL of aprotinin, leupeptin, and pepstatin.
4. BC100 buffer: 20 mM Tris-HCl (pH 7.8), 50 mM KCl, 0.2 mM EDTA, 10% glycerol, 10 mM β-mercaptoethanol (pH 7.8), 0.2 mM PMSF, and 1 µg/mL of aprotinin, leupeptin, and pepstatin.
5. 10 mL poly-prep chromatography column (BioRad, Hercules, CA).
6. FLAG peptide (5 µg/µL stock in ddH$_2$O) (Sigma).

2.2.3. Silver Staining

1. Methanol.
2. Acetic acid.
3. Glutaraldehyde.
4. 10 N sodium hydroxide (NaOH).
5. Ammonium hydroxide (NH$_4$OH).
6. Silver nitrate (AgNO$_3$).
7. 1% (w/v) citric acid.
8. 38% (v/v) formaldehyde.
9. ddH$_2$O.

2.2.4. Size Fractionation by Gel Filtration

1. Fast-protein liquid chromatography system (Amersham Biosciences, Uppsala, Sweden).
2. Prepoured columns (Superose 6 HR 1030; Amersham Biosciences).
3. BC500 buffer: 20 mM Tris-HCl (pH 7.8), 500 mM KCl, 0.2 mM EDTA, 10% glycerol, 10 mM β-mercaptoethanol (pH 7.8), 0.2% NP40, 0.2 mM PMSF, and 1 µg/mL of aprotinin, leupeptin, and pepstatin.

2.2.5. TCA Precipitation

1. TCA.
2. Ice-cold acetone.
3. 2X SDS gel-loading buffer: 100 mM Tris-HCl (pH 6.8), 200 mM DTT, 4% SDS, 20% glycerol, and 0.2% bromophenol blue.

2.3. Preparing Pri-miRNA Substrates

2.3.1. In Vitro Transcription of Pri-miRNAs

1. Linearized plasmid DNA template.
2. Riboprobe in vitro transcription system (Promega).
3. α^{32}P-CTP (10 µCi/µL; specific activity: 3000 Ci/mmol) (Amersham, Piscataway, NJ).
4. Phenol:chloroform (5:1) with isoamyl alcohol (pH 4.3) (Fisher Biotech, Hampton, NH).
5. Chloroform.
6. 3 M sodium acetate.
7. Ice-cold ethanol.
8. Ice-cold 70% (v/v) ethanol.

2.3.2. Gel Purification of Pri-miRNAs

1. 2X TBE–urea sample-loading buffer (Invitrogen).
2. 100-bp to 1-kb RNA size marker, e.g., Century (Ambion, Austin, TX).

3. TBE–urea 6% polyacrylamide precast gels (Invitrogen).
4. TBE: 100 mM Tris-borate, 2 mM EDTA (pH 7.6).
5. Reagents (**Subheading 2.3.1.**, **steps 4–8**) for RNA purification and precipitation.
6. X-ray films (Kodak Biomax MS).

2.4. Pri-miRNA Processing Assays

1. Pri-miRNA (in vitro transcribed, uniformly ^{32}P labeled).
2. Immunopurified and dialyzed Drosha complex.
3. Reaction buffer: 20 mM Tris-HCl (pH 7.8), 50 mM KCl, 10% glycerol, 0.5 mM DTT, and 0.2 mM PMSF.
4. 10X energy buffer: 32 mM MgCl$_2$, 10 mM ATP, 200 mM creatine phosphate, and 100 U of RNase inhibitor (Takara).
5. Reagents (**Subheading 2.3.1.**, **steps 4–7**) for RNA purification and precipitation.
6. 10 µg/µL glycogen (Roche).
7. 80% (v/v) ice-cold ethanol.
8. TBE–urea 15% acrylamide precast gels.
9. 10- to 100-bp RNA size marker, e.g., Decade (Ambion).
10. TBE: 100 mM Tris-borate and 2 mM EDTA.
11. X-ray films.

3. Methods

3.1. Generating a FLAG–Drosha Stable Cell Line

3.1.1. Transfection and Colony Selection

1. Transfect one 10-cm plate of HEK293 cells at approx 50% confluence with 5 µg of FLAG-tagged cDNA plasmid and 0.5 µg of puromycin-resistant plasmid DNA using Fugene□ transfection reagent (or similar transfection reagent).
2. After approx 48 h, aspirate culture media and replace with media supplemented with 2.5 µg/mL puromycin (cells will begin to die ~2 d after puromycin addition).
3. For the next 10 to 14 d, change the culture media (adding puromycin) daily to remove dead cells. Individual puromycin-resistant colonies, each deriving from a single transfected cell, will form and be visible after approx 10 d.
4. Once colonies reach 1 to 3 mm in diameter, mark the location of 10 to 20 colonies on the underside of the culture plate with a marker pen.
5. Aspirate media from the plate and wash the cells with approx 5 mL PBS, aspirate PBS.
6. Pick up a Pyrex cloning cylinder with forceps and touch the end to the surface of the silicone grease (silicone helps make a seal with the plate). Place the cloning cylinder over a single colony.
7. Repeat **Subheading 3.1.1.**, **step 6** for the remaining colonies, taking care not to take too long to avoid drying of the cells.
8. Add 50-µL trypsin to each cylinder and leave for 1 to 2 min at room temperature. Pipet several times and transfer the cell-containing trypsin to a well of a 24-well plate (each well already containing 1 mL of puromycin-containing media).
9. Repeat step **Subheading 3.1.1.**, **step 8** for the remaining colonies, remembering to change the pipet tip for each colony.
10. As the cell lines reach confluence, transfer to 6-well plates containing 3 mL media, then subsequently to two 10-cm plates (each with 10–12 mL media). For each of the 10 to 20 cell

lines, one of the two plates is used for screening, whereas the other is expanded. We screen cells by immunoprecipitation followed by Western blot.

3.1.2. Screening Cell Lines by Immunoprecipitation and Western Blot

1. Once cells become confluent (in 10-cm plates) aspirate the culture media and rinse the cells with PBS.
2. Add 700 µL of lysis buffer directly to the cells and transfer the cell lysate by pipet to 1.5-mL Eppendorf tubes.
3. Incubate on ice for 10 min.
4. Centrifuge at 20,000g for 15 min in a microcentrifuge at 4°C.
5. Collect the supernatant. This whole-cell lysate can be stored at –80°C or used directly for immunoprecipitation.
6. For each immunoprecipitation, take 50 µL of 50% (w/v) FLAG beads and rinse with a few milliliters of PBS.
7. Pellet the beads by centrifugation at 100g for 3 min.
8. Aspirate the PBS, carefully leaving the pelleted beads.
9. Add an equal volume of PBS (i.e., 25 µL) to the pelleted beads.
10. Add 50 µL of this 50% (w/v) suspension to the cell lysate and incubate at 4°C with rotation for 2 h.
11. Centrifuge the beads at 100g for 3 min, aspirate the media, and wash with 1 mL of BC500.
12. Centrifuge at 100g for 3 min, aspirate the BC500 wash, and repeat the wash with 1 mL of BC500.
13. Centrifuge the beads at 100g for 3 min, and wash by resuspending in 1 mL of PBS. Pellet the beads by centrifugation at 100g for 3 min.
14. Elute the affinity-purified FLAG–proteins by adding 25 µL FLAG peptide (0.5 µg/µL in PBS) to the beads, mix, and incubate on ice for 20 min.
15. Centrifuge at 2500g for 5 min and decant the affinity eluate, leaving behind the pelleted beads.
16. Add an equal volume (25 µL) of 2X gel-loading buffer to each of the affinity-purified protein samples, mix by vortexing, and heat denature (95°C for 2 min). Load directly onto a Tris-Glycine (TG) SDS-PAGE gel. We use precast 4 to 12% or 4 to 20% gels, depending on the size of the protein of interest.
17. After gel electrophoresis, the proteins are electrotransferred in transfer buffer at 4°C (175 mA for >2 h) onto a polyvinylidene fluoride membrane (e.g., Immobilon-P, Millipore).
18. After transfer, block the membranes with 5% (w/v) nonfat dry milk for approx 30 min.
19. Rinse in TTBS, and incubate with a 1:5000 dilution (in TTBS) of monoclonal FLAG antibody (Sigma) for longer than 1 h.
20. Wash three times for 7 min with TTBS.
21. Incubate with a 1:5000 dilution (in TTBS) of calf intestinal AP-conjugated, anti-mouse IgG secondary antibody in TTBS for 40 min.
22. Wash with TTBS three times for 5 min.
23. Add 10 mL of AP buffer containing 33 µL of 5-bromo-4-chloro-3-indolyl phosphate *p*-toluidine salt and 66 µL of *p*-nitro blue tetrazolium chloride (final concentrations, 165 µg/mL and 330 µg/mL, respectively) until the protein bands on the membrane can be visualized. Based on this initial immunoprecipitation and Western blot screening of the stable cell lines, we discard cells that do not express the FLAG protein of interest. The stable cell line with the highest level of expression is selected and expanded for large-scale nuclear extract preparation.

3.2. Purification of Drosha-Associated Complexes

3.2.1. Preparing Nuclear Extract

1. We suggest purifying Microprocessor from no less than 100 15-cm culture plates of the stable FLAG–Drosha HEK293 cell line grown to confluence. Collect cells by trypsinization.
2. Centrifuge cells at 1500*g* for 5 min at 4°C.
3. Resuspend in ice-cold PBS.
4. Repeat **Subheading 3.2.1.**, **steps 2** and **3**, twice.
5. Resuspend cells in one pellet-volume of PBS and transfer to a 50-mL conical tube (Falcon).
6. Centrifuge cells at 1500*g* for 10 min at 4°C.
7. Pour off the supernatant and measure the packed-cell volume.
8. Add 5 volumes of ice-cold buffer A and resuspend the cells.
9. Swell at 4°C with rotation for 10 min.
10. Centrifuge at 1000*g* for 10 min at 4°C.
11. Pipet off the supernatant, being careful not to disturb the cell pellet.
12. Add 2 volumes of ice-cold buffer A.
13. Homogenize in a glass dounce (with pestle type B) with 10 to 15 strokes.
14. Centrifuge the homogenized cells at 1000*g* for 10 min at 4°C.
15. Remove supernatant with a pipet. This supernatant is the S100 fraction and represents the soluble fraction, comprising mainly of components of the cytosol. The S100 fraction can be frozen on dry ice stored at –80°C.
16. Add 1 volume of buffer C to the nuclear pellet and resuspend by pipetting.
17. Homogenize with 10 to 15 strokes with the glass dounce (B pestle).
18. Rotate for 30 min at 4°C.
19. Centrifuge at 10,000*g* for 30 min at 4°C.
20. Collect the supernatant (comprising the soluble nuclear extract).
21. Dialyze for 4 h to overnight against 50 to 100 volumes of immunoprecipitation buffer.
22. Centrifuge at 10,000*g* for 20 min at 4°C.
23. Collect the supernatant (nuclear extract).

3.2.2. Immunoprecipitation

1. Add anti-FLAG agarose beads (Sigma) to the nuclear extract. Use 0.5 mL of beads per 100 mg of nuclear extract (determined by a standard Bradford assay). Beads should be washed with PBS before immunoprecipitation.
2. Incubate beads with FLAG–Drosha nuclear extract for 2 h to overnight, with rotation.
3. Pellet beads by centrifugation at 500*g* for 5 min in a refrigerated centrifuge.
4. Decant supernatant and save unbound fraction.
5. Incubate beads with 50 mL of buffer BC500. Rotate for 10 min at 4°C.
6. Pellet beads by centrifugation at 500*g* for 5 min in a refrigerated centrifuge.
7. Repeat **Subheading 3.2.2.**, **steps 5** and **6**, three times (a total of four washes with buffer BC500).
8. Pellets beads (500*g* for 5 min at 4°C), aspirate supernatant, and incubate beads with 50 mL of buffer BC100.
9. Load beads onto a 10-mL poly-prep chromatography column (BioRad) and allow buffer to elute at the column's gravimetric flow rate.
10. Buffer exchange the beads into low salt by passing five column volumes of buffer BC100 (100 m*M* KCl) over the beads.
11. FLAG–Drosha-associated complexes can now be eluted using FLAG peptide. Add one column volume of BC100 supplemented with 400 µg/mL of FLAG peptide. Allow half of

the bed volume of buffer to elute and cap the column. Incubate the beads and elution buffer for 15 min before elution.

12. Collect four more elutions, with 15-min incubation intervals between each elution.

13. Fractions can be analyzed by Western blot, assaying for immunoreactivity to Drosha, FLAG, or DGCR8. *See* **Subheading 3.1.2.** for details of the Western blot protocol. Importantly, if the unbound fraction contains a large quantity of FLAG–Drosha, a second immunoprecipitation on the flow-through may be performed. Fractions should be analyzed for purity by silver stain (**Subheading 3.2.3.**).

3.2.3. Silver Staining

1. Load 10 to 15 µL of affinity-purified proteins with an equal volume of 2X SDS loading dye on a 4 to 12% TG SDS-PAGE gel. Run the gel at 120 V, approx 1.5 to 2 h.

2. The gel is first fixed in 250 mL of 50% methanol and 10% acetic acid for 15 to 60 min.

3. Pour off the fix, and add 250 mL of 10% methanol and 7% acetic acid for 10 min.

4. Pour off the solution and add 250 mL of a 1:10 dilution of glutaraldehyde for 15 min.

5. Wash the gel with ddH$_2$O three times for 15 min each.

6. Prepare silver stain A (0.37 mL of 10 N NaOH, 5.6 mL NH$_4$OH, and ddH$_2$O to 45 mL), and add and silver stain B (2 g AgNO$_3$ in 10 mL ddH$_2$O).

7. Add silver stain B drop-wise to silver stain A in a stirring conical flask. Once all of the silver stain B has been added to the silver stain A, bring the volume to 200 mL with ddH$_2$O.

8. Add the stain to the fixed gel and incubate for 15 min.

9. Wash the gel three times for 5 min.

10. Prepare the silver-developing solution (2.5 mL of 1% [w/v] citric acid plus 0.2 mL of 38% [v/v] formaldehyde; bring volume to 500 mL with ddH$_2$O); proteins on the gel will become visible.

11. Once the desired level of development is reached, add 50% methanol and 5% acetic acid for 10 min to stop further development, then replace solution with ddH$_2$O.

3.2.4. Size Fractionation by Gel Filtration

Fractionation of the affinity eluate via a Superose 6 HR 1030 gel filtration column is carried out according to the manufacturer's instructions and has been described previously. Briefly, the column is equilibrated in buffer BC500 before loading 0.5 to 1 mL of protein sample. We run the column at 0.5 mL/min and collect 0.5-mL fractions.

3.2.5. TCA Precipitation

1. Add 1/10 volume of TCA to the protein sample.

2. Incubate on ice for 15 min.

3. Centrifuge at 20,000g for 15 min.

4. Remove supernatant and wash the protein pellet with 1 mL of ice-cold acetone.

5. Centrifuge at 20,000g for 15 min.

6. Remove supernatant and dry the pellet on ice.

7. Resuspend in 15 to 20 µL of 2X SDS gel-loading dye. If the dye in the loading buffer turns yellow after resuspending the precipitated proteins, adjust the pH with a small amount of Tris-HCl, pH 8.0.

8. Vortex the samples, then heat to 95°C for 1 min, and vortex.

9. Run the samples on a precast 4 to 12% TG SDS-PAGE gel.

3.3. Preparing Pri-miRNA Substrates

3.3.1. In Vitro Transcription of Pri-miRNAs

1. Set up a reaction containing 0.2 to 1.0 µg of SpeI-linearized pGemT Easy (Promega) plasmid containing mir-23a~27a~24-2 DNA sequence; 4 µL of 5X transcription buffer; 2 µL of 100 mM DTT; 40 U RNasin® RNase inhibitor; 1 µL each of rATP, ribose-guanosine triphosphate, and ribose-uridine triphosphate (10 mM); 1 µL of 250 µM rCTP; 5 µL of 10 µCi/µL α32P-rCTP; and 20 U of T7 polymerase, bring to a final volume of 20 µL with ddH$_2$O.
2. Incubate at 37°C for 60 min.
3. Add 1 µL (10 U) deoxyribonuclease I and incubate at 37°C for 15 min.
4. Add an equal volume of phenol:chloroform (5:1) with isoamyl alcohol (pH 4.3) to the reaction mix.
5. Vortex to mix.
6. Centrifuge at 20,000g for 1 min.
7. Carefully collect the upper aqueous phase and transfer to a fresh 1.5-mL Eppendorf tube.
8. Add an equal volume of chloroform.
9. Vortex to mix.
10. Centrifuge at 20,000g for 1 min.
11. Carefully collect the upper aqueous phase and transfer to a fresh 1.5-mL Eppendorf tube.
12. Precipitate the RNA by adding 1/10 volume of 3 M sodium acetate and 3 volumes of ice-cold ethanol.
13. Incubate at –80°C for 30 min.
14. Centrifuge at 20,000g at 4°C for 20 min.
15. Pipet off the supernatant.
16. Wash the pellet with 70% ethanol and centrifuge at 20,000g at 4°C for 1 min.
17. Remove the supernatant, being careful not to disturb the RNA pellet.
18. Air-dry for a few minutes on ice.
19. Resuspend in 50 µL ddH$_2$O.

3.3.2. Gel Purification of Pri-miRNA

1. Prepare RNA as described in **Subheading 3.3.1.**
2. Add an equal volume of 2X TBE–urea sample-loading buffer and heat denature by incubation at 65°C for 3 min.
3. Load samples onto a 6% TBE–urea precast polyacrylamide gel, include one lane of the gel with labeled Century™ (prepared according to manufacturers instructions), and run at 240 V until the xylene cyanol marker reaches the bottom of the gel.
4. Transfer the gel to Whatman paper and cover with plastic wrap.
5. Expose the gel to X-ray film (usually <1 min).
6. Using a clean blade, excise a gel slice containing the band corresponding to the RNA of the correct length.
7. Place the gel slice in an Eppendorf tube and break into pieces using a pipet tip.
8. Add 300 µL of ddH$_2$O and incubate at 65°C for approx 2 h.
9. Using a pipet, collect the water containing the eluted RNA and transfer to a clean 1.5-mL tube (measure the activity of the solution compared with that of the remaining gel pieces to determine the extent of RNA recovery. We usually achieve >50% recovery).
10. Perform RNA phenol/chloroform purification and precipitation by following **Subheading 3.3.1., steps 4–19.**

3.4. Pri-miRNA Processing Assays

1. For activity assays, we dialyze immunopurified Drosha complexes in reaction buffer for longer than 2 h at 4°C.
2. For activity assays, aliquot 4 µL of a master reaction mix containing 0.1 to 0.3 µL of pri-miRNA (corresponding to ~0.1 pmoles, or 30,000 cpm); 3 µL of 10X energy buffer (containing 10 mM ATP, 200 mM creatine phosphate, 32 mM MgCl$_2$, and 10 U of RNase inhibitor); and reaction buffer to a total of 4 µL, into 1.5-mL tubes.
3. To each of the tubes containing 4 µL of a reaction mix, add 2 to 26 µL of immunopurified and dialyzed protein complex. Add an appropriate volume of reaction buffer to each tube to bring the final reaction volume to 30 µL.
4. Incubate 37°C for 90 min.
5. Follow **Subheading 3.3.1.**, **steps 4** to **15**.
6. Wash the pellet with 80% ethanol, and centrifuge at 20,000g at 4°C for 1 min.
7. Remove the supernatant, being careful not to disturb the RNA pellet.
8. Resuspend the RNA pellets in 10 µL of 1X TBE–urea sample-loading buffer.
9. Heat to 65°C for 3 min.
10. Load samples onto a 15% TBE–urea precast polyacrylamide gel, include one lane with a labeled Decade™ size marker (prepared according to the manufacturer's instructions), and run at 240 V until the xylene cyanol marker reaches the bottom of the gel.
11. Transfer the gel to Whatman paper and cover with plastic wrap.
12. Expose the gel to X-ray film (usually 1–12 h).

4. Notes

1. Use sterile conditions for cell culture to avoid contamination.
2. To avoid protein degradation by endogenous proteases, all steps of the purification procedure (**Subheading 2.2.**) should be performed on ice or at 4°C (precool the centrifuge rotor).
3. Where required, add PMSF, DTT, and protease inhibitors immediately before using buffers.
4. Use wide-bore pipet tips for transfer of FLAG agarose beads.
5. Aliquot purified proteins and avoid multiple freeze/thaws. Snap-freeze using dry ice, and rapid thaw at room temperature.
6. Wear gloves throughout all procedures and respect other usual safety precautions, in particular when handling phenol, chloroform, acrylamide, and glutaraldehyde solutions, and the ^{32}P radioactive isotope.
7. Take care to avoid RNase contamination, follow normal precautions, including the use of filter tips.

Acknowledgments

We thank the Jane Coffin Childs Memorial Fund for Medical Research for a postdoctoral fellowship to R.I.G. Thanks to Neil Cooch for comments.

References

1. Bartel, D. P. (2004) MicroRNAs: genomics, biogenesis, mechanism, and function. *Cell* **116,** 281–297.
2. Grishok, A., Pasquinelli, A. E., Conte, D., et al. (2001) Genes and mechanisms related to RNA interference regulate expression of the small temporal RNAs that control C. elegans developmental timing. *Cell* **106,** 23–34.

3. Sontheimer, E. J. (2005) Assembly and function of RNA silencing complexes. *Nat. Rev. Mol. Cell Biol.* **6,** 127–138.

4. Hammond, S. M., Boettcher, S., Caudy, A. A., Kobayashi, R., and Hannon, G. J. (2001) Argonaute2, a link between genetic and biochemical analyses of RNAi. *Science* **293,** 1146–1150.

5. Liu, J., Carmell, M. A., Rivas, F. V., et al. (2004) Argonaute2 is the catalytic engine of mammalian RNAi. *Science* **305,** 1437–1441.

6. Meister, G., Landthaler, M., Patkaniowska, A., Dorsett, Y., Teng, G., and Tuschl, T. (2004) Human Argonaute2 mediates RNA cleavage targeted by miRNAs and siRNAs. *Mol. Cell* **15,** 185–197.

7. Olsen, P. H. and Ambros, V. (1999) The lin-4 regulatory RNA controls developmental timing in Caenorhabditis elegans by blocking LIN-14 protein synthesis after the initiation of translation. *Dev. Biol.* **216,** 671–680.

8. Zeng, Y., Yi, R., and Cullen, B. R. (2003) MicroRNAs and small interfering RNAs can inhibit mRNA expression by similar mechanisms. *Proc. Natl. Acad. Sci. USA* **100,** 9779–9784.

9. Lee, Y., Jeon, K., Lee, J. T., Kim, S., and Kim, V. N. (2002) MicroRNA maturation: stepwise processing and subcellular localization. *EMBO J.* **21,** 4663–4670.

10. Lee, Y., Ahn, C., Han, J., et al. (2003) The nuclear RNase III Drosha initiates microRNA processing. *Nature* **425,** 415–419.

11. Bernstein, E., Caudy, A. A., Hammond, S. M., and Hannon, G. J. (2001) Role for a bidentate ribonuclease in the initiation step of RNA interference. *Nature* **409,** 363–366.

12. Ketting, R. F., Fischer, S. E., Bernstein, E., Sijen, T., Hannon, G. J., and Plasterk, R.H. (2001) Dicer functions in RNA interference and in synthesis of small RNA involved in developmental timing in C. elegans. *Genes Dev.* **15,** 2654–2659.

13. Hutvagner, G., McLachlan, J., Pasquinelli, A. E., Balint, E., Tuschl, T., and Zamore, P. D. (2001) A cellular function for the RNA-interference enzyme Dicer in the maturation of the let-7 small temporal RNA. *Science* **293,** 834–838.

14. Gregory, R. I., Yan, K. P., Amuthan, G., et al. (2004) The Microprocessor complex mediates the genesis of microRNAs. *Nature* **432,** 235–240.

15. Shiohama, A., Sasaki, T., Noda, S., Minoshima, S., and Shimizu, N. (2003) Molecular cloning and expression analysis of a novel gene DGCR8 located in the DiGeorge syndrome chromosomal region. *Biochem. Biophys. Res. Commun.* **304,** 184–190.

16. Lindsay, E. A. (2001) Chromosomal microdeletions: dissecting del22q11 syndrome. *Nat. Rev. Genet.* **2,** 58–68.

17. Bochar, D. A., Wang, L., Beniya, H., et al. (2000) BRCA1 is associated with a human SWI/SNF-related complex: linking chromatin remodeling to breast cancer. *Cell* **102,** 257–265.

18. Barak, O., Lazzaro, M. A., Lane, W. S., Speicher, D. W., Picketts, D. J., and Shiekhattar, R. (2003) Isolation of human NURF: a regulator of Engrailed gene expression. *EMBO J.* **22,** 6089–6100.

19. Dignam, J. D., Lebovitz, R. M., and Roeder, R. G. (1983) Accurate transcription initiation by RNA polymerase II in a soluble extract from isolated mammalian nuclei. *Nucleic Acids Res.* **11,** 1475–1489.

4

Recognition and Cleavage of Primary MicroRNA Transcripts

Yan Zeng and Bryan R. Cullen

Summary

MicroRNAs (miRNAs) are approx 22-nucleotide (nt)-long, single-stranded, endogenous, noncoding RNAs that are widely expressed in multicellular organisms. This chapter describes methods that allow the overexpression of human miRNAs and also discusses how primary miRNAs (pri-miRNAs), the much longer precursors of mature miRNAs, are processed in human cells, as well as in vitro.

Key Words: RNA processing; RNA interference; microRNA; Drosha.

1. Introduction

miRNAs regulate gene expression by hybridizing to messenger RNAs containing sequences that are perfectly or imperfectly complementary to the miRNA (reviewed in **ref. *1***). Increasing the concentration of certain miRNAs or inhibiting their function by antisense oligonucleotides can profoundly alter gene expression patterns and change the physiological responses of cells *(2–5)*. Thus, it is important to understand the mechanisms underlying miRNA biogenesis.

miRNAs are first synthesized as part of a much longer transcript called a pri-miRNA *(6)*. In animal cells, a nuclear ribonuclease (RNase) called Drosha, together with a protein partner called DiGeorge syndrome critical region 8 (DGCR8) in humans, cleaves the pri-miRNA to generate an approx 60-nt-long hairpin RNA called the precursor miRNA or pre-miRNA *(7–10)*, which is then transported from the nucleus to the cytoplasm by the export factor, Exportin-5 *(11–13)*. In the cytoplasm, another RNase, Dicer, cleaves the pre-miRNA hairpin to liberate an approx 22-nt-long imperfect miRNA duplex intermediate from the stem region *(14–16)*. Both Drosha and Dicer are RNase III family enzymes that produce RNA duplex products with characteristic approx 2-nt 3' overhangs. The miRNA duplex intermediate then goes through a further strand selection step, during which the strand with less stable hydrogen bonding at its 5' end is incorporated into a ribonucleoprotein complex, whereas the other RNA strand is usually released and degraded *(17,18)*. Thus, the stable strand represents the mature miRNA product.

There is generally little sequence homology among the hundreds of pri-miRNAs, pre-miRNAs, or mature miRNAs that have been identified, thus suggesting that the cellular

From: *Methods in Molecular Biology, vol. 342: MicroRNA Protocols*
Edited by: S. Ying © Humana Press Inc., Totowa, NJ

miRNA processing machinery recognizes only the common structural features of these RNAs. The most conserved feature is found within the approx 60 nt pre-miRNA, which is predicted to form a stable stem-loop structure. Although necessary, however, such a short structure is not sufficient for miRNA maturation when transcribed as part of a longer RNA transcript. However, we and others have successfully overproduced mature miRNAs in mammalian cells by using heterologous promoters to transcribe miRNA transcripts that are much longer than the approx 60-nt pre-miRNAs, i.e., artificial pri-miRNAs *(19–22)*. These pri-miRNAs represent truncated versions of endogenous primary transcripts and often contain arbitrary flanking sequences. By overexpressing miRNAs, one can study their functions and define the structural features that not only are important for substrate recognition by cellular processing enzymes, but also affect enzyme cleavage site selection on pri-miRNAs and pre-miRNAs. Such in vivo studies, coupled with in vitro Drosha cleavage assays *(7–10,20,22)*, have revealed a great deal of detail regarding the mechanism and specificity of miRNA processing. Using these in vivo and in vitro systems to further study miRNA biogenesis and function will tell us more regarding how miRNAs regulate gene expression, how miRNAs themselves are regulated, and also add to our knowledge of RNA processing in general.

2. Materials

1. Standard molecular cloning equipment and reagents.
2. Human 293T cells (*see* **Note 1**) and standard tissue culture medium.
3. Maxiprep kit (Qiagen, Valencia, CA).
4. Fugene 6 (Roche, Indianapolis, IN; *see* **Note 2**).
5. Trizol reagent (Invitrogen, Carlsbad, CA).
6. 8 *M* urea/15% polyacrylamide Ready-Gels and minigel apparatus (Bio-Rad, Hercules, CA).
7. Hybond-N membrane (Amersham, Piscataway, NJ).
8. UV Stratalinker 2400 (Stratagene, La Jolla, CA).
9. ExpressHyb solution (BD Biosciences Clontech, Palo Alto, CA).
10. [γ-^{32}P] adenosine triphosphate and [α-^{32}P] cytidine triphosphate (10 μCi/μL, Amersham).
11. Riboprobe system-T7, including RNasin (Promega, Madison, WI).
12. T4 polynucleotide kinase (Promega or New England Biolabs, Beverly, MA).
13. Centrisep spin columns (Princeton Separations, Adelphia, NJ).
14. NETN lysis buffer: 20 m*M* Tris-HC1, pH 7.6, 150 m*M* NaCl, 1 m*M* ethylenediaminetetraacetic acid (EDTA), and 0.4% Nonidet P-40. Stored at room temperature, and supplement with protease inhibitors (Roche) before use.
15. Reaction buffer: 20 m*M* HEPES-KOH, pH 7.6, 100 m*M* KCl, 0.2 m*M* EDTA, and 5% glycerol. Prepare reaction buffer as a 5X stock solution and store at 4°C.
16. Anti-FLAG M2 agarose affinity gel and 3X FLAG peptide (Sigma, St. Louis, MO).
17. 2X loading buffer: 98% formamide, 20 m*M* EDTA, and 0.1% bromophenol blue.
18. PhosphorImager (Amersham).

3. Methods

We first describe procedures that allow overexpression of mature miRNAs in transfected human cells. Next, we introduce assays that examine the processing of pri-miRNAs to generate pre-miRNAs in vitro.

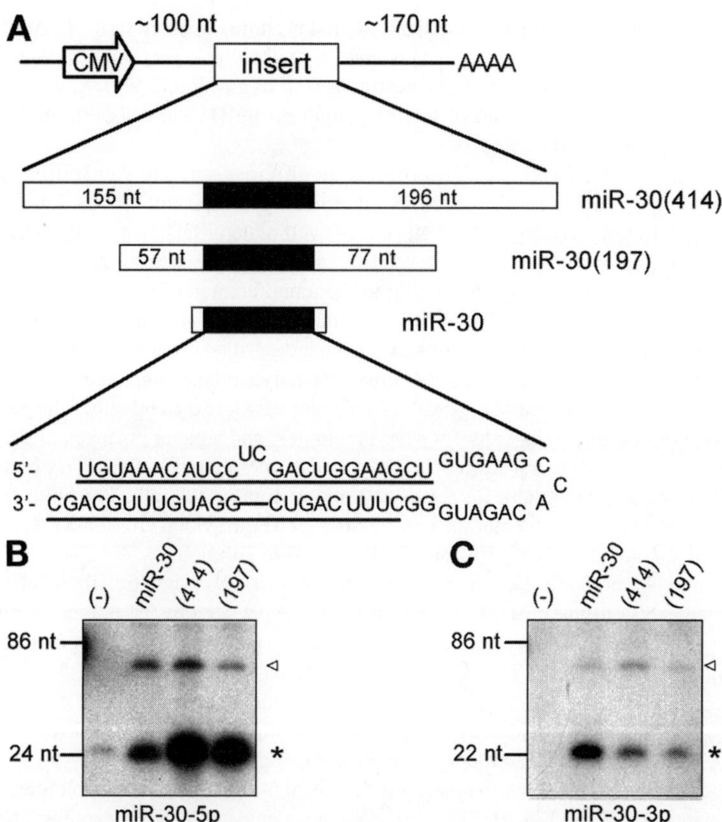

Fig. 1. Overexpression of microRNAs (miRNAs) in transfected human cells. (**A**) Schematic of human miRNA expression plasmids and the miRNA gene insertions. The three miR-30 inserts were cloned into the XhoI site of the vector. The black box represents pre-miR-30, whose predicted secondary structure is shown below. Underlined are the predominant, mature miRNA sequences, miR-30-5p in the 5' arm, and miR-30-3p in the 3' arm. (**B**) Northern analysis of RNAs isolated from nontransfected 293T cells or from cells transfected with the indicated plasmids, with a probe complementary to miR-30-5p. Positions of DNA standards are shown at the left. The asterisk indicates mature miR-30-5p, and the arrowhead points to the pre-miR-30 precursor. (**C**) The same blot used in panel B was stripped and reprobed for miR-30-3p. Symbols and labeling are the same as in B.

3.1. Overexpression of miRNAs in Transfected Cells

1. **Figure 1A** shows a schematic of a plasmid that uses the cytomegalovirus (CMV) immediate early promoter, an RNA polymerase II-dependent promoter, to transcribe pri-miRNAs in human tissue culture cells (*see* **Note 3**). Three constructs were made that each incorporated different lengths of genomic DNA encoding a human miRNA, termed miR-30a (miR-30) (**Fig. 1A**). The first construct, miR-30(414), contains 414 bp of human genomic DNA, whereas the second construct, miR-30(197), contains 197 bp. The third construct has only 71 bp, which include the eventual 63-nt-long pre-miR-30 sequence (shown by the black

box) as well as several adjacent nucleotides, and is simply denoted miR-30. All three miR-30 insertions have restriction sites appended for subcloning purposes and have 5' and 3' flanking sequences derived from the vector, as well as a genomic poly(A) tail addition site that will be transcribed as part of the full-length pri-miRNA in cells. Plasmids were prepared using Qiagen Maxiprep kits.

2. Transfection of 293T cells can be performed in different scales to yield different amounts of RNA. For the purpose of a single Northern analysis (*see* **Note 4**), as detailed in **Subheading 3.4.**, transfection in one well of a 24-well plate is sufficient. For such a transfection, approx 2.5×10^5 293T cells are seeded, and 0.4 µg of plasmid DNA and approx 1 µL of Fugene 6 reagent are used according to the manufacturer's instructions (*see* **Note 5**).

3. Total RNA is isolated using Trizol, 2 d after transfection. In general, approx 20 µg of RNA can be obtained from one transfection experiment described in **Subheading 3.2.** For Northern blotting, the RNA is run on an 8 *M* urea/15% polyacrylamide gel until the bromophenol blue dye is close to the end of the gel (~240 V, generally less than 60 min). The gel is stained with ethidium bromide in water for several minutes, and a picture is taken afterwards (*see* **Note 6**). RNA is then transferred to a Hybond-N membrane in 0.5X Tris-borate-EDTA buffer inside a minigel tank for approx 30 min at approx 400 mA. The blot is dried, and RNA crosslinked to the membrane using a Stratagene ultraviolet crosslinker. Prehybridization and hybridization are performed in ExpressHyb solution.

4. To prepare the probe for Northern analysis, 0.5 to 1 µg of a synthetic oligonucleotide fully complementary to the miRNA of interest is phosphorylated by T4 polynucleotide kinase with [γ-^{32}P] adenosine triphosphate, and purified by passing the reaction mixture through a Centrisep spin column. The probe is used at a concentration of approx 5×10^6 cpm/mL during hybridization. After hybridization, the membrane is washed at the eventual stringency of 0.1X standard sodium citrate, 0.1% sodium dodecylsulfate (twice for ~20 min each), and analyzed by autoradiography or a PhosphorImager.

5. For the three miR-30 expression plasmids described in **Fig. 1A**, Northern blotting results are shown in **Fig. 1B** and **Fig. 1C**. The *miR-30* gene is unusual in that it expresses two mature miRNAs, miR-30-5p and miR-30-3p, derived from the 5' and 3' arms of the precursor stem, respectively (**Fig. 1A**). In untransfected 293T cells, only miR-30-5p is expressed at low but detectable levels (**Fig. 1B**, marked by an asterisk). The miR-30(414) construct and the smaller miR-30(197) construct greatly overexpress miR-30-5p (**Fig. 1B**) and produce lower but still readily detectable amounts of miR-30-3p (**Fig. 1C**, marked by an asterisk). In addition, expression of the approx 60-nt pre-miR-30 processing intermediate is apparent in this Northern analysis (marked by arrowheads in **Fig. 1B** and **C**), indicating that artificial pri-miRNAs go through the normal miRNA maturation pathway. For the smallest miR-30 construct, however, both miR-30-5p and miR-30-3p are produced at similar levels. This change in the relative ratio of miR-30-5p and miR-30-3p expression, from both the endogenous situation and the other two longer miR-30 expression plasmids, is caused by a minor, 1-nt shift in the precise site of the Drosha cleavage in the shortest pri-miR-30, thus, generating versions of the pre-miR-30 duplex intermediate with different nucleotides at the ends *(22)*. Therefore, sequences/structures flanking a pre-miRNA can clearly affect precisely how the pre-miRNA is processed out of the pri-miRNA, which is not surprising, and merits further attention. However, the main message here is that pri-miRNA stem-loops, together with a small amount of flanking genomic sequence, contain all of the *cis*-acting signals required for accurate excision of a mature human miRNA in vivo. As a result, one can readily construct plasmids that encode mature human miRNAs and then detect the expression of these miRNAs in transfected cells.

3.2. Drosha Cleavage Assays In Vitro

1. Biochemical analyses using purified or partially purified components in vitro have been instrumental in dissecting the mechanistic details of many biological processes. For the generation of pre-miRNAs from pri-miRNAs, an RNase called Drosha, along with an accessory subunit, DGCR8 in humans, fulfills such a role in vivo, and one can recapitulate the processing reaction in a test tube *(7–10,22)*.

2. The plasmid pCK-Drosha-FLAG expresses a C-terminal FLAG-tagged human Drosha protein *(7)*. The plasmid pCMV-influenza hemaglutinin (HA)-DGCR8 expresses an amino-terminally HA-tagged DGCR8 and was made by polymerase chain reaction subcloning from a DGCR8 expression plasmid *(9)*.

3. To prepare the Drosha enzyme (*see* **Note 7**), 293T cells in a 6-well plate are transfected with pCK-Drosha-FLAG alone or in combination with pCMV-HA-DGCR8. Two days later, cells are lysed in NETN buffer, and extracts are incubated with anti-FLAG agarose beads at 4°C for approx 1 h. Beads are washed four times with NETN buffer and once with reaction buffer. To elute the immunoprecipitate, 150 ng/mL of 3X FLAG peptide in the same reaction buffer is used according to instructions from Sigma. The resultant immunoprecipitate contains the target Drosha-FLAG protein as well as endogenous DGCR8 and/or overexpressed HA-DGCR8, and is stored at –80°C until used.

4. DNA templates for RNA synthesis are prepared by the polymerase chain reaction method with primers containing recognition sites for T7 RNA polymerase, and isolated by gel electrophoresis. RNA substrates are made by in vitro transcription (Promega) in the presence of $[\alpha\text{-}^{32}P]$ cytidine triphosphate and purified by passing through Centrisep spin columns.

5. Drosha-processing reactions are set up by mixing on ice the eluted immunoprecipitate with approx 10^4 cpm of ^{32}P-labeled RNA in reaction buffer supplemented with 2 m*M* DTT, 7 m*M* $MgCl_2$, and 0.5 U/µL RNasin, and allowed to proceed at 37°C for 60 to 90 min. An equal volume of 2X loading buffer is subsequently added, and after denaturation at 95°C for approx 10 min, RNA is fractionated on an 8 *M* urea/10% polyacrylamide gel. Results are analyzed by autoradiography or a PhosphorImager.

6. **Figure 2** shows representative data of Drosha-mediated pri-miRNA processing in vitro. The RNA substrate is a fragment of human pri-miR-223 that has 24 nt at the 5' side, and 21 nt at the 3' side, flanking the pre-miR-223 RNA hairpin intermediate (**Fig. 2A**). Drosha cleavage generated a major pre-miRNA product of approx 60 nt (**Fig. 2B**, marked by an asterisk), as well as an approx 90-nt RNA (marked by an arrowhead), which probably represents a singly cut intermediate(s). It is clear that the enzyme prepared from the Drosha/DGCR8 cotransfection was significantly more active than the one prepared from transfection with Drosha alone. Such a disparity in pre-miRNA production cannot be attributed to different concentrations of the Drosha subunit in the two enzyme preparations; instead, it reflects the stimulatory or even essential role of the DGCR8 subunit in this specific cleavage reaction.

4. Notes

1. In addition to 293T cells, other cell lines have also been used to overexpress miRNAs. Different cell lines may have different transfection efficiencies and also different endogenous miRNA expression patterns.

2. There are many other applicable transfection methods/reagents, such as Lipofectamine 2000. The amounts of DNA and lipid agent used are very similar for Fugene 6 and Lipofectamine 2000. Fugene 6 is less toxic to cells and, thus, can be used to transfect cells at lower density.

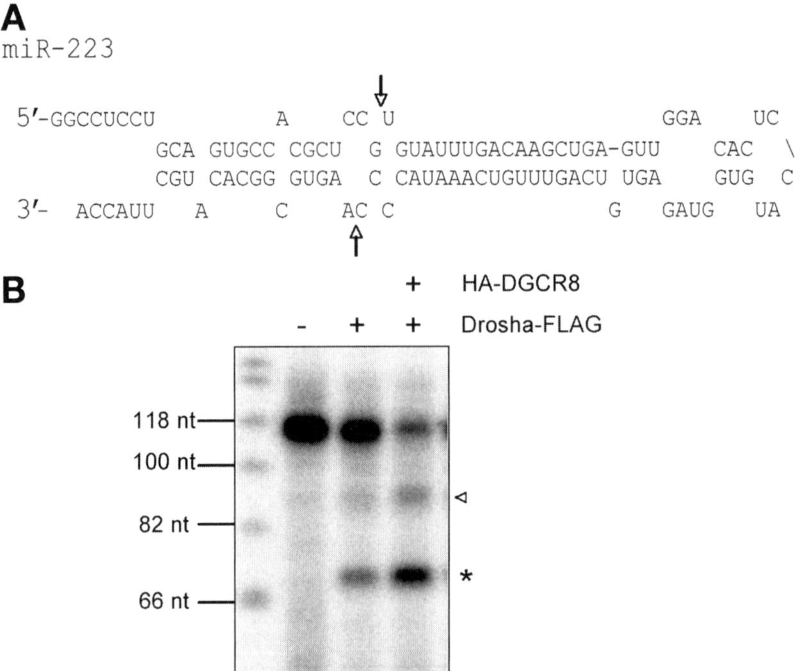

Fig. 2. Drosha-mediated primary (pri)-microRNA cleavage in vitro. (**A**) The predicted secondary structure of an RNA substrate, which encodes human precursor miR-223 flanked by 24 nt on the 5' side and 21 nt on the 3' side. Deduced Drosha cleavage sites are indicated by arrows. (**B**) The ^{32}P-labeled RNA is incubated with buffer alone, FLAG immunoprecipitate from 293T cells transfected with pCK-Drosha-FLAG alone, or with FLAG immunoprecipitate from cells cotransfected with pCK-Drosha-FLAG and pCMV-HA-DGCR8. The asterisk indicates the position of the pre-miR-223 RNA hairpin, and the arrowhead indicates a processing intermediate(s). The DNA size markers used do not accurately comigrate with RNAs of the same size.

3. Both RNA polymerase II and III promoters are compatible with overexpressing miRNAs.
4. Other miRNA detection methods include primer extension and the RNase protection assay.
5. It saves time to perform transfection experiments immediately after or several hours after seeding cells at a relatively high density. Use of Fugene 6 or Lipofectamine 2000 allows efficient transfection with less DNA, and one can isolate enough RNA for subsequent analysis from a single well in a 24-well plate. For cell types that are less susceptible to transfection, more cells and DNA may be needed.
6. A photograph is taken to verify equal amounts of RNA loading in all of the relevant lanes. One can also perform Northern analysis on the membrane for an endogenous RNA species or a cotransfected gene that expresses a control RNA.
7. Baculoviruses encoding Drosha and a plasmid that expresses DGCR8 in bacteria have been generated (*9*). They can be used to yield recombinant proteins as well.

Acknowledgments

We thank V. N. Kim for providing the pCK-Drosha-FLAG plasmid and R. Shiekhattar for the DGCR8 plasmid. This work was supported by the National Institutes of Health grant GM071408 to Bryan Cullen.

References

1. Bartel, D. P. (2004) MicroRNAs: genomics, biogenesis, mechanism, and function. *Cell* **116,** 281–297.
2. Esau, C., Kang, X., Peralta, E., et al. (2004) MicroRNA-143 regulates adipocyte differentiation. *J. Biol. Chem.* **279,** 52,361–52,365.
3. Poy, M. N., Eliasson, L., Krutzfeldt, J., et al. (2004) A pancreatic islet-specific microRNA regulates insulin secretion. *Nature* **432,** 226–230.
4. Cheng, A. M., Byrom, M. W., Shelton, J., and Ford, L. P. (2005) Antisense inhibition of human miRNAs and indications for an involvement of miRNA in cell growth and apoptosis. *Nucleic Acids Res.* **33,** 1290–1297.
5. Lim, L. P., Lau, N. C., Garrett-Engele, P., et al. (2005) Microarray analysis shows that some microRNAs downregulate large numbers of target mRNAs. *Nature* **433,** 769–773.
6. Cullen, B. R. (2004) Transcription and processing of human microRNA precursors. *Mol. Cell* **16,** 861–865.
7. Lee, Y., Ahn, C., Han, J., et al. (2003) The nuclear RNase III Drosha initiates microRNA processing. *Nature* **425,** 415–419.
8. Denli, A. M., Tops, B., Plasterk, R. H. A., Ketting, R. F., and Hannon, G. J. (2004) Processing of pri-microRNAs by the microprocessor complex. *Nature* **432,** 231–235.
9. Gregory, R. I., Yan, K. P., Amuthan, G., et al. (2004) The Microprocessor complex mediates the genesis of microRNAs. *Nature* **432,** 235–240.
10. Han, J., Lee, Y., Yeom, K. H., Kim, Y. K., Jin, H., and Kim, V. N. (2004) The Drosha-DGCR8 complex in primary microRNA processing. *Genes Dev.* **18,** 3016–3027.
11. Yi, R., Qin, Y., Macara, I. G., and Cullen, B. R. (2003) Exportin-5 mediates the nuclear export of pre-microRNAs and short hairpin RNAs. *Genes Dev.* **17,** 3011–3016.
12. Bohnsack, M. T., Czaplinski, K., and Görlich, D. (2004) Exportin 5 is a RanGTP-dependent dsRNA-binding protein that mediates nuclear export of pre-miRNAs. *RNA* **10,** 185–191.
13. Lund, E., Güttinger, S., Calado, A., Dahlberg, J. E., and Kutay, U. (2004) Nuclear export of microRNA precursors. *Science* **303,** 95–98.
14. Grishok, A., Pasquinelli, A. E., Conte, D., et al. (2001) Genes and mechanisms related to RNA interference regulate expression of the small temporal RNAs that control *C. elegans* developmental timing. *Cell* **106,** 23–34.
15. Hutvágner, G., McLachlan, J., Pasquinelli, A. E., Balint, E., Tuschl, T., and Zamore, P. D. (2001) A cellular function for the RNA-interference enzyme Dicer in the maturation of the let-7 small temporal RNA. *Science* **293,** 834–838.
16. Ketting, R. F., Haverkamp, T. H., van Luenen, H. G., and Plasterk, R. H. A. (2001) Dicer functions in RNA interference and in synthesis of small RNA involved in developmental timing in *C. elegans*. *Genes Dev.* **15,** 2654–2659.
17. Khvorova, A., Reynolds, A., and Jayasena, S. D. (2003) Functional siRNAs and miRNAs exhibit strand bias. *Cell* **115,** 209–216.
18. Schwarz, D. S., Hutvágner, G., Du, T., Xu, Z., Aronin, N., and Zamore, P. D. (2003) Asymmetry in the assembly of the RNAi enzyme complex. *Cell* **115,** 199–208.

19. Zeng, Y., Wagner, E. J., and Cullen, B. R. (2002) Both natural and designed microRNAs can inhibit the expression of cognate mRNAs when expressed in human cells. *Mol. Cell* **9,** 1327–1333.
20. Zeng, Y. and Cullen B. R. (2003) Sequence requirements for microRNA processing and function in human cells. *RNA* **9,** 112–123.
21. Chen, C. Z., Li, L., Lodish, H. F., and Bartel, D. P. (2004) MicroRNAs modulate hematopoietic lineage differentiation. *Science* **303,** 83–86.
22. Zeng, Y., Yi, R., and Cullen, B. R. (2005) Recognition and cleavage of primary microRNA precursors by the nuclear processing enzyme Drosha. *EMBO J.* **24,** 138–148.

5

Mouse Embryonic Stem Cells as a Model Genetic System to Dissect and Exploit the RNA Interference Machinery

Stefan A. Muljo and Chryssa Kanellopoulou

Summary

Conditional gene targeting is often a useful approach to elucidate the in vivo function of a gene. We use this approach to investigate the biological role of the RNA interference (RNAi) pathway in mammals. In addition, the RNAi machinery in mammalian cells can be exploited for gene knock-down experiments. In this chapter, we discuss the variety of experiments that can be performed using genetically engineered embryonic stem (ES) cells. ES cells provide a mammalian genetic system that is physiological, and tractable for mutagenesis and experimentation. This approach is economical and rapid, because it does not require production and breeding of genetically engineered mice.

Key Words: Embryonic stem cells; gene targeting; RNA interference; microRNA.

1. Introduction

Mouse embryonic stem (ES) cells are pluripotent cells derived from the inner cell mass of the preimplantation mouse blastocyst (3.5 d postcoitus). They are untransformed, undifferentiated primary cells that undergo seemingly unlimited self-renewal in culture, but still maintain a normal karyotype. In addition, ES cells undergo a higher rate of homologous recombination than somatic cells, and, thus, are practical for gene targeting. Finally, they can be directed to differentiate into many somatic cell types in vitro: adipocytes *(1)*, chondrocytes *(2,3)*, dendritic cells *(4)*, endothelial cells *(5)*, erythrocytes *(6)*, keratinocytes *(7)*, lymphocytes *(6,8,9)*, mast cells *(10)*, myocytes *(11)*, neurons *(12,13)*, osteoblasts *(2,3,14)*, and pancreatic islet cells *(15)*. Although we work with mouse ES cells, in principle, this approach could be applied to human ES cells.

To understand the RNAi pathway, we engineered a mutant ES cell line that cannot carry out processing of double-stranded RNA (dsRNA), a key step in this pathway *(16)*. RNAi is an evolutionarily conserved pathway that has been implicated in a broad spectrum of biological phenomena, including development, stem cell maintenance, viral host–pathogen interactions, tumorigenesis, heterochromatin formation, genome rearrangements, and transposon silencing *(17)*. Dicer is a key enzyme in RNA-based silencing, because it is responsible for the cleavage of long dsRNAs and precursor (pre)-microRNAs (miRNAs) into small interfering RNAs and miRNAs, respectively *(18–22)*. Dicer-pro-

From: *Methods in Molecular Biology, vol. 342: MicroRNA Protocols*
Edited by: S. Ying © Humana Press Inc., Totowa, NJ

cessed short dsRNAs are then incorporated into multicomponent ribonucleoprotein complexes that mediate RNA-induced silencing before and/or after transcription *(17)*.

1.1. Designing Gene Targeting Experiments

We perform our experiments in the C57BL/6 mouse-derived ES cell line, Bruce-4 *(23)*. The advantages of genetically defined ES cell lines have been reviewed *(24)*. If one plans to generate mice and has access to tetraploid blastocyst complementation technology for generating completely ES cell-derived mice, then one should consider using F1 (e.g., C57BL/6 × 129) hybrid ES cells *(25,26)*. Although multiple gene targeting may be required to introduce all of the required alleles, the time and cost for breeding of mice is no longer necessary. The procedure that we use for gene targeting by homologous recombination in ES cells has been extensively detailed *(27)*.

When targeting a gene that may be essential for mouse development, it is advisable to design a conditional gene-targeting vector. The increase in effort is not substantial, and one has the possibility to generate both conventional and conditional knockouts *(28)*. For conditional gene targeting, we incorporate loxP sites into our targeting construct, such that we can excise part or all of our gene of interest using Cre recombinase. Because some genes are too large to be flanked by loxP sites ("floxed") using a single plasmid-based targeting construct, an essential portion of the gene is targeted such that, after Cre-mediated deletion, a null allele would result, or at the very least, would result in the translation of a nonfunctional gene product. With the advent of bacterial artificial chromosome (BAC)-based gene targeting, it is now possible to flox larger DNA segments. Typically, the loxP sites are strategically inserted in regions of the gene that are predicted to be nonessential (e.g., an intronic sequence that is not evolutionarily conserved). Generally, we prefer to use a drug selection cassette that is flanked by Flp recombinase target (FRT) sites. This allows us to selectively delete the drug cassette from the targeted allele using Flp recombinase and leave the gene of interest intact (except for the two loxP sites and one FRT site; also *see* **Subheading 3.2.2.**).

Deletion of *dcr-1* in the mouse germline results in early embryonic lethality *(29)*. For this reason, we generated a conditional mutation of the *dcr-1* gene by inserting loxP sites in the introns flanking exons 18 to 20, which encode for part of the Piwi-Argonaute-Zwille (PAZ) domain and the first ribonuclease III domain *(16)*. The targeting strategy is schematically shown in **Fig. 1**. The possible alleles that can be generated from the gene targeting are depicted in **Fig. 2**.

Fig. 1. *(Opposite page)* Conditional gene targeting strategy for mouse *dcr-1*. Depicted at the **top** is a partial structure of the wild-type *dcr-1* gene (the 3' terminus). **Below**, the structure of the conditional targeting vector and the lengths of homology are shown. Exons 18 to 20, encoding half of the PAZ domain and the first ribonuclease III domain, are flanked by loxP sites (*black triangles*). An FRT-flanked phosphoglycerate kinase-neomycin cassette (neo) is inserted into intron 17 to allow positive selection using G418. FRT sites are denoted by *open ovals*. A thymidine kinase (TK) cassette is included to enable use of ganciclovir to select against random integration of the targeting vector. 5' and 3' probes used for screening of homologous recombinants are indicated as *thick lines* labeled *a* and *b*, respectively. The predicted structure of the targeted allele is shown at the **bottom**. Lengths of BglI restriction fragments for Southern analyses of the wild-type and targeted allele are indicated in kilobases (kb) by *horizontal dashed lines*.

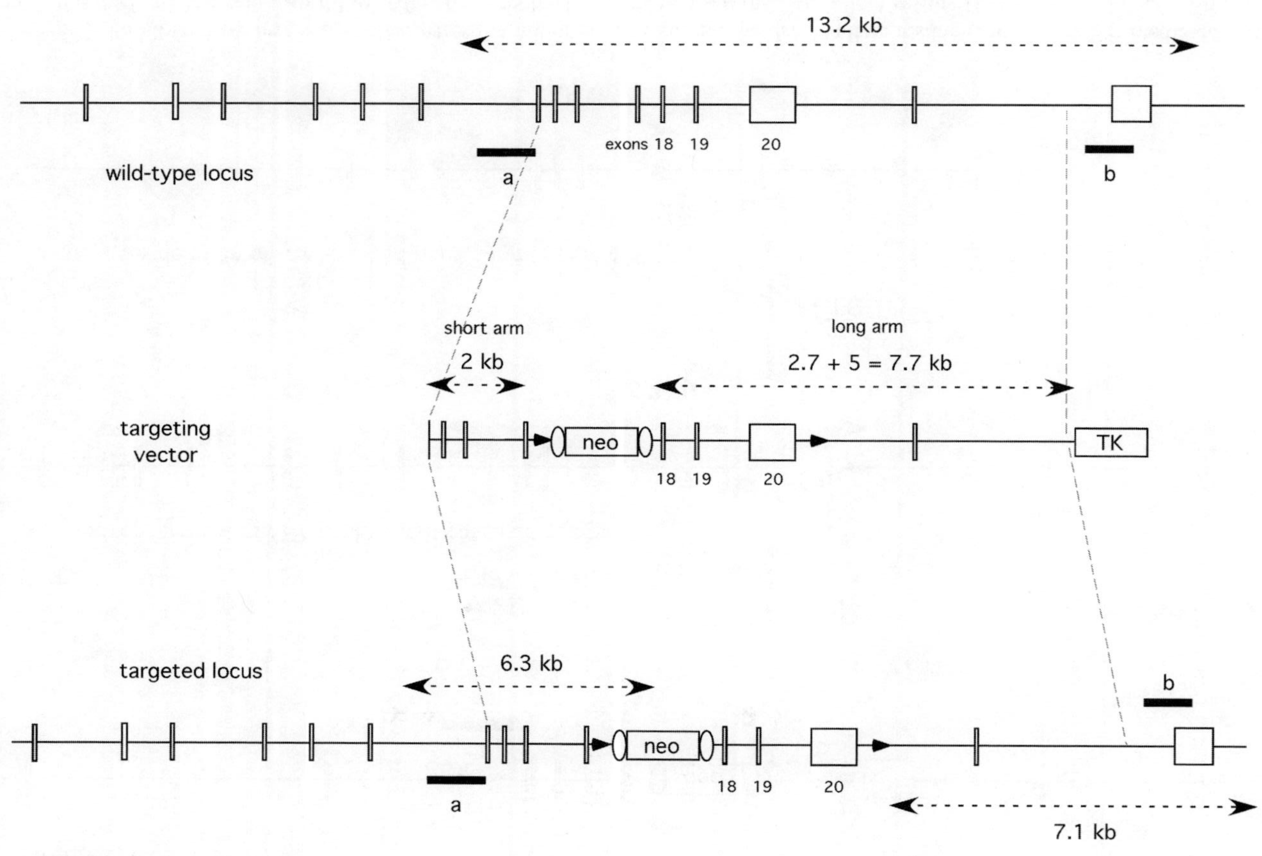

13.2 kb
wild-type locus
exons 18 19 20
a
b
short arm
2 kb
long arm
2.7 + 5 = 7.7 kb
targeting vector
neo
18 19 20
TK
targeted locus
6.3 kb
a
neo
18 19 20
b
7.1 kb

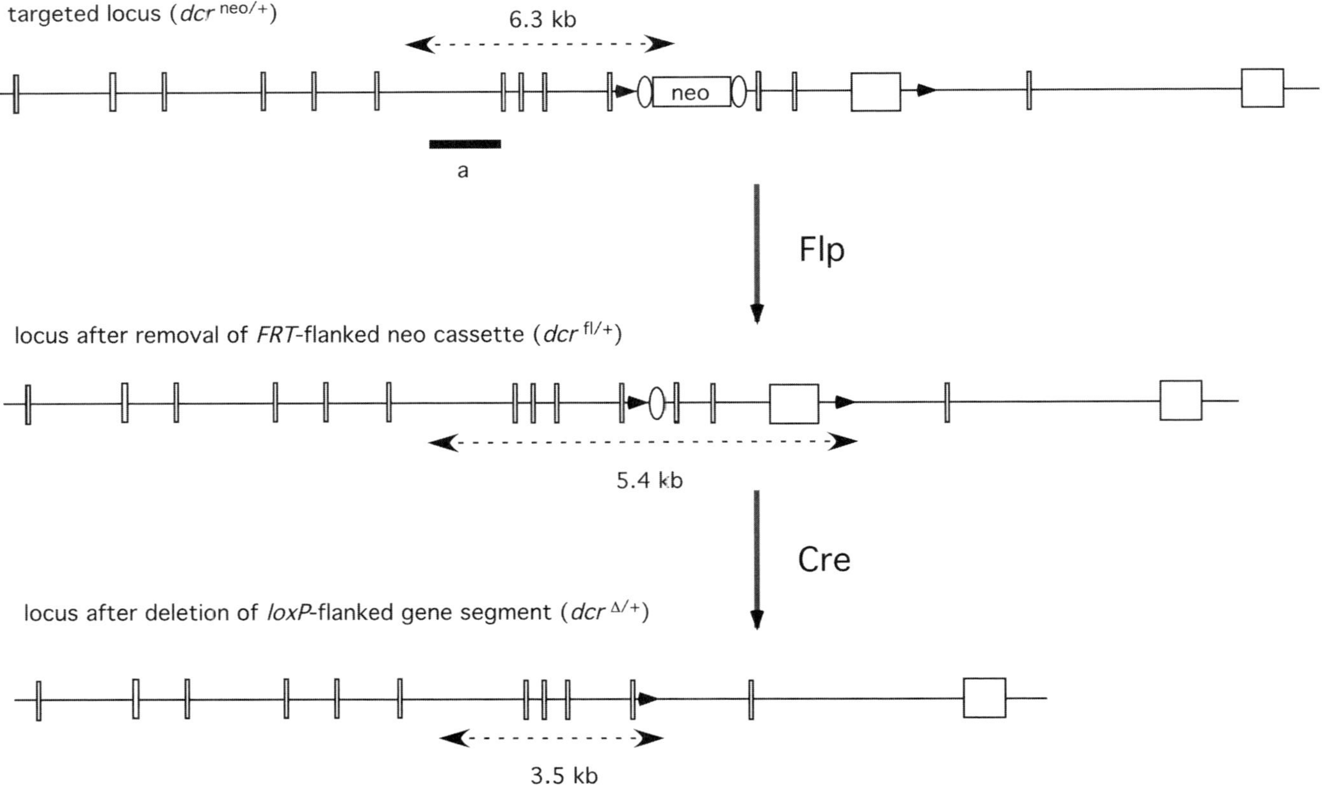

Fig. 2. Possible *dcr-1* targeted alleles. After the initial gene targeting, the *dcr*neo allele results (**top**). After Flp-mediated recombination, the *dcr*fl allele results (**middle**). After Cre-mediated recombination, the *dcr*Δ allele results (**bottom**). Lengths of BglI restriction fragments in kilobases (kb) for the different alleles are indicated by *horizontal dashed lines* (not drawn to scale).

2. Materials

2.1. Gene Targeting

1. BAC clones (CHORI, Oakland, CA; http://bacpac.chori.org/ or Invitrogen, Carlsbad, CA).
2. KOD HiFi XL DNA polymerase (Novagen, San Diego, CA).

2.2. ES Cell Culture

1. Chicken serum (Invitrogen).
2. Trypsin (Invitrogen).
3. ESGRO®/Leukemia inhibitory factor (LIF) (Chemicon, Temecula, CA).
4. Geneticin®/G418 (Invitrogen).
5. PD98509 (Cell Signaling Technology, Danvers, MA).
6. Proteinase K (Roche, Indianapolis, IN).

2.3. Superovulation

1. Pregnant mare serum gonadotropin (Calbiochem, San Diego, CA).
2. Human chorionic gonadotropin (Calbiochem).

2.4. RNA Isolation

1. Trizol® (Invitrogen).
2. MirVana™ RNA isolation kit (Ambion, Austin, TX).

2.5. Solutions

1. ES cell lysis buffer: 10 mM NaCl, 10 mM Tris-HCl (pH 7.5), 0.5% Sarcosyl, and 0.4 mg/mL proteinase K (add fresh before use).
2. NETN: 150 mM NaCl, 20 mM Tris-HCl (pH 8.0), 1 mM ethylenediaminetetraacetic acid, and 0.5% Nonidet P-40.
3. Leupeptin and aprotinin (Roche). Prepare 1000X solution (2 mg/mL) and freeze in small aliquots.
4. 4% paraformaldehyde in phosphate-buffered saline (PBS). Store aliquots at –20°C and thaw just before use. Do not freeze–thaw aliquots. Alternatively, a 20% solution of paraformaldehyde can be purchased from Pierce and diluted in PBS just before use.
5. Vectashield® mounting medium with diamidino phenyl indole (Vector Labs, Burlingame, CA).

3. Methods

3.1. Conditional Gene Targeting

As an example, we discuss our gene targeting of *dcr-1*. Long and short arms of homology and the floxed region that includes exons 18 to 20 of murine *dcr-1* were amplified by polymerase chain reaction (PCR) from a BAC containing the *dcr-1* genomic locus (*see* **Note 1**). Primers containing the appropriate restriction sites to facilitate cloning into targeting vector were used (*see* **Note 2**). High-fidelity, long-range PCR conditions may need to be established for individual PCRs, but generally, KOD HiFi XL DNA polymerase (Novagen) and approx 20 to 25 cycles of amplification worked best. PCR fragments were cut with the respective restriction enzymes and cloned sequentially into the pEASY-FLIRTneo targeting vector *(27)* and sequenced. Alternatively, regions of homology can be subcloned from a BAC using standard recombinant DNA procedures or by more sophisticated BAC "recombineering" techniques (e.g., E–T cloning *[30]*). ES cell culture, transfection and identification of homologous recombinants have been described elsewhere *(27)*.

In addition, Oberdoerffer et al. designed a type III RNA polymerase promoter-based knock-in strategy that could be used to conditionally express pre-miRNAs or short hairpin RNA (shRNA) for knock-down in ES cells or mice *(31)*. This entails a targeting into hypoxanthine phosphoribosyl transferase-deficient ES cells (HM-1 line), which, after selection in hypoxanthine aminopterin thymidine medium, results in a 100% frequency of homologous recombination *(32,33)*. This type III RNA polymerase promoter system has the advantage of containing a floxed transcriptional stop cassette before the shRNA cloning site. Therefore, expression of the small RNA of interest requires Cre-mediated recombination. Different inducible or tissue-specific Cre transgenes can be used to reproducibly express shRNAs in a conditional manner. In this way, one can avoid position effects that may result from transgenesis using stable transfection or retroviral transduction.

3.2. Generating Homozygous ES Cell Lines

3.2.1. Selection Under High G418 Concentration

If a neomycin-resistance cassette has been incorporated as a positive-selection marker for the gene targeting, then singly targeted ES cell clones can be cultured in increasing concentrations of G418 to promote a gene conversion event, whereby the other allele of the gene in interest acquires the neomycin-resistance cassette from its sister targeted allele. Several concentrations of G418 should be tested. This method has been previously described *(34,35)*. A criticism of this technique is that the ES cells are subjected to high concentrations of a drug. It is not known what effect(s) this may have on ES cells, and, occasionally, duplication of the neomycin-resistance cassette occurs at random sites or a linked gene is mutated as a result of the DNA duplication event (*see* **Note 3**). In our case, we used this technique to generate several *dcr*[neo/neo] ES cell clones, and then we deleted Dicer using a Cre-expressing adenovirus to obtain *dcr*[Δ/Δ] ES cells. The *dcr*[neo/neo] clones did not exhibit any of the defects observed in the *dcr*[Δ/Δ] ES cells *(16)*. To further demonstrate that the mutant phenotype is specific to Dicer ablation, we rescued the Dicer-deficient ES cells by reintroducing Dicer. This was accomplished by using the same gene-targeting vector to retarget *dcr-1* in *dcr*[Δ/Δ] ES cells *(16)*. Alternatively, an expression construct containing a complementary DNA could be used; however, it is unlikely that expression of the gene in question will be restored to physiological levels.

1. ES cells harboring a targeted allele are thawed (depending on the concentration of frozen aliquots, they should be plated on appropriate feeder-containing plates).
2. Cells are harvested when subconfluent (*see* **Note 4**).
3. 10^4 ES cells are plated in 6-well plates coated with inactivated mouse embryonic fibroblasts (MEFs) (*see* **Note 5**).
4. A day later, G418-containing medium is added. Different concentrations of G418 should be tested, but an original titration curve of 2, 4, 8, 16, and 32X G418 can be applied ("X"

is the concentration of G418 used for the original targeting, which may vary for different ES cell lines and different neomycin-resistance cassettes; *see* **Note 6**). The concentration of G418 at which ES cells start to die after 2 to 3 d is likely to yield homozygous convertants. The cells grown under this concentration of G418 should be harvested 3 to 4 d later and replated into 10-cm dishes (~10^3 cells/plate). The concentration of G418 can be reduced to 2X (*see* **Note 7**).

5. ES cell colonies are picked after 8 to 10 d and screened as described elsewhere *(27)*.
6. If the colonies seem mosaic from the Southern analysis, they may need to be subcloned to isolate homozygous clones.

3.2.2. Double Gene Targeting

A second strategy for the generation of double-targeted ES cells is to construct two variants of a gene targeting vector: one using the commonly used neomycin-resistance cassette and a second using another drug-resistance marker for positive selection (e.g., hygromycin or puromycin). This is commonly performed in the chicken DT40 B cell line, in which genes are also targeted by homologous recombination. Similarly, homozygous ES cells can be obtained by two consecutive gene targetings. Alternatively, if a conditional gene targeting is planned, it should be possible to delete the drug-resistance cassette (either by Cre or Flp recombinase, as appropriate) and, thus, the singly targeted ES cells would again be sensitive to the drug. A second targeting of the other allele with the same targeting construct can then be performed using the same drug for positive selection.

3.2.3. Isolation of Primary ES Cells From Homozygous Mouse Blastocysts

If mice have already been generated as a result of the gene targeting, then homozygous ES cells can be derived anew from the inner cell mass of homozygous mouse blastocysts. Such ES cells may be desirable because they have not undergone numerous passages in vitro and have not been cultured in high concentrations of G418. If embryonic development is dramatically affected, as in the case of Dicer deficiency, it may not be possible to derive ES cells by this method. Because we generated conditional *dcr-1* knock-out mice, we were able to derive $dcr^{fl/fl}$ ES cells from blastocysts and introduce Cre in vitro to generate $dcr^{\Delta/\Delta}$ ES cells (unpublished data).

1. Timed matings of mice of the appropriate genotypes must be arranged. Set up 3 to 10 natural matings using well-rested males and females in estrus. To obtain more blastocysts, young female mice (~4 wk old) may be superovulated. Intraperitoneally inject female mice with pregnant mare serum, and 48-h later with human chorionic gonadotropin, and promptly set up breeding.
2. The next morning, check for plugs and set aside the females with plugs for harvesting of blastocysts 3 d later.
3. At 3.5 d postcoitus, blastocysts may be isolated from pregnant female mice. In a tissue culture hood, sterilize the abdomen with 70% ethanol. Locate the uterus within the peritoneal cavity and carefully cut it out. Wash the uterus in PBS to remove blood and flush with medium, using a 1-mL syringe and 26-gage needle.
4. Locate the blastocysts under a stereo dissecting microscope (×20 or ×40 magnification) and transfer using a mouth pipet. Alternatively, a P2 pipetman (Gilson) may be used if mouth

pipetting is absolutely prohibited by institutional guidelines. Wash each blastocyst in medium twice.

5. Transfer each blastocyst into an individual well of a 48-well plate that was precoated with gelatin and preplated with a confluent monolayer of inactivated MEFs in ES cell medium supplemented with 50 μM MEK1 inhibitor, PD98509 (Cell Signaling Technology; *see* **Note 8**). It is best not to disturb the plates until the embryos have attached.

6. The next day, do not change the medium, but gently add some fresh ES cell medium containing PD98059.

7. The third day, the embryos should have "hatched," lost their zona pellucida, and adhered to the feeder layer. The trophoblast cells spread out to form a monolayer and the inner cell mass cells appear as a clump of cells. The ES cells will derive from the inner cell mass cells. It is now safe to replace the medium with fresh ES cell medium containing PD98059.

8. The next day, gently trypsinize the whole well and transfer to 6-well plates that were precoated with gelatin and preplated with a feeder layer. Trypsinization at this stage may take up to 10 min at 37°C.

9. Change medium every day.

10. Primary ES cell colonies should appear after approx 1 wk. Otherwise, wells may be retrypsinized every 3 d, until ES cell colonies appear. Not all blastocysts give rise to ES cells and, generally, if ES cell colonies do not start appearing after 2 wk in culture it is unlikely that they will at all (*see* **Note 9**).

11. ES cells can be trypsinized once more and passaged onto 10-cm dishes. At this point, it would be advisable to freeze some cells and passage a small fraction of the cells onto gelatin-coated dishes without any feeder cells. The ES cells grown on gelatin can be harvested for DNA isolation such that they can be genotyped (*see* **Subheading 3.3.1.**, **item 1** and **Note 10**).

12. Individual colonies may be picked to establish clonal ES cell lines.

13. ES cell lines should be karyotyped and tested for *Mycoplasma* contamination.

14. To test their pluripotency, ES cells may be injected back into blastocysts. They should be able to give rise to good chimeras and germline transmission. This is especially important if you plan to retarget the cells and use the resulting cells to generate mice.

3.2.4. Cre-Mediated Deletion of Floxed Alleles in ES Cells

Cre-mediated deletion of a floxed allele in ES cells is relatively easy and efficient (*see* **Note 11**).

1. The ES cells harboring floxed allele(s) are plated on MEF-coated plates, *see* **Note 5**.

2. If cells were previously frozen, it is advisable to passage them once before subjecting them to a transfection.

3. Cre recombinase can be expressed using either an adenovirus or a plasmid. If an adenoviral vector is used, 500 to 1000 cells are plated on a 10-cm plate coated with MEFs, and incubated with the virus overnight in 5 mL of ES cell medium. Medium is replaced the day after (*see* **Notes 12** and **13**). If an adenovirus expressing Cre is not available, a Cre expression plasmid can be used. Cotransfection with a puromycin acetyltransferase-bearing plasmid can be used for selection (*see* **Note 14**). Transfection is performed by electroporation, as previously described *(27)*, and a transient selection with puromycin (1.25 µg/mL for 36 h, starting 5 h after transfection) is sufficient.

4. Colonies should be ready for picking 8 to 10 d after either infection or transfection.

3.3. Experimenting With ES Cells

3.3.1. ES Cell Differentiation Assays

ES cells are pluripotent and can differentiate in vivo and in vitro to multiple lineages. For immunologists, injection of mutant and control ES cells into recombinase activating gene-deficient blastocysts facilitate study of B- and T-lymphocyte development in chimeric mice *(36)*. Subcutaneous injection of ES cells into immunocompromised (e.g., nude) mice leads to the formation of teratocarcinomas, whose growth can be monitored over time and gives an indication of the differentiation and growth capacity of the ES cells. In vitro assays of ES cell differentiation obviate the need for blastocyst isolation and microinjection, embryo transfer into pseudopregnant mice, or the use of animals. Often, but not always, the first step in an in vitro differentiation process is the generation of embryoid bodies (EBs), in which the first signs of endoderm, mesoderm, and ectoderm differentiation are recapitulated. There are various protocols for EB generation, and the simplest one is outlined here.

1. Exponentially growing ES cells are harvested, and MEFs are removed by selective adherence (MEFs tend to stick to plastic more than undifferentiated ES cells); the cells are plated after trypsinization on a nongelatinized 10-cm plate in 8 mL of ES cell medium and transferred back to the incubator for 30 to 40 min. The supernatant is gently collected and the plate (containing most of the attached MEFs) is discarded. The process can be repeated if more stringent removal of MEFs is desired (*see* **Note 15**).
2. After removal of the majority of the contaminating MEFs, ES cells are resuspended in 2 mL of MEF medium and plated on a low-adherence 6-well plate (Costar, Ultra Low Cluster) at a concentration of 10^5 cells/mL (*see* **Note 16**). The cells do not adhere to the plate and start forming clumps floating in the medium. The clumps should be partially dispersed by vigorous pipetting with a P1000 pipetman (Gilson) for the first 2 d, and the medium can be partially replenished if it starts turning acidic.
3. The cell clumps will grow slowly, and 12 to 13 d later, differentiation can be visualized by harvesting the EBs and preparing histological sections. However, it is easier to follow the differentiation process via monitoring the expression of markers associated with mesoderm, endoderm, or ectoderm differentiation by reverse transcriptase-PCR. EBs can be harvested at different time points (one well of a 6-well plate can be harvested per time point; *see* **Note 17**) and RNA prepared using Trizol reagent, according to the manufacturer's instructions. No homogenization is required, because vigorous pipetting should disrupt the EBs.

3.3.2. Preparation of ES Cell DNA

When isolating genomic DNA, RNA, or protein from ES cells, contaminating feeder cells should be depleted as much as possible (*see* **Subheading 3.3.1.**, **step 1**). Specifically, for DNA isolation (because the differentiation status of the ES cells is not critical), we use the following protocol:

1. Coat 10- or 15-cm plastic dishes with gelatin (0.1% gelatin in PBS) for 20 to 30 min at room temperature (RT).
2. Split ES cells on these plates at a dilution of 1:10. A second passage on gelatin plates can be performed if more complete removal of MEFs is desired.

3. Before harvesting, wash plates twice with PBS (10 mL for a 10-cm plate), and add 5 mL of lysis buffer containing 400 µg/mL proteinase K directly to the cells.
4. Incubate plates overnight at 56°C in a humidified chamber.
5. Add two volumes of 100% ethanol to each plate to precipitate the DNA. Harvest DNA with a pipet tip, wash once in 70% ethanol, air-dry, and resuspend in an appropriate volume of TE buffer (usually 300 µL per 10-cm plate). Allow DNA to dissolve overnight at 56°C, and store at 4°C for up to 6 mo.

3.3.3. Preparation of ES Cell RNA or Protein Lysates

RNA and protein isolation, on the other hand, may require undifferentiated ES cells, especially for analysis of ES cell-specific markers. Therefore, ES cells can be grown on MEFs until subconfluent and harvested by trypsinization. MEFs can be subsequently depleted by selective adherence, as previously described (*see* **Subheading 3.3.1.**, **step 1**). The harvested ES cells are washed once with PBS.

For RNA isolation, either Trizol reagent or MirVana RNA isolation kit can be used, according to the manufacturer's instructions. Trizol isolation is easy and reproducible and does not lead to loss of small RNAs as with conventional spin column RNA isolation kits. The MirVana kit has the advantage of allowing fractionation of RNA into a large and small fraction (more and less than 200-nucleotides long, respectively). The RNA from Dicer-deficient ES cells is useful for Northern analyses to confirm whether predicted miRNAs or other small dsRNAs are *bona fide* miRNAs or Dicer products; if so, the mature miRNA or processed dsRNAs (21–28 nucleotides) should be absent or dramatically reduced, and occasionally (but not always), accumulation of the pre-miRNA or dsRNA precursor should become evident.

1. For protein isolation, the ES cell pellet is resuspended in 150 m*M* NETN buffer containing protease inhibitors (leupeptin/aprotinin). Depending on the number of cells, the volume of the NETN buffer is adjusted. Typically, cells harvested from a 10-cm dish were resuspended in 200 µL of lysis buffer.
2. Lysate is incubated on ice for 30 min. For cytoplasmic/soluble extract preparation, centrifuge the lysate at top speed on a tabletop microcentrifuge at 4°C and transfer supernatant to a fresh tube. For whole cell extract, sonicate the lysate (20 s, setting 7 of the sonicator), and centrifuge again.
3. Store cell lysates at –80°C.

3.3.4. Immunofluorescence Microscopy of ES Cells

Indirect immunofluorescence of ES cells is complicated because of their size (small compared with most cells) and the fact that usually they grow in compact three-dimensional structures and not as a monolayer.

1. In our experience, immunofluorescence is optimal when the cells are prepared by one of the following two methods. Subconfluent ES cell cultures are harvested, and MEFs are depleted as previously described (*see* **Subheading 3.3.1.**, **step 1**). Resuspend ES cells in PBS (10^6 cells/mL), and load 200 µL of the cell suspension on a Cytospin holder. Gently centrifuge cells onto a slide (200 rpm for 2 min). Alternatively, allow ES cells to passively attach to a positively charged glass slide by incubating them at 4°C in a humidified chamber for 2 to 3 h.

2. Circle cells attached to the slide with a liquid blocker "Super PAP" pen (Cedarlane) to mark the area where the cells are concentrated on the slide.
3. Fix cells in 4% paraformaldehyde for 30 min at RT.
4. Permeabilize cells with 0.1% Triton X-100 in paraformaldehyde.
5. Wash cells three times in PBS-Tween-20 (PBS-T) with 50 mM glycine.
6. Before antibody incubation, incubate cells in blocking buffer (PBS-T, 50 mM glycine, 2% bovine serum albumin, and 0.2% gelatin) for 1 h at RT. Alternatively, block at 4°C overnight, in a humidified chamber.
7. Dilute antibodies appropriately in blocking buffer. Incubate with primary antibody for 1 h at RT.
8. Wash cells six times (5 min/wash) in PBS-T.
9. Incubate with secondary antibody for 45 min at RT.
10. Wash cells as described in **step 8**.
11. Quickly rinse cells in H$_2$O. Add one drop of mounting solution (Vectashield with diamidino phenyl indole) carefully place cover slips on top of cells. Remove excess mounting solution and air bubbles by inverting slides and gently pressing them on Whatman paper.
12. Seal cover slips with clear nail polish and image slides as soon as possible with a fluorescence microscope.

4. Notes

1. BACs containing your gene of interest can be found using the University of California, Santa Cruz genome browser (http://genome.ucsc.edu/). The *dcr-1* gene is used as an example in **Fig. 3**. The RP23 BAC library was constructed from genomic DNA isolated from the brain and kidney of three female C57BL/6J mice *(37)*. The RP24 library was constructed from genomic DNA isolated from the brain and spleen of a male C57BL/6J mouse. Alternatively, as template for PCR, one can use the genomic DNA from the ES cell line that will be used for gene targeting. However, establishment of PCR conditions might be more difficult when using genomic DNA as template.
2. Appropriate restriction sites for cloning and also subsequent screening of ES cell colonies should be included. It is also essential to ensure that a unique restriction site, at the end of the long or the short arm of homology is present, because the final targeting vector needs to be linearized before transfection.
3. It is advisable, therefore, to isolate multiple double-targeted clones, and also to screen for random integrants by Southern blot analysis, using a probe specific for the neomycin-resistance cassette.
4. ES cells should be harvested when they are in the exponential growth phase, but before colonies start touching each other. Colonies should be plump and undifferentiated. Usually, ES cells do not grow well at a low cell density.
5. MEFs are inactivated either by irradiation (3000 rad) or mitomycin C treatment. We prefer irradiating the cells, because mitomycin C has to be washed off extensively before plating ES cells on the MEFs.
6. Many of the commonly used gene targeting vectors contain an "attenuated" neomycin-resistance cassette (i.e., a neomycin-resistance gene harboring a mutation). This attenuated neomycin-resistance gene confers resistance to G418 at the concentrations normally used for selection of ES cells but does not allow cells to tolerate increased concentrations of G418. If homozygous mutant ES cells are desired, an attenuated neomycin gene should be used in the original targeting vector.

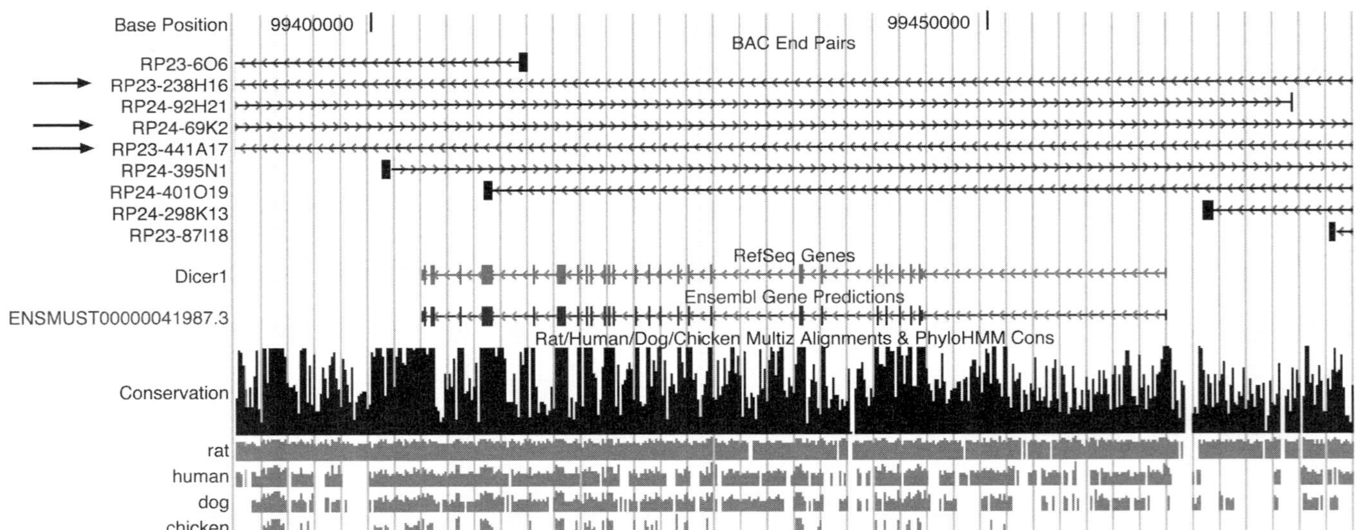

Fig. 3. Screenshot of the University of California, Santa Cruz Genome Browser annotation tracks display showing a view of *dcr-1* on mouse chromosome 12 from the May 2004 assembly *(43)*. Bacterial artificial chromosomes containing the entire *dcr-1* gene are indicated by arrows.

7. MEFs usually do not tolerate the high G418 concentration and start dying. Therefore, it is preferable to reduce the concentration of G418 as soon as possible and to replate onto fresh MEFs.
8. Because mitogen-activated protein kinase–extracellular signal-regulated kinase signaling counteracts LIF–signal transducer and activator of transcription 3 signaling, blastocysts are cultured on MEFs in ES medium supplemented with the MEK-1 inhibitor (PD98509) to promote maintenance of *oct-4* expression *(38,39)*.
9. Genetic background and introduced mutations may influence the derivation of ES cells *(40,41)*. However, we have successfully generated ES cells from C57BL/6 and F1 hybrid mice. One should try with at least 30 blastocysts.
10. To determine the sex of the ES cells, a PCR assay for a gene on the Y chromosome (e.g., *Sry* or *Zfy*) is usually sufficient *(42)*.
11. Usually 20 to 40 ES cell colonies are sufficient to obtain Cre-deleted ES cell clones. Flp-mediated deletion, on the other hand, is not as efficient (~3% deletion efficiency), because Flp recombinase does not work as well at 37°C. If Flp deletion is required, one should plan to pick more colonies.
12. The number of cells plated is critical. If the cells are too dense, picking colonies will be impossible. If cells are too sparse, increased differentiation will occur. Therefore, cells should be counted carefully before infection or plating.
13. Although adenoviral titers differ, a good efficiency of Cre-mediated recombination was usually obtained ranging from 10 to 90%. Small aliquots of the virus should be stored at –20°C, and aliquots should be discarded after thawing.
14. Cotransfection by electroporation works reasonably well in ES cells. A 10-fold excess of the plasmid of interest (i.e., Cre-expression vector) to the puromycin selection plasmid should be used.
15. For us, one of the biggest drawbacks of using ES cells for experiments was the fact that MEFs could never be completely removed from our preparations. Other ES cell lines (e.g., E14) can be adapted to grow on gelatin-coated plates without significant differentiation if a higher concentration of LIF is supplied; unfortunately, Bruce-4 ES cells exhibit a greater requirement for MEFs and we were never able to culture them on gelatin without significant differentiation.
16. If large numbers of EBs are not needed, then one can also prevent ES cells from adhering to the plastic dish by performing hanging drop cultures (~750 ES cells per 20-μL drop).
17. If RNA is to be prepared for the earlier time points of differentiation (e.g., days 3 and 5), more wells should be plated, because there are not as many cells per well. Two to four wells of a 6-well plate should be sufficient for RNA preparation at days 3 and 5, and one well for any subsequent time point.

Acknowledgments

S. A. M. is in Klaus Rajewsky's laboratory and is supported by a Ruth L. Kirschstein National Research Service Award postdoctoral fellowship. This work is supported by grants from the National Institutes of Health (AI064345 to K. Rajewski). C. K. is in David M. Livingston's laboratory. We thank K. Rajewski for reading this manuscript; P. Oberdoerffer, Y. Sasaki, and S. Willms for discussion; A. Kung for help with EBs, and D. Ghitza for her expertise in isolating mouse blastocysts. We are indebted to D. M. Livingston and K. Rajewski for support.

References

1. Dani, C., Smith, A. G., Dessolin, S., et al. (1997) Differentiation of embryonic stem cells into adipocytes in vitro. *J. Cell. Sci.* **110(Pt 11),** 1279–1285.
2. Kramer, J., Hegert, C., and Rohwedel, J. (2003) In vitro differentiation of mouse ES cells: bone and cartilage. *Methods Enzymol.* **365,** 251–268.
3. Kawaguchi, J., Mee, P. J., and Smith, A. G. (2005) Osteogenic and chondrogenic differentiation of embryonic stem cells in response to specific growth factors. *Bone* **36,** 758–769.
4. Fairchild, P. J., Brook, F. A., Gardner, R. L., et al. (2000) Directed differentiation of dendritic cells from mouse embryonic stem cells. *Curr. Biol.* **10,** 1515–1518.
5. Yamashita, J., Itoh, H., Hirashima, M., et al. (2000) Flk1-positive cells derived from embryonic stem cells serve as vascular progenitors. *Nature* **408,** 92–96.
6. Nakano, T., Kodama, H., and Honjo, T. (1994) Generation of lymphohematopoietic cells from embryonic stem cells in culture. *Science* **265,** 1098–1101.
7. Bagutti, C., Wobus, A. M., Fassler, R., and Watt, F. M. (1996) Differentiation of embryonal stem cells into keratinocytes: comparison of wild-type and beta 1 integrin-deficient cells. *Dev. Biol.* **179,** 184–196.
8. Cho, S. K. and Zuniga-Pflucker, J. C. (2003) Development of lymphoid lineages from embryonic stem cells in vitro. *Methods Enzymol.* **365,** 158–169.
9. de Pooter, R. F., Cho, S. K., and Zuniga-Pflucker, J. C. (2005) In vitro generation of lymphocytes from embryonic stem cells. *Methods Mol. Biol.* **290,** 135–147.
10. Tsai, M., Tam, S. Y., Wedemeyer, J., and Galli, S. J. (2002) Mast cells derived from embryonic stem cells: a model system for studying the effects of genetic manipulations on mast cell development, phenotype, and function in vitro and in vivo. *Int. J. Hematol.* **75,** 345–349.
11. Rohwedel, J., Maltsev, V., Bober, E., Arnold, H. H., Hescheler, J., and Wobus, A. M. (1994) Muscle cell differentiation of embryonic stem cells reflects myogenesis in vivo: developmentally regulated expression of myogenic determination genes and functional expression of ionic currents. *Dev. Biol.* **164,** 87–101.
12. Strubing, C., Ahnert-Hilger, G., Shan, J., Wiedenmann, B., Hescheler, J., and Wobus, A. M. (1995) Differentiation of pluripotent embryonic stem cells into the neuronal lineage in vitro gives rise to mature inhibitory and excitatory neurons. *Mech. Dev.* **53,** 275–287.
13. Ying, Q. L., Stavridis, M., Griffiths, D., Li, M., and Smith, A. (2003) Conversion of embryonic stem cells into neuroectodermal precursors in adherent monoculture. *Nat. Biotechnol.* **21,** 183–186.
14. Buttery, L. D., Bourne, S., Xynos, J. D., et al. (2001) Differentiation of osteoblasts and in vitro bone formation from murine embryonic stem cells. *Tissue Eng.* **7,** 89–99.
15. Lumelsky, N., Blondel, O., Laeng, P., Velasco, I., Ravin, R., and McKay, R. (2001) Differentiation of embryonic stem cells to insulin-secreting structures similar to pancreatic islets. *Science* **292,** 1389–1394.
16. Kanellopoulou, C., Muljo, S. A., Kung, A. L., et al. (2005) Dicer-deficient mouse embryonic stem cells are defective in differentiation and centromeric silencing. *Genes Dev.* **19,** 489–501.
17. Denli, A. M. and Hannon, G. J. (2003) RNAi: an ever-growing puzzle. *Trends Biochem. Sci.* **28,** 196–201.
18. Bernstein, E., Caudy, A. A., Hammond, S. M., and Hannon, G. J. (2001) Role for a bidentate ribonuclease in the initiation step of RNA interference. *Nature* **409,** 363–366.
19. Hutvagner, G., McLachlan, J., Pasquinelli, A. E., Balint, E., Tuschl, T., and Zamore, P. D. (2001) A cellular function for the RNA-interference enzyme Dicer in the maturation of the let-7 small temporal RNA. *Science* **293,** 834–838.

20. Ketting, R. F., Fischer, S. E., Bernstein, E., Sijen, T., Hannon, G. J., and Plasterk, R. H. (2001) Dicer functions in RNA interference and in synthesis of small RNA involved in developmental timing in C. elegans. *Genes Dev.* **15,** 2654–2659.

21. Knight, S. W. and Bass, B. L. (2001) A role for the RNase III enzyme DCR-1 in RNA interference and germ line development in Caenorhabditis elegans. *Science* **293,** 2269–2271.

22. Grishok, A., Pasquinelli, A. E., Conte, D., et al. (2001) Genes and mechanisms related to RNA interference regulate expression of the small temporal RNAs that control C. elegans developmental timing. *Cell* **106,** 23–34.

23. Kontgen, F., Suss, G., Stewart, C., Steinmetz, M., and Bluethmann, H. (1993) Targeted disruption of the MHC class II Aa gene in C57BL/6 mice. *Int. Immunol.* **5,** 957–964.

24. Seong, E., Saunders, T. L., Stewart, C. L., and Burmeister, M. (2004) To knockout in 129 or in C57BL/6: that is the question. *Trends Genet.* **20,** 59–62.

25. Eggan, K., Akutsu, H., Loring, J., et al. (2001) Hybrid vigor, fetal overgrowth, and viability of mice derived by nuclear cloning and tetraploid embryo complementation. *Proc. Natl. Acad. Sci. USA* **98,** 6209–6214.

26. Seibler, J., Zevnik, B., Kuter-Luks, B., et al. (2003) Rapid generation of inducible mouse mutants. *Nucleic Acids Res.* **31,** e12.

27. Casola, S. (2004) Conditional gene mutagenesis in B-lineage cells. *Methods Mol. Biol.* **271,** 91–109.

28. Rajewsky, K., Gu, H., Kuhn, R., et al. (1996) Conditional gene targeting. *J. Clin. Invest.* **98,** 600–603.

29. Bernstein, E., Kim, S. Y., Carmell, M. A., et al. (2003) Dicer is essential for mouse development. *Nat. Genet.* **35,** 215–217.

30. Testa, G., Vintersten, K., Zhang, Y., Benes, V., Muyrers, J. P., and Stewart, A. F. (2004) BAC engineering for the generation of ES cell-targeting constructs and mouse transgenes. *Methods Mol. Biol.* **256,** 123–139.

31. Oberdoerffer, P. (2005) Efficiency of RNA interference in the mouse hematopoietic system varies between cell types and developmental stages. *Mol. Cell. Biol.* **25,** 3896–3905.

32. Magin, T. M., McWhir, J., and Melton, D. W. (1992) A new mouse embryonic stem cell line with good germ line contribution and gene targeting frequency. *Nucleic Acids Res.* **20,** 3795–3796.

33. Bronson, S. K., Plaehn, E. G., Kluckman, K. D., Hagaman, J. R., Maeda, N., and Smithies, O. (1996) Single-copy transgenic mice with chosen-site integration. *Proc. Natl. Acad. Sci. USA* **93,** 9067–9072.

34. Mortensen, R. M. (2000) Production of a homozygous mutant embryonic stem cell line (double knockout). In: *Current Protocols in Molecular Biology* (Ausubel, F. M., Brent, R., Kingston, R. E., et al., eds.), John Wiley & Sons, New York, pp. 23.26.21–23.26.23.

35. Mortensen, R. M., Conner, D. A., Chao, S., Geisterfer-Lowrance, A. A., and Seidman, J. G. (1992) Production of homozygous mutant ES cells with a single targeting construct. *Mol. Cell. Biol.* **12,** 2391–2395.

36. Chen, J., Lansford, R., Stewart, V., Young, F., and Alt, F. W. (1993) RAG-2-deficient blastocyst complementation: an assay of gene function in lymphocyte development. *Proc. Natl. Acad. Sci. USA* **90,** 4528–4532.

37. Osoegawa, K., Tateno, M., Woon, P. Y., et al. (2000) Bacterial artificial chromosome libraries for mouse sequencing and functional analysis. *Genome Res.* **10,** 116–128.

38. Buehr, M. and Smith, A. (2003) Genesis of embryonic stem cells. *Philos. Trans. R. Soc. Lond. B Biol. Sci.* **358,** 1397–1402; discussion 1402.

39. Burdon, T., Stracey, C., Chambers, I., Nichols, J., and Smith, A. (1999) Suppression of SHP-2 and ERK signalling promotes self-renewal of mouse embryonic stem cells. *Dev. Biol.* **210,** 30–43.
40. Smith, A. G. (2001) Embryo-derived stem cells: of mice and men. *Annu. Rev. Cell. Dev. Biol.* **17,** 435–462.
41. Brook, F. A. and Gardner, R. L. (1997) The origin and efficient derivation of embryonic stem cells in the mouse. *Proc. Natl. Acad. Sci. USA* **94,** 5709–5712.
42. Kunieda, T., Xian, M., Kobayashi, E., Imamichi, T., Moriwaki, K., and Toyoda, Y. (1992) Sexing of mouse preimplantation embryos by detection of Y chromosome-specific sequences using polymerase chain reaction. *Biol. Reprod.* **46,** 692–697.
43. Karolchik, D., Baertsch, R., Diekhans, M., et al. (2003) The UCSC Genome Browser Database. *Nucleic Acids Res.* **31,** 51–54.

6

MicroRNAs and Messenger RNA Turnover

Julia A. Chekanova and Dmitry A. Belostotsky

Summary

Although initially believed to act exclusively as translational repressors, microRNAs (miRNAs) are now known to target complementary messenger RNA (mRNA) transcripts for either translational repression or cleavage via the RNA-induced silencing complex (RISC) (*[1]*, reviewed in **ref. *2***). The current model postulates that mature miRNAs are incorporated into the RISC, bind target mRNAs based on complementarity, and guide cleavage of mRNA targets with perfect or nearly perfect complementarity and translational repression of targets with lower complementarity *(2)*. The translational repression mechanism of miRNA-mediated gene regulation, which is common in animals but also exists in plants, is not well understood mechanistically. Conversely, miRNA-directed mRNA cleavage by RISC is common in plants, but also occurs in animals *(3)*. This chapter focuses on the mRNA cleavage by miRNA-programmed RISC, and, specifically, on characterizing the products of such cleavage.

Key Words: RISC; miRNA; mRNA; 5'-cap; poly(A) tail; exoribonuclease.

1. Introduction

RNA-induced silencing complexes (RISCs) are multiple-turnover entities that direct many rounds of site-specific target mRNA cleavage *(1)*. A principal RISC component in all eukaryotes is a member of the Argonaute (AGO) protein family *(4)*. AGO contains the conserved PAZ and PIWI domains, and seems to be the sole protein required for RISC-mediated activities *(5)*. The discovery that the PIWI domain adopts a ribonuclease (RNase) H fold *(6–8)* has led to a concept of AGO as an "mRNA slicer" component of the miRNA-programmed or small interfering RNA (siRNA)-programmed RISC. The cleavage of the mRNA target occurs between the nucleotides that are complementary to positions 10 and 11 of the miRNA that guides the RISC to cleave its target mRNA, and is defined by the 5' end of the guide RNA strand *(9,10)*. This distance-dependent mechanism is now beginning to be understood in precise terms of structural constraints imposed on the target mRNA recognition by the molecular architecture of the AGO/guide RNA complex *(11,12)*.

From: *Methods in Molecular Biology, vol. 342: MicroRNA Protocols*
Edited by: S. Ying © Humana Press Inc., Totowa, NJ

The characterization of the mRNA turnover events accompanying and following the initial endonucleolytic mRNA cleavage by RISC is an area of intense scrutiny *(13–16)*. That such cleavage products must be removed is dictated by several reasons. For instance, the 5' fragments, if translated, would result in truncated, and therefore, potentially toxic, polypeptides. Indeed, the existence of a specialized "nonstop" pathway of mRNA decay, which specifically targets mRNAs lacking stop codons *(17)*, is indicative of an evolutionary pressure to prevent such truncated mRNAs from being translated. In addition, the products of the mRNA cleavage by RISC that are not promptly removed may engage RNA-dependent RNA polymerases and, thus, initiate a chain of events resulting in gene silencing (e.g., **ref. *14***). In this chapter, we outline procedures for characterizing the products of the mRNA cleavage by RISC, including:

a. Mapping the 5' end of the 3' fragment resulting from the RISC-mediated cleavage (**Subheading 3.1.**, **Fig. 1B**, top).
b. Mapping of the 3' end of the 5' fragment resulting from the RISC-mediated cleavage (**Subheading 3.2.**, **Fig. 1B**, bottom).
c. Assessing the 5'-cap status of the 5' fragment resulting from the RISC-mediated cleavage (**Subheading 4.1.**, **Fig. 2A**).
d. Assessing the poly(A) status and poly(A) tail length of the 3' fragment resulting from the RISC-mediated cleavage (**Subheadings 4.2.** and **4.3.**, **Fig. 2B,C**).

To facilitate downstream analyses, it is helpful to devise strategies to enrich for the products of mRNA cleavage by the RISC complex and/or stabilize them. Such strategies include overexpression of the mRNA whose RISC-mediated cleavage is being studied, to saturate the exonuclease systems that degrade them, and therefore increase the steady state level of the primary products of the endonucleolytic cleavage by RISC. Alternatively (or additionally), one might engineer a genetic depletion of the exonucleases that might be responsible for the degradation of the mRNA cleavage products. In either scenario, the relative abundance of the products of the endonucleolytic cleavage of mRNA by RISC will determine the degree of sensitivity that is required to detect them.

An obvious benefit of the exonuclease depletion strategy is an immediate insight into the pathways of degradation of the primary mRNA cleavage products. Indeed, the key criterion in the identification of the factors responsible for the decay of the products of the RISC-mediated cleavage is their stabilization after the depletion of such factors. Based on the current literature, the list of possible factors includes (but is not limited to) the 5'–3' exonucleases of the XRN1 family and several 3'–5' exonucleases, such as the exosome (and its associated SKI2/3/8 complex), CCR4/POP2, and PARN (**Fig. 1A**). For instance, in the *Drosophila* S2 cells, the 5' and 3' products of the mRNA cleavage by the siRNA-programmed RISC are degraded exonucleolytically by exosome and XRN1, respectively, without previous decapping or deadenylation *(15)*. It remains to be determined whether this is also true in other systems, as well as in the case of the miRNA-programmed RISC. The choice of the exonuclease depletion method depends on particular features and constraints of a given model system. The range of possibilities includes the use of repressible promoters and specific enzyme inhibitors, as well as targeting the enzyme in question via RNA interference (reviewed in **ref. *18***).

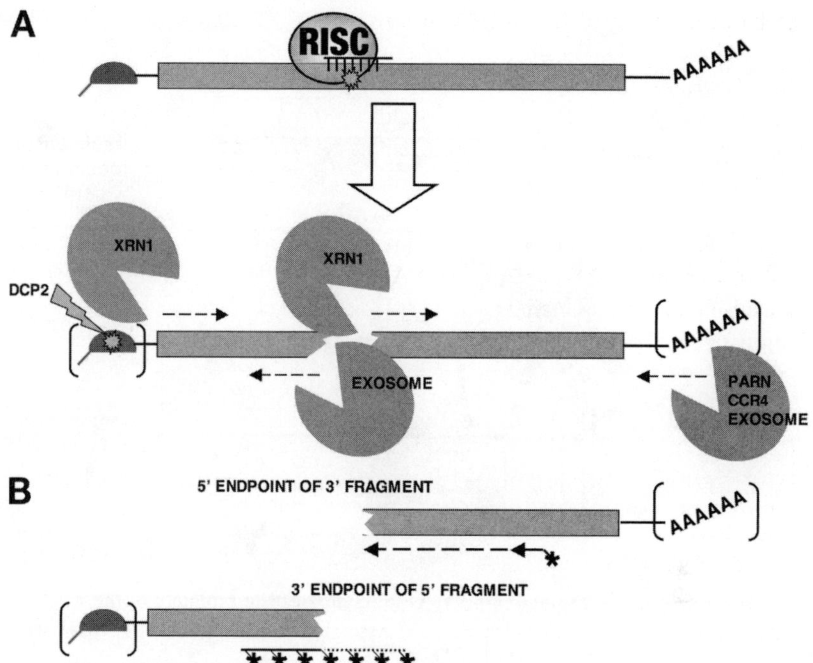

Fig. 1. Mapping the position of the messenger RNA (mRNA) cleavage by RNA-induced silencing complex (RISC). (**A**) A scheme illustrating the possible fates of the 5' and 3' mRNA fragments resulting from the RISC-mediated cleavage. The exonucleases that are known or suspected to degrade the 5' and 3' mRNA fragments are indicated. (**B**) A scheme illustrating the use of the primer extension and ribonuclease protection to map the 5' endpoint of the 3' fragment and the 3' endpoint of the 5' fragment, respectively.

2. Materials

2.1. Primer Extension

1. RNA extraction reagent (e.g., Trizol reagent, Invitrogen, Carlsbad, CA).
2. Chloroform.
3. Isopropanol.
4. 75% EtOH.
5. T4 polynucleotide kinase and 10X kinase buffer (New England Biolabs, Beverly, MA).
6. Primer design software Primer3.0 (web interface at http://frodo.wi.mit.edu).
7. Diethylpyrocarbonate (DEPC)-treated H_2O.
8. 6000 Ci/mmol $[\gamma\text{-}^{32}P]$ adenosine triphosphate (ATP).
9. TE (pH 7.5).
10. AMV reverse transcriptase and 10X AMV buffer (Promega, Madison, WI).
11. Deoxyribonucleoside triphosphates (dNTPs) (100 mM stocks).
12. 1 M dithiothreitol (DTT).
13. 1 M $MgCl_2$.
14. Formamide loading dye: 95% formamide, 0.025% bromophenol blue, 0.025% xylene cyanol FF, and 5 mM ethylenediaminetetraacetic acid (EDTA).

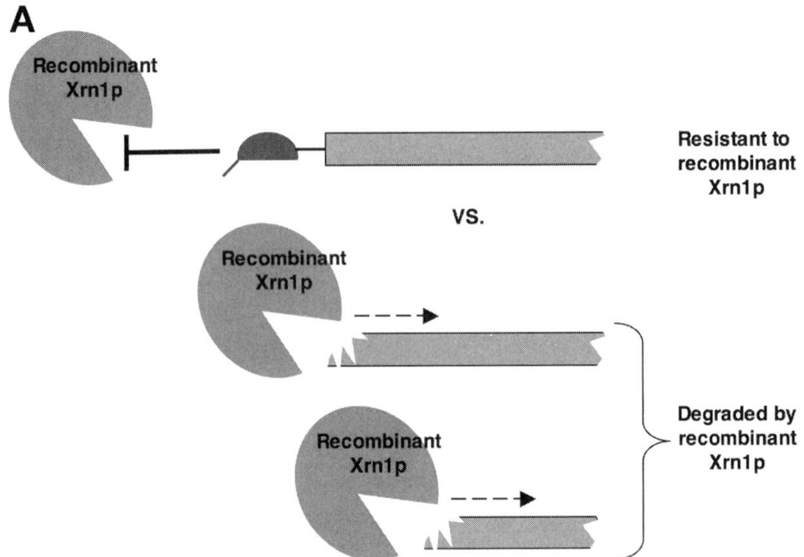

Fig. 2. Assessing the 5'-cap and 3'-poly(A) tail status of the products of the RNA-induced silencing complex (RISC)-mediated cleavage. (**A**) Assessing the 5'-cap status by XRN1 sensitivity.

15. Denaturing polyacrylamide gel (e.g., commercial SequaGel, National Diagnostics; www.nationaldiagnostics.com).
16. X-ray film or/and PhosphorImager (Molecular Dynamics, Sunnyvale, CA).

2.2. Ribonuclease Protection

1. Reagents for in vitro transcription (Promega): 5X transcription buffer, DTT, RNasin, ribonucleoside triphosphates, and T7 RNA polymerase.
2. DEPC-treated H_2O.
3. 10 mCi/mL [α-^{32}P] uridine triphosphate (UTP) (3000 Ci/mmol).
4. RQ1 RNase-free deoxyribonuclease (DNase) (Promega).
5. 5 µg/µL glycogen carrier (Ambion, Austin, TX).
6. Phenol/chloroform/isoamyl alcohol.
7. 3 *M* Na acetate (pH 5.2).
8. 100% EtOH.
9. Cold 75% EtOH.
10. Dry ice.
11. Hybridization buffer: 80% deionized formamide, 10 m*M* Na citrate, 300 m*M* Na acetate, pH 6.4, and 1 m*M* EDTA.
12. 10X RNase ONE buffer and RNAse ONE (Promega).
13. 10% sodium dodecylsulfate (SDS).

2.3. XRN1 Assay

1. Recombinant Xrn1p. If the recombinant Xrn1p must be purified in-house, express and purify as described *(19)* on a Ni^{2+} column (we use the Ni-NTA kit from Qiagen [Valencia, CA] and follow the manufacturer's protocol).

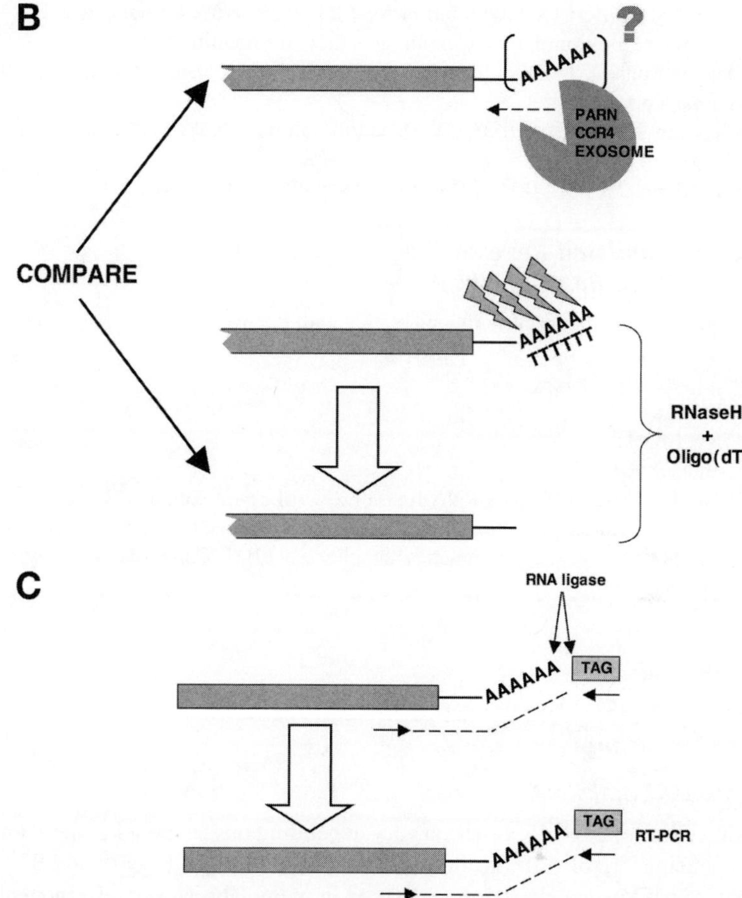

Fig. 2. (**B**) Analysis of the poly(A) tail status of the 3' fragment by oligo(dT)/ribonuclease H cleavage. (**C**) Analysis of the poly(A) tail status of the 3' fragment using ligation-mediated reverse transcriptase polymerase chain reaction.

2. Xrn1p reaction buffer: 33 mM Tris-HCl (pH 8.0), 50 mM NaCl, 2.5 mM MgCl$_2$, 0.2 mM DTT, with and without 5 mM EDTA.
3. Phenol/chloroform/isoamyl alcohol.
4. 100% EtOH.

2.4. RNase H Assay

1. Oligo(dT)$_{15}$.
2. 10X RNase H buffer and RNase H (Promega).
3. Hybridization membrane (BioTrans Plus, MP Biomedicals, Irvine, CA).
4. Phenol/chloroform/isoamyl alcohol.
5. 100% EtOH.
6. Formamide loading dye.

7. Electrophoresis buffer: 1X MOPS buffer for 1.2% agarose/6% formaldehyde gels or 0.5X TBE for high-resolution polyacrylamide gels (*see* **Subheading 4.2.3.**).
8. Transfer solution: 1X TAE (for polyacrylamide gels) or 10X standard sodium citrate (SSC) (for agarose gels).
9. Hybridization solution: 6X SSC, 5X Denhardt solution, 0.5% SDS, and 100 µg/mL of salmon sperm DNA.
10. Wash solutions: 2X SSC, 0.1% SDS plus 0.2X SSC, and 0.1% SDS.

2.5. Ligation-Mediated Reverse Transcriptase Polymerase Chain Reaction (PCR)

1. 5'-Phosphorylated adaptor oligoribonucleotide with the inverted deoxynucleotide in the 3' position (Dharmacon Inc, Lafayette, CO).
2. Phenol/chloroform/isoamyl alcohol.
3. 100% EtOH.
4. Cold 75% EtOH.
5. DEPC-treated H_2O.
6. 10X T4 RNA ligase buffer and RNA ligase (20 U/µL, New England Biolabs).
7. MMLV reverse transcriptase Superscript II and 10X Superscript II buffer (Invitrogen).
8. Appropriate DNA oligos, any commercial supplier (e.g., IDT, Coralville, IA or Sigma-Genosys, St. Louis, MO).

3. Methods

3.1. Mapping of the 5' Endpoint of the 3' Fragment by Primer Extension (see Note 1)

3.1.1. Prepare Total RNA

Procedures for total RNA extraction vary depending on the model system; an example protocol using Trizol (Life Technologies) follows (Qiagen Rneasy and BD Biosciences NucleoSpin kits are also commonly used in many laboratories). Homogenize 100 mg of tissue in 1 mL Trizol reagent and let samples stand for 3 min at room temperature (if necessary, remove the insoluble material from the homogenate by centrifugation at 12,000*g* for 10 min at 4°C). Add 0.2 mL chloroform per 1 mL Trizol, mix well, let stand for 10 min at room temperature. Centrifuge at 12,000*g* for 15 min at 4°C. Transfer upper aqueous phase into new tubes. Add 0.5 mL isopropanol per 1 mL Trizol, mix, and incubate at room temperature for 10 min. Centrifuge at 12,000*g* for 10 min at 4°C. Wash with 75% EtOH (use at least 1 mL of 75% EtOH per 1 mL of Trizol used for homogenization). Air-dry for 10 min. Dissolve in DEPC-treated H_2O and determine the optical density of the samples (high-purity RNA should have an $A_{260/280}$ ratio of approx 2:1).

3.1.2. Prepare the Labeled Oligo for Primer Extension

Combine 0.5 µL oligo (1 µg/µL), 1 µL of 10X kinase buffer, 2 µL of ^{32}P γ-ATP (6000 Ci/mmol), 5.5 µL of DEPC-treated H_2O, and 1 µL of T4 polynucleotide kinase (sufficient for 10 extension reactions). Incubate at 37°C for 30 to 60 min. To stop the reaction, add 40 µL of TE and heat at 95°C for 3 min.

3.1.3. Anneal the Labeled Oligonucleotide

Combine 10 to 20 µg of total RNA with 2 µL of the 5X AMV reverse transcriptase buffer (Promega) and 0.5 µL of the labeled oligonucleotide (*see* **Note 2**), and bring the total reaction volume to 8 µL with DEPC-treated H_2O. Incubate at 65°C for 10 min, transfer to a 42°C water bath, and incubate for 30 to 60 min to allow annealing.

3.1.4. Conduct the Primer Extension Reaction

For 10 primer extensions, make up a cocktail containing 5 µL of 0.2 M $MgCl_2$, 5 µL of 20 mM DTT, 2.5 µL of dNTPs (2.5 mM each), 5.5 µL of DEPC-treated H_2O, and 2 µL of AMV reverse transcriptase (Promega). Add 2 µL of this cocktail to the 8 µL annealing mix (**Subheading 3.1.3.**) and incubate at 42°C for 30 to 60 min. Add 10 µL of formamide loading dye to terminate the reaction, heat at 75°C, and resolve by electrophoresis on a denaturing polyacrylamide gel (6–20%, depending on the size of the expected extended product). Expose to a X-ray film or, for quantitation, to a Phosphorscreen, scan on a PhosphorImager, and analyze with ImageQuant software (Molecular Dynamics).

3.2. Mapping the 3' Endpoint of the 5' Fragment by Ribonuclease Protection

A detailed protocol using RNase ONE (Promega) is provided next (*see* **Notes 3** and **4** for general considerations regarding the use of ribonuclease protection). Alternatively, the RNase ONE kit (Promega) or the RPA III kit (Ambion) could be used, as described by the respective manufacturers (*see* **Note 5** on differences in the properties of the RNase A/T1 that is used in the RPA III kit compared with the RNase ONE kit).

3.2.1. Prepare the Appropriate Body-Labeled Probes by In Vitro Transcription

For example, in the case of a T7 promoter-driven run-off probe, combine 1 µL of linearized template DNA (at 1 µg/µL) with 4 µL of 5X in vitro transcription buffer (Promega); 2 µL of 100 mM DTT; 1 µL of 40 U/µL RNasin; 1 µL each of 10 mM ATP, GTP, and CTP; 0.6 µL of 100 µM UTP; 5 µL of 10 mCi/mL [α-^{32}P] UTP (3000 Ci/mmol); 2.4 µL of DEPC-treated H_2O; and 1 µL of T7 RNA polymerase. Incubate the reaction for 60 min at 37°C. Add 1 µL of RQ1 RNase-free DNase and incubate for another 15 min at 37°C to digest away the template DNA.

3.2.2. Purify the RNA Probe

To each RQ1 DNase-treated sample, add 100 µL of DEPC-treated H_2O, 2 µL of 5 µg/µL glycogen as a carrier, and extract with phenol/chloroform/isoamyl alcohol (*see* **Note 6**). To the aqueous phase, add 1/10 volume of 3 M Na acetate (pH 5.2) and 2.5 volumes of EtOH and incubate for 15 min on dry ice, followed by centrifugation for 15 min at 12,000g. Carefully wash the pellet with cold 75% EtOH, air-dry, and resuspend in the DEPC-treated H_2O at 1×10^6 cpm/µL (for the specific probe against the RISC-cleaved mRNA fragment), or at 2×10^5 cpm (for the internal control probe directed against a suitable housekeeping message, such as actin or a ribosomal protein).

3.2.3. Hybridize the RNase Protection Probe With Target RNA

For each reaction, combine the RNA sample to be analyzed (5–20 µg RNA in a total volume of 8 µL or less) with 20 µL of the hybridization buffer, 1 µL of a specific probe directed against the RISC-cleaved mRNA fragment (1×10^6 cpm), and 1 µL of an internal control probe for normalization purposes (2×10^5 cpm). For each specific probe, also prepare two control reactions, via substituting transfer RNA (tRNA) for the target sample RNA. Mix, denature at 75°C to 80°C for 3 min (avoid prolonged incubation at 75°C to 80°C, because it may lead to nonspecific RNA fragmentation). Incubate at 45°C overnight.

3.2.4. Perform the RNase Digestion

To each hybridization reaction, add 270 µL of DEPC-treated H_2O, 30 µL of 10X RNase ONE buffer, and 5 U of RNAse ONE (Promega). Incubate at 37°C for 60 min. To one of the two "tRNA only" control reactions, add 270 µL of DEPC-treated H_2O and 30 µL of 10X RNase ONE buffer ("no RNase" sample). Add all three components to the second "tRNA only" control reaction.

3.2.5. Terminate the RNase Digestion

To each sample, add 5 µL of 10% SDS, 800 µL EtOH, and 1 µL glycogen (5 µg/µL), mix, incubate for 15 min on dry ice, and centrifuge at 12,000g for 15 min. Carefully wash the RNA pellet with cold 75% EtOH and air-dry the pellet for several minutes. Carefully resuspend the RNA in the 8 µL of the formamide loading dye, denature at 75°C to 80°C for 3 min, tap-spin, and load onto the denaturing polyacrylamide gel (6–20% acrylamide, depending on the size of the expected extended product). Expose the dried gel to a Phosphorscreen, scan on a PhosphorImager, and analyze with ImageQuant software (Molecular Dynamics).

4. Assessing the 5'-Cap and 3'-Poly(A) Tail Status of the Products of the RISC-Mediated Cleavage

4.1. Assessing the 5'-Cap Status by XRN1 Sensitivity

In this approach, the cap status of the 5' cleavage product is revealed by testing its sensitivity to the action of the recombinant 5'–3' exonuclease Xrn1p that is purified from yeast. Only the uncapped, but not the capped, RNA species are degraded by Xrn1p (*see* **Note 7**).

4.1.1. Purification of Xrn1p

Express the His-tagged Xrn1p encoded by the construct pAJ95 (2 µ/*LEU2*/pGAL10-*XRN1*-HA-His$_6$) in the yeast strain BJ5464, as described *(19)*, and purify on a Ni^{2+} column (Ni-NTA, Qiagen) as suggested by the manufacturer.

4.1.2. Digest RNA With Xrn1p

Digest the total RNA samples containing the RISC-mediated mRNA cleavage products of interest with the purified Xrn1p *(20)*. Combine 5 to 10 µg of total RNA with 400 ng of purified Xrn1p in a final volume of 10 µL of 33 m*M* Tris-HCl (pH 8.0), 50 m*M*

NaCl, 2.5 m*M* MgCl$_2$, and 0.2 m*M* DTT, in the presence or absence of 5 m*M* EDTA (*see* **Note 8**). Incubate the Xrn1p reactions for 30 min at 37°C. Terminate the reactions by phenol extraction followed by EtOH precipitation (*see* **Note 9**).

4.1.3. Analysis of Xrn1p Reaction Products

Visualize the 5' RISC cleavage product by ribonuclease protection as described in **Subheading 3.2.** or by Northern blotting (**Subheading 4.2.**). Disappearance of the 5' cleavage products after the Xrn1p treatment serves as an indication that they are uncapped and, thus, conversely, their resistance to this treatment attests to their capped status (*see* **Note 10**).

4.2. Analysis of the Poly(A) Tail Status
of the 3' Fragment by Oligo(dT)/RNase H Cleavage

A straightforward way to detect the presence, as well as to assess the size, of the poly(A) tail on the 3'-fragment involves oligo(dT)/RNase H cleavage, followed by the Northern blot analysis (obviously, this is possible only if the 3' fragment is abundant enough to be detected by Northern blot; alternatively, one must use ligation-mediated PCR, as described in **Subheading 4.3.**). A characteristic increase in the electrophoretic mobility of the 3' cleavage fragment as a result of RNase H treatment indicates that it is polyadenylated. Furthermore, judicious choice of the molecular weight markers allows determination of its poly(A) tail length distribution and comparison with the poly(A) tail length of intact, full-length mRNA, and, thereby, allows inference of whether a significant amount of deadenylation precedes the RISC-mediated cleavage.

4.2.1. Assemble the RNase H Cleavage Reaction

Combine 25 μg of total RNA with 500 ng of oligo(dT)$_{15}$, denature at 75°C for 5 min, and allow to anneal for 20 min. Add the 10X RNase H buffer to achieve final concentrations of 20 m*M* Tris-HCl, pH 7.4, 10 m*M* MgCl$_2$, 0.5 m*M* EDTA, 50 m*M* NaCl, 1 m*M* DTT, and 30 μg of bovine serum albumin per milliliter. Add 0.25 U of RNase H (Promega) and digest for 1 h at 37°C.

4.2.2. Terminate the RNase H Cleavage

Stop the RNase H reaction by conducting phenol extraction followed by EtOH precipitation. Alternatively, stop the reaction by directly adding an equal volume of the formamide loading dye (but *see* **Note 9**).

4.2.3. Conduct Northern Blotting

Denature the RNA samples for 3 min in the formamide loading dye at 75°C to 80°C. Separate the RNA cleavage products via polyacrylamide or agarose gel electrophoresis, depending on the expected product size. For analysis by polyacrylamide gel electrophoresis, aliquots (≥10 μg) of treated and control (no RNase H and oligo[dT]$_{15}$) samples are loaded onto 6 to 20% (depending on the expected product sizes) polyacrylamide/8 *M* urea gel in 0.5X TBE. For agarose gel electrophoresis, at least 10 μg of total RNA is loaded onto 1.2% agarose/6% formaldehyde gel in 1X MOPS buffer (20 m*M* MOPS, 8 m*M* sodium acetate, and 1 m*M* EDTA, pH 7.0). RNA is then transferred either electrophoretically in 1X TAE (for high-resolution polyacrylamide gels) or with a vacuum blotter in 10X SSC (for formaldehyde/agarose gels) onto a BioTrans Plus membrane (ICN). In the case of formaldehyde/agarose gels, reverse the formaldehyde modifications by baking the membrane at 80°C for 1 hr. To fix the RNA, crosslink the membrane, when it is still slightly damp, for 1 min on an ultraviolet transilluminator (254 nm), or using a commercial ultraviolet crosslinker set at 120 mJ/cm^2.

4.2.4. Hybridize the Membrane

Hybridize the membrane in 6X SSC, 5X Denhardt solution, and 0.5% SDS plus 100 µg/mL of salmon sperm DNA at 65°C (if a random hexamer-labeled DNA fragment is used as a probe) or at 40°C to 48°C (if an oligonucleotide probe is used, the hybridization temperature should be calculated according to **ref. 21**). After overnight hybridization, wash the membranes twice in 2X SSC plus 0.5% SDS for 10 min at the temperature of hybridization, followed by high-stringency washes in 0.2X SSC plus 0.5% SDS. Expose the membranes to a Phosphor storage screen, scan on a PhosphorImager, and process and quantitate images using ImageQuant software (Molecular Dynamics).

4.3. Poly(A) Tail Status Analysis Via Ligation-Mediated Reverse Transcriptase-PCR

This method, modified from the ligation-mediated poly(A) tail assay *(22)*, was developed to address the need for a more sensitive alternative method for analyzing the poly(A) tail length distribution. In **Subheading 4.3.**, we describe a modified ligation-mediated poly(A) tail assay that we have developed *(23)* from the published protocol for the identification of the 3' ends of siRNAs *(24)*. In this method, the mRNA is first tagged at its 3' end via ligation of a RNA oligonucleotide of arbitrary sequence. The resulting tag is used as a priming site for reverse transcription, which is then followed by PCR across the poly(A) tail with a tag-specific and a gene-specific primer pair. The length distribution of the resulting population of PCR products reflects the poly(A) tail length distribution of the 3' cleavage product.

4.3.1. Separate the mRNA 3' Cleavage Products

Separate the mRNA 3' cleavage products away from the full-length (uncleaved) transcripts by size fractionation on a denaturing (polyacrylamide *[25]* or agarose *[26]*, depending on the expected size) gel. Elute the RNA in the target size range, extract with phenol/chloroform/isoamyl alcohol, precipitate with EtOH, wash with ice-cold 75% EtOH, air-dry, and dissolve in DEPC-treated H$_2$O at approx 1 µg/µL.

4.3.2. Ligate the Oligonucleotide Tag to the 3' End of RNA

Ligate the appropriate RNA size fractions with the 5'-phosphorylated adaptor oligo-ribonucleotide of arbitrary sequence that contains an inverted deoxynucleotide at its 3' end (e.g., 5'-UACUCAUCAUACGUUGUAGAGUACCUUGUAidT; *see* **Note 11**). Combine 1 to 5 µg of size-fractionated RNA with 100 pmol of the adaptor oligo in 17 µL of DEPC-treated H$_2$O, denature for 3 min at 75°C to 80°C, and chill on ice. Add 2 µL of 10X T4 RNA ligase buffer, mix, and add 1 µL (20 U) of T4 RNA ligase (New England Biolabs). Incubate for 1 h at 37°C.

4.3.3. Conduct Reverse Transcriptase Reaction

Reverse-transcribe 1 to 5 µL of the ligated RNA using a primer complementary to the adaptor oligonucleotide and SuperScript II reverse transcriptase (Life Technologies), according to the manufacturer's protocol.

4.3.4. Carry Out the PCR

Dilute the complementary DNA 10-fold with DEPC-treated H_2O. Use 1 µL of the diluted complementary DNA as a template for the PCR, using the oligo that is complementary to the adaptor oligonucleotide as an antisense primer, and using an appropriate gene-specific primer as a sense primer (*see* **Note 12**). If necessary, diluted first-round products can be subjected to nested PCR under the same conditions.

4.3.5. Analyze the PCR Products

Resolve the products on nondenaturing agarose or polyacrylamide gel and authenticate by Southern hybridization with an internal, gene-specific oligonucleotide as a probe (*see* **Note 13**).

5. Notes

1. Mapping the endpoints of the mRNA cleavage products by Northern blotting is also possible provided that the products are sufficiently abundant (e.g., **ref. 24**), however, the precision that is afforded by even high-resolution polyacrylamide Northern blots is inferior.
2. For normalization in quantitative assays, include a second-labeled oligo targeted against a transcript that is not subject to RISC-mediated cleavage.
3. This protocol is also suitable for mapping the 5' endpoint of the 3' fragment, in addition to the primer extension protocol.
4. Nuclease S1 and DNA probes can be used for this purpose, as well. However, S1 nuclease is prone to nonspecific cleavage in AU-rich regions, as well as to nibbling (i.e., acting as a double-stranded exonuclease) artifacts.
5. RNAses ONE (Promega) and A/T1 (Ambion) have different properties. RNase ONE cleaves at a position immediately 3' to either C, A, U, or G, whereas RNAse A and RNAse T1 cleave at positions immediately 3' to pyrimidines and to G residues, respectively. Also, RNase ONE is easily inactivated by 0.1% SDS.
6. If premature polymerase stops are observed, purify the full-length RNA probe away from the truncated species by denaturing gel electrophoresis *(25)*.
7. Alternatively, one can assess the cap status of the 5' cleavage product by immunoprecipitation with anticap antibody. The monoclonal antibody H20 (Biodesign International, Saco, ME; www.biodesign.com) was originally generated against the 2,2,7-trimethylguanosine cap, but it also crossreacts with the 7-methylguanosine-cap *(27)*. However, we find the Xrn1p resistance assay to be more quantitative and reproducible.
8. EDTA chelates Mg^{2+}, which is absolutely required for the Xrn1p activity. Therefore, target RNA species should remain intact in the control reactions containing EDTA.
9. We prefer to purify RNA by phenol extraction because carryover of EDTA and Mg^{2+} from the reactions tend to affect the electrophoretic mobility of the RNA fragments, especially on high-resolution polyacrylamide gels.
10. Completeness of the Xrn1p digestion can be verified by Northern hybridization or RNase protection using a probe directed against an RNA species that is known to be naturally uncapped, such as the 7S rRNA precursor species.

11. The inverted residue at the 3' end prevents formation of oligonucleotide multimers.
12. We prefer to use the touchdown profile (initial annealing at 59°C, then decreasing by 1°C per cycle until the annealing temperature of 48°C is reached, followed by another 25 annealing cycles at 48°C).
13. With appropriate oligos, the ligation-mediated PCR protocol can also be applied to mapping the 3' endpoint of the 5'-fragment produced by RISC. In this case, the poly(A) RNA fraction must be first isolated (e.g., using an Oligotex kit from Qiagen), to remove the polyadenylated full-length species and the cleavage 3' fragments.

Acknowledgments

This work was supported by grants from the National Science Foundation (9874580 and 0424651) and the US Department of Agriculture (2003-53504-13210) to D. A. B.

References

1. Hutvagner, G. and Zamore, P. D. (2002) A microRNA in a multiple-turnover RNAi enzyme complex. *Science* **297,** 2056–2060.
2. Bartel, D. P. (2004) MicroRNAs: genomics, biogenesis, mechanism, and function. *Cell* **116,** 281–297.
3. Yekta, S., Shih, I. H., and Bartel, D. P. (2004) MicroRNA-directed cleavage of HOXB8 mRNA. *Science* **304,** 594–596.
4. Hammond, S. M., Boettcher, S., Caudy, A. A., Kobayashi, R., and Hannon, G. J. (2001) Argonaute2, a link between genetic and biochemical analyses of RNAi. *Science* **293,** 1146–1150.
5. Rand, T. A., Ginalski, K., Grishin, N. V., and Wang, X. (2004) Biochemical identification of Argonaute 2 as the sole protein required for RNA-induced silencing complex activity. *Proc. Natl. Acad. Sci. USA* **101,** 14,385–14,389.
6. Liu, J., Carmell, M. A., Rivas, F. V., et al. (2004) Argonaute2 is the catalytic engine of mammalian RNAi. *Science* **305,** 1437–1441.
7. Parker, J. S., Roe, S. M., and Barford, D. (2004) Crystal structure of a PIWI protein suggests mechanisms for siRNA recognition and slicer activity. *EMBO J.* **23,** 4727–4737.
8. Song, J. J., Smith, S. K., Hannon, G. J., and Joshua-Tor, L. (2004) Crystal structure of Argonaute and its implications for RISC slicer activity. *Science* **305,** 1434–1437.
9. Elbashir, S. M., Martinez, J., Patkaniowska, A., Lendeckel, W., and Tuschl, T. (2001) Functional anatomy of siRNAs for mediating efficient RNAi in Drosophila melanogaster embryo lysate. *EMBO J.* **20,** 6877–6888.
10. Elbashir, S. M., Lendeckel, W., and Tuschl, T. (2001) RNA interference is mediated by 21- and 22-nucleotide RNAs. *Genes Dev.* **15,** 188–200.
11. Ma, J. B., Yuan, Y. R., Meister, G., Pei, Y., Tuschl, T., and Patel, D. J. (2005) Structural basis for 5'-end-specific recognition of guide RNA by the A. fulgidus Piwi protein. *Nature* **434,** 666–670.
12. Parker, J. S., Roe, S. M., and Barford, D. (2005) Structural insights into mRNA recognition from a PIWI domain-siRNA guide complex. *Nature* **434,** 663–666.
13. Belostotsky, D. A. (2004) mRNA turnover meets RNA interference. *Mol. Cell.* **16,** 498–500.
14. Gazzani, S., Lawrenson, T., Woodward, C., Headon, D., and Sablowski, R. (2004) A link between mRNA turnover and RNA interference in Arabidopsis. *Science* **306,** 1046–1048.
15. Orban, T. I. and Izaurralde, E. (2005) Decay of mRNAs targeted by RISC requires XRN1, the Ski complex, and the exosome. *RNA* **11,** 459–469.

16. Souret, F. F., Kastenmayer, J. P., and Green, P. J. (2004) AtXRN4 degrades mRNA in Arabidopsis and its substrates include selected miRNA targets. *Mol. Cell* **15,** 173–183.

17. Maquat, L. E. (2002) Molecular biology. Skiing toward nonstop mRNA decay. *Science* **295,** 2221–2222.

18. Baulcombe, D. (2004) Overview of RNA interference and related processes. In: *Current Protocols in Molecular Biology* (Ausubel, F. M., Brent, R., Kingston, R. E., et al., eds.), John Wiley & Sons, New York, 26.21.21–26.21.26.

19. Johnson, A. W. and Kolodner, R. D. (1991) Strand exchange protein 1 from Saccharomyces cerevisiae. A novel multifunctional protein that contains DNA strand exchange and exonuclease activities. *J. Biol. Chem.* **266,** 14,046–14,054.

20. Boeck, R., Lapeyre, B., Brown, C. E., and Sachs, A. B. (1998) Capped mRNA degradation intermediates accumulate in the yeast spb8-2 mutant. *Mol. Cell. Biol.* **18,** 5062–5072.

21. Casey, J. and Davidson, N. (1977) Rates of formation and thermal stabilities of RNA:DNA and DNA:DNA duplexes at high concentrations of formamide. *Nucleic Acids Res.* **4,** 1539–1552.

22. Salles, F. J., Richards, W. G., and Strickland, S. (1999) Assaying the polyadenylation state of mRNAs. *Methods* **17,** 38–45.

23. Reverdatto, S. V., Dutko, J. A., Chekanova, J. A., Hamilton, D. A., and Belostotsky, D. A. (2004) mRNA deadenylation by PARN is essential for embryogenesis in higher plants. *RNA* **10,** 1200–1214.

24. Xie, Z., Kasschau, K. D., and Carrington, J. C. (2003) Negative Feedback Regulation of Dicer-Like1 in Arabidopsis by microRNA-Guided mRNA Degradation. *Curr. Biol.* **13,** 784–789.

25. Pfeffer, S., Lagos-Quintana, M., and Tuschl, T. (2004) Cloning of small RNA molecules. In: *Current Protocols in Molecular Biology* (Ausubel, F. M., Brent, R., Kingston, R. E., et al., eds.), John Wiley & Sons, New York, 26.4.1–26.4.18.

26. Jackson, A., Jiao, P. E., Ni, I., and Fu, G. K. (2003) Agarose gel size fractionation of RNA for the cloning of full-length cDNAs. *Anal. Biochem.* **323,** 252–255.

27. Bochnig, P., Reuter, R., Bringmann, P., and Luhrmann, R. (1987) A monoclonal antibody against 2,2,7-trimethylguanosine that reacts with intact, class U, small nuclear ribonucleoproteins as well as with 7-methylguanosine-capped RNAs. *Eur. J. Biochem.* **168,** 461–467.

7

Prediction of MicroRNA Targets

Marc Rehmsmeier

Summary

I describe the use of RNAhybrid, a program that predicts multiple potential binding sites of microRNAs (miRNAs) in large target RNAs. The core algorithm finds the energetically most favorable hybridization sites of a miRNA in a large potential target RNA. Intramolecular hybridizations, i.e., base pairings between target nucleotides or between miRNA nucleotides are, not allowed. For large targets, the time complexity of the algorithm is linear in the target length, allowing many long targets to be searched in a short time. Starting from the observation that the binding energies are results from an optimization procedure, we can model them as following an extreme value distribution. From this, we can calculate the statistical significance of individual binding sites, of multiple binding sites in a single target sequence, and of binding sites in comparative analyses of orthologous sequences across species. The latter involves the calculation of the effective number of orthologous sequences, which can be considerably smaller than the actual number, reflecting the statistical dependence of evolutionarily related sequences.

Key Words: miRNA target prediction; minimum free energy (mfe); dynamic programming; statistical significance; p-value; E-value; multiple binding sites; statistical dependence.

1. Introduction

In this section, I review the key concepts of the RNAhybrid approach (for a more detailed explanation, *see* **ref.** *1*). For other methods, *see* **Note 1**.

1.1. Energy Minimization

RNAhybrid is an extension of the classic RNA secondary structure prediction algorithm *(2)* to two sequences. The miRNA is hybridized to the target in an energetically optimal way, thus yielding the minimum free energy (mfe). Intramolecular base pairings and branching structures (multiloops) are not allowed. In contrast to the Zuker algorithm, in which the calculation starts inside the one sequence and proceeds outward, RNAhybrid proceeds from left to right for both sequences. Thus, technically,

From: *Methods in Molecular Biology, vol. 342: MicroRNA Protocols*
Edited by: S. Ying © Humana Press Inc., Totowa, NJ

the RNAhybrid algorithm can be seen as a mixture between pairwise sequence alignment and RNA folding according to the nearest-neighbor model. Energy parameters are described previously *(3)*.

1.2. Length Normalization of Mfes

Because of the shortness of miRNAs, good mfes can occur frequently by chance. The longer a putative target sequence, the better such random energies will be. Thus, large negative mfes can be statistically insignificant if they result from searching large sequences. Although the mfe itself might look good, suggesting the biochemical possibility of a functional miRNA/target interaction, the possibility of the mfe having occurred by chance cannot be excluded with confidence. We normalize mfes to eliminate the influence of the sequence length.

1.3. Extreme Value Statistics of Normalized Mfes

Predicted binding sites for miRNAs are the results of an optimization procedure (the Dynamic Programming approach of RNAhybrid). In analogy to the score statistics of pairwise sequence alignment, we can model duplex energies with extreme value distribution (evds). The two parameters of such an evd, location and scale, depend on the dinucleotide distributions of the target database and the miRNA itself. Because miRNAs can vary considerably in their GC-content, a miRNA-specific modeling of random energies is important. RNAhybrid can determine miRNA-specific evd parameters in a number of ways (*see* **Subheading 3.**). The parameters then allow the calculation of significance levels (*p*-values) of observed duplex energies in a miRNA target prediction experiment.

1.4. Poisson Statistics of Multiple Binding Sites

Multiple binding sites of a miRNA in a single target sequence are additional evidence (in comparison to only one binding site) that the target gene is under control of the miRNA. This is not only a biological consideration, but also a statistical consideration, because the chance occurrence of several good binding sites is much rarer than the occurrence of a single site. We model multiple binding sites in a given target with a Poisson statistics, which assigns better *p*-values to larger numbers of binding sites, thus rendering these likely to have a biological meaning.

1.5. Comparative Analysis of Orthologous Targets

It has been noted that it is difficult to make significant target predictions when searching sequences from a single organism, and that targets should be predicted in a comparative analysis of multiple organisms. If two orthologous sequences, e.g., one from *Drosophila melanogaster* and the other from *Drosophila pseudoobscura*, show binding sites for the same miRNA, one could conclude that these binding sites are evolutionarily conserved and, thus, functional. Consequently, finding binding sites in a number of orthologous sequences across various species usually considerably increases statistical significance and, thus, the confidence in a biological meaning. However, one has to be careful if orthologous sequences are very similar, either because they are closely related on an evolutionary scale, or because larger stretches of a regulatory sequence (unrelated to the miRNA pathway) have been conserved during evolution. The occurrence of binding sites across species could then be an artifact of the overall sequence conservation: if a miRNA has some good predicted binding sites in one sequence, it is not surprising that it has binding sites in the other sequence, given that these sequences are very similar. RNAhybrid takes this statistical dependence into account by calculating the effective number of orthologous sequences, which, for similar sequences, is lower than the actual number. Neglecting this dependence can easily result in a huge overestimation of the statistical significance and, thus, in a large number of false-positive predictions.

2. Materials

2.1. Accessing the RNAhybrid Web Interface

An online version of RNAhybrid can be accessed on the Bielefeld Bioinformatics Server at http://bibiserv.techfak.uni-bielefeld.de/rnahybrid/. The first page is a welcome page. On the right-hand side, you will find links to other sections, such as "Download," "References," and "Submission." Follow the link titled Submission to get to the page where you can easily submit sequences.

An expert version of the RNAhybrid web server is also available (follow the link "Expert Submission"), which allows the use of all of the RNAhybrid options presented in this chapter. However, to avoid server overloads, the amount of sequence data that can be analyzed is restricted. *See* **Fig. 1** for a sample screenshot.

2.2. Downloading the RNAhybrid Software

RNAhybrid is freely available from the following URL: http://bibiserv.techfak.uni-bielefeld.de/download/tools/rnahybrid.html. Choose the appropriate platform for a binary distribution or "src" for the source distribution. You may enter some personal data to receive information in the future, but this is not required.

2.3. Installing a Binary Distribution

2.3.1. Windows and Macintosh

After you have downloaded the installer file (*see* **Subheading 2.2.**), execute the file (double-click on the file). The installation procedure is self-explanatory.

2.3.2 Unix

After you have downloaded the binary distribution that is appropriate for your platform, unpack it, and copy the binary and the manual page to the desired directories. For unpacking, *see* also **Subheading 2.4.**

2.4. Compiling and Installing RNAhybrid Under Unix

This section explains the compilation and installation of the RNAhybrid source distribution in a Unix environment, such as Solaris, Linux, Windows Cygwin, or Mac OS X.

The downloaded archive will be titled something similar to RNAhybrid-2.2.tar.gz. The .gz suffix indicates that the archive is compressed, the .tar suggests that the file is a tar archive. Throughout the next steps, we assume the above name. Note that the version

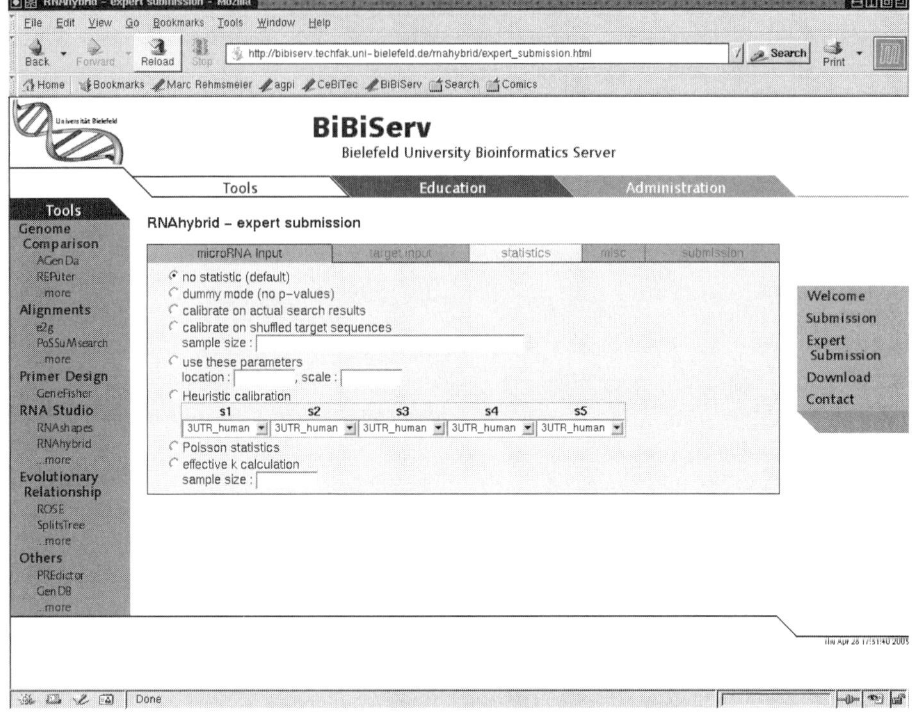

Fig. 1. A screenshot of the RNAhybrid web server expert submission.

number (version 2.2 at the time this chapter was written) might have changed. Also assume that you have downloaded this file to the directory /homes/juser, and that you are in this directory (type: cd /homes/juser).

1. Unzip the archive: gunzip RNAhybrid-2.2.tar.gz.
2. Extract files from the archive: tar -xvf RNAhybrid-2.2.tar. This should create a directory named RNAhybrid-2.2, which contains the whole distribution.
3. Create a directory named build (or any other name you find appropriate): mkdir build.
4. Enter the build directory and configure your RNAhybrid installation: cd /homes/juser/build, /homes/juser/RNAhybrid-2.2/configure. If you do not have superuser rights on your computer, you will probably not be allowed to write to directories such as /usr/bin. In that case, you might want to install RNAhybrid somewhere under your home directory. This can be done by giving configure the appropriate prefix: /homes/juser/RNAhybrid-2.2/configure --prefix=/homes/juser. The effect is that the binaries will be installed in /homes/juser/bin and the man pages in /homes/juser/man. For other configure options, type /homes/juser/RNAhybrid-2.2/configure --help.
5. Compile the program: make (*see* also **Note 2**).
6. Install binary and man page: make install.
   Check that the files have been copied to the binary and man page directories.
7. Delete the build directory: cd /homes/juser, rm -r -f build.

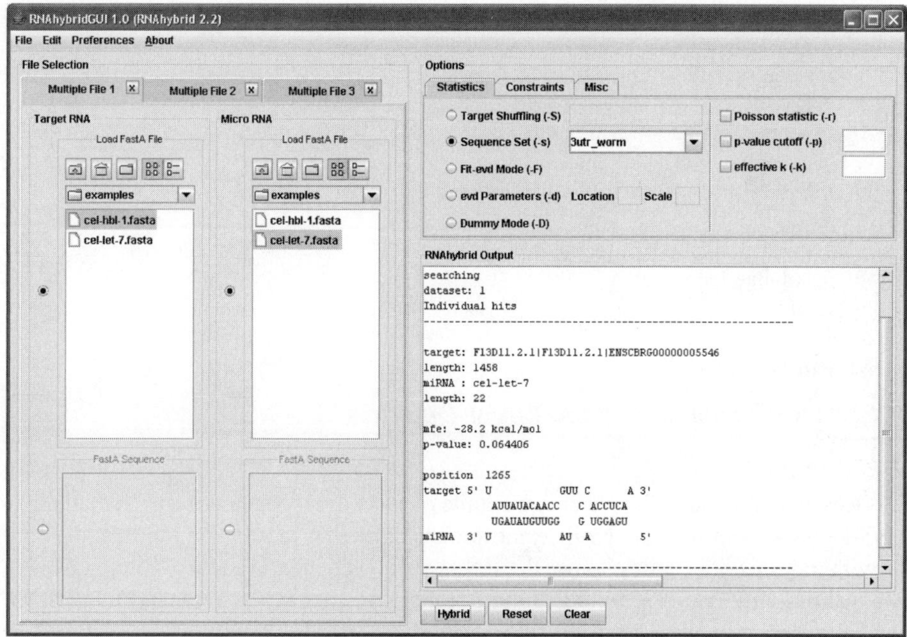

Fig. 2. A screenshot of the RNAhybrid graphical user interface.

2.5. Graphical User Interface

Part of the distribution is a graphical user interface (GUI), which offers all options presented in this chapter in an easy-to-use program. The GUI itself is written in Java. *See* **Fig. 2** for a sample screenshot. Instead of using the command line options as given in this chapter, choose the corresponding GUI options.

2.6. RNAhybrid Options

This is a summary of the RNAhybrid options that are referred to in the following text (*see* also **Note 3**):

```
-a <target focus key>,<query focus key>
-b <number of hits per target>
-c compact output
-d <xi>, <theta>
-D dummy mode (no p-values)
-e <energy cut-off>
-f helix constraint
-g (ps|png|jpg|all)
-h help
-k <sample size> calculate effective ks
-m <max target length>
```

-n <max query length>
-o <output order>
-p <*p*-value cut-off>
-q <query file>
-r use poisson statistics (for multiple hits)
-s (3utr_fly|3utr_worm|3utr_human)
-S <sample size> perform calibration on randomized target sequences
-t <target file>
-u <max internal loop size (per side)>
-v <max bulge loop size>
-w weighting

3. Methods

3.1. A Quick Look at miRNA/Target Duplexes

3.1.1. Web Server

Occasionally, you will have only a couple of potential target genes and a small number of miRNAs in hand and will want to check whether reasonable binding sites are present. For this, it is easiest to use the RNAhybrid web interface (for accession details, *see* **Subheading 2.1.**). Go to the "Submission" page (nonexpert version) and perform the following steps:

1. Paste the miRNA sequences in Fasta format into the miRNA sequence field. Alternatively, you can upload a file that contains the sequences. For an explanation of the Fasta format, *see* **Note 4**.
2. Paste your potential target sequences (e.g., 3' untranslated regions [UTRs]) in Fasta format into the target sequence field. Alternatively, you can upload a file that contains the sequences.
3. Click on the "Submit" button. After a short time, the web server will reply with the results. An example is shown in **Fig. 3**.
4. If you are new to target prediction and just want to know what it is about, click on the "Example" button on the "Submission" page. This will insert example target and miRNA sequences into the appropriate fields. Then click on "Submit."

3.1.2. Local Version

Alternatively, you can use your local version of RNAhybrid (*see* **Subheadings 2.2.** and **2.3.**, or **2.4.**; *see* also **Notes 5** and **6**):

1. miRNA preparation. Save the miRNA sequences in Fasta format. Let us assume the filename queries.fasta.
2. Target preparation. Save the potential target sequences in Fasta format. Let us assume the filename targets.fasta.
3. Search. Start RNAhybrid with the following options: RNAhybrid -D -t targets.fasta -q queries.fasta. For every miRNA/target combination, this gives you the best (i.e., the energetically most favorable) hybridization site, if a hybridization is possible. Option -D starts RNAhybrid in "dummy mode," in which no *p*-values are calculated (if you want *p*-values, *see* **Subheadings 3.2.** and **3.3.**). If you would like to see more sites per miRNA/target combination, use the -b option. For example, to get up to five binding sites, use: RNAhybrid

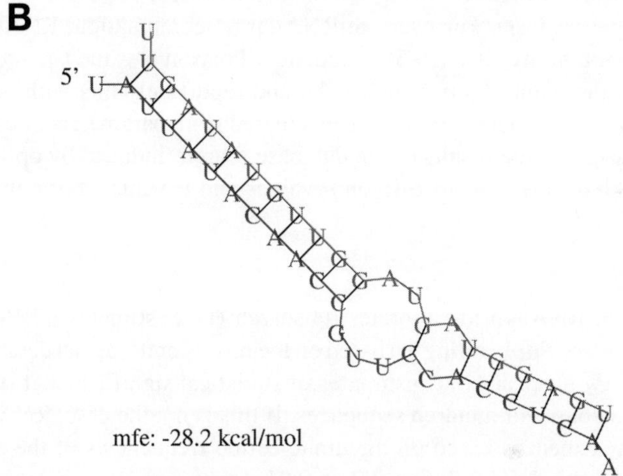

Fig. 3. Example of an RNAhybrid output. (**A**) This is a hit between the target sequence F13D11.2.1 (length 1458) and microRNA (miRNA) cel-let-7 (length 22). The minimum free energy of the duplex is –28.2 kcal/mol, and this energy has a *p*-value of 0.064406 (there is no *p*-value calculation in the simple web version). The duplex starts at position 1265 in the target sequence (letter U). Paired bases are written directly on top of each other, unpaired bases are two lines apart. (**B**) Graphical representation of the same hit. The miRNA is shown in gray, the target in black (with an additionally marked 5' end). *See* also **Note 16**.

-D -b 5 -t targets.fasta -q queries.fasta. If you are only interested in hybridizations that have a certain level of free energy, use the -e option. For example, to get only sites with an mfe of –20 kcal/mol or better, use: RNAhybrid -e -20.0 -D -b 5 -t targets.fasta -q queries.fasta. For further useful options, *see* **Notes 7, 8**, and **9**. For output redirection, *see* **Note 10**. For a discussion of runtimes, *see* **Notes 11** and **12**.

3.2. Whole-Genome Target Prediction

This section discusses the prediction of miRNA targets in a single genome (this does not necessarily mean that all genes of an organism have to be analyzed).

3.2.1. miRNA Preparation

Save the miRNAs in which you are interested in Fasta format (for Fasta format, *see* **Note 4**). If you do not have miRNAs of special interest in hand already, you can download miRNAs, e.g., from the miRNA registry (*see* **Note 13**). Let us assume for the remainder of this section that the filename is queries.fasta.

3.2.2. Target Preparation

Save the potential target sequences in Fasta format. If you do not have sequences in hand already, you can download them from a multitude of internet addresses (*see* **Note 14**). Let us assume for the remainder of this section, that the filename is targets.fasta.

3.2.3. Search

Start RNAhybrid with the following options: RNAhybrid -F -b 5 -r -o 1 -p 0.01 -t targets.fasta -q queries.fasta. For every miRNA/target combination, RNAhybrid will look for up to five binding sites (-b 5), calculate a Poisson p-value (-r, *see* also **Subheading 1.**), sort the output by p-value (-o 1), and report only hits with p-values not larger than 0.01 (-p 0.01). The p-values are calculated from parameters of evds, which, in turn, are estimated on the results of the database search (induced by option -F). For interpreting search results, *see* **Note 15** on p-values and E-values. For output redirection, *see* **Note 10**.

3.2.4. Shuffling

With option -F, RNAhybrid calibrates its search (i.e., estimates miRNA-specific parameters of evds, *see* **Subheading 1.**) based on the results of the actual database search. This, however, only gives accurate estimates of statistical significance if the database contains at least a couple of hundred sequences. If this is not the case, RNAhybrid can generate random sequences based on the dinucleotide frequencies of the target database, e.g., RNAhybrid -S 1000 -b 5 -r -o 1 -p 0.01 -t targets.fasta -q queries.fasta. The option -S 1000 tells RNAhybrid to generate 1000 random sequences for each miRNA. The calibration is performed in the beginning and protocoled in the output. This approach assumes that dinucleotide distributions do not vary much over target sequences. Should you observe a strong deviation, you are advised to repeat the analysis with the target in question and to perform a calibration that is specific for this target (use this single sequence as the argument to the -t option).

3.2.5. Heuristic Parameter Estimate

A quick alternative to using the -S option is a quick estimate of parameters that is based on maximal duplex energies of the miRNAs. This requires telling RNAhybrid the sequence set from which the targets are chosen. For example: RNAhybrid -s 3utr_human -b 5 -r -o 1 -p 0.01 -t targets.fasta -q queries.fasta. Option -s 3utr_human determines the basic parameters that underly the heuristics, and has to be chosen appropriately. A number of such sequence sets (and parameters) are hard-coded into the RNAhybrid program. *See* RNAhybrid help (RNAhybrid -h) for possible options. Note that these sets assume that no seed constraint is given, i.e., no -f option (on seeds, *see* **Note 8**).

3.3. Large-Scale Multispecies Target Prediction

This section discusses the prediction of targets in multiple genomes. As outlined in **Subheading 1.**, the occurrence of binding sites in orthologous genes across species increases the likelihood that the predicted miRNA/target relationship is real. In this section, how to enter multiple sequence files into RNAhybrid is presented, as well as how to tell the program which genes (targets and miRNAs) are orthologous.

3.3.1. miRNA Preparation

Save the miRNAs in which you are interested in Fasta format, as described in **Subheading 3.2.** As an example, we assume that you have a set of human miRNAs named hsa-miRNAs.fasta and a set of mouse miRNAs named mmu-miRNAs.fasta.

3.3.2. Target Preparation

Save the targets in which you are interested in Fasta format, as described in **Subheading 3.2.** As an example, we assume that you have a set of human targets named human_3 utr.fasta and a set of mouse targets named mouse_3utr.fasta.

To tell RNAhybrid which genes are orthologous, the genes have to be annotated with unique keys. If, for example, the human sequences have Ensembl ids (such as ENSG 00000139618), you can annotate the mouse sequences with the human ids:

```
>ENSG00000139618 3'UTR
CTCACCATGGATGATGATACTGCCGTGCTCGTCATTGACAACGGCTCTGGCATGTG
   CAAGGCCGGCTTTGCAGGTGACGA ...
>ENSMUSG00000041147–ENSG00000139618 3'UTR
AGGAAAGAAGACTCTCAGTTGTACAGTGCTGGAAGCACACACGCTTCTCTGCACC
   CGACTGTGTCGTAGAGCTTGATTTC ...
```

In this case, the key is the human Ensembl gene id, written as a regular expression as "ENSG[0–9]*" meaning "ENSG" followed by an arbitrary number of digits.

If your miRNA ids look like hsa-miR101 and mmu-miR101, the corresponding key would be "-.*" meaning a dash followed by an arbitrary number of arbitrary characters.

Another easy possibility would be to assign numbers to target genes, such as

```
>100_ENSG00000139618 3'UTR
CTCACCATGGATGATGATACTGCCGTGCTCGTCATTGACAACGGCTCTGGCATG
   TGCAAGGCCGGCTTTGCAGGTGACGA ...
>100_ENSMUSG00000041147 3'UTR
AGGAAAGAAGACTCTCAGTTGTACAGTGCTGGAAGCACACACGCTTCTCTGCAC
   CCGACTGTGTCGTAGAGCTTGATTTC ...
```

The corresponding target key would be "[0–9]*_" meaning an arbitrary number of digits followed by an underscore. Note that the keys have to be part of the sequence identifiers, which are only the characters up to the first white space.

3.3.3. Search

You can now start RNAhybrid as follows: RNAhybrid -F -b 5 -o 1 -p 0.01 -t human_ 3utr.fasta,mouse_3utr.fasta. -q hsa-miRNAs.fasta,mmu-miRNAs.fasta -a "ENSG[0– 9]*","-.*"

```
target:  ENSG00000165152.1  mirna:  hsa-let-7b  hits:  1  poisson  p-value:

0.000076

target:  ENSG00000165152.1|ENSMUSG00000039611.1  mirna:  mmu-let-7b  hits:  1

poisson p-value: 0.002079

effective k: 1.7

multi-species p-value: 0.000028

multi-species p-value without effective-k calculation: 0.000004
```

Fig. 4. RNAhybrid multispecies hit. RNAhybrid has found one hit of human microRNA (miRNA) let-7b in human gene ENSG00000165152 and one hit of mouse miRNA let-7b in mouse gene ENSMUSG00000039611 (additionally annotated with the human id). Although the actual number of target genes is 2, the effective number ("effective k") is only 1.7, leading to the more accurate multispecies *p*-value of 0.000028 (the multispecies *p*-value that does not consider the effective k, 0.000004, in this example, is output for illustrative purposes). For a brief discussion of the effective number of orthologous sequences, *see* **Subheading 1.**

Be careful that the comma-separated file lists do not contain any blank characters. Option -a gives the target and miRNA keys. For an explanation of other options (especially -S and -s), *see* **Subheading 3.2.** The option -r is not necessary here, because Poisson *p*-values are automatically calculated if there is more than one target file.

If you have just one miRNA set with which you would like to search multiple genomes, you can give just that one set (however, you also have to provide a miRNA key):

> RNAhybrid -F -b 5 -o 1 -p 0.01 -t human_3utr.fasta,mouse_3utr.fasta
> -q miRNAs.fasta -a "ENSG[0-9]*","-.*"

For interpreting search results, *see* **Note 15** on *p*-values and E-values. For output redirection, *see* **Note 10**.

3.3.4. Effective k

For an accurate assessment of statistical significance, it is of great importance to consider the statistical dependence of orthologous target sequences (*see* **Subheading 1.**). This is done by calculating the effective number of orthologous sequences. This calculation is performed if you enter the option -k:

> RNAhybrid -k 500 -F -b 5 -o 1 -p 0.01 -t human_3utr.fasta,mouse_3utr.fasta
> -q hsa-miRNAs.fasta,mmu-miRNAs.fasta -a "ENSG[0-9]*","-.*"

The effective number of orthologous sequences ("effective k") is determined by another shuffling procedure. Here, 500 shuffles of the miRNA in hand are performed for each prospective set of orthologous target sequences (larger values give more accurate results, but 500 should be sufficient). **Figure 4** shows an example output.

4. Notes

1. Other prediction methods. There is a number of other miRNA target prediction methods, the majority of which, however, are not available as a tool. Instead, predicted miRNA/target interactions are presented on the web:

- *Drosophila* target prediction at EMBL at http://www.russell.embl.de/miRNAs.
- The miRBase target database at the Sanger Institute: http://microrna.sanger.ac.uk/targets.
- The core program (called miRanda) can also by downloaded from: http://www.microrna.org/miranda.html.
- A human subset of miRanda predictions at http://www.cbio.mskcc.org/mirnaviewer.
- The PicTar database at http://pictar.bio.nyu.edu.
- The TargetScan website at http://genes.mit.edu/targetscan/index.html.

2. Compiler version. The RNAhybrid source code should be compliant with the ISO C89 standard and can easily be compiled, e.g., with the GNU C compiler gcc in version 3.1. If this does not work, ask your system administrator or inquire with the BiBiServ help team at: http://bibiserv.techfak.uni-bielefeld.de/rnahybrid/contact.html.

3. RNAhybrid manual. The RNAhybrid distribution contains manual pages for RNAhybrid that explain all parameters. If you follow the installation procedure of **Subheading 2.3.** or **2.4.**, they will be installed in a directory named man under the prefix directory (*see* **Subheading 2.4.**).

4. Fasta format. In the Fasta format, each sequence entry consists of a line beginning with the symbol ">" (the description line) and followed by the sequence's identifier and description, and one or more lines with the sequence itself. For example: >F13D11.2 Caenorhabditis elegans hunchback like (hbl-1) 3'UTR TGAGGACGTCCTCGTTAAGGAAACACTTCCCA TAGCCCCTTACCCTCGTCTAGTGACCCATTCTGAAATCGGCAGATAGACTTTCATGT AGCTGGTTTAAGTTTTCTCTTCATTTTCTTTAACTTATCAATGTTCGGGCGT TACCACTTT... A Fasta file can contain many such entries, which are just pasted one after the other (also called a multiple Fasta file). Note that the relevant characters of the description line are only the characters up to the first white space, the so-called identifier (F13D11.2 in the entry sample given here). Be careful that every sequence has a unique identifier.

5. Path. To use RNAhybrid in the locally installed Unix version, make sure that the PATH environment variable is set such that RNAhybrid can be found. If you work in a bash shell, this would be accomplished by export PATH=/homes/juser/bin: ${PATH}, assuming that RNAhybrid has been installed in /homes/juser/bin. In a cshell (or tcshell), the command would be setenv PATH /homes/juser/bin: ${PATH}. If this does not work, contact your system administrator.

6. Example sequences. Example sequences can be found in the RNAhybrid source distribution (*see* **Subheading 2.2.**) in the examples directory.

7. Sequence length restrictions. To prevent RNAhybrid from consuming too much memory, the maximal length of a target sequence is set to 2000 nucleotides by default. If your computer has enough memory, you can change this limit by using the -m option, e.g., RNAhybrid -m 50000 -D -q queries.fasta -t targets.fasta. This tells RNAhybrid to search sequences of lengths up to 50,000 nucleotides. There is an analogous option for query sequence lengths, which is -n (default is 30 nucleotides), e.g., RNAhybrid -n 100 -D -q queries.fasta -t targets.fasta. This would allow query sequences of lengths up to 100 nucleotides to be analyzed. If a sequence (target or query) exceeds the limit, RNAhybrid prints an error message and ignores the sequence. Note also that individual lines of sequence data must not be longer than 1000 characters, regardless of overall length restrictions.

8. Seed forcing. It has been suggested that miRNAs usually bind perfectly to their target with their 5'-region, e.g., from nucleotides 2 to 7 or 8 (called seed or nucleus, *see*, e.g., **ref. 4**). Although there are experimentally verified exceptions (*see* targets for let-7 and lin-4 in *C. elegans [5]*), many true binding sites should be found with this restriction, and these should have a better statistical significance, because chance occurrences of such binding sites are

less likely than chance occurrences of arbitrary good binding sites. In the local version of RNAhybrid, this can be achieved with the option -f, which takes the start and end position of the seed, e.g., RNAhybrid -f 2,7 -D -q queries.fasta -t targets.fasta. Note that this still allows G:U base pairs.

9. Plant targets. miRNA/target interactions in plants (*see* e.g., **ref. 6**) are, in general, different from those in animals: first, plant miRNAs usually bind in coding regions of mRNAs, second, the hybridization is stronger, especially around nucleotides 10 and 11 in the miRNA, which leads to cleavage of the targeted mRNA, not to a translational repression as in animals. These requirements can be met by using RNAhybrid with the following options: RNAhybrid -f 8,12 -u 1 -v 1 -D -q queries.fasta -t targets.fasta. Option -f 8,12 forces RNAhybrid to perfect hybridizations between miRNA and target at positions 8–12 in the miRNA, -u 1 restricts the size of internal loops to a maximum of 1 nucleotide (on each side), -v 1 restricts the size of bulge loops to a maximum of 1 nucleotide.

10. Output redirection. Note that, when using the local Unix version of RNAhybrid, results are output to stdout, therefore, you should redirect them to a file, e.g., RNAhybrid -D -t targets.fasta -q queries.fasta > rnahybrid_output. For large data sets, it might be required to save disk space by using RNAhybrid's compact output mode (option -c), in which individual hit reports, such as the one in **Fig. 3**, are written onto single lines: RNAhybrid -c -D -t targets.fasta -q queries.fasta > rnahybrid_output.

11. Approximate runtime. The runtime of RNAhybrid depends very much on the search mode. For example, in dummy mode (option -D, no *p*-values), searching 50 sequences of 24,000-bp total length with one miRNA (length 22 bp) takes 1.5 s on a Sun Fire V20z (AMD Opteron processor). Searching a set of 25,000 human 3' UTRs takes 33 min. A complete prediction of human/mouse/rat targets (141 conserved miRNAs; 57,000 targets in total), using the approach described in **Subheading 3.3.** on a cluster of 60 Opterons is accomplished in 2 d. For such large amounts of data, using a distributed computing system is advisable (*see* **Note 15**).

12. Distributed computing. Although RNAhybrid is a fast program, the analysis of hundreds of miRNAs and tens of thousands of potential targets is extremely time intensive (*see* **Note 14**). For such large amounts of data, you are advised to distribute the calculations onto several machines. This is easiest with a scheduler system, such as Sun Grid Engine (SGE, http://gridengine.sunsource.net) or Load Sharing Facility (LSF, http://www.platform.com). Ask your system administrator if you have access to such a system. To distribute RNAhybrid jobs, you can either chop your set of miRNAs into smaller sets, or do the same with your target sequence set. In any case, if you are performing a multispecies analysis, as in **Subheading 3.3.**, be careful that orthologous sequences (either miRNAs or targets) are analyzed in the same job.

13. Obtaining miRNA sequences. Sequences of experimentally confirmed miRNAs can be obtained from the miRNA registry at the Sanger Institute: http://www.sanger.ac.uk/Software/Rfam/mirna/index.shtml. You can browse miRNAs by species, select the ones you want (e.g., all human miRNAs), and download their sequences at one time.

14. Obtaining target sequences. Potential target sequences can be downloaded from a variety of sources on the internet. One possibility would be the Ensembl database: http://www.ensembl.org. If you want to download many sequences, it is best to use Ensembl's MartView: http://www.ensembl.org/Multi/martview. There, you can also easily select sequences of 3' UTRs from a number of model organisms. For flies, an excellent resource is http://www.flybase.org. For *Arabidopsis*, go to http://www.arabidopsis.org. For other plant genomes (or eukary-

otic genomes in general), have a look at http://www.tigr.org/tdb/euk. If you are interested in worm genes, this is a good address: http://www.wormbase.org.

15. The p-values and E-values. The p-values occur at different stages of an miRNA target prediction: they are assigned to individual hits, to multiple hits of the same miRNA to one target (Poisson p-values), and to hits in orthologous genes across species (multispecies p-values). The p-values are important, because they assess the statistical significance of the search results, thereby providing a guide to which predictions one can be confident in. Small p-values indicate that observations (in our case good binding sites) can not easily be explained as random events, therefore, are likely to carry a biological meaning. RNAhybrid p-values always refer to target genes, e.g., an individual hit p-value is the probability of a hit of the observed quality or better under a random model, given the one miRNA and the one target. Because usually we want to analyze many targets and many miRNAs, this is a multiple testing scenario, testing combination after combination. In the end, what we would like to know is the expected number of hits of a certain quality, the so-called E-value. We can calculate E-values by multiplying p-values with the number of tests. For example, if we analyze 10,000 targets and 100 miRNAs, each p-value has to be multiplied by 1,000,000 (10,000 × 100). On the other hand, if we have only a very small set of potential targets (maybe experimentally defined), E-values will be much smaller, thus, increasing our confidence in the predictions.

16. Graphics support. RNAhybrid can produce graphics of predicted miRNA/target duplexes in ps, png, and jpg format. For this, you need the graphics library g2, which you can download from http://g2.sourceforge.net, and the library gd from http://www.boutell.com/gd. If you have compiled and installed everything successfully (*see* **Subheading 2.4.**), you can give RNAhybrid the option -g, with the argument being either ps, png, jpg, or all. For an example, *see* **Fig. 3**. Using the appropriate setting of RNAhybrid options, be careful that not too many graphics are generated, because this can easily lead to an exhaustion of disk space.

Acknowledgments

I thank Leonie Ringrose for advice concerning the language of this chapter, and Robert Heinen and Alexander Sczyrba for reading the manuscript and testing the methods.

References

1. Rehmsmeier, M., Steffen, P., Höchsmann, M., and Giegerich, R. (2004) Fast and effective prediction of microRNA/target duplexes. *RNA* **10,** 1507–1517.
2. Zuker, M. and Stiegler, P. (1981) Optimal computer folding of large RNA sequences using thermodynamics and auxiliary information. *Nucleic Acids Res.* **9,** 133–148.
3. Mathews, D. H., Sabina, J., Zuker, M., and Turner, D. H. (1999) Expanded sequence dependence of thermodynamic parameters improves prediction of RNA secondary structure. *J. Mol. Biol.* **288,** 911–940.
4. Lewis, B. P., Shih, I., Jones-Rhoades, M. W., Bartel, D. P., and Burge, C. B. (2003) Prediction of mammalian MicroRNA Targets. *Cell* **115,** 787–798.
5. Grosshans, H. and Slack, F. J. (2002) Micro-RNAs: small is plentiful. *J. Cell Biol.* **156,** 17–21.
6. Rhoades, M. W., Reinhart, B. J., Lim, L. P., Burge, C. B., Bartel, B., and Bartel, D. P. (2002) Prediction of plant MicroRNA targets. *Cell* **110,** 513–520.

8

Prediction of Human MicroRNA Targets

Bino John, Chris Sander, and Debora S. Marks

Summary

MicroRNAs (miRNAs) are small, nonprotein-coding RNAs that regulate gene expression. Although hundreds of human miRNA genes have been discovered, the functions of most of these are unknown. Computational predictions indicate that miRNAs, which account for at least 1% of human protein-coding genes, regulate protein production for thousands of or possibly all of human genes. We discuss the functions of mammalian miRNAs and the experimental and computational methods used to detect and predict human miRNA target genes. Anticipating their impact on genome-wide discovery of miRNA targets, we describe the various computational tools and web-based resources available to predict miRNA targets.

Key Words: MicroRNA; microRNA targets; gene regulation; gene silencing; translational repression; computational prediction.

1. Introduction

miRNAs are small (~22 nucleotides) RNAs that mediate posttranscriptional silencing of genes by base pairing with target messenger RNAs (mRNAs) *(1)*. Animal miRNAs are known to either inhibit translation initiation *(2)* or direct the target mRNA degradation *(3,4)*. The study of miRNAs may revolutionize our view of genes and open up a new world of molecular networks. To date, approx 300 miRNAs have been identified in the human genome *(5)* and hundreds more have been predicted computationally *(6–8)*. Computational predictions of miRNA target genes reveal the potential scope and scale of gene regulation by miRNAs. In particular, miRNAs are predicted to regulate translation of thousands or possibly all of human genes. The regulation of genes by miRNAs is likely to generally involve the modulation of multiple mRNAs by a given miRNA ("multiplicity") and cooperative interactions of multiple miRNAs ("cooperativity") to regulate a given gene *(9–12)*. The emerging complexity of miRNA-mediated gene regulation is reminiscent of transcriptional regulation in promoter regions of DNA in which one-to-many and many-to-one relations exist between regulatory

From: *Methods in Molecular Biology, vol. 342: MicroRNA Protocols*
Edited by: S. Ying © Humana Press Inc., Totowa, NJ

factors and regulated genes *(13,14)*. The combinatorial relationships influence the methods to determine the likelihood that a particular gene is a target of a given miRNA.

Differential expressions of mammalian miRNAs have been shown to occur in specific cell types, tissues, and embryonic stem cells *(15–26)*. Distinct miRNA expression profiles are associated with diseases, such as human B-cell chronic lymphocytic leukemia *(27)*, lung cancer *(28)* and diabetes mellitus *(29)*. Recently, miRNAs were also identified in human pathogens such as, Epstein–Barr virus *(30)*, HIV *(31)*, cytomegalovirus *(32)*, and Kaposi's sarcoma virus *(32,33)*. The observed dynamic range of expression of miRNAs underscores their functional importance and suggests that their expression profile could be useful to predict their function.

Although the molecular mechanisms behind miRNA-mediated gene regulation are largely unknown, the principles of miRNA target recognition are emerging. Experimentally verified miRNA target sites indicate that the 5' end of the miRNA tends to have more bases complementary to the target than its 3' end *(34)*. The 5' end of an miRNA: mRNA duplex does not seem to generally tolerate G:U wobble basepairs *(12,34)*. However, some miRNA target sites with G:U basepairs are also known to be functional *(3,10,35)*. Interestingly, the regions near the miRNA-binding site may also be important for miRNA target recognition. In *lin-41,* a 27-nucleotide intervening sequence between two consecutive *let-7* sites is necessary for its regulation *(36)*. We anticipate that other regions in the target mRNA (e.g., RNA sequence motifs that bind protein complexes) may also be important for the function of miRNAs.

In this chapter, the known functions of mammalian miRNAs are briefly discussed, followed by the experimental and computational methods used to detect human miRNA targets. In general, computational methods have been a key factor in the identification of miRNA-regulated genes in several species *(34,37–42)*. Therefore, we provide a detailed description of the steps involved in the prediction of human miRNA targets.

1.1. The Known Functions of Mammalian miRNAs

Genetic and molecular studies in mammals have identified the biological functions of several mammalian miRNAs. Experiments in mouse have shown that *miR-181a* modulates hematopoietic differentiation *(43)*; *miR-196* negatively regulates the expression of *Hoxb8 (3,44)*; *miR-375* inhibits glucose-stimulated insulin secretion by targeting the pancreatic endocrine protein, myotrophin *(39)*; *miR-1* downregulates a transcription factor (*Hand2*) that promotes ventricular cardiomyocyte expansion *(45)*; and *miR-122a* reduces the expression of the germ cell transition protein 2 (*Tnp2*) via the cleavage of the *Tnp2* mRNA transcript *(46)*. Additionally, *miR-122a* is thought to negatively regulate *CAT-1*, an essential gene that encodes an endogenous ecotropic murine retrovirus receptor, which is associated with leukemia *(47)*. Experiments conducted using human cell lines and tissues indicate that the *let-7* miRNA family negatively regulates the *NRAS* and *KRAS* oncogenes *(48)*. The expression of *let-7* inversely correlates with expression of the NRAS protein in lung cancer tissues, suggesting a possible causal relationship *(48)*. In HeLa cells, *miR-17-5p* and *miR-20a*, which are located within a 500-nucleotide region (*miR-17-92* cluster) and are under the transcriptional control of *c-Myc*, negatively regulate the transcription factor, *E2F1 (49),* possibly buffering the mutual positive activation of *E2F1* and *c-Myc* *(50)*. The overexpression of *miR-17-19b*, a member of the *miR-17-92* cluster, accelerates *c-Myc*-induced lymphomagenesis in mice *(51)*. Current evidence indicates that miRNAs could act as potential human oncogenes or tumor suppressors. In cultured human preadipocytes, *miR-143* promotes adipocyte differentiation, possibly by increasing the level of its suggested target gene, *ERK5* *(52)*. Human miRNAs are also thought to have antiviral potential *(53)*. For instance, the accumulation of the retrovirus primate foamy virus type 1 in human cells is effectively restricted by *miR-32* *(53)*.

A number of studies have linked specific miRNAs to cancer *(17,27,54–61)*, Fragile X syndrome *(10,62–65)*, and neurodegenerative diseases *(18)*. Recent analysis of the genomic location of known miRNA genes suggests that 50% of miRNA genes may be located in cancer-associated genomic regions or in fragile sites *(58)*. For instance, the miRNAs *miR-15* and *miR-16* are located within a 30-kb region at chromosome 13q14, a region deleted in 50% of B-cell chronic lymphocytic leukemias, 50% of mantle cell lymphoma, 16 to 40% of multiple myeloma, and 60% of prostate cancers *(54,55,66)*. This raises the possibility that loss of *miR-15* and *miR-16* contributes to tumorigenesis. Similarly, *miR-143* and *miR-145* are downregulated at the adenomatous and cancer stages of colorectal neoplasia *(56)*. Additionally, *miR-155* is upregulated in children with Burkitt lymphoma *(57)*. The clinical isolates of several types of B-cell lymphomas, including diffuse large B-cell lymphoma, have 10- to 30-fold higher copy numbers of *miR-155* than do normal circulating B-cells. Interestingly, the mRNA of the transcription factor PU.1, which is required for late differentiation of B-cells, contains potential *miR-155* regulatory sites that are conserved in human, mouse, rat, dog, and chicken *(10,59)*. A recent study of global expression levels of miRNAs in normal and tumor-tissue samples, using beads marked with fluorescent tags, suggested that miRNA profiles reflect the developmental lineage and differentiation state of the tumors *(60)*. The study also showed that miRNA expression patterns may be generally more accurate than mRNA profiles for the classification of poorly differentiated tumors.

Several miRNAs are also known to be important factors in the development or maintenance of the neoplastic state. In adult differentiated cancer cells, depletion of *miR-125b* profoundly decreases cell proliferation *(67)*, and the knock-down of the strongly overexpressed *miR-21* in cultured glioblastoma cells triggers the activation of caspases, which leads to increased apoptotic cell death *(68)*. Additionally, several miRNAs that mediate the regulation of cell growth and apoptosis were identified in HeLa cells *(69)*. A growing amount of evidence suggests that miRNAs are associated with a multitude of biological processes. However, the details of the regulation by miRNAs are still largely unknown. Although a few miRNA target genes have been experimentally identified, the details of their precise binding sites are largely unknown. We anticipate that many more miRNA-regulated genes will be identified in the near future.

1.2. Experimental Methods to Identify miRNA Functions

The genes regulated by hundreds of human miRNAs must be experimentally identified. Most experimental protocols that probe a specific miRNA–target interaction assess the regulatory capacity of the 3' untranslated region (UTR) that contains the predicted miRNA binding sites. Such protocols fuse the regions of the 3' UTR from predicted targets to a reporter construct *(38,41,48)*. The predicted UTR targets tested by the reporter constructs generally seem to confer significant repression on the reporter, with respect to a control UTR *(38,41)*. However, the reporter-based assays fall short of establishing whether the observed regulation would occur with the full-length UTR in vivo or whether other endogenous miRNAs regulate the candidate gene of interest. In addition, if the miRNA is exogenously introduced, its concentration may exceed the physiological levels in the cell. The abnormal miRNA levels may cause aberrant cellular functions, which may result in the indirect regulation of the gene. The problem can be partially overcome if the effects of point mutations in the target site are assessed using an assay that makes use of the full-length 3' UTR.

Overexpression of endogenous miRNAs may be used to provide additional evidence to validate a potential miRNA target *(28,39,45)*. Recent evidence suggests that miRNAs can affect transcript levels, as well as protein levels of target genes *(4)*. Therefore, microarray-based profiling of miRNA-transfected cells may also be useful for the identification of the functions of miRNAs *(4)*.

Loss-of-function-based experiments are among the definitive tests to validate miRNA-mediated gene regulation. A given miRNA loss-of-function mutant must cause corresponding deregulation of its genuine targets, and the mutation of miRNA-binding sites must at least partially phenocopy the corresponding miRNA loss of function *(70)*. The loss of function of a miRNA can be achieved by small interfering RNA knockdown, in which the small interfering RNA is targeted to the loop region of the precursor miRNA *(71)*. Loss of function may also be achieved by inhibiting miRNAs via chemical inhibitors, such as 2'-*O*-methyl oligoribonucleotides *(72)*, locked nucleic acids *(73,74)*, and morpholinos *(75)*.

1.3. Computational Methods to Identify miRNA Functions

Experimental identification of miRNA-regulated genes is mainly dependent on computationally predicted miRNA targets or on conjectures based on miRNAs associated with specific biological pathways. Most computational methods for the prediction of miRNA targets are based on models of the nature of the pairing between the miRNA and the target gene. Computational predictions indicate that miRNAs may regulate protein production for thousands of human genes. Because of the importance of computational methods for the identification of miRNA targets, we describe them in greater step-by-step detail (**Subheading 2.**).

2. Methods

The three main steps involved in most computational approaches to predict miRNA targets are (**Fig. 1A**):

1. To obtain miRNA and 3' UTR sequences.
2. To scan for potential miRNA target sites.
3. To analyze evolutionary conservation of the target sites.

We next describe these steps in detail.

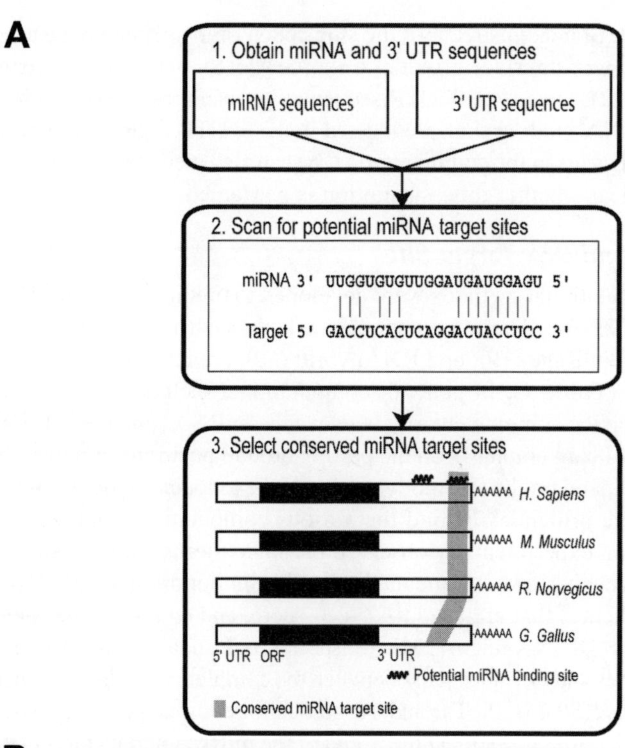

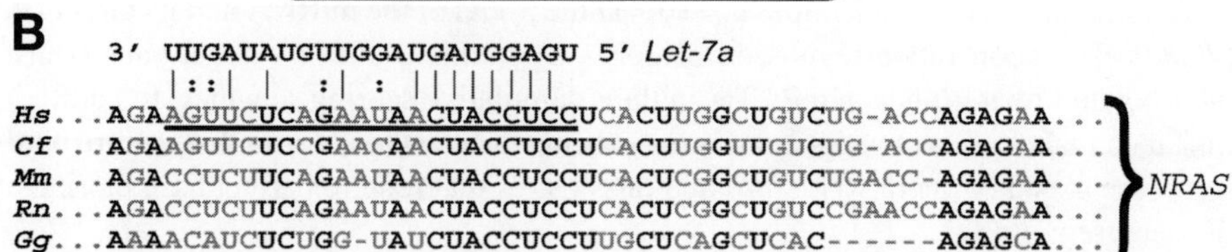

Fig. 1. Prediction of human microRNA (miRNA) targets. Steps involved in computational prediction of miRNA targets and an example of the conservation pattern of an miRNA target site in distantly related species. (**A**) The mature miRNAs are used to scan the 3' untranslated regions (UTRs) of human genes using a computational method (**steps 1** and **2**). The candidate miRNA target sites are then analyzed for their conservation in distantly related species (**step 3**), such as *Canis familiaris* (dog), *Mus musculus* (mouse), *Rattus norvegicus* (rat), and *Gallus gallus* (chicken). (**B**) An example for a conserved miRNA target site; a *let-7* target site (underscore) in the 3' UTR of the protooncogene, *NRAS*, is conserved between human, mouse, rat, and chicken. The 5' end of the miRNA-binding site has more completely conserved nucleotides (solid black) than at the 3' end of the miRNA. The predicted mode of binding between *let-7* and the human *NRAS* 3' UTR is also indicated.

2.1. Obtain the miRNA and 3' UTR Sequences

The known human miRNA sequences (*see* **Note 1**) can be obtained from public data repositories, such as RFAM (*5*). The 3' UTR sequences of human genes can be extracted using the Entrez nucleotide database (*76*). If a 3' UTR sequence of a given human gene is unknown, the genomic region downstream of the stop codon of the gene may be used instead. The Ensembl *(77)* web interface provides a simple way to extract downstream genomic regions (*see* **Note 2**). The use of 3' UTR sequences to scan for miRNA binding sites assumes that the miRNA-binding sites are located in the 3' UTR region. However, the observation that binding sites in the coding region *(78)* can also mediate translational suppression leaves it unclear whether this assumption is warranted.

2.2. Scan for Potential miRNA Target Sites

Recently, several computational methods were developed to predict animal miRNA target sites *(9–11,37,41,42,79–84)*. The computational methods, such as DIANA-microT *(41)*, MicroInspector *(85)*, miRanda *(9)*, and RNAhybrid *(80)*, are readily available to the scientific community (**Table 1**). In general, computational methods that predict miRNA targets are based on the complementarity between the miRNAs and the 3' UTRs of their potential targets, with an emphasis on the pairing around positions two to eight at the 5' end of the miRNA, and on the thermodynamics of the association between the miRNA and its target. The principles behind the various computational approaches are similar and are based on experimentally observed pairing patterns between animal miRNAs and their target genes. However, the methods differ in important details, specifically in the scoring schemes that are used to detect, score, and rank the target sites. For instance, methods such as DIANA-microT, MicroInspector, miRanda, and RNAhybrid allow occasional mismatches and G:U basepairs between the complete miRNA sequence to the 3' UTR sequence *(9,41,80,85)*. PicTar and TargetScanS require a perfectly base-paired stretch of 6 to 7 nucleotides ("seed") at the 5' end of the miRNA and its target site *(40,84)*. The cooperative regulation of genes by multiple miRNA target sites is also incorporated by miRanda and PicTar in their cumulative scoring schemes. In addition, miRanda makes use of a weighted scoring scheme to detect target sites that require binding at the 3' end of the miRNA *(86)* and target sites that require perfect base pairing at the seed region *(34)*.

Among these methods, the miRanda software was the first open-source software made available. It is one of the commonly used tools to scan for miRNA target sites *(9,10,30, 33,86,87)*. The miRanda (v1.9) algorithm searches for stretches of complementary nucleotides that correspond to a double-stranded antiparallel duplex between a given miRNA and its target sequence. The complementarity scores at positions two to eight are multiplied by a scaling factor (currently set to 4.0), so as to reflect the observed 5' to 3' asymmetry in miRNA–target interaction. The method also calculates the free energy of duplex formation using the Vienna package *(9)*. miRanda may be used through a graphical user interface on Mac OS X via the command line on UNIX-based systems, and via a web browser. The software also provides ways to adjust the parameters used for detecting candidate target sites.

2.3. Select Conserved Target Sites

Biologically relevant animal miRNA regulatory sites generally do not have a statistically significant level of pairing between the miRNA and its target. Therefore, additional information, such as evolutionary conservation of the candidate target sites in

Table 1

Resources for the Prediction of Human MicroRNA Targets[a]

Resource	Availability	Targets	Program	Server	References
DIANA-MicroT	http://diana.pcbi.upenn.edu/DIANA-microT			✓	*(41)*
MicroInspector	http://mirna.imbb.forth.gr/microinspector			✓	*(85)*
miRanda	http://www.microrna.org	✓	✓	✓	*(9,10,30)*
MovingTargets	Program is made available on request		✓		*(95)*
PicTar	http://pictar.bio.nyu.edu	✓			*(40)*
RNAhybrid	http://bibiserv.techfak.uni-bielefeld.de/rnahybrid		✓	✓	*(80)*
TargetScan	http://genes.mit.edu/targetscan/index.html	✓			*(38,84)*

[a]The checked lists of resources are freely accessible. Targets, predicted mammalian miRNA targets; program, a downloadable program to scan for miRNA target sites in 3' UTRs; and server, a computational server to identify candidate miRNA targets.

distantly related species, could be useful to limit the list of candidate targets. For instance, 12 of the 22 nucleotides of the *let-7* target site in human *NRAS* are conserved in dog, mouse, rat, and chicken (**Fig. 1B**). The use of evolutionary conservation may aid in indirectly incorporating other unknown requirements for miRNA–target recognition.

To analyze the evolutionary conservation of the human miRNA–target interaction in other species, such as mouse or chicken, the orthologous target gene and the orthologous miRNA must be identified. The Ensembl web interface *(77)* and the National Center for Biotechnology Information HomoloGene *(76)* are valuable resources to identify homologs of human genes in several other species (*see* **Note 3**). The orthologs of human miRNAs in other genomes may be obtained from RFAM *(88)* or identified *(89)* by an alignment search program, such as BLAST, the basic local alignment search tool *(76,90)*. Once the ortholog of a candidate target human gene is identified, the simplest approach to analyze the evolutionary conservation of the target site is to check whether the 3' UTR of the orthologous gene also contains target sites for the given miRNA ortholog (**Subheading 2.2.**). More stringently, multiple sequence alignment programs, such as MAVID *(91,92)*, can be used to align the 3' UTR sequences (**Fig. 1B**), or pre-computed multiple sequence alignments may be used (e.g., University of California, Santa Cruz genome browser *[93]*). The multiple sequence alignment tool can then be used to analyze the positional conservation of the target sites in the 3' UTR sequences.

Current methods for prediction of miRNA targets generally rely on conservation filters to enhance the significance of their predictions. However, some of the biological processes that require a specific miRNA–target interaction may be specific to humans *(8)*; such miRNA–gene interactions are evolutionarily not conserved in other species. Therefore, other considerations are essential to add confidence to the list of candidate miRNA–target interactions (*see* **Notes 4–7**).

3. Notes

1. Distinct strategies (e.g., cloning of miRNAs) used to clone a given miRNA may cause variations in the reported sequence composition of the miRNA at its terminal ends. The computational prediction methods are sensitive to sequence variations at the 5' end of the miRNA. Hence, the sequences of mature miRNAs must be carefully selected, preferably based on the most frequently observed mature form.
2. The average length of mammalian 3' UTRs is approx 1000 nucleotides. Therefore, when 3' UTR sequences are arbitrarily assigned by extracting downstream sequences of the stop codon (**Subheading 2.1.**), it is prudent not to extend them far beyond 1000 nucleotides, so that the number of false predictions is minimized.
3. In some cases, for a given gene, computational tools (**Subheading 2.3.**) may not identify the functionally equivalent orthologous gene or may predict several orthologs. In such cases, additional information must be used to identify orthologs.
4. The miRNA and the gene must be coexpressed to interact physically. Therefore, the co-expression pattern of the miRNA and the potential target gene may be useful to increase the accuracy of the predictions. However, if the miRNA directs the degradation of the target mRNA, their expression patterns will be anticorrelated.
5. A number of experimentally validated miRNA targets contain multiple predicted miRNA-binding sites. Thus, in addition to evolutionary conservation of the target sites, the presence

of multiple sites in a 3' UTR may also be used as a confidence measure to evaluate target genes. However, single miRNA-binding sites are also known to confer regulation of mRNAs in vivo, hence, they should not be disregarded.

6. The predicted regulation of multiple mRNAs by a given miRNA in a common biological process is a useful feature for identifying compelling miRNA target candidates. For example, *miR-196* is thought to repress the expression of several of the *HOX* genes during vertebrate development *(3,44)*.
7. The secondary structure of the mRNA can be calculated using RNA folding programs *(94)*. The information regarding accessibility of the target site to the miRNA based on the mRNA secondary structure may be used to eliminate false predictions *(42,45)*.

References

1. Lee, R. C., Feinbaum, R. L., and Ambros, V. (1993). The C. elegans heterochronic gene lin-4 encodes small RNAs with antisense complementarity to lin-14. *Cell* **75,** 843–854.
2. Pillai, R. S., Bhattacharyya, S. N., Artus, C. G., et al. (2005) Inhibition of translational initiation by let-7 MicroRNA in human cells. *Science* **309,** 1573–1576.
3. Yekta, S., Shih, I. H., and Bartel, D. P. (2004) MicroRNA-directed cleavage of HOXB8 mRNA. *Science* **304,** 594–596.
4. Lim, L. P., Lau, N. C., Garrett-Engele, P., et al. (2005) Microarray analysis shows that some microRNAs downregulate large numbers of target mRNAs. *Nature* **433,** 769–773.
5. Griffiths-Jones, S. (2004) The microRNA registry. *Nucleic Acids Res.* **32,** D109–D111.
6. Berezikov, E., Guryev, V., van de Belt, J., Wienholds, E., Plasterk, R. H., and Cuppen, E. (2005) Phylogenetic shadowing and computational identification of human microRNA genes. *Cell* **120,** 21–24.
7. Xie, X., Lu, J., Kulbokas, E. J., et al. (2005) Systematic discovery of regulatory motifs in human promoters and 3' UTRs by comparison of several mammals. *Nature* **434,** 338–345.
8. Bentwich, I., Avniel, A., Karov, Y., et al. (2005) Identification of hundreds of conserved and nonconserved human microRNAs. *Nat. Genet.* **37,** 766–770.
9. Enright, A. J., John, B., Gaul, U., Tuschl, T., Sander, C., and Marks, D. S. (2003) MicroRNA targets in Drosophila. *Genome Biol.* **5,** R1.
10. John, B., Enright, A. J., Aravin, A., Tuschl, T., Sander, C., and Marks, D. S. (2004) Human microRNA targets. *PLoS Biology* **2,** e363.
11. Krek, A., Grun, D., Poy, M. N., et al. (2005) Combinatorial microRNA target predictions. *Nat. Genet.* **37,** 495–500.
12. Doench, J. G. and Sharp, P. A. (2004) Specificity of microRNA target selection in translational repression. *Genes Dev.* **18,** 504–511.
13. Kadonaga, J. T. (2004) Regulation of RNA polymerase II transcription by sequence-specific DNA binding factors. *Cell* **116,** 247–257.
14. Hobert, O. (2004) Common logic of transcription factor and microRNA action. *Trends Biochem. Sci.* **29,** 462–468.
15. Lagos-Quintana, M., Rauhut, R., Yalcin, A., Meyer, J., Lendeckel, W., and Tuschl, T. (2002) Identification of tissue-specific microRNAs from mouse. *Curr. Biol.* **12,** 735–739.
16. Krichevsky, A. M., King, K. S., Donahue, C. P., Khrapko, K., and Kosik, K. S. (2003) A microRNA array reveals extensive regulation of microRNAs during brain development. *RNA* **9,** 1274–1281.

17. Lagos-Quintana, M., Rauhut, R., Meyer, J., Borkhardt, A., and Tuschl, T. (2003) New microRNAs from mouse and human. *RNA* **9,** 175–179.

18. Dostie, J., Mourelatos, Z., Yang, M., Sharma, A., and Dreyfuss, G. (2003) Numerous microRNPs in neuronal cells containing novel microRNAs. *RNA* **9,** 180–186.

19. Sempere, L. F., Freemantle, S., Pitha-Rowe, I., Moss, E., Dmitrovsky, E., and Ambros, V. (2004) Expression profiling of mammalian microRNAs uncovers a subset of brain-expressed microRNAs with possible roles in murine and human neuronal differentiation. *Genome Biol.* **5,** R13.

20. Miska, E. A., Alvarez-Saavedra, E., Townsend, M., et al. (2004) Microarray analysis of microRNA expression in the developing mammalian brain. *Genome Biol.* **5,** R68.

21. Babak, T., Zhang, W., Morris, Q., Blencowe, B. J., and Hughes, T. R. (2004) Probing microRNAs with microarrays: tissue specificity and functional inference. *RNA* **10,** 1813–1819.

22. Liu, C. G., Calin, G. A., Meloon, B., et al. (2004) An oligonucleotide microchip for genome-wide microRNA profiling in human and mouse tissues. *Proc. Natl. Acad. Sci. USA* **101,** 9740–9744.

23. Thomson, J. M., Parker, J., Perou, C. M., and Hammond, S. M. (2004) A custom micro-array platform for analysis of microRNA gene expression. *Nat. Methods* **1,** 47–53.

24. Baskerville, S. and Bartel, D. P. (2005) Microarray profiling of microRNAs reveals frequent coexpression with neighboring miRNAs and host genes. *RNA* **11,** 241–247.

25. Houbaviy, H. B., Murray, M. F., and Sharp, P. A. (2003) Embryonic stem cell-specific MicroRNAs. *Dev. Cell* **5,** 351–358.

26. Suh, M. R., Lee, Y., Kim, J. Y., et al. (2004) Human embryonic stem cells express a unique set of microRNAs. *Dev. Biol.* **270,** 488–498.

27. Calin, G. A., Liu, C. G., Sevignani, C., et al. (2004) MicroRNA profiling reveals distinct signatures in B cell chronic lymphocytic leukemias. *Proc. Natl. Acad. Sci. USA* **101,** 11,755–11,760.

28. Takamizawa, J., Konishi, H., Yanagisawa, K., et al. (2004) Reduced expression of the let-7 microRNAs in human lung cancers in association with shortened postoperative survival. *Cancer Res.* **64,** 3753–3756.

29. Poy, M. N., Eliasson, L., Krutzfeldt, J., et al. (2004) A pancreatic islet-specific microRNA regulates insulin secretion. *Nature* **432,** 226–230.

30. Pfeffer, S., Zavolan, M., Grasser, F. A., et al. (2004) Identification of virus-encoded microRNAs. *Science* **304,** 734–736.

31. Omoto, S., Ito, M., Tsutsumi, Y., et al. (2004) HIV-1 nef suppression by virally encoded microRNA. *Retrovirology* **1,** 44.

32. Pfeffer, S., Sewer, A., Lagos-Quintana, M., et al. (2005) Identification of microRNAs of the herpesvirus family. *Nat. Methods* **2,** 269–276.

33. Cai, X., Lu, S., Zhang, Z., Gonzalez, C. M., Damania, B., and Cullen, B. R. (2005) Kaposi's sarcoma-associated herpesvirus expresses an array of viral microRNAs in latently infected cells. *Proc. Natl. Acad. Sci. USA* **102,** 5570–5575.

34. Brennecke, J., Stark, A., Russell, R. B., and Cohen, S. M. (2005) Principles of MicroRNA-Target Recognition. *PLoS. Biol.* **3,** e85.

35. Vella, M. C., Reinert, K., and Slack, F. J. (2004) Architecture of a validated microRNA::target interaction. *Chem. Biol.* **11,** 1619–1623.

36. Vella, M. C., Choi, E. Y., Lin, S. Y., Reinert, K., and Slack, F. J. (2004) The C. elegans microRNA let-7 binds to imperfect let-7 complementary sites from the lin-41 3'UTR. *Genes Dev.* **18,** 132–137.

37. Stark, A., Brennecke, J., Russell, R. B., and Cohen, S. M. (2003) Identification of Drosophila microRNA targets. *PLoS. Biol.* **3,** e60.
38. Lewis, B. P., Shih, I., Jones-Rhoades, M. W., Bartel, D. P., and Burge, C. B. (2003) Prediction of mammalian microRNA targets. *Cell* **115,** 787–798.
39. Poy, M. N., Eliasson, L., Krutzfeldt, J., et al. (2004) A pancreatic islet-specific microRNA regulates insulin secretion. *Nature* **432,** 226–230.
40. Krek, A., Grün, D., Poy, P., et al. (2005) Combinatorial microRNA target predictions. *Nat. Genet.* **37,** 226–230.
41. Kiriakidou, M., Nelson, P. T., Kouranov, A., et al. (2004) A combined computational-experimental approach predicts human microRNA targets. *Genes Dev.* **18,** 1165–1178.
42. Robins, H., Li, Y., and Padgett, R. W. (2005) Incorporating structure to predict microRNA targets. *Proc. Natl. Acad. Sci. USA* **102,** 4006–4009.
43. Chen, C. Z., Li, L., Lodish, H. F., and Bartel, D. P. (2004) MicroRNAs modulate hematopoietic lineage differentiation. *Science* **303,** 83–86.
44. Mansfield, J. H., Harfe, B. D., Nissen, R., et al. (2004) MicroRNA-responsive 'sensor' transgenes uncover Hox-like and other developmentally regulated patterns of vertebrate microRNA expression. *Nat. Genet.* **36,** 1079–1083.
45. Zhao, Y., Samal, E., and Srivastava, D. (2005) Serum response factor regulates a muscle-specific microRNA that targets Hand2 during cardiogenesis. *Nature* **436,** 214–220.
46. Yu, Z., Raabe, T., and Hecht, N. B. (2005) MicroRNA122a reduces expression of the post-transcriptionally regulated germ cell transition protein 2 (Tnp2) messenger RNA (mRNA) by mRNA cleavage. *Biol. Reprod.* **73,** 427–433.
47. Chang, J., Nicolas, E., Marks, D., et al. (2004) miR-122, a mammalian liver-specific microRNA, is processed from hcr mRNA and may down-regulate the high affinity cationic amino acid transporter CAT-1. *RNA Biology* **1,** 106–113.
48. Johnson, S. M., Grosshans, H., Shingara, J., et al. (2005) RAS is regulated by the let-7 microRNA family. *Cell* **120,** 635–647.
49. O'Donnell, K. A., Wentzel, E. A., Zeller, K. I., Dang, C. V., and Mendell, J. T. (2005) c-Myc-regulated microRNAs modulate E2F1 expression. *Nature* **435,** 839–843.
50. Matsumura, I., Tanaka, H., and Kanakura, Y. (2003) E2F1 and c-Myc in cell growth and death. *Cell Cycle* **2,** 333–338.
51. He, L., Thomson, J. M., Hemann, M. T., et al. (2005) A microRNA polycistron as a potential human oncogene. *Nature* **435,** 828–833.
52. Esau, C., Kang, X., Peralta, E., et al. (2004) MicroRNA-143 regulates adipocyte differentiation. *J. Biol. Chem.* **279,** 52,361–52,365.
53. Lecellier, C. H., Dunoyer, P., Arar, K., et al. (2005) A cellular microRNA mediates antiviral defense in human cells. *Science* **308,** 557–560.
54. Bullrich, F. and Croce, C. M. (2001) *Chronic Lymphoid Leukemia,* Dekker, New York, pp. 6640–6648.
55. Calin, G. A., Dumitru, C. D., Shimizu, M., et al. (2002) Frequent deletions and down-regulation of microRNA genes miR-15 and miR-16 at 13q14 in chronic lymphocytic leukemia. *Proc. Natl. Acad. Sci. USA* **99,** 15,524–15,529.
56. Michael, M. Z., O'Connor, S. M., van Holst Pellekaan, N. G., Young, G. P., and James, R. J. (2003) Reduced accumulation of specific microRNAs in colorectal neoplasia. *Mol. Cancer Res.* **1,** 882–891.
57. Metzler, M., Wilda, M., Busch, K., Viehmann, S., and Borkhardt, A. (2004) High expression of precursor microRNA-155/BIC RNA in children with Burkitt lymphoma. *Genes Chromosomes Cancer* **39,** 167–169.

58. Calin, G. A., Sevignani, C., Dumitru, C. D., et al. (2004) Human microRNA genes are frequently located at fragile sites and genomic regions involved in cancers. *Proc. Natl. Acad. Sci. USA* **101,** 2999–3004.

59. Eis, P. S., Tam, W., Sun, L., et al. (2005) Accumulation of miR-155 and BIC RNA in human B cell lymphomas. *Proc. Natl. Acad. Sci. USA* **102,** 3627–3632.

60. Lu, J., Getz, G., Miska, E. A., et al. (2005) MicroRNA expression profiles classify human cancers. *Nature* **435,** 834–838.

61. Ciafre, S. A., Galardi, S., Mangiola, A., et al. (2005) Extensive modulation of a set of microRNAs in primary glioblastoma. *Biochem. Biophys. Res. Commun.* **334,** 1351–1358.

62. Caudy, A. A., Myers, M., Hannon, G. J., and Hammond, S. M. (2002) Fragile X-related protein and VIG associate with the RNA interference machinery. *Genes Dev.* **16,** 2491–2496.

63. Jin, P., Zarnescu, D. C., Ceman, S., et al. (2004) Biochemical and genetic interaction between the fragile X mental retardation protein and the microRNA pathway. *Nat. Neurosci.* **7,** 113–117.

64. Jin, P., Alisch, R. S., and Warren, S. T. (2004) RNA and microRNAs in fragile X mental retardation. *Nat. Cell Biol.* **6,** 1048–1053.

65. Veneri, M., Zalfa, F., and Bagni, C. (2004) FMRP and its target RNAs: fishing for the specificity. *Neuroreport* **15,** 2447–2450.

66. Dong, J. T., Boyd, J. C., and Frierson, H. F. Jr. (2001) Loss of heterozygosity at 13q14 and 13q21 in high grade, high stage prostate cancer. *Prostate* **49,** 166–171.

67. Lee, Y. S., Kim, H. K., Chung, S., Kim, K. S., and Dutta, A. (2005) Depletion of human micro-RNA miR-125b reveals that it is critical for the proliferation of differentiated cells but not for the down-regulation of putative targets during differentiation. *J. Biol. Chem.* **280,** 16,635–16,641.

68. Chan, J. A., Krichevsky, A. M., and Kosik, K. S. (2005) MicroRNA-21 is an antiapoptotic factor in human glioblastoma cells. *Cancer Res.* **65,** 6029–6033.

69. Cheng, A. M., Byrom, M. W., Shelton, J., and Ford, L. P. (2005) Antisense inhibition of human miRNAs and indications for an involvement of miRNA in cell growth and apoptosis. *Nucleic Acids Res.* **33,** 1290–1297.

70. Lai, E. C. (2004) Predicting and validating microRNA targets. *Genome Biol.* **5,** 115.

71. Lee, Y. S., Kim, H. K., Chung, S., Kim, K. S., and Dutta, A. (2005) Depletion of human microRNA miR-125b reveals that it is critical for the proliferation of differentiated cells but not for the down-regulation of putative targets during differentiation. *J. Biol. Chem.* **280,** 16,635–16,641.

72. Meister, G., Landthaler, M., Dorsett, Y., and Tuschl, T. (2004) Sequence-specific inhibition of microRNA- and siRNA-induced RNA silencing. *RNA* **10,** 544–550.

73. Braasch, D. A. and Corey, D. R. (2001) Locked nucleic acid (LNA): fine-tuning the recognition of DNA and RNA. *Chem. Biol.* **8,** 1–7.

74. Valoczi, A., Hornyik, C., Varga, N., Burgyan, J., Kauppinen, S., and Havelda, Z. (2004) Sensitive and specific detection of microRNAs by northern blot analysis using LNA-modified oligonucleotide probes. *Nucleic Acids Res.* **32,** e175.

75. Summerton, J. and Weller, D. (1997) Morpholino antisense oligomers: design, preparation, and properties. *Antisense Nucleic Acid Drug Dev.* **7,** 187–195.

76. Wheeler, D. L., Barrett, T., Benson, D. A., et al. (2005) Database resources of the National Center for Biotechnology Information. *Nucleic Acids Res.* **33,** D39–D45.

77. Birney, E., Andrews, D., Bevan, P., et al. (2004) Ensembl 2004. *Nucleic Acids Res.* **32 (Database issue),** D468–D470.

78. Saxena, S., Jonsson, Z. O., and Dutta, A. (2003) Small RNAs with imperfect match to endogenous mRNA repress translation. Implications for off-target activity of small inhibitory RNA in mammalian cells. *J. Biol. Chem.* **278,** 44,312–44,319.
79. Lewis, B. P., Shih, I. H., Jones-Rhoades, M. W., Bartel, D. P., and Burge, C. B. (2003) Prediction of mammalian microRNA targets. *Cell* **115,** 787–798.
80. Rehmsmeier, M., Steffen, P., Hochsmann, M., and Giegerich, R. (2004) Fast and effective prediction of microRNA/target duplexes. *RNA* **10,** 1507–1517.
81. Rajewsky, N. and Socci, N. D. (2004) Computational identification of microRNA targets. *Dev. Biol.* **267,** 529–535.
82. Grosshans, H., Johnson, T., Reinert, K. L., Gerstein, M., and Slack, F. J. (2005) The temporal patterning microRNA let-7 regulates several transcription factors at the larval to adult transition in C. elegans. *Dev. Cell* **8,** 321–330.
83. Smalheiser, N. R. and Torvik, V. I. (2004) A population-based statistical approach identifies parameters characteristic of human microRNA-mRNA interactions. *BMC Bioinformatics* **5,** 139.
84. Lewis, B. P., Burge, C. B., and Bartel, D. P. (2005) Conserved seed pairing, often flanked by adenosines, indicates that thousands of human genes are microRNA targets. *Cell* **120,** 15–20.
85. Rusinov, V., Baev, V., Minkov, I. N., and Tabler, M. (2005) MicroInspector: a web tool for detection of miRNA binding sites in an RNA sequence. *Nucleic Acids Res.* **33,** W696–W700.
86. Leaman, D., Chen, P. Y., Fak, J., et al. (2005) Antisense-mediated depletion reveals essential and specific functions of microRNAs in Drosophila development. *Cell* **121,** 1097–1108.
87. Chen, P. Y., Manninga, H., Slanchev, K., et al. (2005) The developmental miRNA profiles of zebrafish as determined by small RNA cloning. *Genes Dev.* **19,** 1288–1293.
88. Griffiths-Jones, S., Bateman, A., Marshall, M., Khanna, A., and Eddy, S. R. (2003) Rfam: an RNA family database. *Nucleic Acids Res.* **31,** 439–441.
89. Weber, M. J. (2005) New human and mouse microRNA genes found by homology search. *FEBS J.* **272,** 59–73.
90. Altschul, S. F., Madden, T. L., Schaffer, A. A., et al. (1997) Gapped BLAST and PSI-BLAST: a new generation of protein database search programs. *Nucleic Acids Res.* **25,** 3389–3402.
91. Bray, N. and Pachter, L. (2004) MAVID: constrained ancestral alignment of multiple sequences. *Genome Res.* **14,** 693–699.
92. Bray, N. and Pachter, L. (2003) MAVID multiple alignment server. *Nucleic Acids Res.* **31,** 3525–3526.
93. Kent, W. J., Sugnet, C. W., Furey, T. S., et al. (2002) The human genome browser at UCSC. *Genome Res.* **12,** 996–1006.
94. Wuchty, S., Fontana, W., Hofacker, I. L., and Schuster, P. (1999) Complete suboptimal folding of RNA and the stability of secondary structures. *Biopolymers* **49,** 145–165.
95. Burgler, C. and Macdonald, P. M. (2005) Prediction and verification of microRNA targets by MovingTargets, a highly adaptable prediction method. *BMC Genomics* **6,** 88.

9

Complications in Mammalian MicroRNA Target Prediction

Neil R. Smalheiser and Vetle I. Torvik

Summary

In this chapter, we review evidence that at least three different types of microRNA (miRNA)–messenger RNA (mRNA) target interactions exist in mammals: short seeds, long seeds, and "perfect" hits (allowing G:U matches). Because new types of miRNAs are still being discovered, this list may not yet be complete.

Key Words: MicroRNA; microRNA target prediction; RNA interference; LINE-2; genomic repeats.

1. Introduction

The phenomena of RNA interference were first defined in plants and *Caenorhabditis elegans*, and have subsequently been studied in all living phyla, including mammals *(1)*. Among several different populations of small RNAs that have been identified, the miRNAs have perhaps received the most attention because they arise from well-defined genomic precursors, because they appear to regulate mRNA stability and/or translation, and because they are clearly important for development and cell differentiation (*see* reviews in **refs.** *2–4*).

During the past few years, a growing number of biologically validated mRNA targets have been identified for specific miRNAs. In plants, many of the mRNA targets appear to encode transcription factors; the miRNAs often show perfect or nearly perfect "long-seed" complementarity with its target, and miRNAs bind within the protein-coding region as well as in untranscribed regions *(5,6)*. In *C. elegans* and *Drosophila*, the situation appears to be quite different: the 5' end of the miRNA generally exhibits a short, perfect "seed" of 6 to 8 nucleotides in length, excluding G:U matches, which appears to be targeted to the 3' untranslated region (UTR) of the mRNA *(2–4)*.

A number of studies have used biologically validated mRNA targets in *C. elegans* and *Drosophila* as a training set for machine-learning algorithms to predict additional mRNA targets that follow the same rules in a variety of species, including mammals *(7–15)*. Most of these studies focused attention on 3' UTR regions that are well-conserved across species to minimize the chance of false-positive predictions. Indeed, based

From: *Methods in Molecular Biology, vol. 342: MicroRNA Protocols*
Edited by: S. Ying © Humana Press Inc., Totowa, NJ

on these rules, each miRNA appears to have approx 10 to 100 plausible mRNA targets. Studies of miRNA–mRNA binding have confirmed the importance of short seeds having a 5' end location within certain miRNAs *(16)*.

However, it does not appear that all mammalian miRNAs interact with their targets via short seeds. Xie et al. *(17)* identified a large number of 8-mer motifs within 3' UTRs that were conserved across multiple mammalian species, which correspond to short-seed mRNA target regions. Only approximately half of currently identified mammalian miRNAs mapped to one of these motifs, suggesting that the remaining miRNAs may obey different types of binding interactions with their targets.

In a recent study, we asked whether mammalian miRNAs may exhibit long-seed complementarity interactions with their mRNA targets *(18)*. Although no biologically validated mammalian miRNA–mRNA pairs were known at the time, we took the statistical approach of looking at the entire set of potential binding interactions among all known miRNAs and all mRNAs in the human RefSeq database. To define the level of binding interactions that would be expected by chance, each miRNA sequence was scrambled 10 times (either by random permutation or by maintaining the dinucleotide composition; both methods gave similar results) and each of the scrambled miRNAs was tested. Our underlying assumption is that scrambled sequences will hit mRNA at random and define the noise level in any given situation, whereas miRNA sequences will hit the same number of noise interactions plus any true targets.

2. Methods

2.1. Retrieving the miRNA and RefSeq mRNA Sequences

The set of mature miRNA sequences are available in FASTA format in a plain text file from the miRNA Registry (http://www.sanger.ac.uk/Software/Rfam/mirna/). This file contains all miRNA sequences from all species, and the human sequences are identified by lines beginning with ">hsa." The most recent set of human mRNA sequences in the National Center for Biotechnology Information (NCBI) RefSeq database (http://www.ncbi.nlm.nih.gov/RefSeq/) can be retrieved by submitting the query "srcdb_refseq [prop] AND biomol_mrna[prop] AND homo sapiens[orgn]" to the Entrez Nucleotide (http://www.ncbi.nlm.nih.gov/entrez/query.fcgi?db=Nucleotide) database, and saving the results to a local file. The RefSeq database is updated often, therefore, one is not likely to retrieve the same set of records for the same query performed twice, e.g., a month apart. Some records are deleted, some are temporarily removed while being annotated, and some are replaced by newer versions (although the actual sequence may not be changed). However, the status of any given record can be found by searching via the GI or accession numbers.

2.2. Preprocessing

Many miRNA sequences are similar (some even differ only in 1 or 2 nucleotides), a fact that could potentially affect the statistics in this study. To remove redundant miRNAs, we compared all miRNA sequences pair-wise, removing the shorter miRNAs from consideration if they overlapped with 10 or more nucleotides. Because we only

```perl
$mrna = 'ACTTTGGGACGAGCTT';
$mrna =~ s/T/U/g;      #replace Ts with Us
$mirna = 'UUGG';
$mirna = reverse $mirna;   #reverse the sequence
$mirna =~ tr/ACUG/UGAC/;   #find the complement

if ($GUs_allowed) {
        $mirna =~ s/C/[CU]/g;      #Gs will now match either Cs or Us
        $mirna =~ s/A/[AG]/g;      #Us will now match either As or Gs
}

while ($mrna =~ /$mirna/g) {
    $hit_lngth = length($mirna);
    $hit_pos = pos($mrna) - $hit_lngth;
    substr($mrna,$hit_pos,$hit_lngth) = 'X' x $hit_lngth;
}
```

Fig. 1. Perl script to match a subsequence of a microRNA with a messenger RNA. *See* **Subheading 2.** for details.

count exact hits of at least 10 nucleotides, no hits on the same mRNA at the same location will be counted more than once.

To create a population of "negative control" sequences to represent what is expected by chance, we created 10 scrambled versions of each miRNA sequence by randomly permuting its nucleotides. This maintains the base composition but not the order. Alternatively, we also scrambled the sequences but preserved the dinucleotide composition by first splitting each miRNA sequence into chunks of two nucleotides analogous to a reading frame: once starting with the first nucleotide and once starting with the second nucleotide. We then permuted these chunks to create a second set of scrambled miRNA sequences.

Note that RefSeq mRNA sequences use a "T", whereas the miRNA Registry files use a "U." The regular expression $sequence =~ s/T/U/g substitutes each occurrence of a T with a U, which is necessary to be able to match the two sequences (**Fig. 1**).

2.3. Aligning miRNAs With mRNA Sequences

Because the standard basic local alignment search tool (BLAST) server at NCBI is unable to find imperfect alignments of the nature studied here (potentially with large gaps and multiple mismatches per matched nucleotide) *(19)*, we wrote a Perl script to perform a custom-gapped BLAST alignment. The procedure comprises two main steps:

2.3.1. Identifying Exact Hits

Because we are looking for sequence complementarity (in which miRNAs bind to mRNAs), each miRNA sequence (and their scrambled counterparts) are first reversed and then complemented (i.e., A→U, C→G, U→A, and G→C). Complementation can be accomplished with the regular expression $sequence =~ tr/ACUG/UGAC/g. For each pair of miRNA and mRNA sequences, take all subsequences of the miRNA in decreasing length, starting with the entire sequence and going down to 10 nucleotides. Search for this subsequence within the mRNA sequence (*see* Perl code in **Fig. 1**). If an exact match is found, then the hit site on the mRNA is replaced with Xs, therefore, only the longest hit by the miRNA at this site will be counted. The hits are then recorded in a hit file identifying the two sequences, the length of the hit and the location on each of the two sequences.

Often, several different RefSeq records represent close variants of the same mRNA. To prevent this redundancy effect from inflating the statistics on exact hits, we only count the longest mRNA and do not count hits on other mRNAs whose sequences matched exactly on the 25 nucleotides on each side of the hit. This removes hits that have long stretches of exactly the same sequences, and preserves the hits that only share the hit region and not the flanks. We also remove hits having low complexity sequences by using the regular expression $sequence =~ s/((.+)\2{4,})/'N' x length $1/eg (Lincoln Stein, Bioperl: Repetitive DNA, http://bioperl.org/pipermail/bioperl-l/1999-November/003313.html).

2.3.2. Extending the Exact Hits

Given an exact hit of 10 or more nucleotides, with no gaps, mismatches, or G:U matches, the seed region is extended in both directions to find the optimal alignment allowing for large gaps and multiple mismatches. This is achieved by penalizing gaps at only a fraction of the reward of a match, and making the mismatch penalty a fraction of the reward of a match. Note that the BLAST program from NCBI tends to not identify good alignments in this scenario, probably because of the method of calculating significance (i.e., "Expect Values"). We allow a ratio of up to 4 to 1 between mismatches and matches, and allow a 4-nucleotide gap between matches, and allow a longer gap as long as multiple matches are obtained as a result. This is achieved with the parameters: match reward, $r = 10$; mismatch penalty, $q = -2.5$; open-gap penalty, $G = 8$; extend-gap penalty, $E = 0.5$.

Given a pair of sequences x and y of lengths m and n, respectively, let x_i, y_j denote their i-th and j-th nucleotide, respectively. Then, the alignment score is calculated as follows:

Start by assigning Score(0,0) = 0. Then, for $i = 0,1..., m$ and $j = 0,1, ..., n$ compute the score using the following equation:

$$Score(i,j) = \max \begin{cases} Score(i-1, j-1) + (r-q) \times Match(x_i, y_j) + q \\ Score(k, j) - G - E \times (i-k), k = 0,..., i-1 \\ Score(i, k) - G - E \times (j-k), k = 0,..., j-1 \end{cases}$$

where $Match(x_i, y_j) = 1$ if $x_i + y_j$, and 0 otherwise.

The greatest score is then given by Score(m,n). If the actual alignment is to be found, one needs to also keep track of the path from (0,0) to (m,n) in the Score array.

For each record identified in the hit file, a sequence alignment is performed between the right flank of the miRNA vs the right flank of the mRNA using the recursive equation given, ensuring that the first nucleotides are either gap or mismatch scored. The same procedure is performed on the left flanks, after which the total score is tallied and recorded in a file. When allowing for G:U matches, nucleotide C in the miRNA

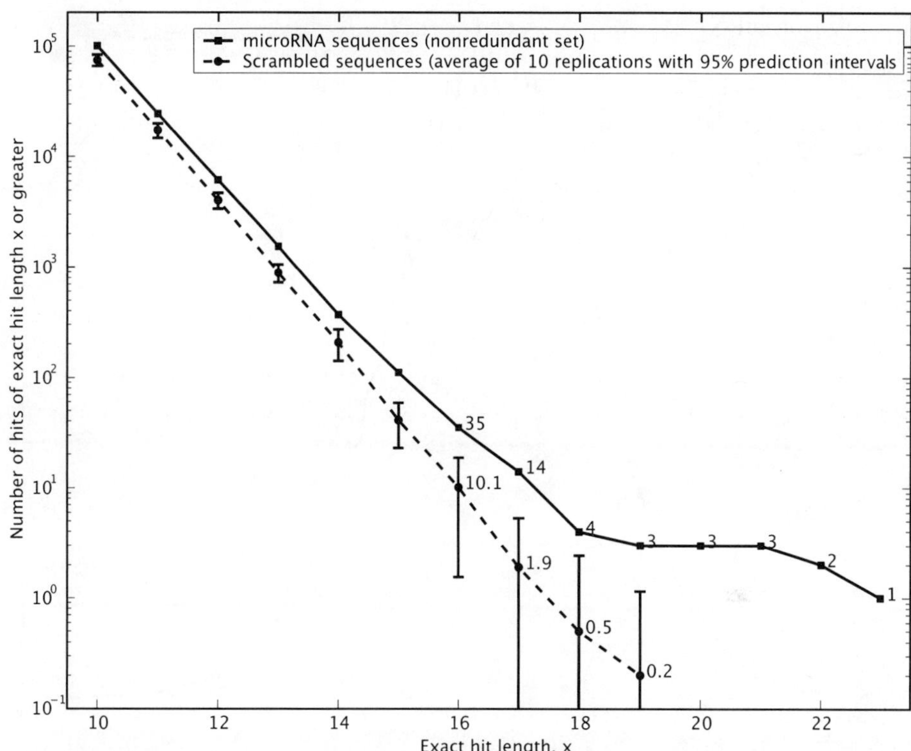

Fig. 2. MicroRNAs (miRNAs) and their scrambled counterparts interact differently with the population of human mRNAs. Shown are all exact hits of at least 10 bases long (not counting G:U matches) produced on human RefSeq mRNAs by the set of nonredundant miRNAs vs the average of 10 replications of scrambled control sequences. Shown is the number of hits as a function of exact hit length. Only the longest hit was counted, e.g., for a hit of length 18, the two subsets of length 17 in the same hit position were not counted. (Reproduced with permission from **ref. *18*.**)

reverse-complement sequence is replaced by C or U, and nucleotide A is replaced by A or G (**Fig. 1**) indicating that multiple combinations should receive a match reward.

3. An Analysis of Long-Seed Interactions Between Mammalian miRNAs and Their Targets

As shown in **Fig. 2**, a large number of long-seed complementary interactions existed between miRNA sequences and mRNA sequences having 10 or more exact matches (excluding G:U matches), which differed significantly from the level expected by chance. Strikingly, at longer seed lengths, the difference between the miRNA set and the scrambled set became more and more pronounced; at a seed length of 16 or greater, there were 3.5 times more examples of potential target interactions in the miRNA set than in the scrambled set, and at a seed length of 17 or greater, the ratio was greater than 7 to 1 (**Fig. 2**).

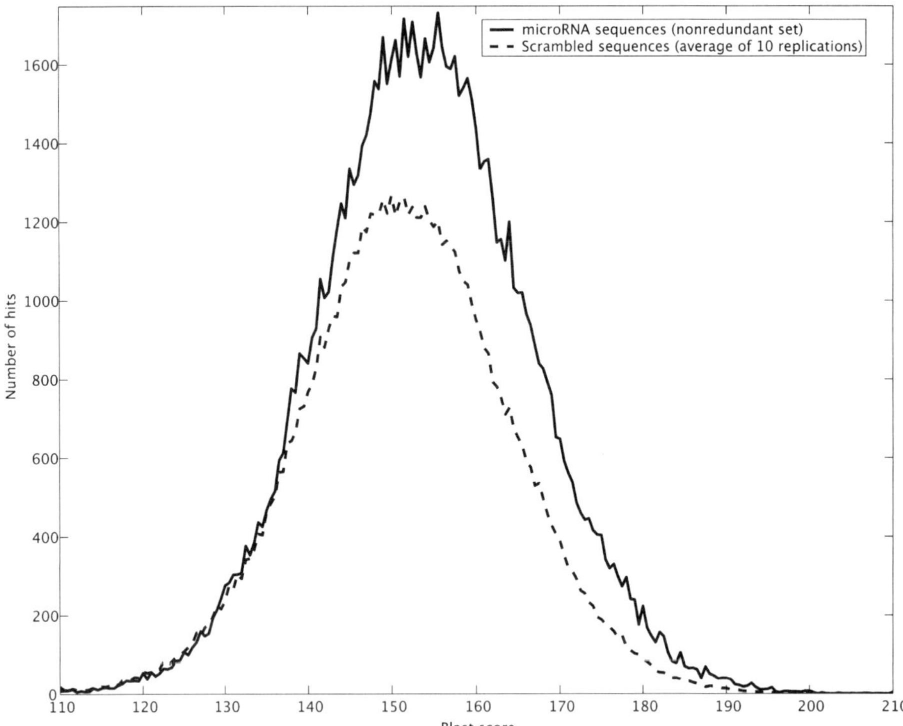

Fig. 3. Distribution of gapped basic local alignment search tool (BLAST) scores in hits made by miRNAs and scrambled counterparts. Without permitting G:U matches in the extension phase, the miRNAs had better average gapped BLAST scores than scrambled counterparts across all messenger RNAs in the "10+ set" (153.00 ± 0.03 vs 150.98 ± 0.01; mean ± SEM, p < 0.0001). Permitting G:U matches in the extension phase, the miRNA set showed significantly fewer G:U matches overall relative to scrambled counterparts, even when holding constant the length of the exact hit (2.891 ± 0.004 vs 2.939 ± 0.001; p < 0.0001). (Reproduced with permission from **ref. *18*.)

This finding suggested that some true miRNA–mRNA target interactions may involve long seeds. To further define a list of candidate mRNA targets with high confidence, we further analyzed the set of interactions having 10 or more matches in a row (the "10+ set") to see whether they would also exhibit other statistically significant differences at the population level. Indeed, we defined a gapped BLAST score for miRNA–mRNA interactions, taking into account gaps, mismatches, and G:U matches, and found that the gapped BLAST scores in the 10+ set were significantly better overall than expected by chance (**Fig. 3**). Furthermore, for those mRNAs that received multiple hits from different miRNAs within the 10+ set, we examined the minimum distance between hits. Again, there was a striking difference between the minimum distance seen in the miRNA population vs the population of scrambled sequences (**Fig. 4**).

By combining these three criteria (seed length, gapped BLAST score, and minimum distance between hits) we created a list of 71 candidate mRNA targets which

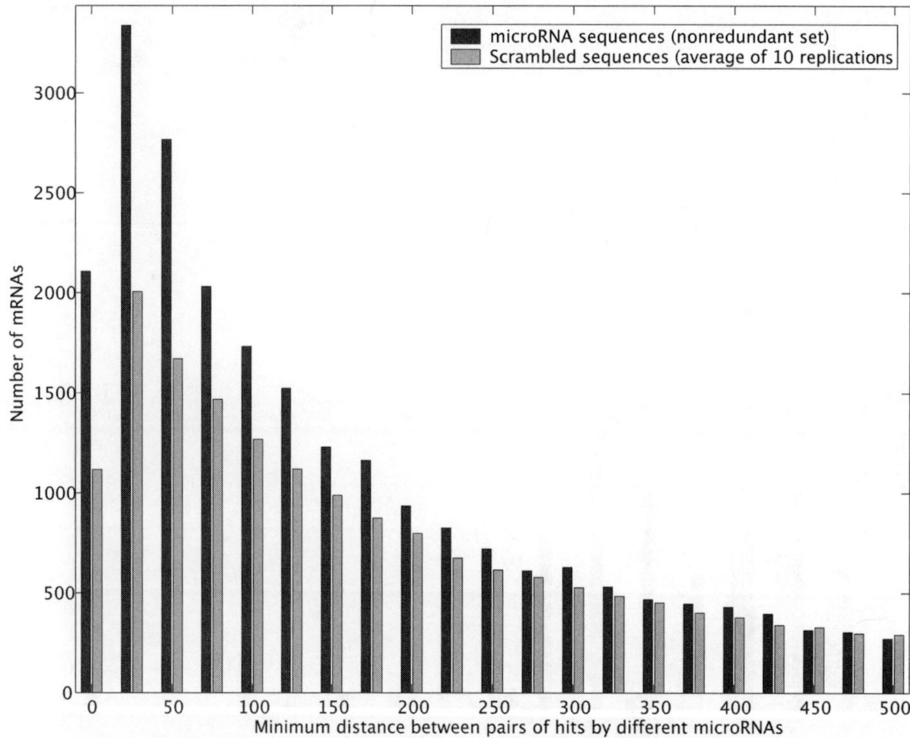

Fig. 4. Number of distinct mRNA sequences that received hits from two or more distinct miRNAs, as a function of the minimum distance between hits. Distances of 0 or 1 were excluded because they might be produced by partial overlap of miRNA sequences. (Reproduced with permission from **ref. *18*.**)

were unlikely to be chosen by chance—with a discrimination ratio of 5.2 to 1, which indicates that more than 80% of the targets on the list are expected to be biologically valid targets. The 71 mRNAs had a larger number of miRNA hits per kilobase of target sequence than did the scrambled sequences. Additionally, individual miRNAs hit multiple (up to 17) distinct members of the candidate set, which again happened significantly more often than by chance (**Fig. 5**). These findings indicate that the outlier mRNAs are different as a whole from the mRNAs that were hit by scrambled counterparts, even those that satisfied the same cut-off criteria.

Our candidate target list contained very similar types of targets as predicted by the short-seed computational studies, including members of the same gene families: transcription factors (including homeobox genes), nucleic acid-binding proteins, and many other functional categories, including kinases, receptors, and other signal transduction proteins, membrane and cytoskeletal proteins, and effectors of differentiation. In addition, our study was in concordance with other studies showing that some individual miRNAs may hit multiple mRNA targets residing in the same metabolic pathway *(18)*. However, surprisingly, we found that the long-seed candidate mRNA target list had

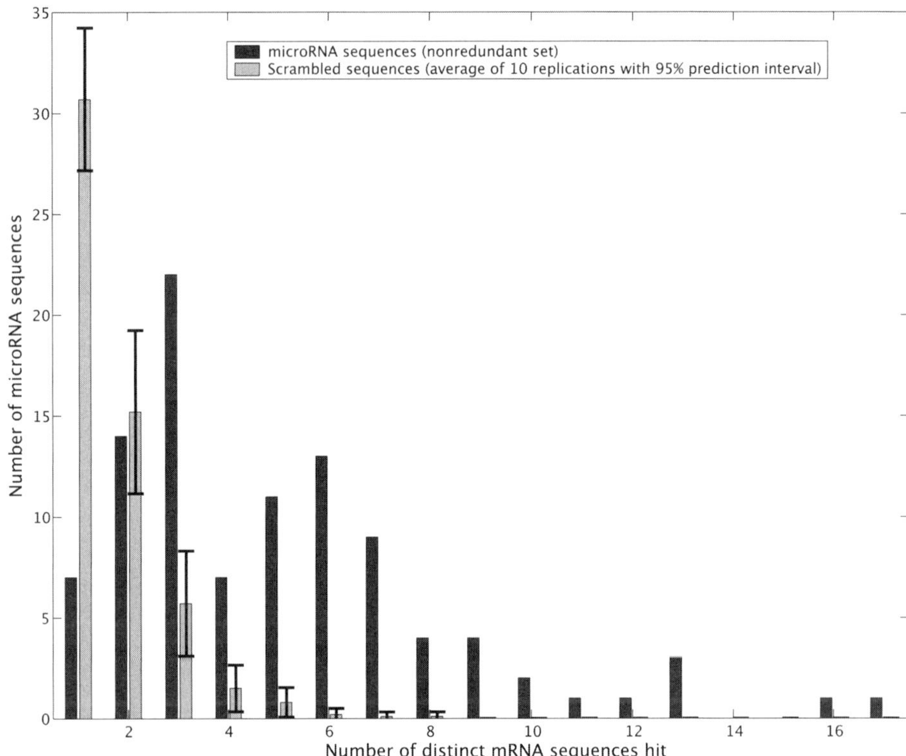

Fig. 5. Individual miRNAs hit multiple targets on the candidate list, more often than expected by chance. (Reproduced with permission from **ref. *18*.**)

no preferences for miRNA hits to be located within 3' UTRs, but hit within the protein coding region in approx two-thirds of the cases. In addition, the best miRNA hits on candidate mRNA targets did *not* have relatively better target complementarity near their 5' end. These considerations suggest that short-seed and long-seed target interactions both exist in mammals, and that they may follow different rules.

4. "Perfect" Target Interactions (Allowing G:U Matches)

A few examples of miRNAs exhibiting perfect complementarity have been described (miR-196 *[20]*, miR-127, and miR-136 *[21,22]*). During our analysis of long-seed interactions, we were struck by the existence of targets that had perfect complementarity to miRNAs along their full length (**Fig. 2**) *(18)*, and we wondered whether they could be representatives of a larger, distinct class of targets.

Whereas long-seeds are defined as having exact Watson-Crick base pairing with no G:U matches, recent studies suggest that complementarity interactions that contain up to approx five to seven G:U matches (but no frank mismatches) could still be deemed "perfect" in gene silencing *(23)*. In particular, we noted that human miR-95 was perfectly complementary (including up to four G:U matches) with scores of human mRNAs and expressed sequence tags (ESTs) (**Fig. 6**). Similarly, miR-151* was perfectly com-

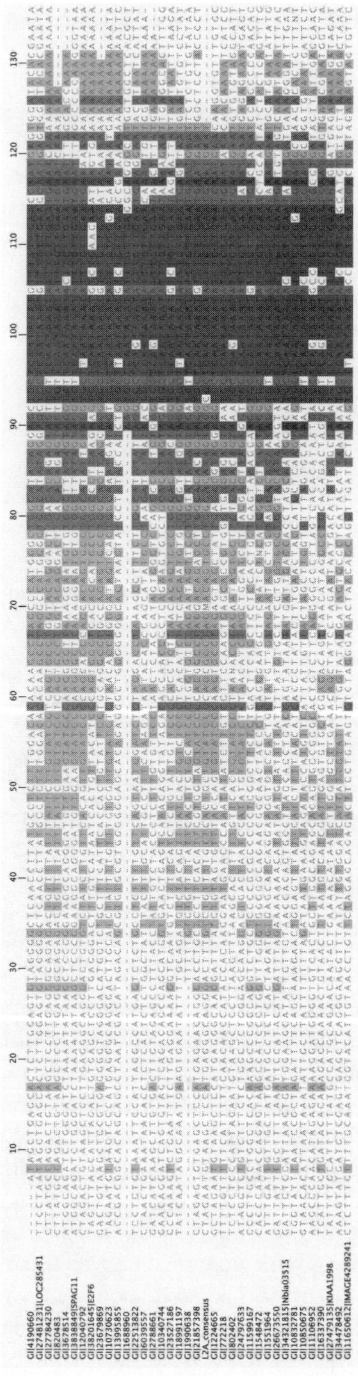

Fig. 6. Multiple sequence alignment of messenger RNAs (mRNAs) and expressed sequence tags (ESTs) that exhibited perfect complementarity to miR-95. miR-95 hit perfectly (including 2 to 4 G:U matches) on 3 mRNAs, and 94 ESTs comprising 31 distinct clusters (Unigene clusters or singletons when not belonging to a Unigene cluster). Multiple sequence alignment performed using ClustalW (http://www.ebi.ac.uk/clustalw) shows that these putative targets are not related to each other except in the microRNA hit region and in nearby LINE-2 homologous sequences (L2A consensus from Repbase; http://www.girinst.org). (Reproduced with permission from **ref. 24**).

plementary to six transcripts, which was significantly greater than the level expected by chance.

The reason for these perfect hits turned out to be simple and intriguing: the precursors of these two miRNAs, as well as two others (miR-28 and miR-325), turned out to derive entirely from genomic repeats *(24)*. In particular, the hairpin fold backs were formed by the junction of two adjacent long interspersed nucleotide repeat-2 (LINE-2) repeat segments apposed in opposite orientation (**Fig. 7**). Insofar as MIR repeats and other LINE-2-derived elements are present in the 3' UTR of many different mRNAs and EST transcripts, when aligned in the proper orientation, they are natural generic targets for the repeat-derived miRNAs—in some cases having perfect complementarity, and in other cases (because there is divergence among LINE-2 elements) having imperfect complementarity *(24)*.

5. Discussion

Computer and genomic analyses of mammalian miRNA–mRNA target interactions suggest that at least three distinctly different types of interactions exist: short seeds, long seeds, and perfect hits (allowing G:U matches). By their nature, one would expect that short-seed interactions are likely to have weak effects, to inhibit protein translation, and to affect large numbers of genes in parallel, whereas long-seed interactions might be expected to have stronger effects and involve fewer targets. The LINE-2 repeat-derived miRNAs seem to recognize transcripts that share repeats in their 3' UTR regions, and when they bind with perfect or nearly perfect complementarity, they may be expected to lead to degradation of the transcripts. This could serve as a mechanism for detecting and neutralizing aberrant transcripts (having read-through transcription from retained introns or neighboring genomic regions), as well as serving to regulate specific mRNAs *(24)*.

It should be cautioned that complementarity between miRNAs and their targets is not the only factor that may govern which miRNA–mRNA target interactions are effective in vivo. One must consider the potential importance of mRNA target secondary structure *(25)*, as well as the strong possibility that RNA-binding proteins may participate in miRNA recognition *(26)*. Furthermore, both miRNA and mRNA need to be coexpressed in proper amounts within the same cell for effective interaction to occur, and A-to-I editing of RNA might abrogate potential mRNA targets from being effectively silenced by the RNA-induced silencing complex complex *(27)*.

Finally, it is likely that new types of miRNA–mRNA target interactions still remain to be uncovered. A number of viruses have been shown to encode miRNA precursors *(28–31)* that are not conserved in their host genomes or across different viruses, and their targets have not been fully defined. Furthermore, a population of small RNAs that shares some, but not all, of the features of miRNAs has been described in *C. elegans* *(32)*; these so-called tiny noncoding RNAs are not conserved across species, and their targets (if any) have not been identified yet. Therefore, new types of target interactions, and indeed new types of small RNAs, may be identified in mammalian species within the near future.

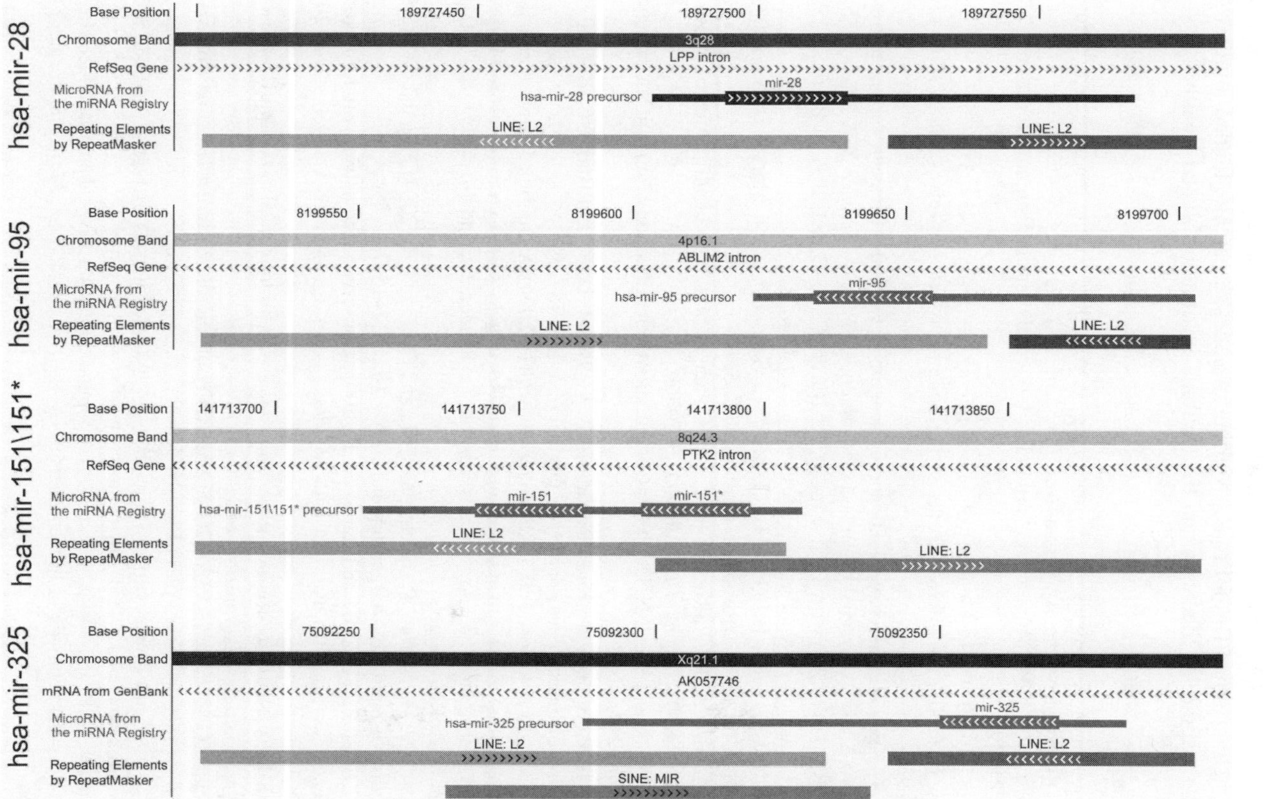

Fig. 7. Genomic structure of human LINE-2-derived miRNA precursors. Information was downloaded and edited from the University of California, Santa Cruz Genome Browser. Each of the precursors resides within an intron, and each flanks the junction of two L2 repeats in opposite orientation (darker shading indicates less divergence from the L2 consensus sequence). (Reproduced with permission from **ref. 24**).

125

Acknowledgments

This work was supported by the National Institutes of Health grants DA15450 and LM07292. This Human Brain Project/Neuroinformatics research is funded jointly by the National Library of Medicine and the National Institute of Mental Health.

References

1. Dykxhoorn, D. M., Novina, C. D., and Sharp, P. A. (2003) Killing the messenger: short RNAs that silence gene expression. *Nat. Rev. Mol. Cell Biol.* **4,** 457–467.
2. Bartel, D. P. (2004) MicroRNAs: genomics, biogenesis, mechanism, and function. *Cell* **116,** 281–297.
3. Ambros, V. (2004) The functions of animal microRNAs. *Nature* **431,** 350–355.
4. Lai, E. C. (2003) microRNAs: runts of the genome assert themselves. *Curr. Biol.* **13,** R925–936.
5. Llave, C., Xie, Z., Kasschau, K. D., and Carrington, J. C. (2002) Cleavage of Scarecrow-like mRNA targets directed by a class of Arabidopsis miRNA. *Science* **297,** 2053–2056.
6. Rhoades, M. W., Reinhart, B. J., Lim, L. P., Burge, C. B., Bartel, B., and Bartel, D. P. (2002) Prediction of plant microRNA targets. *Cell* **110,** 513–520.
7. Enright, A. J., John, B., Gaul, U., Tuschl, T., Sander, C., and Marks, D. S. (2003) MicroRNA targets in Drosophila. *Genome Biol.* **5,** R1.
8. Stark, A., Brennecke, J., Russell, R. B., and Cohen, S. M. (2003) Identification of Drosophila MicroRNA Targets. *PLOS Biol.* **1,** 397–409.
9. Rajewsky, N. and Socci, N. D. (2004) Computational identification of microRNA targets. *Dev. Biol.* **267,** 529–535.
10. Lewis, B. P., Shih, I. H., Jones-Rhoades, M. W., Bartel, D. P., and Burge, C. B. (2003) Prediction of mammalian microRNA targets. *Cell* **115,** 787–798.
11. Kiriakidou, M., Nelson, P. T., Kouranov, A., et al. (2004) A combined computational-experimental approach predicts human microRNA targets. *Genes Dev.* **18,** 1165–1178.
12. John, B., Enright, A. J., Aravin, A., Tuschl, T., Sander, C., and Marks, D. S. (2004) Human MicroRNA targets. *PLoS Biol.* **2,** e363.
13. Rehmsmeier, M., Steffen, P., Hochsmann, M., and Giegerich, R. (2004) Fast and effective prediction of microRNA/target duplexes. *RNA* **10,** 1507–1517.
14. Lewis, B. P., Burge, C. B., and Bartel, D. P. (2005) Conserved seed pairing, often flanked by adenosines, indicates that thousands of human genes are microRNA targets. *Cell* **120,** 15–20.
15. Brennecke, J., Stark, A., Russell, R. B., and Cohen, S. M. (2005) Principles of microRNA-target recognition. *PLoS Biol.* **3,** e85.
16. Doench, J. G. and Sharp, P. A. (2004) Specificity of microRNA target selection in translational repression. *Genes Dev.* **18,** 504–511.
17. Xie, X., Lu, J., Kulbokas, E. J., et al. (2005) Systematic discovery of regulatory motifs in human promoters and 3' UTRs by comparison of several mammals. *Nature* **434,** 338–345.
18. Smalheiser, N. R. and Torvik, V. I. (2004) A population-based statistical approach identifies parameters characteristic of human microRNA–mRNA interactions. *BMC Bioinformatics* **5,** 139.
19. Altschul, S. F., Madden, T. L., Schaffer, A. A., et al. (1997) Gapped BLAST and PSI-BLAST: a new generation of protein database search programs. *Nucleic Acids Res.* **25,** 3389–3402.

20. Yekta, S., Shih, I. H., and Bartel, D. P. (2004) MicroRNA-directed cleavage of HOXB8 mRNA. *Science* **304,** 594–596.
21. Seitz, H., Youngson, N., Lin, S. P., et al. (2003) Imprinted microRNA genes transcribed antisense to a reciprocally imprinted retrotransposon-like gene. *Nat. Genet.* **34,** 261–262.
22. Smalheiser, N. R. (2003) EST analyses predict the existence of a population of chimeric microRNA precursor–mRNA transcripts expressed in normal human and mouse tissues. *Genome Biol.* **4,** 403.
23. Miyagishi, M., Sumimoto, H., Miyoshi, H., Kawakami,Y., and Taira, K. (2004) Optimization of an siRNA-expression system with an improved hairpin and its significant suppressive effects in mammalian cells. *J. Gene Med.* **6,** 715–723.
24. Smalheiser, N. R. and Torvik, V. I. (2005) Mammalian microRNAs derived from genomic repeats. *Trends Genet.* **21,** 322–326.
25. Bohula, E. A., Salisbury, A. J., Sohail, M., et al. (2003) The efficacy of small interfering RNAs targeted to the type 1 insulin-like growth factor receptor (IGF1R) is influenced by secondary structure in the IGF1R transcript. *J. Biol. Chem.* **278,** 15,991–15,997.
26. Jing, Q., Huang, S., Guth, S., et al. (2005) Involvement of microRNA in AU-rich element-mediated mRNA instability. *Cell* **120,** 623–634.
27. Scadden, A. D. and Smith, C. W. (2001) RNAi is antagonized by A—>I hyper-editing. *EMBO Rep.* **2,** 1107–1111.
28. Pfeffer, S., Zavolan, M., Grasser, F. A., et al. (2004) Identification of virus-encoded microRNAs. *Science* **304,** 734–736.
29. Bennasser, Y., Le, S. Y., Yeung, M. L., and Jeang, K. T. (2004) HIV-1 encoded candidate micro-RNAs and their cellular targets. *Retrovirology* **1,** 43.
30. Pfeffer, S., Sewer, A., Lagos-Quintana, M., et al. (2005) Identification of microRNAs of the herpesvirus family. *Nat. Methods* **2,** 269–276.
31. Cai, X., Lu, S., Zhang, Z., Gonzalez, C. M., Damania, B., and Cullen, B. R. (2005) Kaposi's sarcoma-associated herpesvirus expresses an array of viral microRNAs in latently infected cells. *Proc. Natl. Acad. Sci. USA* **102,** 5570–5575.
32. Ambros, V., Lee, R. C., Lavanway, A., Williams, P. T., and Jewell, D. (2003) MicroRNAs and other tiny endogenous RNAs in C. elegans. *Curr. Biol.* **13,** 807–818.

10

miRBase

The MicroRNA Sequence Database

Sam Griffiths-Jones

Summary

The miRBase Sequence database is the primary repository for published microRNA (miRNA) sequence and annotation data. miRBase provides a user-friendly web interface for miRNA data, allowing the user to search using key words or sequences, trace links to the primary literature referencing the miRNA discoveries, analyze genomic coordinates and context, and mine relationships between miRNA sequences. miRBase also provides a confidential gene-naming service, assigning official miRNA names to novel genes before their publication. The methods outlined in this chapter describe these functions. miRBase is freely available to all at http://microrna.sanger.ac.uk/.

Key Words: MicroRNA; homolog; gene names; noncoding RNA.

1. Introduction

The miRBase Sequence database is the online repository for miRNA sequence information and annotation, hosted by the Wellcome Trust Sanger Institute. Its main goals are:

a. To provide a centralized, searchable database of all published miRNA sequence information and annotation.
b. To provide researchers with consistent names for novel miRNA gene discoveries before publication, while maintaining privacy of unpublished data.

miRBase rationalizes data and functionality previously provided by the miRNA Registry *(1)* in "miRBase Sequences," provides an miRNA gene nomenclature and naming function in "miRBase Registry," and is expanded to include data on predicted miRNA target genes in "miRBase Targets." Functionality of the miRBase Target database is currently under active development using recently published methods *(2,3)* and will be described elsewhere.

From: *Methods in Molecular Biology, vol. 342: MicroRNA Protocols*
Edited by: S. Ying © Humana Press Inc., Totowa, NJ

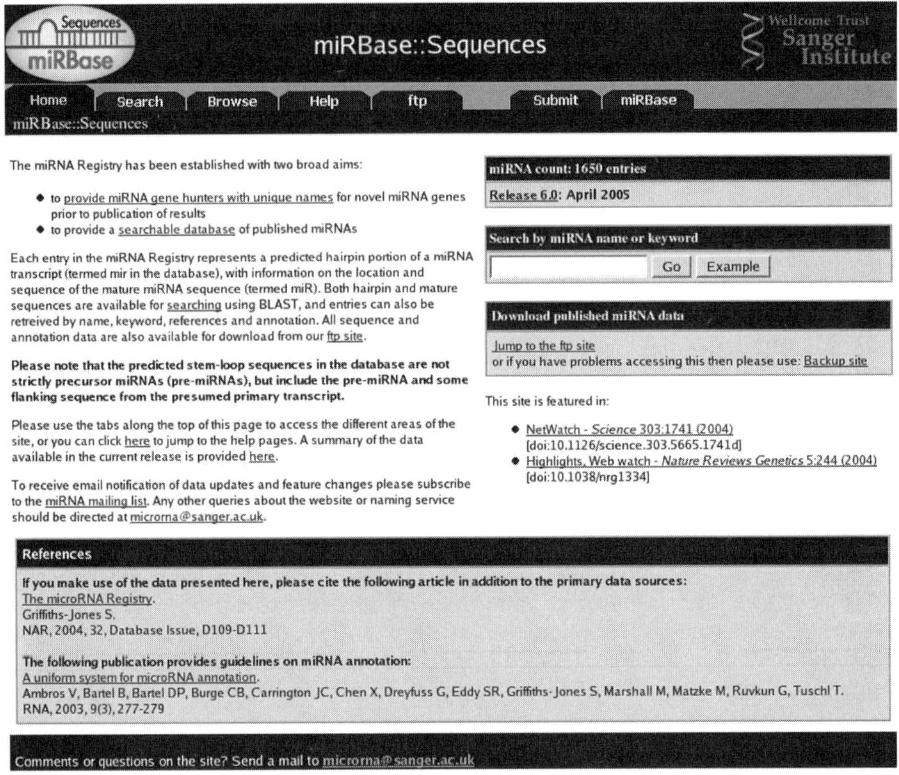

Fig. 1. miRBase Sequence front page. Tabs for navigation to the main areas of the site are provided along the top.

The database is available for web-based browsing and searching at http://microrna.sanger.ac.uk/, and can be downloaded for local installation and querying from our FTP site (ftp://ftp.sanger.ac.uk/pub/mirbase). Please note that the data and protocols discussed in this chapter are current as of miRBase Sequence release 6.0 in May 2005. The design and format of the web pages described in this chapter and shown in **Figs. 1–3** is subject to change, but the core data concepts and formats are largely stable.

It may be useful to understand the core miRBase data structure and the concept of an entry before examining the methods in this chapter. These principles are briefly described in **Note 1** *(1)*.

2. Materials

Methods presented in this chapter deal with both web-based functionality and installing the data for manipulation in your local environment. The website has further help pages and resources that should be referred to alongside this guide.

Matches for your nucleotide sequence

miRNA	Query Start	Query End	Subject Start	Subject End	Strand	Bits score	Evalue	Alignment
gga-mir-15a	9	84	9	82	+	206	3.9e-06	Align
hsa-mir-15a	1	84	1	82	+	203	5.4e-06	Align
mmu-mir-15a	1	80	2	81	+	197	9.9e-06	Align
hsa-mir-15b	8	69	14	75	+	114	0.048	Align
rno-mir-15b	8	32	14	38	+	107	0.099	Align
mmu-mir-15b	11	32	1	22	+	92	0.72	Align

Alignment of Query to hairpin miRNAs

▶Alignment of Query to gga-mir-15a

```
UserSeq      9 UACUGUAGCAGCACAGAAUGGUUUGUGAGUUAUAACGGGGGUGCAGGCCGUACUGUGCUGCGGCAACAACGACAGG  84
               ||  |||||||||||  |||||||||||  |||  |  |    ||  |||||||| || ||||||||  ||| ||  |||  |
gga-mir-15a  9 UAACGUAGCAGCACAUAAUGGUUUGUGGGGUUUUGAAAAGG-UGCAGGCCAUAUUGUGCUGCCUCAAAAAU-ACAAG  82
```

▶Alignment of Query to hsa-mir-15a

```
UserSeq      1 CCUGUCG-GUACUGUAGCAGCACAGAAUGGUUUGUGAGUUAUAACGGGGGUGCAGGCCGUACUGUGCUGCGGCAACAACGACAGG  84
               ||| | | |||  |||||||||||  |||||||||||  || | |   || |||||||| || ||||||||  ||| ||  |||  |
hsa-mir-15a  1 CCU-UGGAGUAAAGUAGCAGCACAUAAUGGUUUGUGGAUUUUGAAAAGG-UGCAGGCCAUAUUGUGCUGCCUCAAAAAU-ACAAG  82
```

▶Alignment of Query to mmu-mir-15a

```
UserSeq      1 CCUGUCG-GUACUGUAGCAGCACAGAAUGGUUUGUGAGUUAUAACGGGGGUGCAGGCCGUACUGUGCUGCGGCAACA-ACGA  80
               ||| | | |||  |||||||||||  |||||||||||  | | |   || |||||||| |||||||||||  ||| | ||  |
mmu-mir-15a  2 CCU-UGGAGUAAAGUAGCAGCACAUAAUGGUUUGUGGAUGUUGAAAAGG-UGCAGGCCAUACUGUGCUGCCUCAAAAUACAA  81
```

▶Alignment of Query to hsa-mir-15b

```
UserSeq      8 GUACUGUAGCAGCACAGAAUGGUUUGUGAGUUAUAACGGGGGUGC-AGGCCGUACUGUGCUGC  69
               ||||||||||||||||  |||||||  | ||| |  | ||| |  || |  || | ||||||
hsa-mir-15b 14 GUACUGUAGCAGCACAUCAUGGUUUACAUGCUACAGUCAAGAUGCGAAUCAUUAUU-UGCUGC  75
```

▶Alignment of Query to rno-mir-15b

```
UserSeq      8 GUACUGUAGCAGCACAGAAUGGUUU  32
               |||||||||||||||||  |||||||
rno-mir-15b 14 GUACUGUAGCAGCACAUCAUGGUUU  38
```

▶Alignment of Query to mmu-mir-15b

```
UserSeq     11 CUGUAGCAGCACAGAAUGGUUU  32
               ||||||||||||||  |||||||
mmu-mir-15b  1 CUGUAGCAGCACAUCAUGGUUU  22
```

Fig. 2. Results of searching a query sequence against the database hairpin precursor sequences using BLASTN. A summary of the results is shown in the table, followed by alignments of the query sequence to each hit.

2.1. Web-Based Protocols

a. A computer with an internet connection.
b. Sequences of interest (optional).

2.2. For Local Installation

The miRNA sequence and annotation data underlying the website is held in a MySQL relational database. MySQL table dumps are provided on the FTP site for ease of local database creation, but the data should be portable to other relational databases, such as ORACLE, POSTGRES, SQLSERVER, and many others.

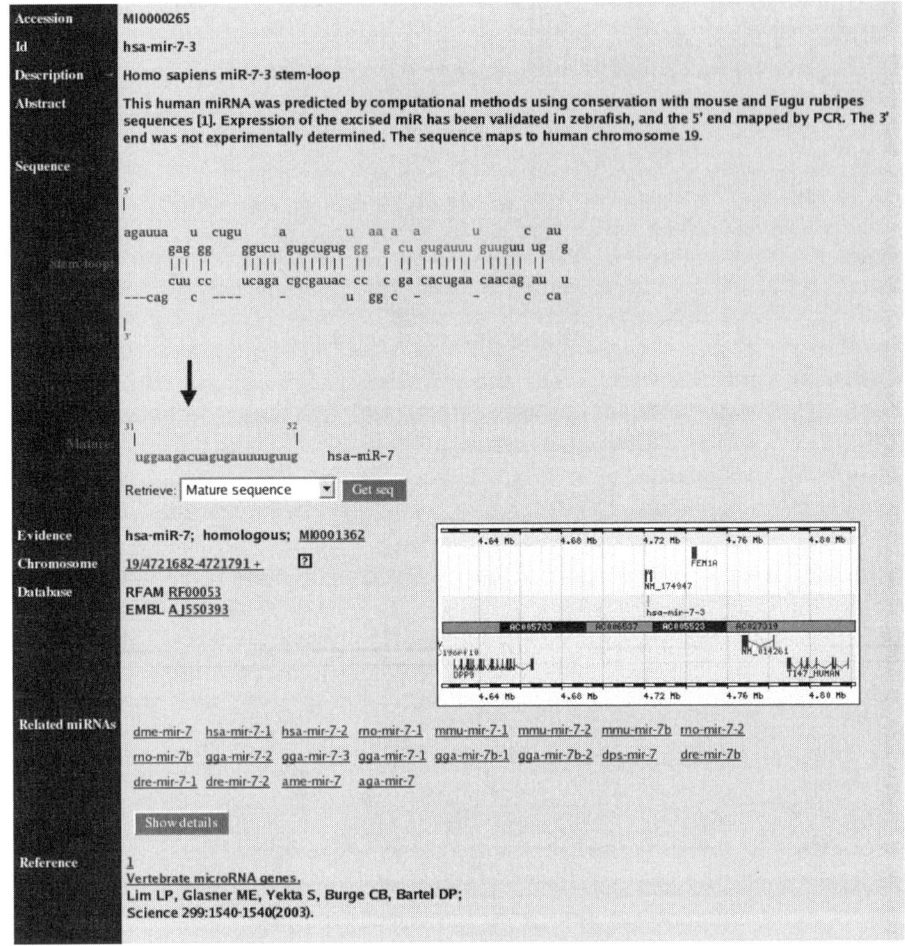

Fig. 3. The entry page for hsa-mir-7-3, showing the hairpin flanking regions, mature sequence, annotation, and genomic context.

a. miRBase release files, described in **Note 2** (ftp://ftp.sanger.ac.uk/pub/mirbase/sequences/).
b. MySQL (http://www.mysql.com/).
c. Sequence similarity software, such as basic local alignment search tool (BLAST) (http://www.ncbi.nlm.nih.gov/BLAST/; http://blast.wustl.edu/) or FASTA (ftp://ftp.virginia.edu/pub/fasta/).

3. Methods

The methods presented in this chapter describe how to use the miRBase web interface to locate an miRNA sequence entry by browsing (*see* **Subheading 3.1.**) or by searching by gene name, key word, or sequence (*see* **Subheading 3.2.**), and take the user through the information that is available for each miRNA entry (*see* **Subheading 3.3.**). **Sub-**

heading 3.4. describes how to install a local copy of the data in a MySQL relational database.

3.1. Browsing the Published miRNA Gene List

Figure 1 shows the miRBase Sequence main page. Tabs along the top navigate to different sections of the database.

1. Click the "Browse" link to view a list of organisms.
2. Choose an organism of interest from the tree shown. Click the "+" icons to view a list of sequences. For example, choose the *"Homo sapiens"* link to see a list of all known miRNAs in human. At the time of writing, the table contains 227 entries. The columns show the miRNA name (*see* **Note 3** for more information), the chromosomal coordinates in the latest genome assembly (chromosome, start, end, and strand), followed by the lengths of the stem-loop hairpin and the mature sequence.
3. Click the miRNA name to view detailed information regarding that miRNA on the entry page, which is described in detail in **Subheading 3.3.**
4. From the browse page, click one or more tick box in the "Get Sequence" column to retrieve sequences from the database—stem-loop flanking regions or mature sequences may be selected from the drop-down menus at the bottom of the page. Choose unaligned FASTA sequences or CLUSTALW aligned multiple sequences and click the "Fetch Sequences" button. miRNAs from multiple organisms may be viewed and selected for retrieval simultaneously.

3.2. Searching the miRBase Sequence Database

The miRBase Sequence database may be queried online by a variety of methods.

1. Navigate to the search page using the "Search" tab in the navigation bar. The results of all searches are shown in tabular form as in the "Browse" tables described in **Subheading 3.1.**

    a. Input an miRNA name, accession number, or key word into the "By identifier or key word" section of the search page. The tick boxes allow restriction of the search to particular fields, including miRNA gene names, literature references, and evidence.
    b. The search "By genomic location" portion of the search page allows the user to ask for all miRNAs located between 1 Mb and 2 Mb on chromosome 1 in human, for example. Use the drop-down menus to choose an organism, chromosome, and start and end coordinates.
    c. The search "By sequence" section of the search page allows the user to search a query sequence for relationships with known miRNAs. Paste your sequence in the box provided, choose your options on the right, and click "Search." Searches for both mature miRNAs and stem-loop flanking regions are available. Use BLASTN to search a longer sequence for the presence of miRNA homologs. SSEARCH is available to search for shorter sequences or motifs in the library of miRNA sequences. *See* **Note 4** for a note on scores and E-values. **Figure 2** shows the results page for a typical BLASTN search of a query sequence for miRNA homologs. The table summarizes the results, followed by views of the alignments of the query sequence against the miRNA hits.

3.3. Finding Information Regarding a Specific miRNA

The miRNA entry page is the central source of information regarding any given miRNA, accessible by clicking an miRNA gene name or accession number from any page. An example entry page is shown in **Fig. 3**. The page contains accession and name information, together with a short description of contextual and functional information. The structure of the stem-loop precursor is shown, and links to external databases and literature references are provided. Specific functions available from the entry page are described:

1. Click the "Get sequence" button to retrieve the mature or precursor sequence in FASTA format.
2. Click the genome coordinates to view the genomic context of the miRNA gene locus in the EnsEMBL genome browser (http://www.ensembl.org/) *(4)*.
3. The "Related miRNAs" section of the entry page expands into a table of miRNAs with significant sequence similarity to the current entry. The table contains the same information and sequence retrieval options as the browse table described in **Subheading 3.1.**
4. The "evidence" section of the entry page references the evidence for the miRNA discovery. Each mature miRNA may have "experimental" evidence, in the form of a cloning experiment or Northern blot, for example, or it may be homologous to a verified miRNA in another organism.
5. The literature references link to the PUBMED database to enable retrieval of the primary articles discovering, validating, and characterizing the miRNA.

3.4. Submitting Novel miRNAs for the Assignment of Gene Names

The miRBase Registry provides a straightforward web form for submission of miRNA sequences for the assignment of names. Please note that stable gene names are assigned after a publication describing their discovery has been accepted for publication, but before the final proofs are returned. This takes advantage of the peer review process to ensure that sequences meet miRNA annotation guidelines *(1,5)* and minimizes the gaps in the naming scheme caused by unpublished data. **Note 3** has more information regarding miRNA gene nomenclature.

1. Navigate to the miRBase Registry page (http://microrna.sanger.ac.uk/registry/).
2. Complete the sections on the web form, including the sequences for both the mature miRNA and their flanking precursor regions.
3. Names are assigned in consultation with the author by email.

3.5. Installing a Local Copy of the MySQL Database

Some users may require local access to the miRNA data available in miRBase, for large-scale sequence searching or for complex and customized queries. All data are available for download from the FTP site (ftp://ftp.sanger.ac.uk/pub/mirbase/sequences/), and may then be subject to many different analyses. For example, the FASTA format sequence files hairpin.fa and mature.fa allow the user to use standard sequence similarity algorithms, such as BLAST or FASTA, to find homologs of the known miRNAs in a query sequence, such as an unannotated completed genome sequence. Refer to the documentation for such sequence search algorithms for more information (*see* for example http://blast.wustl.edu/ and http://www.ncbi.nlm.nih.gov/BLAST/).

This protocol demonstrates how to install a local copy of the data in a MySQL relational database. This method assumes that you have MySQL installed, and that you have permission to create databases and tables and upload data. Some understanding of computing and informatics is required, and this method should be considered significantly more advanced than **Subheadings 3.1.** to **3.4.** The commands shown here are for example use only—refer to the database documentation (for example http://www.mysql.com/) for more information.

1. Download the miRBase release files. In particular, you require the database dump files in the database_files directory on the FTP site.
2. Unzip each of the rdb_TABLENAME.dat.gz files.
3. Start the mysql client with a command like: mysql –u <user> -h <host> -p.
4. At the mysql prompt, create a database with a command such as: create database microrna.
5. Run each create table command stored in the tables.sql file by pasting them at the mysql prompt.
6. Upload each of the rdb_TABLENAME.dat files to the correct table with a command such as: load data infile '/DIR/rdb_TABLENAME.dat' into table TABLENAME; replace TABLENAME with the name of the each table in turn. DIR should be replaced with the full path to the downloaded files.

The data are now available for a wide range of local queries, including any question that the web interface allows. Because the database schema is subject to change, a list of up-to-date example queries is shown in the help section on the website.

4. Notes

1. Each entry in the database is based on a genomic locus, and represents the stem-loop portion of the primary transcript, which includes the hairpin precursor product of Drosha cleavage. Every entry has a name, of the form hsa-mir-142. The nomenclature is explained in detail in **Note 3.** In addition, each entry has a unique accession number. The accession number is the only truly stable identifier for an entry—miRNA names may change from those published as relationships between sequences become clear. The advantage of the accessioned system is that such changes can be tracked in the database allowing names to evolve to remain consistent, and providing the user with full access to the data and history. However, accession numbers convey little biological meaning, and it is expected that miRNAs are referred to by name in publications.

   The end functional product of miRNA biogenesis (reviewed in **ref. 6**), the mature miRNA (termed miR), is processed from the stem-loop sequence represented by a database entry. One precursor may give rise to two mature miRNAs, and one mature miRNA may be processed from more than one precursor. Mature miR sequences also have a name (*see* **Note 3**) and an accession number.

   The database contains data from two fundamental sources: miRNAs that have been experimentally verified (for instance, by cloning), and those that are homologs of known miRNAs. For example, the database contains many miRNA sequences that have been experimentally confirmed in mouse, and their human homologs, which are often easily identified by sequence search methods. miRBase does not currently contain predicted sequences without experimental evidence. Every mature miRNA has an evidence tag with its evidence type, source, and literature reference if applicable.

2. Every miRBase Sequence database release contains the sequence and annotation data in various formats. These files are available from the FTP site (ftp://ftp.sanger.ac.uk/pub/mirbase/sequences/). The README file available from this address contains important up-to-date information regarding format changes and differences between releases.

```
ID   cel-mir-1              standard; RNA; CEL; 96 BP.
XX
AC   MI0000003;
XX
DE   Caenorhabditis elegans miR-1 stem-loop
XX
RN   [1]
RX   PUBMED; 11679671.
RA   Lau NC, Lim LP, Weinstein EG, Bartel DP;
RT   "An abundant class of tiny RNAs with probable regulatory roles in
RT   Caenorhabditis elegans";
RL   Science 294:858-862(2001).
XX
RN   [2]
RX   PUBMED; 11679672.
RA   Lee RC, Ambros V;
RT   "An extensive class of small RNAs in Caenorhabditis elegans";
RL   Science 294:862-864(2001).
XX
RN   [3]
RX   PUBMED; 11679670.
RA   Lagos-Quintana M, Rauhut R, Lendeckel W, Tuschl T;
RT   "Identification of novel genes coding for small expressed RNAs";
RL   Science 294:853-858(2001).
XX
DR   EMBL; AJ487556; .
DR   RFAM; RF00103; mir-1.
DR   WORMBASE; T09B4/23107-23012; .
XX
CC   miR-1 was independently identified in C. elegans [1,2] and Drosophila
CC   melanogaster (MIR:MI0000116) [3].  The sequence is also conserved in C.
CC   briggsae (MIR:MI0000493).  miR-1 maps to chromosome I in C. elegans.
XX
FH   Key             Location/Qualifiers
FH
FT   miRNA           61..81
FT                   /product="cel-miR-1"
FT                   /accession="MIMAT0000003"
FT                   /evidence=experimental
FT                   /experiment="cloned [1-2], Northern [1]"
XX
SQ   Sequence 96 BP; 32 A; 16 C; 23 G; 0 T; 25 other;
     aaagugaccg uaccgagcug cauacuuccu uacaugccca uacuauauca uaaauggaua       60
     uggaauguaa agaaguaugu agaacggggu gguagu                                 96
//
```

Fig. 4. The full representation of a microRNA entry from the miRNA.dat file.

a. The miRNA.dat file contains (almost) all of the data in the database. The format is based on the EMBL database distribution format; a single entry from the file is shown in **Fig. 4**. Each line has a tag; for example, the AC line contains the miRNA entry accession, the CC lines contain comments, the R lines contain literature references, and the SQ lines contain the nucleotide sequence. Of particular note are the FT (feature table) lines, which contain information regarding the mature miRNA sequence(s) for the entry. In the example shown in **Fig. 4**, nucleotides 61 to 81 of the hairpin precursor entry represent the derived mature miRNA sequence named cel-miR-1, accession number MIMAT 0000003. This mature sequence is experimentally verified by cloning and Northern blot. For more information about this file format, please see the miRBase help files and the EMBL distribution documentation (http://www.ebi.ac.uk/embl/).

b. Stem-loop precursor flanking regions and the mature miR sequences are available FASTA format in the hairpin.fa and mature.fa files. These files are ready for indexing and searching using search algorithms, such as BLAST.

```
hsa-miR-302a  UAAGUGCUUCCAUGUUUUGGUGA
hsa-miR-302b  UAAGUGCUUCCAUGUUUUAGUAG
hsa-miR-302c  UAAGUGCUUCCAUGUUUCAGUGG
hsa-miR-302d  UAAGUGCUUCCAUGUUUGAGUGU
```

Fig. 5. Multiple sequence alignment of four related mature miRNA sequences. Darker shaded boxes represent more conserved bases.

   c. Genome coordinates for all miRNA sequences are available in GFF format in the genomes directory. The genome assembly versions used are kept up-to-date with those in the ENSEMBL genome database (http://www.ensembl.org/).

   d. All data are also available as MySQL table dumps ready for import into a relational database (as described in **Subheading 3.5.**). The format of these data is particularly prone to change, but the tables.sql file provided should always reflect these changes.

3. Criteria and conventions for miRNA identification and naming have been published *(5)*. miRNA gene names are of the form mir-143. The numbering is simply sequential. miRBase also includes a three letter organism abbreviation in the name, derived, if possible, from the first letter of the genus and the first two of the species, thus, hsa-mir-143 refers to human (Homo sapiens) mir-143.

In miRBase and much of the primary literature, the approx 22-nucleotide mature product is designated miR-143. Names of the form mir-143 are used to refer to the precursor hairpin that is the product of Drosha cleavage, and also the gene (when it is usually italicized: *mir-143*). These conventions have some use when rigorously applied, but it is unwise to rely on such subtleties to convey meaning. For clarity, the primary miRNA transcript is sometimes explicitly called pri-mir-143 and the precursor hairpin pre-mir-143.

Cleavage of the mature miRNA from the precursor produces a double-stranded complex of the miRNA with the base-paired sequence from the opposite arm of the hairpin, called the miR* sequence *(6)*. The miR* sequence is generally discarded, but is sometimes detected in cloning studies. Sometimes it is unclear which arm of the precursor hairpin gives rise to the functional product, and in some cases, two functional miRNAs may result. Sequences arising from the 5' and 3' arms of the precursor hairpin have been named miR-142-5p and miR-142-3p, respectively.

Names are also used to encode rudimentary information about relationships between sequences. Orthologous miRNAs in different organisms are assigned the same number; at the time of writing, the database contains entries named hsa-mir-143, mmu-mir-143 (*Mus musculus*) and rno-mir-143 (*Rattus novegicus*). Identical mature miRNAs may be expressed from more than one genomic locus (and hairpin precursor). The loci are then named mir-143-1 and mir-143-2. Lettered suffixes are used to denote closely related mature miRNAs from the same organism. For example, **Fig. 5** shows a multiple sequence alignment of four mature miRNAs, named miR-302a, -b, -c, and -d. It is important to note that names cannot encode complex relationships between sequences. The web pages contain information regarding related sequences (*see* **Subheading 3.3.**), and allow searchs of any sequence to find homologs (*see* **Subheading 3.2.**).

Plant miRNAs adopt a slightly different nomenclature: precursor sequences have names of the form MIR156a, and lettered suffixes are used for all loci that give rise to identical and closely related mature miRNA products.

A few exceptions to the numbering scheme exist; let-7 and lin-4 are obvious examples. Novel miRNAs from well-characterized loci are sometimes published with names related to these loci. *See*, for example, bantam miRNA, and mir-iab-4 from *Drosophila melanogaster*.

4. The results of sequence similarity searches using software such as BLAST *(7)* or FASTA *(8)*, as used on the website and described in **Subheading 3.2.**, include scores to judge the significance of each hit. These scores warrant a short discussion when applied to searching query sequences for miRNA relationships.

   Figure 2 shows the results of a BLASTN search of a query sequence against hairpin miRNA sequences. For each hit, a raw score and an E-value are reported. These values are those reported by the sequence search algorithm. The higher the raw score, the more significant the match. The E-value gives some measure of the statistical significance of the score, taking into account the chances that the sequences match by chance. A lower E-value indicates a more significant match. Typically, an E-value of less than 0.01 might be considered a significant match. Shorter query sequences and matches to the target contain less information, leading to a lower raw score (and higher E-value). Mature, approx 22-nucleotide sequences contain very little information, and the search algorithms are not designed to work with such short sequences. Therefore, when searching for miRNA homologs in large sequences, it is important to use the miRNA precursor flanking sequence to increase confidence in the results. The facility to search just the mature sequence can be useful, but it is important not to overinterpret the statistics of such hits. For more information regarding search statistics, *see* **refs.** *9* and *10*.

Acknowledgments

This work is funded by the Wellcome Trust. The miRBase authors are keen to hear from users with suggestions for improvement of both the data and the web interface. This feedback and any questions should be directed to microrna@sanger.ac.uk.

References

1. Griffiths-Jones, S. (2004) The microRNA Registry. *Nucleic Acids Res.* **32,** D109–D111.
2. Enright, A. J., John, B., Gaul, U., Tuschl, T., Sander, C., and Marks, D. S. (2003) MicroRNA targets in Drosophila. *Genome Biol.* **5,** R1.
3. John, B., Enright, A. J., Aravin, A., Tuschl, T., Sander, C., and Marks, D. S. (2004) Human microRNA targets. *PLoS Biol.* **2,** e363.
4. Hubbard, T., Andrews, D., Caccamo, M., et al. (2005) Ensembl 2005. *Nucleic Acids Res.* **33,** D447–D453.
5. Ambros, V., Bartel, B., Bartel, D. P., et al. (2003) A uniform system for microRNA annotation. *RNA* **9,** 277–279.
6. Bartel, D. P. (2004) MicroRNAs: genomics, biogenesis, mechanism, and function. *Cell* **116,** 281–297.
7. Altschul, S. F., Madden, T. L., Schaffer, A. A., et al. (1997) Gapped BLAST and PSI-BLAST: a new generation of protein database search programs. *Nucleic Acids Res.* **25,** 3389–3402.
8. Pearson, W. R. (2000) Flexible sequence similarity searching with the FASTA3 program package. *Methods Mol. Biol.* **132,** 185–219.
9. Durbin, R., Eddy, S., Krogh, A., and Mitchison, G. (1998) *Biological Sequence Analysis: Probabilistic Models of Proteins and Nucleic Acids.* Cambridge University Press, Cambridge, UK.
10. Korf, I., Yandell, M., and Bedell, J. (2003) *BLAST.* O'Reilly & Associates, Sebastopol, CA.

Methodologies for High-Throughput Expression Profiling of MicroRNAs

Paz Einat

Summary

MicroRNAs (miRNAs) have recently emerged as important regulators of gene expression controlling central biological processes. These small, approx 22-nucleotide (nt)-long RNA molecules induce translational suppression when they are imperfectly matched to their target messenger RNA (mRNA) or direct mRNA cleavage when perfectly, or nearly perfectly, matched to their target. Direct roles in developmental processes have been described in a variety of species, and involvement in human diseases, such as cancer and diabetes, has been implied. These studies highlight the need to obtain detailed expression profiles of miRNAs in tissues, during development, and in disease. Their small size and the existence of miRNA families of related sequences pose critical problems in approaching expression analysis of miRNAs, especially using high-throughput approaches. All methodologies presented here address the special requirements for the analysis of miRNA expression using a variety of platforms, including cloning, microarrays, and microbeads. The different variables, as well as the different approaches, used by various laboratories are detailed and general recommendations are provided.

Key Words: MicroRNA; microarray; high-throughput; expression profiling; microbead; real-time RT-PCR.

1. Introduction

Since the initial observation of sequence-specific gene silencing by the introduction of double-stranded RNA into *Caenorhabditis elegans (1)*, the phenomena of RNA interference has been widely studied and used. In parallel to the enormous popularity of artificial RNA as specific gene silencers in a wide variety of species, a novel group of endogenous regulators of gene expression, the miRNAs, has been discovered. The first miRNA to be discovered was the *lin-4* miRNA *(2)* followed, after a 7-yr delay, by the identification of *let-7 (3)*. These miRNAs are heterochronic switching genes essential for the normal temporal control of diverse developmental events in the roundworm *C. elegans*. Only after the discovery of *let-7*, and the identification of fly and human

From: *Methods in Molecular Biology, vol. 342: MicroRNA Protocols*
Edited by: S. Ying © Humana Press Inc., Totowa, NJ

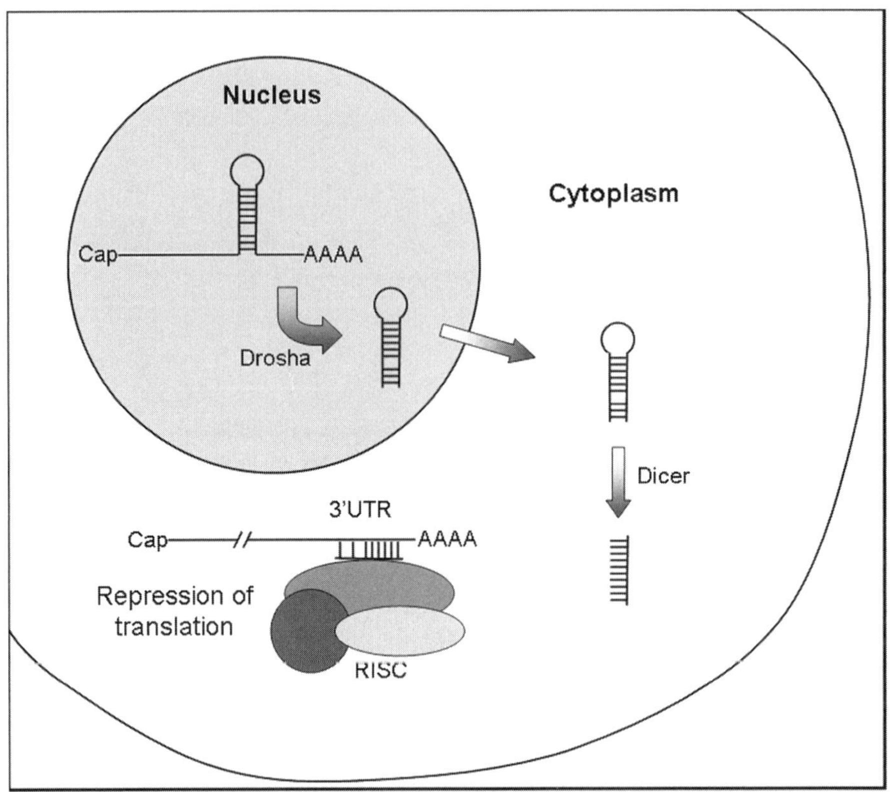

Fig. 1. MicroRNA biogenesis.

let-7 homologs *(4)*, did it gradually become clear that there are many miRNA genes and that they are not unique to lower organisms but actually exist in all multicellular organisms examined to date, from worms up to humans. In humans, the number of miRNAs in the central miRNA database, the miRBase at the Sanger Center (http://microrna.sanger. ac.uk/sequences/index.shtml), is 326, with similar numbers in the genomes of other mammals. Although these are experimentally verified miRNAs, several studies suggest that the number is much higher *(5–7)*, probably approaching 1000 miRNA genes in the human genome. This also suggests that the number of miRNA genes in nonmammalian and nonvertebrate organisms is much higher then known today. There are several excellent reviews and theoretical papers on all aspects of miRNA biology *(8–17)* that can provide more details on this highly interesting group of genes.

miRNAs are derived by a two-step process from long, type II RNA polymerase-transcribed, primary miRNA transcripts that are capped and polyadenylated *(18)* (**Fig. 1**). First, the primary miRNA transcripts are processed in the nucleus into 60- to 120-nt-long hairpin structures (precursor miRNA) by the ribonuclease (RNase) III enzyme, Drosha *(19)*. This processing step is thought to be mediated by Microprocessor *(20,21)*, a multiunit complex that contains the Drosha enzyme. The precursor miRNAs are then transported to the cytoplasm, where they are processed into 18- to 25-nt mature miRNAs by the RNAse III enzyme, Dicer *(22,23)*. One of the strands is then incorporated into the RNA-induced silencing complex, which mediates miRNA activity.

The miRNAs exert their suppressive function by binding to complementary sites on target mRNAs (mainly on the 3' untranslated region) and either cleaving the mRNA or suppressing its translation *(8)*. Cleavage takes place when the miRNAs have perfect or nearly perfect complementarities to their target. This was found mainly in plants *(24)*, but one example was observed in mammals *(25)*. Most miRNAs, however, are not perfectly complementary to their binding sites and regulate gene expression by suppressing translation. It should be noted, however, that it was recently suggested that mRNA levels are also reduced *(26)*.

miRNA regulation influences a variety of central biological processes in many different organisms. This includes a variety of developmental processes, cell growth, differentiation, apoptosis, and metabolism in organisms as varied as worms, insects, plants, and mammals (reviewed in **refs.** *8* and *10*). More recently, miRNA involvement in insulin secretion and adipocyte differentiation in mammals was reported *(27,28)*, suggesting important functions in clinically relevant biological systems. Reports on the possible involvement of miRNAs in cancer started to appear in 2002, reporting deletion or downregulation of specific miRNAs in cancer cells *(29)*. This was followed by many additional reports showing mainly reduced expression of a variety of miRNAs in various cancer types *(30–33)*, but also elevated expression of other miRNAs *(34,35)*. More recently, it was shown that miRNA expression profiles can be uniquely used to classify several human cancers *(36)*. Although the exact biological role of miRNAs in cancer is unknown, it was recently shown that some miRNAs are regulated by *c-Myc*, a gene whose dysregulation or function is one of the most common abnormalities in human malignancy. These miRNAs, in turn, were shown to negatively regulate the transcription factor E2F1, a promoter of cell cycle progression, which is in itself a target of *c-Myc* *(37)*. An even more direct study has shown that one of the miRNA clusters functioned as an oncogene and accelerated tumor development in a mouse B-cell lymphoma model *(35)*.

The involvement of miRNAs in such a vast array of biological processes, both normal and abnormal, indicates that reliable methodologies for high-throughput expression profiling of miRNAs are essential in the study of miRNA function. Several approaches have been used to profile miRNA expression. These include miRNA cloning, microarray analysis, microbead expression analysis, and other approaches. In this chapter I detail each approach, examine the various modes undertaken by different groups when applicable, and analyze the pros and cons of each approach. The use of microarrays has been the most popular approach, and eight articles and work from two companies have attempted to develop robust protocols for miRNA expression profiling. Thus, a major part of this chapter is dedicated to description of the efforts in the microarray platform.

The small size of the miRNAs requires special consideration in approaching high-throughput analysis of their expression. Additionally, the existence of miRNA families in which the members have high sequence similarity complicates matters even more. Therefore, every methodology must withstand strong scrutiny regarding its specificity. Only then comes the issue of sensitivity, namely, the relation between the amount of starting material and the signal obtained.

2. Working With miRNAs: General Technical Issues

In almost all applications of miRNAs, a size fractionation step is implemented. This step is mostly performed by separation using denaturing polyacrylamide gel electrophoresis (PAGE). A recent advance in the field is the flashPAGE™ fractionator developed by Ambion (http://www.ambion.com/catalog/ProdGrp.html?fkApp=29&fkSubApp=175&fkProdGrp=353). This device is a miniaturized electrophoresis instrument designed for rapid PAGE purification of small nucleic acids. Another option is the use of column or filter-based devices, such as that available in the mirVANA miRNA isolation kit from Ambion that isolates RNAs of approx 200 nt or fewer, using a modified glass fiber filter.

miRNAs have the hallmarks of RNAse III cleavage: they have 5'-phosphate and 3'-OH groups. This is in contrast to RNAs cleaved by other enzymes, which produce 5'-OH and 3'-phosphate groups. This feature is used to differentiate miRNAs from degradation products of mRNAs or other RNAs. Thus, a combination of size fractionation and ligation of adaptors to the unique ends (**Fig. 2**) is used in most applications to enrich the RNA population for miRNAs.

3. miRNA Expression Profiling Methodologies

3.1. miRNA Expression Profiling by Cloning and Sequencing

The realization that small RNAs are actually abundant in the cells, and that there are numerous miRNAs in many organisms, stemmed from the pioneering works from the laboratories of Tuschl, Ambros, and Bartel *(38–40)*. Later on, the massive cloning efforts in the Tuschl lab were also carried out to obtain expression profiles of the miRNAs *(41–43)*. This was achieved by establishing libraries from a variety of tissues and developmental stages. The small RNAs from each library were sequenced and the number of times each miRNA appeared in the library was noted.

The cloning of small RNAs is achieved by ligating adaptors to both ends of the RNA molecules using T4 RNA ligase (**Fig. 2**). This is followed by reverse transcription and derivation of a double-stranded complementary DNA (cDNA) library. For cloning, the molecules are first concatenated, and only then ligated into the plasmid vector *(38, 39)*. Thus, each sequenced plasmid contains several copies of the small RNAs and each sequencing reaction provides sequence data of several different molecules.

The greatest advantage of "expression profiling by cloning" is in its accuracy regarding miRNA identity. There are several known miRNA families, with members showing high sequence similarity with differences of only 1 nt between some members. Thus, direct sequencing provides the highest accuracy. Another advantage is that knowledge of the miRNAs sequences is not a requirement. This can be a significant consideration when approaching analysis of organisms never studied before and for which no genomic information exists.

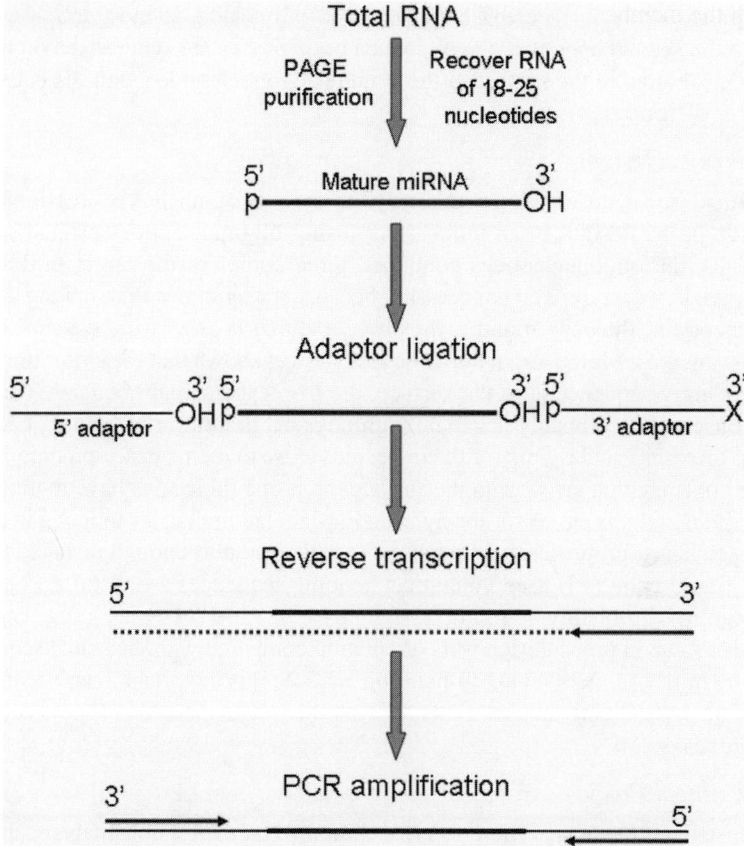

Fig. 2. Preparation of microRNA-enriched complementary DNA libraries.

The major disadvantages of the method are in its low speed, low sensitivity, and low cost effectiveness. The construction of the libraries is a lengthy procedure and many thousands of sequencing reactions must be performed on each library to obtain enough data. The low sensitivity stems from the fact that, even with thousands of sequencing reactions, the highly expressed miRNAs are represented by only tens of clones. One of the reasons is that the percentage of miRNAs in the libraries is relatively low, usually in the range of 5 to 20%.

3.2. Microarray Analysis

The adaptation of microarray analysis to profile miRNA expression is not straightforward. Several technical obstacles had to be dealt with and the questions of specificity and sensitivity critically examined. To this end, two variants of the microarray platform were used: fabricated (printed) microarrays and *in situ* synthesized microarrays. The first requires standard synthesis of the selected oligonucleotide probes that are then printed on the array surface and bound to it, usually at the 5' end through an amino group. In the second approach, the oligonucleotide probes are synthesized on the array and are thus bound to the surface at the 3' end (oligonucleotide synthesis is carried in the 3' to 5' direction).

3.2.1. Probe Design

The first issue in designing a microarray for analysis of miRNA expression is oligonucleotide probe design. In an initial study using oligonucleotides printed on nylon membranes, the oligonucleotides contained three copies of the target miRNA *(44)*. This design, however, proved unnecessary because it was shown that, in long (~60mer) oligonucleotides, the copy found at the probe end that is away from the surface is the most relevant *(45)*. Moreover, in the same study it was shown that the closer the miRNA complementary sequence is to the surface, the lower the signal obtained. The reason for this observation probably has to do with physical hindrance of binding because of the close proximity and rigidity of the molecules close to their surface-binding position. One can envisage that away from the surface the probe molecules have more freedom of movement and it is easier for the hybridizing-labeled molecules to move in and find their target. Thus, probe design must make sure that there is enough distance from the surface. Barad et al. *(45)* used nonhuman genome sequences as a "stuffer," but other linkers can most probably be used.

Another issue in probe design is its orientation compared with the actual sequence of the mature miRNAs. As seen in **Subheading 3.2.3.2.**, it is important to ensure the orientation of the hybridizing-labeled material. This then determines the desired orientation of the probes.

3.2.2. Control Probes

Because the issue of specificity is critical in miRNA expression analysis, the use of proper controls can increase the confidence of data analysis. The most basic control probes are for abundant RNAs, such as transfer RNAs and ribosomal RNAs. These controls would show how much of these RNAs exist in the hybridizing-labeled material. More important control probes are mismatch controls. Much like the probes in the Affimetrix GeneChips, which include mismatch controls in nucleotide 13 on the 25-mer probes to ensure hybridization specificity, similar types of controls can significantly increase confidence in data interpretation. The most extensive mismatch controls were used in the study by Barad et al. *(45)*. For 60 of the miRNAs in their study, an extensive set of mismatch probes were used, showing that even a single mismatch can cause a significant decrease in signal intensity. In comparison, mismatches in the probe sequences outside the miRNA complementary region had no effect on signal intensity.

Another class of controls is spike-in control probes. These are common in mRNA expression profiling by microarrays. In the miRNA-profiling applications, these controls were used in only a few studies, but they can be beneficial in controlling some aspects of the methodology, including labeling efficiency, hybridization efficiency, and accuracy in measuring differential expression.

3.2.3. Preparation of Labeled Material From RNA Samples

The development of new labeling procedures is an important part in the application of the microarray platform to miRNA expression analysis. Because the methodologies used for mRNA labeling, which are based on oligo-dT-driven reverse transcription, cannot be applied, new methodologies had to be developed. Several labeling methods directly label the RNA sample and do not require any amplification. Other methods use various means of amplification to obtain labeled material. **Table 1** summarizes all of the labeling procedures and the various microarray platforms used.

3.2.3.1. LABELING PROCEDURES REQUIRING NO AMPLIFICATION

The most direct approach involves direct labeling of total RNA by reverse transcription using random 8-mers as primers *(46)*. In their application, Liu et al. used biotin-labeled random 8-mer primers. In principle, however, one could incorporate fluorescent dyes as in the usual application of microarray-labeling procedures. Here, the detection is performed after addition of streptavidin–phycoerythrin that binds the biotin moiety. This labeling approach enables the use of as little as 2.5 μg of total RNA. However, clearly, the vast majority of the labeled material, probably as much as 99% of it, is ribosomal RNA and transfer RNA, and, thus, miRNAs are a very small minority in the population of labeled molecules. This seems to lead to accurate detection of highly abundant miRNAs, but to inaccuracies in many miRNAs expressed at lower levels *(46)*.

Another direct-labeling approach uses ligation of fluorescent dinucleotides to the 3' end of RNA molecules using T4 RNA ligase *(47)*. This reaction requires the presence of 3'-OH, one of the hallmarks of mature miRNAs, and, thus, other RNAs, especially degradation products, are not labeled. The procedure requires the use of 25 μg of total RNA that is precipitated through polyethylene glycol to remove high molecular weight RNA. Labeling PAGE size-fractionated RNAs also worked well, but not any better than the other procedure. This approach seems to be efficient, specific, and of significant sensitivity.

Babak et al. *(48)* adopted a method for covalently labeling RNA with fluorescent labels *(49)*. In their study, a 7-μg sample of nonsize-fractionated total RNA was used for labeling. The labeling reaction adds the fluorescent labels onto G residues, and analysis of miRNA sequences revealed that all miRNAs studied had at least one G residue. The labeling places either Ulysis Alexa Fluor 546 or Ulysis Alexa Fluor 647 (Molecular Probes) on the RNA. These dyes are read much like the regular Cy3 and Cy5 dyes in the common microarray scanners. The advantage of this approach is that two-color hybridization, namely, hybridizing two samples, each labeled with a different dye, to one microarray, can be used. This is not possible in the first two methods described here, in which labeling is performed with biotin. This study reported good sensitivity and a good correlation (0.7) to previous Northern blot data *(50)*. As in the study of Liu et al. *(46)*, here, too, miRNAs make up a very small fraction of the labeled material, possibly less than 1%. However, correlation with the Northern blot data reported here is similar to that reported by Barad et al. *(45)* and much higher than the 0.1 correlation calculated for the Liu et al. work. Because of the labeling of the RNA on G residues, one should

Table 1

Microarray Platforms and Labeling Procedures

Study	Microarray platform	Labeling procedure	Amplification
Liu et al., 2004 (*46*)	GeneMachine OmniGrid 100 Microarrayer using Amersham Bioscience CodeLink-activated slides	Reverse transcription with biotin-labeled random 8-mer primers	No
Thomson et al., 2004 (*47*)	GeneMachine OmniGrid 100 Microarrayer using Corning GAPS-2 slides	Ligation of fluorescent dinucleotides to the 3' end of RNA molecules using T4 RNA ligase. Label - Alexa 647 (Cy5).	No
Babak et al., 2004 (*48*)	Agilent Technologies *in-situ* synthesized microarrays	Covalently labeling RNA with fluorescent labels on G residues - Ulysis Alexa Fluor 546 or Ulysis Alexa Fluor 647 (MolecularProbes)	No
Ambion, *see* web site	Not disclosed; user defined	Addition of poly-A stretches to 3'-OH end using poly-A polymerase. Fluorescently labeled or amino-modified nucleotides can be used. mirVANA™ miRNA labeling kit.	No
Nelson et al., 2004 (*51*)	GeneMachine OmniGrid 100 Microarrayer using Amersham Bioscience CodeLink-activated slides	The RAKE technique: labeling on-chip using Klenow to add three biotinylated dATPs to probes to which miRNAs specifically hybridized. Detection with streptavidin-conjugated fluorophore.	No
Liang et al., 2005 (*52*)	Glycidyloxipropyltrimethoxysilane-(GOPTS) activated glass slides (Sigma). PixSys 5500 spotting robot (Cartesian Technology), in which ArrayIt SMP3 spotting pin from Tele-Chem was used.	Chemical modification of 3'-OH and addition of biotin. Quantum Dot-labeled (or gold-labeled) streptavidin used for detection.	No

Genisphere, *see* web site	User defined	Ligation of capture oligonucleotide to miRNA 3'-end through the use of an oligo-dT bridge. Hybridization of the ligated miRNAs to the microarray followed by hybridization of 3DNA moieties, carrying either Cy3 or Cy5, to the capture oligonucleotide.	No, but compatible with amplified material
Miska et al., 2004 *(53)*	MicroGrid TAS II arrayer (BioRobotics) using Amersham Bioscience CodeLink-activated slides	Amplification of adaptor ligated miRNA enriched sample with adaptor-specific primers, one of which is labeled with Cy3. Double-stranded material denatured and used for hybridization.	Yes
Baskerville and Bartel, 2005 *(54)*	Probes spotted onto Amersham Bioscience CodeLink-activated slide; undisclosed spotter.	Similar to Miska et al. *(53)* but isolating the labeled strad after strand separation enabled by artificial lengthening of one strand. Cy3 and Cy5 used.	Yes
Barad et al., 2004 *(45)*	Agilent Technologies *in situ* synthesized microarrays	Ligation of adaptors with the T7 RNA polymerase promoter on a 3'-adaptor. Amplification by PCR followed by T7 RNA polymerase reaction incorporating either Cy3-UTP or Cy5-UTP.	Yes

be cautious in comparing miRNA abundance across different miRNAs, because the number of G residues should be considered.

Ambion has developed a different labeling method that uses poly-A polymerase as its anchor (the mirVANA™ miRNA-labeling kit). This polymerase can append tens of nucleotides to the 3' end of RNA molecules bearing a 3'-OH. Thus, many fluorescently labeled or amine-modified nucleotides can be added to each miRNA molecule, resulting in high sensitivity. Labeling is performed on miRNAs purified by size fractionation, but reportedly, a quantity equivalent to purification from 10 µg of total RNA can be used. The use of this labeling kit is reported in Ambion's website (http://www.ambion.com/techlib/tn/116/8.html).

A highly novel approach, termed RAKE for array-based Klenow enzyme assay, was reported by Nelson et al. *(51)*, using an ingenious on-slide labeling reaction. The microarray platform used involved printing of presynthesized oligonucleotides with attachment through the 5' end. This enabled placing miRNA complementary sequences at the 3'-half of the probes and a fixed sequence of 21 nucleotides at the 5'-half, separated by three thymidines from the 3'-half. After hybridization of the RNA sample to the microarray, all single-stranded molecules are degraded using exonuclease I. Thus, all probes to which an miRNA hybridized to the 3'-half are available for the next step. A reaction mixture including the Klenow enzyme and biotinylated deoxyadenosine triphosphate (dATP) is added to the microarray slide. This results in the incorporation of three biotinylated dATP molecules to match the three thymidine nucleotides that follow the miRNA complementary sequences in the probes. Detection is then performed by addition of streptavidin-conjugated fluorophore. The protocol uses Ambion's mirVANA miRNA isolation kit to enrich for miRNAs (cutoff of ~200 nucleotides), and 4 µg of the enriched RNA was used for hybridization. The advantage of this approach is in its ability to achieve high discrimination of the 3' end of the miRNAs because of the specificity required by the Klenow enzyme. It is conceivable that the use of RNases, such as RNase A and RNase T1, as used in RNase protection assays, might enhance the overall specificity. The choice of the mirVANA miRNA isolation kit for miRNA enrichment allows some enrichment while keeping the procedure simple and quick.

Liang et al. *(52)* presented an approach for the chemical modification of miRNAs and addition of the label directly to the miRNA in the sample. miRNA enrichment is performed by size fractionation of 90 µg of total RNA on PAGE, and the recovered fraction is treated for chemical modification and label addition. This enables the direct addition of a biotin group to the miRNAs and, therefore, the next steps in their protocol can be adapted to any method that adds biotin to the material that will be hybridized to the microarray. The distinct innovation in this work is the use of Quantum Dot (QD) particles added via streptavidin in a posthybridization processing step. QDs are fluorescent moieties introduced relatively recently into biomedical research. Information regarding QDs can be found in the Quantum Dot Corp. website (http://www.qdots.com/live/index.asp). The use of QDs by Liang et al. seems to have resulted in significant sensitivity, allowing efficient detection of miRNA expression. It should be noted, however, that the comparison made by the authors has shown sensitivity similar to that measured by Miska et al. *(53)* (*see* **Subheading 3.2.3.2.**), who used Cy3 for labeling but used amplification in their procedure. The same study also examined the use of the colorimetric gold–silver detection method. In this application, streptavidin-conjugated gold is used and detection is performed by a silver-enhancer kit. The sensitivity obtained with this method was comparable with that of the QD labeling. Thus, this offers a cost-effective labeling alternative.

An interesting alternative of potentially supreme sensitivity is offered by Genisphere (http://www.genisphere.com/array_detection_900mirna.html). At the heart of their procedure is a "3DNA" moiety that contains approx 900 fluorescent labels, either Cy3 or Cy5. The principle of this approach is that the 3DNA contains many identical single-stranded arms that are ligated to the target RNAs. To achieve this, specifically for miRNA applications, a poly-A tail is added to the miRNA molecules (as described above for Ambion's mirVANA miRNA-labeling kit), allowing ligation of a specific capture oligonucleotide through the use of an oligo-dT bridge. Importantly, the capture oligonucleotide contains a region that is complementary to the single-stranded arms of the 3DNA moieties. These capture oligonucleotide-ligated miRNA molecules are hybridized to the microarray. In a posthybridization processing step, the labeled 3DNA is added and is able to hybridize specifically to the capture oligonucleotide, thus adding the label, and the fluorescence can be detected using regular means. As detailed in the company's protocol, the procedure works well with the simple enrichment obtained with Ambion's mirVANA miRNA isolation kit. Other means of enrichment, such as PAGE size fractionation, also work well. Although there are no publications using this procedure yet, it seems to offer potentially high sensitivity and requiring only reasonable additional manipulations.

3.2.3.2. Labeling Procedures Requiring Amplification

The first steps in all miRNA amplification procedures follow the adaptor ligation procedure described in **Subheadings 2.** and **3.1.** (**Fig. 2**). This also involves size fractionation of the total RNA to enrich for miRNAs.

Miska et al. *(53)* used a simple approach in which one of the primers used in the amplification is fluorescently labeled with Cy3. The labeled double-stranded polymerase chain reaction (PCR) products are then simply denatured and hybridized to the microarray. An obvious criticism would be that the relatively rapid reannealing of the strands can cause significant depletion of the labeled molecules available for hybridization to the microarray probes. Still, Miska et al. reported the successful analysis of miRNA expression, most probably with compromised sensitivity. Importantly, they included control mismatch probes in their microarray and observed that their hybridization condition, which reached a hybridization temperature maximum of 50°C, did not allow differentiation between two probes that are different in two nucleotides. Indeed, at 50°C, similar results were observed by Barad et al. *(45)*, but increasing the hybridization temperature to 60°C allowed differentiation between probes having one mismatch.

Baskerville and Bartel *(54)* used the same basic approach as Miska et al. *(53)*, but for hybridization used only the labeled strand of the PCR products. To produce single-stranded labeled material they artificially lengthened one of the strands *(55)* and were, thus, able to efficiently purify the fluorescently labeled strand using denaturing polyacrylamide gels. The amount of material used for hybridization was 10 pmol, which is approx 100 ng. Because minimal amplification was used, obtaining this amount would require more than 100 µg of total RNA as starting material. The use of this labeling approach enables the two-color hybridization strategy. In their study, Baskerville and Bartel used Cy3 to label the sample and Cy5 to label a reference oligonucleotide set. This set contained synthetic oligonucleotides matching each miRNA probe on the array. This enabled a faithful comparison of all hybridizations by normalizing each miRNA to its reference signal. Overall, this approach seems specific and of significant sensitivity, and the use of the reference set, possible in all cases in which a two-color strategy can be used, greatly increases the accuracy of comparing many different hybridizations. However, the labeling approach, requiring an additional step of gel purification, seems time consuming and, in my opinion, does not provide a significant advantage over other methods. The fact that only one fluorescent molecule exists per each nucleic acid molecule is an advantage in terms of equal labeling of all miRNAs, but compromises sensitivity.

A different approach introduced a T7 RNA polymerase promoter sequence into the adaptor ligated to the 3' end of the miRNAs *(45)*. The labeling protocol used a double-stranded cDNA library as the starting material and a T7 RNA polymerase reaction, which included either Cy3-uridine triphosphate (UTP) or Cy5-UTP, was performed. Using this approach, the labeled material is in the antisense orientation and the microarray probes should be in the sense orientation, same as the original miRNA sequence. The amount of material used for hybridization was 17 µg of labeled artificial RNA (aRNA), similar to the amounts used in standard Affymetrix GeneChip® hybridization applications. However, the preparation of the double-stranded cDNA library required 300 µg (!) of total RNA. It is reasonable that this amount can be reduced to 100 µg, but this is still a considerable amount of starting material. On the other hand, this study most probably shows the highest sensitivity and was able to accurately monitor the expression of low abundance miRNAs. It should also be noted that the T7 RNA polymerase promoter sequence can be introduced to the 5' adaptor and that this would be suitable for a microarray containing antisense probes.

3.2.4. Microarray Processing

The profiling of miRNA expression also requires deviation from the standard microarray procedures developed for mRNA expression profiling in the processing step. The main parameters are hybridization temperature, washing temperature, and conditions. None of the studies carefully examined all parameters, therefore, I compared the conditions used in the variety of studies and tried to reach some recommendations. All details are summarized in **Table 2.**

It seems that most groups have taken a cautious approach in determining hybridization and washing conditions. These were probably chosen to ensure efficient hybridization of short molecules and prevent unwanted loss of signal. However, the works by Baskerville and Bartel *(54)* and Barad et al. *(45)* have shown that hybridizations can be performed at higher temperatures (57°C and 60°C, respectively). Some groups also used washing conditions that were more stringent, raising the temperature up to 42°C (usually with a relatively high salt concentration) and washing at low salt concentrations

Table 2

Microarray Hybridization and Washing Conditions[a]

Study	Hybridization conditions	Washing conditions
Liu et al., 2004 (46)	6X SSPE (0.9 M sodium chloride, 60 mM sodium phosphate, 8 mM EDTA, pH 7.4) and 30% formamide at 25°C for 18 h	0.75 TNT (Tris-HCl, sodium chloride, and Tween-20) at 37°C for 40 minutes
Thomson et al., 2004 (47)	400 mM Na$_2$PO$_4$, pH, 7.0; 0.8% BSA; 5% SDS; and 12% formamide for 2 h at 37°C	Once in 2X SSC, and 0.025% SDS; three times in 8X SSC; three times in 4X SSC at 25°C.
Babak et al., 2004 (48)	1 M NaCl; 0.5% sodium sarcosine; 50 mM methyl ethane sulfonate, pH 6.5; 33% formamide; and 40 µg of salmon sperm DNA for 16–24 h at 42°C	30 s in 6X SSPE, 0.005% sarcosine, then 30 s in 0.06X SSPE
Ambion	No details	No details
Nelson et al., 2004 (51)	5X SSC and 5% formamide for 18 h at 25°C	Three 1-min rinses in 2X SSC at 37°C
Liang et al., 2005 (52)	Formamide prehybridization/hybridization solution (no details) at 37°C overnight	1X SSC and 0.5% SDS at 37°C for 10 min
Genisphere	Hybridization solution (no details), overnight (16–20 h) at 50°C–54°C	15 min in prewarmed 2X SSC, and 0.2% SDS at 42°C; 10–15 min in 2X SSC at room temperature; 10–15 min in 0.2X SSC at room temperature
Miska et al., 2004 (53)	5X SSC, 0.1% SDS, and 0.1 mg/mL of sheared denatured salmon sperm DNA at 50°C for 6 h.	No details
Baskerville and Bartel, 2005 (54)	3.5X SSC, 1% BSA, 0.1% SDS, 0.1 mg/mL of herring sperm DNA (Sigma), 0.2 mg/mL of yeast tRNA (Sigma), and 0.4 mg/mL of poly-A RNA at 57°C for 6 h	2X SSC, and 0.1%, SDS at 50°C for 5 min; 0.1X SSC, and 0.1% SDS for 10 min; wash 3X; washes with 0.1X SSC for 1 min at Temp not disclosed
Barad et al., 2004 (45)	Hybridization solution: Agilent protocols; overnight at 60°C	No details

[a]EDTA, ethylenediaminetetraacetic acid; BSA, bovine serum albumin; SDS, sodium dodecylsulfate; SSC, standard sodium citrate.

in lower temperatures. My recommendation would be to use a hybridization that is more stringent and washing conditions that are more stringent, because the issue of specificity is, in my opinion, more important than sensitivity. It is better to obtain lower signal levels but to have more robust results.

4. Microbead Expression Analysis

Of the several attempts to develop microbead (microsphere) technologies for expression analysis, the methodological platform developed by Luminex is the most successful. In general, while the location on the array provides identity in the microarray approach, in the microbead approach, each microbead must have its own easily and reliably detectable identity. In the heart of the technology developed by Luminex is the ability to provide identity to many different microbeads. This technology, termed xMAP (http://www.luminexcorp.com/01_xMAPTechnology/index.html), involves 100 different microbeads. Each microbead type is color coded, namely, has a distinct mix of fluorescent dyes that can be uniquely detected after excitation with a laser beam. The microbeads can be coated with the reagent of choice and, thus, 100 different reagents can be assayed in one reaction. One of the obvious applications of this platform is the use of oligonucleotide probe coating for the examination of gene expression. In this application, the microbeads bearing the oligonucleotide probes are hybridized with a fluorescently labeled library derived from mRNA. The detection step is performed in the Luminex reader that can read one microbead at a time. Each microbead is read twice: once to determine its identity and a second time to determine the amount of labeled nucleic acid molecules that hybridized to the oligonucleotide probes.

A recent study has taken a direct approach in the use of the xMAP technology *(36)*. Oligonucleotides probes complementary to selected miRNAs were attached to the microbeads and hybridized with a biotin-labeled PCR-amplified miRNA-enriched library. After the hybridization and washing steps, the beads are incubated with streptavidin–phycoerythrin and are loaded into the reader. The amount of fluorescence derived from the phycoerythrin is indicative of the expression level of each miRNA, as determined by deciphering the identity of each bead by the reader. In their study, Lu et al. *(36)* examined the expression of 217 miRNAs across 334 human tumor samples and obtained highly informative results regarding developmental lineage and differentiation state of the tumors.

A different approach was undertaken by GENACO, who developed the mirMASA methodology (http://gene.genaco.com/mirmasa.html). This methodology differs in two aspects. First, locked nucleic acid derivatives were spiked along the oligonucleotides used. Second, two oligonucleotides are used: a capture oligonucleotide bound to the bead and a detection oligonucleotide that is labeled with biotin. The capture oligonucleotide is complementary to approximately half of the target miRNA and the detection oligonucleotide is complementary to the other half. After the binding of both the target miRNA to the capture oligonucleotide and the detection oligonucleotide to the target miRNA, the presence of the target miRNAs in the complex RNA population can be detected. Again, streptavidin–phycoerythrin is added for detection. The mirMASA method was successfully used to validate miRNA expression after microarray and Northern blot analysis *(45)*.

The advantages of the approach of Lu et al. *(36)* are its simplicity and the fact that they multiplex together 75 different miRNAs in one reaction. An additional advantage is the fact that the oligonucleotide probe bound to the beads is complementary to the entire miRNA target and, thus, has the highest specificity. However, this approach requires the production of a labeled PCR product, namely, preparing a full miRNA-enriched library and amplifying using a primer pair in which one of the primers is labeled with biotin.

The greatest advantage of the GENACO mirMASA approach is that total RNA can be directly assayed for the expression of the targeted miRNAs. As advertised by the company, only between 100 and 500 ng of total RNA is required. This is a significant advantage, especially in cases in which the amount of starting material is limited, e.g., in clinical samples. The use of total RNA also ensures that the results are not biased by amplification, as in the Lu et al. *(36)* approach. On the other hand, mirMASA uses short detection oligonucleotides, possibly the main reason for the need for locked nucleic acid spiking to increase specificity. This also limits the number of different miRNAs that can be assayed in one reaction, which is usually only approx 10. Thus, to profile 150 different miRNAs, one would need to perform 2 reactions using the Lu et al. approach and 15 reactions using mirMASA. As always, there is a balance between the various advantages and disadvantages, and the user will choose according to the specific needs and capabilities of the laboratory.

5. Other Approaches

Several other methodologies potentially enabling high-throughput profiling of miRNA expression have been either reported in the scientific literature or developed by companies. Because these methods are somewhat outside the scope of this chapter, I will review them only briefly and refer the reader to the relevant publications for more details.

An approach using signal-amplifying ribozymes was developed by Hartig et al. *(56)*. The idea is based on miRNA-dependant ribozyme activity that will direct the cleavage of a TaqMan-like probe. Such probes carry both fluorescent and quencher moieties on one single-stranded oligonucleotide, and its cleavage enables detection of the fluorescence. An interesting potential application of this method is the detection of miRNA *in situ* or in vivo.

The developers of the TaqMan technology, Applied Biosystems Inc. (ABI), presented posters in conferences describing the development of quantitative reverse transcriptase PCR methodology for the analysis of miRNA expression. The posters can be obtained at http://www.appliedbiosystems.com/search/?collection=&queryText=microrna. The short size of the miRNAs poses a tough hurdle in approaching amplification of specific miRNAs. ABI's method includes the ligation of a primer containing a loop to the 3' end of miRNA molecules. The loop provides room for a general reverse primer and for a TaqMan probe that covers several nucleotides of the target miRNA and several nucleotides of the ligated primer. The forward primer is specific to the 5' portion of the miRNA. Together, these three primers are used for the real-time reverse transcriptase PCR analysis of any selected miRNA. At the time this chapter is written, this kit is not yet available from ABI.

A unique approach for the sequencing of library clones was developed by Lynx Therapeutics, Inc. (http://www.lynxgen.com). This process, termed "massive parallel signature sequencing," does not use standard sequencing but uses a unique bead-based technology for the rapid sequencing of up to 20 bases from hundred of thousands of library clones *(57)*. It may provide a time- and cost-effective alternative for the straightforward cloning approach described in **Subheading 3.5.** However, peer-reviewed studies using this technology in its application to miRNAs have not yet been published, therefore, it is difficult to assess its advantages over other technologies. This method might be useful for a whole genome survey of miRNA expression, especially in organisms for which no miRNA data exists.

I end with a different technology that is not high-throughput in its essence but seems to have significant potential in miRNA expression analysis. An approach for miRNA detection by solution hybridization, without the need for amplification, was developed by US Genomics (http://www.usgenomics.com/index.php?option=com_content&task =view&id=77&Itemid=82&m=t). Briefly, their Trilogy technology is based on the ability of their special reader to detect single molecules. For every miRNA, two oligonucleotides are designed, each covering one-half of the miRNA sequence. These two oligonucleotides are labeled with different fluorescent tags. After hybridization, the reader is able to detect single molecules containing both fluorescent tags and only these are counted as positive signals.

6. Conclusions

In this chapter I presented a wide variety of alternative methodologies that can be used for the high-throughput analysis of miRNA expression. I do not intend to provide specific recommendations of which methodologies are preferable, but leave it to the readers to find the technology most suitable to their specific needs. Because the number of miRNAs seems to be higher than previously estimated, probably approaching the 1000 mark (for human and most probably for vertebrates in general), one consideration would be how many miRNAs are to be assayed. Thus, for assaying a few tens of miRNAs, one may choose to use the microbead-based method of Genaco, the approach described by Lu et al. *(36)*, or the TaqMan approaches of ABI and Hartig et al. *(56)*. For the analysis of hundreds of miRNAs, the various microarray approaches or the bead technology of Lu et al. *(36)* seem more suitable. Finally, in cases in which the sequences of many (or all) miRNAs of a certain organism are unknown, one may choose the cloning methodologies, either the straightforward approach or the methodology developed by Lynx.

Acknowledgments

I thank my son Tal Einat and my wife Dr. Miriam Friedman-Einat for their help in finalizing this chapter.

References

1. Fire, A., Xu, S., Montgomery, M. K., Kostas, S. A., Driver, S. E., and Mello, C. C. (1998) Potent and specific genetic interference by double-stranded RNA in Caenorhabditis elegans. *Nature* **391**, 806–811.
2. Lee, R. C., Feinbaum, R. L., and Ambros, V. (1993) The C. elegans heterochronic gene lin-4 encodes small RNAs with antisense complementarity to lin-14. *Cell* **75**, 843–854.
3. Reinhart, B. J., Slack, F. J., Basson, H., et al. (2000) The 21-nucleotide let-7 RNA regulates developmental timing in Caenorhabditis elegans. *Nature* **403**, 901–906.
4. Pasquinelli, A. E., Reinhart, B. J., Slack, F., et al. (2000) Conservation of the sequence and temporal expression of let-7 heterochronic regulatory RNA. *Nature* **408**, 86–89.
5. Berezikov, E., Guryev, V., van de Belt, J., Weinholds, E., Plasterk, R. H., and Cuppen, E. (2005) Phylogenetic shadowing and computational identification of human microRNA genes. *Cell* **120**, 21–24.
6. Xie, X., Lu, J., Kulbokas, E. J., et al. (2005) Systematic discovery of regulatory motifs in human promoters and 3' UTRs by comparison of several mammals. *Nature* **434**, 338–345.
7. Bentwich, I., Avniel, A., Karov, Y., et al. (2005) Identification of hundreds of conserved and nonconserved human microRNAs. *Nat. Genet.* **37**, 766–770.
8. Carrington, J. C. and Ambros, V. (2003) Role of microRNAs in plant and animal development. *Science* **301**, 336–338.
9. Bartel, B. and Bartel, D. P. (2003) MicroRNAs: at the root of plant development? *Plant Physiol.* **132**, 709–717.
10. Bartel, D. P. (2004) MicroRNAs: genomics, biogenesis, mechanism, and function. *Cell* **116**, 281–297.
11. Ambros, V. (2004) The functions of animal microRNAs. *Nature* **431**, 350–355.
12. Bartel, D. P. and Chen, C. Z. (2004) Micromanagers of gene expression: the potentially widespread influence of metazoan microRNAs. *Nat. Rev. Genet.* **5**, 396–400.
13. Hobert, O. (2004) Common logic of transcription factor and microRNA action. *Trends Biochem. Sci.* **29**, 462–468.
14. Murchison, E. P. and Hannon, G. J. (2004) miRNAs on the move: miRNA biogenesis and the RNAi machinery. *Curr. Opin. Cell Biol.* **16**, 223–229.
15. Mattick, J. S. and Makunin, I. V. (2005) Small regulatory RNAs in mammals. *Hum. Mol. Genet.* **14(Spec 1)**, R121–R132.
16. Bentwich, I. (2005) A postulated role for microRNA in cellular differentiation. *FASEB J.* In press.
17. Kim, V. N. (2005) MicroRNA biogenesis: coordinated cropping and dicing. *Nat. Rev. Mol. Cell Biol.* **6**, 376–385.
18. Lee, Y., Jeon, K., Lee, J. T., Kim, S., and Kim, V. N. (2002) MicroRNA maturation: stepwise processing and subcellular localization. *EMBO J.* **21**, 4663–4670.
19. Lee, Y., Ahn, C., Han, J., et al. (2003) The nuclear RNase III Drosha initiates microRNA processing. *Nature* **425**, 415–419.
20. Denli, A. M., Tops, B. B., Plasterk, R. H., Ketting, R. F., and Hannon, G. J. (2004) Processing of primary microRNAs by the Microprocessor complex. *Nature* **432**, 231–235.
21. Gregory, R. I., Yan, K. P., Amuthan, G., et al. (2004) The Microprocessor complex mediates the genesis of microRNAs. *Nature* **432**, 235–240.
22. Ketting, R. F., Fischer, S. E., Bernstein, E., Sijen, T., Hannon, G. J., and Plasterk, R. (2001) Dicer functions in RNA interference and in synthesis of small RNA involved in developmental timing in C. elegans. *Genes Dev.* **15**, 2654–2659.

23. Hutvagner, G. and Zamore, P. D. (2002) A microRNA in a multiple-turnover RNAi enzyme complex. *Science* **297,** 2056–2060.
24. Hake, S. (2003) MicroRNAs: a role in plant development. *Curr. Biol.* **13,** R851–R852.
25. Yekta, S., Shih, I. H., and Bartel, D. P. (2004) MicroRNA-directed cleavage of HOXB8 mRNA. *Science* **304,** 594–596.
26. Lim, L. P., Lau, N. C., Garrett-Engele, P., et al. (2005) Microarray analysis shows that some microRNAs downregulate large numbers of target mRNAs. *Nature* **433,** 769–773.
27. Esau, C., Kang, X., Peralta, E., et al. (2004) MicroRNA-143 regulates adipocyte differentiation. *J. Biol. Chem.* **279,** 52,361–52,365.
28. Poy, M. N., Eliasson, L., Krutzfeldt, J., et al. (2004) A pancreatic islet-specific microRNA regulates insulin secretion. *Nature* **432,** 226–230.
29. Calin, G. A., Dumitru, C. D., Shimizu, M., et al. (2002) Frequent deletions and down-regulation of micro-RNA genes miR15 and miR16 at 13q14 in chronic lymphocytic leukemia. *Proc. Natl. Acad. Sci. USA* **99,** 15,524–15,529.
30. Michael, M. Z., O'Connor, S. M., van Holst Pellekaan, N. G., Young, G. P., and James, R. J. (2003) Reduced accumulation of specific microRNAs in colorectal neoplasia. *Mol. Cancer Res.* **1,** 882–891.
31. Calin, G. A., Liu, C. G., Sevignani, C., et al. (2004) MicroRNA profiling reveals distinct signatures in B cell chronic lymphocytic leukemias. *Proc. Natl. Acad. Sci. USA* **101,** 11,755–11,760.
32. Takamizawa, J., Konishi, H., Yanagisawa, K., et al. (2004) Reduced expression of the let-7 microRNAs in human lung cancers in association with shortened postoperative survival. *Cancer Res.* **64,** 3753–3756.
33. Calin, G. A., Sevignani, C., Dumitru, C. D., et al. (2004) Human microRNA genes are frequently located at fragile sites and genomic regions involved in cancers. *Proc. Natl. Acad. Sci. USA* **101(9),** 2999–3004.
34. Metzler, M., Wilda, M., Busch, K., Viehmann, S., and Borkhardt, A. (2004) High expression of precursor microRNA-155/BIC RNA in children with Burkitt lymphoma. *Genes Chromosomes Cancer* **39,** 167–169.
35. He, L., Thomson, J. M., Hemann, M. T., et al. (2005) A microRNA polycistron as a potential human oncogene. *Nature* **435,** 828–833.
36. Lu, J., Getz, G., Miska, E. A., et al. (2005) MicroRNA expression profiles classify human cancers. *Nature* **435,** 834–838.
37. O'Donnell, K. A., Wentzel, E. A., Zeller, K. I., Dang, C. V., and Mendell, J. T. (2005) c-Myc-regulated microRNAs modulate E2F1 expression. *Nature* **435,** 839–843.
38. Lagos-Quintana, M., Rauhut, R., Lendeckel, W., and Tuschl, T. (2001) Identification of novel genes coding for small expressed RNAs. *Science* **294,** 853–858.
39. Lau, N. C., Lim, L. P., Weinstein, E. G., and Bartel, D. P. (2001) An abundant class of tiny RNAs with probable regulatory roles in Caenorhabditis elegans. *Science* **294,** 858–862.
40. Lee, R. C. and Ambros, V. (2001) An extensive class of small RNAs in Caenorhabditis elegans. *Science* **294,** 862–864.
41. Lagos-Quintana, M., Rauhut, R., Yalcin, A., Meyer, J., Lendeckel, W., and Tuschl, T. (2002) Identification of tissue-specific microRNAs from mouse. *Curr. Biol.* **12,** 735–739.
42. Lagos-Quintana, M., Rauhut, R., Meyer, J., Borkhardt, A., and Tuschl, T. (2003) New microRNAs from mouse and human. *RNA* **9,** 175–179.
43. Chen, P. Y., Manninga, H., Slanchev, K., et al. (2005) The developmental miRNA profiles of zebrafish as determined by small RNA cloning. *Genes Dev.* **19,** 1288–1293.

44. Krichevsky, A. M., King, K. S., Donahue, C. P., Khrapko, K., and Kosik, K. S. (2003) A microRNA array reveals extensive regulation of microRNAs during brain development. *RNA* **9,** 1274–1281.

45. Barad, O., Meiri, E., Avniel, A., et al. (2004) MicroRNA expression detected by oligonucleotide microarrays: System establishment and expression profiling in human tissues. *Genome Res.* **14,** 2486–2494.

46. Liu, C. G., Calin, G. A., Meloon, B., et al. (2004) An oligonucleotide microchip for genome-wide microRNA profiling in human and mouse tissues. *Proc. Natl. Acad. Sci. USA* **101,** 9740–9744.

47. Thomson, J. M., Parker, J., Perou, C. M., and Hammond, S. M. (2004) A custom microarray platform for analysis of microRNA gene expression. *Nat. Methods* **1,** 47–53.

48. Babak, T., Zhang, W., Morris, Q., Blencowe, B. J., and Hughes, T. R. (2004) Probing microRNAs with microarrays: tissue specificity and functional inference. *RNA* **10,** 1813–1819.

49. Peng, W. T., Robinson, M. D., Mnaimneh, S., et al. (2003) A panoramic view of yeast noncoding RNA processing. *Cell* **113,** 919–933.

50. Sempere, L. F., Freemantle, S., Pitha-Rowe, I., Moss, E., Dmitrovsky, E. and Ambros, V. (2004) Expression profiling of mammalian microRNAs uncovers a subset of brain-expressed microRNAs with possible roles in murine and human neuronal differentiation. *Genome Biol.* **5,** R13.

51. Nelson, P. T., Baldwin, D. A., Scearce, L. M., Oberholtzer, J. C., Tobias, J. W., and Mourelatos, Z. (2004) Microarray-based, high-throughput gene expression profiling of microRNAs. *Nat Methods* **1,** 155–161.

52. Liang, R. Q., Li, W., Li, Y., et al. (2005) An oligonucleotide microarray for microRNA expression analysis based on labeling RNA with quantum dot and nanogold probe. *Nucleic Acids Res.* **33,** e17.

53. Miska, E. A., Alvarez-Saavedra, E., Townsend, M. et al. (2004) Microarray analysis of microRNA expression in the developing mammalian brain. *Genome Biol.* **5,** R68.

54. Baskerville, S. and Bartel, D. P. (2005) Microarray profiling of microRNAs reveals frequent coexpression with neighboring miRNAs and host genes. *RNA* **11,** 241–247.

55. Williams, K. P. and Bartel, D. P. (1995) PCR product with strands of unequal length. *Nucleic Acids Res.* **23,** 4220–4221.

56. Hartig, J. S., Grune, I., Najafi-Shoushtarai, S. H., and Famulok, M. (2004) Sequence-specific detection of MicroRNAs by signal-amplifying ribozymes. *J. Am. Chem. Soc.* **126,** 722–723.

57. Brenner, S., Johnson, M., Bridgham, J., et al. (2000) Gene expression analysis by massively parallel signature sequencing (MPSS) on microbead arrays. *Nat Biotechnol.* **18,** 630–634.

12

In Situ Hybridization as a Tool to Study
the Role of MicroRNAs in Plant Development

Catherine Kidner and Marja Timmermans

Summary

MicroRNAs (miRNAs) have a vital role in the generation of plant forms through post-transcriptional regulation of the accumulation of developmental regulators. Analysis of their roles requires detailed knowledge of their expression patterns. We describe an *in situ* hybrid-iz-ation technique we have used to study the patterns of miRNA accumulation in *Arabidopsis* and in maize.

Key Words: *In situ* hybridization; microRNA; plants.

1. Introduction

miRNAs are small (~22mer) single-stranded RNA molecules that guide RNA-induced silencing complexes to target transcripts and facilitate their site-specific cleavage or translational repression. The first miRNAs were discovered in *Caenorhabditis elegans* in a screen for heterochronic mutations that alter the timing of developmental events *(1,2)*. They have since been found in both metazoans and plants (for review, *see* **ref. 3**). However, the miRNAs identified in these lineages are quite distinct. Most animal miRNAs interact with weak complementarity to multiple sites in the 3' untranslated region of target transcripts and act at the translational level. In contrast, plant miRNAs and their targets frequently possess near perfect complementarity, and most plant miRNA–messenger RNA (mRNA) interactions lead to cleavage of the target transcript at a position corresponding to nucleotides 10 and 11 of the miRNA. The realization that plant miRNAs display near perfect complementarity to target mRNAs has enabled the identification of many target genes using computational approaches *(4–6)*. Interestingly, the known plant miRNAs show a strong propensity to target transcription factor families or other genes controlling development.

The significance of miRNA-mediated gene regulation in plant development is exemplified by the range of developmental processes affected by mutations in genes required for miRNA biogenesis or function: e.g., *dicer-like1 (7)*, *argonaute1 (8–11)*, *hen1 (12,13)*, *hyponastic leaves1 (14–16)*, and *zippy (17)*. Elucidation of the precise developmental

From: *Methods in Molecular Biology, vol. 342: MicroRNA Protocols*
Edited by: S. Ying © Humana Press Inc., Totowa, NJ

roles of individual miRNAs is, however, complicated by the presence of extensive redundancy. Nearly all miRNAs identified in plants are encoded by multigene families. Consequently, few recessive loss-of-function alleles of miRNA genes (*MIR*) have been identified that give rise to developmental phenotypes *(18)*. The developmental roles of several miRNAs have been revealed through characterization of dominant miRNA-overexpressing mutations. For instance, miR-JAW was identified in a collection of activation-tagged lines based on its leaf morphology defects *(19)*. miR-JAW regulates a subset of *TCP* genes required for the proper temporal transition from cell division to differentiation *(20,21)*. Overexpression of miR-JAW in the *jaw-D* mutant leads to decreased expression of the *TCP* targets, which prolongs cell proliferation and alters leaf shape. Similar gain-of-function mutations for miR159, miR164, miR165, and miR172 lead to defects in organ separation, meristem function, vascular patterning, flowering, and floral organ development *(18,22–29)*.

A second approach to studying miRNA function involves the phenotypic analysis of plants expressing a miRNA-resistant allele of a target locus. For example, mutations that reduce the complementarity of class III homeodomain leucine zipper (*HD-ZIPIII*) transcripts to miR165/166 were shown to interfere with miRNA-directed transcript cleavage leading to ectopic *HD-ZIPIII* expression *(28,30–34)*. Analysis of the phenotypes caused by these gain-of-function mutations indicates that miR165/166-mediated regulation of *HD-ZIPIII* genes is required for normal meristem function and axis specification in developing lateral organs and vascular strands. Transgenic approaches have also been used to analyze the developmental phenotypes conferred by expression of miRNA-resistant transcripts of genes regulated by miR-JAW, miR160, miR164, miR168, and miR172 *(18,19,25,35–37)*. In total, these studies have revealed that miRNAs are important regulatory signals in plant development that may direct changes in cell fate by "clearing out" transcripts of regulatory genes. In addition, because the miRNA pathway itself is regulated by miRNAs, a feedback mechanism is established that may act as a rheostat of gene expression *(11,38,39)*.

The identification of miRNAs as important regulators of developmental genes raised the question of how the spatial and temporal patterns of miRNA expression are established. The miRNA loci generate long noncoding transcripts called primary (pri)-miRNA that undergo several processing steps to yield the mature miRNA. Pri-miRNA processing involves slightly different mechanisms in animals and plants, which have been outlined in several recent reviews *(3,40,41)*. However, in both lineages, the long transcript is first cleaved to yield an approx 70 to 300-nucleotide (nt) stem-loop intermediate, termed precursor (pre)-miRNA. Processing of the stem-loop pre-miRNA by Dicer activity releases an approx 22-bp duplex that comprises the mature miRNA and the imperfectly complemented miRNA* strand. Only the mature miRNA strand becomes incorporated into a RNA-induced silencing complex, which mediates the cleavage or translational repression of target mRNAs.

miRNA expression patterns were initially determined by Northern blot hybridization *(12,42,43)*. More recently, microarray technologies have been developed to analyze miRNA accumulation patterns (*see* **refs. *44*** and ***45*** and references therein). Both of these approaches examine expression at the bulk tissue level and, therefore, cannot be used to address how miRNA expression patterns establish patterns of tissue organization during development. A more detailed miRNA expression pattern can be inferred using so-called "miRNA-sensors" *(46,47)*. Sensor constructs drive the constitutive expression of a reporter gene that contains a miRNA complementary sequence in the 3' untranslated region. Reporter gene expression will be limited to those cells lacking the complementary miRNA. However, miRNA processing in plants can lead to the production of short interfering RNAs from sequences downstream of the miRNA cleavage site that can traffic between cells. Expression of miRNA sensors must, therefore, be observed in an *sde1* background, which blocks the production of secondary short interfering RNAs *(46)*. As for many other transcripts, detailed expression patterns of miRNAs at the cellular level can be studied directly using *in situ* hybridization. Two different methods have been described. Chen *(37)* performed low-stringency hybridizations with a probe that comprised concatamers of miR172. In contrast, we used probes containing fragments of *MIR165* and *MIR166* that include a single copy of the miRNA *(10,31)* (**Fig. 1**), and used an *in situ* hybridization method modified from that of Jackson *(48)*. In plants, both pri-miRNAs and pre-miRNAs are processed very efficiently to yield the mature miRNA. As a result, neither precursor accumulates to levels that can be detected by Northern blot analysis. Similarly, pri-miRNA probes that exclude the miRNA are not detectable in *in situ* hybridization experiments. The *in situ* hybridization method we use for the expression analysis of miRNAs is also being used for the expression analysis of normal transcripts, and is outlined below.

2. Materials

All solutions are prepared using ribonuclease (RNase)-free glassware and chemicals in diethylpyrocarbonate (DEPC)-treated dH_2O (water with 0.05% DEPC is stirred overnight at room temperature and subsequently autoclaved). *See* **Note 1**.

2.1. Tissue Preparation

2.1.1. Fixation

Four percent paraformaldehyde (Sigma P6148, Sigma, St. Louis, MO) fixative must be prepared fresh on the day of use. Make up the required amount of phosphate buffered saline (PBS) (130 mM NaCL, 7 mM Na_2HPO_4, and 3 mM NaH_2PO_4) in DEPC-treated water. Adjust the pH to 11.0 with NaOH. The pH can be checked with pH papers and disposable RNase-free plastic pipets. Heat the solution to 60°C to 70°C. In a fume hood, add paraformaldehyde (final concentration, 4%) and mix thoroughly until dissolved. Place the solution on ice and, when cooled, adjust the pH to 7.0 with H_2SO_4 (1–2 drops for 100 mL). Do not use HCl to adjust the pH, because this will release highly toxic fumes. To improve the infiltration of the fixative, the following detergents can be added: dimethylsulfoxide (DMSO) (up to 4%), Triton X-100 (up to 0.1%), or Tween-20 (up to 0.1–0.3%).

2.1.2. Embedding

1. PBS.
2. 100% EtOH.

 Kidner and Timmermans

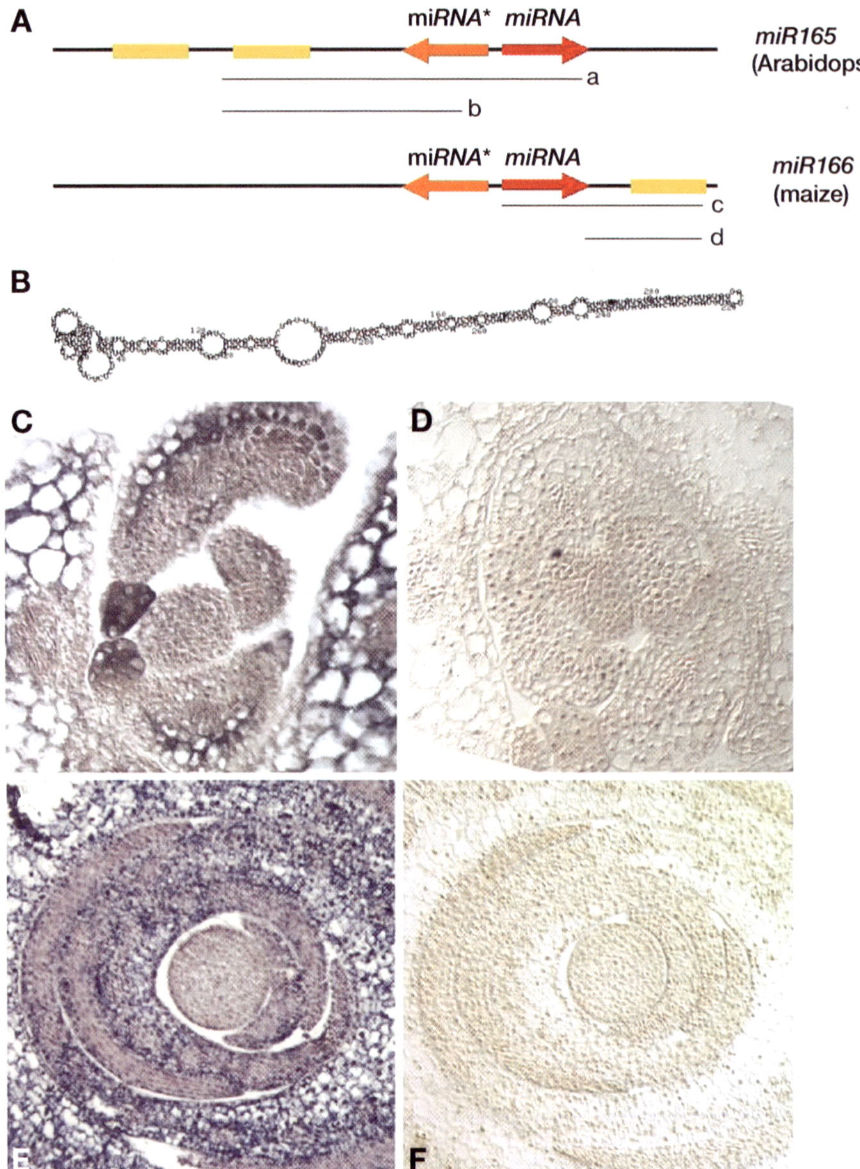

Fig. 1. *In situ* hybridization analysis of miRNAs in *Arabidopsis* and maize. (**A**) Primers were designed to amplify the precursor (pre)-microRNA (miRNA) sequences from the genomic template. The pre-miRNA was identified by sequences conserved between different loci/different species (in yellow). Probes for miR165 in *Arabidopsis* contained either the miRNA and miRNA* (a) or the miRNA* alone (b). Probes for miR166 in maize contained either the miRNA (c) or only precursor sequence (d). (**B**) Transcription through the miRNA and miRNA* was not possible in the 3' to 5' direction but was possible in the 5' to 3' direction. This is probably because of extensive secondary structure—see the folding of (a) from the miR165b precursor (as predicted

3. 1 L 8.5% NaCl.
4. Histoclear (National Diagnostics, Atlanta, GA; cat. no. HS-200).
5. Tissuepath paraplast X-tra (Fisher, Pittsburg, PA; cat. no. 23-021-401). Paraplast should be freshly melted before use, in an oven at 58°C to 60°C. However, prolonged heating above 60°C should be avoided.
6. Base moulds (EMS, Fort Washington, PA; cat. no. 62352-15).
7. Embedding rings (Fisher; cat. no. 22-038-197).

2.1.3. Sectioning

1. Probe-on-plus slides (Fisher; cat. no. 15-188-52).
2. 0.2 N NaOH.

2.2. Probe Preparation

2.2.1. In Vitro Transcription

1. Phenol/chloroform.
2. Digoxygenin (DIG) RNA-labeling kit (Roche, Indianapolis, IN; cat. no. 1-175-025).
3. RNasin.
4. RNA polymerase.

Transcripts are made from linearized plasmid templates that typically carry promoters for one of the following RNA polymerases: T3, T7, or Sp6.

2.2.2. Deoxyribonuclease Treatment

1. RNase-free deoxyribonuclease (DNase) (RQ1) (Promega, Madison, WI; cat. no. M610A).
2. 100 mg/mL of transfer RNA (tRNA) (store at −20°C) (Roche; cat. no. 109541).
3. 100 mL of 4 M NH_4Ac.
4. 100% EtOH.

2.2.3. Carbonate Hydrolysis

1. 50 mL of 2X CO_3 buffer: 80 mM $NaHCO_3$, 120 mM Na_2CO_3.
2. 50 mL of 10% acetic acid.
3. 100 mL of 3 M NaAc, pH 5.2.
4. 50% deionized formamide (store at 4°C) (Sigma; cat. no. F9037).

2.3. In Situ *Hybridization*

The following general stock solutions should be prepared. Again, all solutions are prepared using RNase-free chemicals and DEPC-treated dH_2O. In addition, approximately 12 L of DEPC-treated dH_2O is needed in 1-L RNase-free bottles for diluting stock solutions.

Fig. 1. (*Continued*) by mfold, M. Zuker, 2003). (**C**) *In situ* hybridization analysis of miR165b in *Arabidopsis* using the (a) probe at a 1X concentration. Signal is seen on the abaxial side of the leaf primordia. (**D**) *In situ* hybridization analysis of miR165b in *Arabidopsis* using the (b) probe at a 1X concentration. No signal is seen. (**E**) *In situ* hybridization analysis of miR166 in maize using the (c) probe at 5X concentration. Signal is seen in the abaxial side of the first leaf, and expression extends gradually during leaf development. (**F**) *In situ* hybridization analysis of miR166 in maize using the (d) probe at a 5X concentration. No signal is seen, consistent with the low abundance of miR precursors.

1. 1 L of 10X PBS, pH 7.0.
   a. 1.3 *M* NaCl.
   b. 70 m*M* Na$_2$HPO$_4$.
   c. 30 m*M* NaH$_2$PO$_4$.
   This solution should come out to pH 7.0, but, if necessary, the pH can be adjusted with H$_3$PO$_4$ or NaOH. Check the pH with pH paper.
2. 500 mL of 0.5 *M* ethylenediaminetetraacetic acid (EDTA), pH 8.0 (adjust the pH with NaOH).
3. 1 L of 1 *M* Tris-HCl solution, pH 9.5, pH 8.0, and pH 7.5 (adjust the pH with concentrated HCl). Tris-HCl contains an amino group, which inactivates DEPC, so it is best made up with Tris-HCl powder from a dedicated clean stock and dissolved in DEPC-treated water.
4. 500 mL of 5 *M* NaCl.
5. 100 m*M* Phosphate buffer, pH 6.8. For 200 mL, mix 51 mL of 200 m*M* NaH$_2$PO$_4$, 49 mL of 200 m*M* Na$_2$HPO$_4$, and 100 mL of dH$_2$O.
6. 500 mL of 1 *M* MgCl$_2$.

2.3.1. Section Pretreatment

1. Histoclear.
2. 100% ethanol.
3. 1 L of 20X standard sodium citrate (SSC).
   a. 3 *M* NaCl.
   b. 300 m*M* Na citrate.
4. 10 mg/mL proteinase K. Proteinase K does not need to be predigested. Aliquots of this stock solution are stored at –20°C. For maize tissues, we frequently use pronase instead of proteinase K; 40 mg/mL pronase (Sigma type XIV) is dissolved in water and predigested to remove nucleases by incubating at 37°C for 4 h. Aliquots are stored at –20°C (*see* **Note 2**).
5. 20% glycine in 10X PBS (store at –20°C).
6. 4% paraformaldehyde in PBS, made fresh, as detailed in **Subheading 2.1.1.**
7. 4 mL of acetic anhydride in 800 mL of 0.1 *M* triethanolamine-HCl, pH 8.0. Acetic anhydride is unstable in water, thus, this solution should be made fresh immediately before use. Place an RNase-free glass container over a magnetic stirrer in the fume hood and add the following solutions while stirring vigorously: 786 mL DEPC-treated dH$_2$O, 10.4 mL triethanolamine (Sigma T1377), and 3.2 mL HCl. After the solution is mixed, add 4 mL acetic anhydrite (Sigma A6404). Lower the mixing speed and immediately lower the slide rack into the solution. Whereas the other solutions can be used for multiple slide racks, this solution should be made fresh for each rack of slides.

2.3.2. Hybridization

1. 50 mL of 10X *in situ* hybridization salts.
   a. 3 *M* NaCl.
   b. 100 m*M* Tris-HCl, pH 8.0.
   c. 100 m*M* Na phosphate, pH 6.8.
   d. 50 m*M* EDTA.
2. 100 mg/mL tRNA (store at –20°C) (Roche 109541).

3. 40 mL of 50% dextran sulfate (molecular weight > 500,000) (store at −20°C) (Sigma D8906-5G). Dextran sulfate should be heated to 80°C to dissolve.
4. 50X Denhardts (store at −20°C) (Sigma D2532).
5. Formamide (store at 4°C) (Sigma F9037).

2.3.3. Posthybridization Treatment

1. 1 L of 20X SSC: 3 *M* NaCl, 300 m*M* Na citrate.
2. 1 L of 5X NaCl, Tris-HCl, EDTA (NTE): 2.5 *M* NaCl, 50 m*M* Tris-HCl, pH 8.0, 5 m*M* EDTA.
3. 20 mg/mL RNase-A (store at −20°C) (Roche 109142).

2.3.4. Detection of the Hybridization Signal

1. 1 L Tris-buffered saline (TBS): 100 m*M* Tris-HCl, pH 7.5, 150 m*M* NaCl.
2. 1% blocking reagent (Roche 1096176) in 200 mL TBS.
   TBS should be heated to 60°C, blocking reagent should be added on top of the solution and stirred for at least 1 h to dissolve completely.
3. 1% bovine serum albumin (BSA) (Sigma A7906) and 0.3% Triton X-100 in 500 mL TBS.
4. Anti-DIG-alkaline phosphatase, Fab fragments (Roche 1093274).
5. 250 mL Tris saline (TN): 100 m*M* Tris-HCl, pH 9.5, 100 m*M* NaCl.
6. Nitroblue tetrazolium (NBT) plus bromochloroindolyl phosphate (BCIP) mix (store at −20°C) (Roche 1681451). Just before use, add 200 µL NBT/BCIP mix to 10 mL TN. Alternatively, a premix of NBT/BCIP called "Western Blue" (Promega S3841) can be used.
7. 500 mL Tris-HCl and EDTA, pH 8.0: 10 m*M* Tris-HCl, 1 m*M* EDTA.
8. 100% EtOH.
9. Histoclear.
10. Cytoseal (EMS 18006).

2.4. Equipment

Vacuum system.
Fume hood.
Oven at 58°C to 60°C to melt the paraplast.
Ovens for 50°C, 55°C, and 37°C (two ovens are needed for the quick change between temperatures).
Slide warmer.
Microtome.
Metal slide rack to fit in glass trough.
Three glass troughs baked at 250°C overnight.
Stir bars, spatulas, and glass measuring cylinders baked at 250°C overnight.
21 plastic boxes, soaked overnight in 0.2 *M* NaOH and rinsed in DEPC-treated water (*see* **Note 3**).
Two large flat plastic boxes with sealable lids for hybridization and antibody treatment.
Plastic disposable pipets, individually wrapped.
Disposable plastic Pasteur pipets.

3. Methods

3.1. Tissue Preparation

Before beginning, assess the expression levels of the miRNA of interest in the various tissues of the plant via small RNA Northern blots. Alternatively, the expression pattern of the pri-miRNAs can be determined by reverse transcriptase polymerase chain reaction (PCR) to ensure that appropriate tissues or developmental stages are analyzed.

3.1.1. Fixation

1. Harvest samples and place as quickly as possible in fresh fixative on ice, either in 15-mL blue Falcon tubes or glass scintillation vials. If dissection is required, this is best done on ice in cold fixative. For instance, maize apices are dissected into small 4 × 4 × 3-mm blocks to optimize the infiltration of fixative and subsequent solutions.
2. Apply vacuum (~400 mmHg) to samples while the samples are on ice. Small bubbles should be released from the samples. Hold the vacuum for 15 to 20 min and release slowly. Ensure that the fixative does not boil. Repeat this step until the tissues sink. Tissue samples that are more difficult to infiltrate can be placed in special tissue holders such that the tissue is fully submerged in fixative.
3. Replace the paraformaldehyde with fresh fixative and gently shake overnight at 4°C. Use a large excess of each solution, e.g., for 8 to 10 maize apices or *Arabidopsis* seedlings use 10 to 15 mL.

3.1.2. Embedding

Machines for automatic wax embedding are available and can be used to simplify this step.

1. Precool the following solutions by keeping them in the cold room.
   All steps are performed at 4°C with gentle shaking or rotation.
   a. 1X PBS 30 min.
   b. 1X PBS 30 min.
   c. 30% EtOH 60 min.
   d. 40% EtOH 60 min.
   e. 50% EtOH 60 min.
   f. 60% EtOH 60 min.
   g. 70% EtOH 60 min.
   h. 85% EtOH 60 min.
   i. 95% EtOH overnight.
   Addition of 0.1% eosin to the final step helps to visualize small samples when sectioning. 0.85% NaCl can be added to the 30 to 85% EtOH solutions to avoid excessive swelling and shrinking of the tissue. Tissue can be stored for several months in 70% EtOH at 4°C.
2. If the initial steps are performed in 15-mL blue Falcon tubes, the samples should be transferred to glass vials before the histoclear is added because static can otherwise be a problem.
   All steps are performed at room temperature with gentle shaking.
   a. 100% EtOH + eosin 30 min.
   b. 100% EtOH + eosin 30 min.
   c. 100% EtOH + eosin 60 min.
   d. 100% EtOH + eosin 60 min.
   e. 25% histoclear, 75% EtOH 30 min.

    f. 50% histoclear, 50% EtOH 30 min.

    g. 75% histoclear, 25% EtOH 30 min.

    h. 100% histoclear 60 min.

    i. 100% histoclear 60 min.

    j. 100% histoclear + 1/4 volume of paraplast chips overnight.

3. Place the samples at 42°C until the chips are completely melted (this may take several hours).

4. Add more chips and move to 60°C. At the end of the day, replace the wax/histoclear with freshly melted wax and leave the vials open overnight at 60°C. An RNase-free beaker of wax should be set up and replenished at each change so there is always freshly melted wax at hand.

5. Change the wax each morning and evening of days 5 and 6. Leave the vials open at 60°C overnight.

6. In the morning of day 7, replace the wax once more. Samples can be embedded later on day 7. Pour paraplast into a mold and arrange the tissue sample in the mold, using warmed forceps. Place the molds on ice to aid rapid setting. We orientate plant tissues carefully in the molds to fit onto the microtome to be sectioned directly. Alternatively, we embed samples randomly and in bulk in unused pie dishes (aluminium tins ~5 cm in diameter). Individual samples can later be cut out and, using more hot wax, can be mounted in the correct orientation onto the microtome blocks.

    If wax infiltration seems to be a problem, as evidenced by holes in the tissue sections, samples can be vacuum infiltrated once more immediately before making the blocks. However, make sure that the vacuum system is warmed up to 58°C to 60°C. Special hotplates are available that maintain temperature at 60°C and simplify the embedding process. Blocks can be stored in plastic bags at 4°C for 1 yr or longer.

3.1.3. Sectioning

Sectioning can be tricky in very dry conditions, in which case static becomes a problem, or in warmer temperatures, in which case the ribbon may buckle in the heat. The wax blocks can be sectioned from cold and grounding the microtome with a wire sometimes helps to reduce static electricity. Slides used are Probe-On Plus from Fisher Biotechnology. They are precleaned and charged. They also have a white paint label that provides a capillary space when two slides are sandwiched together.

1. Prewarm the slide warmer to 42°C. Clean the microtome and slide warmer by wiping with 0.2 *M* NaOH. Lay clean filter paper next to the microtome on which to place the wax ribbons.

2. Trim the block into a trapezoid shape, leaving approx 2 mm of wax around the plant tissue. Place the block into the microtome such that the longer of the two parallel faces is at the bottom. Section through the region of interest. Sections 8- to 10-μm thick are reasonable, depending on the size of the cells in the tissue. The sections should make long wax ribbons.

3. Place a Probe-On Plus slide on the slide warmer and apply several drops of DEPC-treated water. Slides can be marked with pencil, because pencil marks will not dissolve in later EtOH incubations.

4. Float the wax ribbon on the water, shiny side down (the bottom side as the ribbon comes off of the microtome). Let the ribbon warm for approximately a minute to allow it to flatten out completely.

5. Before the edges of the wax contact the warm slide, tip off the water carefully but in one smooth movement, so the ribbon is lowered down onto the slide. Hold the slide upright and use a twist of tissue to drain off any excess water from the edge of the ribbon.

6. Leave the slides at a slight angle on the slide warmer at 42°C overnight so that the tissue adheres. Sectioned tissue can be stored in a box with silica desiccant for several weeks at 4°C.

3.2. Probe Preparation

3.2.1. Designing the Probe

Because only the mature miRNA seems to accumulate in plants, any DNA fragment that includes the miRNA sequence can serve as a probe for *in situ* hybridization. However, the probes we used originally for expression analysis of miR165 and miR166 were derived from the actual pri-miRNAs (**Fig. 1A**). Many miRNA loci are members of gene families and show sequence conservation in the miRNA* sequence. Pair-wise comparisons between the *Arabidopsis MIR165* or *MIR166* family members revealed extensive sequence conservation also surrounding the predicted miRNA:miRNA* duplex. Primers derived from regions conserved between *MIR165a* and *MIR165b* allowed the amplification of pri-miRNA transcripts by reverse transcriptase PCR *(10)*. Pri-miRNA levels varied considerable between different tissues and developmental stages, as well as between the different loci, in accordance with what was known from small RNA gels.

miRNA and miRNA* sequences are often conserved between distantly related species *(45)*. We identified one additional sequence motif that is conserved between *MIR166* loci from *Arabidopsis* and rice, and this conservation allowed us to clone pri-miRNA transcripts for miR166 from maize *(31)*. Fragments of the *Arabidopsis* and maize pri-miRNAs that include the miRNA were used as *in situ* hybridization probes (**Fig. 1C,E**). Similar fragments that excluded the miRNA were used as negative controls in the experiments (**Fig. 1D,F**).

More recently, we use fragments of genomic DNA as *in situ* hybridization probes. Primers are designed to genomic sequences surrounding the miRNA that allow the amplification of approx 300- to 500-bp fragments (this size fragment works well in the in vitro transcription reaction). To avoid potential complications with secondary structure, we exclude the miRNA* from the probe fragment by placing one primer within the pre-miRNA.

The PCR products, whether derived from pri-miRNA transcripts or genomic DNA, were cloned into the pCRII-TOPO vector (Invitrogen). This vector includes an Sp6 and a T7 promoter, allowing in vitro transcription in either direction across the insert. Several other vectors are available that contain T7, T3, or Sp6 promoters.

3.2.2. In Vitro Transcription

1. Linearize the plasmid by digesting approx 5 μg DNA with a restriction enzyme that digests at the end of the insert opposite the site of the promoter. Do not use restriction enzymes that leave a 3' overhang. This can lead to transcription artifacts because the polymerase can use the 3' overhang as a substrate to continue transcription. Digest for 3 h and use extra enzyme to be sure of a complete digest.

2. Check an aliquot of the digest on a gel to verify that the reaction has gone to completion.
3. Extract the DNA with phenol/chloroform, precipitate with EtOH, and resuspend in DEPC-treated dH$_2$O to a concentration of 0.5 µg/µL. Alternatively, the digest can be cleaned using standard DNA purification columns.
4. Set up the transcription reaction as follows:
   a. 4 µL of DNA (0.5 µg/µL).
   b. 5 µL of 5X buffer.
   c. 5 µL of 5X nucleotides.
   d. RNase inhibitor, to 1 U/µL.
   e. RNA polymerase, to 0.4 U/µL.
   f. H$_2$O to 25 µL.

   5X nucleotides are 2.5 m*M* adenosine triphosphate, guanosine triphosphate, cytidine triphosphate, and uridine triphosphate (UTP)/DIG-UTP in H$_2$O. Incubate at 37°C for 30 to 60 min. We use a 1:1 DIG-UTP:regular UTP ratio because this gives a much better RNA yield. In our experience, longer incubations times (up to 2 h) can improve the RNA yield for certain miRNA probes.
5. Treat a gel box and comb with RNase zap (Sigma) or 0.2 *N* NaOH for 30 min. Make up a fresh 1% gel that contains ethidium bromide. Run 1 µL of the transcription reaction at 80 V for approx 15 min. For a good in vitro transcription reaction, the RNA band will be at least as intense in brightness as the DNA band. Use a control RNA, which is usually provided with the in vitro transcription kit, to estimate the amount of probe synthesized. Alternatively, the relative intensity of the RNA and DNA bands can be used to estimate the probe yield. Depending on the concentration at which the probe will be used (which will vary for different genes) 2 µg of probe is usually sufficient for 80 slides.

3.2.3. DNase Treatment

To remove the DNA template from the *in situ* hybridization probe, the in vitro transcription reaction is treated with DNaseI.

1. To the transcription reaction add:
   a. DEPC-treated H$_2$O 75 µL.
   b. tRNA (100 mg/mL) 1 µL.
   c. RNase-free DNase (RQ1) 5 U.
   Incubate for 10 min at 37°C. The tRNA serves as a carrier RNA in the subsequent precipitation reactions.
2. Add an equal volume of 4 *M* NH$_4$Ac plus two volumes of EtOH, and precipitate the RNA at −20°C for 1 h. Centrifuge the RNA pellet at 4°C for 30 min. Rinse the pellet with 70% EtOH and let it air-dry for 15 to 30 min on ice.
3. Resuspend the pellet in 100 µL DEPC-treated H$_2$O.

3.2.4. Carbonate Hydrolysis

The probe is usually partially hydrolyzed to yield fragments of approx 150 nt. Shorter probes can better penetrate the tissue and, consequently, improve the hybridization signal and reduce the background. Because some of our miRNA probes are approximately this length, we sometimes skip this step.

The length of time required to hydrolyze probes of different sizes is calculated using the formula:

$$\text{Time} = (Li - Lf) \, / \, (\text{K} \times Li \times Lf),$$

where *Li* is the initial length of probe (in kilobases); *Lf* is the final length of probe (0.150 kb); and K is 0.11 kb/min.

1. Add 100 µL 2X CO_3 buffer and incubate at 60°C for the calculated length of time.
2. Neutralize the reaction with 10 µL of 10% acetic acid.
3. Add 1/10 volume of 3 *M* NaAc, pH 5.2, plus 2 volumes EtOH and precipitate the RNA at −20°C for 1 h. Centrifuge the RNA pellet at 4°C for 30 min. Rinse the pellet with 70% EtOH and let the pellet air-dry for 15 to 30 min on ice.
4. Resuspend the RNA in 50% formamide at a final concentration of 50 ng/kb/µL.

Most probes are used at a final concentration of 0.5 ng/kb/µL probe complexity, so this gives a 100X stock for making up the hybridization solution. Hybridizations are performed with 100 µL per slide. Thus, if a probe is 0.5-kb long, the probe should be resuspended at a concentration of 25 ng/µL (50 ng × 1 µL × 0.5 kb) to obtain a 100X stock. If the probe is 1-kb long, 50 ng/µL probe will make a 100X stock.

Probes can be stored for months at −80°C, allowing the same probe to be used as a control in different experiments.

3.3. In Situ *Hybridization*

3.3.1. Section Pretreatment

Before the hybridization, sections are pretreated to optimize the signal intensity and specificity. Tissue sections are first dewaxed and rehydrated through an ethanol series. The sections are subsequently treated with proteinase K, which increases the permeability of the tissues, thus enhancing the infiltration with the RNA probe. Some experimentation may be needed to determine the optimum conditions, time, and temperature to maximize the hybridization signal without breakdown of the tissue. Proteinase K activity is stopped with glycine. The sections are fixed again with paraformaldehyde, and then treated with acetic anhydride to neutralize positive charges that may lead to nonspecific binding of the probe.

The volume required for each solution will obviously depend on the number of slides to be treated and the container size used. The sections should always be completely submerged. For a 50-slide rack and a neatly fitting container, 600 mL should be sufficient. Because many of the incubation steps are very short, we usually prepare all possible solutions, including the 4% paraformaldehyde (*see* **Subheading 2.1.1.**), first, before beginning the slide pretreatments (*see* **Note 4**). However, the acetic anhydride solution will need to be prepared immediately before use, and proteinase K is added at the time of use.

All steps are performed at room temperature unless noted otherwise (*see* **Note 5**).

1. Select the slides and label each in pencil with the probe to be used. Be sure to pick pairs for each probe because the hybridization steps are performed with sandwiched slides.
2. Warm 600 mL of 100 m*M* Tris-HCl, pH 8.0, and 50 m*M* EDTA to 37°C (60 mL of 1 *M* Tris-HCl, pH 8.0 and 60 mL of 0.5 *M* EDTA for 600 mL). Add 60 µL of 10 mg/mL proteinase K just before **step 3**.

3. Deparaffinize and rehydrate the tissue sections:
   a. Histoclear 10 min (use a glass dish).
   b. Histoclear 10 min (use a glass dish).
   c. 100% EtOH 1 min.
   d. 100% EtOH 1 min.
   e. 95% EtOH 1 min.
   f. 90% EtOH 1 min.
   g. 80% EtOH 1 min.
   h. 60% EtOH 1 min.
   i. 30% EtOH 1 min.
   j. H_2O 1 min.
4. 2X SSC for 15 to 20 min.
5. 100 m*M* Tris-HCl, pH 8.0, and 50 m*M* EDTA, with freshly added proteinase K (1 µg/mL) for 30 min at 37°C (*see* **Note 2**).
6. 0.2% glycine in PBS for 2 min.
7. PBS for 2 min.
8. PBS for 2 min.
9. 4% paraformaldehyde, pH 7.0 (made fresh), for 10 min.
10. PBS for 5 min.
11. PBS for 5 min.
12. Acetic anhydride for 10 min. While the slides are in the PBS washes, make up 0.1 *M* triethanolamine buffer, pH 8.0, in a glass dish (*see* **Subheading 2.3.1.**) by mixing on a magnetic stirrer in the fume hood:
    a. 786.4 mL DEPC-treated H_2O.
    b. 10.4 mL Triethanolamine.
    c. 3.2 mL Concentrated HCl.
    Add 4 mL acetic anhydride into the triethanolamine immediately before putting the slides in, and stir well. Reduce the speed of the stirrer and elevate the slide rack in the container of triethanolamine/acetic anhydride (we use a second inverted slide rack to support the samples). After adding the slides, continue to stir slowly for 10 min.
13. PBS for 5 min.
14. PBS for 5 min.
15. Dehydrate again:
    a. 30% EtOH 30 s.
    b. 60% EtOH 30 s.
    c. 80% EtOH 30 s.
    d. 90% EtOH 30 s.
    e. 95% EtOH 30 s.
    f. 100% EtOH 30 s.
    g. 100% EtOH 30 s.
16. Slides can be stored in container with a small amount of 100% EtOH at the bottom for up to several hours at 4°C.

Both paraformaldehyde and acetic anhydride are toxic, therefore, these solutions should be prepared in a fume hood and disposed of properly.

3.3.2. Hybridization

We do not usually include a sense "control" probe because this RNA is entirely different in sequence and not a true negative control. However, if a RNA-null mutant exists,

Table 1
Hybridization Solutions Table[a]

Pairs of slides	Probe (µL)	50% Formamide (µL)		Hyb solution (µL)	Final volume (µL)	
1	2	38		160	200	Apply 200 µL to each pair of slides
2	4	76		320	400	
3	6	114	80°C	480	600	
4	8	152	2 min	640	800	
5	10	190		720	1000	
1[b]	10	30		160	200	

[a]This table assumes that the probe is at 50 ng/kb/µL. Hyb, hybridization.
[b]5X probe.

such tissues would be an excellent negative control. For miRNA *in situ* hybridizations, we include an antisense probe specific for the pri-miRNA as a negative control. We also always include a positive control, most often *SHOOTMERISTEMLESS* or *knotted1*, which are relatively abundant. As mentioned in **Subheading 3.2.4.**, most probes are used at a probe complexity of 0.5 ng/kb/µL. However, for new probes or new tissues, a dilution series of the probe should be evaluated. We often use 1, 5, and 20X concentrations.

1. Decide what slides to use with which probe. Determine how much hybridization solution to make based on the total number of slide pairs.
   Hybridization Solution (enough for five slide pairs) total volume: 800 µL:
   a. 100 µL of 10X *in situ* hybridization salts.
   b. 400 µL of deionized formamide.
   c. 200 µL of 50% dextran sulfate.
   d. 20 µL of 50X Denhardt solution.
   e. 10 µL of tRNA (100 mg/mL).
   f. 70 µL of DEPC-treated H_2O.
   This solution is very viscous because of the dextran sulfate. Either warm it up before use, or make more than you need to overcome loss in dispensing. Hybridization solution can be made up in bulk and stored in aliquots at −20°C.
2. Air-dry the slides by leaving the slide rack covered with a Kimwipe in a clean dry box while you prepare the solutions. The slides must be completely dry.
3. For each pair of slides, probe should be added to 50% formamide, such that the total volume is 40 µL. Heat to 80°C for 2 min, immediately chill on ice, centrifuge briefly, and keep on ice.
4. Add 160 µL of hybridization solution for each pair of slides, such that the volume is now 200 µL (hybridization solution + probe) for each slide pair (*see* **Table 1** for mixing volumes of hybridization solutions). Mix slowly and carefully to avoid bubbles.
5. Apply the probe to the slides. Because the sections are dried and the probe is viscous, care should be taken to infiltrate all sections and to avoid air bubbles. We use one of three methods:
   a. Excess amounts of the hybridization solution are placed in a plastic trough designed for multiwell pipettors (Matrix Technologies). Two slides are sandwiched together

and the slide sandwich is dripped into the tough on its side. This allows the solution to be pulled up by capillary action.

    b. A second technique is to apply 200 µL probe to the long edge of one slide, then make a sandwich by gradually lowering the second slide down. Tap on the slides if the probe seems to exclude a section.

    c. A third technique is to apply 100 µL probe to each slide, carefully spreading it over the entire slide with the side of a pipet tip so that all sections are covered. Then slowly sandwich the two slides together without getting air bubbles. If bubbles do arise, do not pull the slide apart but tap the slides to displace the bubbles from all tissue sections, add additional hybridization solution, if needed.

6. Line a plastic box with damp tissue paper and use plastic pipets to make racks for the pairs of slides. The slide sandwiches can be stacked on top of each other, but they should not touch on the side, because this will lead to mixing of the probes. Seal the box tightly.

7. Hybridize at 50°C overnight.

3.3.3. Posthybridization Treatment

The hybridization solution is washed off the slides and the slides are treated with RNase A to remove single-stranded RNA and to increase the specificity of the probe. RNase A will cleave at mismatches in RNA:RNA hybrids. As a result, probe that cross-hybridizes with potential closely related sequences will be fragmented and washed off in the subsequent washes.

1. Warm 0.2X SSC to 55°C (need ~3 L).
2. Warm NTE solution to 37°C (need ~3 L). These solutions are usually prepared the evening before and warmed up overnight.

During one of the wash steps, 200 mL of blocking solution should be prepared (*see* **Subheading 2.3.4.**; 1% blocking reagent [Roche] in 200 mL TBS).

The TBS should be heated to 60°C. The blocking reagent should be added on top of the solution and stirred for at least 1 h to dissolve completely. The solution will remain cloudy. Do not heat higher than 60°C.

All washes are performed with prewarmed solutions and with gentle shaking.

1. Dip pairs of slides into a dish of prewarmed 0.2X SSC to separate and rinse the slides before placing in a rack.
2. Wash slides in 0.2X SSC at 55°C for 60 min.
3. Replace the 0.2X SSC and wash at 55°C for 60 min.
4. Wash in NTE at 37°C for 5 min.
5. Replace the NTE and wash at 37°C for 5 min.
6. Incubate with RNase (20 µg/mL) in NTE with gentle shaking at 37°C for 30 min. Add RNase to prewarmed NTE immediately before use.
7. Wash in NTE at 37°C for 5 min.
8. Replace the NTE and wash at 37°C for 5 min.
9. Wash in 0.2X SSC at 55°C for 60 min.
10. Rinse in PBS at room temp for 5 min.

3.3.4. Detection of the Hybridization Signal

The slides are first blocked to prevent nonspecific crossreaction with the anti-DIG antibody.

1. Place slides on the bottom of a large flat plastic container, tissue side up. Add 1.0% Roche block (*see* **Subheading 2.3.4.**); use just enough blocking solution to cover the slides. Place the container on a rocking platform, rock gently, and incubate at room temperature for 45 min. At this time, make up 500 mL of 1% BSA and 0.3% Triton X-100 in TBS (*see* **Subheading 2.3.4.**):
   a. 5 g of BSA.
   b. 50 mL of 1 *M* Tris-HCl, pH 7.5.
   c. 15 mL of 5 *M* NaCl.
   d. 1.5 mL of Triton X-100.
2. Replace blocking solution with 1% BSA and 0.3% Triton X-100 in TBS, and wash for 45 min, as in **Subheading 3.3.4.**, **step 1**.
3. Dilute the anti-DIG antibody (1:1250) in the 1% BSA and 0.3% Triton X-100 in TBS solution. For 25 pairs of slides, 10 µL of antibody in 12.5 mL is sufficient.
4. Place a few milliliters of antibody solution in a small dish. We often use plastic multipipetting or weighing dishes. Sandwich slides together and dip one long side in the solution, allowing capillary action to pull up the solution. Drain the slides on a Kimwipe and fill the slides with antibody solution again. You may need to tap the slides as the solution flows in to avoid bubbles.
5. Arrange slides on racks of plastic pipets above wet tissue in a tightly sealed plastic container and leave overnight at 4°C.
6. Drain slides on Kimwipes and separate the slides. Place the slides on the bottom of a plastic container, as in **Subheading 3.3.4.**, **step 1**. Wash four times in 1% BSA and 0.3% Triton X-100 in TBS solution on a rocking platform at room temperature for 15 min each.
7. Wash in TN (100 m*M* Tris-HCl, pH 9.5, and 100 m*M* NaCl) for 10 min.
8. Dip each slide in TN solution to ensure that all detergent is washed off and the pH in the sections is raised to 9.5 for optimum alkaline phosphatase activity.
9. Prepare the substrate solution immediately before use by adding 200 µL of premixed NBT/BCIP (Roche 1681451) to 10 mL of TN solution. This is sufficient for 25 slide pairs.
10. Sandwich two slides and draw up the substrate solution as in **Subheading 3.3.4.**, **step 4**. Repeat.
11. Place the slides in a plastic container above wet paper towels in total darkness for 1 to 5 d. Check the development on a dissection microscope with the slide sandwich balanced on an opened Petri dish to avoid having capillary forces drain the substrate. Replace the substrate solution every other day by pulling out the old solution onto Kimwipes and drawing up fresh substrate via capillary action as in **Subheading 3.3.4.**, **step 4**.
12. When the signal is clear, drain the slide pairs, separate the slides, and rinse them in Tris-HCl and EDTA to stop the alkaline phosphatase reaction.
13. Dehydrate the sections through an EtOH series:
   a. 30% EtOH 5 s.
   b. 50% EtOH 5 s.
   c. 70% EtOH 5 s.
   d. 85% EtOH 5 s.
   e. 95% EtOH 5 s.
   f. 100% EtOH 5 s.
   g. Histoclear 2 min.
   h. Histoclear 2 min.
   It is important to keep the time in EtOH to a minimum because the color product is alcohol soluble.

14. Dry the slides in a fume hood and mount them with a few drops of Cytoseal. Leave the slides flat overnight to dry.

The dehydrating EtOH series can be skipped. Instead, rinse the slides in milli-Q water and dry at 37°C in a box with Kimwipes to ensure thorough dryness. Then proceed with the mounting in cytoseal as above.

4. Notes

1. It is usual to make all solutions RNase-free by DEPC treatment. However, if you have good clean milli-Q water, this may not be necessary; DEPC does interfere to some extent with transcription reactions and is a potent carcinogen, therefore, it is best to do without it if possible. We use Falcon tubes to measure most RNase-free solutions.
2. Some researchers prefer to use pronase instead of proteinase K to permeabilize the tissue sections. To do so, the pretreatment steps after the 1 min incubation in H_2O, **Subheading 3.3.1.**, **steps 4** and **5**, can be modified as follows:

   4. PBS for 5 min.
   5. Pronase for 10 min.

   Predigested pronase (*see* **Subheading 2.3.1.**) is diluted to a final concentration of 0.125 mg/mL in 50 mM Tris-HCl, pH 7.5, and 5 mM EDTA.
3. Treat plastic containers with 0.2 M NaOH overnight and rinse with DEPC-treated water. They can be kept from experiment to experiment as long as they are not stored for more than a week or so. We keep boxes that are used before the RNase step separated from those boxes used for RNase treatment or thereafter.
4. Because of the number of solutions used and the length of the protocol, it is important to have everything to hand before you begin to avoid hurriedly making solutions during a 5-min wash. The timetable below is the one we use, although the protocol can be worked through in 2 long days by reducing the washes in **Subheading 3.3.3.** to 30 min and the antibody incubation step to 4 h at room temperature.

    Timetable
        Day 0
            Prepare the probes.
            Prepare and label slides.
            Made up stock solutions.
            Prepare 21 RNase-free boxes.
            Bake slide rack, stir bars, three glass boxes, and one 500-mL glass measuring cylinder.
        Day 1
            Preparation before lunch:
                Make up EtOH series and histoclear.
                Make up 2X SSC, PBS, and PBS/glycine.
                Warm proteinase-K buffer.
                Make up paraformaldehyde.
            12 to 3 PM
                Pretreat the slides as outlined in **Subheading 3.3.1.**
            4 PM
                Aliquot the probes and hybridization solutions, *see* **Subheading 3.3.2.**

Add probes to the slides (~30 min for 10 slide pairs).
Incubate slides at 50°C overnight.
Make up 3 L each of NTE (37°C) and 0.2X SSC (55°C) and set to warm.

Day 2

Before noon:

Start the posthybridization washes, *see* **Subheading 3.3.3.**
Make up blocking solution.

Approximately 4 h later:

Place slides in blocking solution.
Wash with BSA/Triton X-100/TBS solution.
Add antibody solution to slide sandwiches (~30 min for 10 slide pairs).
Incubate at 4°C overnight.

Day 3

Wash excess antibody off of the slides.

Approximately 2 h later:

Set up the color reaction.
Add the alkaline phosphate substrate to the sandwiched slides (~30 min for 10 slide pairs).
Leave slides in a sealed box above damp towels in the dark at room temperature for 1 to 5 d.

5. A dedicated *in situ* hybridization space is very useful and lessens the worry regarding RNase contamination from adjacent experiments. An entire clean lab bench is necessary to lay out all of the boxes of solutions during the dehydration and rehydration steps, and quick access to a fume hood for the histoclear, acetic anhydride, and paraformaldehyde steps is also necessary.

Acknowledgments

C. K. thanks Rob Martienssen, in whose lab at Cold Spring Harbor Laboratory these *in situ* hybridizations were first performed. M. T. thanks Michelle Juarez and Jonathan Kui for their invaluable contributions to the expression analysis of miR166 in maize. This research was funded by a grant from the National Science Foundation to M. T.

References

1. Lee, R. C., Feinbaum, R. L., and Ambros, V. (1993) The C. elegans heterochronic gene lin-4 encodes small RNAs with antisense complementarity to lin-14. *Cell* **75,** 843–854.
2. Reinhart, B. J., Slack, F. J., Basson, M., et al. (2000) The 21-nucleotide let-7 RNA regulates developmental timing in Caenorhabditis elegans. *Nature* **403,** 901–906.
3. Bartel, D. P. (2004) MicroRNAs: genomics, biogenesis, mechanism and function. *Cell* **116,** 281–297.
4. Bonnet, E., Wuyts, J., Rouze, P., and Van De Peer, Y. (2004) Detection of 91 potential conserved plant microRNAs in Arabidopsis thaliana and Oryza sativa identifies important target genes. *Proc. Natl. Acad. Sci. USA* **101,** 11,511–11,516.
5. Jones-Rhoades, M. W. and Bartel, D. P. (2004) Computational identification of plant microRNAs and their targets, including a stress-induced miRNA. *Mol. Cell* **14,** 787–799.
6. Rhoades, M. W., Reinhart, B. J., Lim, L. P., Burge, C. B., Bartel, B., and Bartel, D. P. (2002) Prediction of plant microRNA targets. *Cell* **110,** 513–520.
7. Schauer, S. E., Jacobsen, S. E., Meinke, D. W., and Ray, A. (2002) DICER-LIKE1: blind men and elephants in *Arabidopsis* development. *Trends Plant Sciences* **7,** 487–492.

8. Bohmert, K., Camus, I., Bellini, C., Bouchez, D., Caboche, M., and Benning, C. (1998) AGO1 defines a novel locus of Arabidopsis controlling leaf development. *EMBO J.* **17,** 170–180.

9. Lynn, K., Fernandez, A., Aida, M., et al. (1999) The PINHEAD/ZWILLE gene acts pleiotropically in Arabidopsis development and has overlapping functions with the ARGONAUTE1 gene. *Development* **126,** 469–481.

10. Kidner, C. A. and Martienssen, R. A. (2004) Spatially restricted microRNA directs leaf polarity through ARGONAUTE1. *Nature* **428,** 81–84.

11. Vaucheret, H., Vazquez, F., Crete, P., and Bartel, D. P. (2004) The action of ARGONAUTE1 in the miRNA pathway and its regulation by the miRNA pathway are crucial for plant development. *Genes Dev.* **18,** 1187–1197.

12. Park, W., Li, J., Song, R., Messing, J., and Chen, X. (2002) CARPEL FACTORY, a Dicer homolog, and HEN1, a novel protein, act in microRNA metabolism in Arabidopsis thaliana. *Curr. Biol.* **12,** 1484–1495.

13. Boutet, S., Vasquez, F., Liuy, J., et al. (2003) Arabidopsis HEN1: a genetic link between endogenous miRNA controlling development and siRNA controlling transgene silencing and virus resistance. *Curr. Biol.* **13,** 843–848.

14. Han, M. H., Goud, S., Song, L., and Fedoroff, N. (2004) The Arabidopsis double-stranded RNA-binding protein HYL1 plays a role in microRNA-mediated gene regulation. *Proc. Natl. Acad. Sci. USA* **101,** 1093–1098.

15. Vazquez, F., Gasciolli, V., Crete, P., and Vaucheret, H. (2004) The nuclear dsRNA binding protein HYL1 is required for microRNA accumulation and plant development, but not posttranscriptional transgene silencing. *Curr. Biol.* **14,** 346–351.

16. Lu, C. and Fedoroff, N. (2000) A mutation in the Arabidopsis HYL1 gene encoding a dsRNA binding protein affects responses to abscisic acid, auxin, and cytokinin. *Plant Cell* **12,** 2351–2366.

17. Hunter, C., Sun, H., and Poethig, R. S. (2003) The Arabidopsis heterochronic gene ZIPPY is an ARGONAUTE family member. *Curr. Biol.* **13,** 1734–1739.

18. Baker, C. C., Sieber, P., Wellmer, F., and Meyerowitz, E. M. (2005) The early extra petals1 mutant uncovers a role for microRNA miR164c in regulating petal number in Arabidopsis. *Curr. Biol.* **15,** 303–315.

19. Palatnik, J. F., Allen, E., Wu, X., et al. (2003) Control of leaf morphogenesis by microRNAs. *Nature* **425,** 257–263.

20. Nath, U., Crawford, B. C., Carpenter, R., and Coen, E. (2003) Genetic control of surface curvature. *Science* **299,** 1404–1407.

21. Crawford, B. C., Nath, U., Carpenter, R., and Coen, E. S. (2004) CINCINNATA controls both cell differentiation and growth in petal lobes and leaves of Antirrhinum. *Plant. Physiol.* **135,** 244–253.

22. Schwab, R., Palatnik, J. F., Riester, M., Schommer, C., Schmid, M., and Weigel, D. (2005) Specific effects of microRNAs on the plant transcriptome. *Dev. Cell* **8,** 517–527.

23. Achard, P., Herr, A., Baulcombe, D. C., and Harberd, N. P. (2004) Modulation of floral development by a gibberellin-regulated microRNA. *Development* **131,** 3357–3365.

24. Mallory, A. C., Reinhart, B. J., and Jones-Rhoades, M. W. (2004) MicroRNA control of PHABULOSA in leaf development: importance of pairing to the microRNA 5' region. *EMBO J.* **23,** 1360–1375.

25. Mallory, A. C., Dugas, D. V., Bartel, D. P., and Bartel, B. (2004) MicroRNA regulation of NAC-domain targets is required for proper formation and separation of adjacent embryonic, vegetative, and floral organs. *Curr. Biol.* **14,** 1035–1046.

26. Mallory, A. C., Bartel, D. P., and Bartel, B. (2005) MicroRNA-directed regulation of arabidopsis AUXIN RESPONSE FACTOR17 is essential for proper development and modulates expression of early auxin response genes. *Plant Cell.* **17,** 1360–1375.

27. Laufs, P., Peaucelle, A., Morin, H., and Traas, J. (2004) MicroRNA regulation of the CUC genes is required for boundary size control in Arabidopsis meristems. *Development* **131,** 4311–4322.

28. Kim, J., Jung, J . H., Reyes, J. L., et al. (2005) microRNA-directed cleavage of ATHB15 mRNA regulates vascular development in Arabidopsis inflorescence stems. *Plant J.* **42,** 84–94.

29. Aukerman, M. J. and Sakai, H. (2003) Regulation of flowering time and floral organ identity by a MicroRNA and its APETALA2-like target genes. *Plant Cell.* **15,** 2730–2741.

30. Zhong, R. and Ye, Z. H. (2001) Alteration of auxin polar transport in the Arabidopsis ifl1 mutants. *Plant Physiol.* **126,** 549–563.

31. Juarez, M. T., Kui, J. S., Thomas, J., Heller, B. A., and Timmermans, M. C. (2004) MicroRNA-mediated repression of rolled leaf1 specifies maize leaf polarity. *Nature* **428,** 84–88.

32. McHale, N. A. and Koning, R. E. (2004) MicroRNA-directed cleavage of nicotiana sylvestris PHAVOLUTA mRNA regulates the vascular cambium and structure of apical meristems. *Plant Cell* **16,** 1730–1740.

33. Emery, J. F., Floyd, S. K., Alvarez, J., et al. (2003) Radial patterning of Arabidopsis shoots by class III HD-ZIP and KANADI genes. *Curr. Biol.* **13,** 1768–1774.

34. McConnell, J. R., Emery, J., Eshed, Y., Bao, N., Bowman, J., and Barton, M. K. (2001) Role of *PHABULOSA* and *PHAVOLUTA* in determining radial patterning in shoots. *Nature* **411,** 709–713.

35. Millar, A. A. and Gubler, F. (2005) The Arabidopsis GAMYB-like genes, MYB33 and MYB65, are microRNA-regulated genes that redundantly facilitate anther development. *Plant Cell.* **17,** 705–721.

36. Laufs, P., Peaucelle, A., Morin, H., and Traas, J. (2004) MicroRNA regulation of the CUC genes is required for boundary size control in Arabidopsis meristems. *Development* **131,** 4311–4322.

37. Chen, X. (2004) A microRNA as a translational repressor of APETALA2 in Arabidopsis flower development. *Science* **303,** 2022–2025.

38. Bartel, D. P. and Chen, C.-Z. (2004) Micromanagers ofgene expression: the potentially widespread influence ofmetazoan microRNAs. *Nat. Rev. Genet.* **5,** 396–400.

39. Xie, Z., Kasschau, K. D., and Carrington, J. C. (2003) Negative feedback regulation of Dicer-Like1 in Arabidopsis by microRNA-guided mRNA degradation. *Curr. Biol.* **13,** 784–789.

40. Kidner, C. A. and Martienssen, R. A. (2005) The developmental role of microRNA in plants. *Curr. Opin. Plant Biol.* **8,** 38–44.

41. Murchison, E. P. and Hannon, G. J. (2004) miRNAs on the move: miRNA biogenesis and the RNAi machinery. *Curr. Opin. Cell. Biol.* **16,** 223–229.

42. Reinhart, B. J., Weinstein, E. G., Rhoades, M. W., Bartel, B., and Bartel, D. P. (2002) MicroRNAs in plants. *Genes Dev.* **16,** 1616–1626.

43. Llave, C., Kasschau, K. D., Rector, M. A., and Carrington, J. C. (2002) Endogenous and silencing-associated small RNAs in plants. *Plant Cell* **14,** 1605–1619.

44. Nelson, P. T., Baldwin, D. A., Scearce, L. M., Oberholtzer, J. C., Tobias, J. W., and Mourelatos, Z. (2004) Microarray-based, high-throughput gene expression profiling of microRNAs. *Nat. Methods* **1,** 155–161.

45. Axtell, M. J. and Bartel, D. P. (2005) Antiquity of microRNAs and their targets in land plants. *Plant Cell.* **17,** 1658–1673.
46. Parizotto, E. A., Dunoyer, P., Rahm, N., Himber, C., and Voinnet, O. (2004) In vivo investigation of the transcription, processing, endonucleolytic activity and functional relevance of the spatial distribution of a plant miRNA. *Genes and Development* **18,** 2237–2242.
47. Mansfield, J. H., Harfe, B. D., Nissen, R., et al. (2004) MicroRNA-responsive 'sensor' transgenes uncover Hox-like and other developmentally regulated patterns of vertebrate microRNA expression. *Nat. Genet.* **36,** 1079–1083.
48. Jackson, D. (1991) In situ hybridization in plants. In: *Molecular Plant Pathology: A Practical Approach* (Bowles, D. J., Gurr, S. J., and McPherson, M., eds.), Oxford University Press, Oxford, pp. 163–174.

13

Usefulness of the Luciferase Reporter System to Test the Efficacy of siRNA

Fengfeng Zhuang and Yi-Hsin Liu

Summary

Small interefence RNA (siRNA) has revamped the technology of gene silencing in cultured mammalian cells after its first demonstration by Tushl et al. 4 yr ago. To circumvent the cost and the inconvenience in identifying a unique siRNA duplex that can quench target gene expression, we devised a reporter-based system to test knockdown efficiency of selected siRNAs. We demonstrated that this luciferase-based siRNA testing system can be used to evaluate the knockdown efficiency of a directly transfected siRNA duplex or an siRNA expressed from a lentiviral vector.

Key Words: siRNA; luciferase assay; gene silencing; *Eaf2*; lentiviral vector; C2C12 myofibroblast.

1. Introduction

RNA interference (RNAi) is a gene-silencing mechanism that uses double-stranded RNA (dsRNA) molecules. RNAi seems to be a widely used gene-silencing mechanism, being present in plants and animals *(1–3)*. In fact, RNAi was first discovered in plants; the presence of either a sense or an antisense transgene leads to simultaneous silencing of exogenous transgenes and homologous endogenous genes *(4,5)*. This cosuppression phenomenon has since been found to work in invertebrates, such as the worm and the fruit fly *(6–8)*. The RNAi machinery has been also been found to be conserved in vertebrates, including the fish and the mouse. It serves as an important mechanism in regulating developmental processes *(9,10)*.

Recent studies demonstrated that RNAi is mediated by dsRNA molecules that are 21- to 23-nucleotides in length. To be effective in silencing homologous gene activity, these dsRNAs are processed by the ribonuclease III-like nuclease, Dicer, to generate siRNA *(11)*. It is thought that the resulting small dsRNA fragments, in association with a multimeric nuclease complex called RNA-induced silencing complex, guide the complex to their homologous messenger (mRNA) targets, leading to their degradation *(11)*.

From: *Methods in Molecular Biology, vol. 342: MicroRNA Protocols*
Edited by: S. Ying © Humana Press Inc., Totowa, NJ

Since the first demonstration by Tuschl et al. *(12)* that synthetic siRNA duplexes can repress target gene expression in mammalian cells in a sequence-specific manner, siRNA has become a method of choice for gene knockdown in cultured cells and in simple model organisms, such as the nematode *Caenorhabditis elegans*. A large number of genes in a variety of mammalian cell lines have been targeted successfully in this fashion.

Although siRNA has proven to be an effective tool in degrading endogenous mRNA targets, defining an optimal siRNA sequence for a specific endogenous target remains a limiting step. The current method uses computer algorithms to first select plausible candidate sequences for generating siRNAs. Several siRNAs are then synthesized and experimental validated to identify an optimal siRNA for the subsequent gene knockdown experiment. This is normally achieved by Northern blot hybridization, quantitative reverse transcriptase polymerase chain reaction (PCR), or by Western blot, if antibody is available. All of these methodology are time consuming if the assay conditions are not optimized.

In this chapter, we describe a quantitative method of validating siRNA for silencing *ELL* associated factor 2 (*Eaf2*) expression in the C2C12 myofibroblast cell line. *Eaf2* encodes a cofactor for RNA polymerase II elongation factor, eleven-nineteen lysine-rich leukemia gene (*ELL*) *(13,14)*. We showed that its expression is temporally and spatially regulated during embryonic development *(13)*. Its expression profile in the developing mouse embryo strongly suggests that it may play an important role in regulating the process of cell differentiation. Recent studies on its *Xenopus* homolog demonstrated that *Eaf2* is required for eye formation in the frog *(15)*. To demonstrate its function in controlling cell differentiation, we chose the C2C12 myofibroblast cell line as our model system. C2C12 can differentiate into muscle or bone cell lineages when provided with appropriate stimuli.

To test the efficacy of siRNA in silencing the *Eaf2* gene, a modified firefly luciferase expression vector was used to create an in-frame fusion between the target gene, *Eaf2*, and the luciferase reporter. The Eaf2–luciferase fusion plasmid was cotransfected with each testing siRNA and pCVM-lacZ expression plasmid as an internal control. For negative siRNA control, we used a siRNA targeting the Alkaline phosphatase (*ALP*) transcripts. The gene-silencing activity of each siRNA was measured by a performing dual luciferase/β-galactosidase assay.

We designed three siRNAs against *Eaf2* mRNA. We tested two siRNAs by transfecting synthetic siRNA duplexes together with pEaf2-luc. We also tested one siRNA by expressing it from a lentiviral vector. The luciferase assay showed that siRNA Eaf2-147 and Eaf-368 could specifically suppress the reporter gene expression by knocking down the luciferase activity to 30 and 6%, respectively, in comparison with a nongene specific siRNA (ALP) (**Fig. 1**). As an internal control, the activities of the cotransfected β-galactosidase reporter were comparable based on raw data.

To evaluate whether this luciferase-based reporter system can also be adapted for use in testing siRNAs that are expressed from a lentiviral vector, we inserted an Eaf2-619 duplex into pll3.7, in which the cytomegalovirus (CMV) promoter was replaced by the human U6 promoter. Pll3.7-Eaf2-619 was cotransfected into C2C12 cells with

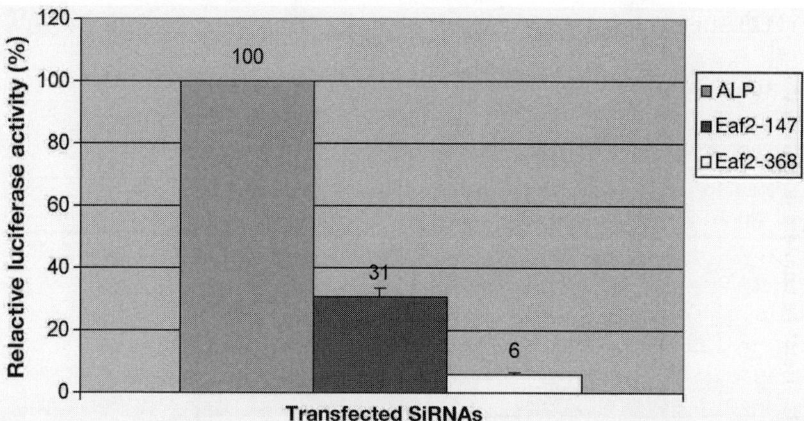

Fig. 1. Efficient knockdown of *Eaf2*–luciferase gene fusion was achieved with two small interfering RNA (siRNA) duplexes against the *Eaf2* mRNA targets, Eaf2-147 and Eaf2-368. Eaf2-368 was far more efficient in quenching luciferase activity. No inhibition was observed with the recombinant *Eaf2*–luciferase gene fusion using an irrelevant siRNA, alkaline phosphatase. Each data set represents an average value from triplicate transfections.

pEaf2-luc and pCMV-lacZ. For a negative control, empty pll3.7 lentiviral vector was used for cotransfection with pEaf2-luc and pCMV-lacZ. Measurement of luciferase activity showed that Eaf2-619 was capable of quenching Eaf2–luc expression by 91%. This gene-silencing effect specifically depends on the *Eaf2* sequence, because the luciferase activity was not altered significantly when the pGL3-control was cotransfected with pll3.7-Eaf2-619 (**Fig. 2**).

In summary, we established a siRNA validation system in which the efficacy of an siRNA could be measured quantitatively. Knowing the quantitative efficacy of each siRNA allows flexibility in performing the task of dose-dependent gene silencing. It will not be difficult to broaden the usefulness of this system in validating siRNAs against partial complementary DNA (cDNA) sequences for genes that are large or for genes for which the full-length cDNAs are not readily available. To circumvent the in-frame cloning, a cDNA fragment can be cloned in front of a luciferase reporter whose translation is controlled by an internal ribosomal entry site (IRES), or the cDNA can be inserted downstream of the luciferase reporter and followed by a transcriptional termination site.

2. Materials

2.1. Construction of In-Frame Eaf2–Luciferase Fusion Plasmid

The open-reading frame encoding luciferase and the polyadenylation sequence was amplified via PCR from the pGL3-Control plasmid (Promega, Madison, WI; cat. no. E1741) and cloned into the XhoI and MluI sites of pIRES-hrGFP 1a (Stratagene, La Jolla, CA; cat. no. 240031) to create pLUC-c1. To construct the pEaf2–luc reporter, a PCR-generated DNA fragment of the mouse *Eaf2* coding region was inserted into the BamHI and XhoI sites of the pLUC-c1 plasmid.

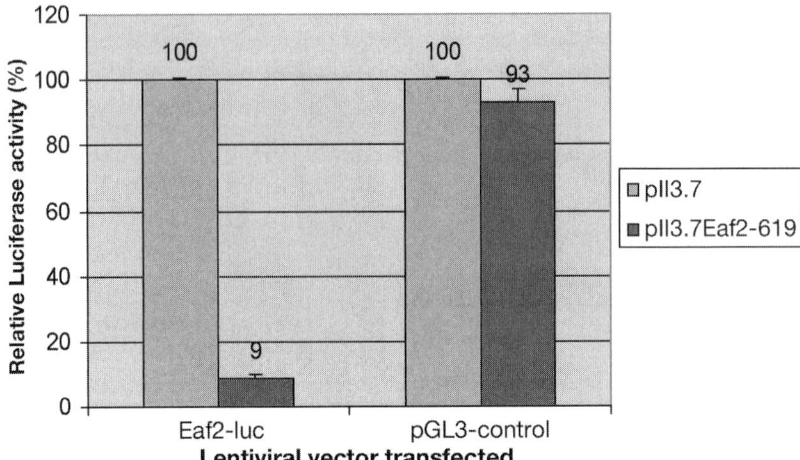

Fig. 2. Silencing of reporter gene activity was accomplished by small interfering RNA (siRNA) expressed using a lentiviral vector. pEaf2-luc was cotransfected with either a pll3.7 empty vector or a pll3.7Eaf2-619 that carried the Eaf2-specific siRNA expression cassette. An efficient knockdown of Eaf2–luc expression was observed in cultures that received pll3.7Eaf2-619. The gene-silencing activity of vector-expressed siRNA was sequence specific. This was demonstrated by the robustness of luciferase activities in cultures that were cotransfected a luciferase expression plasmid, pGL3-control, and the siRNA-expressing lentiviral vector, pll3.7Eaf2-619. Results were plotted as averages of triplicate transfections.

2.2. Construction of siRNA Lentiviral Vector

To construct the lentiviral vector that carries siRNA targeting the *Eaf2* gene, pEaf2-619, a sense oligonucleotide (5'-TGGACCAGATGAGTAGTTGTTTCAAGAGAACA ACTACTCATCTGGTCCTTTTTTC-3') and a complementary antisense oligonucleotide (5'-TCGAGAAAAAAGGACCAGATGAGTAGTTGTTCTCTTGAAACAACTACTCA TCTGGTCCA-3') were chemically synthesized and annealed to make a double-stranded oligonucleotide. The annealed siRNA duplex was inserted into HpaI/XhoI sites downstream of the U6 promoter in the lentiviral vector pll3.7 (from Dr. Luk Van Parijs, Massachusetts Institute of Technology).

2.3. Synthetic siRNA

All siRNA were synthesized by the University of Southern California Kenneth Norris Cancer Center Microchemical Core Facility. Target sequences of each siRNA are listed:

Eaf2-147: 5'-GACCGTCGCGAGCGGGTTCTC-3'.
Eaf2-368: 5'-AAAGAATGCATTTTGATTATT-3'.
ALP: 5'-AATGTCATCATGTTCCTGGGA-3' used as a negative control.

2.4. Cell Line and Transfection

The C2C12 cell line was obtained from the American Type Culture Collection and maintained in Dulbecco's Modified Eagle Medium (DMEM) plus 10% fetal calf serum

(Invitrogen). All plasmids used in the transient transfections were purified by using an Eppendorf Fast Plasmid mini Kit (Brinkmann, Westbury, NY; cat. no. 955150601). For transfection of double-stranded siRNA and reporter plasmids into cells, Oligofectamine reagent (Invitrogen; cat. no. 12252-011) was used. For transfection of lentiviral vector and plamids, lipofectamine (Invitrogen; cat. no. 18324-012) and the Plus reagent (Invitrogen; cat. no. 11514-015; Invitrogen) were used. The Dual-Light kit (Applied Biosystems, Foster City, CA; cat. no. T1003) was used to assay luciferase and β-galactosidase activities in cell lysates. Measurement of light output in cell lysates was performed using a LB9501 Lumat luminometer (Berthold, Oak Ridge, TN).

3. Methods

3.1. Selection of siRNA Sequences

Candidate siRNAs for target gene sequences can be obtained using free online siRNA screening tools (*see* **Note 1**). Custom sense and antisense RNA oligonucleotides can be purchased from commercial sources (*see* **Note 2**). We routinely purchase oligonucleotides from Integrated DNA Technology (www.idtdna.com).

3.2. Anneal Sense and Antisense siRNA Oligo Pairs

1. Prepare 2X annealing buffer (200 mM potassium acetate, 4 mM magnesium acetate, and 60 mM HEPES-KOH, pH 7.4).
2. To make a siRNA duplex stock solution at a final concentration of 20 μM, combine sense and antisense siRNA olignucleotides at equal molar ratio in sterile water. Add annealing buffer and sterile water to bring up to the final volume.
3. Heat at 95°C for 5 min.
4. Incubate at 70°C for 1 min.
5. Allow to gradually cool down to room temperature.
6. Store at −80°C until ready to use.

3.3. Cotransfection of siRNA Duplex and Reporter Plasmids

1. The day before transfection, C2C12 cells were plated at a density of 50 to 70% confluency onto a 12-well plate. It is important to optimize the plating density and transfection efficiency. Do not add antibiotics into the culture medium (*see* **Note 3**).
2. Add 2.5 μL (20 μM) of siRNA duplex, 50 ng of pEaf2–luc, and 50 ng of pCMV-lacZ into 85 μL of Opti-MEM I (Invitrogen).
3. Dilute 2 μL of Oligofectamine reagent into 7 μL of Opti-MEM I without serum.
4. Allow diluted reagent to incubate for 10 min.
5. Add diluted Oligofectamine reagent to diluted siRNA and reporter mixture. Mix gently and incubate for 20 min.
6. Wash cells once with medium without serum.
7. Add 400 μL of serum-free medium to each well containing cells.
8. Mix gently and overlay the Oligofectamine/siRNA/reporter complex onto the cells.
9. Incubate the cells for 4 h in the CO_2 incubator.
10. Add DMEM plus 30% fetal calf serum.
11. Harvest cell 24 h after transfection.

3.4. Cotransfection of siRNA-Expressing Lentiviral Vectors and Reporter Plasmid

1. The day before transfection, plate cells in 12-well plates so that they are 50 to 70% confluent on the day of transfection. Omit antibiotics in the culture medium.
2. Precomplex the DNA with the Plus reagent:
   a. Dilute 0.7 µg DNA (200 ng pll3.7Eaf2-619 or pll3.7, 100 ng pEaf2–luc, 100 ng pCMV-lacZ, or 300 ng pCRII) into 50 µL DMEM.
   b. Add 4 µL of Plus reagent to diluted DNA, mix, and incubate at room temperature for 15 min.
3. Dilute 2 µL lipofectamine reagent into 50 µL DMEM in a separate tube and mix.
4. Combine precomplexed DNA and diluted lipofectamine reagent, mix, and incubate for 15 min at room temperature.
5. Replace the medium on the cells with 0.4 mL DMEM without serum (cell growth medium without serum).
6. Add the DNA/Plus/lipofectamine reagent complexes to cells in each well. Mix complexes into the medium gently; incubate in CO_2 incubator for 3 h.
7. Replace transfection medium with serum-containing growth medium.
8. Harvest cells 18 h after transfection.

3.5. Luciferase and β-Galactosidase Assay by Chemiluminescent Detection

1. Remove culture medium.
2. Rinse transfected cells twice with phosphate-buffered saline.
3. Add 80 µL of lysis solution per well of a 12-well plate to cover the cells.
4. Transfer the cell lysates to microcentrifuge tubes and centrifuge for 5 min to pellet the debris.
5. Transfer supernatant into a glass test tube.
6. Equilibrate Buffer A and B to room temperature.
7. Dilute Galacton-Plus substrate 1:100 in Buffer B.
8. Transfer 10 µL of extracts to luminometer tubes.
9. Add 25 µL of Buffer A to the extract samples.
10. Within 10 min, add 100 µL of Buffer B. After a 1 to 2 s delay, read the light units produced by the hydrolysis of luciferin by luciferase for 1 s per sample.
11. Incubate for 30 to 60 min at room temperature.
12. Add 100 µL of Accelerator-II. After a 1 to 2 s delay, read the light units produced by the hydrolysis of β-galactosidase substrates for 1 s per sample.

4. Notes

1. Selection of siRNA sequences: We used the Dharmacon Si*Design* Tool (http://www.dharmacon.com/SiDESIGN/SMARTpool.aspx) to identify potential siRNAs for *Eaf2*. Some cDNA sequences may not yield excellent siRNA candidates. Choose the best ones that fit the selection criteria. Make sure to perform a basic local alignment search tool (BLAST) search to eliminate siRNAs that may potentially form duplexes with transcripts of different gene targets.
2. When ordering siRNA oligos for cloning into expression vectors, be sure to specify 5' phosphorylation. 5' phosphorylation of oligos is required for the ligation to work. Tuschl's lab web site: http://www.rockefeller.edu/labheads/tuschl/sirna.html is an excellent resource for siRNA-related questions.

3. Transfection. The amount of transfection reagents used in the transfection protocol is cell-type specific. One can refer to manufacturer's product manuals for detail instructions on how to optimize the transfection. It is critical to eliminate antibacterial and antifungal agents from the culture medium when using lipofectamine and Oligofectamine.

References

1. Bass, B. L. (2000) Double-stranded RNA as a template for gene silencing. *Cell* **101,** 235–238.
2. Ketting, R. F. and Plasterk, R. H. (2000) A genetic link between co-suppression and RNA interference in C. elegans. *Nature* **16,** 296–298.
3. Hannon, G. J. and Rossi, J. J. (2004). Unlocking the potential of the human genome with RNA interference. *Nature* **431,** 371–378.
4. Napoli, C., Lemieux, C., and Jorgensen, R. A. (1990) Introduction of a chimeric chalcone synthase gene into *Petunia* results in reversible co-suppression of homologous genes in trans. *Plant Cell* **2,** 279–289.
5. van der Krol, A. R., Mur, L. A., Beld, M., Mol, J. N., and Stuitje, A. R. (1990) Flavonoid genes in *Petunia*: addition of a limited number of gene copies may lead to a suppression of gene expression. *Plant Cell* **2,** 291–299.
6. Fire, A., Albertson, D., Harrison, S., and Moerman, D. (1991) Production of antisense RNA leads to effective and specific inhibition of gene expression in *C. elegans* muscle. *Development* **113,** 503–514.
7. Guo, S. and Kemphues, K. (1995) *par-1*, a gene required for establishing polarity in *C. elegans* embryos, encodes a putative Ser/Thr kinase that is asymmetrically distributed. *Cell* **81,** 611–620.
8. Fire, A., Xu, S., Montgomery, M. K., Kostas, S. A., Driver, S. E., and Mello, C. C. (1998) Potent and specific genetic interference by double-stranded RNA in *Caenorhabditis elegans*. *Nature* **391,** 806–811.
9. Bernstein, E., Kim, S. Y., Carmell, M. A., et al. (2003) Dicer is essential for mouse development. *Nat. Genet.* **35,** 215–217.
10. Wienholds, E., Koudijs, M. J., van Eeden, F. J., Cuppen, E., and Plasterk, R. H. (2003) The microRNA-producing enzyme Dicer1 is essential for zebrafish development. *Nat. Genet.* **35,** 217–218.
11. He, L. and Hannon, G. J. (2004) MicroRNAs: small RNAs with a big role in gene regulation. *Nat. Rev. Genet.* **5,** 522–531.
12. Elbashir, S. M., Harborth, J., Lendeckel, W., Yalcin, A., Weber, K., and Tuschl, T. (2001) Duplexes of 21-nucleotide RNAs mediate RNA interference in cultured mammalian cells. *Nature* **411,** 494–498.
13. Li, M., Wu, X., Zhuang, F., Jiang, S., Jiang, M., and Liu, Y. H. (2003) Expression of murine *ELL-associated factor 2* (*Eaf2*) is developmentally regulated. *Dev. Dyn.* **228,** 273–280.
14. Simone, F., Luo, R. T., Polak, P. E., Kaberlein, J. J., and Thirman, M. J. (2003) ELL-associated factor 2 (EAF2), a functional homolog of EAF1 with alternative ELL binding properties. *Blood* **101,** 2355–2362.
15. Maurus, D., Heligon, C., Burger-Schwarzler, A., Brandli, A. W., and Kuhl, M. (2005) Noncanonical Wnt-4 signaling and EAF2 are required for eye development in Xenopus laevis. *EMBO J.* **24,**1181–1191.

14

Cloning MicroRNAs From Mammalian Tissues

Michael Z. Michael

Summary

MicroRNAs (miRNAs) are ubiquitous regulators of gene expression in plants and animals. Their distinctive structure, as very short RNAs with a 5'-phosphate and 3'-hydroxyl group, has enabled the development of protocols to clone miRNAs. After enrichment of these small molecules by size, serial ligation of adapter oligonucleotides to each terminus allows amplification using reverse transcription (RT)-polymerase chain reaction (PCR). Plasmid cloning of multiple miRNA sequences and subsequent DNA sequence analysis enable both bioinformatic characterization of the various miRNAs and experimental validation of their accumulation in cells.

Key Words: MicroRNA; RNA; cDNA; cloning; gene expression; development; Northern blot analysis.

1. Introduction

miRNAs are a class of small cytoplasmic RNAs that regulate the expression of other genes, by either inhibiting translation or directing transcript degradation (1). In mammals, mature miRNA sequences range between 19 and 24 nucleotides (nt) in length (usually 21–22 nt) and are the products of Dicer ribonuclease (RNase) III cleavage of longer (~70 nt) precursor molecules, called precursor (pre)-miRNAs, that adopt a hairpin conformation because of (imperfect) indirect repeat sequences. The pre-miRNAs are, themselves, the products of cleavage from longer RNA polymerase II-generated transcripts, by the Drosha RNase III (within the Microprocessor complex) before export from the nucleus (2,3).

The first miRNAs were identified in *Caenorhabditis elegans*, as a result of genetic screens to identify mutants with altered timing of development (4). Subsequently, miRNAs have been shown to regulate a diverse range of eukaryotic developmental and metabolic processes, including bilateral asymmetry, apoptosis, cellular proliferation, lipid metabolism, insulin secretion, stress response, and flowering (5–7). In mammals, miRNAs are being assessed for their roles in the onset of diseases. The recent discoveries of viral miRNAs encoded by human pathogens suggest that infection of host cells involves not

From: *Methods in Molecular Biology, vol. 342: MicroRNA Protocols*
Edited by: S. Ying © Humana Press Inc., Totowa, NJ

only miRNA regulation of viral genes, but also, potentially, the host transcriptome *(8)*. The fundamental cellular processes that are regulated by mammalian miRNAs, such as cellular differentiation and proliferation, and the knowledge that many miRNA genes are near disease-associated loci and are differentially expressed in neoplasia, also suggest their involvement in a variety of diseases, including cancer *(9–13)*. Current efforts are directed to identifying all of the miRNA sequences in mammalian genomes, using bioinformatic and direct cloning approaches.

While studying the mechanism of RNA interference, Thomas Tuschl's group developed a method for cloning small interfering RNAs, the products generated by Dicer-cleavage of exogenous double-stranded RNA *(14,15)*. A consequence of these experiments was the development of a protocol that could also clone the endogenous products of Dicer activity, namely miRNAs. This approach has been used to clone miRNAs from a variety of plant and animal species. It has also inspired the development of alternative miRNA cloning protocols, notably one developed by David Bartel's group *(16)* (*see* **Note 1**). We describe a variation of the original Elbashir *(14)* protocol, with modifications showing the influence of the Lau *(16)* protocol.

The miRNA cloning procedure requires size selection of 18- to 24-nt RNA purified by polyacrylamide gel electrophoresis (PAGE). The small RNA is then dephosphorylated to enable directional ligation of an adapter sequence, first to the 3' end of the RNA, and, after PAGE purification of ligated products and rephosphorylation of the 5' terminus, ligation of a second adapter to the 5' end. The resultant miRNA sequence is inserted between two known sequences and can be amplified by standard RT-PCR. Restriction enzyme cleavage of the amplified products, at a site present in both adaptor sequences, allows the concatamerization of multiple PCR products before cloning into a plasmid vector. The cloning of complementary DNA (cDNA) concatamers reduces the number of clones and sequencing reactions required. Sequence data generated are scrutinized *in silico* for their genomic origin and for the ability of a putative precursor transcript to adopt a hairpin configuration. Northern analysis is also used to validate the in vivo accumulation of a particular miRNA. A flow diagram that summarizes the protocol is presented in **Fig. 1.**

2. Materials

2.1. RNA Isolation

1. Trizol® reagent (Invitrogen, Carlsbad, CA).
2. Chloroform.
3. Isopropyl alcohol.
4. Formamide.
5. 3 *M* sodium acetate.
6. 100% ethanol.
7. Cold (0°C–4°C) 75% ethanol.
8. Nuclease-free water.
9. 10X MOPS buffer: 200 m*M* 3-(*N*-morpholino)propanesulphonic acid (MOPS; pH 7.0), 10 m*M* ethylenediaminetetraacetic acid (EDTA), and 50 m*M* sodium acetate.
10. 1.2% agarose gel containing 1X MOPS buffer and 2% (v/v) 12.3 *M* formaldehyde.

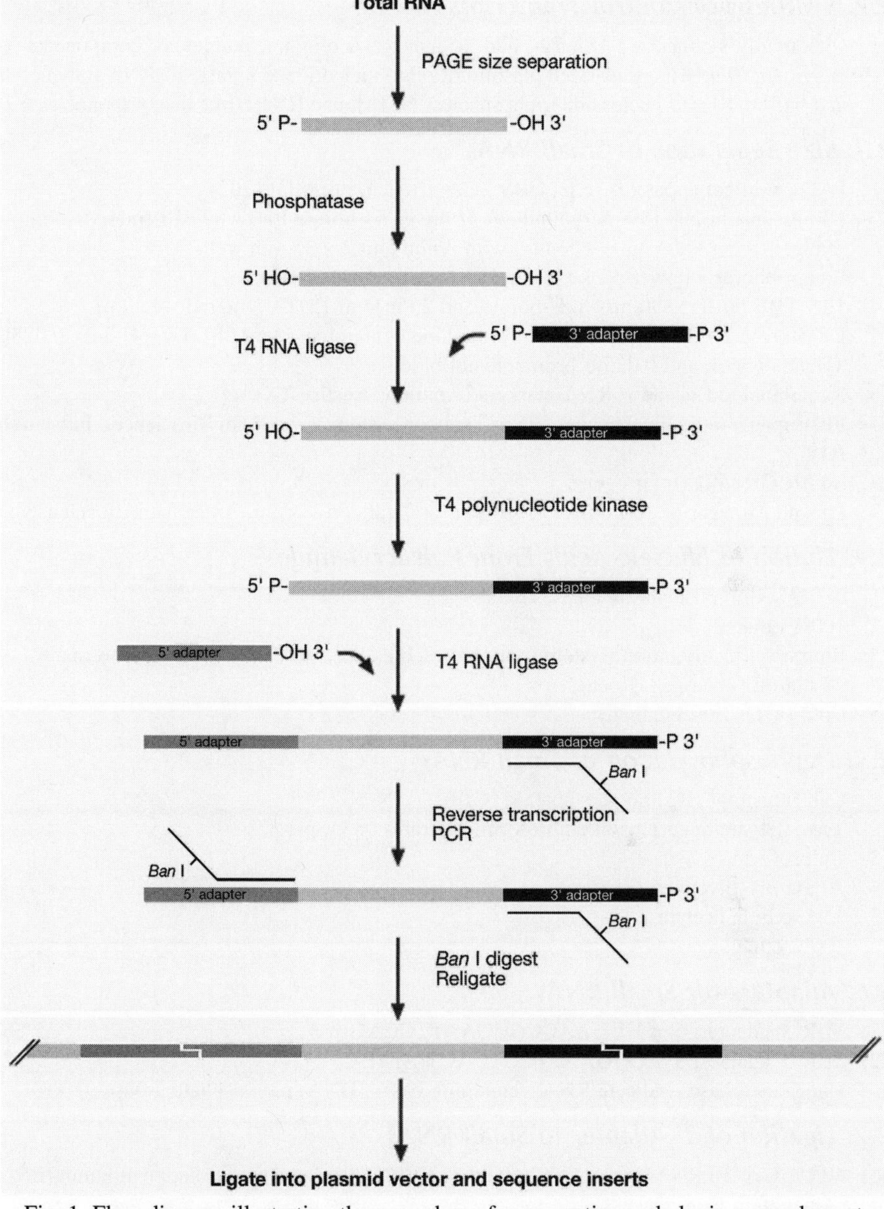

Fig. 1. Flow diagram illustrating the procedures for generating and cloning complementary DNAs from microRNAs.

11. 5X RNA loading buffer: 35% formamide, 4X MOPS buffer (*see* **Subheading 2.1., item 9**), 4 mM EDTA, 0.9 M formaldehyde, 0.16% (v/v) saturated bromophenol blue and xylene cyanol aqueous solutions, and 2 µg/mL ethidium bromide.
12. 20 mg/mL glycogen (Roche, Indianapolis, IN).

2.2. Synthesis of Control Transcripts

1. Chemically synthesized 18-, 22-, and 24-mer RNA oligonucleotides, or components for enzymatic synthesis (linearized plasmid or oligonucleotide template, T7 RNA polymerase and buffer, 10 mM nucleoside triphosphates [NTPs], and RNase-free deoxyribonuclease I).

2.3. Size Separation of Small RNAs

1. PAGE minigel apparatus (e.g., CBS Scientific cat. no. MGV-202).
2. 10-mL denaturing 15% acrylamide/8 M urea/Tris-borate-EDTA (TBE; filtered solution) minigel (8 cm × 8.5 cm × 1.5 mm) with 3 mm and 2 × 35 mm wells.
3. Electrophoresis power pack (preferably with thermal sensor).
4. 10X TBE buffer: 890 mM Tris-borate and 20 mM of EDTA (filtered solution).
5. Denaturing PAGE loading buffer: formamide containing 18 mM EDTA (pH 8.0), 0.025% xylene cyanol, and 0.025% bromophenol blue.
6. Radiolabeled Decade™ RNA markers (Ambion, Austin, TX).
7. Fluorimager (e.g., FluorImager 595 or Typhoon system; Amersham Biosciences, Pittsburgh, PA).
8. SYBR Green II (Invitrogen).
9. PhosphorImager (e.g., FujiBas, FujiFilm; or Typhoon system, Amersham Biosciences).

2.4. Elution of Nucleic Acids From Polyacrylamide

1. 0.3 M sodium acetate (nuclease-free).
2. 100% ethanol.
3. Elutrap® Electroelution System (optional; Schleicher and Schuell, Dassel, Germany).
4. 20 mg/mL glycogen (Roche).
5. Cold (4°C) 75% ethanol.

2.5. Dephosphorylation of Small RNAs

1. Calf intestinal alkaline phosphatase (CIP).
2. Tris-HCl-saturated phenol/chloroform, 1:1 ratio (v/v), pH 8.0.
3. Chloroform.
4. 20 mg/mL glycogen (Roche).
5. 3 M sodium acetate.
6. 100% ethanol.

2.6. Adapters for Small RNAs

1. MIR 3' adapter: 5' p-UUUAACCGCGAATTCCAG-p 3'.
2. MIR 5' adapter: 5' ACGGAATTCCTCACTrArArA 3'.
   Underlined bases indicate RNA; remaining bases, DNA; p, phosphate group.

2.7. Ligation of 3' Adapter to Small RNAs

1. 40 U/µL of T4 RNA ligase, 10X buffer, and 0.1% acetylated bovine serum albumin (BSA) (Amersham Biosciences).
2. RNasin RNase inhibitor (Promega, Madison, WI).

2.8. PAGE Purification of 3' Adapter-Ligated Small RNAs

1. 15% acrylamide/8 M urea minigel.
2. Denaturing PAGE loading buffer (as in **Subheading 2.3.**, **item 5**).
3. SYBR Green II (Invitrogen).

4. 0.3 *M* sodium acetate.
5. 20 mg/mL glycogen (Roche).
6. 100% ethanol.

2.9. 5′ Phosphorylation of 3′ Adapter-Ligated RNA

1. 9 U/μL of T4 polynucleotide kinase (PNK) and 10X buffer (USB, Amersham Biosciences).
2. Tris-HCl-saturated phenol/chloroform, 1:1 ratio (v/v), pH 8.0.
3. Chloroform.
4. 20 mg/mL glycogen (Roche).
5. 3 *M* sodium acetate.
6. 100% ethanol.

2.10. 5′ Adapter Ligation

1. MIR 5′ adapter.
2. 40 U/μL of T4 RNA ligase (Amersham Biosciences).
3. 10X T4 RNA ligase buffer (Amersham Biosciences).
4. 0.1% acetylated BSA.
5. RNasin RNase inhibitor (Promega).

2.11. PAGE Separation of Double Adapter-Ligated RNA

1. Stop solution: 8 *M* urea and 50 m*M* EDTA.
2. 12% acrylamide/8 *M* urea minigel.
3. SYBR Green II (Invitrogen).

2.12. Reverse Transcription

1. Superscript II and 5X buffer (Invitrogen).
2. 0.1 *M* dithiothreitol.
3. RNasin RNase inhibitor (Promega).
4. 10 m*M* deoxy NTPs (dNTPs).

2.13. PCR Amplification of Small RNAs

1. BanI-MIR 3′ primer: 5′-CTAGCTTGGTGCCTGGAATTCGCGGTTAAA-3′.
2. BanI-MIR 5′ primer: 5′-CCAACAGGCACCACGGAATTCCTCACTAAA-3′.
3. 5 U/μL of Taq DNA polymerase and 10X buffer.
4. 25 m*M* MgCl$_2$ (if using magnesium-free PCR buffer).
5. Thermal cycler.
6. Tris-HCl-saturated phenol/chloroform, 1:1 ratio (v/v), pH 8.0.
7. Chloroform.
8. 3 *M* sodium acetate.
9. 100% ethanol.
10. 2% agarose/Tris-acetate-EDTA (TAE) gel with 0.2 μg/mL ethidium bromide.
11. Low molecular weight DNA markers (e.g., pUC19/HpaII).

2.14. Restriction of PCR Products

1. 20 U/μL BanI restriction endonuclease and 10X buffer (New England Biolabs, Ipswich, MA).
2. Tris-HCl-saturated phenol/chloroform, 1:1 ratio (v/v), pH 8.0.
3. Chloroform.

4. 3 *M* sodium acetate.
5. 100% ethanol.

2.15. Concatamerization of PCR Products

1. 3 U/μL of T4 DNA ligase (Promega).
2. 2X rapid ligation buffer (Promega).
3. 100-bp DNA ladder (e.g., 2-Log DNA Ladder; New England Biolabs).
4. 1.5% agarose/TAE gel containing 0.2 μg/mL ethidium bromide. If Elutrap system is not available, will require 1.5% low-melt agarose/TAE gel, Tris-HCl-buffered phenol, pH 8.0, phenol/chloroform, and chloroform (as in **Subheading 2.14.**), 20 mg/mL glycogen, 3 *M* sodium acetate, and ethanol.

2.16. Taq DNA Polymerase Processing of Concatamer Ends

As in **Subheading 2.13.**, no primers are required.

2.17. Cloning and Sequence Analysis of miRNAs

1. 50 ng/μL of pGEM®-T Easy cloning vector (Promega).
2. 3 U/μL of T4 DNA ligase (Promega).
3. 2X rapid ligation buffer (Promega).
4. Transformation competent *Escherichia coli* cells (e.g., DH5α or XL1-blue).
5. Luria-Bertani (LB) agar: LB medium (10 g/L bacto-tryptone, 5 g/L yeast extract, and 10 g/L NaCl) with 15 g/L agar; autoclave solution and add 100 μg/mL ampicillin or 50 μg/mL carbenicillin before pouring the plates.
6. 100 m*M* isopropylthiogalactoside.
7. 2% X-gal in dimethylformamide.

2.18. PCR Screening of Bacterial Colonies

1. LB agar + carbenicillin plates (as in **Subheading 2.17.**).
2. 10 μ*M* M13 forward primer: 5'-CGCCAGGGTTTTCCCAGTCACGAC-3'.
3. 10 μ*M* M13 reverse primer: 5'-TCACACAGGAAACAGCTATGAC-3'.
4. 5 U/μL of Taq DNA polymerase and 10X buffer.
5. 25 m*M* MgCl$_2$ (if using magnesium-free buffer).
6. Thermal cycler.
7. 1.2% agarose/TAE gel with 0.2 μg/mL ethidium bromide.
8. 100-bp DNA ladder (e.g., 2-Log DNA Ladder; New England Biolabs).

2.19. Exo/Shrimp Alkaline Phosphatase Preparation of Sequencing Templates

1. 20 U/μL of *E. coli* exonuclease I (New England Biolabs).
2. 1 U/μL of shrimp alkaline phosphatase (USB, Amersham Biosciences).

2.20. Validation of miRNAs: Northern Analysis

1. Radiolabeled Decade RNA markers (Ambion).
2. 15% acrylamide/8 *M* urea/TBE gel.
3. Hybond N+ nylon transfer membrane (Amersham Biosciences).
4. Semi-dry electroblotter (e.g., Panther™; OWL Separation Systems, Portsmouth, NH).
5. QuikHybe™ hybridization solution (Stratagene, La Jolla, CA).
6. Hybridization incubator.

7. 3,000 Ci/mmol (10 mCi/mL) of γ-^{32}P adenosine triphosphate (ATP).
8. 10 U/μL of T4 PNK and 10X PNK buffer (New England Biolabs).
9. Microspin G-25 Sephadex columns (Amersham Biosciences) or homemade equivalents.
10. Liquid scintillation counter and handheld Geiger monitor.
11. Wash solutions: 2X standard sodium citrate (SSC), 0.1% sodium dodecylsulfate (SDS) plus 0.2X SSC, and 0.1% SDS.
12. PhosphorImager or X-ray film.

3. Methods

3.1. RNA Isolation

Several methods are suitable for obtaining high-quality total RNA from mammalian tissues and cultured cells (*see* **Note 2**). The following Trizol protocol is commonly used and provides a sufficient yield of intact small RNAs.

1. Homogenize tissues thoroughly in Trizol reagent (Invitrogen) (100 mg of tissue per milliliter of Trizol) using a Polytron power homogenizer. Cell pellets can be lysed by pipetting, then vortexing, in 1 mL Trizol/10^7 cells. Adherent cells are lysed directly in the culture dish or flask (after removal of growth medium) by the addition of 1 mL Trizol/10 cm^2 of growth area, then pipetting repeatedly, transferring to a microcentrifuge tube, and vortexing for 30 s.
2. Centrifuge lysates at 12,000g for 10 min at 4°C to pellet debris.
3. If a pellet forms, transfer the supernatant to a fresh tube (avoid lipids that may result from fatty tissues) and keep at room temperature for 10 min. Add 0.2 mL chloroform per 1 mL Trizol reagent and shake vigorously by hand to mix; incubate at room temperature for 3 min. Centrifuge tubes at 12,000g for 15 min at 4°C to separate phases. Remove the upper aqueous phase (avoiding interface contamination) and transfer the aqueous phase into a fresh tube.
4. Precipitate RNA in the aqueous phase by adding 0.5 volume of isopropyl alcohol (per original Trizol volume), vortex briefly, then incubate at room temperature for 10 min and centrifuge at 12,000g for 10 min at 4°C. Remove the supernatant and wash pellet with 0.5 mL of cold 75% ethanol. Centrifuge at 12,000g for 5 min at 4°C. Carefully remove the ethanol solution, centrifuge briefly, and aspirate off the remaining ethanol. Air-dry the pellet briefly (3–5 min), then resuspend in nuclease-free water or, preferably, formamide (*see* **Note 3**).
5. Add 2 to 5 μg of total RNA to 5X RNA loading buffer, heat at 70°C for 5 min, and chill on ice. Load onto a 1.2% agarose/MOPS/formaldehyde gel. Inspect on an ultraviolet (UV) transilluminator.

As a rule, RNA quality can be assessed by the integrity of the 28S and 18S ribosomal RNA bands (no smearing). The intensity of the 28S band should be at least double that of the 18S ribosomal RNA band.

3.2. Control Transcripts for Gel Standards and Ligation

Synthetic 18- and 24-mer RNA oligonucleotides (as used in **Subheading 3.2.**) are required, both as markers for comparative sizing on gels and as controls for subsequent RNA manipulations. They are recommended for optimizing later reaction conditions to avoid wasting precious small RNA samples (*see* **Note 4**). The sequence of the oligonucleotides is unimportant, except that guanosine should be avoided at the 5' terminus, because guanosine is a less-efficient donor for T4 RNA ligase-mediated ligation to the 5' adapter *(14)*.

In the following procedure (**Subheading 3.7.**) it is wise to add the control transcript to ligations in larger amounts than the sample RNA, to aid SYBR Green II-stained/fluorimager detection.

3.3. Size Separation of Small RNAs

PAGE is suitable for separating small (18–24 nt) RNAs from the remaining total RNA preparations (*see* **Note 3**).

1. Add 500 µg of total RNA to an equal volume of PAGE loading buffer and heat at 90°C for 5 min. Load into prerinsed, wide (35 mm) wells of a prewarmed gel (45°C). Load marker/control 18- and 24-mer oligoribonucleotides (*see* **Note 4**) into the 3-mm well, taking care not to contaminate the total RNA samples.
2. Run the gel with a power level to maintain a constant temperature of between 40°C and 45°C (2–5 W). When the bromophenol blue nears the end of the gel, remove the gel, stain with SYBR Green II (1:10,000 dilution in 0.5X TBE; Molecular Probes), and visualize the gel on a fluorimager.
3. Alignment of an actual size (100% scale) print of the image with the gel allows excision of the sample area within the 18- to 24-nt size range (*see* **Note 5**).

3.4. Elution From Gels (Passive vs Electroelution)

RNA can be reclaimed from the gel, either by passive elution or electroelution.

3.4.1. Passive Elution

1. Passive elution involves covering the gel slice with 0.3 *M* RNase-free sodium acetate, then heating the tube at 95°C for 5 min, followed by overnight incubation at 4°C.

3.4.2. Electroelution (Preferred)

1. Cut gel strips into 1-cm long fragments and perform electrophoresis in 0.5X TBE using an Elutrap system (Schleicher and Schuell), run at a constant 4 W for 45 min, with a final 20 s reversal of polarity. The eluent, trapped between separation membranes, is then carefully transferred to a microcentrifuge tube and adjusted to 0.3 *M* sodium acetate.
2. RNA is precipitated from either passive or electroeluents, by addition of 2.5 volumes of ethanol, and incubation at −20°C overnight. Precipitation efficiency can be enhanced by the addition of 20 µg glycogen as a carrier.
3. After overnight precipitation, RNA (and glycogen) are pelleted in a microcentrifuge at 14,000*g* for 20 min at 4°C. The pellet is rinsed with cold (4°C) 75% ethanol and briefly air-dried.
4. The RNA pellet is redissolved in 20 µL water and the RNA concentration determined either by spectrophotometry (OD_{260}) or SYBR Green II staining and comparison with standards.

3.5. Dephosphorylation of Small RNAs

To ensure directional ligation of the 3' adapter to the miRNAs using RNA ligase, the miRNA 5' phosphate, which is characteristic of Dicer-cleaved fragments, is removed using alkaline phosphatase.

1. Add the following components to the PAGE-purified small RNA in a 26 μL volume: 3 μL of 10X CIP buffer (Amersham Biosciences), 0.5 μL of 20 U/μL calf intestinal alkaline phosphatase (Amersham Biosciences).
2. Incubate at 50°C for 30 min, then increase the reaction volume to 100 μL with water and extract once with 100 μL phenol/chloroform. Transfer the aqueous phase to a fresh tube and re-extract with 70 μL chloroform.
3. Precipitate the aqueous phase by adding 1 μL of 20 μg/mL glycogen (Roche), 10 μL of 3 *M* sodium acetate and 250 μL ethanol. Incubate at −20°C, 2 h to overnight.
4. Pellet RNA in a microcentrifuge at 16,000*g* for 20 min at 4°C, rinse pellet with 200 μL of cold 75% ethanol, and air-dry.
5. Resuspend RNA pellet in 10 μL of nuclease-free water.

3.6. Adapters and Their Ligation to miRNAs

Removal of the 5'-phosphate group on miRNAs allows directional ligation of an RNA: DNA chimeric oligonucleotide adapter (*see* **Note 6**) to their 3' termini. RNA sequences at the 5' end of the adapter provide an efficient donor substrate for T4 RNA ligase-mediated ligation to the miRNA. Ligation to the 3' end of the 3' adapter is blocked by the incorporation of a 3'-phosphate group on the oligonucleotide. The adapters also incorporate restriction sites to allow cleavage and subsequent religation of the products into concatamers before final cloning. This restriction site may, however, be redundant because additional BanI sites are introduced during PCR amplification (*see* **Note 6**).

The adapter sequences (similar to those described by Elbashir et al., **ref.** *14*) are:

1. MIR 3' adapter: 5' p-<u>UUU</u>AACCGCGAATTCCAG-p 3'.
2. MIR 5' adapter: 5' ACGGAATTCCTCACT<u>rArArA</u> 3'.
   Underlined bases indicate RNA; remaining bases, DNA; p, phosphate group.

3.7. Ligation of 3' Adapter to Small RNAs

1. Combine the following in a PCR tube:
   a. 4 μL (≥0.4 μg) dephosphorylated small RNA prep (or RNA controls).
   b. 1 μL 100 μ*M* MIR 3' adapter oligonucleotide.
2. Heat at 65°C for 3 min, then chill on ice and centrifuge briefly.
3. Add:
   a. 1 μL 10X RNA ligase buffer (Amersham Biosciences).
   b. 0.5 μL (40 U/μL) RNasin RNase inhibitor (Promega).
   c. 0.5 μL (40 U/μL) T4 RNA ligase (Amersham Biosciences).
   d. 2 μL nuclease-free water.
   e. 1 μL 0.1% BSA.
4. Incubate at 14°C overnight.

Include 3' adapter-only control ligation.

3.8. PAGE Purification of 3' Adapter-Ligated Small RNAs

1. After ligation, add 1.5 volumes of denaturing PAGE loading buffer and separate fragments on prewarmed 15% acrylamide/8 *M* urea preparative minigel with 1.5-mm spacers and 5-mm wells. Also load Decade RNA markers, the 3' adapter-ligated control, and unligated transcript controls to enable detection of the appropriate ligation products.

2. Stain gel with SYBR Green II (1:10,000 dilution in 0.5X TBE) for 10 min, then scan on a fluorimager. The sensitivity of detection can generally be increased by raising the photomultiplier tube level, or by using the accompanying imaging software to enhance the image and visualize bands. Comparison of the gel with an actual size 100% scale print of the fluorimage allows detection of the ligated products. Excise bands that correspond to the expected ligation product (approx 40 nt). Also excise bands of control transcript ligations. Rescan gel after band excision to ensure that the appropriate fragments were removed. Decade RNA markers (4 µL, prepared per manufacturer's instructions) can be directly visualized by SYBR Green II staining and also detected by phosphorimaging after excision of bands (if the Decade markers are radiolabeled).
3. Place excised gel bands in 300 µL of 0.3 M sodium acetate in a microcentrifuge tube, heat at 95°C for 5 min, then allow to elute overnight at 4°C.
4. After overnight elution, transfer the eluents into fresh tubes, add 40 µg glycogen and 750 µL ethanol, vortex, and precipitate at −20°C for 2 h to overnight.
5. Pellet DNA by centrifugation, 16,000g for 20 min at 4°C, then rinse pellet with cold 200 µL of 75% ethanol, and air-dry briefly.

3.9. 5' Phosphorylation of 3' Adapter-Ligated RNAs

1. Resuspend the 3' adapter-ligated RNA pellets in 17 µL of nuclease-free water, add 2 µL of 10X PNK buffer and 0.5 µL of 9 U/µL T4 PNK (USB, Amersham Biosciences). Mix gently and incubate at 37°C for 30 min, then inactivate by heating at 68°C for 5 min.
2. Adjust volume to 100 µL with nuclease-free water, then extract once with an equal volume of phenol/chloroform and re-extract the aqueous phase with 60 µL chloroform, transfer the aqueous phase to a fresh tube, and add 10 µL of 3 M sodium acetate, 20 µg glycogen, and 300 µL ethanol, vortex, and precipitate at −20°C for at least 2 h.
3. Pellet nucleic acids, 16,000g for 20 min at 4°C, then rinse with cold 75% ethanol and air-dry briefly.
4. Resuspend in 6 µL of nuclease-free water.

3.10. Ligation of 5' Adapter

1. Heat the 3' adapter-ligated RNA solution at 70°C for 3 min, chill on ice, then add:
   a. 1 µL 10X T4 RNA ligase buffer (Amersham Biosciences).
   b. 1 µL 100 µM MIR 5' adapter oligonucleotide.
   c. 0.5 µL 40 U/µL RNasin RNase inhibitor (Promega).
   d. 0.5 µL 40 µ/L T4 RNA ligase (Amersham Biosciences).
   e. 1 µL 0.1% acetylated BSA (Amersham Biosciences) (add BSA last).
2. Incubate at 14°C, overnight.

Include positive-control ligations of 3' adapter/control transcripts with 5' adapter, as well as 5' adapter-only negative controls.

3.11. PAGE Separation of RNAs Ligated to Both 3' and 5' Adapters

1. After ligation, stop the reaction by adding an equal volume of stop solution (8 M urea and 50 mM EDTA), heat at 95°C for 2 min, then load onto a prewarmed, preparative 12% acrylamide/8 M urea minigel (with 1.5-mm spacers). Run the gel at a constant temperature, 45°C, until the bromophenol blue band nears the end of the gel.
2. Stain the gel with SYBR Green II (1:10,000 dilution in 0.5X TBE) for 10 min, destain briefly, and view on fluorimager. Excise the ligation products (approx 60 nt). Place the

excised gel fragments in 300 µL of 0.3 *M* sodium acetate, heat at 95°C for 5 min, then allow to elute overnight at 4°C.

3. Precipitate the nucleic acids from the eluent by adding 2 µL of 20 mg/mL glycogen and 900 µL ethanol. Incubate at –20°C for at least 2 h.

4. Pellet the nucleic acids/glycogen by centrifugation at 16,000*g* for 20 min at 4°C. Rinse pellet with cold 75% ethanol, air-dry briefly, and resuspend in 20 µL of nuclease-free water. Use 5 µL as a template for RT.

3.12. Reverse Transcription

To generate cDNA for PCR amplification, reverse transcribe the RNA/adaptor molecules in the following reactions:

1. Combine 5 µL of PAGE-purified double-adapter-ligated RNA, 0.5 µL of 100 µ*M* BanI-MIR-3' primer, 1 µL of 10 m*M* dNTPs, and 6 µL of nuclease-free water.

2. Heat at 70°C for 5 min, chill on ice, pulse centrifuge, then add 4 µL of 5X Superscript II First Strand buffer (Invitrogen), 2 µL of 0.1 *M* dithiothreitol, and 0.5 µL of RNasin RNase inhibitor (Promega).

3. Mix reagents, centrifuge briefly, and allow to equilibrate at 42°C for 2 min. Add 1 µL of 200 U/µL Superscript II reverse transcriptase (Invitrogen) and incubate at 42°C for 50 min, then heat at 70°C for 10 min to inactivate the enzyme. Keep the reaction on ice for use as a template in the PCR reactions.

3.13. PCR Amplification of Adapted Small RNAs

1. In PCR tubes, assemble the following amplification reactions:
   a. 4 µL template cDNA.
   b. 1 µL 10 µ*M* BanI-MIR3' primer.
   c. 1 µL 10 µ*M* BanI-MIR5' primer.
   d. 5 µL 10X *Taq* polymerase buffer.
   e. 1 µL 10 m*M* dNTPs.
   f. 3 µL 25 m*M* MgCl$_2$.
   g. 0.5 µL 5 U/µL *Taq* DNA polymerase.
   h. 35.5 µL nuclease-free water.
2. Thermal cycler program:
   a. Hold at 94°C for 3 min.
   b. 35 cycles of: 94°C for 30 s (denaturation); 55°C for 30 s (annealing); 72°C for 60 s (extension).
   c. 72°C for 7 min (final extension).
   d. Hold at 4°C.
3. Run 5 µL of each PCR reaction on a 2% agarose/TAE gel with ethidium bromide to analyze the products. Expect to see PCR products of approx 80 bp, however, smaller products may also be visible (*see* **Note 7**).
4. To the remaining PCR reactions, add nuclease-free water for a final volume of 100 µL. Extract once with an equal volume phenol/chloroform, and re-extract the aqueous phase with 60 µL chloroform. Precipitate the second aqueous phase by adding 10 µL of 3 *M* sodium acetate and 250 µL ethanol. Incubate at –20°C for 2 h to overnight.

3.14. Restriction of PCR Products

1. After precipitation of the PCR products, pellet the DNA at 4°C, 16,000*g* for 15 min. Rinse the pellet with 75% ethanol and allow to air-dry.

2. Resuspend the pellet in 17.5 µL of nuclease-free water and add 2 µL of 10X BanI endonuclease buffer (RE buffer 4; New England Biolabs) and 0.5 µL of 20 U/µL BanI restriction endonuclease (New England Biolabs).
3. Incubate at 37°C for 3 h, then heat-kill the endonuclease at 70°C for 20 min.
4. Increase the reaction volume to 100 µL with nuclease-free water, then extract with an equal volume of phenol/chloroform, re-extract the aqueous phase with 60 µL chloroform, and precipitate the subsequent aqueous phase by adding 10 µL of 3 M sodium acetate and 250 µL ethanol and incubating at −20°C for longer than 2 h.
5. Pellet BanI-restricted PCR products: 4°C, 16,000g for 15 min. Rinse pellets with 75% ethanol and air-dry. Resuspend DNA in 8.5 µL of nuclease-free water.

3.15. Concatamerization of cDNAs

1. To 8.5 µL of BanI-restricted PCR products, add 8 µL 2X rapid ligation buffer (Promega) and 0.5 µL of 3 U/µL T4 DNA Ligase (Promega).
2. Ligate at room temperature for 90 min. Load onto a 1.5% low-melt agarose/TAE gel containing ethidium bromide. Also load a 100-bp DNA ladder. Run the gel far enough to clearly distinguish 200- from 600-bp DNA. An optimal ligation time should be empirically determined for each experiment.
3. Excise agarose fragments containing ligation products between 200 and 600 bp in length, with minimum exposure to UV light.
4. Electroelute concatamers in TAE buffer, using the Elutrap apparatus (Schleicher and Schuell), at 150 V for 60 min, then reverse polarity at 50 V for 30 s. Transfer the eluents from between the separating membranes (~300 µL) into a microcentrifuge tube and add 1 µL of 20 mg/mL glycogen (Roche), 30 µL of 3 M sodium acetate, and 750 µL ethanol. Precipitate at −20°C for 1 h to overnight.

If an electroelution apparatus is not available, other agarose gel–DNA purification procedures, such as low-melt agarose/phenol extraction (*see* **Note 8**) can be used.

3.16. Taq DNA Polymerase Processing of Concatamer Ends

The ends of the concatamers are repaired and A-tailed using *Taq* DNA polymerase to allow ligation into T-tailed PCR cloning plasmid vectors.

1. Pellet concatamers/glycogen: 16,000g for 20 min at 4°C. Wash pellets with 400 µL of 75% ethanol and air-dry.
2. Resuspend each sample in a final volume of 10 µL with nuclease-free water (each sample pooled into one PCR tube). Add 2.5 µL of 10X *Taq* DNA polymerase buffer, 0.5 µL of 10 mM dNTPs, 0.5 µL of 2 U/µL *Taq* DNA polymerase, and 11.5 µL water. Incubate at 37°C for 30 min.
3. Increase the reaction volume to 100 µL with nuclease-free water. Extract with an equal volume of phenol/chloroform, transfer the aqueous phase, and re-extract with 80 µL chloroform. Transfer the aqueous phase to a fresh tube, precipitate by adding 10 µL of 3 M sodium acetate and 300 µL ethanol, incubate at −20°C for at least 1 h.
4. Pellet DNA at 16,000g for 15 min at 4°C, wash pellets with 75% ethanol, and air-dry. Resuspend each pellet in 10 µL of nuclease-free water and use as insert in the following ligations.

3.17. Ligation of Concatamers Into Plasmid Vector

1. Prepare the following ligation reactions:

   a. 4 μL small RNA concatamers (*Taq* polymerase processed).
   b. 0.5 μL 50 ng/μL linear pGEM®-T Easy vector (Promega).
   c. 5 μL 2X Rapid Ligation Buffer (Promega).
   d. 0.5 μL 3 U/μL T4 DNA ligase (Promega).
   Include a vector-only control ligation. Allow ligations to proceed at 4°C overnight.

2. Transform one-half (5 μL) of each ligation into competent *E. coli* cells (e.g., strain DH5α) and plate on LB plates with carbenicillin (or ampicillin) and blue/white (isopropylthio-galactoside and X-gal) selection. Incubate plates at 37°C overnight.

3.18. PCR Screening of Bacterial Colonies

To screen for colonies that contain the cloned concatamers and generate templates for DNA sequencing, bacterial colonies are lysed by heating, then PCR is used to amplify the plasmid inserts.

3.18.1. Colony Lysis

1. Pick white (or light blue) colonies from the *E. coli* transformation plates, using sterile yellow micropipette tips. Briefly spot the tips onto a fresh LB plus carbenicillin plate (in a defined grid to allow later identification of resultant colonies; grow overnight at 37°C) and swizzle the tip into 50 μL of sterile water in PCR tubes/strips.
2. Lyse the bacteria in water by heating at 99°C for 5 min, and centrifuge the tubes for at least 2 min to pellet the cell debris. The supernatant serves as the template for the PCR reactions.

3.18.2. Colony PCR Reactions

1. The following reagents are combined in PCR tubes:
   a. 5 μL bacterial lysate.
   b. 0.5 μL 10 μ*M* M13 forward primer.
   c. 0.5 μL 10 μ*M* M13 reverse primer.
   d. 0.5 μL 10 m*M* dNTPs.
   e. 2.5 μL 10X *Taq* polymerase buffer.
   f. 1.5 μL 25 m*M* MgCl$_2$.
   g. 0.2 μL 5 U/μL *Taq* DNA polymerase.
   h. 14.3 μL nuclease-free water.
   Thermal cycler program:
   a. Hold for 2 min at 94°C.
   b. 35 cycles of: 94°C for 30 s (denaturation); 55°C for 30 s (annealing); and 72°C for 1 min (extension).
   c. 72°C for 7 min (final extension).
   d. Hold at 4°C.
2. Run 5 μL of each reaction on a 1.2% agarose/TAE minigel with ethidium bromide. Compare migration with pUC19/HpaII DNA markers. Select clones that generate a single PCR product longer than 300 bp.

3.19. Exonuclease/Shrimp Alkaline Phosphatase Treatment of PCR Product to Prepare Sequencing Template

1. Transfer 6 μL of the PCR reaction to a fresh PCR tube, then add 0.5 μL of 20 U/μL *E. coli* exonuclease 1 (New England Biolabs) and 1.5 μL of 1 U/μL shrimp alkaline phosphatase (USB, Amersham Biosciences). Incubate at 37°C for 30 min, then at 80°C for 15 min to inactivate enzymes.

2. Use between 2 and 4 µL of reaction as a template in the sequencing reactions. Sequence data should confirm the presence of several small RNA species in each clone interspersed with adapter sequences. Generally, each clone will contain between three and eight small RNA sequences.

3.20. Validation of miRNAs

The small RNA sequences generated are first placed through a bioinformatics screen to determine:

1. Whether they represent degradation products of known transcripts (ribosomal RNAs, transfer RNAs, messenger RNAs, and so on).
2. Whether they represent previously identified miRNAs (by searching the miRNA registry (**Subheading 3.22.**).
3. The genomic origin of the transcript (by basic local alignment search tool [BLAST] searching genome databases) and to define whether a transcript from the surrounding genomic sequence (approx 70 bp either side of the miRNA) is predicted to fold into a pre-miRNA hairpin structure, using algorithms such as Mfold *(17)*. The Mfold web server can be found at http://www.bioinfo.rpi.edu/applications/mfold.

   Experimental validation of novel miRNAs is of particular importance. Northern analysis allows a qualitative, as well as quantitative, assessment of miRNA levels in vivo (*see* **Note 9**).

3.21. Northern Analysis

3.21.1. Generation of Radiolabeled Oligonucleotide Probes

1. Working behind a Perspex screen, combine the following reagents in a PCR tube: 1 µL of 10 µ*M* antisense oligonucleotide, 1 µL of 10X PNK buffer, 5 µL of nuclease-free water, 1 µL of 10 U/µL T4 PNK (New England Biolabs), and 2 µL of 3,000 Ci/mmol γ-^{32}P ATP (10 mCi/mL). Incubate at 37°C for 30 min, then heat at 95°C for 2 min to inactivate enzyme. Chill on ice.
2. Increase the reaction volume to 50 µL with 50 m*M* EDTA, then add probe onto a prepacked Microspin G-25 column (Amersham Biosciences) and centrifuge at 700*g* for 2 min at room temperature. Using a hand-held Geiger monitor, ensure that labeled probe is in the collection tube, whereas unincorporated isotope remains in the Sephadex column.
3. Remove 1 µL of probe into appropriate scintillant and determine the radioactivity (in counts per minute) using a liquid scintillation counter. Freeze the probe at −20°C until ready to use, but use within 1 wk.

3.21.2. Northern Blot Transfer and Hybridization

1. Combine up to 20 µg of total RNA in a final 10 µL volume with an equal volume of formamide loading buffer, heat at 95°C for 5 min and separate on a preheated 15% acrylamide/8 *M* urea minigel, along with radiolabeled Decade RNA markers (Ambion). As the bromophenol blue dye front nears the end of the gel, remove the gel, stain with ethidium bromide, and photograph to record the loading uniformity.
2. Transfer the RNA to a Hybond N+ membrane (Amersham Biosciences) with 0.5X TBE using a semidry blotting apparatus (e.g., Panther semidry electroblotter; OWL Separation Systems, NH) at constant 1 mA/cm^2 of gel for 2 h.
3. Briefly rinse the filter in 2X SSC, blot dry, and UV crosslink the RNA to the filter. Prehybridize the filter in QuikHybe solution (Stratagene) for 30 min, then add ^{32}P-labeled

antisense oligonucleotide probe (10^6 cpm/mL QuikHybe solution) and hybridize for 1 to 2 h. Both the prehybridization and hybridization temperatures should be approx 5°C less than the calculated melting temperature (Tm) of the probe sequence.

4. Wash the filter twice in 2X SSC and 0.1% SDS at room temperature for 10 min, then wash once for 20 min at room temperature in 2X SSC and 0.1% SDS. Blot the solution from the filter, cover in plastic wrap, and expose to a phosphorimaging screen or autoradiography film. The filter can be returned to more stringent washing conditions (using less SSC or a higher temperature) if the background signal is high.

Mature miRNAs should be visible at approx 21 to 22 nt, as compared with Decade markers. Hybridization to a band of 60 to 80 nt is also often detected, which may represent the pre-miRNA hairpin molecule.

3.22. miRNA Registry

The miRNA Registry (http://www.sanger.ac.uk/Software/Rfam/mirna/index.shtml) acts as a repository for miRNA sequences, annotating the sequences and providing relevant information *(18,19)*. Briefly, novel miRNA sequences (and their predicted hairpin precursors) are submitted to the registry online and after a publication describing the miRNAs has been accepted, the sequences are released onto the database with new accession titles. Further information regarding the miRNA Registry is available on the website.

3.23. High-Throughput Sequencing of MicroRNAs

Recent advances in high-throughput nucleotide sequencing offer alternative approaches for qualitative and quantitative analysis of miRNA profiles in mammalian cells. Services, such as those provided by 454 Life Sciences Corp. (http://www.454.com), enable the identification of miRNAs without cloning into plasmid vectors.

4. Notes

1. The Lau protocol *(16)* forgoes the need to dephosphorylate the miRNAs before ligation of the 3' adapter. By incorporating a preadenylated 3' adapter in the first ligation, ATP is not required for ligation, thereby preventing circularization of the small RNAs. This procedure has recently become more convenient, because of the commercial availability of the preadenylated 3' adapter (IDT DNA Technologies; www.idtdna.com). The Lau protocol is available online at the Bartel lab web site (http://web.wi.mit.edu/bartel/pub) and, more recently, through the Ambros lab web site (http://banjo.dartmouth.edu/lab/microRNAs/Ambros_microRNAcloning.htm). Modifications of the Elbashir and Lau protocols have also been described elsewhere *(14,20)*.
2. The isolation of ribonucleic acids from any tissue or cultured cell requires a rapid and methodical approach because of the presence of RNases. Tissue must be processed or frozen immediately after harvesting from the animal. Once lysed, cellular RNases rapidly degrade RNA, therefore, most procedures use chaotropic agents, such as guanidinium thiocyanate in the lysis solution. Degraded total RNA is naturally a concern for miRNA procedures, because the degradation products mask *bona fide* small RNA species. Guanidinium inactivates RNases and removes proteins that are bound to nucleic acids. Critical for the purifi-

cation of miRNAs, is the efficient isolation of small RNA species. Many ion exchange and silicon-based separation techniques do not isolate small RNAs (less than 200 nt) and are, therefore, unsuitable RNA isolation procedures.

The early RNA isolation procedure of Chomczynski and Sacchi *(21)* provides cellular lysis by homogenization in 4 *M* guanidinium thiocyanate solution followed by extraction with acid phenol. This procedure preferentially retains RNA in the aqueous phase, and is followed by a series of ethanol precipitations to further purify RNA. Although we have found this procedure suitable for isolation of RNA and miRNAs from human colorectal tissues, the requirement for multiple precipitations may compromise the proportion of miRNA recovered, because small RNAs precipitate less efficiently. This is especially true for LiCl precipitation, which biases against the precipitation of short RNAs and should be replaced with sodium salt-assisted precipitation.

Recent commercial preparations that are based on the procedure of Chomczynski *(22)* and combine chaotropic disruption with organic solvent extraction are convenient and useful for a variety of tissues and, particularly, for adherent cell cultures in which cells can be lysed directly on the plate. Organic solvent preparations, such as Trizol (Invitrogen), or methods designed to enrich for small RNAs (*mir*Vana™ Isolation kit; Ambion) are suitable. Each of these procedures provides clean RNA with a useful representation of small RNAs.

3. Many animal organs, such as the pancreas, are particularly rich in RNases and are difficult sources of intact RNA. Storage in formamide reduces the risk of degradation during storage. After isolation and final ethanol precipitation, RNA should be resuspended and stored in 100% formamide, rather than as an aqucous solution. For spcctrophotomctric quantitation, dilute 1 μL RNA/formamide in 500 μL water and measure the optical density against a blank solution with the same formamide/water dilution. RNA in formamide is ready for PAGE separation. RNA can also be precipitated from formamide solution by addition of one-tenth volume 3 *M* sodium acetate and four volumes of ethanol.

4. Although dependent on the amount of RNA required, small 15% acrylamide/8 *M* urea minigels are usually suitable for this procedure, although multiple (>2) samples may be run on larger format gels. Because these gels will be used at several stages of the miRNA cloning procedure, a considerable volume (200 mL) of gel solution can be prepared before the experiment and stored at 4°C.

For repeated isolations, it is worth considering the flashPAGE™ Fractionator system (Ambion), which uses cartridge-format PAGE gels and is specifically designed for small RNA (<40 nt) isolation.

Suitable markers include commercially synthesized, 18- and 24-mer oligoribonucleotides, or in vitro (T7 RNA polymerase) generated 18- and 24-nt transcripts. Suitable markers can be generated using commercial T7 RNA polymerase-based kits (e.g., MEGAshortscript™; Ambion) or the standard protocols *(23)*. Enzymatically generated transcripts should be treated with RNase-free deoxyribonuclease I, and PAGE-purified to ensure only full-length transcripts are used. An aliquot of the transcripts will also require dephosphorylation (with calf intestinal phosphatase in the presence of RNase inhibitor) before ligation with the 3' adapter oligonucleotide.

Commercial RNA ladders, such as Decade markers (Ambion) can be used also (for determining RNA size) but are less accurate for defining the 18- to 24-nt size range. With SYBR Green II staining/fluorimaging, a significant amount of Decade markers (>4 μL) is required. DNA oligonucleotides are not suitable markers, because their PAGE migration differs from that of RNA with similar length.

5. Radiolabeled RNA markers can be used as an alternative to fluorescence imaging of the gel, if a fluorimager is not available, or if sensitivity is problematic. Lau et al. *(16)* combine radiolabeled 18- to 24-nt RNA markers with the total RNA sample before separation on 15% acrylamide/urea gel. This allows imaging of the gel using a phosphorimager and excision of the gel encompassing the region between the radioactive fragments. The incorporation of radiolabeled control fragments within the RNA sample also allows assessment of ligation efficiencies and visualization of cloning products in later cloning steps.

6. The quality of adapter oligonucleotides is critical, and mass spectrometric analysis should be requested, when available, from suppliers. If this is not available, and perhaps in addition to these data, adapters should be examined for purity on a 15% polyacrylamide/urea gel and, if necessary, PAGE purified to ensure that full-length adapter molecules are used. The choice of restriction site incorporated into the adapter sequence is flexible. The original protocol of Elbashir et al. *(14)* used EcoRI sites, whereas Lau et al. *(16)* incorporated BanI sites (G|GYRCC). BanI digestion offers the benefit of later concatamerization without monomer recircularization and is, therefore, preferred. In this protocol, EcoRI sites are present in the adapter sequences, but BanI sites are introduced later, during PCR.

7. Shorter products of 60 bp (likely adapter sequences without small RNA) may also be seen. If the level of these products is high, it may be worth gel purifying the larger (~80 bp) fragments before the next step. A second round of PCR amplification might also be necessary to generate sufficient PCR products for BanI digestion before concatamerization.

8. To isolate PCR-concatamers from low-melt agarose, perform electrophoresis on the samples through a 2% low-melt agarose/TAE gel and isolate the desired fragments as described (**Subheading 3.15.3.**). Assuming that the volume of a gel slice is approx 0.5 mL, add 1 mL melt buffer (20 m*M* Tris-HCl, pH 8.0, and 1 m*M* EDTA) and heat at 65°C for 10 min. Extract with 1 mL of Tris-HCl-saturated phenol, pH 8.0, then re-extract the aqueous phase with 800 μL phenol/chloroform. Extract the aqueous phase with 500 μL chloroform. Divide the aqueous phase between two 2-mL microcentrifuge tubes and to each tube add 2 μL of 20 mg/mL glycogen, 60 μL of 3 *M* sodium acetate, and 1.4 mL ethanol. Precipitate at –20°C overnight. Wash the pellets with 75% ethanol, air-dry the pellets, resuspend each pellet in 5 μL of nuclease-free water, and continue with **Subheading 3.16.** of the protocol.

9. Quantitative analyses of miRNAs can be achieved using RNase protection assays (e.g., *mir*Vana™ Detection kit, Ambion), RT-PCR *(24)*, and microarray-based approaches *(25, 26)*. However, the additional qualitative information (size of hybridizing band(s) and pre-miRNA detection) provided by Northern blot analysis is desirable for the initial assignment of any small RNA sequence as a miRNA.

Acknowledgments

The pioneering efforts of the Tuschl, and later the Bartel and Ambros groups in the development and refinement of the miRNA cloning methods are gratefully acknowledged. Thanks to R. James, S. Fitter, and G. Young for critical reading of the manuscript. M. Michael is supported, in part, by the Flinders Medical Centre Foundation.

Disclaimer

The descriptions of commercial services and products in this article are indicative of suitable materials for these protocols. The author has no affiliation with the companies listed and researchers are encouraged to compare the benefits of competitive services and products.

References

1. Meister, G. and Tuschl, T. (2004) Mechanisms of gene silencing by double-stranded RNA. *Nature* **431,** 343–349.
2. Denli, A. M., Tops, B. B., Plasterk, R. H., Ketting, R. F., and Hannon, G. J. (2004) Processing of primary microRNAs by the Microprocessor complex. *Nature* **432,** 231–235.
3. Gregory, R. I., Yan, K. P., Amuthan, G., et al. (2004) The Microprocessor complex mediates the genesis of microRNAs. *Nature* **432,** 235–240.
4. Bannerjee, D. and Slack, F. (2002) Control of developmental timing by small temporal RNAs: a paradigm for RNA-mediated regulation of gene expression. *Bioessays* **24,** 119–129.
5. Ambros, V. (2004) The functions of animal microRNAs. *Nature* **431,** 350–355.
6. Bartel, D. (2004) MicroRNAs: genomics, biogenesis, mechanism and function. *Cell* **116,** 281–297.
7. Poy, M. N., Eliasson, L., Krutzfeldt, J., et al. (2004) A pancreatic islet-specific microRNA regulates insulin secretion. *Nature* **432,** 226–230.
8. Pfeffer, S., Zavolan, M., Grasser, F. A., et al. (2004) Identification of virus-encoded microRNAs. *Science* **304,** 734–736.
9. Calin, G. A., Sevignani, C., Dumitru, C. D., et al. (2004) Human microRNA genes are frequently located at fragile sites and genomic regions involved in cancers. *Proc. Natl. Acad. Sci. USA* **101,** 2999–3004.
10. Calin, G. A., Liu, C. G., Sevignani, C., et al. (2004) MicroRNA profiling reveals distinct signatures in B cell chronic lymphocytic leukemias. *Proc. Natl. Acad. Sci. USA* **101,** 11,755–11,760.
11. Michael, M. Z., O'Connor, S. M., van Holst Pellekaan, N. G., Young, G. P., and James, R. J. (2003) Reduced accumulation of specific microRNAs in colorectal neoplasia. *Mol. Cancer Res.* **1,** 882–891.
12. Eis, P. S., Tam, W., Sun, L., et al. (2005) Accumulation of miR-155 and BIC RNA in human B cell lymphomas. *Proc. Natl. Acad. Sci. USA* **102,** 3627–3632.
13. Takamizawa, J., Konishi, H., Yanagisawa, K., et al. (2004) Reduced expression of the let-7 microRNAs in human lung cancers in association with shortened postoperative survival. *Cancer Res.* **64,** 3753–3756.
14. Elbashir, S. M., Lendeckel, W., and Tuschl, T. (2001) RNA interference is mediated by 21- and 22-nucleotide RNAs. *Genes Dev.* **15,** 188–200.
15. Pfeffer, S., Lagos-Quintana, M., and Tuschl, T. (2003) Cloning of small RNA molecules. In: *Current Protocols in Molecular Biology* (Ausubel, F. M., Brent, R., Kingston, R. E., et al., eds.), Wiley, New York, pp. 26.4.1–26.4.18.
16. Lau, N. C., Lim, L. P., Weinstein, E. G., and Bartel, D. P. (2001) An abundant class of tiny RNAs with probable regulatory roles in *Caenorhabditis elegans*. *Science* **294,** 858–862.
17. Zucker, M. (2003) Mfold web server for nucleic acid folding and hybridization prediction. *Nucl. Acids Res.* **31,** 3406–3415.
18. Ambros, V., Bartel, B., Bartel, D. P., et al. (2003) A uniform system for microRNA annotation. *RNA* **9,** 277–279.
19. Griffiths-Jones, S. (2004) The microRNA registry. *Nucl. Acids Res.* **32,** D109–D111.
20. Ambros, V. and Lee, R. C. (2004) Identification of microRNAs and other tiny noncoding RNAs by cDNA cloning. In: *Methods in Molecular Biology*, vol. 265, RNA Interference, Editing, and Modification (Gott, J. M., ed.), Humana, Totowa, NJ, pp. 131–158.
21. Chomczynski, P. and Saachi, N. (1987) Single-step method of RNA isolation by acid guanidinium thiocyanate-phenol-chloroform extraction. *Anal. Biochem.* **162,** 156–159.

22. Chomczynski, P. (1993) A reagent for the single-step simultaneous isolation of RNA, DNA and proteins from cell and tissue samples. *Biotechniques* **15,** 532–534, 536–537.
23. Milligan, J. F. and Uhlenbeck, O. C. (1989) Synthesis of small RNAs using T7 RNA polymerase. In: *Methods in Enzymology*, vol. 180, RNA Processing Part A (Dahlberg, J., Abelson, J., and Simon, M., eds.), Academic, New York, pp 51–62.
24. Schmittgen, T. D., Jiang, J., Liu, Q., and Yang, L. (2004) A high-throughput method to monitor the expression of microRNA precursors. *Nucl. Acids Res.* **32,** e43.
25. Liu, C.-G., Calin, G. A., Meloon, B., et al. (2004) An oligonucleotide microchip for genome-wide microRNA profiling in human and mouse tissues. *Proc. Natl. Acad. Sci USA* **101,** 9740–9744.
26. Barad, O., Meiri, E., Avniel, A., et al. (2004) MicroRNA expression detected by oligonucleotide microarrays: system establishment and expression profiling in human tissues. *Genome Res.* **14,** 2486–2494.

15

Methods for Analyzing MicroRNA Expression and Function During Hematopoietic Lineage Differentiation

Hyeyoung Min and Chang-Zheng Chen

Summary

MicroRNAs (miRNAs), an abundant class of approx 22-nucleotide (nt) small RNAs that control gene expression at the posttranscriptional level, may play important roles during normal hematopoiesis and leukemogenesis. This chapter focuses on the methods and strategies for dissecting miRNA function during hematopoietic lineage differentiation. We describe a modified miRNA cloning method and expression analysis approach for determining miRNA expression during hematopoietic lineage differentiation. We illustrate a retroviral vector and a general strategy for the ectopic expression of miRNAs in hematopoietic stem/progenitor cells. We discuss in vitro and in vivo functional assays that can be used to examine the roles of miRNAs during hematopoietic lineage differentiation. The methods and principles described here should also be applicable to study the roles of miRNAs in the differentiation and function of nonhematopoietic cell types.

Key Words: MicroRNA; noncoding RNA; hematopoiesis; retroviral expression; bone marrow transplantation; hematopoietic lineage differentiation.

1. Introduction

The discovery of the *lin-4* small noncoding RNA (ncRNA) revealed the posttranscriptional genetic programs that are controlled by small ncRNAs and the importance of such genetic programs in controlling the timing of worm development *(1,2)*. Now, nearly a decade later with the identification of a large number of miRNAs—an abundant class of approx 22-nt *lin-4*-like endogenous small ncRNAs—from animals and plants, it is apparent that miRNA-mediated gene regulatory programs may represent a fundamental layer of genetic regulation that is conserved throughout the animal and plant kingdoms *(3–5)*.

Hundreds of miRNAs have been identified through experimental and computational approaches and many of them are expressed in high copy numbers in cells, suggesting that miRNAs are an abundant class of gene regulatory molecules in animal and plant genomes *(6–20)*. More importantly, some miRNAs have been shown to play important

From: *Methods in Molecular Biology, vol. 342: MicroRNA Protocols*
Edited by: S. Ying © Humana Press Inc., Totowa, NJ

functional roles in plants and animals. In plants, some miRNAs control leaf and flower development *(21–24)*. In *Caenorhabditis elegans,* the *lin-4* and *let-7* miRNAs control the timing of larval development *(1,2,25,26)*, and the *lsy-6* and *mir-273* miRNAs act sequentially to control neuronal asymmetry *(27,28)*. In *Drosophila,* the *Bantam* miRNA regulates fly growth by controlling cell proliferation and cell death *(29,30)*, and the *mir-14* miRNA represses apoptosis and affects fat metabolism *(31)*. In mammals, some miRNAs have been shown to regulate hematopoietic lineage differentiation, insulin secretion, and adipocyte differentiation *(32–34)*. Furthermore, as elegantly exemplified by the genetic studies of *lin-4* and *lin-14* interactions, animal miRNAs are likely to control gene expression at the posttranscriptional level through imperfect base pairing to the complementary site(s) in the 3' untranslated region of their target gene(s) *(1,2)*. It has been predicted that each miRNA can potentially regulate large numbers of target genes *(35–43)*. Therefore, miRNAs seem to have diverse functional roles and regulate a broad spectrum of protein-coding genes. This suggests that miRNA-mediated gene regulation represents a fundamental mode of posttranscriptional gene regulation that is potentially involved in all biological processes. Nevertheless, the biological functions and relevant target genes of the majority of known miRNAs remain elusive.

In an earlier study, we illustrated a systematic approach to identify and examine miRNA functions during hematopoietic lineage differentiation processes *(32)*. The approach we used can be summarized in three basic steps:

1. The identification of candidate miRNAs.
2. The generation of miRNA expression constructs.
3. The characterization of miRNA function during hematopoietic lineage differentiation (**Fig. 1**).

In this chapter, we describe detailed protocols for identifying and testing the function(s) of miRNAs in mouse hematopoiesis. We discuss methods for analyzing the expression of miRNAs in mouse hematopoietic tissues or lineage-specific hematopoietic cells. We describe a strategy to generate viral constructs expressing miRNAs and also explain the use of in vitro and in vivo assay systems to assess the roles of miRNAs during hematopoietic stem/progenitor cell differentiation. The methods and principles we describe here can be applied to study the roles of miRNAs in the differentiation and function of nonhematopoietic cell types.

2. Materials

2.1. Common Reagents for Total RNA Preparation

Rnase-free plastic bottles, Eppendorf tubes, and pipet tips. Trizol reagent (Invitrogen, Carlsbad, CA; cat. no. 15596-018), Chloroform, RNase free water, 100% Isopropyl alcohol, 100% Ethanol, 75% Ethanol (*see* **Note 1**).

2.2. Radiolabeling of Oligonucelotide Probes and Markers

1. 6000 Ci/mmole [γ-^{32}P] adenosine triphosphate (ATP) (NEN Life Sciences, Boston, MA; cat. no. BLU502Z).

Identification of Candidate miRNAs

(1) Identification of cell or tissue-specific miRNAs by cDNA cloning
(2) Northern-blot analyses to determine miRNA expression
(3) Expression profiling using miRNA microarrays
(4) Determine miRNA gene expression by ribonuclease protection assays

Generation of miRNA Expression Constructs

(1) Amplify miRNA genes
(2) Clone miRNA genes into retroviral vectors
(3) Prepare retroviral supernatant and infect cells
(4) Analyze miRNA expression in infected cells

Examine miRNA Functions in Hematopoietic Lineage Differentiation

(1) S17 stromal culture assay
(2) Bone marrow transplantation assay

Fig. 1. Overall experimental design for analyzing the roles of microRNAs in hematopoietic lineage differentiation.

2. 3000 Ci/mmole [γ-^{33}P] ATP (NEN Life Sciences; cat. no. NEG602H).
3. 10 U/μL T4 polynucleotide kinase (New England Biolabs, Ipswich, MA; cat. no. M0201S).
4. 10X kinase reaction buffer (New England Biolabs).
5. G-25 MicroSpin columns (Amersham Biosciences; cat. no. 27-5325 01).
6. 100 ng/μL Decade marker RNA (Ambion, Austin, TX; cat. no. 7778).
7. 10X cleavage reagent (supplied in the Decade marker system kit).

2.3. miRNA Cloning (see Note 2)

1 Carrier oligonucleotides: 5'-UGUCAGUUUGUUAAUUAACCCAA-3'.
2. Restriction enzymes from New England Biolabs: PacI (cat. no. R0547S), BanI (R0118S).

2.4. Northern Blot

1. Vertical slab gel electrophoresis apparatus, glass plates, gel spacers, binder clips, combs, and aluminum plates. Aluminum plates are used to evenly distribute the heat generated during electrophoresis and eliminate the "smile" effects.
2. Acrylamide gel system (National Diagnostics Sequagel or equivalent): 10X gel buffer (8.3 M urea in 1 M Tris-borate and 20 mM ethylenediaminetetraacetic acid [EDTA]; 10X TBE buffer, pH 8.3; National Diagnostics cat. no. EC-835), gel concentrate (19% acrylamide, 1% *bis* acrylamide, and 8 M urea; National Diagnostics, Atlanta, GA; cat. no. EC-830), gel diluent (8 M urea; National Diagnostics cat. no. EC-840).
3. 5X TBE buffer: dissolve 54 g of Tris-base and 27.5 g of boric acid in H_2O. Add 20 mL of 0.5 M EDTA, pH 8.0. Adjust final volume to 1 L.
4. 10% ammonium persulfate; store at -20°C.
5. *N,N,N',N'*-tetramethylethylene diamine (National Diagnostics; cat. no. EC-503).

6. 4 µg/mL ethidium bromide (EtBr) in 0.5X TBE.
7. 2X gel-loading buffer: 8 *M* urea, 20 m*M* EDTA, pH 8.0, 1 mg/mL xylene cyanole FF, and 1 mg/mL bromophenol blue. To make 1 L of 2X gel-loading buffer, mix 480 g of urea, 40 mL of 0.5 *M* EDTA, 2 mL of 1 *M* Tris-HCl, 1 g of xylene cyanole FF, and 1 g of bromophenol blue.
8. Nylon membrane (GeneScreen Plus, NEN Life Science; cat. no. NEF1017).
9. 20% sodium dodecyl sulfate (SDS).
10. 20X standard sodium citrate (SSC): 3 *M* NaCl and 0.3 *M* sodium citrate, pH 7.0. Dissolve 175.3 g of NaCl and 88.2 g of sodium citrate in 800 mL H_2O, adjust pH to 7.0 with 1 *M* HCl, and adjust the volume to 1 L with H_2O.
11. 50X Denhardt solution: dissolve 1 g (1% w/v) of Ficoll-400, 1 g (1% w/v) of polyvinylpyrrolidone, and 1 g (1% w/v) of bovine serum albumin in 100 mL H_2O. Store at −20°C.
12. 1 *M* phosphate buffer (pH 7.2): dissolve 268.07 g of $NaPO_4$ in 800 mL H_2O, add 4 mL of 85% phosphoric acid, and adjust the volume to 1 L.
13. Prehybridization/hybridization (prehyb/hyb) solution: 5X SSC, 20 m*M* Na_2HPO_4, pH 7.2, 7% (w/v) SDS, and 2X Denhardt solution in H_2O.
14. Nonstringent wash solution: 3X SSC, 25 m*M* Na_2PO_4, pH 7.5, 5% SDS, and 10X Denhardt solution in H_2O.
15. Stringent wash solution: 1X SSC and 1% SDS in H_2O.
16. Phosphoimager screen.

2.5. Preparation of Hematopoietic Cells for RNA Isolation and Immunochemistry

1. Bone marrow washing medium: Dulbecco's Modified Eagle Medium (DMEM), 2% fetal bovine serum (FBS), and 10 m*M* HEPES, pH 7.2.
2. 1X phosphate-buffered saline (PBS): dissolve 8 g NaCl, 0.2g KCl, 1.44 g Na_2HPO_4, and 0.24 g KH_2PO_4 in 800 mL of H_2O. Adjust pH to 7.2 and add H_2O to a final volume of 1 L.
3. Turk's staining solution: 0.01% (w/v) crystal violet in 3% (v/v) acetic acids (*see* **Note 3**).

2.6. Reagents for Magnetic Activated Cell Sorting and Fluorescence Activated Cell Sorting (see Note 4)

1. Magnetic-activated cell sorting (MACS) labeling buffer: PBS, pH 7.2, and 2 m*M* EDTA.
2. MACS separation buffer: PBS, 2 m*M* EDTA, and 0.5% bovine serum albumin.
3. Antibodies for MACS: purified anti-mouse CD16/32 antibody, biotinylated antibodies against lineage-specific surface antigens: anti-CD3e, anti-Mac1, anti-Gr-1, anti-Ter-119, and anti-B220 (lineage panel; BD Biosciences Pharmingen, San Diego, CA; cat. no. 559971).
4. MACS streptavidin microbeads (Miltenyi Biotec, Auburn, CA; cat. no. 30-048-101), anti-Sca-1 microbeads (Miltenyi Biotec; cat. no. 120-001-503), or microbead-conjugated antibodies against lineage-specific antigens.
5. Fluorescence-activated cell sorting (FACS) buffer: PBS with 2% FBS.
6. Fluorescence-labeled FACS antibodies: anti-CD4–phycoerythrin (PE), anti-CD8–allophycocyanin (APC), anti-CD19–PE, anti-Thy-1.2–APC, anti-Gr-1–PE, anti-Mac1–APC, anti-Ter-119–PE, and anti-CD71–APC (BD Biosciences Pharmingen).
7. 1 mg/mL propidium iodide (PI) stock.

2.7. Generation of miRNA Expression Constructs

1. Lysis buffer: 100 m*M* Tris-HCl, pH 8.5, 5 m*M* EDTA, 0.2% SDS, and 200 m*M* NaCl. Sterilize the solution by filtering through a 0.45-µm nitrocellulose filter. Store the sterile

solution at room temperature. Adjust the proteinase K concentration to 0.2 mg/mL before use.

2. Proteinase K: 20 mg/mL stock solution; 0.2 mg/mL final concentration.
3. Isopropanol.
4. Nuclease-free water.
5. Sequencing primer for MDH1–3-phosphoglycerate kinase promoter (PGK)–green fluorescent protein (GFP) 2.0: 5'-GGATCCCAATATTTGCATGTCGC-3'.

2.8. Generate Retrovirus by Transient Transfection

1. Culture medium for 293T and BOSC 23 cells: DMEM, 10% FBS, and penicillin/streptomycin (Pen/Strep).
2. FuGene 6 (Roche Diagnostics; cat. no. 1 815 091).
3. pCLeco packaging vector *(44)*.

2.9. Hematopoietic Lineage Differentiation Assays

1. 30 mg/mL 5-fluorouracil in saline.
2. S17 culture medium: Minimum Essential Medium Eagle, α-Modification (α-MEM), 20% FBS, and Pen/Strep.
3. B cell growth medium: α-MEM supplemented with 20% FBS, Pen/Strep, 2 m*M* L-glutamine, 10 ng/mL interleukin (IL)-3, 10 ng/mL IL-6, 10 ng/mL IL-7, and 50 ng/mL stem cell factor (SCF).
4. 0.05% Trypsin–EDTA.
5. 4 mg/mL polybrene (hexadimethrine bromide).
6. 0.5 *M* EDTA, pH 8.0.
7. PBS in 5 m*M* EDTA.
8. C57BL/6J (CD45.2 or Ly5.2) mice (Jackson Laboratory, Bar Harbor, ME).
9. B6.SJL-CD45a-Pep3b mice (CD45.1 or Ly5.1) (Jackson Laboratory).
10. Hematopoietic stem cell infection medium: α-MEM supplemented with 20% FBS, Pen/Strep, 2 m*M* L-glutamine, 10 ng/mL IL-3, 10 ng/mL IL-6, 10 ng/mL IL-7, and 100 ng/mL SCF.
11. Heparinized capillary tube.
12. 2 U/mL heparin.
13. Ammonium chloride potassium (ACK) red blood cell lysis buffer (10X): to 500 mL of H_2O, add 40.15 g NH_4Cl, 5.0 g $KHCO_3$, and 185.1 mg Na_2–EDTA. Adjust the pH to 7.2 to 7.4. Make 1X buffer by diluting with H_2O before use.

3. Methods

3.1. Identification of Candidate miRNAs for Functional Analyses

The spatial and temporal patterns of miRNA expression provide clues regarding their biological functions. Many approaches have been developed to examine miRNA expression, including miRNA cloning *(6–8)*, Northern blot analysis *(1)*, miRNA microarray analysis *(45–51)*, the invader assay *(52)*, and the ribonuclease protection assay. Although multiple miRNA array platforms have been reported, these platforms all have certain limitations. Many miRNA array platforms use probes or amplification methods that simultaneously measure the mature and precursor (pre)-miRNA forms rather than the functional mature miRNAs only. Furthermore, because miRNAs are short and have a wide-range of melting temperatures, it is intrinsically difficult to design antisense probes that have similar hybridization kinetics that also ensure the sensitivity and specificity of the arrays. Lastly, these arrays may be incomplete because additional miRNA genes in human and mouse genomes are yet to be identified *(53)*. Thus, to design a miRNA array with probe sets relevant to the cells of interests, it may first require systematic cloning to identify the miRNAs expressed in these cell populations. Because of limited space, we only provide detailed protocols for a modified cloning method and Northern Blot analysis in this chapter.

3.1.1. Cloning of miRNAs From Hematopoietic Progenitor Cells

Direct cloning of miRNAs from tissues or enriched cell populations offers a sensitive approach to identify new miRNAs. One can also use the cloning frequency, the number of times a miRNA is identified from a miRNA library, as a reliable indicator for the relative abundance of the cloned miRNA *(54)*. Because most miRNA cloning experiments were carried out using cell lines and tissues, miRNAs expressed in rare progenitor cell populations are likely to be underrepresented or missed in previous studies. Therefore, the cloning approach may offer an alternative method for identifying new miRNAs and determining miRNA expression in purified hematopoietic progenitor cell populations. The drawback, however, is that the cloning method is relatively tedious and costly.

The original cloning methods from the Ambros, Bartel, and Tuschl laboratories all require a large amount of starting material (~100 µg of total RNA) *(6–8)*. To increase the sensitivity of the cloning procedure, we made a slight modification to the original method *(6–8)* and successfully cloned miRNAs from as few as 100,000 purified progenitor cells *(see* **Note 5**). In this chapter, we describe only the modifications we made to the protocol. A detailed description of the original cloning protocol can be found in an early publication by Nelson et al. *(7)* and on the Bartel lab website (http://web.wi. mit.edu/bartel/pub).

In brief, we extract the total RNA from sorted hematopoietic stem/progenitor cell populations (>100,000 cells) using the Trizol reagent and following the manufacturer's instructions (Invitrogen). To isolate the small RNAs, of 18- to 26-nt in length, from the purified cell populations, we spike 1 pmol of a ^{32}P-labeled 23-mer carrier oligo (5'-UGUCAGUUUGUUAAUUAACCCAA-3') into the total RNA samples and carry out RNA size fractionation on a 15% acrylamide/8 *M* urea gel. The radiolabeled oligo serves as a carrier and tracer during the subsequent precipitation, ligation, and gel purification steps. The carrier also contains a PacI restriction site that allows for the subsequent removal of the ligation product containing the carrier in later cloning stages. Following the original protocol, we ligate size-fractionated small RNAs first to a 3' adaptor oligonucleotide (5' preadenylated) without the presence of ATP, then to a 5' adaptor oligonucleotide, and carry out reverse transcriptase polymerase chain reaction (PCR) to amplify the final ligation products. After reverse transcriptase PCR amplification, we digest the PCR product with PacI to eliminate the carrier sequences, then purify the undigested products on a 15% nondenaturing acrylamide gel, and amplify the PacI-digested PCR products with 10 to 20 rounds of PCR. Typically, one round of PacI digestion can remove more than 90% of the carrier-containing amplification products. One can carry out another round of digestion to further reduce the carrier-containing PCR products, but no gel purification is necessary. We then digest the PCR products with the BanI restriction enzyme, concatermerize the BanI-digested products, ligate them into TOPO vectors (Invitrogen), and submit the miRNA libraries for sequencing analyses. Bioinformatics analyses will then be carried out to identify new miRNAs and to determine miRNA abundance *(6–8)*.

3.1.2. Northern Blot to Analyze miRNA Expression

Northern blotting is a routine lab method for analyzing miRNA expression. It reveals information regarding miRNA size and the relative abundance of both the mature and pre-miRNAs. However, it has limited sensitivity (at least 5 µg of total RNA is required for detection) that precludes its application in detecting miRNA expression of many rare hematopoietic stem/progenitor cell populations.

3.1.2.1. PREPARE A SINGLE-CELL SUSPENSION FROM HEMATOPOIETIC TISSUES

Isolate bone marrow cells by flushing femurs and tibias with bone marrow washing medium (*see* **Note 6**). Pipet bone marrow cells up and down several times to produce a single-cell suspension and filter through a 70-µm nylon mesh cell strainer. For the preparation of thymocyte or splenocyte suspensions, place the thymus or spleen in a 35-mm Petri dish containing PBS (cut tissues into several pieces if necessary), and mince by gently pressing the thymus or spleen between the frosted ends of two glass slides. Wash glass slides with cold PBS and filter through a 70-µm nylon mesh cell strainer (*see* **Note 6**). Wash cells with cold PBS. Count enucleated hematopoietic cells by staining with Turk's solution. Cells are now ready for immunochemistry or RNA preparation.

3.1.2.2. ISOLATE HEMATOPOIETIC PROGENITOR CELL POPULATIONS BY MACS OR FACS

Label cells with fluorescence-conjugated antibodies against lineage-specific antigens. For example, use anti CD45R or CD19 for B-lineage cells; Mac1 or Gr-1 for myeloid lineage cells; and CD3 or Thy-1.2 (CD90.2) for T-lineage cells. Determine the appropriate dilution for each antibody before use. For MACS separation, add microbead-conjugated antibodies against lineage-specific antigens (*see* **Subheadings 3.3.1.3.** and **3.3.2.4.** for detailed protocols for MACS separation and immunofluorescence staining). Proceed to MACS or FACS cell separation.

3.1.2.3. TOTAL RNA PREPARATION

Trizol reagent (Invitrogen) was used to isolate total RNA from hematopoietic tissues and cell populations. Compared with other commercial column- or resin-based RNA purification kits, the Trizol protocol gives a better yield and is more reliable in isolating small RNAs. To prepare RNA samples for gel electrophoresis, dissolve RNA samples (5 to 20 µg of total RNA) in 15 µL of water (or less) and add an equal volume of 2X gel-loading dye. Heat samples at 80°C for 5 to 10 min and centrifuge.

3.1.2.4. Preparation of Radiolabeled RNA Marker

Label the Decade marker (Ambion,) with γ-^{33}P ATP according to the manufacturer's instructions. ^{33}P-labeled marker can be stored at $-20°C$ and used for a month. Heat at $95°C$ for 5 min before use.

3.1.2.5. Electrophoresis of RNA Samples

Prepare a 15% acrylamide/8 *M* urea gel with the Sequagel sequencing system solutions (National Diagnostics). Prerun the gel at 25 W for 15 min in 0.5X TBE. Load the RNA samples and ^{33}P-labeled RNA ladder and run the gel at 25 W for approx 1 h, until the bromophenol blue band reaches the end of the gel. Separate the gel onto plastic wrap and stain the gel with 4 µg/mL EtBr in 0.5X TBE for 5 to 10 min. Examine the EtBr-stained image to evaluate the RNA quality and loading consistency. Discrete transfer RNA (78-nt) and 5S ribosomal RNA (120-nt) bands indicate a good quality of RNA preparation. The 5S ribosomal RNA bands can be used as loading controls in publication. Take a digital picture and save the EtBr-stained image.

3.1.2.6. Gel Transfer

Reduce the gel size by cutting off the loading wells and empty lanes. Cut the nylon membrane (GenScreen Plus) and six sheets of 3M Whatman filter paper to the size of the gel. Soak the nylon membrane and filter papers in 0.5X TBE. Assemble the transfer sandwich on the surface of a semi-dry transfer unit in the following order: three sheets of soaked filter paper, nylon membrane, gel, and three sheets of soaked filter paper. Make marks on the RNA side of the nylon membrane with pencil. Remove possible air bubbles within the transfer sandwich by gently rolling a plastic serological pipet over the sandwich. Place the top on the semidry transfer unit, and run the transfer at a constant current (3.3 mA/cm^2) for 35 min. Place the filter with the RNA side up on a dry piece of filter paper and crosslink with ultraviolet light at 1000 µJ of energy. Bake the filter at $80°C$ for 1 h. Store it at $-20°C$ or proceed to the prehybridization step.

3.1.2.7. Preparation of Radiolabeled miRNA Probes

Design and synthesize the antisense oligonucleotide probes against the mature miRNA targets. Prepare a 50-µL reaction mixture by mixing 2 µL of oligonucleotides (20 pmol/µL), 5 µL of 10X T4 polynucleotide kinase buffer, 26 µL H$_2$O, 15 µL of [γ-^{32}P] ATP, and 2 µL of T4 polynucleotide kinase (New England Biolabs). Incubate at $37°C$ for 1 h. Heat the mixture at $68°C$ for 10 min. Use a G-25 column (Amersham) to remove unlabeled radionucleotides.

3.1.2.8. Hybridization

Wet the membrane with water, place it in a hybridization tube, and add 20 mL warm prehyb/hyb solution (~$50°C$). Rotate at $50°C$ for 1 to 2 h. Replace with 20 mL fresh prehyb/hyb solution and add the denatured radiolabeled probe. Cap the tube tightly and rotate in the hybridization oven at $50°C$ overnight. Recover probes and store at $-20°C$ (probes can be reused two to three times within a week). Wash three times with 25 mL of nonstringent wash solution in the hybridization oven at $50°C$ for 30 min. Repeat the wash two more times with 25 mL of nonstringent wash solution in the hybridization oven at 50°C for 1 h. Finally, wash with stringent wash solution in the hybridization oven at 50°C for 5 min. Wrap the membrane with Saran wrap and expose the membrane to a phosphorimager screen at room temperature overnight.

3.2. Ectopic Expression of miRNAs in Hematopoietic Stem/Progenitor Cells

Gain-of-function analysis has been the most fruitful approach for identifying many of the key protein players in hematopoietic lineage differentiation *(55,56)*. In human leukemias, chromosomal translocations often result in aberrant gene expression and can reveal gene function in normal hematopoiesis *(57)*. The ectopic expression of an active Notch in hematopoietic stem/progenitor cells revealed the key role of Notch signaling in T-cell and B-cell fate determination, which is consistent with Notch loss-of-function studies in mice *(55,58)*. Furthermore, ectopic expression seems to be quite effective in revealing miRNA function in animals and plants *(21,29,31,32)*. The high degree of redundancy of miRNA genes may present a unique challenge for elucidating miRNA gene function using a loss-of-function approach in mice. Furthermore, many miRNAs may carry out very fine genetic controls in animals, as was elegantly illustrated in worms, in which *lsy-6* and *mir-273* miRNAs act sequentially to determine the neuronal patterning in merely two neurons *(27,28)*. It would be difficult to discern these functions without well-informed functional guidance. Thus, miRNA gain-of-function analyses in hematopoietic stem/progenitor cells will provide a solid foundation and guidance for future loss-of-function studies in mice.

3.2.1. Design of Retroviral Constructs for miRNA Expression

To ectopically express miRNAs in primary hematopoietic stem/progenitor cells, we have developed a retroviral vector using the murine stem cell virus backbone *(32)*. In one of the configurations, a polymerase (pol) III expression cassette that contains the human H1 promoter and a polyT (T5) termination sequence was placed in the U3 region of the 3' long terminal repeat (LTR). This vector design is termed a "double-copy" configuration because the process of retroviral reverse transcription and integration leads to two copies of the expression cassette to be integrated into the host genome (**Fig. 2A**). We found that the double-copy configuration provides robust and consistent expression of the miRNA hairpins when infecting primary hematopoietic cells. In contrast, when the H1 expression cassette is placed after the 5' LTR, the H1 promoter is silenced when infecting primary hematopoietic cells (data not shown). In addition, as a marker for infection, GFP is introduced under the control of the constitutive murine PGK promoter.

We also noted that functional miRNAs cannot be effectively processed from minimal pre-miRNA stem-loop precursors and that the genomic flanking sequences of pre-miRNAs are essential for miRNA processing and maturation *(32)*. Based on these observations, we designed a general strategy for the ectopic expression of miRNA genes by placing approx 270-nt-long primary (pri)-miRNA transcripts into the H1 expression cassette of MDH1-PGK-GFP 2.0 (**Fig. 2B**). The approx 270-nt pri-miRNA transcript contains the approx 22-nt mature miRNA and the 125-nt corresponding genomic sequences flank-

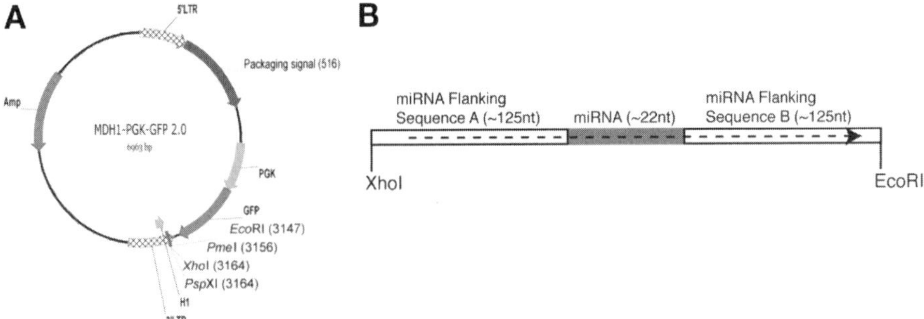

Fig. 2. Retroviral vector for microRNA (miRNA) expression. (**A**) A double-copy retroviral vector for miRNA expression. A polymerase III expression cassette containing the human H1 promoter (H1) and the T5 termination signal is placed in the U3 region of the viral 3' long terminal repeat (LTR). Viral infection can be monitored by the expression of a green fluorescent protein (GFP) marker driven by the constitutive murine 3-phosphoglycerate kinase promoter (PGK). (**B**) A diagram depicting a primary (pri)-miRNA gene fragment that contains the mature miRNA and 125-nucleotide flanking sequences.

ing both sides of the mature miRNA. It is now known that miRNA biogenesis consists of sequential steps that are essential for the production of functional miRNAs *(59)*. The pri-miRNA transcripts are processed into the approx 60-nt pre-miRNA stem-loops by the nuclear RNase III, Drosha, with the facilitation of Parsha *(59,60)*. The pre-miRNA is then actively transported into the cytoplasm by Exportin 5 in a Ran guanosine triphosphate-dependent manner *(61,62)* and further processed into a approx 21-nt duplex by Dicer in the cytoplasm *(63–65)*. The information for the sequential processing and maturation of miRNA is likely to be stored in the sequences of pri-miRNAs *(32,59)*.

3.2.2. Generation of miRNA Expression Constructs

3.2.2.1. DESIGN PCR PRIMERS TO AMPLIFY PRE-MIRNA GENE FRAGMENTS

Obtain mature and pre-miRNA sequences from Rfam—"the miRNA Registry" (http://www.sanger.ac.uk/cgi-bin/Rfam/mirna/browse.pl)—and search the genome database of relevant organisms using the pre-miRNA sequences to extract the pri-miRNA gene fragments containing the corresponding flanking sequences (*see* **Note 7**). Use Primer 3 (http://frodo.wi.mit.edu/cgi-bin/primer3/primer3_www.cgi) to select PCR primers from pri-miRNA gene fragments for amplifying the approx 270-nt PCR products that include the 22-nt mature miRNAs and 125-nt of genomic sequences flanking the mature miRNAs. Add XhoI and EcoRI restriction enzyme sites to the ends of the PCR primers to facilitate cloning of the PCR products into the MDH1–PGK–GFP 2.0 vector (**Fig. 2A**). Use other restriction enzymes when the pri-miRNA gene fragments contain internal EcoRI or XhoI sites.

3.2.2.2. PREPARATION OF GENOMIC DNA

Genomic DNA can be isolated from cultured cells or mouse tissues using the following protocol. Add 0.5 mL of DNA lysis buffer to mouse tissue or cells (~25 mg tissue or 10^9 cells per 1 mL lysis buffer) and digest overnight at 55°C while rotating in the hybridization oven. After overnight incubation, the tissue should no longer be visible. Centrifuge to remove debris, hair, and bone. Precipitate the DNA by adding an equal volume of isopropanol. Use a sterile pipet tip to transfer the precipitated DNA to a clean tube. Add 200 μL water and incubate overnight at 55°C to allow DNA to dissolve. Measure the DNA concentration.

3.2.2.3. GENERATION OF MIRNA EXPRESSION CONSTRUCT

Amplify the pre-miRNA gene fragments from genomic DNA by PCR. Most of the pre-miRNA gene fragments we tried can be easily amplified from mouse genomic DNA. However, in some cases, it is necessary to optimize PCR conditions by varying the annealing temperature or using different *Taq* polymerases. For those that are extremely difficult to amplify, one can try to use bacterial artificial chromosome DNA clones containing the pre-miRNA gene fragments as templates. Digest the PCR products with restriction enzymes and clone into MDH1–PGK–GFP. Verify inserts by DNA sequencing analysis with the following primer (from the H1 promoter side): 5'-GGATCCCA ATATTTGCATGTCGC-3'.

3.2.3. Viral Packaging by Transient Transfection

This protocol is designed for transfecting viral construct and packaging construct into cells on a 6-well plate. Adjust the amount of FuGene 6 reagent and DNA accordingly for larger scale transfections.

1. Prepare 50 to 80% confluent 293T (or BOSC23) cells by plating approx 5×10^5 cells per well in a 6-well plate the day before the transfection.
2. Add 100 μL of serum–free DMEM to a sterile 1.5-mL Eppendorf tube (Tube A) and aliquot 6 μL of FuGene 6 to Tube A (do not touch the pipet tip to the side of the tube because the FuGene 6 will stick to plastic). Mix and let stand for 5 min at room temperature.
3. Mix 2 μg of the miRNA expression vector and 1 μg of the pCLeco packaging vector *(44)* in a separate Eppendorf tube (Tube B).
4. Add diluted FuGene 6 solution (Tube A) to Tube B, mix well by tapping the tube, and incubate for 15 min at room temperature.
5. Remove the media from cells and replace it with 3 mL of fresh media.
6. Drop-wise, add the FuGene 6/DNA mixture (A and B mixture) to the cells and swirl to mix. Culture for 2 d.
7. Check GFP expression at 48 h after transfection and collect the supernatant. Store viral supernatant at −80°C.

3.3. Analysis of miRNAs' Roles in Hematopoietic Lineage Differentiation

As one of the best-studied developmental systems, many in vitro and in vivo assays have been developed to examine the hematopoietic lineage differentiation processes. Some hematopoietic progenitor cells can be grown clonally in a semisolid culture. If provided with the right combination of colony stimulating factors, cultured progenitor cells will differentiate into mature forms, and can be enumerated and characterized based on the size and morphology of the colonies. A variety of myeloid, erythroid, and lymphoid progenitor cells at different stages of differentiation can be identified and scored using this assay *(66)*. Moreover, hematopoietic stem/progenitor cells can be maintained in vitro with some bone marrow stromal cell lines that provide a niche for stem cell maintenance and progenitor differentiation *(67–69)*. With defined culture medium, this culture system can also be used to examine the differentiation potential of hematopoietic stem/progenitor cells. For example, S17, OP9, and MS-5 bone marrow stromal culture assays are commonly used to study B lymphopoiesis, whereas the fetal thymic organ culture and OP9–DL1 stromal culture assays are used to study T lymphopoiesis *(70–72)*. Finally, the self-renewal and differentiation potentials of hematopoietic stem/progenitor cells can be measured by the bone marrow transplantation assay, in which transplanted stem cells are capable of rescuing lethally irradiated mice and repopulating the entire blood system *(73,74)*. With these assays, one can alter the miRNA expression in hematopoietic stem/progenitor cells and then examine the effects of miRNA perturbations on stem cell self-renewal and lineage differentiation using in vitro and in vivo assays described in **Subheadings 3.3.2.** and **3.3.3.** Here, we will only describe the S17 stromal culture assay and the bone marrow transplantation assay.

3.3.1. Enrichment of Lineage-Negative Cells From the Bone Marrows of 5-Fluorouracil-Treated Mice

3.3.1.1. Prime Hematopoietic Stem/Progenitor Cells With the Pyrimidine Analog 5-Fluorouracil

Inject mice (BS.SJL or C57BL/6J) with 5-fluorouracil (FU) (30 mg/mL stock concentration; 150 mg/kg body weight) via the lateral tail vein or retro-orbital vein. Injection of 5-FU kills the cycling hematopoietic cells, stimulates the quiescent stem cells into the cell cycle, and increases the retroviral infection of hematopoietic stem/progenitor cells (*see* **Note 8**).

3.3.1.2. Prepare Bone Marrow Cells for Immunochemistry and Lineage Depletion

Harvest bone marrow cells on day 3 or 4 after 5-FU treatment (*see* **Subheading 3.1.2.1**). Count the enucleated cells by staining with Turk's solution (*see* **Note 3**). Wash the cells with labeling buffer and resuspend in labeling buffer to a final concentration of 10^8 cells/mL.

3.3.1.3. Lineage Depletion by MACS

Add an antibody to CD16/32 to cells (<1 μg/10^6 cells) and incubate on ice for 5 min to block the Fc receptors (optional). Add 200 μL of each biotinylated mouse lineage panel antibody per 10^8 cells (anti-CD3ε, anti-B220, anti-Mac1, anti-Gr-1, and anti-Ter-119) and incubate cells on ice for 20 min (*see* **Note 9**). Wash twice with 10 mL of ice-cold labeling buffer and spin down in a refrigerated centrifuge. Resuspend cells to 10^7 cells/90 μL with labeling buffer. Add 10 μL of MACS streptavidin-microbeads per 10^7 cells and incubate on ice for 20 min. Wash twice with 10 mL of ice-cold labeling buffer and spin down in a refrigerated centrifuge. Resuspend cells in separation buffer (up to 10^8 cells in 500 μL) and proceed to the MACS separation system to isolate lineage-negative cells. Count the lineage negative (Lin⁻) cells with Turk's solution.

3.3.2. S17 Stromal Culture Assay

3.3.2.1. PREPARE S17 STROMAL CELLS

Trypsinize the S17 stromal cells and seed 20,000 cells/well in 24-well plates on the day of 5-FU injection. The S17 stromal cells should be confluent by the time of culture initiation.

3.3.2.2. RETROVIRAL INFECTION OF LIN⁻ CELLS BY SPINOCULATION

Resuspend enriched Lin⁻ cells to 5×10^5 cells/mL in the B-cell culture medium. Mix 1 mL of Lin⁻ cells and 1 mL of virus (at least 10^6 cfu/mL) in a 5-mL FACS tube. Add 2 µL of polybrene to a final concentration of 4 µg/mL. Cap the tube tightly and centrifuge at 900*g* for 2 h at room temperature (*see* **Note 10**).

3.3.2.3. SEED THE INFECTED CELLS ONTO S17 STROMA

Remove the infection supernatant, resuspend cells in B-cell culture medium, and seed them onto the S17 stromal layer (20,000–40,000 infected Lin⁻ cells/0.5 mL/well). Prepare 12 culture replicates for each viral infection. Place the plate in a 37°C, 5% CO_2, humidified incubator. Feed the cells with fresh B-cell culture medium 5 d after initiating the culture.

3.3.2.4. PREPARE CELLS FOR IMMUNOCHEMISTRY

Collect adherent and nonadherent cells from the S17 stromal culture at day 10 after culture initiation. First collect the nonadherent cells from the culture medium into FACS tubes (or 1.2-mL cluster tubes) and centrifuge at 5000*g* for 5 min. Carefully remove the supernatant and save the cell pellets on ice. While centrifuging the nonadherent cells, add 0.5 mL of PBS/5 m*M* EDTA to the remaining adherent cells and incubate on a rocking platform at room temperature for 5 to 10 min. Recover adherent cells by repetitive pipetting to generate a single-cell suspension. Add the adherent cells to the nonadherent cells in the same tube. Wash twice with cold FACS buffer and resuspend cells in 100 µL of FACS staining buffer. When multiple stainings are required for each culture, resuspend cells in a larger volume of FACS buffer and aliquot 100 µL of cells into multiple tubes. When analyzing a large number of culture assays, carry out staining in a 96-well plate.

3.3.2.5. IMMUNOCHEMISTRY AND FACS ANALYSIS OF S17 CULTURE

Add antibodies (anti-CD-19 PE and anti-Thy-1.2 APC) to the cells and incubate at 4°C to 8°C for 15 min (*see* **Note 9**). Spin down the cells in a refrigerated centrifuge and wash twice with cold FACS buffer. Resuspend cells in FACS buffer containing 1 µg/mL PI. PI is used for live/dead cell discrimination because PI cannot permeate the membrane of the live cells, but can enter the nucleus of dead cells and stain the chromatin. Analyze the stained cells by FACS. Viral-infected donor cells are GFP positive. Analyze FACS data with BD CellQuest™ to determine the lineage profiles of the viral-infected cells and compare the lineage profiles of cells that are infected with the control vector and the miRNA-expressing virus.

3.3.3. Bone Marrow Transplantation Assay

3.3.3.1. Retroviral Infection of Hematopoietic Stem Cells

Prepare Lin⁻ bone marrow cells from 5-FU-treated B6/SJL mice and infect them with viruses by spinoculation (*see* **Subheading 3.3.2.2.**). After centrifuging for 2 h, culture the infected cells in hematopoietic stem cell infection medium at 37°C in humidified air with 5% CO_2 for 24 h. Repeat spinoculation and culture for another 24 h.

3.3.3.2. Prepare Sca-1-depleted Bone Marrow Cells

Isolate bone marrow cells from C57BL/6J mice. Stain the bone marrow cells with anti-Sca-1 microbeads following the instructions from Miltenyi Biotec. Proceed to MACS separation to isolate the Sca-1-depleted bone marrow cells. Sca-1-depleted bone marrow cells, which lack of long-term repopulating hematopoietic stem cells, will be used as supporting cells in the bone marrow transplantation assay.

3.3.3.3. Bone Marrow Transplantation

Irradiate recipient mice on the day of transplantation. Recipient C57BL/6J (Ly 5.2) mice of 6- to 8-wk old are subjected to lethal irradiation (10 Gy) 3 to 5 h before transplantation (*see* **Note 11**). About 20 to 40 recipients per group are used for each miRNA construct. Mix 2.5×10^4 infected cells with 4×10^5 C57BL/6J bone marrow cells depleted of Sca-1-positive cells and inject them into lethally irradiated C57BL/6J recipient mice via the retro-orbital route.

3.3.3.4. Prepare Peripheral Blood Cells for Immunochemistry

Bleed the recipient mice from the retro-orbital veins using heparinized capillary tubes at 1, 3, and 4 mo after transplantation. Collect 0.1 to 0.2 mL of peripheral blood into collection tubes containing 30 µL of heparin solution (2 U/mL). Mix the blood and heparin solution to prevent coagulation. Add 1 mL of ACK lysis buffer to the collection tubes and incubate at room temperature for 15 min. Centrifuge at 500*g* at 4°C for 5 min and carefully aspirate out the lysis buffer. Repeat the ACK lysing step if there are still many red blood cells left. Wash cells twice with FACS buffer and resuspend in FACS buffer.

3.3.3.5. Immunochemistry and FACS Analysis (*see* **Note 12**)

To examine the influences of miRNAs on lineage differentiation, peripheral blood cells from the recipient mice are immunoreacted with lineage-specific antibodies to determine the lineage profiles of the viral-infected donor cells (marked by the GFP reporter). Enucleated peripheral blood cells from each recipient are immunoreacted with the following sets of antibodies:

1. Anti-CD4–PE and anti-CD8–APC.
2. Anti-CD19–PE and anti-Thy-1.2–APC.
3. Anti-Gr-1–PE and anti-Mac1–APC.
4. Anti-Ter-119–PE and anti-CD71–APC.

Add antibodies to the cells and incubate at 4°C to 8°C for 15 min. Spin down the cells in a refrigerated centrifuge and wash twice with cold FACS buffer. Resuspend cells in the FACS buffer containing 1 μg/mL PI and subject to FACS analyses. Viral-infected donor cells are GFP positive. Analyze FACS data with BD CellQuest to determine the lineage profiles of the viral-infected cells and compare the lineage profiles of cells infected with the control vector and the miRNA-expressing virus.

4. Notes

1. New and unused plastic bottles, Eppendorf tubes, and pipet tips are generally RNase free. Designate a set of unopened chemicals and solutions for RNA preparation. Wear gloves to handle all RNase-free reagents.
2. A comprehensive list of reagents required for miRNA cloning can be found in the Bartel lab cloning protocol. Preadenylated 3' adaptor oligo is available from Integrated DNA Technologies.
3. Turk's solution is used to count enucleated cells in the peripheral blood. Acetic acid selectively lyses red blood cells. However, Turk's staining does not discriminate dead cells from the live cells. To count the liver cells, use Trypan blue dye staining.
4. Unless otherwise stated, buffers and solutions for MACS and FACS analyses are maintained on ice. Entire staining procedures are carried out on ice (0°C–4°C). Centrifugations are carried out in a refrigerated centrifuge or in the cold room (4°C–8°C).
5. The modified miRNA cloning method is now being tested for cloning miRNAs using as few as 10,000 hematopoietic stem/progenitor cells.
6. Use a 10-mL syringe and 21-gage needles for flushing femurs, and 23-gage needles for flushing tibias. Alternatively, place thymus or spleen on a 70-μm nylon mesh cell strainer, gently mash the thymus or spleen with the rubber end of a plunger from a 3-mL syringe, and wash with cold PBS to release thymocytes or splenocytes into a 50-mL conical tube.
7. Try to avoid a long stretch of Ts when designing primers to amplify the approx 270-nt pri-miRNA gene fragments because the H1 Pol III promoter will terminate at a long stretch of Ts (more than five Ts). miRNAs can also be expressed from a Pol II promoter. However, we noted that a longer pri-miRNA gene (~520-nt in length) containing the 22-nt mature miRNA and approx 250-nt of genomic sequences flanking the mature miRNA is required for higher expression using Pol II promoters.
8. Approximately 10 to 15 × 10^6 cells can be isolated from the bone marrow of a 5-FU-treated mouse.
9. It is recommended that antibodies be titrated to determine their optimal concentration. Once the optimal concentrations are determined, make diluted antibodies stock with FACS staining buffer. If performing multicolor labeling, prepare the antibody mixture in a microcentrifuge tube and add the multiple antibodies simultaneously to the sample. Also, prepare single-color staining controls for adjusting the compensations.
10. Typically, more than 50% of the progenitor cells are infected with the miRNA vector as indicated by GFP expression, and this percentage does not substantially change during the 10-d assay.
11. Irradiation dose will vary depending on the strain and age of the animals and the source of irradiation. Therefore, a preliminary dose-titration experiment is required to determine the optimal irradiation protocol and dose. In general, lethal-dose irradiation can be delivered by exposing mice to two doses of 500 rad, 3 to 4 h apart, or to a single dose of 1000 rad.
12. One can follow the same animal over time by screening peripheral blood. Donor-derived cells will start to appear in the peripheral blood approx 2 wk after reconstitution, when bone marrow chimerism is about to be achieved. An alternative method is to set up multiple sets

of animals, kill animals at various time points, and analyze the lymphoid tissues as well as the peripheral blood. If mice are killed to harvest the lymphoid tissues, prepare a single-cell suspension as described in **Subheading 3.1.2.1.** Then, transfer 10^6 cells/100 µL of FACS buffer into FACS tubes and label with antibodies. For the labeling of bone marrow cells and splenocytes, red blood cells should be lysed by ACK lysing buffer before proceeding to the labeling step.

Acknowledgment

We thank Jacqueline Chau, Gwen Liu, and Giselle Sylvester for comments on the manuscript. miRNA research is supported by a startup fund from Stanford University School of Medicine to C.-Z. Chen.

References

1. Lee, R. C., Feinbaum, R. L., and Ambros, V. (1993) The C. elegans heterochronic gene lin-4 encodes small RNAs with antisense complementarity to lin-14. *Cell* **75,** 843–854.
2. Wightman, B., Ha, I., and Ruvkun, G. (1993) Posttranscriptional regulation of the heterochronic gene lin-14 by lin-4 mediates temporal pattern formation in *C. elegans. Cell* **75,** 855–862.
3. Ambros, V. (2003) MicroRNA pathways in flies and worms: growth, death, fat, stress, and timing. *Cell* **113,** 673–676.
4. Bartel, D. P. and Chen, C. Z. (2004) Micromanagers of gene expression: the potentially widespread influence of metazoan microRNAs. *Nat. Rev. Genet.* **5,** 396–400.
5. Bartel, D. P. (2004) MicroRNAs: genomics, biogenesis, mechanism, and function. *Cell* **116,** 281–297.
6. Lee, R. C. and Ambros, V. (2001) An extensive class of small RNAs in Caenorhabditis elegans. *Science* **294,** 862–864.
7. Lau, N. C., Lim, L. P., Weinstein, E. G., and Bartel, D. P. (2001) An abundant class of tiny RNAs with probable regulatory roles in Caenorhabditis elegans. *Science* **294,** 858–862.
8. Lagos-Quintana, M., Rauhut, R., Lendeckel, W., and Tuschl, T. (2001) Identification of novel genes coding for small expressed RNAs. *Science* **294,** 853–858.
9. Lagos-Quintana, M., Rauhut, R., Meyer, J., Borkhardt, A., and Tuschl, T. (2003) New microRNAs from mouse and human. *RNA* **9,** 175–179.
10. Lagos-Quintana, M., Rauhut, R., Yalcin, A., Meyer, J., Lendeckel, W., and Tuschl, T. (2002) Identification of tissue-specific microRNAs from mouse. *Curr. Biol.* **12,** 735–739.
11. Mourelatos, Z., Dostie, J., Paushkin, S., et al. (2002) miRNPs: a novel class of ribonucleoproteins containing numerous microRNAs. *Genes Dev.* **16,** 720–728.
12. Ambros, V., Lee, R. C., Lavanway, A., Williams, P. T., and Jewell, D. (2003) MicroRNAs and other tiny endogenous RNAs in C. elegans. *Curr. Biol.* **13,** 807–818.
13. Dostie, J., Mourelatos, Z., Yang, M., Sharma, A., and Dreyfuss, G. (2003) Numerous microRNPs in neuronal cells containing novel microRNAs. *RNA* **9,** 180–186.
14. Houbaviy, H. B., Murray, M. F., and Sharp, P. A. (2003) Embryonic stem cell-specific MicroRNAs. *Dev. Cell* **5,** 351–358.
15. Michael, M. Z., O'Connor, S. M., van Holst Pellekaan, N. G., Young, G. P., and James, R. J. (2003) Reduced accumulation of specific microRNAs in colorectal neoplasia. *Mol. Cancer Res.* **1,** 882–891.
16. Lim, L. P., Lau, N. C., Weinstein, E. G., et al. (2003) The microRNAs of Caenorhabditis elegans. *Genes Dev.* **17,** 991–1008.

17. Lim, L. P., Glasner, M. E., Yekta, S., Burge, C. B., and Bartel, D. P. (2003) Vertebrate microRNA genes. *Science* **299,** 1540.
18. Lai, E. C., Tomancak, P., Williams, R. W., and Rubin, G. M. (2003) Computational identification of Drosophila microRNA genes. *Genome Biol.* **4,** R42.
19. Grad, Y., Aach, J., Hayes, G. D., et al. (2003) Computational and experimental identification of C. elegans microRNAs. *Mol. Cell* **11,** 1253–1263.
20. Kim, J., Krichevsky, A., Grad, Y., et al. (2004) Identification of many microRNAs that copurify with polyribosomes in mammalian neurons. *Proc. Natl. Acad. Sci. USA* **101,** 360–365.
21. Aukerman, M. J. and Sakai, H. (2003) Regulation of flowering time and floral organ identity by a MicroRNA and its APETALA2-like target genes. *Plant Cell* **15,** 2730–2741.
22. Chen, X. (2004) A microRNA as a translational repressor of APETALA2 in Arabidopsis flower development. *Science* **303,** 2022–2025.
23. Emery, J. F., Floyd, S. K., Alvarez, J., et al. (2003) Radial patterning of Arabidopsis shoots by class III HD-ZIP and KANADI genes. *Curr. Biol.* **13,** 1768–1774.
24. Palatnik, J. F., Allen, E., Wu, X., et al. (2003) Control of leaf morphogenesis by microRNAs. *Nature* **425,** 257–263.
25. Reinhart, B. J., Slack, F. J., Basson, M., et al. (2000) The 21 nucleotide *let-7* RNA regulates developmental timing in Caenorhabditis elegans. *Nature* **403,** 901–906.
26. Pasquinelli, A. E., Reinhart, B. J., Slack, F., et al. (2000) Conservation across animal phylogeny of the sequence and temporal regulation of the 21 nucleotide let-7 heterochronic regulatory RNA. *Nature* **408,** 86–89.
27. Chang, S., Johnston, R. J. Jr., Frokjaer-Jensen, C., Lockery, S., and Hobert, O. (2004) MicroRNAs act sequentially and asymmetrically to control chemosensory laterality in the nematode. *Nature* **430,** 785–789.
28. Johnston, R. J. and Hobert, O. (2003) A microRNA controlling left/right neuronal asymmetry in Caenorhabditis elegans. *Nature* **426,** 845–849.
29. Brennecke, J., Hipfner, D. R., Stark, A., Russell, R. B., and Cohen, S. M. (2003) bantam encodes a developmentally regulated microRNA that controls cell proliferation and regulates the proapoptotic gene hid in Drosophila. *Cell* **113,** 25–36.
30. Hipfner, D. R., Weigmann, K., and Cohen, S. M. (2002) The bantam gene regulates Drosophila growth. *Genetics* **161,** 1527–1537.
31. Xu, P., Vernooy, S. Y., Guo, M., and Hay, B. A. (2003) The Drosophila microRNA Mir-14 suppresses cell death and is required for normal fat metabolism. *Curr. Biol.* **13,** 790–795.
32. Chen, C. Z., Li, L., Lodish, H. F., and Bartel, D. P. (2004) MicroRNAs modulate hematopoietic lineage differentiation. *Science* **303,** 83–86.
33. Poy, M. N., Eliasson, L., Krutzfeldt, J., et al. (2004) A pancreatic islet-specific microRNA regulates insulin secretion. *Nature* **432,** 226–230.
34. Esau, C., Kang, X., Peralta, E., et al. (2004) MicroRNA-143 regulates adipocyte differentiation. *J. Biol. Chem.* **279,** 52,361–52,365.
35. Lewis, B. P., Burge, C. B., and Bartel, D. P. (2005) Conserved seed pairing, often flanked by adenosines, indicates that thousands of human genes are microRNA targets. *Cell* **120,** 15–20.
36. Lewis, B. P., Shih, I. H., Jones-Rhoades, M. W., Bartel, D. P., and Burge, C. B. (2003) Prediction of mammalian microRNA targets. *Cell* **115,** 787–798.
37. Stark, A., Brennecke, J., Russell, R. B., and Cohen, S. M. (2003) Identification of Drosophila MicroRNA Targets. *PLoS Biol.* **1,** E60.
38. Lai, E. C. (2004) Predicting and validating microRNA targets. *Genome Biol.* **5,** 115.

39. John, B., Enright, A. J., Aravin, A., Tuschl, T., Sander, C., and Marks, D. S. (2004) Human MicroRNA targets. *PLoS Biol.* **2,** e363.
40. Kiriakidou, M., Nelson, P. T., Kouranov, A., et al. (2004) A combined computational-experimental approach predicts human microRNA targets. *Genes Dev.* **18,** 1165–1178.
41. Enright, A. J., John, B., Gaul, U., Tuschl, T., Sander, C., and Marks, D. S. (2003) MicroRNA targets in Drosophila. *Genome Biol.* **5,** R1.
42. Rajewsky, N. and Socci, N. D. (2004) Computational identification of microRNA targets. *Dev. Biol.* **267,** 529–535.
43. Krek, A., Grun, D., Poy, M. N., et al. (2005) Combinatorial microRNA target predictions. *Nat. Genet.* **37,** 495–500.
44. Naviaux, R. K., Costanzi, E., Haas, M., and Verma, I. M. (1996) The pCL vector system: rapid production of helper-free, high-titer, recombinant retroviruses. *J. Virol.* **70,** 5701–5705.
45. Liang, R. Q., Li, W., Li, Y., et al. (2005) An oligonucleotide microarray for microRNA expression analysis based on labeling RNA with quantum dot and nanogold probe. *Nucleic Acids Res.* **33,** e17.
46. Baskerville, S. and Bartel, D. P. (2005) Microarray profiling of microRNAs reveals frequent coexpression with neighboring miRNAs and host genes. *RNA* **11,** 241–247.
47. Sioud, M. and Rosok, O. (2004) Profiling microRNA expression using sensitive cDNA probes and filter arrays. *Biotechniques* **37,** 574–576, 578–580.
48. Miska, E. A., Alvarez-Saavedra, E., Townsend, M., et al. (2004) Microarray analysis of microRNA expression in the developing mammalian brain. *Genome Biol.* **5,** R68.
49. Liu, C. G., Calin, G. A., Meloon, B., et al. (2004) An oligonucleotide microchip for genome-wide microRNA profiling in human and mouse tissues. *Proc. Natl. Acad. Sci. USA* **101,** 9740–9744.
50. Barad, O., Meiri, E., Avniel, A., et al. (2004) MicroRNA expression detected by oligonucleotide microarrays: system establishment and expression profiling in human tissues. *Genome Res.* **14,** 2486–2494.
51. Krichevsky, A. M., King, K. S., Donahue, C. P., Khrapko, K., and Kosik, K. S. (2003) A microRNA array reveals extensive regulation of microRNAs during brain development. *RNA* **9,** 1274–1281.
52. Allawi, H. T., Dahlberg, J. E., Olson, S., et al. (2004) Quantitation of microRNAs using a modified Invader assay. *RNA* **10,** 1153–1161.
53. Berezikov, E., Guryev, V., van de Belt, J., Wienholds, E., Plasterk, R. H., and Cuppen, E. (2005) Phylogenetic shadowing and computational identification of human microRNA genes. *Cell* **120,** 21–24.
54. Aravin, A. A., Lagos-Quintana, M., Yalcin, A., et al. (2003) The small RNA profile during Drosophila melanogaster development. *Dev. Cell* **5,** 337–350.
55. Pui, J. C., Allman, D., Xu, L., et al. (1999) Notch1 expression in early lymphopoiesis influences B versus T lineage determination. *Immunity* **11,** 299–308.
56. Shivdasani, R. A. and Orkin, S. H. (1996) The transcriptional control of hematopoiesis. *Blood* **87,** 4025–4039.
57. Gauwerky, C. E. and Croce, C. M. (1993) Chromosomal translocations in leukaemia. *Semin. Cancer Biol.* **4,** 333–340.
58. Maillard, I., Adler, S. H., and Pear, W. S. (2003) Notch and the immune system. *Immunity* **19,** 781–791.
59. Lee, Y., Ahn, C., Han, J., et al. (2003) The nuclear RNase III Drosha initiates microRNA processing. *Nature* **425,** 415–419.

60. Denli, A. M., Tops, B. B., Plasterk, R. H., Ketting, R. F., and Hannon, G. J. (2004) Processing of primary microRNAs by the Microprocessor complex. *Nature* **432,** 231–235.
61. Yi, R., Qin, Y., Macara, I. G., and Cullen, B. R. (2003) Exportin-5 mediates the nuclear export of pre-microRNAs and short hairpin RNAs. *Genes Dev.* **17,** 3011–3016.
62. Lund, E., Guttinger, S., Calado, A., Dahlberg, J. E., and Kutay, U. (2004) Nuclear export of microRNA precursors. *Science* **303,** 95–98.
63. Grishok, A., Pasquinelli, A. E., Conte, D., et al. (2001) Genes and mechanisms related to RNA interference regulate expression of the small temporal RNAs that control C. elegans developmental timing. *Cell* **106,** 23–24.
64. Ketting, R. F., Fischer, S. E., Bernstein, E., Sijen, T., Hannon, G. J., and Plasterk, R. H. (2001) Dicer functions in RNA interference and in synthesis of small RNA involved in developmental timing in C. elegans. *Genes Dev.* **15,** 2654–2659.
65. Hutvágner, G., McLachlan, J., Pasquinelli, A. E., Balint, E., Tuschl, T., and Zamore, P. D. (2001) A cellular function for the RNA-interference enzyme Dicer in the maturation of the *let-7* small temporal RNA. *Science* **293,** 834–838.
66. Metcalf, D. and Nicola, N. A. (1995) *The Hematopoietic Colony-Stimulating Factors.* In: *Biology to Clinical Applications*, Cambridge University Press, Cambridge, UK.
67. Eaves, A. C. and Eaves, C. J. (1988) Maintenance and proliferation control of primitive hemopoietic progenitors in long-term cultures of human marrow cells. *Blood Cells* **14,** 355–368.
68. Collins, L. S. and Dorshkind, K. (1987) A stromal cell line from myeloid long-term bone marrow cultures can support myelopoiesis and B lymphopoiesis. *J. Immunol.* **138,** 1082–1087.
69. Nakano, T., Kodama, H., and Honjo, T. (1994) Generation of lymphohematopoietic cells from embryonic stem cells in culture. *Science* **265,** 1098–1101.
70. Jenkinson, E. J. and Anderson, G. (1994) Fetal thymic organ cultures. *Curr. Opin. Immunol.* **6,** 293–297.
71. Hare, K. J., Jenkinson, E. J., and Anderson, G. (1999) In vitro models of T cell development. *Semin. Immunol.* **11,** 3–12.
72. Schmitt, T. M., de Pooter, R. F., Gronski, M. A., Cho, S. K., Ohashi, P. S., and Zuniga-Pflucker, J. C. (2004) Induction of T cell development and establishment of T cell competence from embryonic stem cells differentiated in vitro. *Nat. Immunol.* **5,** 410–417.
73. Chen, C. Z., Li, L., Li, M., and Lodish, H. F. (2003) The endoglin (positive) sca-1(positive) rhodamine(low) phenotype defines a near-homogeneous population of long-term repopulating hematopoietic stem cells. *Immunity* **19,** 525–533.
74. Chen, C. Z., Li, M., de Graaf, D., et al. (2002) Identification of endoglin as a functional marker that defines long-term repopulating hematopoietic stem cells. *Proc. Natl. Acad. Sci. USA* **99,** 15,468–15,473.

16

Identifying MicroRNA Regulators
of Cell Death in *Drosophila*

Chun-Hong Chen, Ming Guo, and Bruce A. Hay

Summary

Animal genomes contain on the order of at least hundreds of microRNAs (miRNAs). Although most remain uncharacterized, it is already clear that miRNAs regulate many biological processes. A number of *Drosophila* miRNAs have been identified as likely cell death regulators, but functions for most have simply not been explored. Here we describe a protocol for identifying miRNAs that can act as cell death regulators. We also describe a simple protocol for testing roles for mRNAs identified as candidate miRNA targets using computational or other approaches.

Key Words: *Drosophila*; apoptosis; caspase; microRNA; RNAi; cancer.

1. Introduction

Cell death is an evolutionarily conserved process by which organisms remove cells that are no longer needed or that are dangerous for the survival of the organism (reviewed in **ref. *1***). Almost all cell death regulatory genes identified to date encode proteins. However, within the last several years it has become clear that animal genomes encode on the order of hundreds (*2*), or perhaps thousands (**ref. *3***), of small noncoding RNAs known as miRNAs. The first miRNAs to be identified, *lin-4* and *let-7*, were identified through genetic screens for mutations that disrupt development in the nematode *Caenorhabditis elegans* (reviewed in **ref. *4***). However, most miRNAs have been identified through direct cloning of small RNAs, biochemical purification of ribonucleoprotein particles, or computational approaches that involve searches for evolutionarily conserved stem-loop structures characteristic of miRNA precursors. Lists of validated miRNAs can be found at the MicroRNA Registry [http://www.sanger.ac.uk/Software/Rfam/mirna/index.shtml]. It is generally thought that miRNAs downregulate gene expression by binding to 3' untranslated regions of target transcripts. miRNA binding to target transcripts, as a part of a proteinaceous complex known as the RNA-induced silencing complex, targets these transcripts for translational inhibition if the miRNA and the messenger RNA (mRNA) target show limited complementarity, or for transcript cleavage

From: *Methods in Molecular Biology, vol. 342: MicroRNA Protocols*
Edited by: S. Ying © Humana Press Inc., Totowa, NJ

and degradation if the miRNA and the mRNA target show perfect or nearly perfect complementarity (reviewed in **refs. 2,4,5**). Although the study of miRNA function is at a very early stage, it is already clear that these molecules are used to regulate many different biological processes (reviewed in **ref. 6**). In particular, a number of *Drosophila* miRNAs have been shown to act as cell death inhibitors (**refs. 7–9**; reviewed in **ref. 10**). Death-regulating miRNAs have not yet been identified in mammals. However, given the generally high level of conservation of cell death signaling and effector pathways in flies and mammals (reviewed in **refs. 1** and **11**) it is essentially certain that they exist. For example, the expression of a number of miRNAs is deregulated in various forms of cancer (reviewed in **refs. 10** and **12**). Given that inhibition of cell death is essential for cancer development *(13)*, these miRNAs become good candidates for testing. Our goal in the first half of this chapter is to describe some of the experimental approaches that can be used to identify cell death-regulating miRNAs. Our focus is on experiments that can be carried out in *Drosophila*, a model multicellular organism that carries out cell death in response to many of the developmental and environmental stimuli that are important in mammals (reviewed in **refs. 1** and *14*). Many of the techniques described here can, in principle, be adapted for use in vertebrates, such as mice.

Once miRNAs of interest are identified, an important goal becomes the identification of their mRNA targets. It is not yet possible to isolate specific miRNAs complexed with their mRNA targets. Therefore, current strategies for miRNA target identification use computational approaches based on miRNA–mRNA complementarity to predict likely miRNA–mRNA interaction pairs, which can then be tested experimentally (*see* **Subheading 3.5.**). Unfortunately, computational approaches to target site prediction are not straightforward because most animal miRNAs do not bind their target transcripts with perfect complementarity (we know this without knowing the actual targets because perfectly complementary sites are simply not present in the genomes of interest). In addition, the rules that define characteristics of functional miRNA–mRNA interactions are just being discovered *(15–20)*. A number of target prediction programs are available that make use of various aspects of this information, and, in some cases, of the hypothesis that target sites will be evolutionarily conserved between species *(9,18,20–27)*. However, each of these programs has different assumptions and parameter values. Thus, the lists of candidates often show little overlap. Finally, recent work suggests that many miRNAs may regulate the activity of a number of genes, leaving it somewhat unclear how deep one should go in these lists in searching for biologically significant targets *(20,28)*. These issues will presumably fade as more information is accumulated regarding the characteristics of productive miRNA–mRNA pairs. In the second half of this chapter, we describe an experimental approach for testing the significance of candidate miRNA targets, regardless of how they were identified.

2. Materials

1. Mutants are not available for most *Drosophila* miRNAs. Therefore, tests for roles of specific miRNAs in *Drosophila* will often rely on the characterization of phenotypes associated with miRNA overexpression. Strains of *Drosophila* that express specific miRNAs under the control of promoters that allow for spatial and/or temporal control of expression

are used for these experiments (reviewed in **ref. *29***). Much cell death research in the fly uses vectors that drive expression in the developing fly eye, the most commonly used vector being glass multimer reporter (GMR) *(30)*. The eye is a useful tissue for death research because it is large and easy to score for defects using a dissection microscope, and because the eye is nonessential for viability or fertility. In essence, the eye functions as a living 96-well plate in which levels of cell death can be increased or decreased without consequences for the propagation of the animal as a whole. In cases in which genes need to be expressed in other tissues, an often-used tool is the GAL4-upstream activating sequences (UAS) expression system *(31)*. GAL4 is a yeast transcription factor. It binds to UAS sites. Genes to be expressed are cloned in a P element vector (pUASt *[31]* or pUASp *[32]*) downstream of a multimer of GAL4-UAS and introduced into the germline. Many labs have generated flies with P element transposon insertions carrying the GAL4 transcriptional activator. In these lines, GAL4 expression is driven by an introduced upstream promoter or (in a version of this vector that contains only a basal promoter) by endogenous tissue-specific enhancers. When flies carrying the UAS-driven transgene are crossed with flies that express the GAL4 activator, the transgene is expressed in the pattern of the GAL4 activator. A large number of GAL4 lines are available from FlyBase (http://flybase.bio.indiana.edu/).

2. Strains of *Drosophila* in which specific cell death pathways can be activated in spatial and/or temporal patterns that result in visible, easily scorable phenotypes using a dissection microscope. Much cell death takes the form of apoptosis. Caspase proteases are the central executioners of apoptotic cell death. In *Drosophila*, many cells, including those that normally live, experience chronic activation of the caspase Dronc, mediated by the adaptor, Ark, the *Drosophila* Ced-4/Apaf-1 homolog. If unrestrained, active Dronc cleaves and activates downstream effector caspases, such as Drice, that mediate cell death. Cell survival requires the inhibitor of apoptosis protein (IAP)-family caspase inhibitor, DIAP1, which suppresses the activity of Dronc and of caspases activated by Dronc. Thus, the choice between cell survival and death is critically regulated by the balance between death activators and inhibitors in the cytoplasm (reviewed in **ref. *1***). Apoptotic cell death is, in many situations, brought about by the expression of proteins such as Reaper (Rpr), Head involution defective, Grim, Sickle, and Jafrac2, which disrupt DIAP1–caspase interactions. Interestingly, the transcripts that encode these proteins are important sites for miRNA function in *Drosophila* (reviewed in **ref. *10***). Proteins that perform similar apoptotic functions are present in mammals. Flies that overexpress each of these death activators under GMR control (causing increased cell death and a small eye phenotype) are available. Flies have also been generated that show dominant eye phenotypes caused by expression of death-inducing forms of genes associated with a number of human neurodegenerative conditions (reviewed in **refs. *1*** and ***14***). Finally, in many human diseases, cell death results from loss of function, rather than from gain of function (reviewed in **ref. *33***). Tissue-specific loss-of-function phenotypes can be generated in the eye (or in other tissues) using constructs that drive the expression of double-stranded RNA homologous to the gene of interest, which induces RNA interference. Several vectors are available that facilitate this process *(34,35)*.

This discussion focused on the generation of flies that act as reporters for specific signal transduction pathways. Flies have also been generated that act as living reporters for the survival of particular cell types or tissues. These flies provide ideal genetic backgrounds from which to carry out screens for miRNAs that regulate the steps that drive cell death, but without the requirement that one have previous knowledge regarding which pathways are being targeted. For example, epidermal cells that make up the adult wing normally die shortly after eclosion (hatching from the pupal case). If cells of the wing express green fluorescent protein (GFP) under the control of a constitutive promoter, this death can be visualized as a loss of GFP fluorescence. Conversely, a failure of these cells to die can be visualized as persistent GFP expression *(36)*.

3. A binocular dissection microscope with a white light source that provides illumination from the side or above is used to score flies for cell death phenotypes.
4. A fluorescence microscope, or a dissection microscope with a mercury bulb and GFP attachment, in cases in which GFP is used as a marker for the presence of living cells.
5. A CO_2 tank and a flow regulator. CO_2 is used to anesthetize *Drosophila*.
6. Tygon tubing to connect the CO_2 tank to the anesthesia/scoring platform (the CO_2 pad). Tubing leads from the CO_2 tank to a T connector. One branch coming off of the T connector leads to the anesthesia platform. A second branch connects to a piece of tubing that has a hollow needle inserted into the free end. The CO_2 coming out of this end is used to anesthetize flies in vials or bottles before transferring them to the CO_2 pad.
7. A simple CO_2 platform can be generated by cutting the top off (or drilling a number of holes in) a plastic tissue culture flask. A porous polyethylene mesh is glued over this surface to provide a smooth, porous surface through which CO_2 can flow. The needle from the tubing that connects to the CO_2 tank is pushed through a rubber stopper that fits in the neck of the tissue culture flask, providing a tight seal.
8. Fly husbandry. There are many recipes and sources for fly food, vials, bottles, anesthesia equipment, and other miscellaneous items. An excellent resource for this is the resource page at the Bloomington stock center (http://fly.bio.indiana.edu/supplies.htm).
9. Paintbrush with fine tip, or a feather attached to a stick, for moving flies around.
10. Fly morgue. A flask partly filled with ethanol, methanol, or mineral oil. Unneeded flies are discarded in this flask.

3. Methods

1. Generating transgenic *Drosophila*. Germline transformation of *Drosophila* is carried out, in brief, by injecting early stage embryos with the P element vector of interest and a second plasmid that expresses a source of P element transposase. Transposase cuts and pastes the P element vector into the genomic DNA of cells that will give rise to the germline. Once they are adults, these (hopefully) germline chimeric flies are outcrossed to identify flies heterozygous for an insertion of the P element vector as follows. Transgenic flies are most often generated in a genetic background mutant for the *white* (*w*) gene, which is required to generate the red eye pigment characteristic of wild-type flies. Thus, *w* flies have white eyes. The P element carrying the miRNA of interest carries a wild-type copy of the *w* gene. Thus, flies heterozygous for an insertion of this vector will have pigmented eyes (yellow, orange, or red, depending on the site of P element insertion). Therefore, germline chimeric flies (which are themselves white-eyed), are crossed to *w* flies and the progeny scored for any eye color other than white (yellow, orange, or red). These flies are heterozygous for one or more insertions of the P element (*see* **Notes 1** and **2**). A number of protocols for making the initial germline chimeras are available (c.f. http://www.ceolas.org/fly/protocols.html). Alternatively, this service can now be contracted out (c.f. http://www.rainbowgene.com/).
2. Carrying out the crosses. Crosses can be set up in vials with one male and one to three virgin female flies (*see* **Note 3**). A light sprinkle of dry bakers yeast added to the vial facilitates growth. Young (8 h or less at 25°C) males and females are pale and soft as compared with older adults. Females do not mate their first 8 to 10 h after eclosion. Therefore, if bottles are cleared and newly hatched progeny are collected within 8 to 10 h, the females should all be virgin.

3. Balancing the stocks. Once a germline transformant fly has been identified, it is necessary to generate a stable stock in which the fate of the transposon-carrying chromosome can be followed unambiguously, regardless of whether the flies have normal-looking eyes, or any eyes at all. This process, known as balancing the chromosome, is summarized in **Fig. 1** for the two major autosomes.

4. Testing roles for miRNAs as cell death regulators through overexpression. Once a balanced stock carrying the miRNA transgene has been generated, the effects of miRNA expression on death can be assayed in various ways. The most common of these are summarized in **Fig. 2**. Relevant crosses for several of these schemes are illustrated in **Fig. 3** (*see* **Note 4**). Representative examples of wild-type fly eyes, and eyes in which cell death has been induced, are illustrated in **Fig. 4**.

5. Identifying important mRNA targets for a miRNA. As discussed in the **Introduction**, the rules that define productive miRNA–mRNA interactions are only just being uncovered. Computational approaches to target-site identification that use this information generate lists of candidate target transcripts that must be tested for significance. Evidence that the mRNA constitutes a valid target can be obtained using approaches such as antibodies to detect protein levels in the presence and absence of the miRNA, and reporters that can detect miRNA-dependent translation suppression of constructs that carry the relevant 3' untranslated region, which itself carries the miRNA-binding sites *(8)*. However, none of these approaches are function based in the sense of directly testing roles of the predicted target as a cell death regulator. This point is important because miRNAs, similar to transcription factors, may play different roles in different tissues. Genome-wide target-site prediction programs are blind to this possibility. The most important prediction is that decreased expression of an important target should recapitulate at least some aspect of the phenotypes associated with miRNA overexpression. In some cases, it will be possible to carry out the cell death assay in a homozygous mutant background. However, for many genes, mutants do not exist. Lists of mutants associated with each gene in flies are available at the Flybase web site (http://flybase.net/blast/) (*see* **Note 5**). Mutants may also be homozygous lethal. In this latter case, the twofold reduction in gene activity present in viable heterozygotes will often be insufficient to modify the cell death phenotype. The most straightforward approach to creating strong, tissue-specific decrease in function phenotypes uses RNA interference (RNAi) to drive down target transcript levels in the same pattern in which the miRNA was expressed (*see* **Note 6**). As discussed in **Subheading 2.2.**, several P element vectors are available that facilitate this process. It takes roughly 2 mo to go from germline injection to scoring the progeny of a cross that uses a balanced stock. Most of this time is waiting, interspersed with a few days of collecting virgins and setting up crosses, roughly every 10 to 12 d (*see* **Note 7**). One such test cross is illustrated in **Fig. 5**.

4. Notes

1. Transgenes associated with P element insertions will express at different levels, depending on the site of insertion in the genome. Therefore, it is always a good idea to test multiple, independent transgenic lines in any assay.

2. Often, germline transformation is so efficient that the transformed flies carry multiple, independent insertions of the transgene, which may be located on different chromosomes. These can often be recognized as vials that give rise to flies with multiple eye colors. Single independent insertions can be isolated by outcrossing the transformed fly to *w* for several generations until flies with a uniform eye color are obtained. Also, for any given transgene insertion, males tend to have more *w* pigment (and, thus, darker eye color) than females.

$$\frac{w}{w} \quad \times \quad \frac{w, P^{w+}}{Y} \downarrow$$

$$\frac{w}{w} \qquad \frac{w, P^{w+}}{w} \qquad \frac{w}{Y} \qquad \frac{w}{Y}$$

Only white eyed sons. Red and white eyed daughters. The P^{w+} is on the X.

- -

$$\frac{w}{Y} ; \frac{P^{w+}}{A} \quad \times \quad \frac{w}{w} ; \frac{Cyo}{Tft} \downarrow$$

$$\frac{w}{Y} ; \frac{Cyo}{P^{w+}} \quad \times \quad \frac{w}{w} ; \frac{Cyo}{P^{w+}} \downarrow$$

$$w ; \frac{Cyo}{P^{w+}} \quad \text{and} \quad w ; \frac{P^{w+}}{P^{w+}}$$

Crosses of w ; Cyo/P^{w+} flies to each other yield a balanced stock that gives rise to only w ;Cyo/P^{w+} and P^{w+}/P^{w+} progeny if the P^{w+} is on the second chromosome

$$\frac{w}{w} ; \frac{A}{A} \quad \times \quad \frac{w}{Y} ; \frac{P^{w+}}{+} \downarrow$$

$$\frac{w}{w} ; \frac{P^{w+}}{A} \qquad \frac{w}{w} ; \frac{+}{A} \qquad \frac{w}{Y} ; \frac{P^{w+}}{A} \qquad \frac{w}{Y} ; \frac{+}{A}$$

Red and white eyed sons and daughters. The P^{w+} is on an autosome.

- -

$$\frac{w}{Y} ; \frac{P^{w+}}{A} \quad \times \quad \frac{w}{w} ; \frac{TM3, Sb}{Ser} \downarrow$$

$$\frac{w}{Y} ; \frac{TM3, Sb}{P^{w+}} \quad \times \quad \frac{w}{w} ; \frac{TM3, Sb}{P^{w+}} \downarrow$$

$$w ; \frac{TM3, Sb}{P^{w+}} \quad \text{and} \quad w ; \frac{P^{w+}}{P^{w+}}$$

Crosses of w ; TM3,Sb/P^{w+} flies to each other yield a balanced stock that gives rise to only w ; TM3,Sb/P^{w+} and P^{w+}/P^{w+} progeny if the P^{w+} is on the third chromosome

---

Testing roles for miRNAs as cell death regulators through overexpression.

1. Express the miRNA in some pattern using either tissue-specific promoters directly, or the GAL4/UAS system.

2. Score these animals for dominant phenotypes that might reflect increased or decreased cell death, such as an decrease or increase in tissue size, respectively.

3. Cross animals that express a miRNA into genetic backgrounds that allow one to score for the presence or absence of particular cells or cell deaths (c.f. the GFP-labeled wing epidermal cells discussed in the text and in figure 4). Compare the miRNA-expressing progeny with those that are otherwise wildtype.

4. Cross animals that express a miRNA into genetic backgrounds that are sensitized with respect to particular cell death pathways. These backgrounds are often generated by overexpressing a cell death activator. Compare the miRNA-expressing progeny with those that only carry the sensitized background.

5. Expose miRNA-expressing animals to environmental insults at different developmental stages and compare the survival of miRNA-expressing cells/animals with that of comparable wildtype cells/animals.

Fig. 2. Strategies for identifying miRNAs that can regulate cell death when ectopically expressed. *See* **Subheading 3.–4.** and **Fig. 3** for details.

3. It is important that females used for crosses be virgin, because otherwise the genotype of the progeny can be unclear. For each cross set up, it is a good idea to ask what the consequences would be for the progeny genotypes if the females had mated with their brothers instead of the desired mates. Embryogenesis takes approx 24 h at 25°C. Therefore, if you have any question regarding the status of your females put them in a vial with a little fresh yeast for a few days. If none of their eggs hatch, then they are likely virgin.

4. Temperature is an important variable for many crosses. The *GAL4* gene used in *Drosophila* is from the yeast *Saccharomyces cerevisiae*, which grows best at 30°C. Thus, *GAL4* is much less effective as a transcription factor at 18°C (a standard low temperature for growth

---

Fig. 1. *(Opposite page)* Creating stable stocks of microRNA (miRNA) transgenic flies. P^{w+} refers to the chromosome carrying the transposon. Balancer chromosomes contain multiple inversions. These have the effect of suppressing meiotic exchange with their normal homologs. When a balancer chromosome carries a dominant mutation and is placed *in trans* to a chromosome that carries a genetic element of interest, it becomes a powerful tool for predicting the genotype of progeny. Cyo is a balancer chromosome for the second chromosome. It is lethal as a homozygote and carries a dominant mutation, *Cy* (also lethal as a homozygote), that results in flies having curled wings. Therefore, the presence of the *Cy* wing phenotype signifies the presence of the second chromosome balancer chromosome. Tft is a dominant mutation, lethal as a homozygote, which results in flies having extra bristles on their dorsal thorax. TM3 is a third chromosome balancer that is lethal when homozygous, and Sb is a dominant mutation located on the same chromosome that results in flies having short, stubby bristles (rather than long thin ones) all over their body. Serate (Ser) is a dominant mutation that results in flies having nicked margins on the wing. A, any autosome; Y, the Y chromosome; *w* = the recessive white eye phenotype associated with loss of the *white* (*w*) gene. In the crosses illustrated, *w* is also used to refer to the X chromosome, on which it is located. A semicolon is used to indicate separate chromosomes, whereas a comma is used to indicate separate mutations or other genetic elements on the same chromosome. Only relevant progeny genotypes are shown for these crosses. The upper panel illustrates progeny of crosses of a transformant (P^{w+}) male with an element insertion on the X (left) or autosome (right) to *w*. The lower panel illustrates balancing for the two major autosomes, the second and third chromosomes.

A $\dfrac{w}{Y}$; $\dfrac{\textit{tissue-specific-GAL4}}{\textit{tissue-specific-GAL4,}}$; $\dfrac{+}{+}$ x $\dfrac{w}{w}$; $\dfrac{\textit{UAS-miRNA}}{\textit{Cyo}}$; $\dfrac{+}{+}$

$\downarrow$

$\dfrac{w}{w}$; $\dfrac{\textit{tissue-specific-GAL4}}{\textit{UAS-miRNA}}$; $\dfrac{+}{+}$ and $\dfrac{w}{w}$; $\dfrac{\textit{tissue-specific-GAL4}}{\textit{Cyo}}$; $\dfrac{+}{+}$

- -

B $\dfrac{w}{Y}$; $\dfrac{+}{+}$; $\dfrac{\textit{GMR-Rpr}}{\textit{TM3, Sb}}$ x $\dfrac{w}{w}$; $\dfrac{\textit{GMR-miRNA}}{\textit{Cyo}}$; $\dfrac{+}{+}$

$\downarrow$

$\dfrac{w}{w}$; $\dfrac{\textit{GMR-miRNA}}{+}$; $\dfrac{\textit{GMR-Rpr}}{+}$ and $\dfrac{w}{w}$; $\dfrac{\textit{Cyo}}{+}$; $\dfrac{\textit{GMR-Rpr}}{+}$

- -

C $\dfrac{w}{Y}$; $\dfrac{\textit{en-GAL4, UAS-nGFP}}{\textit{en-GAL4, UAS-nGFP}}$; $\dfrac{+}{+}$ x $\dfrac{w}{w}$; $\dfrac{\textit{UAS-miRNA}}{\textit{Cyo}}$; $\dfrac{+}{+}$

$\downarrow$

$\dfrac{w}{w}$; $\dfrac{\textit{en-GAL4, UAS-nGFP}}{\textit{UAS-miRNA}}$; $\dfrac{+}{+}$ and $\dfrac{w}{w}$; $\dfrac{\textit{en-GAL4, UAS-nGFP}}{\textit{Cyo}}$; $\dfrac{+}{+}$

Fig. 3. Testing roles for microRNAs (miRNAs) as cell death regulators. (**A**) Males homozygous for a transposon that carries a tissue-specific *GAL4* driver, located on the second chromosome, are crossed to females that carry a upstream activating sequences (UAS)–miRNA transposon insertion *in trans* to the Cyo balancer chromosome. Two kinds of interesting progeny are shown: flies that express the miRNA in the pattern of the *GAL4* driver (left), and (wild-type) flies that express *GAL4* alone. Only female progeny are shown. These flies can be examined for death-related phenotypes directly. Alternatively, they can be examined after exposure to environmental insults at different life stages. (**B**) GMR–reaper (*Rpr*) flies, which have small eyes because of eye-specific expression of *Rpr*, are crossed with flies that express a miRNA under *GMR* control. Two kinds of interesting progeny arise from the cross. Straight winged, non-*Sb* flies (on the left) carry both *GMR–Rpr* and *GMR*–miRNA. They are compared with progeny that are *Cy* and non-*Sb* (on the right), and, thus, must carry the *GMR–Rpr*, but not the *GMR*–miRNA. If the presence of the miRNA expression construct enhances or suppresses the *GMR–Rpr* phenotype, this would suggest (but not prove; the modifier could be acting to regulate *GMR*-dependent transcription) that the miRNA could be a regulator of *Rpr*-dependent cell death. (**C**) In this cross, the fate of GFP-expressing cells, which are present in a pattern driven by the *engrailed* (*en*) promoter, are compared in the presence (left) and absence (right) of miRNA overexpression, in the *en* pattern. If expression of the miRNA bocks death, this will be apparent as persistent GFP expression.

and long-term storage of flies) than at 25°C (a standard high temperature for rapid growth with minimal activation of the heat-shock response). Genes expressed under GMR control also typically show much stronger phenotypes at higher temperatures.

5. When testing mutants in candidate miRNA target genes for their ability to recapitulate the miRNA overexpression phenotype, it is important to recognize that *Drosophila* mutants have been generated in many different genetic backgrounds, by many different labs, over

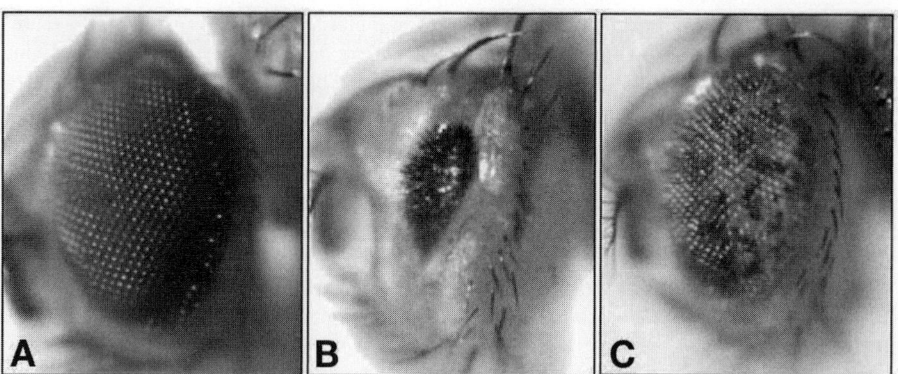

Fig. 4. Fly eye cell death phenotypes. (**A**) Wild-type fly eye. (**B**) Fly eye expressing the cell death activator reaper (*Rpr*) under *GMR* control. (**C**) Fly eye expressing the apical cell death caspase, Dronc, under *GMR* control. Flies expressing *GMR–Rpr* have small eyes because of cell death occurring early in eye development. Flies expressing *GMR*–Dronc have a normal-sized eye, but the eye shows a mottled (or spotted eye) phenotype, in which some areas lack pigment. This phenotype reflects late-onset cell death after retinal cell specification and differentiation. Plastic sections of such eyes (carried out as described in **ref. *41***) would show degenerating photoreceptor and support cells.

Fig. 5. Testing candidate microRNA (miRNA) target transcripts for physiological significance using RNAi. (**A**) Crosses used to identify miRNA regulators of *Rpr*-dependent cell death in the fly eye. (**B**) miRNAs are thought to act by decreasing the expression of their targets. Therefore, decreasing the expression of a physiologically significant miRNA target transcript using an independent strategy, in this case RNAi, should result in a enhancement or suppression of the *GMR–Rpr* small eye phenotype, similar to that seen with miRNA overexpression. As with the cross in A, straight-winged, non-*Sb* flies that express both *GMR–RNAi*-target and *GMR–Rpr* are compared with curly winged flies that express *GMR–Rpr* alone. An important (and untestable) assumption of this strategy is that the miRNA overexpression phenotype reflects action on only (or primarily) a single mRNA target.

many, many years. *Drosophila* cannot be frozen (and successfully reanimated) for routine stock keeping. Therefore, unknown genetic modifiers may also have been introduced into stocks kept for many decades or put through population bottlenecks. It is always a good idea to ask yourself how strong the evidence is that the interesting modifier you have is caused by mutation of the gene you are interested in testing (as opposed to an unknown background mutation). If you observe a similar phenotype in mutants generated through independent screens or screening mechanisms (genomic mutation or RNAi), it is usually a good sign. One of the advantages of using RNAi to test candidate genes is that RNAi transgenes can all be generated in a common genetic background, which can be tested ahead of time for modification of the death phenotype. However, a problem to worry about when using RNAi is protein perdurance. Decreasing the expression of an important target gene at the RNA level may have minimal consequences for some time if the preexisting protein has a long half-life.

6. In cases in which the cell death phenotype being scored for enhancement or suppression is caused by ectopic expression of a cell death activator or inhibitor, it is important to keep in mind that modifier phenotypes can reflect action on processes other than cell death. For example, ectopic miRNA expression, or transgene-driven RNAi of a candidate miRNA target gene, may regulate the expression or activity of the transcription factors that drive the expression of the cell death regulator used to create the sensitized background, rather than the activity of the cell death regulator itself. To identify these uninteresting false positives, it is useful to have flies available that express, under the control of the same promoter, another molecule that results in a dominant phenotype whose basis is unrelated to cell death. If expression of the miRNA or transgene-driven RNAi results in enhancement or suppression of this phenotype similar to that seen in the original sensitized cell death background, chances are that this is not a regulator of cell death.

7. In this review, we focused our description on very general assays for cell death regulators that use whole flies and a dissection microscope. However, it is important to note that these constitute only first-pass assays. Use of other more cell-biological assays is essential if one is to show that cell death (as opposed to proliferation or differentiation) is really being affected. When cells undergo apoptosis, the effector caspase, Drice, becomes cleaved and, thereby, activated. One important target of Drice is a nuclease inhibitor, cleavage of which results in nuclear DNA destruction *(37)*. High-level Drice activation associated with cell death can be visualized with active Drice-specific antibodies, whereas DNA fragmentation associated with apoptosis can be visualized by end labeling of DNA *(38,39)*. Other useful ways of visualizing cell death can be found in *(40)*.

Acknowledgments

This work was supported by Grants from the National Institutes of Health to B. A. H. and M. G., and a Gosney Fellowship to C.-H. Chen.

References

1. Hay, B. A., Huh, J. R., and Guo, M. (2004) The genetics of cell death: approaches, insights and opportunities in Drosophila. *Nat. Rev. Genet.* **5,** 911–922.
2. Bartel, D. P. (2004) MicroRNAs: genomics, biogenesis, mechanism, and function. *Cell* **116,** 281–297.
3. Berezikov, E. Guryev, V., van de Belt, J., Wienholds, E., Plasterk, R. H., and Cuppen, E. (2005) Phylogenetic shadowing and computational identification of human microRNA genes. *Cell* **120,** 21–24.

4. Ambros, V. (2001) MicroRNAs: tiny regulators with great potential. *Cell* **107,** 823–826.

5. Tomari, Y. and Zamore, P. D. (2005) Perspective: machines for RNAi. *Genes Dev.* **19,** 517–529.

6. Ambros, V. (2004) The functions of animal microRNAs. *Nature* **431,** 350–355.

7. Xu, P., Vernooy, S. Y., Guo, M., and Hay, B. A. (2003) The Drosophila microRNA mir-14 suppresses cell death and is required for normal fat metabolism. *Curr. Biol.* **13,** 790–795.

8. Brennecke, J., Hipfner, D. R., Stark, A., Russell, R. B., and Cohen, S. M. (2003) Bantam encodes a developmentally regulated microRNA that controls cell proliferation and regulates the proapoptotic gene hid in Drosophila. *Cell* **113,** 25–36.

9. Stark, A., Brennecke, J., Russell, R. B., and Cohen, S. M. (2003) Identification of Drosophila microRNA targets. *PLOS Biol.* **1,** 397–409.

10. Xu, P., Guo, M., and Hay, B. A. (2004) MicroRNAs and the regulation of cell death. *Trends Genet.* **20,** 617–624.

11. Vernooy, S. Y., Copeland, J., Ghaboosi, N., Griffen, E. E., Yoo, S. J., and Hay, B. A. (2000) Cell death regulation in Drosophila: conservation of mechanism and unique insights. *J. Cell Biol.* **150,** F69–F76.

12. Lu, J., Get, G., Miska, E. A., et al. (2005) MicroRNA expression profiles classify human cancers. *Nature* **435,** 834–838.

13. Green, D. R. and Evan, G. I. (2002) A matter of life and death. *Cancer Cell* **1,** 19–30.

14. Bonini, N. M. and Fortini, M. E. (2003) Human neurodegenerative disease modeling using Drosophila. *Annu. Rev. Neurosci.* **26,** 627–656.

15. Khorova, A., Reynolds, A., and Jayasena, S. D. (2003) Functional siRNAs and miRNAs exhibit strand bias. *Cell* **115,** 209–216.

16. Schwarz, D. S., Hutvagner, G., Du, T., Xu, Z., Aronin, N., and Zamore, P. D. (2003) Asymmetry in the assembly of the RNAi enzyme complex. *Cell* **115,** 199–208.

17. Doench, J. G. and Sharp, P. A. (2004) Specificity of microRNA target selection in translational repression. *Genes Dev.* **18,** 504–511.

18. Kiriakidou, M., Nelson, P. T., Kouranov, A., et al. (2004) A combined computational-experimental approach predicts human microRNA targets. *Genes Dev.* **18,** 1165–1178.

19. Haley, B. and Zamore, P. D. (2004) Kinetic analysis of the RNAi enzyme complex. *Nat. Struct. Mol. Biol.* **11,** 599–606.

20. Brennecke, J., Stark, A., Russell, R. B., and Cohen, S. M. (2005) Principles of microRNA-target recognition. *PloS Biol.* **3,** 404–418.

21. Enright, A. J., John, B., Gaul, U., Tuschl, T., Sander, C., and Marks, D. S. (2003) MicroRNA targets in Drosophila. *Genome Biol.* **5,** R1.

22. Lewis, B. P., Shih, L.-H., Jones-Rhoades, M. W., Bartel, D. P., and Burge, C. B. (2003) Prediction of mammalian microRNA targets. *Cell* **115,** 787–798.

23. Jones-Rhoades, M. W. and Bartel, D. P. (2004) Computational identification of plant microRNAs and their targets, including a stress-induced miRNA. *Mol. Cell* **14,** 787–799.

24. John, B., Enright, A. J., Aravin, A., Tuschl, T., Sander, C., and Marks, D. S. (2004) Human microRNA targets. *PLoS Biol.* **2,** 1862–1879.

25. Krek, A., Grun, D., Poy, M. N., et al. (2005) Combinatorial microRNA target predictions. *Nat. Genet.* **37,** 495–500.

26. Robins, H., Li, Y., and Padgett, R. W. (2005) Incorporating structure to predict microRNA targets. *Proc. Natl. Acad. Sci. USA* **102,** 4006–4009.

27. Burgler, C. and Macdonald, P. M. (2005) Prediction and verification of microRNA targets by MovingTargets, a highly adaptable prediction program. *BMC Genomics* **6,** http://www.biomedcentral.com/1471-2164/6/88. Last accessed Dec. 22, 2005.

28. Lewis, B. P., Burge, C. B., and Bartel, D. P. (2005) Conserved seed pairing, often flanked by adenosines, indicates that thousands of human genes are microRNA targets. *Cell* **120,** 15–20.

29. McGuire, S. E., Roman, G., and Davis, R. L. (2004) Gene expression systems in Drosophila: a synthesis of time and space. *Trends Genet.* **20,** 384–391.

30. Hay, B. A., Wolff, T., and Rubin, G. M. (1994) Expression of baculovirus P35 prevents cell death in Drosophila. *Development* **120,** 2121–2129.

31. Brand, A. H. and Perrimon, N. (1993) Targeted gene expression as a means of altering cell fates and generating dominant phenotypes. *Development* **118,** 401–415.

32. Rorth, P. (1998) Gal4 in the Drosophila female germline. *Mech. Dev.* **78,** 113–118.

33. Bernards, A. and Hariharan, I. K. (2001) Of flies and men—studying human disease in Drosophila. *Curr. Opin. Genet. Dev.* **11,** 274–278.

34. Giordano, E., Rendina, R., Peluso, I., and Furia, M. (2002) RNAi triggered by symmetrically transcribed transgenes in Drosophila melanogaster. *Genetics* **160,** 637–648.

35. Lee, Y. S. and Carthew, R. W. (2003) Making a better RNAi vector for Drosophila: use of intron spacers. *Methods* **30,** 322–329.

36. Kimura, K.-I., Kodama, A., Hayasaka, Y., and Ohta, T. (2004) Activation of the cAMP/PKA signaling pathway is required for post-ecdysial cell death in wing epidermal cells of Drosophila. *Development* **131,** 1597–1606.

37. Nagata, S., Nagase, H., Kawane, K., Mukae, N., and Fukuyama, H. (2003) Degradation of chromosomal DNA during apoptosis. *Cell Death Differ.* **10,** 108–116.

38. Wang, S. L., Hawkins, C. J., Yoo, S. J., Muller, H. A., and Hay, B. A. (1999) The Drosophila caspase inhibitor DIAP1 is essential for cell survival and is negatively regulated by HID. *Cell* **98,** 453–463.

39. Yoo, S. J., et al. (2002) Apoptosis inducers Hid, Rpr and Grim negatively regulate levels of the caspase inhibitor DIAP1 by distinct mechanisms. *Nat. Cell Biol.* **4,** 416–424.

40. McCall, K., Baum, J. S., Cullen, K., and Peterson, J. S. (2004) Visualizing apoptosis. In: *Methods in Molecular Biology*, vol. 247, Drosophila Cytogenetic Protocols Visualizing Apoptosis (Henderson, D. S., ed.), Humana, Totowa, NJ, pp. 431–442.

41. Wolff, T. and Ready, D. F. (1991) Cell death in normal and rough eye mutants of Drosophila. *Development* **113,** 825–839.

17

MicroRNAs in Human Immunodeficiency Virus-1 Infection

Yamina Bennasser, Shu-Yun Le, Man Lung Yeung, and Kuan-Teh Jeang

Summary

Initially reported for *Caenorhabditis elegans*, microRNA (miRNA) has been shown to regulate gene expression in plants, flies, and mammals *(1,2)*. Recently, findings of miRNA have been extended to viruses *(3,4)*. Here, we report on our approaches to investigate the role of miRNAs in human immunodeficiency virus (HIV)-1 infection. Using computer-directed foldings, we first identify potential sequences in HIV-1 that putatively encode miRNAs. Subsquently, we use Northern blotting of RNAs isolated from HIV-infected cells to confirm expression of predicted miRNA sequences. Finally, we use a scanning algorithm to search 3' untranslated regions (UTRs) of human messenger RNAs (mRNAs) in the attempt to predict potential sites targeted by HIV-1 miRNAs.

Key Words: miRNA; bioinformatics; HIV-1; microarray.

1. Introduction

miRNAs are small RNAs of 21 to 25 nucleotides (nt) that regulate cellular gene expression posttranscriptionally *(1,2)*. miRNAs are processed by cellular ribonucleases (RNases) III from imperfect stem-loop precursors of approx 70 nt *(5)*. To date, hundreds of miRNAs have been described in invertebrates, plants, insects, and mammals *(6)*. Although, in some cases, the corresponding miRNA target has not been firmly identified, many miRNAs have been implicated in the regulation of different developmental and physiological processes. Recently, the presence of miRNA in the first human viruses (i.e., herpesviruses) was reported *(3,4)*. To ask whether other human viruses might also specify miRNAs, we investigated miRNAs in a human retrovirus, HIV *(7)*. We previously hypothesized that HIV could encode five precursor (pre)-miRNAs of approx 70 nt in size, with an imperfectly duplexed stem of 21 to 25 bp. These five putative pre-miRNAs are distributed in different regions of the HIV genome: near the transactivation region, in Gag (i.e., capsid), near the *gag-pol* frameshift, in the *nef* gene, and in the 3' long terminal repeat. Moreover, computer searches revealed that, if expressed maturely, the five HIV-1-encoded miRNAs could potentially modulate the expression of 500 to 1000 human target genes *(7)*.

From: *Methods in Molecular Biology, vol. 342: MicroRNA Protocols*
Edited by: S. Ying © Humana Press Inc., Totowa, NJ

In this chapter, we outline protocols starting from the prediction of HIV-encoded miRNA using a new computational algorithm, *StemED*, to the prediction of potential cellular gene targets. We propose the validation of HIV-encoded miRNA by two complementary approaches in ex vivo tissue culture assays:

1. Cloning and sequencing 19- to 25-nt-sized RNAs from HIV-infected cells.
2. Northern blotting to confirm expression using sequence-specific miRNA probes.

2. Materials

1. 25:24:1 (v/v/v) phenol/chloroform/isoamyl alcohol.
2. Chloroform.
3. RNA markers: 18-mer: AGCGUGUAGGGAUCCAAA; 44-mer: GGCCAACGUUCUCA ACAAUAGUGA.
4. 100 m*M* nonradioactive linkers: 5'-phosphorylated linker ATCGTaggcacctgaaa (RNA/DNA version; lowercase, RNA) and 3' linker: pCTGTAGGCACCATCAATx (x: a dideoxy-C base).
5. 100 m*M* adenosine triphosphate (ATP), pH 7.0.
6. 10 U/mL T4 polynucleotide kinase (New England Biolabs, Ipswich, MA).
7. 100 m*M* reverse transcription primer (ATTGATGGTGCCTAC).
8. 0.1 *M* dithiothreitol.
9. 5X first-strand buffer.
10. 10X deoxyribonucleoside triphosphate (dNTP) solution: deoxy-ATP, deoxycytidine triphosphate, deoxyguanosine triphosphate, deoxythymidine triphosphate, 2 m*M* each, pH 7.5 (Invitrogen, Carlsbad, CA).
11. 200 U/mL reverse transcriptase (Superscript III, RNase H(–) M-MLV reverse transcriptase; Invitrogen).
12. 150 m*M* KOH and 20 m*M* Tris base.
13. 150 m*M* HCl.
14. 10X polymerase chain reaction (PCR) buffer.
15. 100 m*M* 5' primer PCR (ATCGTAGGCACCTGAAA) and 3' PCR primer (ATTGATGGT GCCTACAG).
16. 5 U/mL *Taq* polymerase (Roche, Indianapolis, IN).
17. 20 U/mL BanI restriction endonuclease and 10X New England Biolabs buffer 4 (New England Biolabs).
18. 2000 U/mL of T4 DNA ligase, and 10X DNA ligation buffer (New England Biolabs).
19. 25-bp DNA ladder (Invitrogen); 100-bp DNA ladder (New England Biolabs).
20. 2% (w/v) NuSieve (low-melt) agarose gel (Cambrex, East Rutherford, NJ).
21. 10X Tris-acetate-EDTA buffer (TAE).
22. 10X Tris-borate-EDTA (TBE).
23. Ultrahyb hybridization buffer (Ambion, Austin, TX).
24. Sodium chloride sodium citrate (SSC) buffer.
25. TOPO-TA cloning kit with TOP10 cells and pCR2.1 vector (Invitrogen).
26. QIAquick PCR purification kit (Qiagen, Valencia, CA).
27. 0.65-, 1.5-, and 2-mL siliconized Eppendorf tubes (*see* **Note 1**).
28. Plastic wrap.
29. Phosphorimaging screen and phosphorimager.
30. Spectrophotometer and 1-cm quartz cuvette.

31. Thermal cycler.
32. 96-well thermocycler-compatible microtiter plates.
33. 360-nm ultraviolet transilluminator.

3. Methods

3.1. Computational Prediction of HIV-1-Encoded miRNAs and Their Cognate Cellular Targets

Recent computational procedures integrating a routine RNA-folding program, sequence comparisons, machine learning, and statistical inferences have been developed to identify miRNAs *(3,4,8,9)*. In general, these computational methods consist of two steps. In the first step, a stem-loop list is built by RNA folding (e.g., using the mfold program) of highly stable local stem-loop structures generally in UTRs of the genome. Next, the potential miRNA-like candidate stem-loops are selected from the preliminary stem-loop list based on sequence and structural features that may be conserved between miRNA-candidates and known miRNAs. This type of computational methodology has been successfully used for identifying miRNAs in worms, flies, and herpesviruses *(3,4,8,9)*. Here, we present a new version for constructing the stem-loop list from which moieties with defined parameters featured in the stem-loops of pre-miRNAs can be identified.

Our computational test on known stem-loops of pre-miRNAs indicated that the foldback stem-loop of pre-miRNA has a well-ordered conformation that is unlikely to occur by chance *(10)*. The pre-miRNAs possess well-ordered conformations that are both thermodynamically stable and uniquely folded. The well-ordered structural property of a local segment, S_k, can be evaluated by a quantitative measure $E_{diff}(S_k)$ that is defined as the difference of free energies between the routine optimal structure (OS) and its corresponding optimal restrained structure folded by the sequence, in which all previous base pairings in the OS are forbidden *(10)*. That is:

$$E_{diff}(S_k) = E_f(S_k) - E(S_k),$$

where $E(S_k)$ and $E_f(S_k)$ are the lowest free energies of the OS and optimal restrained structure folded by the local segment, S_k, respectively. The greater the $E_{diff}(S_k)$ of the segment, the more well-ordered the folded RNA structure of S_k is expected to be. To extract the signal with statistically high $E_{diff}(S_k)$ computed in a genomic sequence, we also compute a normalized score $Zscr_e(S_k)$ of $E_{diff}(S_i)$ for each segment.

$$Zscr_e(S_k) = [E_{diff}(S_k) - E_{diff}(w)]/std(w),$$

where $E_{diff}(w)$ and $std(w)$ are the sample mean and standard deviation (std), respectively, of the $E_{diff}(S_k)$ computed by sliding a fixed-length window in steps of a few nucleotides from 5' to 3' along the sequence.

The normalized score, $Zscr_e$ is independent of the size of the selected window. It is important to note that the free energy difference between two distinct stem-loops folded from the same segment is used to characterize the unique base order and specific conformations instead of routinely using the lowest free energy only as used in current computational predictions of miRNA *(3,4,8,9)*.

3.1.1 Statistical Inference of Distinct Well-Ordered Stem-Loops

One important question in our approach is how to evaluate the statistical significance of the score E_{diff} computed from a local RNA folding. Statistical inference of the computed data needs to quantify uncertainties involved in the analysis. In the statistical analysis, we adapt Monte Carlo simulations *(11)* to estimate the typical behavior of E_{diff} computed in a random sample that is selected to be related to the local segment.

For a given segment, S_k, we generate a large number of randomly shuffled sequences $(RS_{k,1}, ..., RS_{k,m})$, in which the number "m" is often determined by the length of the segment S_k. $E_{diff}(S_k)$ and $E_{diff}(RS_{k,i})$ of the "m" randomly shuffled sequences are then computed. Similarly, a normalized z-score, $SigZscr_e(S_k)$ can be computed *(12)* by the formula:

$$SigZscr_e(S_k) = [E_{diff}(S_k) - E_{diff}(RS_k)]/std(RS_k),$$

where $E_{diff}(RS_k)$ and $std(RS_k)$ are the sample mean and sample standard deviation computed from the random sample.

In the random sample, the distribution of the random variable $SigZscr_e(RS_{k,i})(i = 1, ..., m)$ is expected to approximately follow a normal distribution. Thus, the statistical significance of $E_{diff}(S_k)$ for the segment S_k can be estimated by means of the classical normal distribution.

In constructing the distinct stem-loop list, the following steps are generally used:

1. Using program StemEd, $Zscr_e$ values are computed by moving a window of approx 80 nt (or another size) along the genomic sequence.
2. The distinct stem-loops in the noncoding region with high $Zscr_e$ can be statistically inferred by the computed distribution.
3. For each segment of the predicted stem-loops determined in **step 2**, an extended fragment of 100-nt (or another size) is selected with an additional 10 nt in both the 5' and 3' end of the segment. Using StemEd, the $SigZscr_e$ values are computed by a set of windows whose sizes are systematically changed with a range of 60 to 100 nt. The most well-ordered stem-loop can be determined by the maximal $SigZscr_e$. It is interesting to note that the pre-miRNA stem-loops have small bulges and internal loops in which the conserved, approx 22-nt miRNA sequence, contains at least 16 base pairings within one arm. The predicted stem-loops in **step 3** are further evaluated by the conserved structural features, so that potential candidates with miRNA-like stem-loop structures can be predicted.

3.1.2. Computation of the Lowest Free Energy for Stem-Loop Formation

It is well-established that, in all RNA molecules, most nucleotide residues interact to form short, intramolecular helical regions and unpaired loops, thereby defining a secondary structure. The helical stems consist of a series of uninterrupted Watson–Crick or wobble G:U basepairs. The loops include hairpin loops, internal loops, bulge loops, and multibranch loops. The energy of a secondary structure is assumed to be the sum of the energy contributions from all of its stacked basepairs and loops *(13,14)*.

For a given RNA segment, S_k, the dynamic programming approach *(14)* recursively calculates the minimum energy structure on progressively longer subsequences. Because our goal is to discover distinct well-ordered stem-loops, we exclude the multibranch loop in the structure prediction. Furthermore, we only consider a secondary structure with a single stem-loop structure within the local segment. Under these restrictions, the optimal energy, $E(i,j)$, in a segment $S_{i,j}$ from base i to j can be computed as follows:

$$E(i,j) = \min[V(i,j), V(i + 1,j) + d(i), V(i,j - 1) + d(j),$$
$$V(i + 1, j - 1) + d(i) + d(j), E(i,j - 1), E(i+1,j)],$$

where $V(i,j)$ is the optimal energy of $S_{i,j}$ in which base i is paired with base j denoted by $i{:}j$; $d(i)$ is the free energy contribution from the dangling base i. From the definition of the various types of loops in a secondary structure, $V(i,j)$ can be computed by:

$$V(i,j) = \min[V_H(i,j), V(i + 1, j - 1) + e_s(i,j), V_{IB}(i,j)],$$

where $V_H(i,j)$ is the free energy of the structure if basepair $i{:}j$ closes a hairpin loop, $e_s(i,j)$ is the stacking energy if $i{:}j$ stacks over $(i + 1){:}(j - 1)$, and $V_{IB}(i,j)$ is the optimal energy if $i{:}j$ closes a bulge or interior loop. We have:

$$V_{IB}(i,j) = \min[e_{ib}(i,j;i',j') + V(i',j'), \ i < i' < j' < j],$$

where $e_{ib}(i,j;I',j')$ is the energy contribution of the bulge or interior loop closed by basepairs $i{:}j$ and $i'{:}j'$.

Thus, the energy matrices V and E can be obtained by the following dynamic programming algorithm:

do j = 1 to n
    do i = j down to 1
        $V(i,j) = min\ \{V_H(i,j), V(i + 1,j - 1) + e_s(i,j), V_{IB}(i,j)\}$
        $E(i,j) = min\ \{V(i,j), V(i + 1,j) + d(i), V(i,j - 1) + d(j),$
               $V(i + 1,j - 1) + d(i) + d(j), E(i,j - 1), E(i + 1,j)\}$
    End do
End do

The energy, $E(S_k)$, of an OS folded by the local fragment $S_{1,k}$ is $E(1,k)$. The basepairs in the optimal stem-loop structure are then determined by a trace-back algorithm, as follows:

To compute $E_f(S_k)$, we need to fold the fragment again under the condition in which all basepairs in the OS are prohibited.

In the calculation of energy matrices, we first assign a large positive value to $V(i,j)$ for each basepair $i{:}j$ in OS. Thus, we need to fold the segment S_k twice to compute E_{diff} of the fragment S_k.

3.1.3. Statistical Inference From Known miRNA Stem-Loops

To date, 227 miRNA stem-loops of the human genome are listed in the database of the miRNA Registry (http://www.sanger.ac.uk/Software/Rfam/mirna). For each of the 227 miRNA stem-loops, to assess the statistical significance of E_{diff} values, the sample mean $E_{diff}(RS_i)$ and sample standard deviation $std(RS_i)$ were computed from 500 randomly shuffled sequences. On the average, $E_{diff}(RS_i)$ and $std(RS_i)$ were 3.50 and 0.55 kcal/mol, respectively. In contrast, the mean and std of E_{diff} computed from 227 pre-miRNAs were 20.52 and 5.89 kcal/mol. The average $SigZscr_e$ computed from these pre-miRNA was 6.11, which is highly significant in a normal distribution. Among them, 90% of the human pre-miRNAs had $SigZscr_e$ greater than 4.0. Our results indicate that

Table 1
**Statistical Analysis of Computed E$_{diff}$ From miRNA Precursor
and Their Corresponding Randomly Shuffled Sequences**

| miRNAs | | Sample mean and standard devision (std) computed from | | | | | | | |
| | | Natural sequence | | | | Randomly shuffled sequence | | | |
Genome	number	E_{diff}	(std)	$SigZscr_e$	(std)	E_{diff}	(std)	$SigZscr_e$	(std)
Human	207	20.52	(5.89)	6.11	(2.25)	3.50	(0.55)	0.0	(1.0)
Mouse	208	19.14	(6.19)	5.76	(2.34)	3.43	(0.52)	0.0	(1.0)
Rat	187	20.40	(6.13)	5.93	(2.15)	3.54	(0.46)	0.0	(1.0)
G. gal.	121	19.81	(5.02)	6.13	(1.77)	3.30	(0.36)	0.0	(1.0)
Fly	78	18.22	(4.68)	5.80	(1.73)	3.14	(0.41)	0.0	(1.0)
C. eleg.	116	20.15	(7.03)	6.09	(2.40)	3.36	(0.41)	0.0	(1.0)
C. brig.	50	21.84	(6.03)	6.77	(2.30)	3.36	(0.34)	0.0	(1.0)
A. tha.	92	30.54	(8.22)	8.48	(2.17)	3.99	(0.80)	0.0	(1.0)
O. sat.	122	30.35	(9.89)	7.72	(2.61)	4.35	(0.66)	0.0	(1.0)

the E_{diff} computed from these miRNA stem-loops are significantly greater than that computed from their corresponding randomly shuffled sequences.

For other known miRNA stem-loops listed in the miRNA database, we used the same approach to evaluate the statistical significance of the distinct stem-loop structures folded by pre-miRNAs in the genomes of mouse, rat, *Gallus gallus*, fly, *C. elegans*, *Caenorhabditis briggsae*, *Arabidopsis thaliana*, and *Oryza sativa*. These statistical analysis data are summarized in **Table 1**. In addition, our prediction data for *C. elegans* premRNAs indicated that approx 90% of worm pre-mRNAs were identified by a threshold of $Zscr_e$ = 4.0 by scanning an approx 85-nt window along the genomic sequence *(15)*.

In general, these thresholds of $Zscr_e$ and $SigZscr_e$ can be used in the prediction of miRNA-like stem-loops in genomic sequences.

3.2. Identification of HIV-1 miRNA by Complementary DNA Cloning and Northern Blotting

To assess whether viral miRNA sequences predicted *in silico* are expressed by HIV in infection of cultured cells, we validate using two complementary approaches (**Fig. 1**):

1. Direct cloning and sequencing a library of small 19- to 24-nt RNAs from infected cells *(16)*.
2. Northern blotting from small RNAs isolated from HIV-infected cells.

3.2.1. HIV Infection of T-Cell Line

HIV virus stock is prepared by transfecting HeLa cells with an HIV molecular clone (e.g., pNL4-3). Cell supernatant is collected 48 h after transfection, clarified by centrifugation, and sterilely filtered to remove residual cellular contaminants. Virus content is quantified in a sample aliquot by measuring reverse transcriptase activity; typically, 3×10^6 cpm of reverse transcriptase activity units are used to infect 5×10^6 MT4 cells at 37°C. After 2 h of exposure to virus, T-cell substrates are washed and resuspended

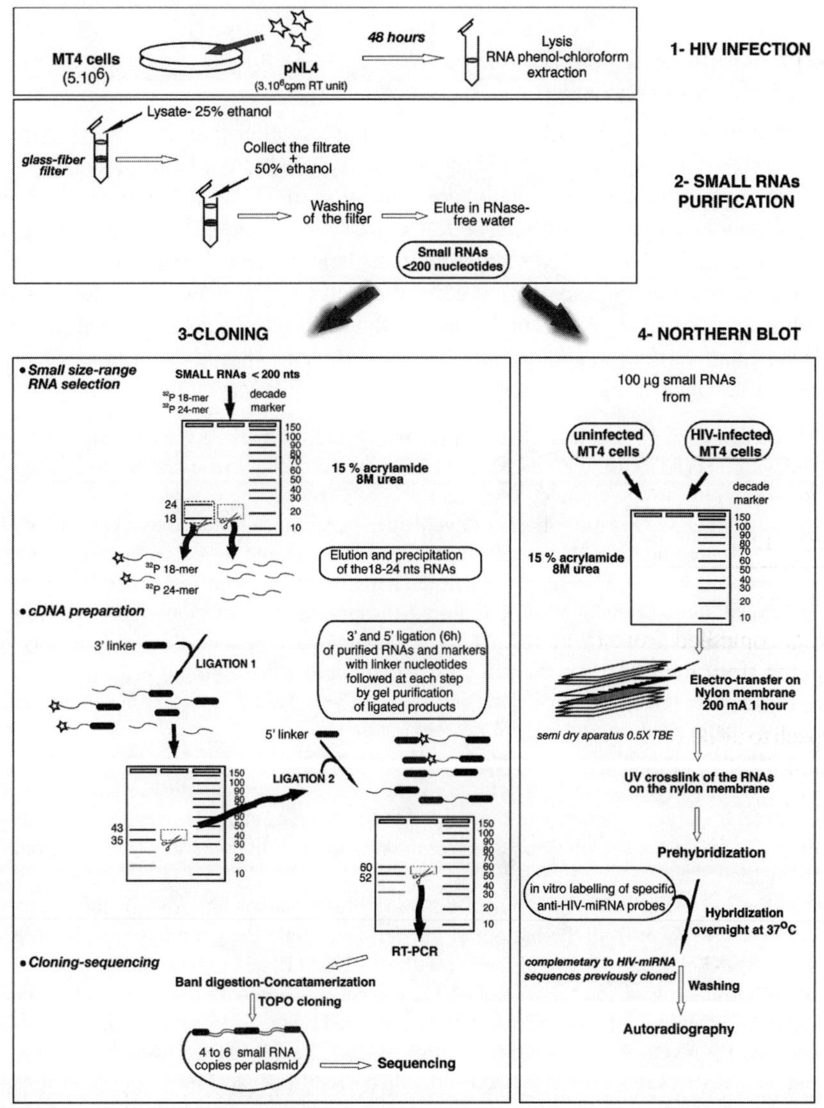

Fig. 1. Overview of HIV-1 miRNA identification. To assess if viral miRNA sequences predicted *in silico* are expressed by HIV in infection of cultured cells, a validation using two complementary approaches was conducted. MT4 cells were infected by 5.10^6 RT units of pNL4-3 HIV molecular clone (1) and the small RNAs of less than 200 nucleotides were purified using *mir*Vana miRNA isolation kit (Ambion) (2). Direct cloning and sequencing a library of small 19–24 nucleotide RNAs (3) and Northern blotting (4) from small RNAs isolated from HIV-infected cells are then conducted.

into RPMI-1640 medium. After 48 h, reverse transcriptase activity is quantified in the supernatant to monitor for successful viral infection; cells are harvested and washed; and the RNA is extracted.

3.2.2. Isolation of Small-Size-Ranged RNAs
From HIV-1 Infected Cells

We routinely size-select our RNA for only those smaller than 200 nt using the *mir Vana*™ miRNA Isolation Kit (Ambion). Basically, absolute ethanol is added first to the lysate sample with a final ethanol concentration of 25%. At this reduced concentration, ethanol precipitates only large RNAs that bind to the glass-fiber filter affixed in a column. Small RNAs (≤200 nt) present in the column flow through are subsequently precipitated by adjusting the ethanol concentration to 55%, and are captured using a second glass-fiber filter. After three washes, the captured RNAs are eluted in RNase-free water; and further size selection of RNAs between 18 and 24 nt is made via gel isolation after denaturing electrophoresis in an urea polyacrylamide gel.

1. 25 pmol of each 18-mer and 24-mer RNA and Decade™ markers are radiolabeled at the 5' end with $^{32}\gamma$P(ATP) using KinaseMax™ (Ambion), according to the manufacturer's protocol.
2. RNA samples are precipitated overnight at –20°C by adding 0.3 *M* NaCl and 3.5 vol of absolute ethanol. One microliter of GlycoBlue™ (Ambion) is added as a carrier for effective RNA precipitation. The next day, RNAs are recovered by centrifugation at 10,000*g* and 4°C for 30 min. Carefully remove the supernatant without disturbing the pellet. An additional short centrifugation is required to remove any salt contamination. However, washing the pellet with 70% ethanol is not recommended because this washing may cause material to be lost. Air-dry the pellet for 10 min before dissolving it in 10 µL of diethyl-pyrocarbonate (DEPC)-treated water and 10 µL of gel-loading buffer. Heat samples at 95°C for 30 s before chilling on ice prior to gel loading.
3. Load the RNA samples equally into the two center wells of a 10-well, 15% denaturing gel (15 × 17 × 0.15-cm; 40-mL gel volume). Load 10 µL of radiolabled RNA makers and 6 µL of Decade marker separately at both sides of the RNA sample. However, leave one well empty between the samples and the size markers to prevent contamination and cloning of the marker RNA sequence.
4. Run the gel using 0.5X TBE buffer until the bromophenol blue dye of the gel-loading buffer is 2 to 3 cm from the bottom of the gel. Dismantle the gel and wrap it with plastic wrap. Spot any three corners of the gel with [γ-^{32}P] ATP, and expose the wrapped gel to a phosphorimaging screen for 30 min. Align the gel position with the spots at three corners to identify the region between 18 and 24 nt identified by the RNA markers. Excise this size-selected RNA region and, in separate tubes, excise the labeled RNA markers.
5. Put the gel slices into preweighed 2.0-mL siliconized Eppendorf tubes and determine their weights. Grind the gel slices into pieces using a melted pipet tip (*see* **Note 2**), and elute the RNAs by adding three volumes of 0.3 *M* NaCl, incubate overnight at 4°C with constant agitation (*see* **Note 3**).
6. The next day, spin down the gel and collect the supernatant into 1.5-mL siliconized Eppendorf tubes. Precipitate the RNAs at –20°C, overnight, by adding 3.5 vol of absolute ethanol (*see* **Note 4**).

3.2.3. Preparation of Complementary DNAs
Corresponding to Small RNAs

To generate complementary (cDNAs) to the small RNAs, individual linkers are ligated to the 3' and 5' ends, respectively, of the isolated small RNAs. The small RNAs are reverse transcribed and PCR amplified before cloning into plasmids.

3.2.3.1. 3' Ligation of RNA With Linker Oligonucleotide

Dissolve the ethanol-precipitated RNAs with 10 µL of DEPC-treated water and use 5 µL for ligation. Set up a 10-µL 3' ligation reaction with 2 µL of 5X RNA ligation buffer, 2 µL of 200 µ*M* 3' linker, 1 µL of T4 RNA ligase (Amersham Pharmacia), and 5 µL of the small RNA sample. In parallel, set up a control reaction using the commercial 18- and 24-mer RNA markers instead of the small RNAs that were isolated. Incubate the ligation reaction at room temperature for 6 h (*see* **Note 5**), and stop the reaction by adding 10 µL of gel-loading buffer with heating at 95°C for 30 s. The samples are placed on ice until loading. Prepare a 15% denaturing gel (15 × 17 × 0.75-cm; 20-mL gel volume) and load the entire 3' linker-ligated small RNA into two center wells. Load 10 µL of the 3' linker-ligated RNA markers and 6 µL of the Decade marker separately on both sides of the RNA sample. Leave one well empty between the samples and the size markers. When visualized, we routinely see the upshift of the ligated RNA markers, but it is not uncommon that unligated material remains. Isolate the 3' linker-ligated small RNAs (35–43 nt) and markers as described in **Subheading 3.2.2**.

3.2.3.2. Ligation With a 5' Linker Oligonucleotide

Dissolve ethanol-precipitated RNAs with 10 µL of DEPC-treated water and use 5 µL for the next ligation. We set up a 10 µL of 5' ligation reaction using 2 µL of 5X RNA ligation buffer, 2 µL of 200 µ*M* 5' linker, 1 µL of 4 m*M* ATP, 1 µL of T4 RNA ligase (Amersham Pharmacia), and 5 µL of 3' linker-ligated small RNAs. In parallel, set up another reaction using the 3' linker-ligated RNA markers (from **Subheading 3.2.3.1.**). Perform the ligation and the isolation steps as described in **Subheading 3.2.3.1.** Then isolate the doubly ligated 5' and 3' linker-ligated small RNAs (52–60 nt) and markers, as described in **Subheading 3.2.2.** Unligated 35- and 43-nt RNA markers should also be observed.

3.2.3.3. Reverse Transcription of Linker-Ligated RNA

Dissolved the ethanol-precipitated RNAs in 10 µL of DEPC-treated water and incubate 5 µL at 95°C for 30 s. Quickly cool samples on ice and add 1.5 µL of 0.1*M* dithiothreitol, 3 µL of 5X first-strand buffer, and 4.2 µL of 10X dNTP, and incubate the entire mixture at 50°C for 3 min before the additional of 0.75 µL of reverse transcriptase. Continue the incubation at 42°C for 30 min. Hydrolyze RNAs by addition of 40 µL of 150 m*M* KOH/20 m*M* Tris base and heating to 95°C for 10 min. The entire mixture is then neutralized by adding 40 µL of 150 m*M* HCl to bring to a pH of approx 7.0, which is required for the next PCR step.

3.2.3.4. PCR Amplification of cDNA

Set up three equal PCR reactions by combining 10 µL of the cDNA products, 10 µL of 10X dNTP (Invitrogen), 10 µL of 10X PCR buffer, 1 µL of 100 µ*M* 5' primer, 1 µL of 100 µ*M* 3' primer, 67 µL water, and 1 µL of *Taq* polymerase (Roche). Also set up a negative-control reaction that has only water instead of the cDNA.

Perform PCRs respectively for 10, 20, and 30 cycles, using the following parameters:

94°C 45 s
50°C 1 min 25 s
72°C 1 min

After the conclusion of the cycles, analyze 15 μL of the PCR products by loading onto a 3% agarose gel using a low molecular weight DNA ladder (New England Biolabs) as reference. Stain the gel with SYBR Gold stain (Molecular Dynamics) for 60 min with constant agitation. A 50-nt band corresponding to the PCR-amplified product of the linker-ligated moiety should be observed. However, it is not uncommon to find a linker-dimerized band (without an insert) at approx 35 nt.

Note that we compare PCR products after the three different cycle conditions and choose the condition with the largest amount of PCR product and the least amount of smear (nonspecific product) to perform PCR for the remaining reverse transcription products (*see* **Note 6**). We combine all of the PCR products (approx 700 μL) in a 1.5-mL Eppendorf tube and add 45 μL of 5 *M* NaCl and 500 μL of 25:24:1 phenol/chloroform/isoamyl alcohol, vortex for 1 min, and centrifuge for 5 min at 10,000*g* at room temperature. Collect the supernatant and repeat the procedure with 500 μL chloroform. Precipitate the DNA by adding 2.5 vol of absolute ethanol and incubating overnight at –20°C.

3.2.4. Cloning of cDNA Into Plasmid

3.2.4.1. CONCATAMERIZATION OF cDNAS

This step allows for the incorporation of several small RNAs into one single cloning plasmid, simplifying subsequent sequencing analysis. The PCR products are digested with the BanI endonuclease, whose restriction sites are designed into in both 5' and 3' linkers. After restriction enzyme digestion, the products are ligated to each other in a head-to-tail fashion. The termini of the ligated products are filled in with *Taq* polymerase.

1. Dissolve the cDNA pellet in 200 μL of buffer 4 (New England Biolabs). Save 10 μL of the undigested DNA for subsequence gel analysis.
2. Add 200 U of BanI endonuclease and incubate for 4 h at 37°C. Confirm the restriction digestion by loading 10 μL of the digested product along with 10 μL of undigested DNA on a 3% agarose gel.
3. Perform one 200-μL (25:24:1) phenol/chloroform/isoamyl alcohol extraction followed by one 200-μL chloroform extraction and an ethanol precipitation.
4. Dissolve the DNA pellets into 12 μL of water.
5. Heat the DNA at 68°C for 10 min to denature small digested products.
6. Add 1.5 μL of 10X DNA ligation buffer and 1.5 μL of T4 DNA ligase (New England Biolabs) to the DNA, and incubate the mixture for 1 h at room temperature.
7. Load the entire reaction mix into one lane of a 3% GTG Nusieve agarose gel and visualize the concatamerized products.
8. Excise the larger than 300-bp smear, collect the gel slices, and purify the DNA using a QIAEX II Gel Extraction Kit. Elute the DNA with two times 20 mL of water.

3.2.4.2. TOPO CLONING OF CONCATAMERIZED cDNAS

1. Setup a *Taq* fill-in reaction by adding 5 μL of 10X PCR buffer, 5 μL of 10X dNTP, and 1 μL of *Taq* polymerase to 40 μL of the concatamerized product, and incubate for 5 min at 72°C.
2. Use 5 μL of the filled-in reaction product to perform TOPO cloning with a pCR2.1-TOPO vector (Invitrogen), as described by the manufacturer's protocol. Successful cloning is usually indicated by white colonies on β-gal plates; these clones are analyzed by PCR and sequenced.

3.2.5. Validation of HIV miRNA Sequences

After sequencing, the cloned small RNAs are assessed by computer alignment to determine whether they are HIV encoded. The cloned sequence should match a sequence within the HIV-1 genome, and should be different from previously identified cellular miRNAs. The latter could be queried using a basic local alignment search tool (BLAST) search of the miRNA registry, http://www.sanger.ac.uk/Software/Rfam/mirna/search. shtml. Additionally, if the cloned sequence matches to a portion of the HIV genome, we would further query whether there is capacity within the HIV genome to encode a precursor for the mature miRNA. This query and secondary structure prediction could be performed using Michael Zucker's mfold program *(14)*. The predicted secondary structure of a putative viral miRNA is then further evaluated against common properties conserved within known miRNA stem-loops (*see* **Subheading 3.1.4.**).

We physically check via Northern blotting for the expression of HIV-encoded miRNAs in infected cells.

1. For each miRNA sequence, design and 5'-end label a complementary antisense DNA oligonucleotide probe.
2. Resolve 100 μg of the small-RNA sample isolated from HIV-infected MT4 cells (as described in **Subheading 3.2.2.**) in a 15% acrylamide/8 *M* urea gel.
3. Electrotransfer the RNA gel to a nylon membrane in a semidry apparatus with a stack of three sheets of blotting paper soaked in 0.25X TBE, for 1 h at 200 mA.
4. Crosslink the RNA to the membrane with ultraviolet light at 120 mJ for 1 min.
5. Prehybridize the membrane for 1 h at 68°C in ultrahyb buffer (Ambion) and incubate overnight at 37°C with 10^6 cpm/mL of in vitro-labeled probe specific to each HIV miRNA sequence.
6. Wash the membrane with agitation at room temperature for 10 min with low-stringency buffer (2X SSC and 0.1% sodium dodecylsulfate) and then for 2 min with high-stringency buffer (0.1X SSC and 0.1% sodium dodecylsulfate).
7. Wrap the membrane in plastic and expose overnight with autoradiography.

3.3. Search for Cellular Genes Targeted by miRNAs

Several computational methods have been recently reported for identifying cellular genes that may be miRNA targets *(15,17–20)*. All of these methods share the same principles based on sequence complementarity, free energy calculation of RNA duplex formation, and statistical inference. As discussed in a recent study *(21)* on the minimal requirements for a functional miRNA target, in vivo target sites can be grouped into two categories, 5' dominant sites in which the 5' end of the miRNAs are base paired well, and 3' compensatory sites that have weak 5' base pairing and strong compensatory pairing in the 3' end of the miRNAs. Moreover, it is suggested that targets containing 7-bp complementarity to the 5' end of a miRNA are subject to in vivo regulation *(21)*. If so, purely ranking miRNA targets based on overall complementarity and free energy of duplex formation might not present the entire picture.

For predicting miRNA targets, we use a simple scanning algorithm that is based on sequence complementarity between the mature miRNA and the target sites, and a simple scoring system in which a G:C base pairing has a score of 3 and both the A:U and G:U pairings have a score of 2. We scan only the 3' UTRs of sequences deposited into the

3' UTR database, and no gap is allowed in either miRNA sequence or target sequence. Potential target sites are selected if the overall score is greater than a predetermined threshold. Currently, we are performing empirical testing to determine what threshold values are physiologically relevant.

4. Notes

There are several points to be aware of when performing small-RNA isolation:

1. Siliconized microcentrifuge tubes should be used whenever handling RNA. The coated surface prevents the loss of material during the isolation process.
2. After excision of acrylamide gel to isolate the size-selected RNA region, it is important to ground the gel into small pieces for efficient RNA elution. If tips are used for grounding, make sure that you round them by melting the peak of the tip to avoid trapping of gel leading to loss of material.
3. Gel elution and RNA precipitation should be performed at 4°C overnight to maximize the RNA recovery.
4. During RNA precipitation, glycoblue was routinely added to the mixture as a carrier, for efficient precipitation and recovery of RNA.
5. Ligation of the small RNA to the linker is more efficient when performed during 6 h at room temperature instead of 1 h at 37°C in the presence of 50% dimethylsulfoxide, as also proposed by many kit manufacturers.
6. It is essential to perform a third PCR amplification of the reverse transcription product to maximize the specific product and minimize the background.

References

1. He, L. and Hannon, G. J. (2004) MicroRNAs: small RNAs with a big role in gene regulation. *Nat. Rev. Genet.* **5,** 522–531.
2. Bartel, D. P. (2004) MicroRNAs: genomics, biogenesis, mechanism, and function. *Cell* **116,** 281–297.
3. Pfeffer, S., Zavolan, M., Grasser, F. A., et al. (2004) Identification of virus-encoded microRNAs. *Science* **304,** 734–736.
4. Pfeffer, S., Sewer, A., Lagos-Quintana, M., et al. (2005) Identification of microRNAs of the herpesvirus family. *Nat. Methods* **2,** 269–276.
5. Tang, G. (2005) siRNA and miRNA: an insight into RISCs. *Trends Biochem. Sci.* **30,** 106–114.
6. Griffiths-Jones, S. (2004) The microRNA registry. *Nucleic Acids Res.* **32 database issue,** D109–D111.
7. Bennasser, Y., Le, S. Y., Yeung, M. L., and Jeang, K. T. (2004) HIV-1 encoded candidate micro-RNAs and their cellular targets. *Retrovirology* **1,** 43.
8. Lim, L. P., Lau, N. C., Weinstein, E. G., et al. (2003) The microRNAs of Caenorhabditis elegans. *Genes Dev.* **17,** 991–1008.
9. Lai, E. C., Tomancak, P., Williams, R. W., and Rubin, G. M. (2003) Computational identification of Drosophila microRNA genes. *Genome Biol.* **4,** R42.
10. Le, S. Y., Chen, J. H., Konings, D., and Maizel, J. V. Jr. (2003) Discovering well-ordered folding patterns in nucleotide sequences. *Bioinformatics* **19,** 354–361.
11. Le, S. Y. and Maizel, J. V. Jr. (1989) A method for assessing the statistical significance of RNA folding. *J. Theor. Biol.* **138,** 495–510.

12. Le, S. Y., Chen, J. H., and Maizel J. V. Jr. (2003) Statistical inference for well-ordered structures in nucleotide sequences. *Proc. IEEE Comput. Soc. Bioinform. Conf.* **CSB2003,** 190–196.

13. Mathews, D. H., Sabina, J., Zuker, M., and Turner, D. H. (1999) Expanded sequence dependence of thermodynamic parameters improves prediction of RNA secondary structure. *J. Mol. Biol.* **288,** 911–940.

14. Zuker, M. and Stiegler, P. (1981) Optimal computer folding of large RNA sequences using thermodynamics and auxiliary information. *Nucleic Acids Res.* **9,** 133–148.

15. Le, S. Y., Maizel, J. V. Jr., and Zhang, K. (2004) Finding conserved well-ordered RNA structures in genomic sequences. *Int. J. Comp. Intell. Appl.* **4,** 417–430.

16. Lau, N. C., Lim, L. P., Weinstein, E. G., and Bartel, D. P. (2001) An abundant class of tiny RNAs with probable regulatory roles in Caenorhabditis elegans. *Science* **294,** 858–862.

17. Lewis, B. P., Shih, I. H., Jones-Rhoades, M. W., Bartel, D. P., and Burge, C. B. (2003) Prediction of mammalian microRNA targets. *Cell* **115,** 787–798.

18. John, B., Enright, A. J., Aravin, A., Tuschl, T., Sander, C., and Marks, D. S. (2004) Human microRNA targets. *PLoS Biol.* **2,** e363.

19. Stark, A., Brennecke, J., Russell, R. B., and Cohen, S. M. (2003) Identification of Drosophila MicroRNA targets. *PLoS Biol.* **1,** E60.

20. Robins, H., Li, Y., and Padgett, R. W. (2005) Incorporating structure to predict microRNA targets. *Proc. Natl. Acad. Sci. USA* **102,** 4006–4009.

21. Brennecke, J., Stark, A., Russell, R. B., and Cohen, S. M. (2005) Principles of microRNA-target recognition. *PLoS Biol.* **3,** e85.

18

Cloning and Detection of HIV-1-Encoded MicroRNA

Shinya Omoto and Yoichi R. Fujii

Summary

MicroRNAs (miRNAs) are 21- to 25-nucleotides (nt) long and interact with messenger RNAs to trigger either translational repression or RNA cleavage through RNA interference (RNAi). We have shown that HIV-1 *nef* double-stranded RNA from AIDS patients who are long-term nonprogressors, inhibits HIV-1 transcription; and that *nef*-derived miRNA, miR-N367, is produced in human T-cells persistently infected with HIV-1. The miR-N367 can block HIV-1 *Nef* expression and long terminal repeat (LTR) transcription, suggesting that miR-N367 might suppress both Nef function and HIV-1 transcription through the RNAi pathway. Protocols are presented here for cloning HIV-1-encoded miRNA and confirming miRNA expression by Northern blot hybridization.

Key Words: HIV-1; *nef*; microRNA; cloning; Northern blot.

1. Introduction

RNAi is an intracellular defense mechanism against aberrant transcripts that may be produced during viral infection and transposon mobilization *(1,2)*. The RNAi pathway has been implicated in transposon silencing in the *Caenorhabditis elegans* germline *(3–5)*, stellate repeat silencing in the *Drosophila* germline *(6)*, and plant response against invading viruses *(7)*. Posttranscriptional and/or transcriptional regulation by RNAi is mediated by small, noncoding, 21- to 25-nt RNAs. These single-stranded miRNAs can bind messenger RNA 3' untranslated regions to produce translational repression with or without target degradation *(8,9)*.

The HIV-1 gene, *nef*, is located at the 3' end of the viral genome and partially overlaps the 3' LTR. The *nef* gene is expressed during HIV infection and often accounts for up to 80% of HIV-1 specific RNA transcripts during the early stages of viral replication *(10,11)*. Our own investigations have shown that defective variants of *nef* double-stranded RNA containing the 3'-LTR regions, obtained from long-term nonprogressor AIDS patients, actually inhibit HIV-1 transcription *(12)*. We also established a link between miRNA and HIV infection by demonstrating that *nef*-derived miRNA, miR-N367, is produced in HIV-1-infected cells *(13)*. Furthermore, miR-N367 can reduce HIV-1

From: *Methods in Molecular Biology, vol. 342: MicroRNA Protocols*
Edited by: S. Ying © Humana Press Inc., Totowa, NJ

LTR promoter activity through the negative responsive element of the U3 region in the 5'-LTR *(14)*.

This protocol describes procedures for cloning HIV-1-encoded miRNA from HIV-1-infected cells and Northern blot analysis of the cloned miRNA. These procedures might be useful for cloning other virus-encoded miRNAs.

2. Materials

2.1. Preparation of HIV-1-Infected Cells

1. RPMI-1640 medium (GIBCO, Grand Island, NY; cat. no. 31800-022).
2. Heat-inactivated fetal bovine serum (GIBCO).
3. Polybrene (Sigma, St. Louis, MO; cat. no. H-9268).
4. HIV-1 virus stocks (IIIB, SF2, and so on).

2.2. Total RNA Extraction From HIV-1-Infected Cells

1. Ribonuclease (RNase)-free water: To prepare RNase-free water, dispense distilled water into RNase-free glass bottles, and add diethylpyrocarbonate to 0.01% (v/v). Let stand overnight and autoclave (*see* **Note 1**).
2. RNase-free 1.5-mL microcentrifuge tubes.
3. Trizol reagent (Invitrogen; San Diego, CA; cat. no. 15596) (*see* **Note 2**).
4. Chloroform.
5. 100% isopropanol.
6. 70% ethanol (in RNase-free water).
7. Deoxyribonuclease I (DNase I) amplification grade (Invitrogen; cat. no. 18068-015).
8. 10X DNase I reaction buffer: 200 mM Tris-HCl (pH 8.4), 20 mM MgCl$_2$, and 500 mM KCl.

2.3. Preparation of Size-Selected RNA From Total RNA

1. Vertical slab gel apparatus (ATTO, Tokyo, Japan; cat. no. AE-6450).
2. 1X TBE buffer: 89 mM Tris base (pH 8.3), 89 mM boric acid, and 2 mM ethylenediamine-tetraacetic acid (EDTA); sterilized by filtration through a 0.22-μm filter.
3. N,N,N',N'-tetramethylethylenediamine (Bio-Rad, Hercules, CA; cat. no. 161-0800) (store at 4°C).
4. 10% ammonium persulfate in RNase-free water (Bio-Rad; cat. no. 161-0700) (store at 4°C).
5. Denaturing gel sample buffer: 95% formamide, 0.025% xylene cyanol, 0.025% bromophenol blue, 20 mM EDTA, and 0.025% sodium dodecylsulfate.
6. Decade Marker (Ambion, Austin, TX; cat. no. 1554).
7. Gel elution buffer: 20 mM Tris-HCl (pH 7.5), 5 mM EDTA, and 400 mM sodium acetate; sterilized by filtration through a 0.22-μm filter.
8. SUPREC-01 (Takara, Kyoto, Japan; cat. no. 9040).
9. 20 μg/mL glycogen in RNase-free water (store at −20°C).
10. 20 mM Tris-HCl (pH 7.5), sterilized by filtration through a 0.22-μm filter.
11. 3 M sodium acetate in RNase-free water.
12. 100% ethanol.

2.4. Ligation of Linker Oligonucleotide

1. 20 U/μL calf intestinal alkaline phosphatase (CIAP) (Roche, Branchburg, NJ; cat. no. 108-138).

2. 10X CIAP buffer: 500 mM Tris-HCl (pH 9.0) and 10 mM MgCl$_2$.
3. 10 U/μL T4 RNA ligase (Amersham, Piscataway, NJ; cat. no. E2050Y).
4. 10X RNA ligase buffer: 500 mM Tris-HCl (pH 7.5), 100 mM MgCl$_2$, 100 mM dithiothreitol, 10 mM adenosine triphosphate, 600 μg/mL bovine serum albumin.
5. 100 μM 3'-linker oligonucleotide A: 5'-P-cuguguAGGC<u>GTCGAC</u>ATG-ddC-3' (P, phosphate; lowercase, RNA; ddC, di-deoxy C; underline, SalI site).

2.5. Reverse Transcription and Preparation of First-Strand Complementary DNA

1. 5' Rapid amplification of cDNA ends system for rapid amplification of complementary DNA (cDNA) ends, version 2.0 (Invitrogen; cat. no. 18374-058).
2. 10 μM oligonucleotide B (5'-TCTGAGCATAGGCGGCCGAGGAGATGTTCAT<u>GTCGAC</u>GCC-3') (underline, SalI site).
3. SuperScript II reverse transcriptase (Invitrogen; cat. no. 18064-014).
4. Terminal deoxynucleotidyl transferase (TdT) (Invitrogen; cat. no. 18374-058).
5. 5X tailing buffer: 50 mM Tris-HCl (pH 8.4), 125 mM KCl, and 7.5 mM MgCl$_2$ (Invitrogen; cat. no. 18374-058).

2.6. Polymerase Chain Reaction of cDNA

1. 10 μM 5' Rapid amplification of cDNA ends abridged anchor primer C (5'-GGCCACGC<u>GTCGAC</u>TAGTACGGGIIGGGIIGGGIIG-3') (I, deoxyinosine [*see* **Note 3**]; underline, SalI site) (Invitrogen; cat. no. 10541-019).
2. 10 μM oligonucleotide D (5'-TCTGAGCATAGGCGGCCGAG-3').
3. 10 μM abridged universal amplification primer E (5'-GGCCACGC<u>GTCGAC</u>TAGTAC-3') (underline, SalI site) (Invitrogen; cat. no. 18382-010).
4. 10 μM oligonucleotide F (5'-GAGATGTTCAT<u>GTCGAC</u>GCC-3') (underline, SalI site).
5. 5 U/μL LA *Taq* polymerase (Takara; cat. no. RR002A).
6. Thermal cycler (Applied Biosystems, Foster City, CA; GeneAmp polymerase chain reaction [PCR] System 9700).
7. 10 mg/mL ethidium bromide (EtBr) in RNase-free water.
8. Agarose NA (Amersham; cat. no. 17-0554-02).

2.7. Restriction Enzyme Digestion of cDNA and Ligation Into a Vector

1. 20 U/μL SalI restriction enzyme (Takara; cat. no. 1080A).
2. QIAEXII Gel Extraction Kit (Qiagen, Valencia, CA; cat. no. 20021).
3. Ligation high (Toyobo, Tokyo, Japan; cat. no. LGK-101).

2.8. Sequencing Analysis

1. Sequencing primers: 10 μM of M13 reverse primer (5'-CAGGAAACAGCTTGACCATG-3'), 10 μM of M13 to 20 forward primer (5'-GTAAAACGACGGCCAGTGA-3').
2. National Center for Biotechnology Information (NCBI) basic local alignment search tool (BLAST) web site: www.ncbi.nih.gov/BLAST/.
3. DNA sequencer (DSQ-2000L; Shimadzu, Kyoto, Japan).

2.9. Northern Blotting

1. Electroblotting apparatus (ATTO; cat. no. AE-6670).
2. Hybond-N+ nylon membrane (Amersham; cat. no. RPN 203 B).
3. Whatman 3M filter paper.

4. Enhanced chemiluminescence (ECL) direct labeling and detection kit (Amersham; cat. no. RPN 3000).
5. ECL 3'-oligolabeling and detection reagent (Amersham; cat. no. RPN 5770).
6. Primary wash buffer: 6 M urea, 0.4% sodium dodecylsulfate, and 0.5X standard sodium citrate (SSC) in RNase-free water.
7. 2X SSC: 30 mM sodium citrate and 300 mM NaCl in RNase-free water.
8. Ultraviolet crosslinker (UVC 500; Amersham; cat. no. 80-6222-31).
9. Hybridization oven (Amersham; cat. no. RPN 2512).
10. LAS-1000 film (Fuji Film, Tokyo, Japan).

3. Methods

As described in **Subheading 3.1.**, total RNA is extracted from HIV-1-infected cells and used to prepare 21- to 25-nt long, size-selected, small RNA. The small RNA is reverse transcribed to cDNA and the cDNA is cloned into a plasmid vector as described in **Subheading 3.2.** A flow chart of these procedures is shown in **Fig. 1.** A method for detection of the cloned miRNA by Northern blotting is described in **Subheading 3.3.** and **Fig. 2.**

3.1. Total RNA Extraction From HIV-1-Infected Cells

3.1.1. Preparation of HIV-1-Infected Cells

1. Prepare 5×10^6 cells (MT-4 HTLV-1-transformed human T lymphoma cell line, and so on).
2. Pellet cells by centrifugation at 300g for 5 min, and resuspend in 10 mL phosphate-buffered saline (PBS).
3. Transfer the cells into a 15-mL centrifuge tube.
4. Pellet cells by centrifugation at 300g for 5 min, and carefully remove the PBS.
5. Resuspend cells in 0.5 mL of virus solution containing 2 mg/mL polybrene and incubate at 37°C for 60 min, with occasional shaking.
6. Wash cells once with PBS, resuspend in 10 mL RPMI-1640 medium containing 10% fetal bovine serum, and culture at 37°C in a CO_2 incubator.
7. Passage the cells every 5 to 6 d.
8. Check the cell viability by trypan blue staining and assess the percentage of HIV-1-infected cells by flow cytometry and/or indirect fluorescence.
9. HIV-1-infected cells cultured for at least 6 mo should be used for the experiments described in this chapter.

3.1.2. Total RNA Extraction From HIV-1-Infected Cells

1. Pellet cells by centrifugation at 300g for 5 min, and lyse in Trizol reagent by pipetting. Use 1 mL Trizol per 5×10^6 cells.
2. Incubate the samples for 5 min at room temperature.
3. Add 0.2 mL chloroform, and shake the sample tubes vigorously for 15 s.
4. Centrifuge the samples at 12,000g for 15 min at 4°C. Because RNA remains in the colorless upper aqueous phase, transfer this phase to a fresh tube.

Fig. 1. *(Opposite page)* Schematic of HIV-1 genome structure and flowchart of the strategy for cloning HIV-1 encoded microRNA (miRNA). The HIV-1 genome contains structural genes, *gag*, *pol*, and *env*, and accessory genes, *vif*, *vpr*, *vpu*, *tat*, *rev*, and *nef*. The *nef* coding region partially overlaps the 3' long terminal repeat (LTR). For cloning HIV-1-encoded miRNA, HIV-1-infected MT-4 cells are prepared (**Subheading 3.1.1.**) and total RNA is extracted from these

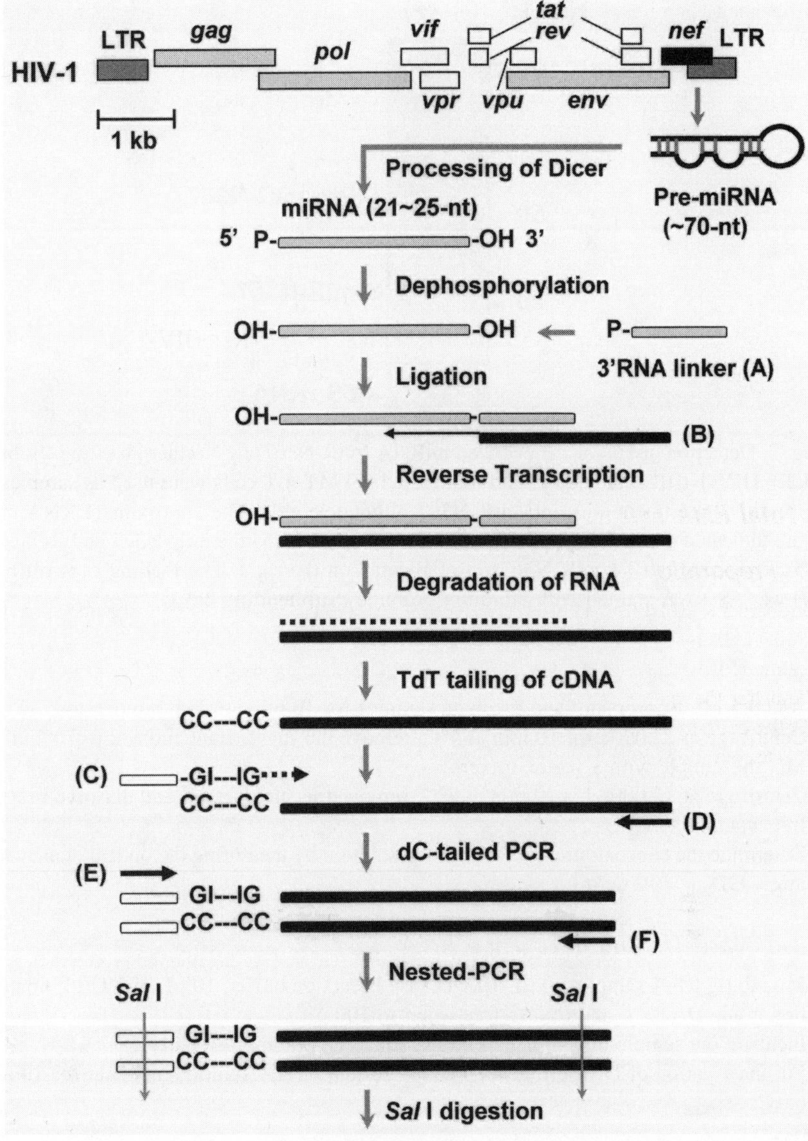

Fig. 1. *(Continued)* infected cells (**Subheading 3.1.2.**). After deoxyribonuclease I treatment (**Subheading 3.1.3.**) and size selection (**Subheading 3.1.4.**), 5'-phosphorylated mature miRNA is dephosphorylated and ligated with 3' linker oligonucleotide A (**Subheading 3.2.1.**). The RNA then is reverse transcribed using oligonucleotide B primer to produce first-strand complementary DNA (cDNA) (**Subheading 3.2.2.**). Deoxycytosine (dC) residues are added to the cDNA by a terminal deoxynucleotidyl transferase (TdT) reaction (**Subheading 3.2.3.**). The dC-tailed cDNA is amplified by polymerase chain reaction (PCR) with primers C and D, followed by nested-PCR with primers E and F (**Subheading 3.2.4.**). Finally, the cDNA is digested with SalI and ligated into a plasmid (**Subheading 3.2.5.**), followed by sequencing analysis (**Subheading 3.2.6.**).

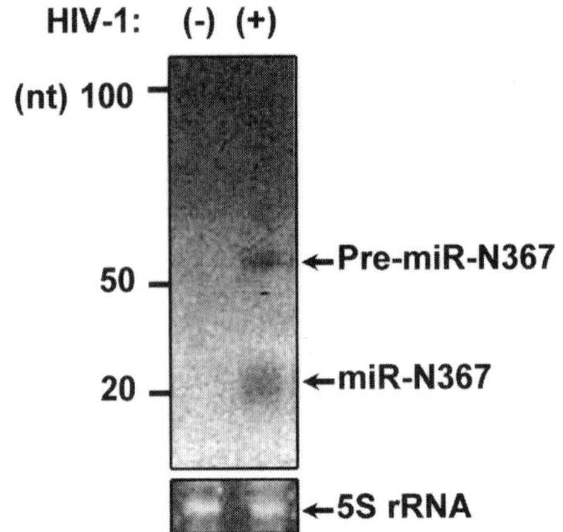

Fig. 2. Detection of HIV-1 *nef* encoded miRNA (miR-N367) by Northern blotting (**Subheading 3.3.**). HIV-1 IIIB-infected (+) and uninfected (−) MT-4 T cells were used as samples. The probe in this experiment was anti-miR-N367 oligonucleotide. The approximate RNA marker sizes are indicated on the left (*upper panel*). The positions of mature miR-N367 and its predicted fold-back precursors (Pre-miR-N367) are indicated on the right. The loading control (*bottom panel*) was 5S RNA stained with ethidium bromide (**Subheading 3.3.1.**).

5. Add 0.5 mL isopropanol and incubate samples for 10 min at room temperature.
6. Centrifuge at 12,000*g* for 10 min at 4°C; remove the supernatant and add to 70% ethanol. Mix the sample with a vortex mixer.
7. Centrifuge at 12,000*g* for 10 min at 4°C, remove the supernatant, and dissolve in RNase-free water.
8. Determine the concentration of RNA in the solution by measuring the optical density at 260 nm; 1 OD_{260} = 40 µg/mL.

3.1.3. DNase Treatment of Total RNA

1. Mix 40 µg RNA sample, 10 µL 10X DNase I reaction buffer, 10 µL of 1 U/µL amplification grade DNase I, and RNase-free water to 100 µL.
2. Incubate the sample tubes for 15 min at room temperature (*see* **Note 4**).
3. For inactivation of DNase I, add 10 µL of 25 m*M* EDTA solution and heat for 10 min at 65°C.

3.1.4. Preparation of Size-Selected RNA From Total RNA

1. Prepare a 15% acrylamide/7 *M* urea gel at room temperature. Use a gel plate that has been washed with 0.5 *M* NaOH, then rinsed thoroughly with RNase-free water.
2. Add 10 µL of denaturing gel sample buffer to a 10-µL sample of total RNA. Heat the sample to 70°C for 5 min, then immediately chill the tube on ice and load the sample onto the gel.
3. Perform electrophoresis at 18 V/cm (i.e., 150 V for an 8-cm gel) until the faster dye (bromophenol blue) reaches the bottom of the gel.

4. Remove the front glass plate and mark the location of the RNA ladder (i.e., Decade Markers; Ambion), and excise the part of the gel corresponding to 21- to 25-nt RNA.
5. Transfer the gel slice into a clean 1.5-mL microcentrifuge tube, add 400 µL (at least four times the volume of the gel slice) gel elution buffer, and agitate vigorously for 10 min with a vortex mixer.
6. Spin the gel slice homogenate through a SUPREC-01 filter.
7. Pool the eluates and, for each 400-µL sample, add 1 µL of 20 µg/mL glycogen solution and 1 mL ethanol.
8. Centrifuge at 12,000g for 10 min at 4°C, decant the supernatant, and air-dry the pellet at room temperature.
9. Dissolve in 400 µL of 20 mM Tris-HCl (pH 7.5) and add 40 µL of 3 M sodium acetate.
10. Add 1 mL ethanol and centrifuge at 12,000g for 10 min at 4°C.
11. Remove the supernatant carefully, air-dry, and dissolve in 20 µL RNase-free water.

3.2. Cloning of miRNAs

3.2.1. Ligation of 3'-Linker Oligonucleotide

1. Set up the following 30-µL reaction mixture: 20 µL RNA (from **Subheading 3.1.4.**), 6 µL RNase-free water, 3 µL 10X CIAP buffer, and 1 µL CIAP (10 U/µL).
2. Incubate the mixture at 37°C for 1 h.
3. Extract with phenol/chloroform.
4. Add three volumes of 100% ethanol, and place at −20°C for 3 h.
5. Centrifuge at 12,000g for 15 min at 4°C.
6. Wash the pellet with 70% ethanol, air-dry, and dissolve in 11 µL RNase-free water.
7. Set up the following 20-µL ligation mixture: 11 µL dephosphorylated RNA from previous step, 2 µL of 10X T4 RNA ligase buffer, 2 µL of 60 µM adenosine triphosphate, 1 µL of 100 µM RNA 3' linker oligonucleotide A, and 2 µL of 10 U/µL T4 RNA ligase.
8. Incubate at 16°C overnight.
9. Extract with phenol/chloroform.
10. Add three volumes of 100% ethanol and place at −20°C for 3 h.
11. Centrifuge at 12,000g for 20 min at 4°C.
12. Wash the pellet with 70% ethanol, air-dry, and dissolve in 10 µL RNase-free water.

3.2.2. Reverse Transcription and Preparation of First-Strand cDNA

1. Set up the following 5-µL first-strand cDNA synthesis mixture: 4 µL of 3' linker ligated product (from **Subheading 3.2.1.**) and 1 µL of 10 µM oligonucleotide B.
2. Incubate at 72°C for 2 min, then chill on ice for 2 min.
3. Add the following reagents: 2 µL 5X first-strand reverse transcription buffer, 1 µL of 20 mM dithiothreitol, 1 µL deoxyribonucleoside triphosphate (dNTP) mix (10 mM of each dNTP), and 1 µL of 200 U/µL SuperScript II reverse transcriptase. Set up an additional identical reaction, but without reverse transcriptase, as a negative control.
4. Incubate at 42°C for 50 min.
5. Incubate at 70°C for 15 min to terminate the reverse transcription reaction.
6. Add 1 µL RNase mix (RNase H and T1) and incubate for 30 min at 37°C, then chill on ice.
7. Extract with phenol/chloroform.
8. Add three volumes of 100% ethanol, and place at −20°C for 3 h.
9. Centrifuge at 12,000g for 20 min at 4°C.
10. Wash the pellet with 70% ethanol, air-dry, and dissolve in 10 µL RNase-free water.

3.2.3. TdT Tailing of cDNA

1. For preparation of deoxycytosine (dC)-tailed cDNA by a TdT reaction, set up the following mixture: 6.5 μL RNase-free water, 5 μL of 5X tailing buffer, 2.5 μL of 2 m*M* deoxycytosine triphosphate, and 10 μL of first-strand cDNA (from **Subheading 3.2.2.**).
2. Incubate for 3 min at 94°C, then chill on ice for 1 min.
3. Add 1 μL TdT and incubate for 10 min at 37°C.
4. Heat to inactivate the TdT for 10 min at 65°C and chill on ice.

3.2.4. PCR of dC-Tailed cDNA

1. Set up the following PCR reaction mixture: 10 μL of dC-tailed cDNA (from **Subheading 3.2.3.**), 1 μL of 10 m*M* dNTP mix, 5 μL of 10X PCR buffer, 2 μL of 10 μ*M* abridged anchor primer C, 2 μL of 10 μ*M* PCR primer D, 31 μL RNase-free water, and 1 μL LA *Taq* polymerase.
2. After 5 min at 94°C, carry out 25 cycles of PCR using the following cycle conditions: 45 s at 94°C, 1 min at 50°C, 1 min at 72°C.
3. Perform nested-PCR using abridged universal amplification primer E and primer F, as described in **Subheading 3.2.4.1.**
4. Run the PCR product on a 2% agarose gel containing EtBr at 100 to 120 V. The size of the PCR product should be approx 70 bp (*see* **Note 5**).
5. Excise the bands at approx 70 bp, isolate the cDNA from the excised gel bands using a QIAEXII DNA Extraction Kit, and dissolve the cDNA in 16 μL RNase-free water.

3.2.5. Restriction Enzyme Digestion of cDNA and Ligation Into a Vector

1. Set up the following SalI digestion reaction mixture: 16 μL of cDNA PCR product, 2 μL of 10X high-salt buffer, and 2 μL of 20 U/μL SalI restriction enzyme. Similarly, a cloning vector, such as a pBluescript, is treated with SalI, and dephosphorylated.
2. Incubate at 37°C for 2 h.
3. Load the sample on a 2% agarose gel containing EtBr, carry out electrophoresis at 100 to 120 V, and excise the SalI-digested cDNA.
4. Isolate the cDNA from the gel using a QIAEXII DNA Extraction Kit, and dissolve in 20 μL RNase-free water.
5. Add 5 μL of ligation high to the cDNA solution, which contains 10 ng of SalI-digested and dephospholyrated pBluescript and 990 ng of SalI-digested insert cDNA.
6. Incubate the tubes at 16°C overnight.
7. Transform an *Escherichia coli* XL-1 Blue strain with the ligated product, and spread the cells onto agar containing X-Gal and isopropylthiogalactoside.
8. Isolate cloned plasmids from white colonies of *E. coli* XL-1 Blue.

3.2.6. Sequencing Analysis

1. Sequencing is performed according to standard methods.
2. Confirm that the cloned miRNA is derived from the HIV-1 genome by a BLAST search.

3.3. Northern Blot Analysis

3.3.1. Electrophoresis of Total RNA Using a Denaturing Gel

1. Prepare a 15% polyacrylamide/7 *M* urea gel, similar to **Subheading 3.1.4.**
2. Dissolve the RNA sample (at least 40 μg of total RNA) in 20 μL of denaturing gel sample buffer, heat at 70°C for 5 min, and chill on ice.

3. Perform electrophoresis at 18 V/cm (i.e., 150 V for an 8-cm gel) until the faster dye (bromophenol blue) reaches the bottom of the gel.
4. Stain the gel with EtBr, and record the image. The fluorescence signal of the 5S RNA band can be used as a measure of the amount of RNA loaded (*see* **Fig. 2**).

3.3.2. Electrophoretic Transfer of RNA to a Nylon Membrane

1. Cut a nylon membrane (Hybond-N+) and six sheets of Whatman 3M filter paper to the size of the gel. Presoak the membrane and filter papers with 0.5X Tris–borate–EDTA (TBE).
2. Place soaked membrane on the gel, and mark the position of wells and loading dye.
3. Flip the gel and membrane/filter and place into the electroblotting apparatus.
4. Smooth out any air bubbles.
5. Add 0.5X TBE buffer to keep the membrane moist.
6. Transfer at a constant current of 400 mA for 4 h.
7. Immediately crosslink with ultraviolet light, with 1×10^3 µJ of energy, then bake for 60 min at 80°C.

3.3.3. Preparation of Probe

1. Design an oligonucleotide probe with a sequence that is precisely antisense (minus strand) to the miRNA sequence.
2. Label the oligonucleotide with the ECL 3'-oligolabeling and detection reagent, according to the manufacturer's instructions.

3.3.4. Hybridization

1. Add sodium chloride to 0.5 *M* in the required volume of hybridization buffer (from the ECL kit).
2. Mix the blocking reagent (from the ECL kit) to a final concentration of 5% (w/v) in the hybridization buffer from the previous step. Immediately mix thoroughly to create a fine suspension of the blocking reagent, and continue mixing at room temperature for 1 h on a magnetic stirrer.
3. Heat the hybridization buffer to 42°C for 30 min.
4. Add hybridization buffer to the blotted membrane, and pack with the hybridization pack.
5. Place in hybridization oven and prehybridize by shaking slowly at 42°C for 90 min.
6. Add the probe (from **Subheading 3.3.3.**) to the blotted membrane, and incubate in the hybridization oven at 42°C for 16 h.
7. Carefully discard the hybridization buffer, then add 40 mL of primary wash buffer to each membrane and shake slowly for 10 min at room temperature.
8. Discard this primary wash buffer and repeat the washing with fresh primary wash buffer for 10 min at room temperature.
9. Discard the wash buffer, add 40 mL of 2X SSC solution, and shake slowly for 10 min at room temperature.

3.3.5. Detection of Chemical Luminescence Signal

1. Mix equal volumes of ECL detection solutions 1 and 2 (from the ECL kit) to yield a sufficient mixture to cover the membrane.
2. Remove excess wash buffer by placing membranes on paper towels for 1 min.
3. In a dark room, add the mixed detection reagents directly to the membranes.
4. Incubate for 1 min at room temperature in the dark.

5. Drain off excess detection buffer and wrap membranes in a fresh hybridization pack in the dark. Gently smooth out any air bubbles and cover with aluminium foil.
6. Remove the aluminium foil and quickly place the membrane on LAS-1000 film to record the fluorescence signal. A typical image from samples of HIV-1-infected and uninfected MT-4 T cells using the miR-N367 probe is shown in **Fig. 2** *(13,14)*.

4. Notes

1. RNases can be introduced accidentally into RNA samples at any point in the isolation and cloning procedure by improper techniques. Disposable gloves should always be worn, and equipment reserved for RNA experiments should be used to prevent contamination by RNases. To inactivate RNase contaminants, glass items should be baked at 180°C for 6 h, and plastic items soaked for 15 min in 0.5 *M* NaOH, rinsed thoroughly with RNase-free water, and autoclaved.
2. Trizol reagent is toxic in contact with skin and causes burns. After contact with skin, the area should be washed immediately with plenty of soap and water.
3. Deoxyinosine can base-pair with all four deoxynucleotides.
4. It is important not to exceed the incubation time and temperature. Higher temperatures and longer times can lead to Mg^{2+}-dependent RNA hydrolysis.
5. Care should be taken to only excise bands containing the approx 70-bp cDNA. Bands at approx 50 bp may be derived from ligation products without small RNA inserts.

Acknowledgments

We thank members of the Fujii Laboratory for helpful assistance. English in the manuscript was proofread by Network Assistance International (NAI), Inc. (Yokohama, Japan). The authors have declared that no conflicts of interest exist.

References

1. Fire, A., Xu, S., Montgomery, M. K., Kostas, S. A., Driver, S. E., and Mello, C. C. (1998) Potent and specific genetic interference by double-stranded RNA in *Caenorhabditis elegans*. *Nature* **391,** 806–811.
2. Tuschl, T., Zamore, P. D., Lehmann, R., Bartel, D. P., and Sharp, P. A. (1999) Targeted mRNA degradation by double-stranded RNA in vitro. *Genes Dev.* **13,** 3191–3197.
3. Ketting, R. F., Haverkamp, T. H., van Luenen, H. G., and Plasterk, R. H. (1999) *mut-7* of *C. elegans*, required for transposon silencing and RNA interference, is a homolog of Werner syndrome helicase and RNaseD. *Cell* **99,** 133–141.
4. Tabara, H., Sarkissian, M., Kelly, W. G., et al. (1999) The *rde-1* gene, RNA interference, and transposon silencing in *C. elegans*. *Cell* **99,** 123–132.
5. Sijen, T. and Plasterk, R. H. (2003). Transposon silencing in the *Caenorhabditis elegans* germ line by natural RNAi. *Nature* **426,** 310–314.
6. Aravin, A. A., Naumova, N. M., Tulin, A. V., Vagin, V. V., Rozovsky, Y. M., and Gvozdev, V. A. (2001) Double-stranded RNA-mediated silencing of genomic tandem repeats and transposable elements in the *D. melanogaster* germline. *Curr. Biol.* **11,** 1017–1027.
7. Baulcombe, D. C. (2001) RNA silencing. Diced defence. *Nature* **409,** 295–296.
8. Zeng, Y., Yi, R., and Cullen, B. R. (2003) MicroRNAs and small interfering RNAs can inhibit mRNA expression by similar mechanisms. *Proc. Natl. Acad. Sci. USA* **100,** 9779–9784.

9. Yekta, S., Shih, I., and Bartel, D. P. (2004) MicroRNA-directed cleavage of *HOXB8* mRNA. *Science* **304,** 594–596.

10. Robert-Guroff, M., Popovic, M., Gartner, S., Markham, P., Gallo, R. C., and Reitz, M. S. (1990) Structure and expression of *tat-*, *rev-*, and *nef*-specific transcripts of human immunodeficiency virus type 1 in infected lymphocytes and macrophages. *J. Virol.* **64,** 3391–3398.

11. Brisibe, E. A., Okada, N., Mizukami, H., Okuyama, H., and Fujii, Y. R. (2003) RNA interference: potentials for the prevention of HIV infections and the challenges ahead. *Trends Biotechnol.* **21,** 306–311.

12. Yamamoto, T., Omoto, S., Mizuguchi, M., et al. (2002) Double-stranded *nef* RNA interferes with human immunodeficiency virus type 1 replication. *Microbiol. Immunol.* **46,** 809–817.

13. Omoto, S., Ito, M., Tsutsumi, Y., et al. (2004) HIV-1 nef suppression by virally encoded microRNA. *Retrovirology* **1,** 44.

14. Omoto, S. and Fujii, Y. R. (2005) Regulation of human immunodeficiency virus type 1 transcription by *nef* microRNA. *J. Gen. Virol.* **86,** 751–755.

## 19

Identification of Messenger RNAs and MicroRNAs Associated With Fragile X Mental Retardation Protein

Ranhui Duan and Peng Jin

Summary

Fragile X syndrome, a common form of inherited mental retardation, is caused by the loss of the Fragile X mental retardation protein (FMRP). FMRP, which may regulate translation in neurons, not only associates with specific messenger RNAs (mRNAs) and with microRNAs (miRNAs), but also associates with the components of the miRNA pathway, including the Dicer and Argonaute proteins. It has been proposed that FMRP regulates the translation of its mRNA targets through miRNAs. In this chapter, we describe the protocol to identify the mRNAs and miRNAs associated with FMRP in vivo. The same method could also be applied to other RNA-binding proteins interacting with specific mRNAs or miRNAs.

Key Words: Fragile X syndrome; FMRP; immunoprecipitation; messenger RNA; microRNA; microarray.

1. Introduction

Fragile X syndrome, a common form of inherited mental retardation, is caused by the loss of an RNA-binding protein, FMRP *(1)*. FMRP, along with its autosomal paralogs, the fragile X-related proteins (FXR1P and FXR2P), compose a small family of RNA-binding proteins (the fragile X-related gene family) that share more than 60% amino acid identity and contain two types of RNA-binding motifs: two ribonucleoprotein (RNP) K homology domains and a cluster of arginine and glycine residues *(2,3)*. FMRP associates with polyribosomes in an RNA-dependent manner via messenger RNP (mRNP) particles and can suppress translation both in vitro and in vivo *(4–7)*. Through use of a nuclear localization signal and a nuclear export signal, FMRP shuttles between the nucleus and cytoplasm *(8)*. A current working model is that FMRP is involved in synaptic plasticity through regulation of mRNA transport and local protein synthesis at synapses *(9)*. To test this model, the identification of the mRNAs specifically bound by FMRP and the structure required for FMRP–RNA interaction in mammals has been extensively investigated. Using different approaches, a number of different groups have identified in vivo mRNA cargos associated with FMRP *(10,11)*. Using in vitro

From: *Methods in Molecular Biology, vol. 342: MicroRNA Protocols*
Edited by: S. Ying © Humana Press Inc., Totowa, NJ

RNA selection approach, an intramolecular G-quartet RNA was identified as a high-affinity target for the arginine and glycine residue cluster of FMRP, whereas a sequence-specific element within a complex tertiary structure, termed the FMRP kissing complex, was identified as the target of the FMRP second K homology domain *(12–14)*.

MiRNAs, a recently discovered class of noncoding RNAs, are believed to control translation of specific target mRNAs by base pairing with complementary sequences in the 3' untranslated region of these messages *(15)*. The accumulation of recent works from several groups strongly supports the idea that FMRP may regulate the translation of its mRNA via the miRNA pathway *(16–18)*. A likely scenario is that once FMRP binds to its specific mRNA ligands, it recruits a RNA-induced silencing complex along with miRNAs and facilitates the recognition between miRNAs and their mRNA ligands. Thus, FMRP might modulate the efficiency of translation of its mRNA targets using miRNAs. This mechanism would allow this activity to be rapid and reversible, as would be needed in protein synthesis-dependent synaptic plasticity. Understanding how FMRP use miRNAs to modulate the translation of its mRNA ligands will help understanding not only of the molecular pathogenesis of fragile X syndrome, but also of miRNA-mediated translational regulation.

To test the hypothesis that translational control involving FMRP is executed in a complex that involves one or more miRNAs interacting with transcripts at specific sites, the identification of mRNAs and miRNAs associated with FMRP will be critical. In this chapter, we describe the immunopurification procedure to characterize the mRNAs and miRNAs in an FMRP-containing mRNP complex. In this method, FMRP-containing mRNP complex is immunoprecipitated with a specific antibody against FMRP. The coimmunoprecipitated RNA is analyzed using different techniques (**Fig. 1**). The same methodology could also be applied to other RNA-binding proteins to identify the co-purifying RNAs.

2. Materials

2.1. Immunoprecipitation of FMRP-Containing mRNP Complex

1. Adult wild-type (WT) and *Fmr1* congenic C57Bl/6J litter mates.
2. Human lymphoblastoid cell lines derived from both individuals with and without fragile X syndrome.
3. Lysis buffer: 10 m*M* HEPES (or Tris-HCl), pH 7.4, 150 m*M* NaCl, 30 m*M* ethylenediaminetetraacetic acid, and 0.5% Triton X-100 with 2X complete protease inhibitors (Roche, Indianapolis, IN; cat. no. 1697498). Prepared fresh and chill on ice.
4. 300 m*M* NaCl. Store at room temperature.
5. Recombinant protein G agarose (Invitrogen, Carlsbad, CA; cat. no. 15920-010).
6. Recombinant RNasin® Ribonuclease Inhibitor (Promega, Madison, WI; cat. no. N2511).
7. 7G1-1 or 6G-2 monoclonal antibody.
8. Trizol (Invitrogen; cat. no. 15596-018).

2.2. Identification of the mRNAs Enriched in the FMRP-Containing mRNP Complex by Microarray

1. RNeasy column (Qiagen, Valencia, CA; cat. no. 74106) for RNA purification.
2. Affymetrix Genechip™.

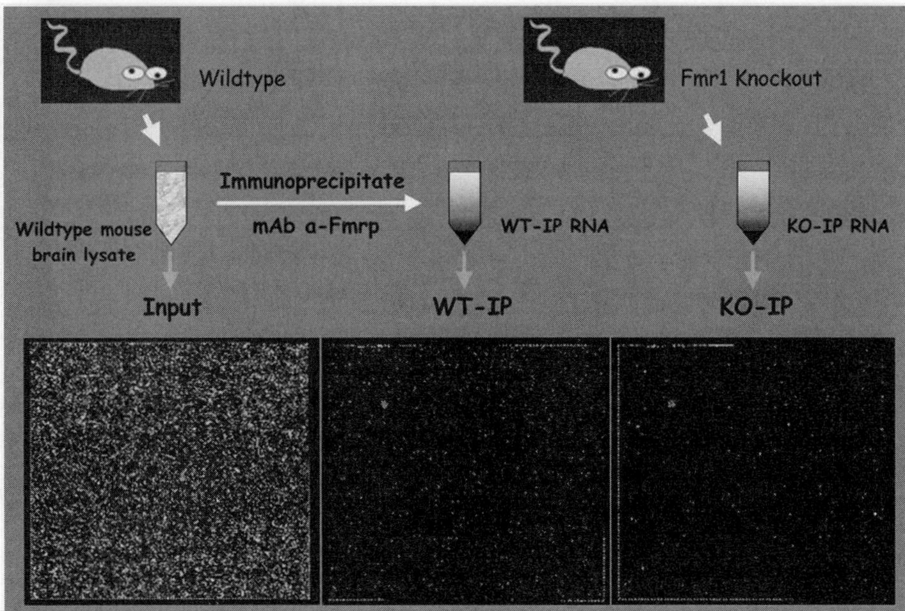

Fig. 1. Affymetrix Genechips were hybridized with targets prepared from the RNA of wild-type (WT) mouse brain INPUT, from the RNA coimmunoprecipitated with fragile X mental retardation protein from WT mouse brain, or from the RNA immunoprecipitated from *Fmr1*-knockout mouse brain.

3. One-cycle target labeling and control reagent (Affymetrix, Santa Clara, CA; cat. no. 900493).
4. T7-oligo(dT) promoter primer kit (Affymetrix; cat. no. 900375).
5. 3 n*M* control oligo B2 (Affymetrix; cat. no. 900301).

2.3. Determination of the Association Between FMRP and Small RNAs In Vivo

1. T4 RNA ligase (New England BioLabs, Ipswich, CA; cat. no. M0204).
2. Isotope: Cytidine 3',5'-bis [α-^{32}P] phosphate (^{32}P-pCp) and γ-^{32}P-adenosine triphosphate (ATP) (Amersham, Piscataway, NJ; cat. no. PB10208 and PB 10218).
3. Bio-Rad Criterion™ precast gel, 15% Tris–borate–ethylenediaminetetraacetic acid (TBE) urea (Bio-Rad, Hercules, CA; cat. no. 345-0092).
4. Decade™ Marker system (Ambion, Austin, TX; cat. no. 7778).
5. Gel dryer.
6. Phosphorimager screen.

2.4. Determination of the Interaction Between FMRP and Specific miRNAs Using Northern Blot Analysis

1. Bio-Rad Criterion precast gel, 15% TBE Urea (Bio-Rad; cat. no. 345-0092).
2. Decade™ Marker system (Ambion; cat. no. 7778).
3. Isotopes: γ-^{32}P-ATP and α-^{32}P-uridine triphosphate (UTP) (Amersham; cat. no. PB 10218 and PB 10203).

4. *Mir*Vana™ miRNA Probe Construction Kit (Ambion; cat. no. 1550).
5. Ribonuclease (RNase)-free 10X TBE. Do not treat TBE with diethylpyrocarbonate.
6. BrightStar®-Plus nylon membrane (Ambion; cat. no. 10100).
7. Ultraviolet (UV) crosslinker (Stratagene, La Jolla, CA).
8. RNase-free deoxyribonuclease I (Ambion; cat. no. 2222).
9. 50X Denhardt solution: add 10 g Ficoll-400, 10 g bovine serum albumin, and 10 g polyvinylpyrrolidone to 1 L nuclease-free water. Store at room temperate.
10. 20X standard sodium citrate (SSC): add 175.3 g NaCl and 88.2 g sodium citrate to 800 mL nuclease-free water. Adjust pH to 7.0 with HCl and the final volume to 1 L. Store at room temperature.
11. Northern blot prehybridization solution: 6X SSC, 10X Denhardt solution, and 0.2% sodium dodecylsulfate (SDS). Filter the solution with a 0.45-μm-pore filter before use to remove particles.
12. Northern blot hybridization solution: 6X SSC, 5X Denhardt solution, the appropriate amount of 5' end-labeled antisense probes, and 0.2% SDS. Filter the solution with a 0.45-μm-pore filter before use to remove particulates.
13. Northern wash solution: 6X SSC and 0.2% SDS.
14. Phosphorimager screen.

3. Methods

The methods described here outline the following:

1. Isolating the FMRP-containing mRNP complex via immunoprecipitation.
2. Identifying the mRNAs enriched in the FMRP-containing mRNP complex via microarray analysis.
3. Determining the association between FMRP and endogenous small RNAs.
4. Determining the association between FMRP and specific miRNAs via Northern blot.

During these procedures, it is essential to develop a program of RNase control involving reagent preparation and testing, routine decontamination, and the use of certified RNase-free reagents and equipment, such as microcentrifuge tubes and pipet tips.

3.1. Immunoprecipitation of FMRP-Containing mRNP Complex

1. Adult WT and *Fmr1* congenic C57Bl/6J litter mates should be CO_2-asphyxiated for 2 min *(19)*. Harvest whole brains and homogenize by 10-stroke dounce homogenization in 2 mL per brain ice-cold lysis buffer. For human cell lines, resuspend the cell pellets with lysis buffer. Perform all further manipulations of the lysates at 4°C or on ice.
2. Nuclei and debris are pelleted at 3000*g* for 10 min. The pellet is then washed with 1 mL lysis buffer, and pelleted again. The supernatants from both spins are pooled, raised to 300 m*M* NaCl, and clarified at 70,000*g* for 30 min.
3. Preclear the resulting supernatant for 1 h with 60 μL recombinant protein G agarose (washed with lysis buffer first). Pellet the preclearing matrix; the supernatant will be used as the precleared input (INPUT). Aliquots of INPUT should be saved for RNA extraction (200 μL) and pro-tein analysis (100 μL).
4. Add RNase inhibitor to the remaining lysates. Immunoprecipitate the lysates with approx 15 μg of monoclonal antibody conjugated to 60 μL of protein G agarose (*see* **Note 1**).
5. Lysates are immunoprecipitated for 2 h and washed three times for 10 min each with 1.5 mL lysis buffer.

6. After the third wash, save 10% of the immunoprecipitate (IP) for protein analysis. Wash the remaining 90% one more time, and resuspend the IP in Trizol reagent for RNA isolation. Use RNAs from INPUT, IP from WT, and IP from knockout (KO) for the following analysis.

3.2. Identification of the mRNAs Enriched in the FMRP-Containing mRNP Complex by Microarray

1. Before microarray analysis, the RNA samples should be further purified with RNeasy columns.
2. Use the RNAs (INPUT, IP from WT, and IP from KO) for target preparation according to the manufacture's protocol from Affymetrix.
3. Hybridize the Affymetrix Genechip arrays overnight, and wash, stain, and scan the arrays according to the Affymetrix protocol.
4. Perform data analysis to identify the mRNAs significantly enriched in IP from WT compared with INPUT, but not in IP from KO (because of space limitation, data analysis is not discussed here; the additional information can be found at the Affymetrix website or in Barr et al., **ref. 20**) (*see* **Note 2**).

3.3. Determination of the Association Between FMRP and Small RNAs In Vivo

To determine the association between FMRP and small RNAs in vivo, the RNA samples are labeled at the 3'-termini with 5'-[^{32}P]pCp and separated by gel electrophoresis.

1. Incubate the RNAs (INPUT, IP from normal cells, and IP from fragile X cells) in 1X T4 RNA ligase reaction buffer with T4 RNA ligase and 5'-[^{32}P]pCp at 37°C for 30 min (*see* **Note 3**).
2. Extract the RNAs with phenol/chloroform and precipitate with sodium acetate and cold ethanol.
3. Suspend the precipitated RNAs in 10 μL gel-loading buffer II.
4. Heat the samples for 2 to 5 min at 95°C to 100°C.
5. Load the samples on a 15% TBE urea Bio-Rad Criterion precast gel and perform electrophoresis at 30 to 45 mA (0.5 h).
6. Stop the electrophoresis when the bromophenol blue dye has migrated to the bottom of the gel.
7. Dry the gel on a gel dryer and expose to X-ray film or a phosphorimager screen, according to the manufacturer's instructions (**Fig. 2**).

3.4. Determination of the Interaction Between FMRP and Specific miRNAs Using Northern Blot Analysis (see Note 4)

3.4.1. Separation of RNAs on Polyacrylamide Gel

1. Mix the RNAs (INPUT, IP from WT, and IP from KO) with an equal volume of gel loading buffer II. For markers, remove 4 μL and heat to 95°C for 5 min.
2. Heat the samples for 2 to 5 min at 95°C to 100°C.
3. Load the samples on a 15% TBE Urea Bio-Rad Criterion precast gel and perform electrophoresis at 30 to 45 mA (0.5 h).
4. Stop the electrophoresis when the bromophenol blue dye has migrated to the bottom of the gel.

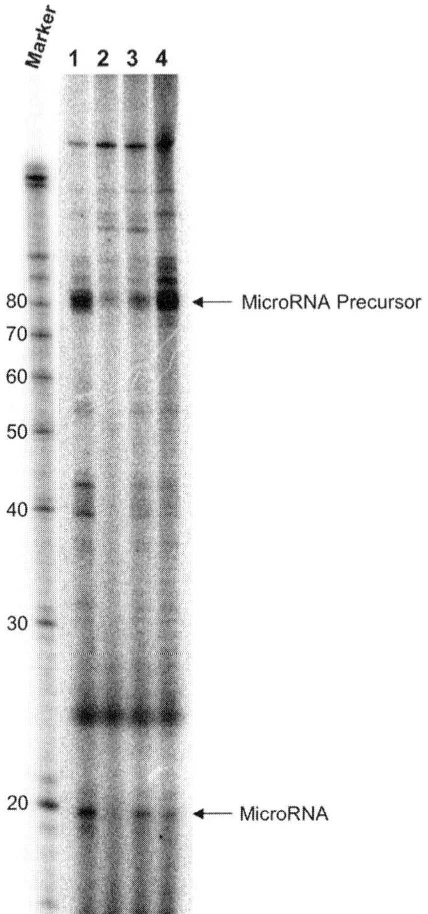

Fig. 2. Immunoprecipitations were performed with anti-Fragile X mental retardation protein (FMRP) (Lane 1), anti-Fragile X-related proteins (FXR)-1P (Lane 3), and anti-FXR2P (Lane 4) antibodies using a human lymphoblastoid cell line from a normal individual. As a negative control, immunoprecipitation was also performed on a fragile X cell line, using an anti-FMRP antibody (Lane 2). The immunoprecipitated RNAs were isolated, 3'-end labeled with [5'-^{32}P]-pCp, and resolved by electrophoresis on 15% denaturing polyacrylamide gels. The bands for microRNAs and their precursors are indicated. The ^{32}P-label RNA size marker (Ambion) for 10 to 100 nucleotides was run in parallel on the left.

3.4.2. Transferring RNA to Membrane

Electroblotting can be performed in a semidry apparatus using a stack of three sheets of blotting paper soaked in 0.25X TBE, placed above and below the gel/membrane.

1. Transfer at 150 to 200 mA for 1 h. After blotting, keep the membrane damp. Rinse in 0.25X TBE for 2 min.

2. Finally, UV crosslink the RNA to the membranes using a UV crosslinker (120 mJ burst during 30 s).

3.4.3. Probe Preparation

3.4.3.1. DOUBLE-STRANDED DNA TRANSCRIPTION TEMPLATE PREPARATION

1. Resuspend the oligonucleotide template to 100 μ*M* (100 pmol/μL).
2. Hybridize the oligonucleotide template to the T7 Promoter Primer.
   a. In a microcentrifuge tube mix the following:

Amount	Component
2 μL	T7 promoter primer
6 μL	DNA hybridization buffer
2 μL	oligonucleotide template (100 μ*M*)

   b. Heat the mixture to 70°C for 5 min, and leave at room temperature for 5 min to allow hybridization.
3. Fill in with Klenow DNA polymerase.
   a. Add the following to the hybridized oligonucleotides:

Amount	Component
2 μL	10X Klenow reaction buffer
2 μL	10X deoxyribonucleoside triphosphate mix
4 μL	Nuclease-free water
2 μL	Exo–Klenow

   b. Incubate for 30 min at 37°C.

3.4.3.2. IN VITRO TRANSCRIPTION

1. Assemble the transcription reactions at room temperature and incubate for 10 to 30 min at 37°C.

Amount	Component
Up to 20 μL	nuclease-free water
1 μL	double-stranded DNA template
2 μL	10X transcription buffer
1 μL	10 m*M* ATP
1 μL	10 m*M* cytidine triphosphate
1 μL	10 m*M* guanosine triphosphate
5 μL	α-^{32}P-uridine triphosphate
2 μL	T7 RNA Polymerase

2. Add 1 μL deoxyribonuclease I to the transcription reaction and incubate for 10 min at 37°C to remove the template DNA.

3.4.4. Prehybridization

Prehybridize the membrane in 10 mL of prehybridization solution for at least 1 h at 65°C. After prehybridizing, remove and discard the prehybridization solution.

3.4.5. Hybridization

Add 10 mL of hybridization solution. Hybridize the blot in approx 10 mL of Northern blot hybridization solution containing at least 4×10^5 cpm of 5' end-labeled antisense probe(s) for 8 to 24 h, with gentle agitation, at room temperature.

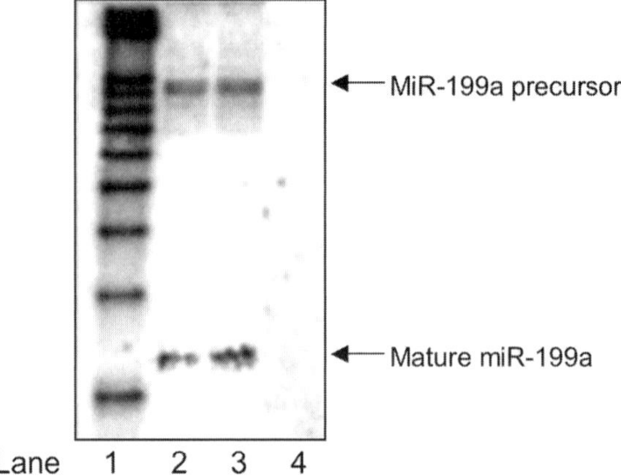

Fig. 3. Northern blot is used to detect the association between Fragile X mental retardation protein and miR-199a in mouse brain. The RNAs of INPUT (Lane 2), immunoprecipitate (IP) from wild type (Lane 3), and IP from knockout (Lane 4) were probed for miR-199a. The ^{32}P-labeled RNA size marker (Ambion) for 10 to 100 nucleotides was run in parallel in Lane 1.

3.4.6. Wash and Expose

After hybridization, remove the hybridization solutions.

1. Wash blot with approx 10 mL wash solution. Agitate at room temperature for 5 min. Remove and discard the wash solution.
2. Repeat the wash two more times.
3. Wash once at 42°C (or ~10°C lower than the estimated melting temperature [Tm] of probe); add approx 10 mL wash solution. Agitate at 42°C for 5–10 min. Remove and discard the wash solution.
4. Wash one more time at 42°C for 20 min.
5. After the final wash, wrap the blots in plastic wrap and expose to X-ray film or a phosphorimager screen, according to the manufacturer's instructions (**Fig. 3**). The latter method allows quantification of the amount of signal present in each band (1 h).

4. Notes

1. Immunoprecipitation. During the immunoprecipitation process, it is critical to control the RNase activity using extra RNase inhibitors. Reducing the time of immunoprecipitation could also effectively prevent RNA degradation. Therefore, immunoprecipitation overnight is not recommended and, in general, 1 to 2 h should be enough. In addition, it is important to include a negative control during the immunoprecipitation. In our case, the negative control is *Fmr1* KO mouse. It is likely that antibody used in immunoprecipitation might also nonspecifically interact with some RNAs. Indeed, some RNAs could also be immunoprecipitated even from *Fmr1* KO mice (**Figs. 1** and **2**).
2. Microarray analysis. Different platforms of microarray could also be used in a similar assay. Before target preparation, RNAs should be purified through RNeasy column (Qiagen). Otherwise, the labeling efficiency will be interfered with. In addition, the fold of enrichment used to determine the mRNAs that specifically interact with FMRP is arbitrary at this stage. Ideally, one or two known mRNA ligands could be used as internal controls to determine how many folds of enrichment should be used.

3. Labeling small RNAs. The RNAs used here should be isolated with Trizol or other RNA isolation reagents that would not remove small RNAs. The RNeasy column, which is required for microarray analysis, should not be used here because it will remove most small RNAs.
4. Northern blot. To prepare the template for in vitro transcription, an oligonucleotide containing specific miRNA sequences along with an 8-base sequence complementary to the 3' end of T7 promoter primer should be designed and synthesized. Because, in general, miRNAs are AU-rich, the hybridization and washing should be less stringent than when probing mRNA. In addition, some miRNAs are almost identical to each other, with only a one- or two-nucleotide difference. In this case, it will be very difficult to distinguish those miRNAs by Northern blot. Alternatively, one could design a probe specifically for each miRNA to perform the RNase protection assay *(21)*.

References

1. Warren, S. T. and Sherman, S. L. (2001) The fragile X syndrome. In: *The Metabolic and Molecular Bases of Inherited Disease*, vol. 1 (Scriver, C. R., Beaudet, A. L., Valle, D., Childs, B., Kinzler, K. W., and Vogelstein, B., eds.), McGraw-Hill, pp. 1257–1290.
2. Siomi, M. C., Siomi, H., Sauer, W. H., Srinivasan, S., Nussbaum, R. L., and Dreyfuss, G. (1995) FXR1, an autosomal homolog of the fragile X mental retardation gene. *EMBO J.* **14,** 2401–2408.
3. Zhang, Y., O'Connor, J. P., Siomi, M. C., et al. (1995) The fragile X mental retardation syndrome protein interacts with novel homologs FXR1 and FXR2. *EMBO J.* **14,** 5358–5366.
4. Ashley, C. T. Jr., Wilkinson, K. D., Reines, D., and Warren, S. T. (1993) FMR1 protein: conserved RNP family domains and selective RNA binding. *Science* **262,** 563–566.
5. Feng, Y., Absher, D., Eberhart, D. E., Brown, V., Malter, H. E., and Warren, S. T. (1997) FMRP associates with polyribosomes as an mRNP, and the I304N mutation of severe fragile X syndrome abolishes this association. *Mol. Cell* **1,** 109–118.
6. Laggerbauer, B., Ostareck, D., Keidel, E. M., Ostareck-Lederer, A., and Fischer, U. (2001) Evidence that fragile X mental retardation protein is a negative regulator of translation. *Hum. Mol. Genet.* **10,** 329–338.
7. Li, Z., Zhang, Y., Ku, L., Wilkinson, K. D., Warren, S. T., and Feng, Y. (2001) The fragile X mental retardation protein inhibits translation via interacting with mRNA. *Nucleic Acids Res.* **29,** 2276–2283.
8. Eberhart, D. E., Malter, H. E., Feng, Y., and Warren, S. T. (1996) The fragile X mental retardation protein is a ribonucleoprotein containing both nuclear localization and nuclear export signals. *Hum. Mol. Genet.* **5,** 1083–1091.
9. Jin, P. and Warren, S. T. (2003) New insights into fragile X syndrome: from molecules to neurobehaviors. *Trends Biochem. Sci.* **28,** 152–158.
10. Brown, V., Jin, P., Ceman, S., et al. (2001) Microarray identification of FMRP-associated brain mRNAs and altered mRNA translational profiles in fragile X syndrome. *Cell* **107,** 477–487.
11. Miyashiro, K. Y., Beckel-Mitchener, A., Purk, T. P., et al. (2003) RNA cargoes associating with FMRP reveal deficits in cellular functioning in Fmr1 null mice. *Neuron* **37,** 417–431.
12. Schaeffer, C., Bardoni, B., Mandel, J. L., Ehresmann, B., Ehresmann, C., and Moine, H. (2001) The fragile X mental retardation protein binds specifically to its mRNA via a purine quartet motif. *EMBO J.* **20,** 4803–4813.

13. Darnell, J. C., Jensen, K. B., Jin, P., Brown, V., Warren, S. T., and Darnell, R. B. (2001) Fragile X mental retardation protein targets G quartet mRNAs important for neuronal function. *Cell* **107,** 489–499.
14. Darnell, J. C., Fraser, C. E., Mostovetsky, O., et al. (2005) Kissing complex RNAs mediate interaction between the Fragile-X mental retardation protein KH2 domain and brain polyribosomes. *Genes Dev.* **19,** 903–918.
15. Bartel, D. P. (2004) MicroRNAs: genomics, biogenesis, mechanism, and function. *Cell* **116,** 281–297.
16. Caudy, A. A., Myers, M., Hannon, G. J., and Hammond, S. M. (2002) Fragile-X-related protein and VIG associate with the RNA interference machinery. *Genes Dev.* **16,** 2491–2496.
17. Jin, P., Zarnescu, D. C., Ceman, S., et al. (2004) Biochemical and genetic interaction between the fragile X mental retardation protein and the microRNA pathway. *Nat. Neurosci.* **7,** 113–117.
18. Ishizuka, A., Siomi, M. C., and Siomi, H. (2002) A Drosophila fragile X protein interacts with components of RNAi and ribosomal proteins. *Genes Dev.* **16,** 2497–2508.
19. The Dutch-Belgian Fragile X Consortium. (1994) Fmr1 knockout mice: a model to study fragile X mental retardation. *Cell* **78,** 23–33.
20. Barr, G. and Gao, P. (2005) Issues for consideration in the analysis of microarray data in behavioural studies. *Addict. Biol.* **10,** 15–21.
21. Lau, A., Teng-Renzelman, C., Vereen, R., et al. (2005) mirMASA, a microsphere array detecting microRNAs with high levels of sensitivity and specificity. *Genome Res.* In press.

## 20

In Vitro Precursor MicroRNA Processing Assays Using *Drosophila* Schneider-2 Cell Lysates

Akira Ishizuka, Kuniaki Saito, Mikiko C. Siomi, and Haruhiko Siomi

Summary

Recent studies have shown that the microRNA (miRNA) pathway is an evolutionarily conserved endogenous pathway that is important for normal development. Mature miRNAs are excised from precursors in a stepwise process and subsequently incorporated into an RNA-induced silencing complex (RISC), which mediates either cleavage of the target messenger RNA (mRNA) or translational repression, depending on the complementarity between the miRNA and its target mRNA. In this chapter, we describe in vitro precursor (pre)-miRNA processing assays using *Drosophila* Schneider-2 (S2) cell lysates and immunopurified materials.

Key Words: miRNA; pre-miRNA; RNAi; Dicer; RISC; *Drosophila*; S2 cell.

1. Introduction

miRNAs are small, single-stranded cellular RNAs consisting of 21 to 23 nucleotides (nt) that function as guide molecules by binding to complementary sites on target mRNAs to control gene expression at the posttranscriptional level in plants and animals *(1–4)*. Many miRNAs show distinctive temporal- and tissue-specific expression patterns in different tissues, including embryonic stem cells and neurons, suggesting an important role for miRNAs in the regulation of endogenous gene expression *(1–4)*. miRNAs are encoded in the genome and transcribed as long primary transcripts (pri-miRNAs) by RNA polymerase II *(4–6)*. miRNAs are excised from pri-miRNAs in a stepwise process. First, the pri-miRNA is cleaved into an approx 70-nt hairpin-shaped precursor, called the pre-miRNA, by the Drosha–Pasha/DiGeorge syndrome critical region 8 complex in the nucleus *(7–10)*. The pair of cuts made by Drosha establishes either the 5' or 3' end of the mature miRNA *(11)*. The pre-miRNA possesses a 3' overhang of 2 nt *(4–6,11)*, and contains the mature miRNA of approx 22 nt in either the 5' or 3' half of its stem *(5)*. Subsequently, the pre-miRNA is exported to the cytoplasm and further processed by Dicer *(12–14)*. Only one of the two strands is then predominantly

From: *Methods in Molecular Biology, vol. 342: MicroRNA Protocols*
Edited by: S. Ying © Humana Press Inc., Totowa, NJ

incorporated into a RISC, which mediates either cleavage of the target mRNA or translational repression, depending on the complementarity between the miRNA and its target mRNA, as is the case for small interfering RNAs *(15–17)*. Every RISC contains a member of the Argonaute protein family, which tightly binds the RNA in the complex *(16,17)*. In addition to Argonaute proteins, a number of other proteins, including fragile X mental retardation protein, have been reported to be associated with RISCs *(18,19)*. Although Argonaute proteins have been shown to be directly responsible for the target mRNA cleavage process *(20,21)*, the mechanism of the translational repression mediated by RISCs remains unknown. Recent studies have shown that Dicer action is not only required for loading small RNAs into RISCs, but also for RISC formation and function *(22–24)*. Therefore, studies of Dicer and its interacting partners will provide clues for how RISCs repress the translation of the target mRNAs.

In this chapter, we describe in vitro pre-miRNA processing assays for characterizing Dicer and its partners. These in vitro assays have enabled us to demonstrate that the processing of *Drosophila* pre-miRNAs to mature miRNAs by Dicer-1 requires the double-stranded RNA-binding domain protein, Loquacious (Loqs) *(25,26)*. These in vitro assays will be useful for studying many aspects of miRNA biogenesis, as well as the expression of genes regulated by miRNAs.

2. Materials

1. Cloning vectors harboring phage promoters: pBluescript SK (Stratagenc, La Jolla, CA) or equivalent.
2. MEGAscript kit (Ambion, Austin, TX).
3. [α-^{32}P]uridine triphosphate (UTP).
4. Gel-filtration columns: Micro Bio-Spin Columns P-30 Tris, RNase-Free (Bio-Rad, Hercules, CA).
5. Precipitation carriers: Quick-Precip Solution (EdgeBioSystems, Gaithersburg, MD), linear acrylamide, glyco-gen, and so on.
6. 7.5% acrylamide denaturing gel: 0.5X Tris–borate–ethylenediaminetetraacetic acid, 7 *M* urea, 1% glycerol, and 7.5% acrylamide.
7. Polyacrylamide gel electrophoresis equipment.
8. Elution buffer: 0.5 *M* ammonium acetate, 1 m*M* ethylenediaminetetraacetic acid, and 0.2% sodium dodecylsulfate.
9. 5X processing buffer: 150 m*M* HEPES-KOH, pH 7.4, 500 m*M* KOAc, 10 m*M* MgOAc, and 25 m*M* dithiothreitol (DTT).
10. *Drosophila* S2 cells.
11. Schneider's *Drosophila* medium (Invitrogen, Carlsbad, CA) supplemented with 10% fetal calf serum.
12. Spinner flasks for large-scale culturing of S2 cells.
13. Protease inhibitors: Pefabloc SC (Roche, Basel, Switzerland); or leupeptin, pepstatin, and aprotinin.
14. Hypotonic buffer: 30 m*M* HEPES-KOH, pH 7.4, 2 m*M* MgOAc, 5 m*M* DTT, and protease inhibitors.
15. Lysis buffer: 30 m*M* HEPES-KOH, pH 7.4, 100 m*M* KOAc, 2 m*M* MgOAc, 5 m*M* DTT, 20% glycerol, and protease inhibitors.
16. Imaging plates: BAS-MS2040 (Fujifilm, Tokyo, Japan).

17. BAS-2500 imaging system (Fujifilm).
18. Anti-Flag M2 agarose beads (Sigma, St. Louis, MO).
19. IP150 buffer: 30 m*M* HEPES-KOH, pH 7.4, 150 m*M* KOAc, 2 m*M* MgOAc, 5 m*M* DTT, 0.1% Nonidet P-40, and protease inhibitors.
20. IP800 buffer: 30 m*M* HEPES-KOH, pH 7.4, 800 m*M* KOAc, 2 m*M* MgOAc, 5 m*M* DTT, 0.1% Nonidet P-40, and protease inhibitors.
21. Wash buffer: 30 m*M* HEPES-KOH, pH 7.4, 100 m*M* KOAc, 2 m*M* MgOAc, 5 m*M* DTT, and protease inhibitors.
22. Peptide elution buffer: 30 m*M* HEPES-KOH, pH 7.4, 100 m*M* KOAc, 2 m*M* MgOAc, 5 m*M* DTT, 400 µg/mL of 3X Flag peptide (Sigma), 10% glycerol, and protease inhibitors.
23. Concentrator columns: Microcon (Millipore), Apollo concentrator (Orbital Biosciences), and so on.

3. Methods

The methods described in this chapter outline:

1. The preparation of pre-miRNA from pri-miRNA.
2. The preparation of lysates from S2 cells for in vitro processing of pre-miRNA.
3. The preparation of immunoprecipitates from S2 cells for in vitro processing of pre-miRNA.
4. In vitro pre-miRNA processing assays.

3.1. Preparation of Pre-miRNA

To prepare pre-miRNA for in vitro processing, three methods can be used:

1. Transcription of the pre-miRNA by phage RNA polymerases.
2. Chemical synthesis of the pre-miRNA.
3. Preparation of the pre-miRNA from its pri-miRNA.

In the first method, the use of phage RNA polymerases, such as T7 and T3 polymerases, and DNA templates containing phage polymerase promoter sequences allow sufficient amounts of pre-miRNAs to be obtained. T7 or T3 transcription is the standard method of producing RNA, because it is easy, quick, and produces relatively good quality RNA compared with solid-phase synthesis. The RNA obtained can be uniformly labeled with [32]P. However, because, for example, T7 strongly prefers to start with a guanine (G) (and GG is even better), this method cannot be used for producing precursors with accurate sequences unless they have a G residue at the 5' end. The second method uses a commercially available chemical synthesis service to make the pre-miRNAs. The synthesized pre-miRNAs are then 5' end-labeled by T4 polynucleotide kinase for in vitro processing, such that only miRNAs located in the 5' half of their precursors can be detected after processing. In other words, one cannot use this method for miRNAs located in the 3' half of their precursors. Furthermore, accurate (5' and 3' ends) sequences for most pre-miRNAs have not yet been determined. The third method uses nuclear lysates to generate pre-miRNAs from pri-miRNAs. Although relatively small amounts of pre-miRNAs can be prepared using this method, the pre-miRNAs will have their natural pre-miRNA characters, including accurate sequence length and characteristic end structures. We describe this third method in detail to demonstrate the pre-miRNA processing activity of S2 cytoplasmic lysates and immunopurified Dicer-1.

3.1.1. Pri-miRNA Transcription

DNA templates for pri-miRNA transcription contain a pre-miRNA stem-loop and its flanking sequence (>50 bases) *(7)* under the control of a phage RNA polymerase promoter, such as T7, T3, or SP6. For example, the template for generating radiolabeled pri-miRNA-bantam by in vitro transcription *(27)* was obtained by nested polymerase chain reaction amplification of *Drosophila* genomic DNA. The gel-purified polymerase chain reaction fragment containing pre-miRNA-bantam and the sequences covering 180 nt upstream and 130 nt downstream from the Drosha-cleavage sites was cloned into the EcoRV site of the pBluescript SK vector in the same direction as the T3 promoter. The plasmid was digested with ClaI at the 3' end of the pri-miRNA and gel purified to create a transcription template (*see* **Note 1**).

The pri-miRNA was transcribed in the presence of [α-^{32}P]UTP, according to the manufacturer's instructions (MEGAscript, Ambion), with the exception of the UTP concentration, which was decreased to 1:200 to enhance the incorporation of radioactive UTP. The detailed protocol follows:

1. Combine the following transcription reaction mixture in a total volume of 20 µL:
   a. 2 µL adenosine triphosphate (ATP) solution.
   b. 2 µL cytidine triphosphate solution.
   c. 2 µL guanosine triphosphate solution.
   d. 1 µL of 1:100-diluted UTP solution.
   e. 2 µL of 10X reaction buffer.
   f. More than 0.5 µg of template DNA.
   g. 1 µL [α-^{32}P]UTP.
   h. 2 µL enzyme mix.
2. Incubate the transcription reaction solution at 37°C for 2 h.
3. Add 1 µL of DNase I and incubate at 37°C for 15 min.
4. Gel filtrate with a P-30 column, according to the manufacturer's instructions (Bio-Rad), to remove any unincorporated nucleotides.
5. Purify the transcribed RNA by phenol extraction followed by ethanol precipitation in the presence of a precipitation carrier.
6. Isolate the pri-miRNA by acrylamide denaturing gel electrophoresis as follows:
   a. Separate the RNA by 7.5% acrylamide denaturing gel electrophoresis.
   b. Excise the gel piece containing the pri-miRNA from the gel.
   c. Crush the gel piece into small pieces with a disposable pipet tip.
   d. Add 400 µL (>two gel volumes) of elution buffer.
   e. Rotate at 37°C overnight to elute the RNA.
   f. Remove the gel pieces and collect the supernatant.
   g. Purify the pri-miRNA by phenol extraction and ethanol precipitation in the presence of a precipitation carrier.
7. Refold the pri-miRNA by heating at 95°C for 2 min, followed by 37°C for 1 h.

3.1.2. Processing of Pri-miRNAs Into Pre-miRNAs Using Nuclear Lysates

Previously, Kim and colleagues showed that nuclear extracts prepared from mammalian cells were capable of releasing pre-miRNAs from pri-miRNAs in vitro *(6,11)*. Subsequently, Hannon and colleagues showed that this pri-miRNA processing activity was also exhibited by *Drosophila* S2 cell extracts *(7)*. In vitro processing of the pri-miRNA was performed according to these previously reported methods, with some modifications *(6,8,11)*. The detailed protocol follows:

1. Prepare the following processing reaction mixture in a total volume of 1 mL:
   a. 0.5X processing buffer.
   b. 0.5 m*M* ATP.
   c. 10 m*M* Creatine phosphate.
   d. 30 µg/mL Creatine kinase (prepare just before use).
   e. 0.1 U/µL RNasin Plus RNase inhibitor (Promega).
   f. 10 ng/µL Yeast RNA.
   g. 500 µL Nuclear lysate (*see* **Subheading 3.2.**).
   h. 1×10^5 cpm pri-miRNA.
2. Incubate at 26°C for 2 h.
3. Purify the RNA by phenol extraction followed by ethanol precipitation in the presence of a precipitation carrier.
4. Isolate the pre-miRNA by gel electrophoresis, as described in **Subheading 3.1.1.**, **step 6**. The pre-miRNA can be detected as a clear band of 60 to 70 nt in length (*see* **Fig. 1**).
5. Refold the pre-miRNA, as described in **Subheading 3.1.1.**, **step 7**.

3.2. Preparation of Drosophila *S2 Cell Lysates* for In Vitro Processing of miRNAs

The *Drosophila melanogaster* S2 cell line has been proven to be a useful system for analyzing gene functions *(28)*. In particular, RNAi-based reverse-genetic methods have been widely applied to study gene functions in S2 cell cultures *(29)*.

S2 cells were grown at room temperature (25°C) under normal atmosphere in Schneider's *Drosophila* medium supplemented with 10% fetal calf serum at a cell density of 5×10^5 to 5×10^6 cells/mL. Nuclear and cytoplasmic lysates of *Drosophila* S2 cells were used for processing the pri- and pre-miRNA, respectively. The detailed protocol follows:

1. Culture 5×10^8 cells (100 mL culture) in a 250-mL spinner flask.
2. Harvest the cells by centrifugation (5 min at 400*g* to 500*g*), and wash twice with phosphate-buffered saline.
3. Suspend the cells in 2 mL of hypotonic buffer.
4. Incubate on ice for 10 to 15 min.
5. Lyse the cells by passing five times through a 30-gage needle attached to a syringe.
6. Centrifuge at 500*g* for 20 min, and separate the supernatant (S500) and precipitate (P500) into two tubes.
7. Add 100 m*M* KOAc to the S500, and centrifuge at maximum speed (17,400*g*) for 15 min to obtain the supernatant as a cytoplasmic lysate.
8. Wash the P500 twice with hypotonic buffer.
9. Suspend the washed materials in 1 mL of lysis buffer.
10. Lyse the nuclei by sonication (*see* **Note 2**).
11. Centrifuge at maximum speed (17,400*g*) for 15 min to obtain the supernatant as a nuclear lysate.

3.3. In Vitro Pre-miRNA Processing

Processing of the pre-miRNA is performed as follows:

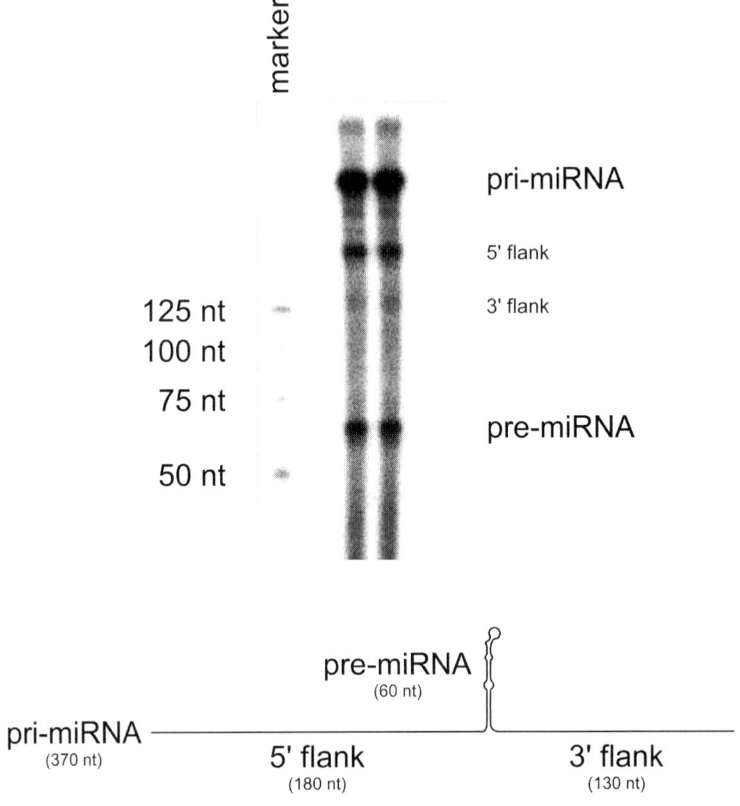

Fig. 1. Processing of the primary (pri)-microRNA (miRNA) into precursor (pre)-miRNA. The products of the processing mixture, in which the pri-miRNA (pri-miR-bantam) had been processed into the pre-miRNA (pre-miR-bantam) by a nuclear lysate, were resolved in a 7.5% acrylamide denaturing gel and visualized by autoradiography. The pre-miRNA is detected as a clear band of 60 nucleotides in length. This pre-miRNA was extracted from the gel, purified, and used for the in vitro processing reaction.

1. Combine the following processing reaction mixture in a total volume of 10 µL:
   a. 0.5X Processing buffer.
   b. 0.5 m*M* ATP.
   c. 10 m*M* Creatine phosphate.
   d. 30 µg/mL Creatine kinase (prepare just before use).
   e. 0.1 U/µL RNasin Plus RNase inhibitor.
   f. 10 ng/µL Yeast RNA.
   g. 5 µL Cytoplasmic lysate.
   h. 200 to 2000 cpm pre-miRNA.
2. Incubate at 26°C for 30 to 60 min.
3. Purify the RNA.
4. Separate in a 12 to 15% acrylamide denaturing gel.
5. Expose the gel to an imaging plate and visualize the signals using the BAS-2500 system.

When purified factors, such as the immunopurified Dicer-1 protein, are used instead of cytoplasmic lysates, use 1X processing buffer to adjust the buffer concentration, and incubate for 2 h (*see* **Subheading 3.4.**).

3.4. Immunopurification of Dicer-1 for Processing of Pre-miRNAs

One way to examine the functional connection between a protein of interest and pre-miRNA processing is to investigate whether depletion of the protein from cells by RNAi has any effect on the production of the mature miRNA from the precursor *(25, 26)*. Another way, which is complementary to the RNAi-based method, is to examine the requirement for a protein of interest in pre-miRNA processing using in vitro processing assays with purified materials. Dicer-1, which is an essential component for pre-miRNA processing in *Drosophila (23)*, will be used to illustrate in vitro pre-miRNA processing assays with purified materials. The detailed protocol follows:

1. Culture S2 cells stably expressing Dicer-1 tagged with a Flag epitope (Flag–Dicer-1) under the control of the metallothionein promoter using the pRmHa-C-FLAG-His vector (*see* **ref. *30***).
2. Harvest 10^8 cells and wash twice with phosphate-buffered saline buffer.
3. Suspend the cells in 1 mL of IP150 buffer.
4. Lyse the cells by sonication.
5. Centrifuge at maximum speed (17,400*g*) for 20 min.
6. Incubate the supernatant with anti-Flag M2 agarose beads for 1 h.
7. Wash the beads twice with IP150 buffer.
8. Wash the beads three times with IP800 buffer.
9. Wash the beads once with wash buffer.
10. Add 500 µL of peptide elution buffer and rotate for 30 min to elute the bound fraction.
11. Concentrate the eluate with a concentrator column.
12. Measure the amount of proteins in the eluate by Western blot analysis or silver staining.
13. For processing of pre-miRNAs use 1X processing buffer to adjust the buffer concentration, and incubate for 2 h.

Flag–Dicer-1 purified under harsher conditions (high salt), in which Dicer-1 is stripped of most of its associated proteins, can be used to examine the requirement for its associated proteins in pre-miRNA processing. Furthermore, purified fractions or recombinant proteins can be added back into in vitro pre-miRNA processing reactions with Flag–Dicer-1 purified under the high-salt conditions to identify and/or characterize proteins that either stimulate or inhibit Dicer-1 action in pre-miRNA processing (*see* **Fig. 2**).

4. Notes

1. Do not use restriction enzymes with activities that leave 3' overhanging ends (such as KpnI, PstI, and so on) to linearize the plasmid template, because these 3' overhanging ends could result in a low level of transcription.
2. Intensive sonication tends to result in a loss of activity for pri-miRNA processing because of heating. To avoid this loss of activity, shorter periods of sonication (e.g., 5 s) with long intervals (>2 min) are recommended. Alternatively, dounce homogenization on ice can be used to prevent the occurrence of heating.

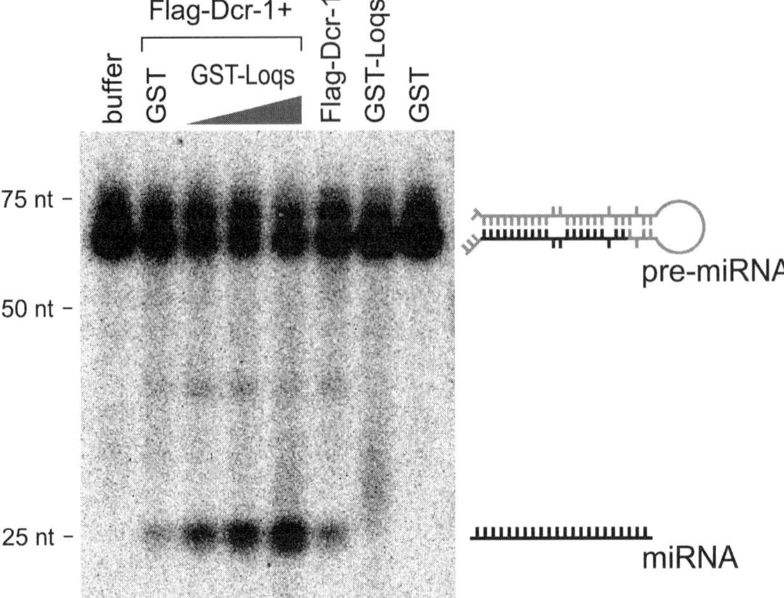

Fig. 2. Processing of the precursor (pre)-microRNA (miRNA) into the mature miRNA by immunopurified Dicer-1 (Dcr-1) complex with recombinant Loquacious (Loqs). The pre-miRNA (pre-miR-bantam) was processed by immunopurified Flag–Dcr-1 complex in the presence or absence of recombinant glutathione-*S*-transferase (GST)–Loqs. The Flag–Dcr-1 complex was purified under high-salt (800 m*M* KOAc) conditions to strip most of the interacting proteins, including Loqs. The purified Flag–Dcr-1 alone shows little activity for processing the pre-miRNA to the mature miRNA (miR-bantam). The addition of GST–Loqs to Flag–Dcr-1 stimulates the processing of the pre-miRNA in a dose-dependent manner (black triangles represent the amounts of GST–Loqs added to the reaction). GST–Loqs alone does not show any activity.

Acknowledgments

A. I. is a predoctoral fellow (DC1) of the Japan Society for the Promotion of Science. This work was supported by grants to M. C. Siomi and H. Siomi from the Ministry of Education, Culture, Sports, Science and Technology of Japan and the Japan Society for the Promotion of Science.

References

1. Ambros, V. (2004) The functions of animal microRNAs. *Nature* **431,** 350–355.
2. Bartel, D. P. (2004) MicroRNAs: genomics, biogenesis, mechanism, and function. *Cell* **116,** 281–297.
3. Baulcombe, D. (2004) RNA silencing in plants. *Nature* **431,** 356–363.
4. Kim, V. N. (2005) MicroRNA biogenesis: coordinated cropping and dicing. *Nature Rev. Mol. Cell Biol.* **6,** 376–385.
5. Lee, Y., Kim, M., Han, J., et al. (2004) MicroRNA genes are transcribed by RNA polymerase II. *EMBO J.* **23,** 4051–4060.

6. Lee, Y., Jeon, K., Lee, J. T., Kim, S., and Kim, V. N. (2002) MicroRNA maturation: stepwise processing and subcellular localization. *EMBO J.* **21,** 4663–4670.

7. Denli, A. M., Tops, B. B., Plasterk, R. H., Ketting, R. F., and Hannon, G. J. (2004) Processing of primary microRNAs by the Microprocessor complex. *Nature* **432,** 231–235.

8. Gregory, R. I., Yan, K. P., Amuthan, G., et al. (2004). The Microprocessor complex mediates the genesis of microRNAs. *Nature* **432,** 235–240.

9. Han, J., Lee, Y., Yeom, K. H., Kim, Y. K., Jin, H., and Kim, V. N. (2005) The Drosha–DGCR8 complex in primary microRNA processing. *Genes Dev.* **18,** 3016–3027.

10. Landthaler, M., Yalcin, A., and Tuschl, T. (2004) The human DiGeorge syndrome critical region gene 8 and its D. melanogaster homolog are required for miRNA biogenesis. *Curr. Biol.* **15,** 2162–2167.

11. Lee, Y., Ahn, C., Han, J., et al. (2003). The nuclear RNase III Drosha initiates microRNA processing. *Nature* **425,** 415–419.

12. Yi, R., Qin, Y., Macara, I. G., and Cullen, B. R. (2003) Exportin-5 mediates the nuclear export of pre-microRNAs and short hairpin RNAs. *Genes Dev.* **17,** 3011–3016.

13. Bohnsack, M. T., Czaplinski, K., and Gorlich, D. (2004) Exportin 5 is a RanGTP-dependent dsRNA-biding protein that mediates nuclear export of pre-miRNAs. *RNA* **10,** 185–191.

14. Lund, E., Guttinger, S., Calado, A., Dahlberg, J. E., and Kutay, U. (2004) Nuclear export of microRNA precursors. *Science* **303,** 95–98.

15. Meister, G. and Tuschl, T. (2004) Mechanisms of gene silencing by double-stranded RNA. *Nature* **431,** 343–349.

16. Sontheimer, E. J. (2005) Assembly and function of RNA silencing complexes. *Nature Rev. Mol. Cell Biol.* **6,** 127–138.

17. Tomari, Y. and Zamore, P. D. (2005) Perspective: machines for RNAi. *Genes Dev.* **19,** 517–529.

18. Ishizuka, A., Siomi, M. C., and Siomi, H. (2002) A *Drosophila* fragile X protein interacts with components of RNAi and ribosomal proteins. *Genes Dev.* **16,** 2497–2508.

19. Caudy, A. A., Myers, M., Hannon, G. J., and Hammond, S. M. (2002) Fragile X-related protein and VIG associate with the RNA interference machinery. *Genes Dev.* **16,** 2491–2496.

20. Liu, J., Carmell, M. A., Rivas, F. V., et al. (2004) Argonaute2 is the catalytic engine of mammalian RNAi. *Science* **305,** 1437–1441.

21. Meister, G., Landthaler, M., Patkaniowska, A., Dorsett, Y., Teng, G., and Tuschl, T. (2004) Human Argonaute2 mediates RNA cleavage targeted by miRNAs and siRNAs. *Mol. Cell* **15,** 185–197.

22. Tabara, H., Yigit, E., Siomi, H., and Mello, C. C. (2002) The dsRNA binding protein RDE-4 interacts with RDE-1, DCR-1, and a DExH-box helicase to direct RNAi in C. elegans. *Cell* **109,** 861–871.

23. Lee, Y. S., Nakahara, K., Pham, J. W., et al. (2004) Distinct roles for Drosophila Dicer-1 and Dicer-2 in the siRNA/miRNA silencing pathways. *Cell* **117,** 69–81.

24. Pham, J. W., Pellino, J. L., Lee, Y. S., Carthew, R. W., and Sontheimer, E. J. (2004) A Dicer-2-dependent 80s complex cleaves targeted mRNAs during RNAi in Drosophila. *Cell* **117,** 83–94.

25. Saito, K., Ishizuka, A., Siomi, H., and Siomi, M. C. (2005) Processing of pre-microRNAs by the Dicer-1-Loquacious complex in Drosophila cells. *PLoS Biol.* **3,** e235.

26. Forstemann, K., Tomari, Y., Du, T., et al. (2005) Normal microRNA maturation by Dicer-1 and germ-line stem cell maintenance requires the double-stranded RNA-binding domain protein, Loquacious. *PLoS Biol.* **3,** e236.

27. Brennecke, J., Hipfner, D. R., Stark, A., Russell, R. B., and Cohen, S. M. (2003) Bantam encodes a developmentally regulated microRNA that controls cell proliferation and regulates the proapoptotic gene hid in Drosophila. *Cell* **113,** 25–36.
28. Towers, P. R. and Sattelle, D. B. (2002) A Drosophila melanogaster cell line (S2) facilitates post-genome functional analysis of receptors and ion channels. *Bioessays* **24,** 1066–1073.
29. Boutros, M., Kiger, A. A., Armknecht, S., et al. (2004) Genome-wide RNAi analysis of growth and viability in Drosophila cells. *Science* **303,** 832–835.
30. Siomi, M. C. and Siomi, H. (2005) Identification of components of RNAi pathways using the tandem affinity purification method. *Methods Mol. Biol.* **309,** 1–9.

## 21

Downregulation of Human Cdc6 Protein Using a Lentivirus RNA Interference Expression Vector

Feng Luo, Jiing-Kuan Yee, Sheng-He Huang, Ling-Tao Wu, and Ambrose Y. Jong

Summary

Eukaryotic *CDC6* gene function is required for the initiation of DNA replication and is a key regulatory protein during cell cycle progression. The human *CDC6* gene is not expressed in most normal tissues, in contrast with its marked expression in proliferating cancer cells. An effective way to explore the gene functions of *CDC6* is to knock-down the *CDC6* messenger RNA (mRNA) and examine the phenotypic consequences. In this chapter, we describe the construction of a lentivirus vector to express a *CDC6* DNA segment. The transcript is able to fold by itself because the sense and antisense regions are complementary. There is a 9-nucleotide (nt) loop region allowing for the short hairpin RNA (shRNA) to form. Cellular ribonucleases process the shRNA into a functional short interfering RNA (siRNA). Downregulation of Cdc6 protein is confirmed by Western blots.

Key Words: Lentivirus vector; shRNA; siRNA; Cdc6; cell cycle progression.

1. Introduction

Eukaryotic Cdc6 is required for the initiation of DNA replication and is a key regulatory protein during cell cycle progression *(1,2)*. In humans, *CDC6* has a very low copy number in normal cells, and the protein has a very short half-life (15–30 min in HeLa cells) *(3)*. Because Cdc6 is an essential component in triggering initiation of DNA replication in human cells, the expression level of human CDC6 could be closely related to the cell growth rate. To knock-down its mRNA may reveal phenotypic consequences, allowing us to explore its gene functions. The human *CDC6* gene has other unique properties that make it a compelling target for cancer therapy. It is not expressed in most normal tissues, in contrast with its marked expression in proliferating cancer cells. As expected, the Cdc6 protein has been used as a marker of brain tumors *(4)* and cervical cancers *(5)*. In those tissues, Cdc6 expression is elevated in highly proliferative cells. Therefore, abrogation of *CDC6* mRNA or Cdc6 protein in cancer cells may effectively block cell proliferation *(6)*.

From: *Methods in Molecular Biology, vol. 342: MicroRNA Protocols*
Edited by: S. Ying © Humana Press Inc., Totowa, NJ

RNA interference (RNAi) is a mechanism of posttranscriptional gene silencing in which double-stranded RNA corresponding to a gene (or a region) of interest is introduced into a cell, resulting in degradation of the corresponding mRNA *(7,8)*. Unlike antisense technology, the RNAi persists for multiple cell divisions. RNAi is, therefore, an extremely simple yet powerful method for assaying gene function. By making a targeted knockout at the RNA level via RNAi, a vast number of genes can be assayed quickly and economically. In many cases, the in vitro RNAi approach can substitute for transgenic knockout mouse studies. Vectors derived from HIV are capable of delivering genes into many different cell types, including primary cells. Recent studies demonstrate that these vectors can mediate stable and high-level siRNA expression in mammalian cells. HIV vectors pseudotyped with the G protein of vesicular stomatitis virus can be concentrated to extremely high titers by ultracentrifugation *(9)*. Because downregulation of *CDC6* mRNA by siRNA may inhibit cell proliferation or lead to cell death, it may not be possible to derive stable siRNA expressing cell lines with low levels of the Cdc6 protein. Thus, highly efficient delivery of the siRNA gene into a majority of the cells by a vector system, such as HIV, may become important to assess the phenotype of Cdc6 downregulation.

In this chapter, we describe the construction of a lentivirus vector to express a *CDC6* DNA segment. The transcript is able to fold onto itself because the sense and antisense regions are able to base pair, forming a shRNA. The cellular ribonuclease (RNase) III enzyme, Dicer, processes the shRNA into a functional siRNA. Downregulation of Cdc6 protein is confirmed by Western blots.

2. Materials

2.1. Molecular Cloning and Plasmid Preparation

1. Plasmid pBP-hTERT/P: a 1.5-kb human telomerase reverse transcriptase (hTERT) promoter is cloned in the vector pBluescript-SK(–) (Stratagene, La Jolla, CA). The DNA fragment contains an MluI site at its 5' end and XhoI sites at its 3' end (**Fig. 1A**).
2. Plasmid pCMV-VSV-G DNA is the expression vector for the G protein of vesicular stomatitis virus (VSV-G) *(9)*.
3. Plasmid pTHTN is the parental plasmid, which contains the HIV-1 genome DNA with *env* and *nef* gene deletions; therefore, it is replication incompetent.
4. Restriction enzymes: MluI, BgLII, BamHI, HindIII, and XhoI.
5. Quick ligation kit (New England Biolabs, Beverly, MA; cat. no. M2200S).
6. *Escherichia coli* competent cells (Stb12; Stratagene; cat. no. 10268-019).
7. Qiagen Maxi prep (cat. no. 12162).

2.2. Cell Culture Media and Transfection

1. Dulbecco's modified Eagle's medium (DMEM).
2. Iscove's modified Dulbecco's medium (IMDM).
3. RPMI-1640 medium.
4. 10% fetal bovine serum.

2.3. Western Blots

1. Bio-Rad sodium dodecylsulfate electrophoresis system and 12.5% sodium dodecylsulfate polyacrylamide.

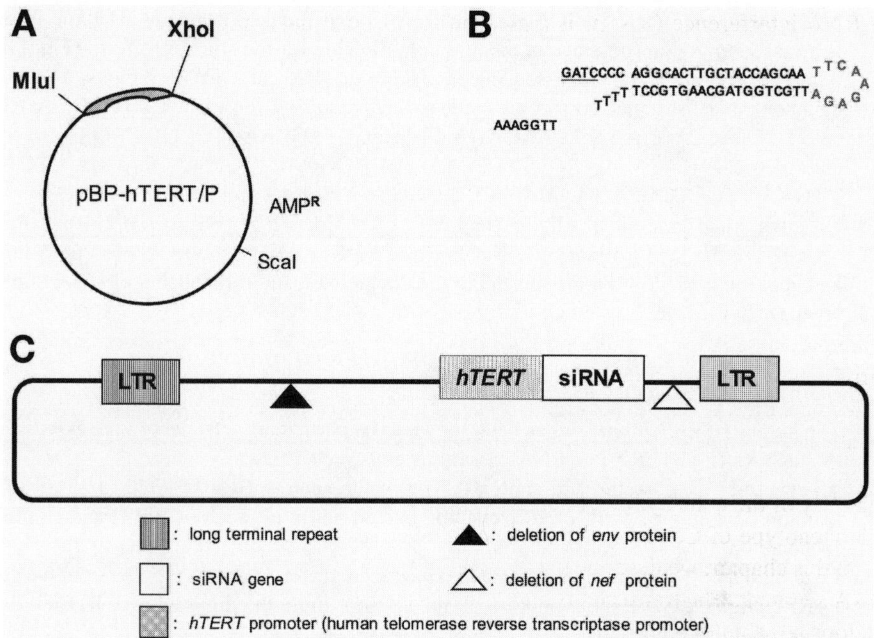

Fig. 1. Construction of anti-Cdc6 RNA interference (RNAi) expression vectors. (**A**) Plasmid pBP-hTERT/P contains a 1.5-kb human telomerase reverse transcriptase promoter, which is cloned in the vector pBluescript-SK(–) (Strategene). The cloning sites are indicated. The shaded bar indicates the hTERT/P promoter region. (**B**) A hairpin structure of oligonucleotide Cdc6_5-A and its complementary strand Cdc6_3-A are blunt ended and inserted into the EcoRV site of the vector, and (**C**) The lentiviral vector pTHTD6Ai that expresses anti-Cdc6 RNAi is shown. This HIV pseudotyped vector contains the HIV-1 genome DNA with *env* and *nef* gene deletions. It is replication incompetent. Its transduction ability is complemented by the G protein of vesicular stomatitis virus (VSV-G).

2. Anti-human CDC6 mouse monoclonal antibody (Sigma; cat. no. C0224).
3. Anti-mouse IgG–horseradish peroxidase conjugate (Kirkegaurd Perry Lab; cat. no. 074-1806).
4. Lumi-Light Western blotting substrate (Roche; cat. no. 12015 200 01).

3. Methods

3.1. Construction of a Lentivirus Vector That Expresses Anti-Cdc6 shRNA

3.1.1. Synthesis of Complementary Oligonucleotides

1. A complementary DNA fragment that can form a hairpin structure is prerequisite for the construction. The basic template is: template-5: <u>GATCCCC</u> {XX} **TTCAAGAGA** {YY} TTTTTGGAAA with a BamHI extrusion (underline) at one end; and template 3: <u>AGCT</u> TTTCCAAAAA {XX} **TCTCTTGAA** {YY} GGG with a HindIII extrusion (underline) at another end. {XX} and {YY} represent the selected DNA fragment. They are complementary, and usually 19-nt long. In our case, two Cdc6 19-nt complement sequences are used:

{XX}: AGGCACTTGCTACCAGCAA and {YY}: TTGCTGGTAGCAAGTGCCT. There is a 9-nt loop region (boldface in the middle), allowing for the shRNA to form (**Fig. 1B**).

2. After incorporating the Cdc6 sequences inside the {XX} and {YY} regions, a pair of complementary oligonucleotides are synthesized: Cdc6_5-A (64-mer): <u>GATCCCC</u> AGGC ACTTGCTACCAGCAA **TTCAAGAGA** TTGCTGGTAGCAAGTGCCT TTTTTGGAAA, and Cdc6_3-A (64-mer): <u>AGCTTTTCCAAAAA</u> AGGCACTTGC TACCAGCAA **TCTC TTGAA** TTGCTGGTAGCAAGTGCCT GGG (*see* **Notes 1** and **2**).

3. Dissolve equal amount of oligonucleotide 10 μ*M* Cdc6_5-A and 10 μ*M* Cdc6_3-A in 50 m*M* Tris-HCl, pH 7.0; 50 m*M* NaCl; 5 m*M* MgCl$_2$; heat denature at 94°C for 5 min; and cool the tube slowly for reannealing the double-stranded oligonucleotides (*see* **Fig. 1** legend).

3.1.2. Link the Reannealed shRNA to the hTERT Promoter to Form an Expression Cassette

1. The human hTERT promoter has been shown to be particularly efficient in the expression of shRNA. The hTERT/P-shRNA cassette is constructed first.

2. To construct the cassette, add approx 0.5 μg of the vector pBP-hTERT/P to 25 μL of a solution containing 2.5 μL of 10X reaction buffer, and 1 μL each of BgLII and HindIII. Incubate the tube at 37°C for 90 min.

3. Load onto a 0.8% agarose gel. Isolate the linearized vector fragment (~5 kb) from the gel, using QIAquick Gel Extraction kit (cat. no. 28706). Elute the digested pBP-hTERT/P in 10 μL of sterile water.

4. Add 10 μL of 2X ligation buffer, 7 μL of digested pBP-hTRET/P, 2 μL of reannealed oligonucleotides, and 1 μL of T4 DNA ligase to a tube. Incubate at room temperature for 10 min.

5. Transform the ligation mixture into Stb12 competent cells: add 5 μL of ligation mixture into a tube with 50 μL of competent cells on ice for 30 min, and heat shock at 37°C for 1 min. Add 0.5 mL SOC, shaking in a 37°C air-shaker for 30 min. Plate the mixture onto a Luria-Bertani plate containing 100 μg/mL ampicillin.

6. Pick single colonies for a plasmid Miniprep. Confirm the insert by DNA sequencing in a 0.5-mL tube containing 0.75 μg of plasmid DNA and 5 pmoles of T7 primer (5'-GTAATA CGACTCACTATAGGGC-3') in a 20-μL reaction mixture.

7. The hTRET/P-D6Ai cassette DNA fragment can be excised from the construct using MluI and XhoI digestion.

3.1.3. Construction of Anti-Cdc6 RNAi HIV Expression Vector

1. Digest the plasmid pTHTN, which is the parental HIV vector, with MluI and XhoI. Both restriction sites are downstream of the *tat* and *rev* genes. Isolate the linearized, approx 14-kb backbone from the agarose gel.

2. In parallel, isolate the approx 1.7-kb hTERT/P-D6Ai cassette from the pBS-hTERT/P-D6Ai with MluI and XhoI digestion.

3. Perform ligation, transformation, and screening as described in **Subheading 3.1.2.**

4. The resulting vector is designated as pTHTD6Ai, as shown in **Fig. 1C**.

3.2. Cell Cultures and Transduction

3.2.1. Cell Lines

1. Human embryonic kidney cell line 293T, maintained in DMEM supplemented with 10% fetal bovine serum, 100 U/mL penicillin, and 100 μg/mL streptomycin, at 37°C in a 5% CO$_2$ incubator.

2. Human neuroblastoma cell line CHLA 255, maintained in a complete Iscove's modified Dulbecco's medium.
3. HeLa cell line, maintained in DMEM.
4. MCF7 cell line, maintained in complete RPMI-1640 medium.

3.2.2. Transfection

1. Two-plasmid cotransfection is used to generate HIV-1-based recombinant virus. The first plasmid, pTHTD6Ai, is described in **Subheading 3.1.3.** The second plasmid, pCMV-VSV-G, provides VSV-G to complement the *env* deletion in the pTHTD6Ai. Both plasmids are purified using a Qiagen Maxi-prep plasmid isolation kit.
2. Seed 5.0×10^6 293T cells in 75-cm^2 tissue culture flasks and culture cells overnight.
3. Transfect 10 µg of pTHTD6Ai and 2 µg of pCMV-VSV-G, using calcium phosphate precipitation.
4. Harvest viral particles from supernatant 36 to 60 h after transfection. Centrifuge the virus-containing medium at 5000*g* for 5 min, pass the supernatant through a 0.45-µm filter, and store at −80°C.
5. The titer of viral particles can be determined using a HIV-1 p24 enzyme-linked immunosorbent assay kit (Coulter Inc., Miami, FL) (*see* **Note 3**).

3.2.3. Transduction

1. Seed 0.2×10^6 of the HeLa, MCF7, or CHLA255 cells in a 60-cm^2 dish. Prepare duplicate dishes for each experiment. Culture cells overnight.
2. Transduce the cells with the VSV-G pseudotyped Cdc6 siRNA HIV vector at a multiplicity of infection (m.o.i.) of 1.0, in the presence of 4 µg/mL polybrene. Change the medium after 16 h of incubation (*see* **Note 4**).
3. Culture cells 2 d before harvesting for the preparation of cell extracts (*see* **Note 5**).
4. The Cdc6 protein is determined by Western blot, using an anti-human CDC6 monoclonal antibody (clone DCS-180; 2 µg of IgG protein per milliliter of blotting buffer; Sigma) (*see* **Note 6**).
5. Detected signal with Lumi-Light Western blotting substrate (Roche).

4. Notes

1. A 19-nt sequence is usually selected for siRNA studies. There are many software programs available to design RNAi segments, either online or from commercial companies. However, the basic principles of designing siRNAs are the same, i.e., the selected region originates at least 50- to 100-nt downstream of the translation start site to avoid regulatory proteins (uridine triphosphate-binding proteins and/or translational initiation complex), the sequence content will be roughly 50% G/C, and the sense strand should have a sequence structure of AA(N19)TT or AA(N21). The addition of two (deoxy)thymidines at the end of a RNA oligo usually makes the oligo more nuclease resistant. The selected sequences should be followed by a search of the National Center for Biotechnology Information database to ensure that only the specific gene (or region) is targeted by the designed siRNA.
2. Even if using the most sophisticated software, there is no guarantee that the designed segment will yield the expected result. We designed another anti-Cdc6 RNAi fragment, CAGGATGACCTTGAGCCAA, following the same procedure. However, the second fragment did not knock-down the Cdc6 protein. Therefore, using two or three regions of a specific gene is recommended for knock-down experiments.

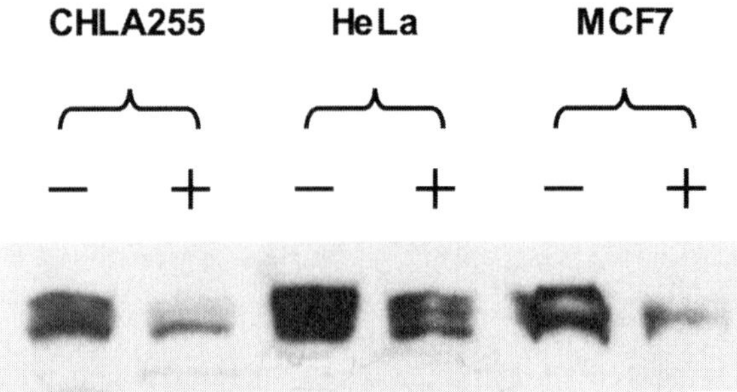

Fig. 2. Suppression of the human CDC6 protein in tested cell lines. The cancer cell lines, CHLA255, HeLa, and MCF7, are transduced with (+) and without (−) anti-Cdc6 short hairpin RNA in parallel. The nuclear extracts are isolated for the Western blot. Twenty micrograms of protein are used in each sample, separated on a 12.5% polyacrylamide-sodium dodecylsulfate gel, transferred to a polyvinylidene fluoride membrane, and probed with an anti-human CDC6 mouse monoclonal antibody.

3. The titer of viral particles can be determined by a HIV-1 p24 enzyme-linked immuno-sorbent assay kit. Usually a range of 0.2 to 1.5 µg/mL of p24 gag protein can be measured, according to our protocol. One HIV virus particle usually contains approx 20 pmoles of p24 gag protein, and 1 pg p24 is approximately equivalent to 5000 infection units. We use a m.o.i of approx 1, because a higher m.o.i may induce apoptosis of the host cells.

4. The infected cells can be selected by adding puromycin (3 µg/mL final concentration), and using a second vector containing a puromycin-resistant gene (at a 1:10 ratio), and recording the drug-resistant colonies. To determine the integration of the recombinant virus in the genome of infected cells, genomic DNA is isolated and is subjected to digesting with the appropriate restriction enzymes. The HIV-1-specific DNA can be detected via Southern blot hybridization.

5. To measure the integrated HIV-1 proviral DNA, generate a long terminal repeat (LTR)-Tag. The quantity of the LTR-Tag can be determined using [^{32}P] radioactivity. To ensure that no replication-competent virus was produced in the infected cells, collect the supernatant and incubate the supernatant with fresh cells. Determine the LTR-Tag from the genomic DNA of the fresh cells. The prepared LTR-Tag can be used in the ligation-mediated polymerase chain reaction for detecting any HIV-1 virus DNA.

6. Our Western blot shows that Cdc6 protein is significantly reduced in all tested cancer cell lines. Particularly, the upper band of Cdc6 (presumably, its phosphorylated form) is abolished in CHLA255 and MCF2 cells. Because of high levels of Cdc6 in HeLa cells, residual Cdc6 is still present in the transfected cells (**Fig. 2**).

References

1. Williams, R. S., Shohet, R. V., and Stillman, B. (1997) A human protein related to yeast Cdc6p. *Proc. Natl. Acad. Sci. USA* **94**, 142–147.
2. Prasanth, S. G., Mendez, J., Prasanth, K. V., and Stillman, B. (2004) Dynamics of pre-replication complex proteins during the cell division cycle. *Philos. Trans. R. Soc. Lond. B Biol. Sci.* **359**, 7–16.

3. Petersen, B. O., Wagener, C., Marinoni, F., et al. (2000) Cell cycle- and cell growth-regulated proteolysis of mammalian CDC6 is dependent on APC-CDH1. *Genes Devel.* **14,** 2330–2343.
4. Ohta, S., Koide, M., Tokuyama, T., Yokota, N., Nishizawa, S., and Namba, H. (2001) Cdc6 expression as a marker of proliferative activity in brain tumors. *Oncol. Rep.* **8,** 1063–1066.
5. Williams, G. H., Romanowski, P., Morris, L., et al. (1998) Improved cervical smear assessment using antibodies against proteins that regulate DNA replication. *Proc. Natl. Acad. Sci. USA* **95,** 14,932–14,937.
6. Feng, D., Tu, Z., Wu, W., and Liang, C. (2003) Inhibiting the expression of DNA replication-initiation proteins induces apoptosis in human cancer cells. *Cancer Res.* **63,** 7356–7364.
7. Gilmore, I. R., Fox, S. P., Hollins, A. J., Sohail, M., and Akhtar, S. (2004) The design and exogenous delivery of siRNA for post-transcriptional gene silencing. *J. Drug Target.* **12,** 315–340.
8. Yee, J. K., Friedmann, T., and Burns, J. C. (1994) Generation of high-titer pseudotyped retroviral vectors with very broad host range. *Methods Cell Biol.* **43(Pt A),** 99–112.
9. Yam, P. Y., Li, S., Wu, J., Hu, J., Zaia, J. A., and Yee, J. K. (2002) Design of HIV vectors for efficient gene delivery into human hematopoietic cells. *Mol. Ther.* **5,** 479–484.

22

Gene Silencing In Vitro and In Vivo
Using Intronic MicroRNAs

Shi-Lung Lin and Shao-Yao Ying

Summary

MicroRNAs (miRNAs), small single-stranded regulatory RNAs capable of interfering with intracellular messenger RNAs (mRNAs) that contain either complete or partial complementarity, are useful for the design of new therapies against cancer polymorphism and viral mutation. Numerous miRNAs have been reported to induce RNA interference (RNAi), a posttranscriptional gene-silencing mechanism. Recent evidence also indicates that they are involved in the transcriptional regulation of genome activities. They were first discovered in *Caenorhabditis elegans* as native RNA fragments that modulate a wide range of genetic regulatory pathways during embryonic development, and are now recognized as small gene silencers transcribed from the noncoding regions of a genome. In humans, nearly 97% of the genome is noncoding DNA, which varies from one individual to another, and changes in these sequences are frequently noted to manifest clinical and circumstantial malfunction. Type 2 myotonic dystrophy and fragile X syndrome were found to be associated with miRNAs derived from introns. Intronic miRNA is a new class of miRNAs derived from the processing of nonprotein-coding regions of gene transcripts. The intronic miRNAs differ uniquely from previously described intergenic miRNAs in the requirement of RNA polymerase (Pol)-II and spliceosomal components for its biogenesis. Several kinds of intronic miRNAs have been identified in *C. elegans*, mouse, and human cells; however, neither function nor application has been reported. Here, we show for the first time that intron-derived miRNA is not only able to induce RNAi in mammalian cells but also in fish, chicken embryos, and adult mice, demonstrating the evolutionary preservation of this gene regulation system in vivo. These miRNA-mediated animal models provide artificial means to reproduce the mechanisms of miRNA-induced disease in vivo and will shed further light on miRNA-related therapies.

Key Words: MicroRNA (miRNA); RNA interference (RNAi); RNA polymerase type II (Pol II); RNA splicing; intron; RNA-induced gene-silencing complex (RISC); gene silencing in vivo.

From: *Methods in Molecular Biology, vol. 342: MicroRNA Protocols*
Edited by: S. Ying © Humana Press Inc., Totowa, NJ

1. Introduction

Nearly 97% of the human genome is noncoding DNA, which varies from one species to another, and changes in these sequences are frequently noted to manifest clinical and circumstantial malfunction. Numerous nonprotein-coding genes are recently found to encode miRNAs, which are responsible for RNA-mediated gene silencing through RNAi-like pathways *(1–3)*. RNAi is a posttranscriptional gene-silencing mechanism that can be triggered by small regulatory RNA molecules, such as miRNA and small interfering RNA (siRNA). miRNAs, small single-stranded regulatory RNAs capable of interfering with intracellular mRNAs that contain either complete or partial complementarity, are useful for the design of new therapies against cancer polymorphism and viral mutation *(4,5)*. This flexible characteristic is different from double-stranded siRNAs because a much more rigid complementarity is required for siRNA-induced RNAi gene silencing. miRNAs were first discovered in *C. elegans* as native RNA fragments that modulate a wide range of genetic regulatory pathways during embryonic development *(6)*. Currently, varieties of natural miRNAs have been found to be derived from hairpin-like RNA precursors in almost all eukaryotes, including yeast (*Schizosaccharomyces pombe*), plant (*Arabidopsis spp.*), nematode (*C. elegans*), fly (*Drosophila melanogaster*), fish, mouse, and human; they have been found to involve intracellular defense against viral infections and regulation of certain gene expressions during development *(7–17)*. In contrast, natural siRNAs were abundantly discovered in plants and low-level animals (worms and flies), but rarely in mammals *(18,19)*. The intronic miRNA is a new class of miRNAs derived from the processing of gene introns. As shown in **Fig. 1**, the intronic miRNAs differ uniquely from previously described intergenic miRNAs in the requirement of Pol II and spliceosomal components for their biogenesis *(20,21)*. We have shown for the first time that these intron-derived miRNAs are able to induce RNA interference in not only human and mouse cells, but also in zebrafish, chicken embryos, and adult mice, demonstrating the evolutionary preservation of the intron-mediated gene regulation through miRNA-associated mechanisms in vertebrates in vitro and in vivo. These findings suggest an intracellular miRNA-mediated gene regulatory system, fine-tuning the degradation of protein-coding mRNAs *(22)*.

The introns occupy the largest proportion of noncoding sequences in the protein-coding DNA of a genome. The transcription of the genomic protein-coding DNA generates precursor (pre)-mRNA, which contains four major parts, including a 5'-untranslated region (UTR), a protein-coding exon, a noncoding intron, and a 3'-UTR *(23)*. In broad definition, both 5'- and 3'-UTRs can be seen as a kind of intron extension; however, their processing during mRNA translation is different from the intron located between two protein-coding exons, termed the in-frame intron. The in-frame intron can be up to several tens of kilobase nucleotides long and was thought to be a huge genetic waste in gene transcripts. Recently, this stereotype misunderstanding was changed with the discovery of intronic miRNAs. Approximately 10 to 30% of some spliced introns are found in the cytoplasm, with moderate half-lives *(24,25)*. The biogenic process of intronic miRNA presumably involves five steps (**Fig. 1**). First, miRNA is generated as a long primary precursor miRNA (pri-miRNA) encoded within a gene transcript (pre-mRNA) by Pol II *(20,26)*. Second, the pre-mRNA is excised by spliceosomal components and/or

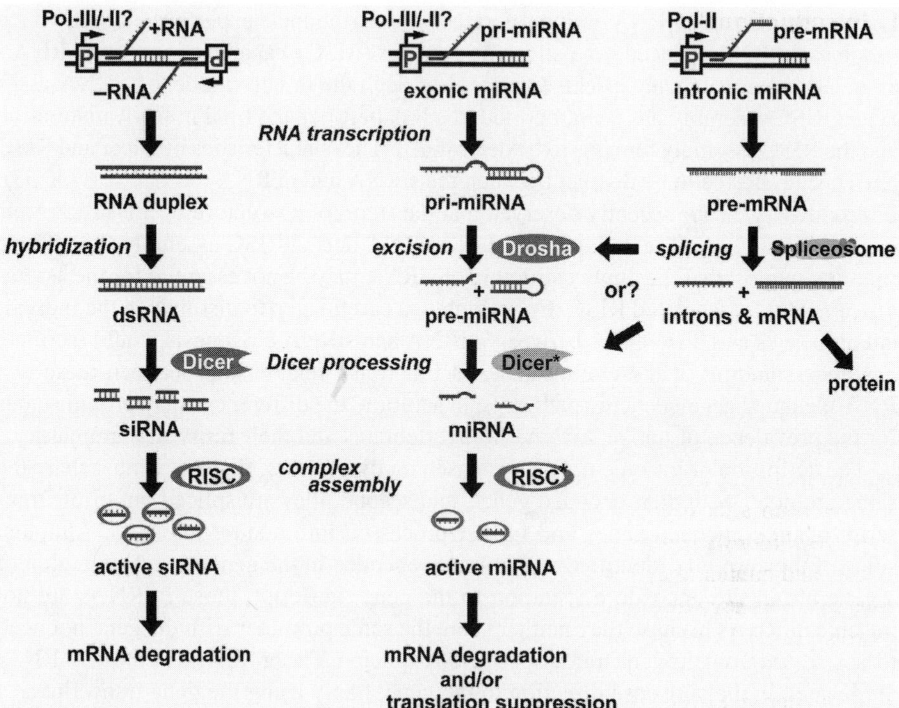

Fig. 1. Comparison of biogenesis and RNA interference (RNAi) mechanisms among small interfering RNA (siRNA), intergenic (exonic) microRNA (miRNA) and intronic miRNA. siRNA is likely formed by two perfectly complementary RNAs transcribed from two different promoters (remains to be determined) and further processing into 19- to 22-bp duplexes by the ribonuclease (RNase) III familial endonuclease, Dicer. The biogenesis of intergenic miRNAs, e.g., *lin*-4 and *let*-7, involves a long transcript primary precursor (pri-miRNA), which is probably generated by RNA polymerase (Pol) II or III RNA promoters, whereas intronic miRNAs are transcribed by the Pol II promoters of its encoded genes and coexpressed in the intron regions of the gene transcripts (pre-messenger RNA [mRNA]). After RNA splicing and further processing, the spliced intron may function as a pri-miRNA for intronic miRNA generation. In the nucleus, the pri-miRNA is excised by Drosha RNase to form a hairpin-like pre-miRNA template and then exported to the cytoplasm for further processing by Dicer* to form mature miRNAs. The Dicers for siRNA and miRNA pathways are different. All three small regulatory RNAs are finally incorporated into a RNA-induced-silencing complex, which contains either strand of siRNA or the single-strand of miRNA. The effect of miRNA is considered more specific and less adverse than that of siRNA because only one strand is involved. However, siRNAs primarily trigger mRNA degradation, whereas miRNAs can induce either mRNA degradation or suppression of protein synthesis depending on the sequence complementarity to the target gene transcripts.

Drosha-like ribonuclease (RNase) III endonucleases to release hairpin-like intronic structures and form pre-miRNA *(20,27)*. Third, the pre-miRNA is exported out of the nucleus, probably by Ran–guanosine triphosphate and a receptor Exportin-5 *(28,29)*. In the cytoplasm, Dicer-like nucleases cleave the pre-miRNA to form mature miRNA.

Lastly, the mature miRNA is incorporated into a ribonuclear particle (RNP), which becomes the RNA-induced gene-silencing complex (RISC), capable of executing RNAi-associated gene-silencing effects *(30,31)*. Although the in vitro model of siRNA-associated RISC assembly has been reported, the link between the final miRNA maturation and the RISC assembly remains to be determined. The characteristics of Dicer and RISC have been reported to be distinct between the siRNA and miRNA mechanisms *(32,33)*. In zebrafish, we have recently observed that the stem-loop structure of pre-miRNAs is involved in the strand selection for mature miRNA during RISC assembly *(21)*. These findings suggest that the duplex structure of siRNA may be not essential for the assembly of miRNA-associated RISC. Conceivably, a careful step to distinguish the individual properties and differences between miRNA and siRNA biogenesis would facilitate our understanding of the evolutional and functional relationship between these two RNA-mediated gene-silencing pathways. In addition, the differences may provide clues for the prevalence of native siRNAs in invertebrates and their rarity in mammals.

The definition of intronic miRNA is based on two factors; first, they must share the same promoter with their encoded genes, and second, they are spliced out of the transcript of their encoded genes and further processed into mature miRNAs. Although some of the currently identified miRNAs are encoded in the genomic intron region of a gene but in the opposite orientation to the gene transcript, those miRNAs are not intronic miRNAs because they neither share the same promoter with the gene nor need to be released from the gene transcript by RNA splicing. The promoters of those miRNAs are located in the antisense direction to the gene, likely using the gene transcript as a potential target for the antisense miRNAs. For example, *let-7c* was found to be an intergenic miRNA located in the antisense region of a gene intron.

To date, more than 90 intronic miRNAs have been identified using bioinformatic approaches *(34,35)*, but the functions of the vast majority of these intronic molecules remain to be determined. According to the strictly expressive correlation of intronic miRNAs to their encoded genes, one may speculate that the levels of condition-specific, time-specific, and individual-specific gene expressions are determined by interactions of different miRNAs on single or multiple genes. This interpretation accounts for a more accurate genetic expression of various traits, and any dysregulation of the interactions, thus, will result in genetic diseases. For instance, monozygotic twins frequently demonstrate slightly, but definitely distinguishing, disease susceptibility and physiological behaviors. For instance, a long CCTG expansion in intron 1 of the zinc finger protein-9 gene has been correlated to type 2 myotonic dystrophy in one twin with a higher susceptibility *(36)*. Although the expansion motif confers high affinity to certain RNA-binding proteins, the interfering role of intron-derived expansion fragments remains to be elucidated. Another more-established example, involving intronic expansion fragments in its pathogenesis, is fragile X syndrome, which represents approx 30% of human inherited mental retardation. An intronic CGG repeat (rCGG) expansion in the 5'-UTR of the *FMR1* gene is the causative mutation in 99% of individuals with fragile X syndrome *(37)*. *FMR1* encodes an RNA-binding protein, fragile X mental retardation protein, which is associated with polyribosome assembly in an RNP-dependent manner, and is capable of suppressing translation through an RNAi-like pathway. Fragile

X mental retardation protein also contains a nuclear localization signal and a nuclear export signal for shuttling certain mRNAs between the nucleus and cytoplasm *(38)*. Jin et al. proposed an RNAi-mediated methylation model in the CpG region of the *FMR1* rCGG expansion, which is targeted by a hairpin RNA derived from the 3'-UTR of the *FMR1* expanded allele transcript *(37)*. The Dicer-processed hairpin RNA triggers the formation of RNA-induced initiator of transcriptional gene silencing on the homologous rCGG sequences and leads to heterochromatin repression of the *FMR1* locus. These examples suggest that natural evolution gives rise to more complexity and more variety of introns in higher animals and plants for coordinating their vast gene expression volumes and interactions; therefore, any dysregulation of miRNAs derived from introns may lead to genetic diseases involving intronic expansion or deletion, such as myotonic dystrophy and fragile X mental retardation.

To understand diseases caused by dysregulation of intronic miRNAs, an artificial expression system is needed to recreate the function and mechanism of the miRNA in vitro and in vivo. The same approach may be used to design and develop therapies for the disease. Using artificial introns carrying hairpin-like pre-miRNA, we successfully generated mature miRNA molecules with a full capacity to trigger RNAi-like gene silencing in human prostate cancer (LNCaP), human cervical cancer (HeLa), and rat neuronal stem (HCN-A94-2) cells *(20,39)*. The artificial intron of **Fig. 2A** was located in a mutated HcRed1 red fluorescent membrane protein (*rGFP*) gene to form a recombined *SpRNAi–rGFP* gene, in which the functional fluorescent structure was disrupted by the splicing-competent RNA intron (SpRNAi) insertion. Thus, we were able to determine the occurrence of intron splicing and rGFP–mRNA maturation through the appearance of red fluorescent emission on the membranes of transfected cells. There is no homology or complementarity between the *SpRNAi–rGFP* gene and its expression vectors. After transfection of *SpRNAi–rGFP* genes containing synthetic inserts homologous to a targeted gene exon, we found that a hairpin insert comprising both sense and antisense exon strands resulted in maximal effects of gene silencing. As shown in **Fig. 2**, the transfection of various *SpRNAi–rGFP* genes targeting the nucleotides 279 to 303 open-reading frame region of the enhanced *Aequorea victoria* green fluorescent protein (eGFP) was found to be highly significant ($n = 4$; $p < 0.01$) in silencing eGFP protein expression. The use of eGFP-positive HCN-A94-2 rat neuronal stem cells offered an excellent visual aid to observe the decreased green fluorescent emission of eGFP in the red fluorescent rGFP reporter gene-expressing cells. Silencing of eGFP was detected 42 to 48 h after transfection, indicating a potential requirement for precise timing of the production of sufficient small interfering intron inserts from the *SpRNAi–rGFP* gene. Quantitative knock-down levels of eGFP protein were significantly altered (**Fig. 2B**), and there were modest reduction rates of $56 \pm 6\%$ for the transfection of inserts homologous to the sense strand of the eGFP target, of $50 \pm 4\%$ for the antisense strand of the GFP target, and a significant rate of $81 \pm 2\%$ for the hairpin inserts containing both strands of the eGFP target. No knockdown specificity to eGFP was detected by the transfection of intron-free *rGFP* gene, or for the *SpRNAi–rGFP* gene containing hairpin inserts homologous to either integrin-β1 exon 1 or to the human immunodeficiency virus (HIV)-1 *gag*-p24 gene. The Western blot results shown in **Fig. 2C** confirmed the knock-

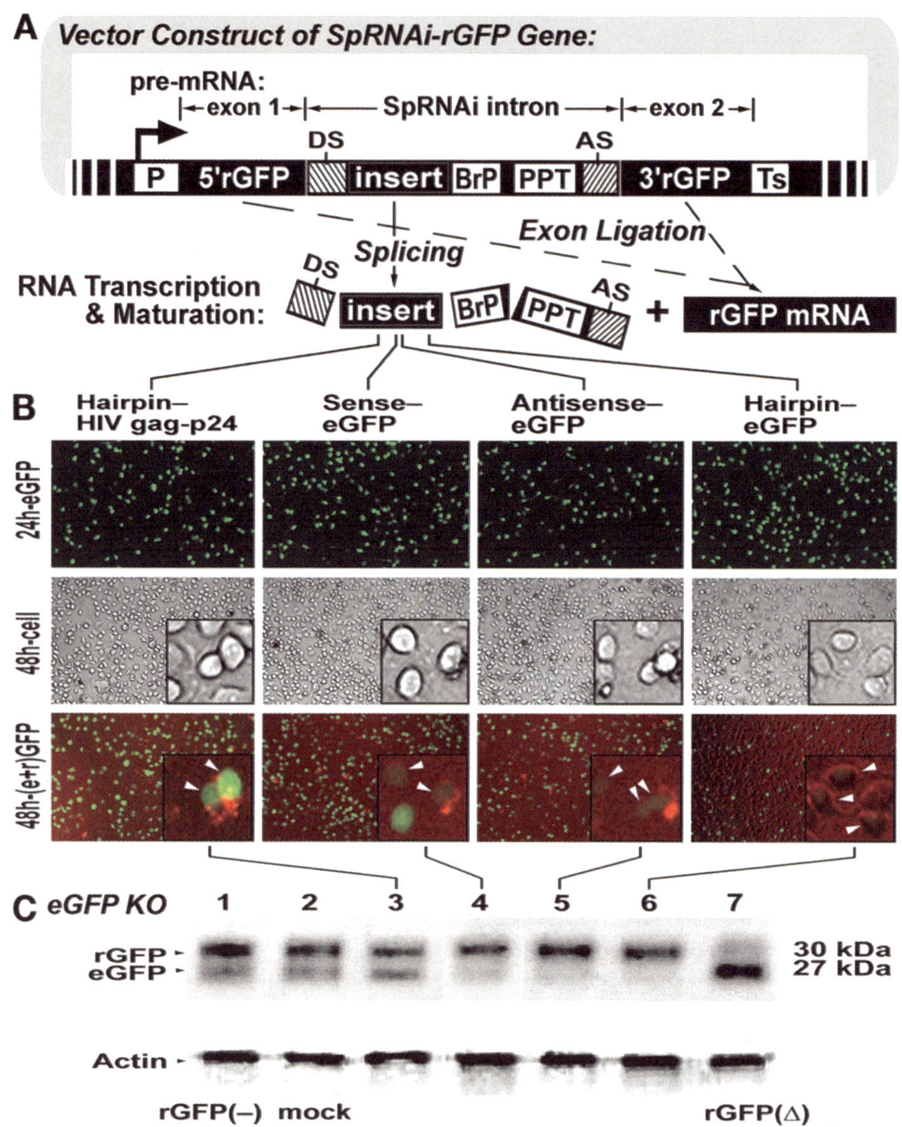

Fig. 2. Strategy for analysis of intronic microRNA (miRNA) mechanisms using artificial *SpRNAi–rGFP* gene vectors. (**A**) The *SpRNAi–rGFP* gene consists of a 5'-RNA promoter (P), an artificial intron (SpRNAi) flanked with two red fluorescent proteins (rGFP) exon fragments, and a 3'-proximity of transcription and translation termination codons (Ts). The construct of SpRNAi includes a 5'-splice donor site (DS), a 3'-splice acceptor site (AS), a poly-pyrimidine tract (PPT), a branch-point domain (BrP) and an inserted pre-miRNA oligonucleotide (insert) in the 5'-proximity of SpRNAi between the DS and BrP sites. During messenger RNA (mRNA) maturation, the SpRNAi is spliced out of the *SpRNAi–rGFP* pre-mRNA and further processed into miRNAs for gene silencing, whereas the mature rGFP mRNA is translated into rGFP for

down specificity observed and demonstrated that such a gene-silencing effect is determined by the hairpin structures of the pre-miRNA inserts.

The intron-derived miRNA system is able to be activated in a specific cell type under the control of a Pol II-directed transcriptional machinery. Our research group was the first to discover the biogenesis of miRNA-like precursors from the 5′-proximal intron regions of gene transcripts (pre-mRNAs) produced by the mammalian Pol II. Depending on the promoter of the miRNA-encoded gene transcript, intronic miRNA is coexpressed with its encoding gene in the specific cell population, which activates the promoter and expresses the gene. This type of miRNA generation relies on the coupled interaction of nascent Pol II-mediated pre-mRNA transcription and intron excision, occurring within certain nuclear regions proximal to genomic perichromatin fibrils *(4,20, 40,41)*. After Pol II RNA processing and splicing excision, some of the intron-derived miRNA fragments can form mature miRNAs and effectively silence the target genes through the RNAi mechanism, whereas the exons of pre-mRNA are ligated together to form a mature mRNA for protein synthesis *(4,20)*. Because miRNAs are single-stranded molecules insensitive to double-stranded RNA-dependent protein kinase (PKR)- and 2′,5′-oligoadenylate synthetase (2-5A)-induced interferon systems, the use of this Pol II-mediated miRNA generation can be safe in vitro and in vivo, preventing the cytotoxic effects of double-stranded RNAs (dsRNAs) and siRNAs. Interferon-induced protein kinase PKR can trigger cell apoptosis, whereas activation of the interferon-induced 2-5A system leads to extensive cleavage of single-stranded RNAs (i.e., mRNAs) *(42, 43)*. Although both the PKR and the 2-5A systems contain dsRNA-binding motifs that are highly conserved for binding to dsRNAs, these motifs do not bind to either single-stranded RNAs or RNA–DNA hybrids. These findings indicate a new function for mammalian introns in intracellular miRNA generation and gene regulation, which can be used as a tool for analysis of gene functions, improvement of current RNAi technology, and development of gene-specific therapeutics against cancers and viral infections.

The components of the Pol II-mediated SpRNAi system include several consensus nucleotide elements, consisting of a 5′-splice site, a branch-point domain, a poly-pyrimidine tract, and a 3′-splice site (**Fig. 2A**). Additionally, a pre-miRNA insert sequence

---

Fig. 2. *(Continued)* target identification. (**B**) Simultaneous expression of rGFP and silencing of *Aequorea victoria* green fluorescent protein (eGFP) by various *SpRNAi–rGFP* transfections. At 24 h after transfection, approximate total cell numbers and eGFP-positive cell populations were observed with very few apoptotic or differentiated cells, whereas no detectable silencing of eGFP occurred. The RNA interference (RNAi) effect was detected 42 h after transfection, showing that the gene knock-down potency of the *SpRNAi–rGFP* genes containing inserts homologous to hairpin-eGFP were much greater than the sense-eGFP, which was approximately equal to the antisense-eGFP, which was much greater than the hairpin-human immunodeficiency virus (HIV) p24 (negative controls). (**C**) Western blot analyses confirmed the knock-down potency of (B). The lanes from left to right indicate the *SpRNAi–rGFP* transfection with genes containing various inserts homologous to the open-reading frame of eGFP, namely: 1, rGFP(–) (blank controls); 2, hairpin-integrin-β1 exon 1 (negative controls); 3, hairpin-HIV *gag*-p24; 4, sense-eGFP; 5, antisense-eGFP; 6, hairpin-eGFP; and 7, rGFPΔ (DS-defective controls).

is placed within the artificial intron between the 5'-splice site and the branch-point domain. This portion of the intron would normally form a lariat structure during RNA splicing and processing. We currently know that spliceosomal U2 and U6 small nuclear RNPs, both helicases, may be involved in the unwinding and excision of the lariat RNA fragment into pre-miRNA; however, the detailed processing remains to be elucidated. Further, the SpRNAi contains translation stop codon domains in its 3'-proximal region to facilitate the accuracy of RNA splicing, which, if present in a cytoplasmic mRNA, would signal the diversion of a splicing-defective pre-mRNA to the nonsense-mediated decay pathway and, thus, cause the elimination of any unspliced pre-mRNA in the cell. For intracellular expression of the SpRNAi, we need to insert the SpRNAi construct into the DraII cleavage site of a *rGFP* gene from mutated chromoproteins of coral reef *Heteractis crispa*. The cleavage of *rGFP* at its 208th nucleotide site by the restriction enzyme, DraII, generates an AG–GN nucleotide break, with three recessing nucleotides in each end, which forms 5' and 3' splice sites, respectively, after the SpRNAi insertion. Because this intronic insertion disrupts the expression of functional *rGFP*, it becomes possible to determine the occurrence of intron splicing and *rGFP*–mRNA maturation via the appearance of red fluorescent emission around the membrane surface of the transfected cells. The *rGFP* also provides multiple exonic splicing enhancers to increase RNA-splicing efficiency.

To test the requirement of a siRNA-like duplex construct in miRNA-associated RISC (miRISC) assembly, the pre-miRNAs were designed to contain perfectly matched stem arm domains. Although most of the native pre-miRNAs contain a mismatched area in their stem arms, it is not necessary for us to construct an imperfectly paired stem arm to trigger RNAi-related gene silencing. Previous studies have demonstrated that a mature miRNA can be generated by placing a perfectly matched siRNA duplex in the miR-30 pre-miRNA structure *(27,44)*. Further, there are many genes not subjected to the regulation of native miRNAs, in particular, *eGFP*, which can be otherwise silenced by intracellular transfection of a pre-miRNA containing a perfectly matched stem arm construct. Therefore, we define a mature miRNA based on its biogenetic function and mechanism, rather than the structural complementarity of its precursor. In this view, any small hairpin RNA can be a pre-miRNA, if a mature miRNA is successfully processed from the small hairpin RNA and further assembled into miRISC for target gene silencing.

This designed miRNA system has been tested in zebrafish in vivo. The foregoing establishes the fact that intronic miRNAs can be used as an effective strategy to silence specific target genes in vivo. We first tried to resolve the structural design of pre-miRNA inserts for the best gene-silencing effect and found that a strong structural bias exists in the selection of a mature miRNA strand during assembly of the RNAi effector, RISC. RISC is a protein–RNA complex that directs either target gene transcript degradation or translational repression through the RNAi mechanism. Formation of siRNA duplexes has been reported to play a key role in assembly of the siRNA-associated RISC. The two strands of the siRNA duplex are functionally asymmetric, but assembly into the RISC complex is preferential for only one strand. Such preference is determined by the thermodynamic stability of each 5'-end base pairing in the strand. Based on this siRNA model, the formation of miRNA and its complementary miRNA (miRNA*) duplexes was thought to be an essential step for the assembly of miRISC. If this were true, no functional bias would be observed in the stem-loop of a pre-miRNA. Nevertheless, we observed that the stem-loop of the intronic pre-miRNA was involved in the strand selection of a mature miRNA for RISC assembly in zebrafish. In these experiments, we constructed miRNA-expressing *SpRNAi–rGFP* vectors, as previously described *(4, 20)*; and two symmetric pre-miRNAs, miRNA–stem-loop–miRNA* (❶) and miRNA* –stem-loop–miRNA (❷), were synthesized and inserted into the vectors, respectively. Both pre-miRNAs contained the same double-stranded stem arm region, which was directed against the *eGFP* nucleotide 280 to 302 sequence. Because the intronic insert region of the *SpRNAi–rGFP* recombined gene is flanked with a PvuI and an MluI restriction site at the 5'- and 3'-ends, respectively, the primary insert can be easily removed and replaced by various gene-specific inserts (e.g., anti-*eGFP*) possessing cohesive ends. By changing the pre-miRNA inserts directed against different gene transcripts, this intronic miRNA generation system provides a valuable tool for genetic and miRNA-associated research in vivo.

To determine the structural preference of the designed pre-miRNAs, we isolated the zebrafish small RNAs by mirVana® miRNA isolation columns (Ambion, Austin, TX) and precipitated all potential miRNAs complementary to the target *eGFP* region by latex beads containing the target RNA sequence. One effective miRNA identity, miR-eGFP (280/302), was verified in the transfections of the 5'-miRNA–stem-loop–miRNA*-3' construct, as shown in **Fig. 3A** (gray-shading sequences). Because the effective mature miRNA was detected only in the zebrafish transfected by the 5'-miRNA–stem-loop–miRNA*-3' construct, the miRISC seems to preferably interact with the ❷ construct rather than the ❶ pre-miRNA. The *eGFP* expression was constitutively driven by the β-actin promoter located in almost all cell types of the zebrafish, whereas **Fig. 3B** shows that transfection of the *SpRNAi–rGFP* vector into the transgenic (*UAS:gfp*) zebrafish coexpressed *rGFP*, serving as a positive indicator for the miRNA generation in the transfected cells. This approach has been successfully used in several mouse and human cell lines to demonstrate RNAi effects *(20,39)*. We applied the liposome-capsulated vector (total 60 μg) to the fish and found that the vector easily penetrated almost all tissues of the 2-wk-old zebrafish larvae within 24 h, achieving fully systemic delivery of the miRNA effect. The indicator rGFP was detected in both of the fish transfected by either 5'-miRNA*–stem-loop–miRNA-3' or 5'-miRNA–stem-loop–miRNA*-3' pre-miRNA, whereas the silencing of target *eGFP* expression (green) was observed only in the fish transfected by the 5'-miRNA–stem-loop–miRNA*-3' pre-miRNA (**Fig. 3B, C**). The suppression level in the gastrointestinal tract was found to be less effective, probably because of the high RNase activity in this region. Because switching the stem-loop position has changed the 5'-end thermostability of the siRNA-like stem arm, resulting in different miRNA maturation patterns, we suggest that the stem-loop of a pre-miRNA may be involved in Dicer recognition and strand selection of a mature miRNA for effective RISC assembly and the resultant gene silencing. Given that the cleavage site of Dicer in the stem arm determines the strand selection of mature miRNA *(27)*, the stem-loop may function as a determinant for the recognition of a special cleavage

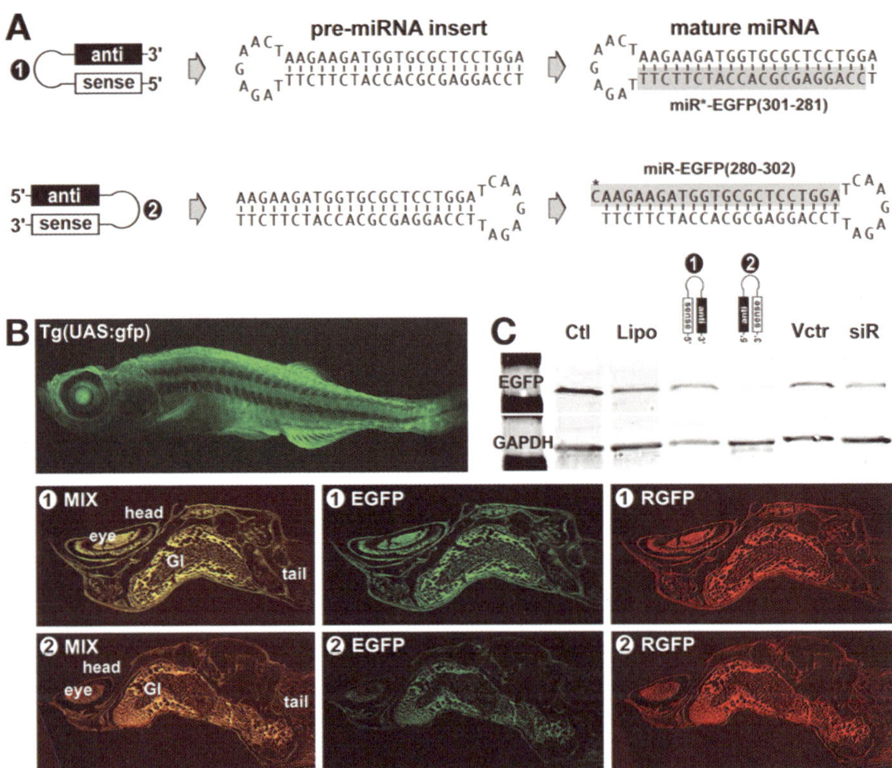

Fig. 3. Structural preference of microRNA (miRNA)–miRNA* asymmetry in miRNA-induced gene-silencing complex (RISC) in vivo. Different preferences of RISC assembly were observed by transfection of 5'-miRNA*–stem loop–miRNA-3' (❶) and 5'-miRNA–stem loop–miRNA*-3' (❷) pre-miRNA constructs in zebrafish, respectively. (**A**) Based on the RISC assembly rule of small interfering RNA (siRNA), the processing of both ❶ and ❷ should result in the same siRNA duplex for RISC assembly; however, the experiments demonstrate that only the ❷ construct was used in RISC assembly for silencing target EGFP. Because the miRNA is predicted to be complementary to its target messenger RNA, the "antisense" (black bar) refers to the miRNA and the "sense" (white bar) refers to its complementarity, miRNA*. One mature miRNA, namely miR-*Aequorea victoria* green fluorescent protein (eGFP)-(280/302), was detected in the ❷-transfected zebrafish, whereas the ❶ transfection produced another kind of miRNA, miR*-EGFP(301/281), which was partially complementary to the miR-eGFP(280/302). (**B**) In vivo gene-silencing efficacy was only observed in the transfection of the ❷ pre-miRNA construct, but not the ❶ construct. Because the color combination of eGFP and rGFP displayed more red than green (as shown in deep orange), the expression level of the target eGFP (green) was significantly reduced in ❷, whereas the miRNA indicator RGFP (red) was evenly present in all vector transfections. (**C**) Western blot analysis of the eGFP protein levels confirmed the specific silencing result seen in (**B**). No detectable gene silencing was observed in fish without (Ctl) and with liposome-only (Lipo) treatments. The transfection of either a U6-driven siRNA vector (siR) or an empty vector (Vctr) without the designed pre-miRNA insert resulted in no gene silencing significance.

site. Therefore, different from the dual open-ends of siRNA, a hairpin-like pre-miRNA has the advantage of using its stem-loop structure to control the asymmetry of the miRNA maturation for more-efficient RISC assembly.

The consistent evidence of miRNA-induced gene-silencing effects in mammalian cell lines and zebrafish demonstrates the preservation of an ancient intron-mediated gene regulation system in eukaryotes. In these in vitro and in vivo models, the intron-derived miRNAs determine the activation of RNAi-associated gene-silencing pathways. We herein provide the first evidence for the biogenesis and function of intronic miRNAs, both in vitro and in vivo. Given that natural evolution gives rise to more complexity and more variety of introns in higher animal and plant species for coordinating their vast gene expression volumes and interactions, dysregulation of these miRNAs because of intronic expansion or deletion will likely cause genetic diseases, such as myotonic dystrophy and fragile X mental retardation. Thus, gene expression produces not only a gene transcript for its own protein synthesis but also intronic miRNAs, capable of interfering with the expression of other genes. Based on this concept, the expression of a gene results in the gain of function of the gene and loss of function of other genes that contain complementarity to the mature intronic miRNAs. An array of genes can swiftly and accurately coordinate their expression patterns with each other through the mediation of their intronic miRNAs, bypassing the time-consuming translation processes under quickly changing environments. Conceivably, intron-mediated gene regulation may be as important as the mechanisms by which transcription factors regulate the gene expression. It is likely that intronic miRNA is able to trigger cell transitions quickly in response to external stimuli without tedious protein synthesis. Undesired gene products are reduced by both transcriptional inhibition and/or translational suppression via miRNA regulation. This could enable a rapid switch to a new gene expression pattern without the need to produce various transcription factors. This regulatory property of miRNAs may serve as one of the most ancient gene modulation systems before the emergence of proteins. According to the variety of miRNAs and the complexity of genomic introns, a thorough investigation of miRNA variants in the human genome will markedly improve the understanding of genetic diseases and improve the design of miRNA-based drugs. Learning how to exploit such a novel gene regulation system for future therapies will be a forthcoming challenge.

2. Materials

2.1. Synthetic Oligonucleotides Used for SpRNAi–rGFP Gene Construction

1. Sense SpRNAi sequence: 5'-dephosphorylated GTAAGTGGTC CGATCGTCGC GACG CGTCAT TACTAACACTAT CATACTTATC CTGTCCCTTT TTTTTCCACA GCTAG GACCT TCGTGCA-3' (100 pmol/μL in autoclaved ddH$_2$O).
2. Antisense SpRNAi sequence: 5'-phosphorylated TGCACGAAGG TCCTAGCTGT GGA AAAAAAA GGGACAGGAT AAGTATGATA GTTAGTAATG ACGCGTCGCG ACG ATCGGAC CACTTAC-3' (100 pmol/μL in autoclaved ddH$_2$O).
3. 2X Hybridization buffer: 200 mM KOAc, 60 mM HEPES-KOH, 4 mM MgOAc, pH 7.4 at 25°C.

4. 0.5 µg/µL pHcRed1-N1/1 plasmid vector (BD Biosciences, Palo Alto, CA).
5. Incubation chambers at 94°C, 65°C, and 4°C.

2.2. Restriction Enzyme Digestion and Sequential Ligation With Cohesive Ends

1. 10X L buffer: 100 m*M* Tris-HCl, pH 7.5 at 37°C, 100 m*M* MgCl$_2$, and 10 m*M* dithiothreitol (DTT).
2. Restriction enzymes, including DraII, BfrI, NheI, and BsmI.
3. DraII digestion reaction mix: 14 µL autoclaved ddH$_2$O, 4 µL of 10X L buffer, and 2 µL DraII; prepare the reaction mix just before use.
4. DraII/BfrI digestion reaction mix: 2 µL autoclaved ddH$_2$O, 4 µL of 10X L buffer, 2 µL DraII, and 2 µL BfrI; prepare the reaction mix just before use.
5. 10X Ligation buffer: 660 m*M* Tris-HCl, pH 7.5 at 20°C, 50 m*M* MgCl$_2$, 50 m*M* DTT, and 10 m*M* adenosine triphosphate (ATP).
6. 5 U/µL T4 DNA ligase.
7. Ligation reaction mix: 4 µL autoclaved ddH$_2$O, 4 µL of 10X ligation buffer, and 2 µL T4 ligase; prepare the reaction mix just before use.
8. 10X M buffer: 100 m*M* Tris-HCl, pH 7.5 at 37°C, 500 m*M* NaCl, 100 m*M* MgCl$_2$, and 10 m*M* DTT.
9. NheI digestion reaxtion mix: 4 µL autoclaved ddH$_2$O, 4 µL of 10X M buffer, and 2 µL NheI; prepare the reaction mix just before use.
10. 10X H buffer: 500 m*M* Tris-HCl, pH 7.5 at 37°C, 1 *M* NaCl, 100 m*M* MgCl$_2$, and 10 m*M* DTT.
11. BsmI digestion reaction mix: 4 µL autoclaved ddH$_2$O, 4 µL of 10X H buffer and 2 µL BsmI; prepare the reaction mix just before use.
12. 10 U/µL T4 polynucleotide kinase.
13. Ligation/phosphorylation reaction mix: 2 µL autoclaved ddH$_2$O, 4 µL of 10X ligation buffer, 2 µL T4 ligase, and 2 µL T4 polynucleotide kinase; prepare the reaction mix just before use.
14. Incubation chambers at 65°C, 37°C, 16°C, and 4°C.
15. 1% agarose gel electrophoresis.
16. Gel extraction kit (Qiagen, Valencia, CA).
17. Microcentrifuge: 17,900*g*.

2.3. Cloning of the SpRNAi–rGFP Gene Construct

1. 10X H buffer: 500 m*M* Tris-HCl, pH 7.5 at 37°C, 1 *M* NaCl, 100 m*M* MgCl$_2$, and 10 m*M* DTT.
2. Restriction enzymes, including XhoI and XbaI.
3. XhoI/XbaI digestion reaction mix: 2 µL autoclaved ddH$_2$O, 4 µL of 10X H buffer, 2 µL XhoI, and 2 µL XbaI; prepare the reaction mix just before use.
4. 10X Ligation buffer: 660 m*M* Tris-HCl, pH 7.5 at 20°C, 50 m*M* MgCl$_2$, 50 m*M* DTT, and 10 m*M* ATP.
5. 5 U/µL T4 DNA ligase.
6. Ligation reaction mix: 4 µL autoclaved ddH$_2$O, 4 µL of 10X ligation buffer, and 2 µL T4 ligase; prepare the reaction mix just before use.
7. Low salt Luria-Bertani culture broth.
8. Expand cloning kit (Roche Diagnostics, Indianapolis, IN).

9. DH5α transformation-competent *E. coli* cells (Roche).
10. 10X MgSO$_4$ solution: 1 *M* MgSO$_4$.
11. 1X CaCl$_2$ solution: 0.1 *M* CaCl$_2$.
12. 10X Glucose solution: 1 *M* glucose.
13. Incubation shaker: 37°C; 285 rpm vortex.
14. Incubation chambers: 37°C, 16°C, and 4°C.
15. Luria-Bertani agar plate containing 50 mg/mL kanamycin.
16. Spin Miniprep kit (Qiagen).
17. Microcentrifuge: 17,900*g*.

2.4. Insertion of Pre-miRNA Into the SpRNAi–rGFP *Gene Construct*

1. Sense pre-miRNA sequence: 5'-GTCCGATCGT CAAGAAGATG GTGCGCTCCT GGA TCAAGAG ATTCCAGGAG CGCACCATCT TCTTCGACGC GTCAT-3' (100 pmol/μL in autoclaved ddH$_2$O).
2. Antisense pre-miRNA sequence: 5'-ATGACGCGTC GAAGAAGATG GTGCGCTCCT GGAATCTCTT GATCCAGGAG CGCACCATCT TCTTGACGAT CGGAC-3' (100 pmol/ μL in autoclaved ddH$_2$O).
3. 2X Hybridization buffer: 200 m*M* KOAc, 60 m*M* HEPES-KOH, and 4 m*M* MgOAc, pH 7.4 at 25°C.
4. 10X H buffer: 500 m*M* Tris-HCl, pH 7.5 at 37°C, 1 *M* NaCl, 100 m*M* MgCl$_2$, and 10 m*M* DTT.
5. Restriction enzymes, including PuvI and MluI.
6. PuvI/MluI digestion reaction mix: 2 μL autoclaved ddH$_2$O, 4 μL of 10X H buffer, 2 μL PuvI, and 2 μL MluI; prepare the reaction mix just before use.
7. 10X Ligation buffer: 660 m*M* Tris-HCl, pH 7.5 at 20°C, 50 m*M* MgCl$_2$, 50 m*M* DTT, and 10 m*M* ATP.
8. 5 U/μL T4 DNA ligase.
9. Ligation reaction mix: 4 μL autoclaved ddH$_2$O, 4 μL of 10X ligation buffer, and 2 μL T4 ligase; prepare the reaction mix just before use.
10. Incubation chambers: 65°C, 37°C, and 16°C.
11. 1% agarose gel electrophoresis.
12. Gel extraction kit (Qiagen).
13. Microcentrifuge: 17,900*g*.

2.5. Liposomal Transfection of the SpRNAi–rGFP *Gene Construct*

1. RPMI-1640 cell culture medium, serum-free.
2. FuGENE transfection reagent (Roche).
3. Cell culture incubator.

3. Methods

3.1. Synthetic Oligonucleotides Used for SpRNAi–rGFP *Gene Construction*

The SpRNAi artificial intron is formed by hybridization of the sense and antisense SpRNAi sequences, which are synthesized to be perfectly complementary to each other. Both of the SpRNAi sequences must be purified by polyacrylamide gel electrophoresis (PAGE) before use and stored at −20°C.

1. Hybridization: mix the sense and antisense SpRNAi sequences (5 µL for each sequence) in 10 µL of 2X hybridization buffer, heat to 94°C for 3 min, and cool to 65°C for 10 min. Stop the reaction on ice.

3.2. Restriction Enzyme Digestion and Sequential Ligation With Cohesive Ends

Two *rGFP* exons are provided by DraII cleavage of the pHcRed1-N1/1 plasmid vector between the 881st and 882nd nucleotide site, forming an AG–GN nucleotide break with 5'-G(T/A)C protruding nucleotides in the cleaved ends. The 5'-GTC protruding nucleotides need to be removed from the end of the first exon for blunt-end ligation, whereas the 5'-GAC protruding end of the second exon is used to ligate with the 3'-DraII-restricted end of the SpRNAi intron. After the ligation of the SpRNAi intron and the second *rGFP* exon, add the first *rGFP* exon to the 5' end of the ligated sequence by blunt-end ligation, so as to form a complete *SpRNAi–rGFP* gene cassette (*see* **Note 1**).

1. DraII cleavage: add the DraII digestion reaction mix to the SpRNAi hybrid. Add the DraII/BfrI digestion reaction mix to 30 µL of the pHcRed1-N1/1 plasmid vector. Incubate both of the reactions at 37°C for 4 h and stop the reaction on ice.
2. Purification of the DraII- and DraII/BfrI-digested sequences: load and run the above reactions from **step 1** in 1% agarose gel electrophoresis and cut out of the DraII-digested SpRNAi hybrid sequence and two other oligonucleotide fragments (one 1760 bp and another 715 bp), which are derived from the DraII/BfrI-cleaved pHcRed1-N1/1 plasmid vector. Separately recover these three oligonucleotide sequences into different tubes in 30 µL autoclaved ddH$_2$O, using the gel extraction columns and following the manufacturer's suggestions. Store the 1760-bp pHcRed1-N1/1 fragment at 4°C for 2 wk before use (*see* **Note 2**).
3. Ligation: mix 15 µL of the DraII-digested SpRNAi hybrid sequence with 15 µL of the 715 bp pHcRed1-N1/1 fragment and add the ligation reaction mix. Incubate the reaction at 16°C for 16 h and stop the reaction on ice.
4. Purification of the ligation product: load and run the ligation in 1% agarose gel electrophoresis and cut out the ligated sequence (~800 bp) using a clean surgical blade. Recover the sequence in one tube of 30 µL autoclaved ddH$_2$O, using the gel extraction column and following the manufacturer's suggestions.
5. Cleavage by NheI and BsmI: add the BsmI digestion reaction mix to the ligation product. Add the NheI digestion reaction mix to the 1760-bp pHcRed1-N1/1 fragment. Incubate both of the reactions at 37°C for 4 h and stop the reaction on ice.
6. Purification of the NheI and BsmI-digested sequences: load and run the reactions in 1% agarose gel electrophoresis and cut out the NheI- and BsmI-digested sequences, respectively, using a clean surgical blade. Recover the two oligonucleotide sequences in one tube of 30 µL autoclaved ddH$_2$O, using the gel extraction columns and following manufacturer's suggestions.
7. Ligation: add the ligation/phosphorylation reaction mix to the extraction. Incubate the reaction at 16°C for 16 h and stop the reaction on ice.
8. Purification of the ligation product: load and run the ligation in 1% agarose gel electrophoresis and cut out the ligated sequences using a clean surgical blade. Recover the sequence in one tube of 30 µL autoclaved ddH$_2$O, using the gel extraction column and following the manufacturer's suggestions. The final ligation product forms the *SpRNAi–rGFP* gene cassette (*see* **Note 1**).

3.3. *Cloning of the* **SpRNAi–rGFP** *Gene Construct*

To express the *SpRNAi–rGFP* gene in transfected cells, clone the *SpRNAi–rGFP* gene cassette into the pHcRed1-N1/1 plasmid vector, replacing the original HcRed protein sequence. Because the functional fluorescent structure of HcRed is disrupted by the SpRNAi intron insertion, one can determine the occurrence of intron splicing and miRNA maturation through the appearance of red fluorescent emission on the cell membranes. The red *rGFP* serves as a visual indicator for the generation of intronic miRNAs. This intron-derived miRNA system is activated under the control of cytomegalovirus-IE promoter.

1. Cleavage by XhoI and XbaI: add the XhoI/XbaI digestion reaction mix to the *SpRNAi–rGFP* gene cassette and the pHcRed1-N1/1 plasmid vector, respectively. Incubate both of the reactions at 37°C for 4 h and stop the reactions on ice.
2. Purification of the XhoI/XbaI-digested sequences: load and run the reactions in 1% agarose gel electrophoresis and cut out the XhoI/XbaI-digested *SpRNAi–rGFP* sequence and the 4000-bp pHcRed1-N1/1 fragment, respectively, using a clean surgical blade. Recover the two oligonucleotide sequences in one tube of 30 μL autoclaved ddH$_2$O, using the gel extraction column and following the manufacturer's suggestions.
3. Ligation: add the ligation reaction mix to the extraction. Incubate the reaction at 16°C for 16 h and stop the reaction on ice.
4. Plasmid amplification: transfect the ligation product into the DH5α transformation-competent *E. coli* cells using the expand cloning kit and following the manufacturer's suggestions.
5. Plasmid recovery: isolate and collect the amplified *SpRNAi–rGFP* plasmid in one tube of 30 μL autoclaved ddH$_2$O, using a spin Miniprep filter and following the manufacturer's suggestions.

3.4. *Insertion of Pre-miRNA Into the* **SpRNAi–rGFP** *Gene Construct*

The *SpRNAi–rGFP* vector does not contain any intronic pre-miRNA structure. Because the intronic insert region of the *SpRNAi–rGFP* vector is flanked with a PvuI and an MluI restriction site at the 5' and 3' ends, respectively, the primary insert can be easily removed and replaced by various gene-specific inserts (e.g., anti-eGFP) possessing cohesive ends (*see* **Note 3**).

1. Hybridization: mix the sense and antisense pre-miRNA sequences (5 μL for each sequence) in 10 μL of 2X hybridization buffer, heat to 94°C for 3 min, and cool to 65°C for 10 min. Stop the reaction on ice.
2. Cleavage by MluI and PvuI: add the MluI/PvuI digestion reaction mix to the *SpRNAi–rGFP* vector and the pre-miRNA hybrid construct, respectively. Incubate the reaction at 37°C for 4 h and stop the reaction on ice.
3. Purification of the MluI/PvuI-digested sequences: load and run the reactions in 1% agarose gel electrophoresis and cut out the MluI/PvuI-digested *SpRNAi–rGFP* sequence and the pre-miRNA fragment, respectively, using a clean surgical blade. Recover the two oligonucleotide sequences in one tube of 30 μL autoclaved ddH$_2$O, using the gel extraction column and following the manufacturer's suggestions.
4. Ligation: add the ligation reaction mix to the extraction. Incubate the reaction at 16°C for 16 h and stop the reaction on ice.
5. Plasmid amplification: transfect the ligation product into the DH5α transformation-competent *E. coli* cells using the expand cloning kit and following the manufacturer's suggestions.

6. Plasmid recovery: isolate and collect the amplified *SpRNAi–rGFP* plasmid in one tube of 30 µL autoclaved ddH$_2$O, using a spin Miniprep filter and following the manufacturer's suggestions (**Note 4**).

3.5. Liposomal Transfection of the SpRNAi–rGFP Gene Construct

To increase transfection efficiency, we use liposomal reagents to facilitate the delivery of the *SpRNAi–rGFP* vector into target cells.

1. Preparation of FuGENE: add 6 µL of the FuGENE reagent into 100 µL of RPMI-1640 medium in a clean tube and gently mix the solution, following the manufacturer's suggestions. Add 20 µg (in less than 50 µL) of the *SpRNAi–rGFP* vector into the liposomal dilution from **Subheading 3.4.**, **step 6**, and gently mix the solution following the manufacturer's suggestions. Store the mixture at 4°C for 30 min.
2. Transfection: add the mixture into the center of the cell culture and gently mix the cell culture medium.
3. Cell culture: culture the treated cells in a cell culture incubator under the condition essential for the cell type.

4. Notes

1. Because of the low efficiency of blunt-end ligation and 5'-nucleotide hydrolysis of the first *rGFP* exon, the chance to obtain a correct *SpRNAi–rGFP* gene sequence is approx 1 in 50 (2%). The final *SpRNAi–rGFP* gene sequence must be confirmed by DNA sequencing.
2. Because there is no enzymatic method to remove the 5'-protruding trinucleotide of the first *rGFP* exon, we need to use hydrolysis, which takes approx 2 to 3 wk to remove three nucleotides from the end of an oligonucleotide sequence.
3. The synthetic pre-miRNA sequences that we present here are directed against the 279 to 303-nt region of enhanced eGFP. The principle for designing an intronic pre-miRNA insert is to synthesize two mutually complementary oligonucleotides, including one 5'-GTCCG ATCGTC, 19- to 27-nt antisense target gene sequence—TCAAGAGAT (stem-loop)—19- to 27-nt sense target gene sequence, CGACGCGTCAT-3'; and another 5'-ATGACGGTCG, 19- to 27-nt antisense target gene sequence—ATCTCTTGA (stem-loop)—19- to 27-nt sense target gene sequence, GACGATCGGAC-3'. The hybridization of these two oligonucleotide sequences forms the intronic pre-miRNA insert, which contains a 5'-PuvI and a 3'-Mlu1 restriction site for further ligation into the intron region of an *SpRNAi–rGFP* gene cassette. All synthetic oligonucleotides must be purified by PAGE to ensure their highest purity and integrity.
4. The sequence of the final *SpRNAi–rGFP* gene cassette and its pre-miRNA insert must be confirmed by DNA sequencing.

Acknowledgments

The work was supported by a grant from the National Institutes of Health, CA 85722.

References

1. Ambros, V. (2004) The functions of animal microRNAs. *Nature* **350,** 431–355.
2. Nelson, P., Kiriakidou, M., Sharma, A., Maniataki, E., and Mourelatos, Z. (2003) The microRNA world: small is mighty. *Trends Biochem. Sci.* **28,** 534–539.

3. Ying, S. Y. and Lin, S. L. (2005) Intronic microRNA (miRNA). *Biochem. Biophys. Res. Commun.* **326,** 515–520.

4. Lin, S. L. and Ying, S. Y. (2004) Novel RNAi therapy—intron-derived microRNA drugs. *Drug Design Reviews* **1,** 247–255.

5. Tuschl, T. and Borkhardt, A. (2002) Small interfering RNAs: a revolutionary tool for the analysis of gene function and gene therapy. *Mol. Interv.* **2,** 158–167.

6. Ambros, V. (1989) A hierarchy of regulatory genes controls a larva-to-adult developmental switch in C. elegans. *Cell* **57,** 49–57.

7. Hall, I. M., Shankaranarayana, G. D., Noma, K., Ayoub, N., Cohen, A., and Grewal, S. I. (2002) Establishment and maintenance of a heterochromatin domain. *Science* **297,** 2232–2237.

8. Llave, C., Xie, Z., Kasschau, K. D., and Carrington, J. C. (2002) Cleavage of Scarecrow-like mRNA targets directed by a class of Arabidopsis miRNA. *Science* **297,** 2053–2056.

9. Rhoades, M. W., Reinhart, B. J., Lim, L. P., Burge, C. B., Bartel, B., and Bartel, D. P. (2002) Prediction of plant microRNA targets. *Cell* **110,** 513–520.

10. Lee, R. C., Feibaum, R. L., and Ambros, V. (1993) The C. elegans heterochromic gene lin-4 encodes small RNAs with antisense complementarity to lin-14. *Cell* **75,** 843–854.

11. Reinhart, B. J., Slack, F. J., Basson, M., et al. (2000) The 21-nucleotide let-7 RNA regulates developmental timing in Caenorhabditis elegans. *Nature* **403,** 901–906.

12. Lau, N. C., Lim, L. P., Weinstein, E. G., and Bartel, D. P. (2001) An abundant class of tiny RNAs with probable regulatory roles in Caenorhabditis elegans. *Science* **294,** 858–862.

13. Brennecke, J., Hipfner, D. R., Stark, A., Russell, R. B., and Cohen, S. M. (2003) Bantam encodes a developmentally regulated microRNA that controls cell proliferation and regulates the proapoptotic gene hid in Drosophila. *Cell* **113,** 25–36.

14. Xu, P., Vernooy, S. Y., Guo, M., and Hay, B. A. (2003) The Drosophila microRNA Mir-14 suppresses cell death and is required for normal fat metabolism. *Curr. Biol.* **13,** 790–795.

15. Lagos-Quintana, M., Rauhut, R., Meyer, J., Borkhardt, A., and Tuschl, T. (2003) New microRNAs from mouse and human. *RNA* **9,** 175–179.

16. Mourelatos, Z., Dostie, J., Paushkin, S., et al. (2002) miRNPs: a novel class of ribonucleoproteins containing numerous microRNAs. *Genes Dev.* **16,** 720–728.

17. Zeng, Y., Wagner, E. J., and Cullen, B. R. (2002) Both natural and designed micro RNAs can inhibit the expression of cognate mRNAs when expressed in human cells. *Mol. Cell* **9,** 1327–1333.

18. Zeng, Y., Yi, R., and Cullen, B. R. (2003) MicroRNAs and small interfering RNAs can inhibit mRNA expression by similar mechanisms. *Proc. Natl. Acad. Sci. USA* **100,** 9779–9784.

19. Carthew, R. W. (2001) Gene silencing by double-stranded RNA. *Curr. Opin. Cell Biol.* **13,** 244–248.

20. Lin, S. L., Chang, D., Wu, D. Y., and Ying, S. Y. (2003) A novel RNA splicing-mediated gene silencing mechanism potential for genome evolution. *Biochem. Biophys. Res. Commun.* **310,** 754–760.

21. Lin, S. L., Chang, D., and Ying, S. Y. (2005) Asymmetry of intronic pre-miRNA structures in functional RISC assembly. *Gene* **356,** 32–38.

22. Ying, S. Y. and Lin, S. L. (2004) Intron-derived microRNAs—fine tuning of gene functions. *Gene* **342,** 25–28.

23. Kramer, A. (1996) The structure and function of proteins involved in mammalian pre-mRNA splicing. *Annu. Rev. Biochem.* **65,** 367–409.

24. Clement, J. Q., Qian, L., Kaplinsky, N., and Wilkinson, M. F. (1999) The stability and fate of a spliced intron from vertebrate cells. *RNA* **5,** 206–220.

25. Nott, A., Meislin, S. H., and Moore, M. J. (2003) A quantitative analysis of intron effects on mammalian gene expression. *RNA* **9,** 607–617.

26. Lee, Y., Kim, M., Han, J., et al. (2004) MicroRNA genes are transcribed by RNA polymerase II. *EMBO J.* **23,** 4051–4060.

27. Lee, Y., Ahn, C., Han, J., et al. (2003) The nuclear RNase III Drosha initiates microRNA processing. *Nature* **425,** 415–419.

28. Lund, E., Guttinger, S., Calado, A., Dahlberg, J. E., and Kutay, U. (2004) Nuclear export of microRNA precursors. *Science* **303,** 95–98.

29. Yi, R., Qin, Y., Macara, I. G., and Cullen, B. R. (2003) Exportin-5 mediates the nuclear export of pre-microRNAs and short hairpin RNAs. *Genes Dev.* **17,** 3011–3016.

30. Schwarz, D. S., Hutvagner, G., Du, T., Xu, Z., Aronin, N., and Zamore, P. D. (2003) Asymmetry in the assembly of the RNAi enzyme complex. *Cell* **115,** 199–208.

31. Khvorova, A., Reynolds, A., and Jayasena, S. D. (2003) Functional siRNAs and miRNAs exhibit strand bias. *Cell* **115,** 209–216.

32. Lee, Y. S., Nakahara, K., Pham, J. W., et al. (2004) Distinct roles for Drosophila Dicer-1 and Dicer-2 in the siRNA/miRNA silencing pathways. *Cell* **117,** 69–81.

33. Tang, G. (2005) siRNA and miRNA: an insight into RISCs. *Trends Biochem. Sci.* **30,** 106–114.

34. Rodriguez, A., Griffiths-Jones, S., Ashurst, J. L., and Bradley, A. (2004) Identification of mammalian microRNA host genes and transcription units. *Genome Res.* **14,** 1902–1910.

35. Ambros, V., Lee, R. C., Lavanway, A., Williams, P. T., and Jewell, D. (2003) MicroRNAs and other tiny endogenous RNAs in C. elegans. *Curr. Biol.* **13,** 807–818.

36. Liquori, C. L., Ricker, K., Moseley, M. L., et al. (2001) Myotinic dystrophy type 2 caused by a CCTG expansion in intron 1 of ZNF9. *Science* **293,** 864–867.

37. Jin, P., Alisch, R. S., and Warren, S. T. (2004) RNA and microRNAs in fragile X mental retardation. *Nat. Cell. Biol.* **6,** 1048–1053.

38. Eberhart, D. E., Malter, H. E., Feng, Y., and Warren, S. T. (1996) The fragile X mental retardation protein is a ribonucleoprotein containing both nuclear localization and nuclear export signals. *Hum. Mol. Genet.* **5,** 1083–1091.

39. Lin, S. L. and Ying, S. Y. (2004) New drug design for gene therapy—taking advantage of introns. *Lett. Drug Design Discovery* **1,** 256–262.

40. Zhang, G., Taneja, K. L., Singer, R. H., and Green, M. R. (1994) Localization of pre-mRNA splicing in mammalian nuclei. *Nature* **372,** 809–812.

41. Ghosh, S. and Garcia-Blanco, M. A. (2000) Coupled in vitro synthesis and splicing of RNA polymerase II transcripts. *RNA* **6,** 1325–1334.

42. Stark, G. R., Kerr, I. M., Williams, B. R., Silverman, R. H., and Schreiber, R. D. (1998) How cells respond to interferons. *Annu. Rev. Biochem.* **67,** 227–264.

43. Sledz, C. A., Holko, M., de Veer, M. J., Silverman, R. H., and Williams, B. R. (2003) Activation of the interferon system by short-interfering RNAs. *Nat. Cell Biol.* **5,** 834–839.

44. Boden, D., Pusch, O., Silbermann, R., Lee, F., Tucker, L., and Ramratnam, B. (2004) Enhanced gene silencing of HIV-1 specific siRNA using microRNA designed hairpins. *Nucleic Acid Res.* **32,** 1154–1158.

23

Isolation and Identification of Gene-Specific MicroRNAs

Shi-Lung Lin, Donald C. Chang, and Shao-Yao Ying

Summary

Prediction of microRNA (miRNA) candidates using computer programming has identified hundreds and hundreds of genomic hairpin sequences, of which, the functions remain to be determined. Because direct transfection of hairpin-like miRNA precursors (pre)-miRNAs in mammalian cells is not always sufficient to trigger effective RNA-induced gene-silencing complex (RISC) assembly, a key step for RNA interference (RNAi)-related gene silencing, we developed an intronic miRNA-expressing system to overcome this problem, and successfully increased the efficiency and effectiveness of miRNA-associated RNAi induction in vitro and in vivo. By insertion of a hairpin-like pre-miRNA structure into the intron region of a gene, this intronic miRNA biogenesis system has been found to depend on a coupled interaction of nascent precursor messenger RNA transcription and intron excision within a specific nuclear region proximal to genomic perichromatin fibrils. The intronic miRNA was transcribed by RNA type II polymerases, coexpressed with a primary gene transcript, and excised out of its encoding gene transcript by intracellular RNA splicing and processing mechanisms. Currently, some ribonuclease III endonucleases have been found to be involved in the processing of spliced introns and probably facilitating the intronic miRNA maturation. Using this miRNA-expressing system, we have shown for the first time that the intron-derived miRNAs were able to induce strong RNAi effects in not only human and mouse cells but also zebrafish, chicken embryos, and adult mice. Based on the strand complementarity between the designed miRNA and its target gene sequence, we have also developed a miRNA isolation protocol to purify and identify the mature miRNAs generated by the intronic miRNA-expressing system. Several intronic miRNA identities and structures are currently confirmed to be active in vitro and in vivo. According to this proof-of-principle method, we now have the knowledge to design pre-miRNA inserts that are more efficient and effective for the intronic miRNA-expressing system.

Key Words: MicroRNA (miRNA) biogenesis; gene cloning; RNA interference (RNAi); RNA-induced gene-silencing complex (RISC); asymmetric assembly; zebrafish.

1. Introduction

More than 90 intronic miRNAs have been identified using bioinformatic approaches to date *(1)*, but the functions of the vast majority of these intronic molecules remain to

From: *Methods in Molecular Biology, vol. 342: MicroRNA Protocols*
Edited by: S. Ying © Humana Press Inc., Totowa, NJ

be determined. According to the strictly expressive correlation of intronic miRNAs to their encoded genes, one may speculate that the levels of condition-specific, time-specific, and individual-specific gene expression are determined by interactions of different miRNAs on single or multiple genes. This interpretation accounts for more-accurate genetic expression of various traits, and any dysregulation of the interactions, thus, will result in genetic disease. For instance, monozygotic twins frequently demonstrate slightly, but definitely distinguishing, disease susceptibility and physiological behaviors. For instance, a long CCTG expansion in intron 1 of the zinc finger protein-9 gene has been correlated to type 2 myotonic dystrophy in one twin with a higher susceptibility *(2)*. Given that the expansion motif confers high affinity to certain RNA-binding proteins, the interfering role of intron-derived expansion fragments remains to be elucidated. Another more-established example, involving intronic expansion fragments in its pathogenesis, is fragile X syndrome, which represents approx 30% of human inherited mental retardation. Intronic CGG repeat (rCGG) expansion in the 5'-untranslated region of the *FMR1* gene is the causative mutation in 99% of individuals with fragile X syndrome *(3)*. *FMR1* encodes an RNA-binding protein, fragile X mental retardation protein, which is associated with polyribosome assembly in an RNP-dependent manner and capable of suppressing translation through an RNAi-like pathway. Fragile X mental retardation protein also contains a nuclear localization signal and a nuclear export signal for shuttling certain mRNAs between the nucleus and cytoplasm *(4)*. Jin et al. proposed an RNAi-mediated methylation model in the CpG region of the *FMR1* rCGG expansion, which is targeted by a hairpin RNA derived from the 3'-untranslated region of the *FMR1* expanded allele transcript *(3)*. The Dicer-processed hairpin RNA triggers the formation of RNA-induced initiator of transcriptional gene silencing on the homologous rCGG sequences and leads to heterochromatin repression of the *FMR1* locus. These examples suggest that natural evolution gives rise to more complexity and more variety of introns in higher animals and plants for coordinating their vast gene expression volumes and interactions; therefore, any dysregulation of miRNAs derived from introns may lead to genetic diseases involving intronic expansion or deletion, such as myotonic dystrophy and fragile X mental retardation.

Fig. 1. Structural preference of microRNA (miRNA)–miRNA* asymmetry in miRNA-induced gene-silencing complex (miRISC) in vivo. (**A**) We demonstrated that only the ❷ construct was used in effective miRISC assembly. Because the miRNA is predicted to be complementary to its target messenger RNA, the "antisense" (black bar) refers to the miRNA and the "sense" (white bar) refers to its complementarity, miRNA*. (**B**) Two designed mature miRNA identities were found only in the ❷-transfected zebrafish, namely miR-green fluorescent protein (EGFP)-(280/302) and miR-EGFP(282/300). (**C**) In vivo gene-silencing efficacy was only observed in the transfection of the ❷ pre-miRNA construct, but not the ❶ construct. Because the mixture color of EGFP and red fluorescent protein (RGFP) displayed more red than green (as shown in deep orange), the expression level of target EGFP (green) was significantly reduced in ❷, whereas the miRNA indicator, RGFP (red), was evenly present in all vector transfections. A strong strand selection was observed in favor of the 5'-stem-loop strand of the designed pre-miRNAs in RISC. (**D**) Western blot analysis of protein expression levels confirmed the specific EGFP-silencing

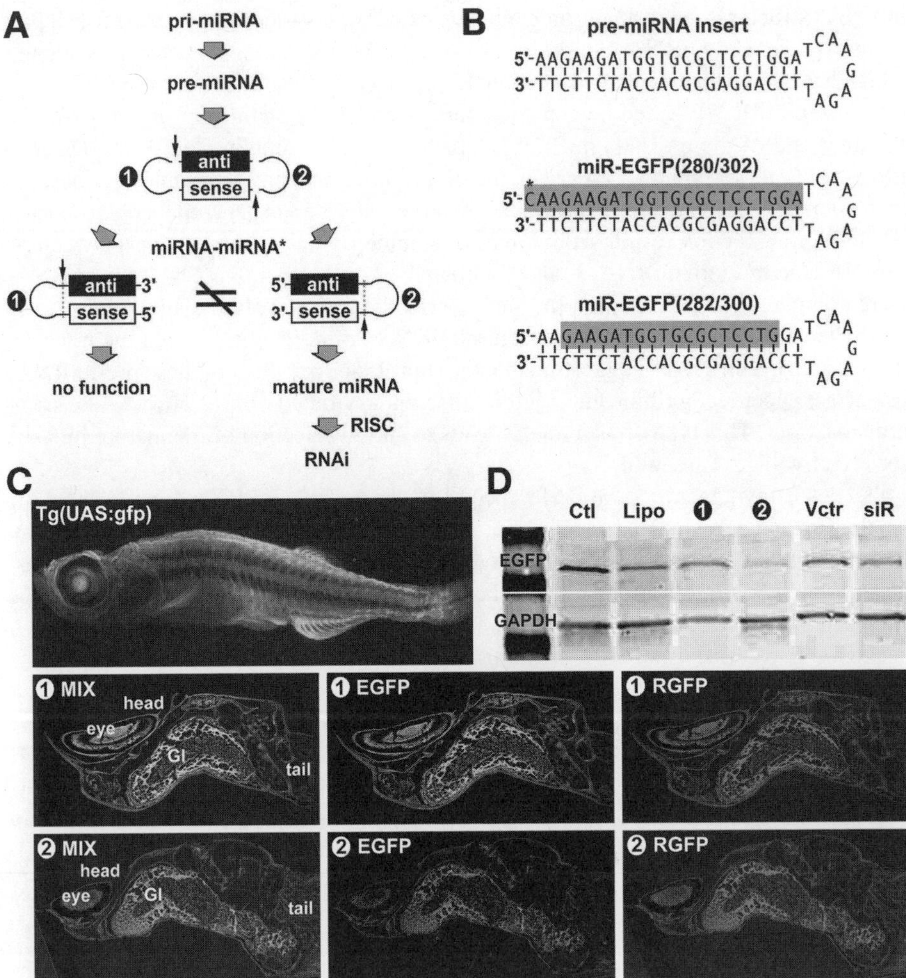

Fig. 1. *(Continued)* result of (**C**). No detectable gene silencing was observed in fish without (Ctl) and with liposome only (Lipo) treatments. The transfection of either a U6-driven small interfering RNA vector (siR) or an empty vector (Vctr) without the designed pre-miRNA insert resulted in no gene-silencing significance.

To understand the diseases caused by dysregulation of intronic miRNAs, an artificial expression system is needed to recreate the function and mechanism of the miRNA in vivo. The same approach may be used to develop and test therapies for the disease. Using artificial introns carrying hairpin-like pre-miRNA, we successfully generated mature miRNA molecules with full function in triggering RNAi-like gene silencing in zebrafish *(5)*. We introduced hairpin-like pre-miRNAs into 2-wk-old zebrafish larvae and successfully tested the processing and functional significance of different miRNA–

miRNA* structures using an intronic miRNA-expressing system that was described previously *(6,7)*. The miRNA expression was driven by a cytomegalovirus IE promoter, which has been well established as a viable approach for manipulation of gene expression in zebrafish *(8)*. Based on conventional reasoning, the stem-loop structure located in either end of the miRNA–miRNA* duplex should be equally cleaved by Dicer to form small interfering RNA (siRNA); therefore, functional bias would not be observed in the stem-loop. However, we unexpectedly observed different gene-silencing responses when the transfection results from a pair of symmetric hairpin constructs between 5'-miRNA*–stem-loop–miRNA-3' and 5'-miRNA–stem-loop–miRNA*-3' pre-miRNAs were compared; both contained the same perfectly matched siRNA-like duplex stem arm (shown in **Fig. 1A**). Different mature miRNAs were identified from the transfections of the pre-miRNAs, suggesting that the stem-loop structures of these pre-miRNAs can affect Dicer recognition and result in different asymmetry of the siRNA-like stem-arm construct. This type of asymmetry leads to strand selection of the mature miRNA for effective RISC assembly.

To determine the structural preference of the hairpin pre-miRNAs, we isolated the small RNAs in zebrafish using mirVana® miRNA isolation columns (Ambion, Austin, TX) and precipitated all potential miRNAs complementary to the target green fluorescent protein *(EGFP)* region using latex beads containing the target RNA sequence. The designed pre-miRNA constructs were directed against the target EGFP messenger RNA sequence nucleotides 280–302 in the transgenic *(UAS:gfp)* zebrafish, of which, the *EGFP* expression was constitutively driven by the β-actin promoter in almost all cell types. As shown in **Fig. 1B**, two major miRNA identities were verified to be active (gray-shading sequences). Because of the fast turn-over rate of small RNAs in vivo *(9, 10)*, the shorter miR-EGFP(282/300) is likely to be a stably degraded form of the miR-EGFP(280/302). The first 5'-cytosine (labeled by an asterisk) of the miR-EGFP(280/302) was not included in the designed target region and probably provided by the original intron sequence because the cytosine (C*) is the most adjacent nucleotide to the 5'-end of the designed pre-miRNA structure in the intron. Because the effective miR-EGFP (280/302) miRNA was detected only in the zebrafish transfected by the 5'-miRNA–stem-loop–miRNA*-3' construct (❷), the stem-loop of the construct ❷, rather than the construct ❶, pre-miRNA is able to determine the correct antisense EGFP domain for micro-RISC (miRISC) assembly. Because Dicer cleavage resulted in distinct mature miRNAs from both pre-miRNA constructs (**Fig. 2**), switching the pre-miRNA stem-loop did not affect the normal process of miRNA maturation; however, the resulting mature miRNAs differed in orientation. One possibility for this preference is that the structure and/or sequence of the stem-loop preferably facilitates miRNA maturation from one orientation over the other. Alternatively, the stem-loop may change the Dicer recognition and, thus, may generate differently asymmetric profiles to the pre-miRNA stem arm. In either case, the cleavage site of Dicer in the pre-miRNA stem arm determines the strand selection of a mature miRNA, and the pre-miRNA stem-loop likely functions as a determinant for the recognition of the special cleavage site. Based on this proven principle of the intronic pre-miRNA structures, we are now able to design correct and effective pre-miRNA inserts for the intronic miRNA-expressing systems.

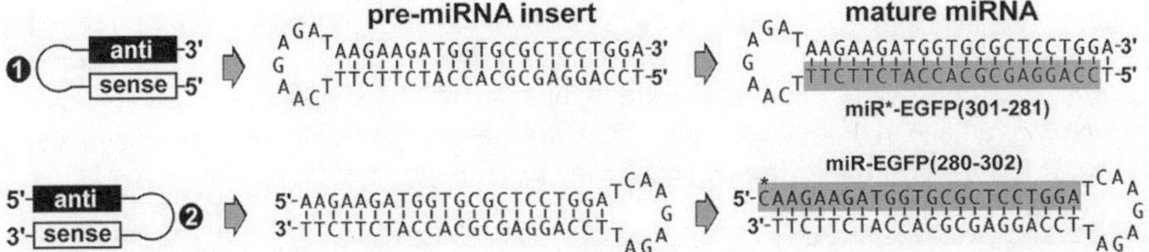

Fig. 2. Bias of microRNA (miRNA)–miRNA* asymmetry in miRNA-induced gene-silencing complex (miRISC) in vivo. Different preferences of RISC assembly were observed in the transfections of 5'-miRNA*–stem-loop–miRNA-3' (❶) and 5'-miRNA–stem-loop–miRNA*-3' (❷) pre-miRNA constructs in zebrafish, respectively. Based on the assembly rule of siRISC assembly, the processing of both ❶ and ❷ pre-miRNAs should result in the same siRISC assembly; however, the present experiments demonstrate that only the ❷ construct was able to silence target *EGFP*. An effective mature miRNA, namely miR-EGFP(280/302), was detected in the ❷-transfected zebrafish directed against target *EGFP*, whereas transfection of the ❶ construct produced a different mature miRNA, miR*-EGFP(301/281), which was partially complementary to the miR-EGFP(280/302) and possessed no gene-silencing effects on EGFP expression.

2. Materials

2.1. Small RNA Isolation

1. mirVana miRNA isolation kit (Ambion, Austin, TX).
2. Incubation chambers: 65°C and 4°C.
3. 1X Nuclease-free hybridization buffer: 100 mM KOAc, 30 mM HEPES-KOH, and 2 mM MgOAc, pH 7.4 at 25°C (*see* **Note 1**).
4. Microcentrifuge: 17,900g (*see* **Note 2**).

2.2. Complementary Affinity Precipitation and Poly(A) Tailing

1. Synthetic 5'-fluorescein-linked oligonucleotides homologous to the target gene sequence (Sigma-Genosys), e.g., as shown here, a synthetic anti-EGFP oligonucleotide 5'-fluorescein-AGAAGATGGT GCGCTCCTGG A-3' (100 pmol/μL in diethylpyrocarbonate [DEPC]-treated ddH$_2$O).
2. Anti-fluorescein monoclonal antibody, biotin-conjugated (Invitrogen, Carlsbad, CA).
3. Streptavidin bead suspension (Invitrogen).
4. Incubation shaker: 25°C, 120 rpm.
5. Incubation chambers: 65°C and 4°C.
6. Microcentrifuge: 17,900g.
7. DEPC-treated H$_2$O: Stir double distilled water with 0.1% DEPC for longer than 12 h and autoclave twice at 120°C under approx 1.2 kgf/cm^2 for 20 min.
8. RNA tailing: Poly(A) tailing kit (Ambion, Austin, TX).

2.3. Complementary DNA Generation and Polyacrylamide Gel Purification

1. Oligo(dT)$_{20}$ primer: 5'-dephosphorylated TTTTTTTTTT TTTTTTTTTT-3' (100 pmol/μL in DEPC-treated ddH$_2$O).
2. 100 U/μL SuperScript II MMLV reverse transcriptase and 5X reverse transcription buffer (250 mM Tris-HCl, pH 8.3, 250 mM KCl, 15 mM MgCl$_2$, and 10 mM dithiothreitol).

3. Reverse transcription mix: 8 μL of DEPC-treated ddH$_2$O, 6 μL of 5X reverse transcription buffer, 2 μL of 10 mM deoxyribonucleoside triphosphate mix (10 mM each for deoxyadenosine triphosphate, deoxyguanosine triphosphate, deoxycytosine triphosphate, and deoxythymidine triphosphate), 1 μL of 25 U/μL ribonuclease inhibitor, 2 μL of SuperScript II MMLV reverse transcriptase; prepare the reaction mix just before use.
4. Incubation chambers: 94°C, 65°C, 42°C, and 4°C.
5. Electrophoresis system for polyacrylamide gel (Bio-Rad, Hercules, CA).
6. 15% Tris–borate–ethylenediaminetetraacetic acid/urea polyacrylamide gel for oligonucleotides (Bio-Rad).
7. Mini whole gel eluter (Bio-Rad).

3. Methods

3.1 Small RNA Isolation

The small intracellular RNAs (fewer than 200 nucleotides) are isolated and collected on a glass-fiber filter using the mirVana miRNA isolation kit. These small RNAs include 5S ribosomal RNA, transfer RNA, small nucleolar RNA (snoRNA), small nuclear RNA, small mitochondrial noncoding RNA (smnRNA), miRNA, and probably siRNA.

1. Small RNA isolation: apply 100 to 10^7 cells to a mirVana miRNA isolation reaction, following the manufacturer's protocol. Collect the final RNAs in 30 μL of 1X nuclease-free hybridization buffer.

3.2. Complementary Affinity Precipitation and Poly(A) Tailing

Small RNAs complementary to the target sequence are recovered by binding to fluorescein-linked target oligonucleotides and then precipitated by further binding to biotin-conjugated anti-fluorescein monoclonal antibodies and streptavidin beads. The resulting small RNAs are protected by adding poly(A) tails in their 3'-termini using *Escherichia coli* poly(A) polymerase I.

1. Complementary annealing: add 2 μL of synthetic 5'-fluorescein-linked oligonucleotides to the isolated small RNAs and mix well. Incubate the mixture in an incubation chamber at 65°C for 5 min, then transfer the mixture to an incubation shaker at 25°C for 30 min.
2. Precipitation: add 10 μL of the biotin-conjugated anti-fluorescein monoclonal antibodies to the mixture and incubate in an incubation shaker at 25°C for 30 min. Add 10 μL of streptavidin bead suspension to the mixture and continue to incubate in an incubation shaker at 25°C for 30 min. Precipitate the bound RNAs by centrifugation at 17,900g for 10 min and discard the supernatant. Dissolve the pellet in 10 μL of DEPC-treated ddH$_2$O.
3. Poly(A) RNA tailing: add poly(A) tails to the 3'-termini of the purified RNAs using *E. coli* poly(A) polymerase I, following the manufacturer's suggestions.
4. Reaction stop: heat the reaction at 94°C for 2 min and cool on ice immediately. Precipitate the beads by centrifugation at 17,900g for 10 min and transfer the supernatant to a clean new tube.

3.3. Complementary DNA Generation and Polyacrylamide Gel Purification

The starting material is approx 1 μg of the poly(A)-tailed small RNAs. The complementary DNAs are synthesized by reverse transcription from the poly(A)-tailed small

RNAs with the oligo(dA) primer. The use of MMLV reverse transcriptase also adds a short poly(dC) tail in the 3'-end of each cDNA sequence, which is used for DNA sequencing in conjunction with a poly(dG)$_{10}$ primer.

1. Primer annealing: mix 10 µL of the RNA supernatant with 1 µL oligo(dT)$_{20}$ primer, heat to 65°C for 5 min to minimize secondary structures, and cool on ice.
2. Complementary DNA (cDNA) synthesis: add 14 µL of the reverse transcriptase mix to the hybrids, heat to 42°C for 20 min and cool on ice.
3. Denaturation of RNA–cDNA hybrids: heat the reaction at 94°C for 2 min and cool on ice immediately.
4. Polyacrylamide gel electrophoresis: load and run the denatured cDNAs on a 15% Tris–borate–ethylenediaminetetraacetic acid/urea gel and recover each cDNA band using the mini whole gel eluter system, following the manufacturer's suggestions. The cDNAs thus obtained are ready for DNA sequencing using the poly(dG)$_{10}$ primer. The resulting cDNA sequences are perfectly complementary to the miRNAs, from which the cDNAs are reverse transcribed (*see* **Note 3**).

4. Notes

1. Autoclave the 1X hybridization buffer twice at 120°C under approx 1.2 kgf/cm^2 for 20 min.
2. Relative centrifugal force (RCF) (g) = (1.12×10^{-5}) (rpm)^{2}r, where r is the radius in centimeters measured from the center of the rotor to the middle of the spin column, and rpm is the speed of the rotor in revolutions per minute.
3. Although most of the native pre-miRNAs contain mismatched areas in their stem arms, it is not necessary for us to construct an imperfect paired stem arm to trigger RNAi-related gene silencing. Previous studies have demonstrated that a mature miRNA can be generated by placing a perfectly matched siRNA duplex in the miR-30 pre-miRNA structure *(11,12)*. Furthermore, there are many genes not subjected to the regulation of native miRNAs, in particular, *EGFP*, which can be otherwise silenced by intracellular transfection of the pre-miRNA containing a perfectly matched stem-arm construct. Therefore, we define a mature miRNA based on its biogenetic function and mechanism, rather than the structural complementarity of its precursor. In this view, any small hairpin RNA can be a pre-miRNA if a mature miRNA is successfully processed from the small hairpin RNA and further assembled into miRISC for target gene silencing.

Acknowledgments

The work was supported by a grant from the National Institutes of Health, CA 85722.

References

1. Rodriguez, A., Griffiths-Jones, S., Ashurst, J. L., and Bradley, A. (2004). Identification of mammalian microRNA host genes and transcription units. *Genome Res.* **14,** 1902–1910.
2. Liquori, C. L., Ricker, K., Moseley, M. L., et al. (2001) Myotinic dystrophy type 2 caused by a CCTG expansion in intron 1 of ZNF9. *Science* **293,** 864–867.
3. Jin, P., Alisch, R. S., and Warren, S. T. (2004) RNA and microRNAs in fragile X mental retardation. *Nat. Cell Biol.* **6,** 1048–1053.
4. Eberhart, D. E., Malter, H. E., Feng, Y., and Warren, S. T. (1996) The fragile X mental retardation protein is a ribonucleoprotein containing both nuclear localization and nuclear export signals. *Hum. Mol. Genet.* **5,** 1083–1091.

5. Lin, S. L., Chang, D., and Ying, S. Y. (2005) Asymmetry of intronic pre-miRNA structures in functional RISC assembly. *Gene* **356,** 32–38.
6. Lin, S. L., Chang, D., Wu, D. Y., and Ying, S. Y. (2003) A novel RNA splicing-mediated gene silencing mechanism potential for genome evolution. *Biochem. Biophys. Res. Commun.* **310,** 754–760.
7. Lin, S. L. and Ying, S. Y. (2004) Novel RNAi therapy—intron-derived microRNA drugs. *Drug Design Reviews* **1,** 247–255.
8. Verri, T., Argenton, F., Tomanin, R., et al. (1997) The bacteriophage T7 binary system activates transient transgene expression in zebrafish (Danio rerio) embryos. *Biochem. Biophys. Res. Commun.* **237,** 492–495.
9. Tourriere, H., Chebli, K., and Tazi, J. (2002) mRNA degradation machines in eukaryotic cells. *Biochimie* **84,** 821–837.
10. Wilusz, C. J. and Wilusz, J. (2004) Bringing the role of mRNA decay in the control of gene expression into focus. *Trends Genet.* **20,** 491–497.
11. Lee, Y., Ahn, C., Han, J., et al. (2003) The nuclear RNase III Drosha initiates microRNA processing. *Nature* **425,** 415–419.
12. Boden, D., Pusch, O., Silbermann, R., Lee, F., Tucker, L., and Ramratnam, B. (2004) Enhanced gene silencing of HIV-1 specific siRNA using microRNA designed hairpins. *Nucleic Acid Res.* **32,** 1154–1158.

## 24

Transgene-Like Animal Models Using Intronic MicroRNAs

Shi-Lung Lin, Shin-Ju E. Chang, and Shao-Yao Ying

Summary

Transgenic animal models are valuable tools for testing gene functions and drug mechanisms in vivo. They are also the best similitude of a human body for etiological and pathological research of diseases. All pharmaceutically developed drugs must be proven safe and effective in animals before approval by the Food and Drug Administration to be used in clinical trials. To this end, the transgenic animal models of human diseases serve as a front line for drug evaluation. However, there is currently no transgenic animal model for microRNA (miRNA) research. miRNAs, small single-stranded regulatory RNAs capable of silencing intracellular gene transcripts that contain either complete or partial complementarity to the miRNAs, are useful for the design and development of new therapies against cancer polymorphism and viral mutation. Recently, varieties of natural miRNAs have been found to be derived from hairpin-like RNA precursors in almost all eukaryotes, including yeast (*Schizosaccharomyces pombe*), plant (*Arabidopsis*), nematode (*Caenorhabditis elegans*), fly (*Drosophila melanogaster*), fish, mouse, and human, involving intracellular defense against viral infections and regulation of certain gene expressions during development. To facilitate the miRNA research in vivo, we have developed a state-of-the-art transgenic strategy for silencing specific genes in zebrafish, chicken, and mouse, using intronic miRNAs. By insertion of a hairpin-like pre-miRNA structure into the intron region of a gene, we have found that mature miRNAs were successfully transcribed by RNA polymerase (Pol)-II, coexpressed with the encoding gene transcript, and excised out of the encoding gene transcript by natural RNA splicing and processing mechanisms. In conjunction with retroviral transfection systems, the hairpin-like pre-miRNA construct was further inserted into the intron of a cellular gene for tissue-specific expression regulated by the gene promoter. Because the retroviral vectors were randomly integrated into the genome of its host cell, the most effective transgenic animal can be selected and propagated to be a stable transgenic line for future research. Here, we have shown for the first time that transgene-like animal models were generated using the intronic miRNA-expressing system described previously, which has been proven to be useful for both miRNA research and in vivo evaluation of miRNA-associated target genes.

Key Words: MicroRNA (miRNA); RNA interference (RNAi); transgenic animal; type II RNA polymerase (Pol II); RNA splicing; intron; embryonic development.

From: *Methods in Molecular Biology, vol. 342: MicroRNA Protocols*
Edited by: S. Ying © Humana Press Inc., Totowa, NJ

1. Introduction

Conventional transgenic animal models rely on the use of antisense oligonucleotide and dominant-negative technologies to generate loss-of-function mutants in vivo. Antisense oligonucleotides complementary to a gene transcript (messenger RNA [mRNA]) directly bind to the mRNA and either degrade the target mRNA or suppress the translation of the gene; whereas dominant-negative methods generate defective proteins to negatively compete with a targeted normal protein function. Both methods contain problems for transgenic animal research. Single-stranded antisense DNA or RNA, including phosphothio-, methylthio-, and morpholino-oligonucleotides, are inefficient, effective only for a short time, and usually require a pharmacological (nearly toxic) dosage to be effective. However, dominant-negative proteins cannot completely eliminate normal protein function and frequently generate inconsistent results because of variable cellular conditions. To circumvent these problems, recent approaches using RNA interference (RNAi) mechanisms provide a stable, effective, and highly specific alternative *(1,2)*. RNAi is a posttranscriptional gene-silencing phenomenon triggered by small regulatory RNAs, such as small interfering RNA (siRNA) and miRNA *(3,4)*. These small RNA molecules usually function as gene silencers, interfering with intracellular expression of genes complementary to the small RNAs. miRNAs, small single-stranded regulatory RNAs capable of interfering with intracellular mRNAs that contain either complete or partial complementarity, are useful for the design of new therapies against cancer polymorphism and viral mutation *(1,4)*. This flexible characteristic is different from double-stranded siRNAs because a much more rigid complementarity is required for siRNA-induced RNAi gene silencing. Currently, varieties of natural miRNAs have been found to be derived from hairpin-like RNA precursors in almost all eukaryotes, including yeast (*Schizosaccharomyces pombe*), plant (*Arabidopsis spp.*), nematode (*Caenorhabditis elegans*), fly (*Drosophila melanogaster*), fish (*Danio rerio*), avian, mouse, and human, and have been found to be involved in intracellular defense against viral infections and regulation of life-essential gene expressions during development *(5–15)*. Because of these advantages, we used miRNA as a tool for transgenic animal research.

Most protein-coding genes are transcribed by Pol II, which is very inefficient in generating short RNA sequences of fewer than 100 nucleotides (nt); thus, the minimal mRNA size in eukaryotes is usually greater than 300 nt *(16,17)*. To generate the short transcripts of siRNA (19–23 bp), current vector-based RNAi systems used Pol III promoters to transcribe the siRNA. The application of Pol III-directed siRNA-expressing vectors has been found to offer better efficacy and stability for RNAi induction in many cell lines in vitro *(2,18–20)*; nevertheless, several in vivo studies *(21,22)* using the Pol III-mediated siRNA system have failed to provide tissue-specific effectiveness in the targeted cell population because of the ubiquitous existence of Pol III activity in almost all cell types. Moreover, because the read-through effect of Pol III frequently occurs on a short transcription template if lacking the proper codon termination, long siRNA could be synthesized and cause unexpected cytotoxicity *(23,24)*. Such a problem can also result from the competitive conflict between the Pol III promoter and another viral promoter of the vector (i.e., long terminal repeat and cytomegalovirus promoters).

Furthermore, Sledz et al. and we have noted that high-dose siRNA (e.g., >250 n*M* in human T-cells) can trigger interferon-induced toxicity similar to that of long double-stranded RNA (dsRNA) *(25,26)*. It is known that interferon-induced double-stranded RNA-dependent protein kinase (PKR) can trigger cell apoptosis, whereas activation of the interferon-induced 2',5'-oligoadenylate synthetase system leads to extensive nonspecific cleavage of single-stranded RNAs (i.e., mRNAs) *(27)*. Both the protein kinase R and 2',5'-oligoadenylate synthetase systems contain dsRNA-binding motifs that are highly conserved for binding to dsRNAs, but these motifs are relatively insensitive to single-stranded RNAs. Because miRNAs are single-stranded RNA molecules, a Pol II-mediated miRNA generation system provides a much safer and less toxic means for both in vitro and in vivo applications of gene regulation *(28)*. These findings indicate the advantages of Pol II-mediated intronic miRNA generation and its related gene regulation, which can be used as a tool for analysis of gene functions, improvement of current RNAi technology, and development of gene-specific therapeutics and transgenic animals.

We are the first research group to discover the biogenesis of miRNA-like precursors (pre-miRNAs) from the 5'-proximal intron regions of primary gene transcripts (pre-mRNAs) produced by the mammalian Pol II *(29)* (**Fig. 1A**). Depending on the promoter of the miRNA-encoded gene transcript, intronic miRNA is coexpressed with its encoding gene in the specific cell population, which activates the promoter and expresses the gene. Using artificial introns carrying pre-miRNA structures, we have successfully generated mature miRNA molecules with full function in triggering RNAi-related gene silencing in human prostate cancer (LNCaP), human cervical cancer (HeLa), and rat neuronal stem cell lines in vitro, and in zebrafish in vivo *(29,30)*. The artificial intron (*SpRNAi*) was placed in a mutated HcRed1 red fluorescent membrane protein (*RGFP*) gene to form a recombined *SpRNAi–RGFP* gene cassette, in which the functional fluorescent structure was disrupted by the intron insertion. Therefore, we were able to determine the occurrence of intron splicing and miRNA maturation through the appearance of red fluorescent emission on the cell membranes. The red RGFP here serves as a visual indicator for the generation of intronic miRNAs. This intron-derived miRNA system is activated under the control of specific Pol II promoters. As shown in **Fig. 1B**, after Pol II RNA processing and splicing excision, some of the intron-derived miRNA fragments form mature miRNAs and effectively silence the target genes through the RNAi mechanism, whereas the exons of the encoding gene transcript are ligated together to form a mature mRNA for protein synthesis (e.g., RGFP). Based on this miRNA generation model, we have tested various pre-miRNA constructs, and observed that the production of intron-derived miRNA fragments originated from the 5'-proximity of the intron sequence between the 5'-splice site and the branching point. These miRNAs were able to trigger strong suppression of genes possessing more than 70% complementarity to the miRNA sequences, whereas nonhomologous miRNAs, i.e., an empty intron without the pre-miRNA insert, an intron with an off-target miRNA insert (negative control), and a splicing-defective intron, showed no silencing effects on the targeted gene. Similar results can be reproduced in the zebrafish directed against target enhanced green fluorescent protein (EGFP) expression (**Fig. 1C**), indicating the consistent preservation of the intronic miRNA biogenesis system in vertebrates. Further, no effect was detected

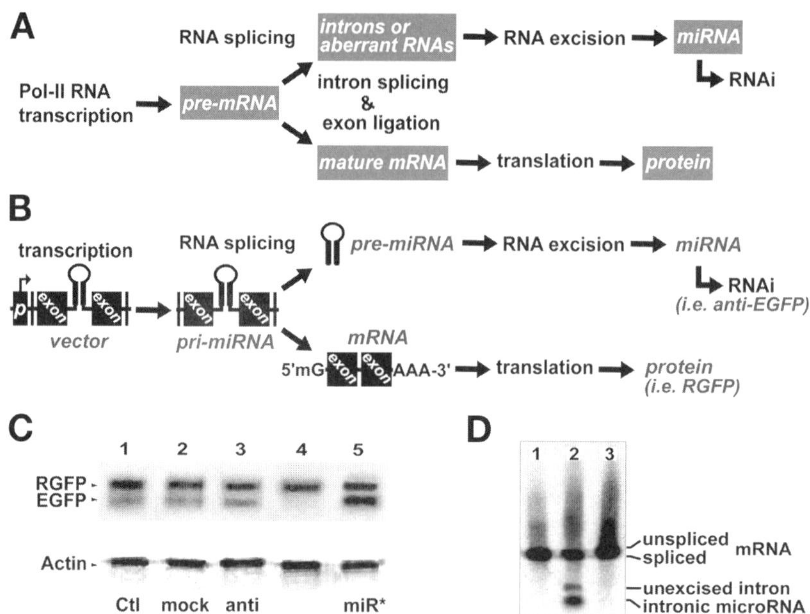

Fig. 1. Biogenesis and function of intronic microRNAs (miRNAs). (**A**) The native intronic miRNA is cotranscribed with a precursor (pre)-messenger RNA (mRNA) by Pol II and cleaved out of the pre-mRNA by the RNA splicing machinery, the spliceosome. The spliced intron with hairpin-like secondary structures is further processed into mature miRNAs capable of triggering RNA interference (RNAi) effects, whereas the ligated exons become a mature mRNA for protein synthesis. (**B**) We designed an artificial intron containing pre-miRNA, namely SpRNAi, mimicking the biogenesis processes of the native intronic miRNAs. (**C**) When a designed miR-EGFP(280/302)–stem-loop RNA construct was tested in the EGFP-expressing transgenic (*UAS: gfp*) zebrafish, we detected a strong RNAi effect only on the target EGFP (lane 4). No detectable gene-silencing effect was observed in other lanes. From left to right: 1, blank vector control (Ctl); 2, miRNA–stem-loop targeting human immunodeficiency virus-p24 (mock); 3, miRNA without stem-loop (anti); and 5, stem-loop–miRNA* complementary to the miR-EGFP(280/302) sequence (miR*). The off-target genes, such as vector red fluorescent membrane protein (RGFP) and fish actin were not affected, indicating the high target specificity of miRNA-mediated gene silencing. (**D**) Three different miR-EGFP(280/302) expression systems were tested for miRNA biogenesis. From left to right: 1, vector expressing intron-free RGFP, no pre-miRNA insert; 2, vector expressing RGFP with an intronic 5'-miRNA–stem-loop–miRNA*-3' insert; and 3, vector similar to the construct in lane 2, but with a defected 5'-splice site in the intron. In Northern blot analysis probing the miR-EGFP(280/302) sequence, the mature miRNA was released only from the spliced intron that resulted from the vector construct in lane 2 in the cell cytoplasm.

on off-target genes, such as RGFP and β-actin, suggesting the high specificity of miRNA-directed RNAi. We have confirmed the identity of the intron-derived miRNAs, which were approx 18- to 25-nt, approximately similar to the newly identified intronic miRNAs in *C. elegans (31)*. Moreover, the intronic small RNAs isolated by guanidinium-chloride ultracentrifugation can elicit strong, but short-term gene-silencing effects on the homologous genes in transfected cells, indicating their temporary RNAi effects *(1)*. Thus, the long-term (>1 mo) gene-silencing effect that we observed in vivo, using the Pol II-mediated intronic miRNA system, is likely maintained by constitutive miRNA production from the vector rather than the from stability of the miRNAs.

We have successfully tested the feasibility of localized gene silencing in chicken embryos in vivo using the intronic miRNA approach and discovered that the interaction between pre-mRNA and genomic DNA may be essential for the miRNA biogenesis. The in vivo model of chicken embryos has been widely used in the research of developmental biology, signal transduction, and flu vaccine development. As an example, the β-catenin gene was selected because it plays a critical role in biological development and ontogenesis *(32)*. β-Catenin is known to be involved in the growth control of skin and liver tissues in chicken embryos. The loss-of-function of β-catenin is lethal in many transgenic animals. As shown in **Fig. 2**, experimental results demonstrated that the miRNAs derived from a predesigned intronic pre-miRNA construct transfected in the cell nucleus were capable of inhibiting β-catenin gene expression in the liver and skin of developing chicken embryos. This is because of the mechanism by which the intronic miRNA generation relies on a coupled interaction of nascent Pol II-directed pre-mRNA transcription and intron excision occurring proximal to genomic perichromatin fibrils. This observation also indicates that the pre-mRNA–genomic DNA recombination may facilitate new miRNA generation by Pol II RNA excision for relatively long-term gene silencing. Alternatively, Pol II may function as an RNA-dependent RNA polymerase for producing more siRNAs, because mammalian Pol II has been reported to possess RNA-dependent RNA polymerase activities *(33,34)*. Taken together, the data suggest that Pol II-mediated RNA generation and excision is involved in intronic miRNA biogenesis, resulting in single-stranded small RNAs of approx 20 nt, comparable to the general sizes of Dicer-processed miRNAs frequently observed in the regulations of numerous developmental events.

To examine the transgenic model of intronic miRNAs, we transfected chicken embryos with the *SpRNAi–RGFP* construct containing a hairpin anti-β-catenin pre-miRNA structure, which was directed against the protein-coding region of the chicken β-catenin gene sequence (*NM205081*) with perfect complementarity. A perfectly complementary miRNA theoretically directs target-mRNA degradation more efficiently than translational repression. Using embryonic day 3 chicken embryos, a dose of 25 n*M* of the *SpRNAi–RGFP* construct was injected into the body region close to where the liver primordia would form (**Fig. 2A**). For efficient delivery into target tissues, the construct was mixed with the FuGENE liposomal transfection reagent (Roche Biomedicals, Indianapolis, IN). A 10% (v/v) fast green solution was concurrently added during the injection as a dye indicator. The mixtures were injected into the ventral side, near the liver primordia, below the heart, using heat-pulled capillary needles. After injection, the embryonic eggs were sealed with sterilized scotch tape and incubated in a humidified incubator at 39°C to 40°C until day 12, when the embryos were examined and photographed under a dissection microscope. Several malformations were observed, however the embryos survived and there was no visible overt toxicity or overall perturbation of embryo development. The liver was the closest organ to the injection site and, thus, was most dramatically

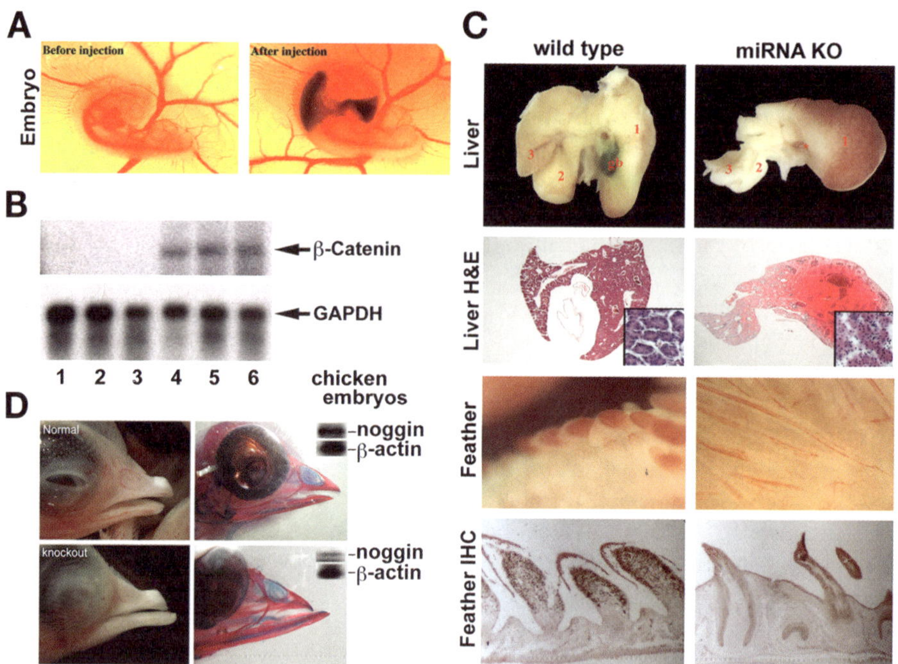

Fig. 2. In vivo gene-silencing effects of anti-β-catenin miRNA and anti-noggin miRNA on special organ development in embryonic chicken. (**A**) The intronic miRNA-expressing construct and fast green dye mixtures were injected into the chicken embryos near the liver primordia below the heart. (**B**) Northern blots of extracted RNAs from chicken embryonic livers with (lanes 1–3) and without (lanes 4–6) anti-β-catenin miRNA treatments were shown. All three knockouts (KO) showed a greater than 98% silencing effect on β-catenin mRNA expression but housekeeping genes, such as *glyceraldehyde phosphate dehydrogenase*, was not affected. (**C**) Liver formation of the β-catenin KOs was significantly hindered (upper right two panels). Microscopic examination revealed a loose structure of hepatocytes, indicating the loss of cell–cell adhesion caused by breaks in adherins junctions formed between β-catenin and cell membrane E-cadherin in early liver development. In severely affected regions, feather growth in the skin close to the injection area was also inhibited (lower right two panels). Immunohistochemistry for β-catenin protein expression (brown) showed a significant decrease in the feather follicle sheaths. H&E, hematoxylin and eosin staining. (**D**) The lower beak development was increased by the mandible injection of the anti-noggin pre-miRNA construct (lower panel) in comparison with the wild type (upper panel). Right panels show bone (alizarin red) and cartilage (alcian blue) staining to demonstrate the outgrowth of bone tissues in the lower beak of the *noggin* KO. Northern blot analysis (insets) confirmed a 60 to 65% decrease of *noggin* mRNA expression in the lower beak area.

affected in its phenotypes. Other regions, particularly the skin close to the injection site, were also affected by the diffused miRNA effects. As shown in **Fig. 2B**, Northern blot analysis detecting the target β-catenin mRNA expression in the dissected livers showed that β-catenin expression in the wild-type livers remained normal (lanes 1–3), whereas those of the miRNA-treated samples was decreased dramatically (lanes 4–6). The miRNA-silencing effect degraded more than 98% of β-catenin mRNA expression in the embryonic chicken, but had no influence on the housekeeping gene, glyceralde-hyde phosphate dehydrogenase (GAPDH) expression, indicating its high target specificity and very limited interferon-related cytotoxicity in vivo.

After 10 d of primordial injection with the anti-β-catenin pre-miRNA construct, the embryonic chicken livers showed an enlarged and engorged first lobe, but the sizes of the second and third lobes of the livers were dramatically decreased (**Fig. 2C**). Histological sections of normal livers showed hepatic cords and sinusoidal space with few blood cells. In the anti-β-catenin miRNA-treated embryos, the general architecture of the hepatic cells in lobes 2 and 3 remained unchanged; however, there were islands of abnormal regions in lobe 1. The endothelium development seemed to be defective, and blood leaked outside of the blood vessels. Abnormal types of hematopoietic cells were also observed between the space of hepatocytes, particularly dominated by a population of small cells with round nuclei and scanty cytoplasm. In severely affected regions, hepatocytes were disrupted (**Fig. 2C**, insets) and the diffused miRNA effect further inhibited the feather growth in the skin area close to the injection site. The results discussed in **Subheading 4.1.** showed that the anti-β-catenin miRNA was very effective in knocking out the targeted gene expression at a very low dose and was effective during a long period of time (≥10 d). Furthermore, the miRNA gene-silencing effect seemed to be very specific, because off-target organs seemed to be normal, indicating that the small, single-stranded composition of miRNA used possessed no overt toxicity. In another attempt to silencing *noggin* expression in the mandible beak area using the same approach (**Fig. 2D**), it was observed that an enlarged lower beak morphology was reminiscent of the previously reported bone morphogenetic protein (BMP)-4-overexpressing chicken embryos *(35,36)*. Skeleton staining showed the outgrowth of bone and cartilage tissues in the injected mandible area (**Fig. 2D**, right panels), and Northern blot analysis further confirmed that approx 60% of *noggin* mRNA expression was knocked out in this region (insets). Because BMP4, a member of the transforming growth factor-β superfamily, is known to promote bone development and *noggin* is an antagonist of *BMP2/4/7* genes, it is not surprising to discover that our miRNA-mediated *noggin* knockouts created a morphological change resembling the *BMP4*-overexpression results previously reported in chicken and other avian models. Thus, the gene silencing in chicken by the pre-miRNA transfection presents a great potential of localized transgene-like approach in creating animal models for developmental biology research.

To test the intronic miRNA effect on adult mammals (**Fig. 3**), we used the vector-based miRNA delivery approach, as previously reported in zebrafish. Patched albino (white) skins of melanin-knockout mice (W-9 black) were created by a succession of intracutaneous transduction of 50 μg of anti-tyrosinase (Tyr) pre-miRNA construct for 4 d (total, 200 μg). Tyr, a type I membrane protein and a copper-containing enzyme, catalyzes the critical and rate-limiting step of tyrosine hydroxylation in the biosynthesis of melanin (black pigment) in skins and hair. After a 13-d incubation, the expression of melanin was blocked because a loss of its intermediates resulted from the anti-Tyr miRNA-silencing effect. Contrarily, the blank control and the U6-directed siRNA-transfected

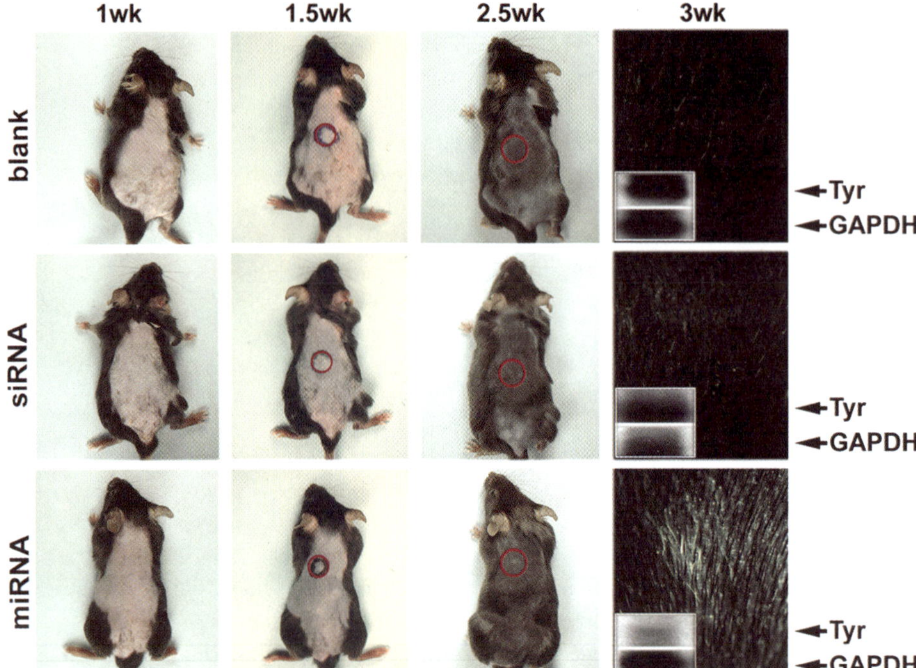

Fig. 3. In vivo effects of anti-tyrosinase (*Tyr*) microRNA (miRNA) on the mouse pigment production of local skins. Transfection of the miRNA induced strong gene silencing of *Tyr* messenger RNA (mRNA) expression but not housekeeping glyceraldehyde phosphate dehydrogenase (*GAPDH*) expression, whereas expression of U6-directed small interfering RNA (siRNA) triggered mild nonspecific RNA degradation of both *Tyr* and *GAPDH* gene transcripts. Because Tyr is an essential enzyme for black pigment melanin production, the success of gene silencing can be observed by a significant loss of the black color in mouse hairs. The red circles indicate the location of intracutaneous injections. Northern blot analysis of *Tyr* mRNA expression in local hair follicles confirmed the effectiveness and specificity of the miRNA-mediated gene-silencing effects (insets).

mice presented normal skin color (black), indicating that the loss of melanin is specifically effective in the miRNA transfections. Moreover, Northern blot analysis using RNA–polymerase chain reaction-amplified mRNAs from hair follicles showed a 76.1 ± 5.3% reduction of Tyr expression 2-d after the miRNA transfection, consistent with the immunohistochemistry results from the same skin area, whereas mild, nonspecific degradation of common gene transcripts was detected in the siRNA-transfected skins (seen from smearing patterns of both the housekeeping control, GAPDH, and target Tyr mRNAs). Thus, the results show that use of intronic miRNA vectors provides a powerful new strategy for in vivo gene therapy, potentially for melanoma treatment. Under the same dosage, the miRNA transfections did not cause a detectable cytotoxicity effect, whereas the induced siRNA transfections showed nonspecific mRNA degradation, as previously reported *(25,26)*. This underscores the fact that the miRNA is effective even under in vivo systems, without the side effects of dsRNA. The results also indicate that this gene-silencing effect is stable and efficient in knocking down the target gene expression during a relatively long period, because the hair regrowth required at least a 10-d recovery. Further, it was observed that nontargeted skin hairs seemed normal, which implies that the intronic miRNA composition possess high specificity and no overt toxicity. Thus, the intronic miRNA approach offers relatively long-term, effective, and safe gene manipulation in local animal tissues or organs, preventing the lethal effects of certain genes in the conventional transgenic animal model.

To date, more than 135 miRNAs have been identified as highly conserved between mammals and other animals *(37)*. This may be an underestimate because the information on unknown 3'-untranslated region sequences in both genomes, nonuntranslated region targets in the internal regions of gene transcripts, and new ortholog annotation, such as intronic miRNAs, were not considered. Approximately 10 to 30% of a spliced intron is exported into the cytoplasm, with moderate half-lives *(38)*. Several types of intronic miRNA have been identified in *C. elegans*, mouse, and human genomes *(29, 31,37)*. Therefore, it is understandable that the current miRNA computing programs do not fully predict the potential miRNA-like molecules. The finding of intronic miRNAs has opened new avenues for predicting miRNA varieties. Although there may be more than one type of new miRNAs to be identified and many new parameters to be generated from different miRNAs, the similarities and differences among these different types of miRNAs will provide better understanding of the small regulatory RNA world. Indeed, a broader definition for various miRNAs in different animal species is needed.

2. Materials

2.1. Preparation of Pre-miRNA Inserts

1. Sense pre-miRNA sequence: 5'-GTCCGATCGTC ATCAAGTCAGCTTGGGTTGCCA TCA AGAGAT TGGCAACCCAAGCTGACTTGAT CGACGCGTCAT-3' (100 pmol/μL in autoclaved ddH$_2$O).
2. Antisense pre-miRNA sequence: 5'-ATGACGCGTCG ATCAAGTCAGCTTGGGTTGCCA ATCTCTTGA TGGCAACCCAAGCTGACTTGAT ACGATCGGAC-3' (100 pmol/μL in autoclaved ddH$_2$O).
3. 2X Hybridization buffer: 200 m*M* KOAc, 60 m*M* HEPES-KOH, and 4 m*M* MgOAc, pH 7.4 at 25°C.
4. Incubation chambers: 94°C, 65°C, and 4°C.

2.2. Change of Pre-miRNA Inserts Located in the SpRNAi–RGFP Gene Cassette

1. *SpRNAi–RGFP* gene vector (University of Southern California File #3443).
2. 10X H buffer: 500 m*M* Tris-HCl, pH 7.5 at 37°C, 1 *M* NaCl, 100 m*M* MgCl$_2$, and 10 m*M* dithiothreitol (DTT).
3. Restriction enzymes, including PuvI and MluI (5 U/μL for each enzyme).
4. PuvI/MluI digestion reaction mix: 12 μL autoclaved ddH$_2$O, 4 μL of 10X H buffer, 2 μL PuvI, and 2 μL MluI; prepare the reaction mix just before use.

5. 10X ligation buffer: 660 mM Tris-HCl, pH 7.5 at 20°C, 50 mM MgCl$_2$, 50 mM DTT, and 10 mM adenosine triphosphate (ATP).
6. 5 U/μL T4 DNA ligase.
7. Ligation reaction mix: 4 μL autoclaved ddH$_2$O, 4 μL of 10X ligation buffer, and 2 μL T4 ligase; prepare the reaction mix just before use.
8. Incubation chambers: 65°C, 37°C, and 16°C.
9. 1% agarose gel electrophoresis.
10. Gel extraction kit (Qiagen, Valencia, CA).
11. Low-salt Luria-Bertani (LB) culture broth.
12. Expand cloning kit (Roche Diagnostics, Indianapolis, IN).
13. DH5α transformation-competent *Escherichia coli* cells (Roche).
14. 10X MgSO$_4$ solution: 1 M MgSO$_4$.
15. 1X CaCl$_2$ solution: 0.1 M CaCl$_2$.
16. 10X Glucose solution: 1 M glucose.
17. Incubation chambers: 42°C and 4°C.
18. Incubation shaker: 37°C, 285 rpm vortex.
19. Luria-Bertani agar plate containing 50 μg/mL kanamycin.
20. Spin Miniprep kit (Qiagen).
21. Microcentrifuge: 17,900g.

2.3. Cloning of the SpRNAi–RGFP Gene Cassette Into a Viral Vector

1. Retroviral vector: e.g., replication-competent avian sarcoma virus (RCAS) vector.
2. 10X H buffer: 500 mM Tris-HCl, pH 7.5 at 37°C, 1 M NaCl, 100 mM MgCl$_2$, and 10 mM DTT.
3. Restriction enzymes, including XhoI and XbaI.
4. XhoI/XbaI digestion reaction mix: 2 μL autoclaved ddH$_2$O, 4 μL of 10X H buffer, 2 μL XhoI, and 2 μL XbaI; prepare the reaction mix just before use.
5. 10X ligation buffer: 660 mM Tris-HCl, pH 7.5 at 20°C, 50 mM MgCl$_2$, 50 mM DTT, and 10 mM ATP.
6. 5 U/μL T4 DNA ligase.
7. Ligation reaction mix: 4 μL autoclaved ddH$_2$O, 4 μL of 10X ligation buffer, and 2 μL T4 ligase; prepare the reaction mix just before use.

2.4. Viral Packaging and Titer Quantitation

1. Serum-free RPMI-1640 cell culture medium.
2. FuGENE transfection reagent (Roche).
3. Chicken embryonic fibroblast cell culture.
4. Cell culture incubator.
5. Lentivirus purification kit (Cell Biolabs).
6. Microcentrifuge: 17,900g.

3. Methods

3.1. Preparation of Pre-miRNA Inserts

The intronic pre-miRNA insert is formed by hybridization of the sense and antisense pre-miRNA sequences, which are synthesized to be perfectly complementary to each other. Both of the SpRNAi sequences must be purified by polyacrylamide gel electrophoresis before use and stored at −20°C.

1. Hybridization: mix the sense and antisense pre-miRNA sequences (5 μL for each sequence) in 10 μL of 2X hybridization buffer, heat to 94°C for 3 min, and cool to 65°C for 10 min. Stop the reaction on ice.

3.2. Change of Pre-miRNA Inserts Located in the SpRNAi–RGFP Gene Cassette

Because the intronic insert region of the *SpRNAi–RGFP* vector is flanked with a PvuI and an MluI restriction site at its 5' and 3' ends, respectively, the primary pre-miRNA insert can be easily removed and replaced by various gene-specific inserts (e.g., anti-EGFP) possessing cohesive ends (*see* **Note 1**).

1. Cleavage by MluI and PvuI: add the PuvI/MluI digestion reaction mix to the 20 μL of *SpRNAi–RGFP* vector and the pre-miRNA hybrid, respectively. Incubate the reaction at 37°C for 4 h and stop the reaction on ice.
2. Purification of MluI and PvuI-digested sequences: load and run the reactions in 1% agarose gel electrophoresis and cut out the MluI- and PvuI-digested *SpRNAi–RGFP* sequence and the pre-miRNA fragment, respectively, using a clean surgical blade. Recover the two oligonucleotide sequences in one tube of 30 μL autoclaved ddH$_2$O, using the gel extraction column and following the manufacturer's suggestions.
3. Ligation: add the ligation reaction mix to the extraction. Incubate the reaction at 16°C for 16 h and stop the reaction on ice.
4. Plasmid amplification: transfect the ligation product into the DH5α transformation-competent *E. coli* cells using the expand cloning kit and following the manufacturer's suggestions.
5. Plasmid recovery: isolate and collect the amplified *SpRNAi–RGFP* plasmid from the DH5α transformation-competent *E. coli* cells into a tube of 30 μL autoclaved ddH$_2$O, using a spin Miniprep filter and following the manufacturer's suggestions (*see* **Note 2**).

3.3. Cloning of the SpRNAi–RGFP Gene Cassette Into a Viral Vector

To express the *SpRNAi–RGFP* gene in chicken embryos, transfer the *SpRNAi–RGFP* gene cassette from the pHcRed1-N1/1 plasmid vector to the RCAS vector. Because the functional fluorescent structure of HcRed is disrupted by the SpRNAi intron insertion, one can determine the occurrence of intron splicing and miRNA maturation through the appearance of red fluorescent RGFP emission on the cell membranes. The RGFP protein also serves as a quantitative marker for measuring the titer activity of the pre-miRNA-expressing RCAS virus using flow cytometry. This intron-derived miRNA system is activated under the control of the *Xenopus* elongation factor 1-α enhancer promoter located in the RCAS vector.

1. Cleavage by XhoI and XbaI: add the XhoI/XbaI digestion reaction mix to the pHcRed1-N1/1 plasmid vector containing an *SpRNAi–RGFP* gene cassette and the RCAS retroviral vector, respectively. Incubate both of the reactions at 37°C for 4 h and stop the reactions on ice.
2. Purification of XhoI/XbaI-digested sequences: load and run the reactions in 1% agarose gel electrophoresis and cut out the XhoI/XbaI-digested *SpRNAi–RGFP* sequence and the large RCAS fragment, respectively, using a clean surgical blade. Recover the two oligonucleotide sequences in one tube of 30 μL autoclaved ddH$_2$O using the gel extraction column and following the manufacturer's suggestions.

3. Ligation: add the ligation reaction mix to the extraction. Incubate the reaction at 16°C for 16 h and stop the reaction on ice.

3.4. Viral Packaging and Titer Quantitation

To increase transfection efficiency, we use liposomal reagents to facilitate the delivery of the *SpRNAi–RGFP* vector into the packaging cells.

1. Preparation of FuGENE: add 6 μL of the FuGENE reagent into 100 μL of RPMI-1640 medium in a clean tube and gently mix the solution, following the manufacturer's suggestions. Add 20 μg (in less than 50 μL) of the *SpRNAi–RGFP* vector into the liposomal dilution and gently mix the solution, following the manufacturer's suggestions. Store the mixture at 4°C for 30 min.
2. Transfection: add the mixture into the center of the chicken embryonic fibroblast cell culture and gently mix the cell culture medium. Culture the transfected cells in a cell culture incubator at 37°C and 5% CO_2 for 48 to 72 h.
3. Purification of viral particles: harvest and concentrate the viral particles from the medium suspension using a lentivirus purification filter, following the manufacturer's protocol (*see* **Note 3**).

4. Notes

1. The synthetic pre-miRNA sequences that we show here are directed against the 5'-coding region of the chicken β-catenin gene sequence (*NM205081*, sense 110–131 nt) with perfect complementarity. The principal rule for designing an intronic pre-miRNA insert is to synthesize two mutually complementary oligonucleotides, including one 5'-GTCCGATC GTC, 19- to 27-nt antisense target gene sequence—TCAAGAGAT (stem-loop)—19- to 27-nt sense target gene sequence, CGACGCGTCAT-3'; and another 5'-ATGACGGTCG, 19- to 27-nt antisense target gene sequence—ATCTCTTGA (stem-loop)—19- to 27-nt sense target gene sequence, GACGATCGGAC-3'. The hybridization of these two oligonucleotide sequences forms the intronic pre-miRNA insert, which contains a 5'-PuvI and a 3'-Mlu1 restriction site for further ligation into the intron region of an *SpRNAi–RGFP* gene cassette. All synthetic oligonucleotides must be purified by polyacrylamide gel electrophoresis to ensure their highest purity and integrity.
2. The sequence of the final *SpRNAi–RGFP* gene cassette and its pre-miRNA insert must be confirmed by DNA sequencing.
3. The RGFP protein can serve as a quantitative marker for measuring the titer levels of the pre-miRNA-expressing RCAS virus using either flow cytometry or the lentivirus quantitation kit (Cell Biolabs). The RGFP-specific monoclonal antibody can be purchased from BD Biosciences (Palo Alto, CA).

Acknowledgments

The work was supported by a grant from the National Institutes of Health, CA 85722.

References

1. Lin, S. L. and Ying, S. Y. (2004) Novel RNAi therapy—intron-derived microRNA drugs. *Drug Design Reviews* **1,** 247–255.
2. Tuschl, T. and Borkhardt, A. (2002) Small interfering RNAs: a revolutionary tool for the analysis of gene function and gene therapy. *Mol. Interv.* **2,** 158–167.

3. Nelson, P., Kiriakidou, M., Sharma, A., Maniataki, E., and Mourelatos, Z. (2003) The microRNA world: small is mighty. *Trends Biochem. Sci.* **28,** 534–539.

4. Ying, S. Y. and Lin, S. L. (2005) Intronic microRNA (miRNA). *Biochem. Biophys. Res. Commun.* **326,** 515–520.

5. Hall, I. M., Shankaranarayana, G. D., Noma, K., Ayoub, N., Cohen, A., and Grewal, S. I. (2002) Establishment and maintenance of a heterochromatin domain. *Science* **297,** 2232–2237.

6. Llave, C., Xie, Z., Kasschau, K. D., and Carrington, J. C. (2002) Cleavage of Scarecrow-like mRNA targets directed by a class of Arabidopsis miRNA. *Science* **297,** 2053–2056.

7. Rhoades, M. W., Reinhart, B. J., Lim, L. P., Burge, C. B., Bartel, B., and Bartel, D. P. (2002) Prediction of plant microRNA targets. *Cell* **110,** 513–520.

8. Lee, R. C., Feibaum, R. L., and Ambros, V. (1993) The C. elegans heterochromic gene lin-4 encodes small RNAs with antisense complementarity to lin-14. *Cell* **75,** 843–854.

9. Reinhart, B. J., Slack, F. J., Basson, M., et al. (2000) The 21-nucleotide let-7 RNA regulates developmental timing in Caenorhabditis elegans. *Nature* **403,** 901–906.

10. Lau, N. C., Lim, L. P., Weinstein, E. G., and Bartel, D. P. (2001) An abundant class of tiny RNAs with probable regulatory roles in Caenorhabditis elegans. *Science* **294,** 858–862.

11. Brennecke, J., Hipfner, D. R., Stark, A., Russell, R. B., and Cohen, S. M. (2003) Bantam encodes a developmentally regulated microRNA that controls cell proliferation and regulates the proapoptotic gene hid in Drosophila. *Cell* **113,** 25–36.

12. Xu, P., Vernooy, S. Y., Guo, M., and Hay, B. A. (2003) The Drosophila microRNA Mir-14 suppresses cell death and is required for normal fat metabolism. *Curr. Biol.* **13,** 790–795.

13. Lagos-Quintana, M., Rauhut, R., Meyer, J., Borkhardt, A., and Tuschl, T. (2003) New microRNAs from mouse and human. *RNA* **9,** 175–179.

14. Mourelatos, Z., Dostie, J., Paushkin, S., et al. (2002) miRNPs: a novel class of ribonucleoproteins containing numerous microRNAs. *Genes Dev.* **16,** 720–728.

15. Zeng, Y., Wagner, E. J., and Cullen, B. R. (2002) Both natural and designed micro RNAs can inhibit the expression of cognate mRNAs when expressed in human cells. *Mol. Cell* **9,** 1327–1333.

16. Hirose, Y. and Manley, J. L. (2000) RNA polymerase II and the integration of nuclear events. *Genes Dev.* **14,** 1415–1429.

17. Kramer, A. (1996) The structure and function of proteins involved in mammalian pre-mRNA splicing. *Annu. Rev. Biochem.* **65,** 367–409.

18. Miyagishi, M. and Taira, K. (2002) U6 promoter-driven siRNAs with four uridine 3' overhangs efficiently suppress targeted gene expression in mammalian cells. *Nat. Biotechnol.* **20,** 497–500.

19. Lee, N. S., Dohjima, T., Bauer, G., et al. (2002) Expression of small interfering RNAs targeted against HIV-1 rev transcripts in human cells. *Nat. Biotechnol.* **20,** 500–505.

20. Paul, C. P., Good, P. D., Winer, I., and Engelke, D. R. (2002) Effective expression of small interfering RNA in human cells. *Nat. Biotechnol.* **20,** 505–508.

21. Xia, H., Mao, Q., Paulson, H. L., and Davidson, B. L. (2002) siRNA-mediated gene silencing in vitro and in vivo. *Nat. Biotechnol.* **20,** 1006–1010.

22. McCaffrey, A. P., Meuse, L., Pham, T. T., Conklin, D. S., Hannon, G. J., and Kay, M. A. (2002) RNA interference in adult mice. *Nature* **418,** 38–39.

23. Gunnery, S., Ma, Y., and Mathews, M. B. (1999) Termination sequence requirements vary among genes transcribed by RNA polymerase III. *J. Mol. Biol.* **286,** 745–757.

24. Schramm, L. and Hernandez, N. (2002) Recruitment of RNA polymerase III to its target promoters. *Genes Dev.* **16,** 2593–2620.

25. Sledz, C. A., Holko, M., de Veer, M. J., Silverman, R. H., and Williams, B. R. (2003) Activation of the interferon system by short-interfering RNAs. *Nat. Cell Biol.* **5,** 834–839.
26. Lin, S. L. and Ying, S. Y. (2004) Combinational therapy for HIV-1 eradication and vaccination. *Intl. J. Oncol.* **24,** 81–88.
27. Stark, G. R., Kerr, I. M., Williams, B. R, Silverman, R. H., and Schreiber, R. D. (1998) How cells respond to interferons. *Annu. Rev. Biochem.* **67,** 227–264.
28. Lin, S. L. and Ying, S. Y. (2004) New drug design for gene therapy—taking advantage of introns. *Lett. Drug Design Discovery* **1,** 256–262.
29. Lin, S. L., Chang, D., Wu, D. Y., and Ying, S. Y. (2003) A novel RNA splicing-mediated gene silencing mechanism potential for genome evolution. *Biochem. Biophys. Res. Commun.* **310,** 754–760.
30. Lin, S. L., Chang, D., and Ying, S. Y. (2005) Asymmetry of intronic pre-miRNA structures in functional RISC assembly. *Gene* **356,** 32–38.
31. Ambros, V., Lee, R. C., Lavanway, A., Williams, P. T., and Jewell, D. (2003) MicroRNAs and other tiny endogenous RNAs in C. elegans. *Curr. Biol.* **13,** 807–818.
32. Butz, S. and Larue, L. (1995) Expression of catenins during mouse embryonic development and in adult tissues. *Cell Adhes. Commun.* **3,** 337–352.
33. Filipovska, J. and Konarska, M. M. (2000) Specific HDV RNA-templated transcription by pol II in vitro. *RNA* **6,** 41–54.
34. Modahl, L. E., Macnaughton, T. B., Zhu, N., Johnson, D. L., and Lai, M. M. (2000) RNA-dependent replication and transcription of hepatitis delta virus RNA involve distinct cellular RNA polymerases. *Mol. Cell Biol.* **20,** 6030–6039.
35. Abzhanov, A., Protas, M., Grant, B. R., Grant, P. R., and Tabin, C. J. (2004) Bmp4 and morphological variation of beaks in Darwin's finches. *Science* **305,** 1462–1465.
36. Wu, P., Jiang, T. X., Suksaweang, S., Widelitz, R. B., and Chuong, C. M. (2004) Molecular shaping of the beak. *Science* **305,** 1465–1466.
37. Rodriguez, A., Griffiths-Jones, S., Ashurst, J. L., and Bradley, A. (2004) Identification of mammalian microRNA host genes and transcription units. *Genome Res.* **14,** 1902–1910.
38. Clement, J. Q., Qian, L., Kaplinsky, N., and Wilkinson, M. F. (1999) The stability and fate of a spliced intron from vertebrate cells. *RNA* **5,** 206–220.

25

Evolution of MicroRNAs

Andrea Tanzer and Peter F. Stadler

Summary

MicroRNAs (miRNAs) form a large class of small regulatory RNAs in eukaryotes. Although they share a common processing pathway and certain structural features, in general, there is no detectable sequence similarity among miRNAs from a given organism. On the other hand, many miRNAs are members of a family of a few, often very similar, paralogs. It is, thus, of interest to trace the evolutionary history of individual miRNAs, to identify the timing of gene duplications, and to study relationships between the histories of different miRNA families. Some miRNAs are transcribed from polycistronic primary transcripts. In these cases, we will study the evolution of entire clusters.

Key Words: MicroRNA; noncoding RNA; clusters; molecular evolution; gene phylogeny.

1. Introduction

1.1. General Features of miRNAs

MicroRNAs form an abundant class of small, noncoding RNAs (ncRNAs). The mature sequences, of 22 nucleotides (nt) in length, are excised from approx 70- to 100-nt-long precursors (pre-miRNA), which fold into stem-loop structures required for the maturation process. First, the nuclear ribonuclease III, Drosha, cuts off the pre-miRNAs from longer primary precursors, and the pre-miRNAs are exported to the cytoplasm via the Exportin-5 pathway. The cytoplasmic ribonuclease III, Dicer, then excises the mature miRNA, which binds to its target sites in messenger RNA (mRNA) or DNA.

There are two major evolutionary constraints on miRNA genes:

1. The mature sequence must recognize its target and, thus, keep its sequence unchanged. Otherwise, the target sequence would have to coevolve. Because miRNAs are believed to target multiple genes, this scenario of coevolution becomes less likely, at least for miRNAs with high numbers of different target genes.
2. Maturation of miRNAs requires a stem-loop fold of the pre-miRNA. Mutations in one arm of the pre-miRNA can be compensated by subsequent changes in the other arm of the imperfect stem.

From: *Methods in Molecular Biology, vol. 342: MicroRNA Protocols*
Edited by: S. Ying © Humana Press Inc., Totowa, NJ

Thus, miRNAs show sufficient variation to provide phylogenetic signals. Nevertheless, high sequence conservation allows detection of homologous genes across genomes by simple basic local alignment search tool (BLAST) searches and subsequent validation by determining the secondary structure and selecting for stem-loops.

Figure 1A shows the multiple sequence alignment of *mir-19b-2* precursors of various vertebrates reflecting the discussed constraints. The mature sequence remains almost unchanged.

1.2. miRNA Detection and Validation

The two properties listed in **Subheading 1.1.** make it relatively simple to detect miRNA genes using comparative genomics. Such an approach is implemented, e.g., in the programs `MiRscan` *(1)* and `miRseeker` *(2)*. Furthermore, miRNAs can be detected based on their increased thermodynamic stability. `Randfold` *(3)* compares the minimum free energy (mfe) structures of a sequence with those inferred from those obtained by randomly shuffling the original sequence. miRNAs exhibit significant lower mfe structures indicated by *p*-values of less than 0.05. miRNAs in plants, in contrast to animals, usually function by binding complementary to their target mRNAs. Thus, plant miRNAs can be found by extracting those hairpin structures that contain sequence motifs complementary to an mRNA *(3–5)*.

However, in this chapter, we do not focus on the discovery of novel miRNA families. To study the phylogeny of miRNAs, we need methods to find additional members of a miRNA family with at least one known member. As we shall see, this can be achieved by more or less straightforward application of `blastn` *(6)*. A recent paper *(7)* shows that `erpin` can be used effectively to discover distant relatives of a given miRNA family. In contrast to `blast`, which performs searches based on sequence information alone, `erpin` searches a combination of sequence and secondary structure patterns *(8)*. Once a number of candidate sequences have been identified, standard methods for computing multiple sequence alignments, in particular `clustalw` *(9)*, can be used (*see* **ref. 10** for a description in the same series).

RNA secondary structures play an important role in miRNA bioinformatics because (1) the pre-miRNAs have characteristic hairpin structures and (2) miRNAs are usually significantly more stable than randomized sequences with the same base composition. miRNA candidates that have been identified based on sequence similarities can, therefore, be validated by checking their secondary structure and, possibly, also their thermodynamic stability.

RNA secondary structure calculations are based on a relatively simple dynamic programming approach that is described in detail, e.g., in **ref. 11**. Two software packages,

---

Fig. 1. *(Opposite page)* The prediction of RNA consensus secondary structures using `RNAalifold` requires a multiple sequence alignment in `Clustalw` format. Such alignment can be viewed using `ClustalX` (**A**). The mature miRNA in this alignment of several *mir-19b-2* homologs is indicated by a run of asterisks in the more 3' half of the sequences. The conventional presentation of a secondary structure (**B**) is also shown as a dot plot (**C**) and a mountain plot (**D**). The basepair probabilities correspond to the intensity of the dots and bars, respectively. The darker they appear, the more likely a base pair is formed.

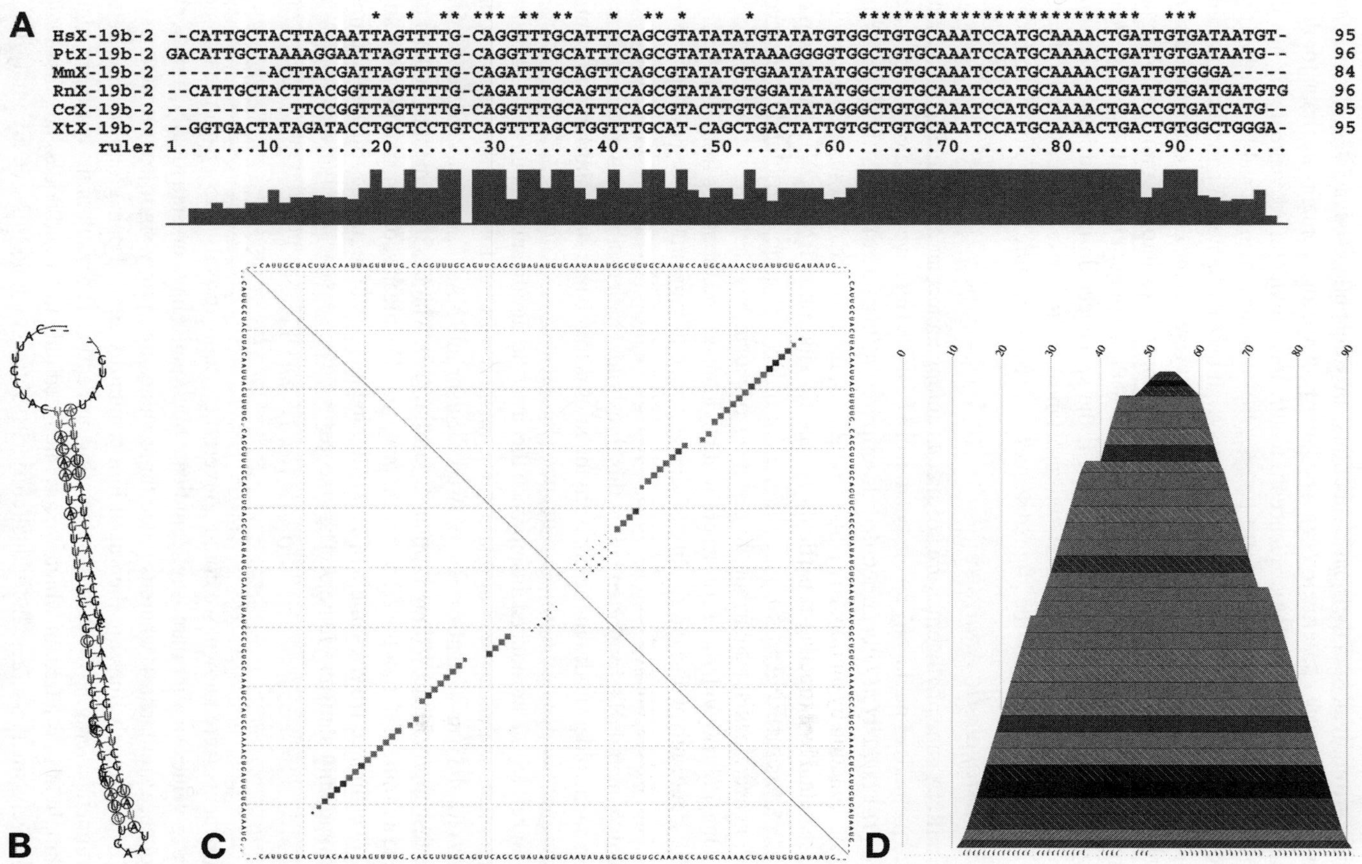

A
HsX-19b-2 --CATTGCTACTTACAATTAGTTTTG-CAGGTTTGCATTTCAGCGTATATATGTATATGTGGCTGTGCAAATCCATGCAAAACTGATTGTGATAATGT-   95
PtX-19b-2 GACATTGCTAAAAGGAATTAGTTTTG-CAGGTTTGCATTTCAGCGTATATATAAAGGGGTGGCTGTGCAAATCCATGCAAAACTGATTGTGATAATG--   96
MmX-19b-2 ---------ACTTACGATTAGTTTTG-CAGATTTGCAGTTCAGCGTATATGTGAATATATGGCTGTGCAAATCCATGCAAAACTGATTGTGGGA-----   84
RnX-19b-2 --CATTGCTACTTACGGTTAGTTTTG-CAGATTTGCAGTTCAGCGTATATGTGGATATATGGCTGTGCAAATCCATGCAAAACTGATTGTGATGATGTG   96
CcX-19b-2 ---------TTCCGGTTAGTTTTG-CAGGTTTGCATTTCAGCGTACTTGTGCATATAGGGCTGTGCAAATCCATGCAAAACTGACCGTGATCATG--   85
XtX-19b-2 --GGTGACTATAGATACCTGCTCCTGTCAGTTTAGCTGGTTTGCAT-CAGCTGACTATTGTGCTGTGCAAATCCATGCAAAACTGACTGTGGCTGGGA-   95
    ruler 1.......10........20........30........40........50........60........70........80........90........

B

C
CAUUGCUACUUACAAUUAGUUUUG_CAGGUUUGCAGUUCAGCGUAUAUGUGAAUAUAUGGCUGUGCAAAUCCAUGCAAAACUGAUUGUGAUAAUG_

D
0 10 20 30 40 50 60 70 80 90

which are equivalent in their basic functions, are frequently used: `mfold` *(12,13)* and the `Vienna RNA Package` *(14)*. The latter package also contains methods for dealing with alignments of RNA sequences, a feature that provides a convenient way of validating miRNA candidates. `RNAalifold` *(15)* computes the most stable structure that can be formed by a group of aligned sequences. It uses the same dynamic programming approach as the folding of a single sequence and averages the energetic contribution of each sequence. If a family of related RNA sequences folds into a common RNA structure, `RNAalifold` will predict this structure with an energy close to the average folding energy of each individual sequence. If the sequences do not fold into a common structure, however, `RNAalifold` returns, at most, the few base pairs that can be formed simultaneously by all of the aligned sequences, i.e., a structure that is nearly unfolded.

1.3. Phylogenetic Analysis

miRNA gene phylogenies are not special among molecular phylogenies. Thus, standard methods of phylogeny reconstruction can be used. Here, we use the `phylip` package *(16)* (*see* **ref. 17** for a detailed description in this series). As is the case for all RNAs that have evolutionarily conserved RNAs, the two sides of a stem do not evolve independently. This is also particularly true for ribosomal RNAs. We can, however, neglect this effect here, because the mature miRNA is almost absolutely conserved and, hence, does not contribute to distances or parsimony scores.

One problem with the reconstruction of phylogenetic relationships from short nucleic acid sequences is that the quality of the sequence alignments rapidly declines when the pair-wise sequence identity falls below 50 or 60%. The precursor sequences of paralogous miRNAs are often below this threshold. One possibility to obtain information on the oldest nodes in the gene phylogenies is to use pair-wise similarity measures that do not depend on multiple sequence alignments.

In **ref. 18**, we introduced an approach that uses the significance of pair-wise sequence alignments as a measure of similarity. The method works as follows: the identity score $s(I,J)$ for the pair-wise alignment of two precursor miRNAs, I and J, is computed using the fast approximate Wilbur-Lipman algorithm *(19)*, which is implemented in the pair-wise alignment step of the `clustalw` program. The mean score, m, and the variance, v, are estimated from a sample of 1000 alignments pairs of sequences that are obtained by randomly shuffling I and J. The z-score:

$$z(I, J) = [s(I, J) - m] / \sqrt{v}$$

is a good statistical measure for relatedness of I and J. If the score distribution of the alignments were known, we could convert the z-score directly into a p-value. In practice, z-values smaller than, say, 2, indicate that I and J have no statistically significant sequence similarities, whereas much large values of z imply significant relatedness.

The z-score values are then used in a standard weighted pair group method using arithmetic averaging (WPGMA) clustering procedure. The result of the clustering algorithm, in turn, is a tree, in which we are interested only in the old nodes, i.e., those with relatively small z-scores. Individual clusters (subtrees) within this tree are analyzed in the conventional way (using multiple sequence alignments). The complete gene phylogeny is then combined from the results of the two methods.

1.4. Typographical Conventions

a. Constant width font is used for program names, variable names, and other literal text, such as input and output in the terminal window.
b. Lines starting with a "#" within a literal text block are commands. You should type the text following the # into your terminal window, finishing by pressing return. (The # signifies the command line prompt, which may look different on your system).
c. All other lines within a literal text block are the output from the command that was typed.

2. Materials

2.1. miRNA Databases

Several ncRNA databases emerged during the past years. For miRNAs, miRBase *(20)* is the most used. It has two aims: a searchable database of published miRNAs and a so-called "gene hunter." New unpublished miRNAs can be uploaded and will be integrated into the database after publication. This strategy provides a stringent nomenclature and, furthermore, the possibility of renaming genes.

MicroRNAs from miRBase can be downloaded either from the ftp site (recommended) or via the web interface. Mature as well as precursor sequences are available in fasta format. The genome positions refer to the University of California, Santa Cruz genome browser *(21)*, in which a separate miRNA track is available.

Another rich source for miRNAs is the noncode database *(22)*, but this registry does not contain a specific miRNA section. Nevertheless, the ncRNAs are assigned to process function classes, providing information regarding their biological functions.

2.2. Genome Databases

The current genome database of choice is definitely the University of California, Santa Cruz database. It serves both classic biologists as well as bioinformaticians. For the selection of genomes available, a large amount of information and genome annotation is provided, even in machine-readable form. Other genomes might be found, e.g., at the National Center for Biotechnology Information *(23)*, Ensembl *(24)*, the Department of Energy Joint Genome Institute *(25)*, and a variety of sequencing centers.

2.3. Software

The Vienna RNA Package v1.5beta contains a variety of programs, including RNAfold, RNAalifold, and RNALfold for RNA secondary structure prediction. The C code, libraries, and Perl modules, as well as a compiled version running under Windows can be downloaded from our web page *(26)*. Furthermore, a web interface is available for sequences of a maximum of 4000 bp (mfe only) or 3000 bp (pair probabilities). A detailed tutorial on the usage of the Vienna RNA Package can be found in **ref. 27**. In this chapter, we use the National Center for Biotechnology Information BLAST algorithm v2.2.6 *(28)*. ClustalW *(29)* and ClustalX *(30)* are available on the internet, including online manuals *(31,32)*. The phylip package *(33)* and documentation *(34)*, as well as NJ-Plot *(35)*, are also freely available. All programs run on several platforms. A test version of randfold *(3)* is ready for download *(36)*. Our z-scoring can be provided by Andrea Tanzer on request *(at@tbi.univie.ac.at.)*.

3. Methods

3.1. Installation of Software

For all programs needed, the documentation provides proper installation instructions. We exclusively use a `Linux`/UNIX environment for our bioinformatics computations. We strongly recommend this for three reasons:

1. Linux is much cheaper than the alternatives.
2. After an initial (admittedly a bit steep) learning curve, using the command line is much more efficient than graphical user interfaces, and powerful scripting languages allow one to automate much of the procedure described in this chapter.
3. Most importantly, most of the more specialized software, i.e., many of the methods that are not already available as web services, are developed in a UNIX environment. In many cases, MS Windows and Mac versions are available as well, or can at least be compiled from the source files for different operating systems. Nevertheless, most of these programs have only command line interfaces.

Mac users: the new Mac OS X has a UNIX-style operating system underneath the aqua user interface, hence, you can work on it similar to a `Linux` box. However, most of the development environment is not installed by default, but the Xcode tools and X11 can be found on the Mac OS X installation CD.

Windows users: the `cygwin` package *(37)* provides a fairly complete development environment for MS Windows, including UNIX-style terminals running the usual command shell programs. This software can be used instead of a generic UNIX operating system. All examples described in this chapter should work without changes in this environment. Note, however, that programs need to be compiled from the source files, downloading `Linux` binaries will not work (*see* **Note 1**).

3.2. Setting Up Databases

Each genome database should be placed in a separate directory. To create blastable databases, go to the directory and type:

```
# formatdb -o T -p F -i db.fa -l db.log
```

where `db.fa` is your fasta file containing the genomic sequence. For large database files, *see* **Note 2.**

3.3. Detection of Homologous miRNAs

3.3.1. BLAST Searches

To begin, choose a precursor miRNA from miRBase or obtain a sequence of interest in fasta format. Here, we describe the procedure for detection of homologs of the human miRNA-17 cluster located on the chromosome X (*HsX-17cl*) in the genome of the frog *Xenopus tropicalis*. You can also search for single miRNAs. The file HsX-17cl.fa is a multi fasta file consisting of five miRNAs. Xt.fa contains the *X. tropicalis* genome (JGI v3; January 2005).

BLAST this sequence against your genome database:

```
# blastall -p blastn -d Xt.fa -i HsX-17cl.fa -e 1e-2 -m8
```

Output:

```
Hs1-20       scaffold_212   100.00  22  0  0   9  30  656642  656663  0.005  44.1
HsX-18       scaffold_212    88.73  71  8  0   1  71  656753  656823  3e-13  77.8
HsX-20       scaffold_212   100.00  26  0  0   7  32  656918  656943  2e-05  52.0
HsX-19b-2    scaffold_212    96.67  30  1  0  59  88  657067  657096  3e-05  52.0
HsX-92-2     scaffold_212   100.00  28  0  0  44  71  657197  657224  1e-06  56.0
```

Usually, the BLAST alignments will generally not cover the entire length of the pre-miRNA. This can be compensated for by extending the blast intervals accordingly. For example, only the sequence positions 7 to 32 of *HsX-20* match scaffold 212. Thus, we have to extract positions $656918 - 7 + 1 = 656912$ to $656943 + (71 - 32) = 656982$, where 71 is the length of *HsX-20*. For our example, we compute the following approximate coordinates for the *Xenopus* candidates:

XtX-106aA	656634	656704	scaffold_212
XtX-18A	656753	656823	scaffold_212
XtX-20A	656912	656982	scaffold_212
XtX-19b-2A	657009	657103	scaffold_212
XtX-92-2A	657154	657228	scaffold_212

Next, we retrieve these subsequences from the genomic sequence:

```
# fastacmd –d Xt.fa –s scaffold_212 –S 1 –L 657009,657103 –l 150
  > XtX-cand.fa
```

Output:

```
>lcl|scaffold_212:657009-657103 No definition line found
GGTGACTATAGATACCTGCTCCTGTCAGTTTAGCTGGTTTGCATCAGCTGACTATTGTGCTGTG
CAAATCCATGCAAAACTGACTGTGGCTGGGA
```

You should also think of some preliminary nomenclature for your sequences, e.g., *Xt-19b-2A* for candidate 1 of *hsa-mir-19b-2* found in *X. tropicalis*. The first 10 characters have to be unique because some programs accept names of this length and truncate longer names. Any text editor can be used to insert a new name into the fasta file just after the >.

Repeat the procedure for all genomes of interest. For distantly related species, you may want to adjust the BLAST parameters (*see* **Note 3**).

3.3.2. Validation of Primary miRNA Candidates

For each miRNA of the cluster, perform a multiple sequence alignment of all candidates using ClustalW, e.g., all *mir-19b-2* genes. It will produce an alignment file, .aln, and a guide tree file, .dnd. Using ClustalW is described in **ref. 10**.

```
# clustalw all-19b-2.fa
```

View the alignment with ClustalX

```
# clustalx all-19b-2.aln
```

The sequence of the mature miRNA should be conserved across different species and, thus, appear as a conserved block of approx 20 nt in the alignment (**Fig. 1A**).

ClustalX indicates conserved positions by asterisks. Those candidates that do not contain this conserved block should be removed and further tested, as described in **Note 4**.

Now we are ready to perform some RNA secondary structure predictions. First, let us calculate the mfe consensus structure of all candidates:

```
# RNAalifold -p -noLP < all-19b-2.aln
__CAUUGCUACUUACAAUUAGUUUUG_CAGGUUUGCAGUUCAGCGUAUAUGUGAAUAUAUGGCUGUGCAAAUCCAUGCAAAACUGAUUGUGAUAAUG__
............(((((((((((((((.(((((((((...(((( ...(((((....)))))))))))))))))))..))))))))))))))).......  (-22.51 = -23.27 + 0.76)
.............,((((((((((((((.(((((((((((...(((( .,,((( ,....,)))))}))))))))))))))..)))))))))))))),.......  [-24.53]
frequency of mfe structure in ensemble 0.0377992
```

RNAalifold produces three files. The secondary structure is drawn in alirna.ps (**Fig. 1B**). alifold.out is a plain text file containing information regarding each plausible pair, ranked by credibility. Each line lists the paired bases i and j, the number of incompatible sequences, the predicted probability, an entropy measure, and the basepair types occurring at this position. The dot plot (**Fig. 1C**) alidot.ps represents these data. Each possible pair (i,j) is represented by a dot in row i and column j, with area proportional to its probability and color representing sequence variation.

To produce another representation, called mountain plot (**Fig. 1D**), run cmount.pl contained in the Alidot package:

```
# cmount.pl < alidot.ps > alimount.ps
```

If you do not get a stem-loop structure, *see* **Note 4**.

In addition to the shape and conservation of the secondary structure, Randfold *(3)* uses the thermodynamic stability for validation of miRNA candidates (*see* **Subheading 1.2.**).

```
# randfold -d XtX-cand.fa 1000
Xt1-92-1    -36.00      0.000999
Xt1-19b-1   -39.00      0.000999
[...]
Xt3-93      -40.10      0.000999
Xt3-25      -43.50      0.001998
```

Here $p = 0.000999$ is the (very small) fraction of randomized sequences that have a folding energy smaller than the actual miRNA candidate. The -d flag refers to dinucleotide shuffling, and 1000 is the sample size, i.e., the number of randomized sequences used. All *X. tropicalis* miRNA candidates show p-values of less than 0.01 and, thus, are considered putative miRNAs.

This test cannot by itself validate miRNA candidates. However, the overwhelming majority of miRNAs exhibit very small p-values. Therefore, it is worthwhile to use this test, particularly if the sequence similarity is low.

3.4. Phylogenetic Analysis

After a set of candidate miRNAs has been detected, phylogenetic analysis is performed. The phylip package is described in detail in **ref. *17***.

3.4.1. Z-Scoring

Our z-scoring procedure *(18)* (*see* **Subheading 1.3.**) reads multisequence fasta files and produces a diagonal matrix of z-scores for all pairs of sequences.

```
# alal12.pl < all_cand.fa > all_cand.zscore
```

In principle, any program for constructing trees from distance matrices will be suitable for drawing the corresponding z-score tree, e.g., `Cluster` *(38)*. We use one of our programs, which converts the z-scoring results into a tree in postscript format.

The z-scoring tree for all members of the mir-17 clusters is shown in **Fig. 2**. For explanation of the unusual directions of some of the branches *see* **Note 5a**.

3.5. Reconstructing the Evolutionary History

Reconstructing the evolutionary history is the most tricky part for those who are not familiar with reading phylogenetic trees. Thus, we will explain in detail how to reconstruct the evolutionary history of the mir-17 cluster based on the z-scoring tree.

3.5.1. Evolution of Subgroups

Reading the z-scoring tree (**Fig. 2**) from the top to the bottom shows that the whole cluster falls into three groups: groups 19, 92, and 17. Thus, we propose that the ancient cluster consisted of three miRNAs. Group 92 is the only one possessing homologs in invertebrates.

Let us now go through the tree from left to right and within each group from top to bottom:

1. Group 19: duplication of *mir-19* led to *19a* and *19b*. After the first cluster duplication, both clusters contained *19a* and *19b*, because *19a* remains in the third cluster of teleost fishes. After the second cluster duplication, *19a* was deleted in cluster 2 and later also lost in the tetrapod cluster 3 (**Fig. 3**).
2. Group 92: *mir-25* arose during the first cluster duplication, *mir-92-1*, and *mir-92-2* during the second. No individual gene duplications were detected for this group.
3. Group 17: the history for this group could not be resolved unambiguously because is it is governed by a series of individual gene duplications and subsequent loss of genes. However, the following scenario might be the most plausible one: *mir-18* arose during the first duplication of the ancestral *mir-17*, and *mir-93* arose during a subsequent duplication. After the first cluster duplication, *mir-93* was deleted from cluster 1 and *mir-18* from the other cluster. After the first cluster duplication, *mir-20* resulted from another duplication of *mir-17*.

3.5.2. Putting the Story Together

Next, we have to take into account that the individual clusters reside on different chromosomes, that miRNAs appear in a certain order within clusters, and that group 17 interleaves with group 19. Taken together, the cluster underwent three duplications. The first duplication resulted in type I and type II clusters, the second duplication in type IAa and type IB clusters. The resulting scenario is shown in **Fig. 4**.

The evolutionary history, however, has to be consistent with the tree of life. To confirm the results, perform a phylogenetic analysis of whole clusters using `Neighbor-joining`. A detailed description of the whole `phylip` package can be found in this series *(17)*.

Type I and type II clusters split early in evolution. Thus, we will analyze them separately. We produce a phylip infile as follows: align all homologous miRNAs (all

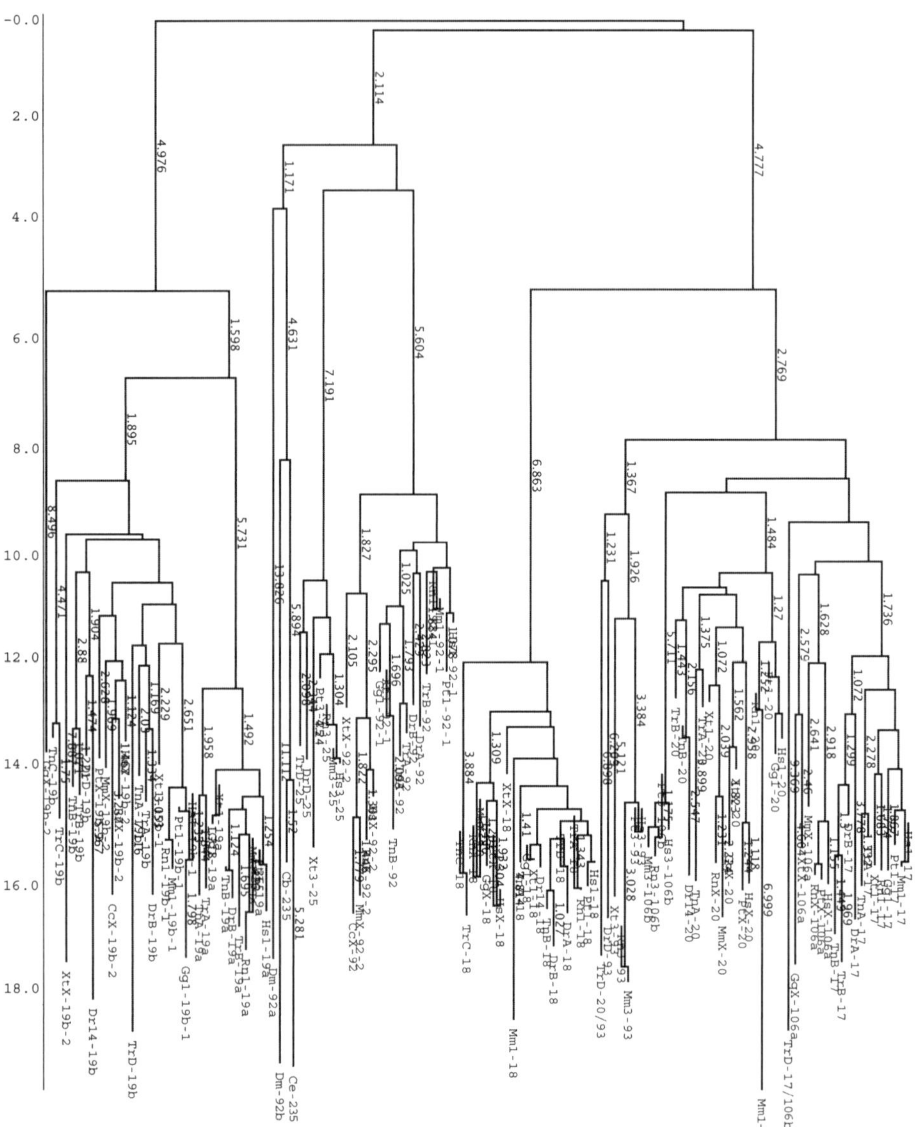

Fig. 2. Phylogeny of miRNAs of mir-17 clusters using z-scoring. The reconstruction of the evolutionary history (**Fig. 4**) of this subgroup of miRNAs is based on this tree.

mir-17/106a, mir-18, mir-20, mir-19a, mir-19b, mir-92, mir-106b, mir-25, and *mir-93*). For those species in which a homolog could not be detected, enter a line of gaps. Make sure that the order of sequences is the same for all multiple alignments. Next, concatenate the alignments, add a header containing the number of clusters and the length of the entire cluster (which is the length of the concatenated sequences), and

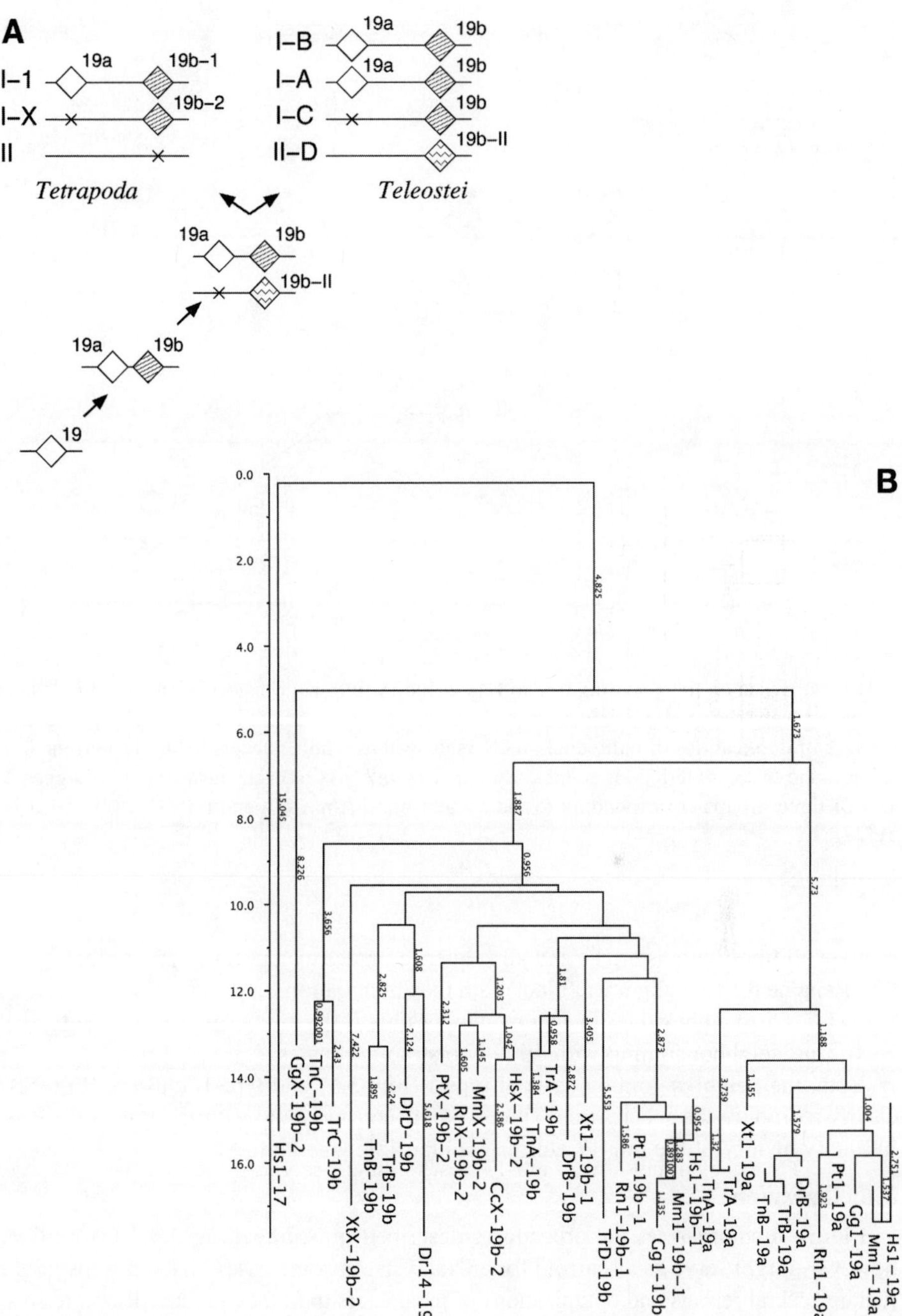

Fig. 3. The reconstruction of the evolutionary history of group 19 miRNAs (**A**) is based on the z-scoring tree (**B**). *Hs1-mir17* was chosen as the outgroup. For details, *see* text in **Subheading 3.5.1.**

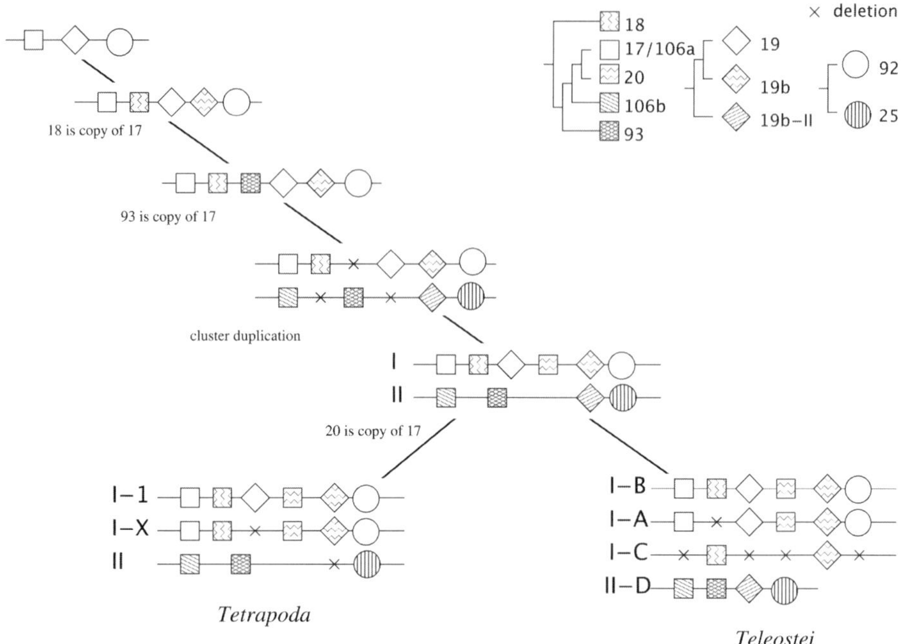

Fig. 4. Based on the z-scoring tree in **Fig. 2**, the evolutionary history of the mir-17 clusters found in several tetrapods was reconstructed. Starting from an ancient cluster of only three genes, a series of duplications of individual miRNAs as well as whole clusters led to the current situation found in recent tetrapods and teleost fish. The miRNAs of each cluster can be assigned to one of three groups corresponding to the ancient mir-17, mir-19, and mir-92. (Revised from **ref. *18*.**)

remove all lines with asterisks and all sequence names except for the first block (*mir-17*). Rename the first alignment block with the abbreviation for the species and clusters, e.g., Hs1. Cross-check the file against the possible infiles for `phylip` (*see* **Note 5b**). Next, run Neighbor-joining with 1000 bootstrap replicates.

Both, the neighbor-joining trees of type I (**Fig. 5A**) and type II clusters (**Fig. 5B**) clearly reproduce the species tree. Thus, we may consider our reconstruction of the evolutionary history of the mir-17 clusters as plausible (*see* **Note 6**).

3.6. Overview

Figure 6 summarizes the procedures described in **Subheading 3.3.** This outline, however, might serve as a scaffold for an analysis. In some cases, distinct steps might require several repeats and optimizations of parameters until they produce useful results. Distantly related sequences, for instance, are more difficult to detect, and, thus, BLAST parameters have to be adjusted such that a sufficient but still feasible amount of candidates is obtained. Furthermore, additional and alternative programs may be used.

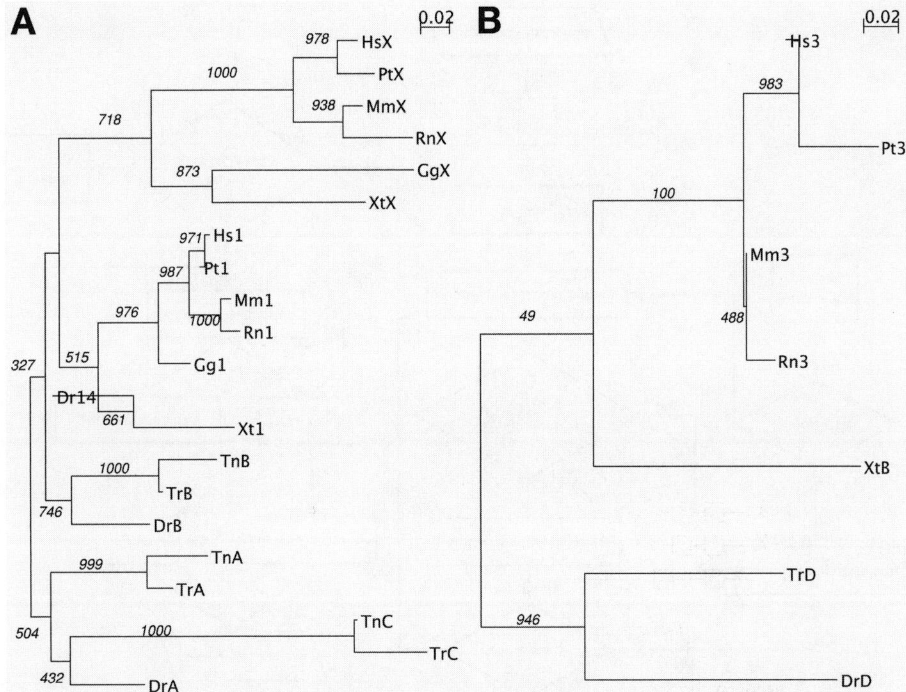

Fig. 5. Neighbor-joining tree of (**A**) type I and (**B**) type II clusters. Bootstrap values are indicated at major branches. The phylogeny of the whole clusters reconstructs the species tree and, thus, proves the correctness of the evolutionary history shown in **Fig. 4**. Trees were drawn using `njplot`.

4. Notes

1. Setting up programs and databases. Windows and Mac users beware: whenever you edit a file using a word processor (such as `MS Word`), you *must* save the file as plain text, not in the word processor's native file format. Otherwise, your file will also contain the word processor's formatting information, which makes it unintelligible to the analysis software, which inevitably expects plain text as input.

2. Setting up databases. Large databases files often come in compressed form. To run the `blast` program you need not unzip the database files. The following command will create a BLASTable database (*see* **Subheading 3.2.**), leaving the original file unchanged:

```
# zcat db.fa.gz | formatdb -o T -p F -i stdin -l db.log -n db
```

3. BLAST searches. In general, BLAST hits with E-values greater than 10^{-2} will not return reliable miRNA candidates (**Subheading 3.3.1.**) In those cases in which species are distantly related, say mouse and nematode, you might want to be less restrictive. There is no general recipe for such cases, rather, try to get as many hits as possible and filter during subsequent alignment and folding steps.

4. Validation of primary miRNA candidates. The miRNA candidates that do not contain the conserved mature miRNA block of approx 20 nt (*see* **Subheading 3.3.2.**) are folded individually.

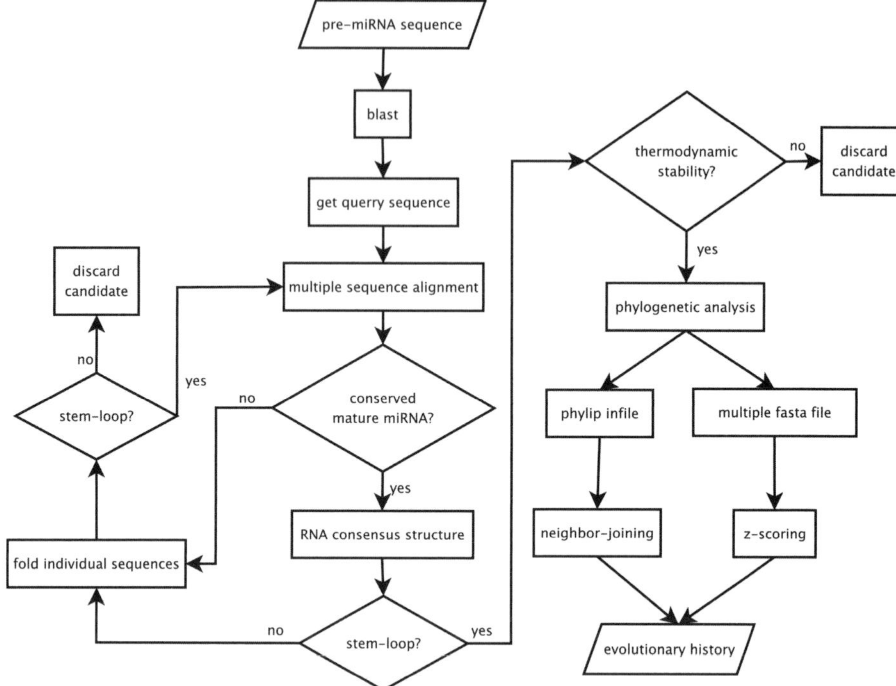

Fig. 6. Overview of methods used in the procedures in this chapter.

In case the consensus structure did not result in a stem-loop, just do the same. RNAfold reads single or multiple fasta files.

```
# RNAfold −d2 −noLP < candX.fa
```

Those that do possess a stem-loop structure are added to the candidate file, cand.fa, others are discarded. In distantly related species, the mature miRNA might simply have introduced compensatory mutations allowing GU/GC pairs such that the miRNA:target duplex structure remains unchanged.

5. Phylogenetic analysis

   a. Z-Scoring. Because z-scoring is based on a sampling method, negative branch length might occur (**Subheading 3.4.1.**). In this case, the branches appear in opposite directions (*see* Hs1-19a and Mm-19a in **Fig. 2B**). For very similar sequences I and J, $s(I,J)$, $s(I,I)$, and $s(J,J)$ have very similar values. Therefore, sampling errors for the means and variances may lead to small negative differences, $z(I,J) - z(I,I)$.

   b. Neighbor-joining. The most prominent reason for errors when running the `phylip` package were incorrect infiles (*see* **Subheading 3.5.2.**). Make sure that the number and length of sequences given in the header are correct and that the individual names are not longer than 10 characters. The manual included in the package provides very good examples of various input formats.

6. Reconstructing the evolutionary history. The last step of the analysis described in **Subheading 3.5.**, however, requires a little intuition. The trees resulting from phylogenetic analysis hardly

ever reflect an unambiguous evolutionary history, especially when there are duplications and deletions of individual genes as well as whole clusters.

The most trivial reason for this observation is, of course, the incompleteness and critical quality of available genome data. Several mammalian genomes have been sequenced thus far, the same holds for teleost fishes. Most other phyla are represented in genome databases by only one species, if at all. Such missing links can complicate or disable phylogenetic reconstructions.

Sequencing errors such as a short stretch of unassigned bases within a sequence or an additional base in a run of As or Ts might cause tremendous changes in the phylogenetic tree. *GgX-19b-2*, for instance, shows evidence of such errors in explaining the unexpected position within group 92. Furthermore, the boundaries of miRNA precursors have not yet been defined. We adjust the length of our miRNA candidates to those of the known homologs used for BLAST searches. This step might be optimized with future knowledge.

Last, but not least, the procedure described in this chapter will serve to describe one of a multitude of possible scenarios of evolutionary events.

References

1. Lim, L. P., Lau, N. C., Weinstein, E. G., et al. (2003) The microRNAs of Caenorhabditis elegans. *Genes Devel.* **17,** 991–1008.
2. Lai, E. C., Tomancak, P., Williams, R. W., and Rubin, G. M. (2003) Computational identification of Drosophila microRNA genes. *Genome Biol.* **4,** R42.
3. Bonnet, E., Wuyts, J., Rouzé, P., and Van de Peer, Y. (2004) Evidence that microRNA precursors, unlike other non-coding RNAs, have lower folding free energies than random sequences. *Bioinformatics* **20,** 2911–2917.
4. Jones-Roades, M. W. and Bartel, D. P. (2004) Computational identification of plant microRNAs and their targets, including a stress-induced miRNA. *Mol. Cell* **14,** 787–799.
5. Adai, A., Johnson, C., Mlotshwa, S., et al. (2005) Computational prediction of miRNAs in Arabidopsis thaliana. *Genome Res.* **15,** 78–91.
6. Altschul, S. F., Gish, W., Miller, W., Myers, E. W., and Lipman, D. J. (1990) Basic local alignment search tool. *J. Mol. Biol.* **215,** 403–410.
7. Legendre, M., Lambert, A., and Gautheret, D. (2005) Profile-based detection of microRNA precursors in animal genomes. *Bioinformatics* **21,** 841–845.
8. Gautheret, D. and Lambert, A. (2001) Direct RNA motif definition and identification from multiple sequence alignments using secondary structure profiles. *J. Mol. Biol.* **313,** 1003–1011.
9. Thompson, J. D., Higgs, D. G., and Gibson, T. J. (1994) CLUSTALW: improving the sensitivity of progressive multiple sequence alignment through sequence weighting, position specific gap penalties, and weight matrix choice. *Nucl. Acids Res.* **22,** 4673–4680.
10. Aiyar, A. (2000) The use of CLUSTAL W and CLUSTAL X for multiple sequence alignment. In: *Bioinformatics Methods and Protocols* (Misener, S. and Krawetz, S. A., eds.), Humana, Totowa, NJ, pp. 221–241.
11. McCaskill, J. (1990) The equilibrium partition function and base pair binding probabilities for RNA secondary structures. *Biopolymers* **29,** 1105–1119.
12. Zuker, M. (2003) Mfold web server for nucleic acid folding and hybridization prediction. *Nucleic Acids Res.* **31,** 3406–3415.
13. Mathews, D., Sabina, J., Zuker, M., and Turner, D. (1999) Expanded sequence dependence of thermodynamic parameters improves prediction of RNA secondary structure. *J. Mol. Biol.* **288,** 911–940.

14. Hofacker, I. L. (2003) Vienna RNA secondary structure server. *Nucl. Acids Res.* **31,** 3429–3431.

15. Hofacker, I. L., Fekete, M., and Stadler, P. F. (2002) Secondary structure prediction for aligned RNA sequences. *J. Mol. Biol.* **319,** 1059–1066.

16. Felsenstein, J. (1989) PHYLIP—phylogeny inference package (version 3.2). *Cladistics* **5,** 164–166.

17. Retief, J. D. (2000) Phylogenetic analysis using PHYLIP. In: *Bioinformatics Methods and Protocols* (Misener, S. and Krawetz, S. A., eds.), Humana, Totowa, NJ, pp. 243–258.

18. Tanzer, A. and Stadler, P. F. (2004) Molecular evolution of a microRNA cluster. *J. Mol. Biol.* **339,** 327–335.

19. Wilbur, W. J. and Lipman, D. J. (1983) Rapid similarity searches of nucleic acid and protein data banks. *Proc. Natl. Acad. Sci. USA* **80,** 726–730.

20. miRBase, http://microrna.sanger.ac.uk. Last accessed Dec. 27, 2005.

21. UCSC Genome Bioinformatics. http://genome.ucsc.edu/. Last accessed Dec. 27, 2005.

22. Noncode. http://www.bioinfo.org.cn/NONCODE/index.htm. Last accessed Dec. 27, 2005.

23. NCBI. http://www.ncbi.nlm.nih.gov/. Last accessed Dec. 27, 2005.

24. Ensembl Genome Browser. http://www.ensembl.org/. Last accessed Dec. 27, 2005.

25. DOE Joint Genome Institute. http://www.jgi.doe.gov/. Last accessed Dec. 27, 2005.

26. Vienna RNA Package. http://www.tbi.univie.ac.at/RNA/. Last accessed Dec. 27, 2005.

27. Flamm, C., Hofacker, I. L., and Stadler, P. F. (2004) RNA folding in silico. In: *Evolutionary Methods in Biotechnology* (Brakmann, S. and Schwienhost, A., eds.), Wiley-VCH, Weinheim, Germany, pp. 177–190.

28. NCBI ftp site for BLAST cxccutablcs. ftp://ftp.ncbi.nlm.nih.gov/blast/executables/release/2.2.6/. Last accessed Dec. 27, 2005.

29. Bioinformatics at IGBMC, ClustalW ftp site. ftp://ftp-igbmc.u-strasbg.fr/pub/ClustalW/. Last accessed Dec. 27, 2005.

30. Bioinformatics at IGBMC, ClustalX ftp site. ftp://ftp-igbmc.u-strasbg.fr/pub/ClustalX/. Last accessed Dec. 27, 2005.

31. Bioinformatics at IGBM, ClustalW help. http://bips.u-strasbg.fr/en/Documentation/ClustalW/. Last accessed Dec. 27, 2005.

32. Bioinformatics at IGBMC, ClustalX help. http://bips.u-strasbg.fr/en/Documentation/ClustalX/. Last accessed Dec. 27, 2005.

33. PHYLIP. http://evolution.genetics.washington.edu/phylip.html. Last accessed Dec. 27, 2005.

34. PHYLIP manual. http://evolution.genetics.washington.edu/phylip/doc/main.html. Last accessed Dec. 27, 2005.

35. NJ Plot at Pole Bioinformatique Lyonnais. http://pbil.univ-lyon1.fr/software/njplot.html. Last accessed Dec. 27, 2005.

36. Bioinformatics and Evolutionary Genomics, Univ. of Ghent. http://bioinformatics.psb.ugent.be/supplementary_data/erbon/nov2003 /downloads/randfold-2.0.tar.gz. Last accessed Dec. 27, 2005.

37. Cygwin. http://www.cygwin.com/. Last accessed Dec. 27, 2005.

38. Spanish National Cancer Center (Cluster v.2.5.2). http://bioinfo.cnio.es/~jherrero/downloads/cluster/. Last accessed Dec. 27, 2005.

26

Perspectives

Shao-Yao Ying, Donald C. Chang, Joseph D. Miller, and Shi-Lung Lin

Summary

The discoveries of microRNAs (miRNAs), a class of noncoding RNAs that can regulate gene expression by translational repression, have opened a new avenue on gene modulation in mammalian cells. Conceivably, this highly effective method of modulation of gene expression would be exploited for numerous prospectives, including human, therapeutics. This chapter offers some perspective, with emphasis on areas that can be further developed.

Key Words: Development; aging; evolution; cancer; gene–gene interaction; gene–environment interaction; addiction; neurological disease; physiology; immune response.

1. Introduction

1. Apart from the obvious perspective of obtaining a molecular understanding of miRNA as listed next, this chapter will focus on potential future perspectives and future directions in miRNA research.
   a. Protein composition of RNA-induced silencing complex (RISC).
   b. Role of the components of RISC in miRNA gene silencing in vivo.
   c. Mechanism by which the maturation of miRNA takes place and how it is regulated.
   d. Cytoplasmic factors that affect the maturation of miRNAs.
   e. How different primary miRNAs are cleaved into precursor miRNA in the cell nucleus.
   f. Means of recognition of primary miRNAs for transport out of the nucleus.
   g. Transcription of native miRNAs, the degradation rate of the mature miRNAs.
   h. Role of miRNA in DNA/RNA methylation in the inactivation of chromosomes.
   i. Biological or molecular methods to identify and test new native miRNAs and their functions.
   j. Generation of a genuine miRNA library.
2. Despite the large body of information available regarding RNA silencing pathways, important questions remain unanswered. Issues such as the total number of endogenous targets of small interfering RNAs and miRNAs in the genome, or the amount of crosstalk between the different manifestations of RNA silencing, are currently being addressed and might yet reveal further surprises.

From: *Methods in Molecular Biology, vol. 342: MicroRNA Protocols*
Edited by: S. Ying © Humana Press Inc., Totowa, NJ

Sequencing of the human and several animal genomes has provided new genetic insights into the predispositions for and causes of human diseases, which may lead to new treatments for patients. The discovery and elaboration of a new class of RNA genes, miRNAs, has provided a tool for determining functional significance of the genes that have been sequenced. Furthermore, miRNAs also offer new opportunities for the regulation of gene function and a probable role in many other yet-to-be-discovered physiological and pathological challenges to the human genome.

2. miRNA and Biological Manifestation

2.1. Gene–Gene and Gene–Environment Interactions

Organisms, including human beings, frequently demonstrate complex quantitative traits. During day-in/day-out adaptation to the environment and during the course of evolution, frequent and continuous gene–gene and gene–environment interactions take place. miRNA genes are most suitable for studying gene–gene and gene–environment interactions in human and animal models. Furthermore, miRNA genes with positive and negative effects on a particular phenotype will certainly be identified in the near future. Each of these miRNA genes will need to be evaluated in relation to potential regulators of the protein-coding gene and environmental modulators in physiological and pharmacogenetic models. Understanding the molecular physiology of such miRNA gene effects is likely to lead to treatments that are more specific, and to allow the selection of more appropriate and effective treatment options against diseases.

2.1.1. Normal Physiological and Behavioral Function is a Result of Gene–Gene and Gene–Environment Interactions

In any particular phase of life, genetic factors explain approx 70% of the variance in a particular phenotype after adjustment for major modulatory and regulatory factors. Hormonal factors, diet, and lifestyle interact with those genetic factors over time. For example, the episodic secretion of gonadotropin-releasing hormone (GnRH) is crucial for fertility, but the cellular mechanisms and network properties generating GnRH pulses are not well understood. This intermittent hormonal signal is thought to reflect the action of a population of synchronized neuronal oscillators, which release a periodic pulse of hormone into the pituitary portal blood. The effects of gene–gene and gene–environment interactions on this neuronal oscillator have not been explored. With the advent of the miRNA era, it is reasonable to hypothesize that miRNAs fine-tune numerous physiological events of such a nature to maintain a dynamic homeostasis. For instance, the intraneuronal oscillator mechanism itself, interneuronal synchronization of the GnRH population, or even the circadian rhythm in GnRH release, are all possible targets of miRNA modulation. Future studies should focus on the identification of miRNAs that modulate burst firing and calcium oscillations, elucidate the roles of miRNAs identified in minute-to-minute intracellular rhythm generation (and in longer period oscillations, i.e., circadian rhythmicity in GnRH release), as well as in the network interactions among protein-coding and miRNA genes that play a crucial role in intercellular synchronization.

Numerous physiological homeostasis events can be studied in similar fashion to determine the role of to-be-identified miRNAs in minute-by-minute fine-tuning of the physiological functions in numerous temporal domains, from milliseconds to years in duration. Another example is our understanding of blood pressure. The search for the genetic basis of hypertension has generated a large number of candidate genes, together with some previously known genes closely associated with various facets of hypertension; indicating potentially quantitative trait loci in people who are susceptible to hypertension. However, this abundance of information can not pinpoint the means by which normal blood pressure is maintained. Indeed, a single protein-coding gene or genes cannot account for the minute-to-minute oscillation of blood pressure, let alone its regulation on a 24-h time base. It is highly likely that the temporal modulation of blood pressure requires polygenic miRNA-mediated fine-tuning of numerous protein-coding genes.

2.1.2. Neurological Disease Is a Result of Gene–Gene and Gene–Environment Interaction

Many neurological diseases, including neurodegenerative disorders, tumors, and retinal disease are potentially a result of gene–gene and gene–environment interaction. It is a great challenge to identify appropriate gene targets in diseases, their modulatory genes (miRNAs), and the biological parameters that determine safe, precise, and effective delivery of functional miRNA-based therapeutic molecules within the unique environment of the nervous system *(1,2)*.

There is increasing evidence to indicate that miRNAs might play a role in many neurological diseases. An excellent example of neurological disease linked to miRNAs is fragile X mental retardation, which is caused by absence or mutations of the fragile X mental retardation protein (FMRP). dFMR1, the *Drosophila* homolog of FMRP, is a component of *Drosophila* RISCs/miRNP *(3)*. FMRP is known to repress the translation of specific messenger RNAs, and the identification of dFMR1 in RISCs might indicate that miRNAs direct dFMR1 against messenger RNAs whose translation must be controlled during the normal development of the nervous system. Another example is the *miR-224* gene, which is located within the minimal candidate region of two different neurological diseases: early onset parkinsonism and X-linked mental retardation. As yet, these data are preliminary, but do suggest fertile ground for future studies.

Another example is hereditary spastic paraplegias, a group of neurodegenerative disorders caused by mutations in the *spastin* gene, which encodes an AAA+ adenosine triphosphatase related to the microtubule-severing protein, katanin. A *Drosophila* homolog of *spastin* (*D-spastin*) was identified recently, and *D-spastin* RNA interference (RNAi)-treated or genetic null flies show neurological defects, with protein overexpression decreasing the density of cellular microtubules. It was observed that D-spastin, similar to katanin, displays ATPase activity and uses energy from ATP hydrolysis to sever and disassemble microtubules; disease mutations abolish or partially interfere with these activities *(4)*.

2.1.3. Addiction Is a Result of Gene–Gene and Gene–Environment Interactions

Some complex behaviors are likely to be influenced by various genes, environmental factors, and gene–gene and gene–environment interactions. Increasing evidence indicates that brain regions (e.g., nucleus accumbens) and genes (dopamine receptors) are associated with addiction. The factors increasing the risk for initiation and continuation of substance use and abuse have been identified. Twin and adoption studies are increasing our understanding of the complex mechanisms involved in substance abuse, including comorbidity and gene–environment interactions. Conceivably, miRNA studies and the understanding of the interactions between miRNAs and protein-coding genes may speed our comprehension of the complex processes involved in drug abuse and addiction. Therefore, a rigorous understanding of both gene–gene and gene–environment interactions will be required to interpret genetic influences on drug addiction and dependence *(5)*.

Indeed, a miRNA-like approach has been used to silence genes associated with drug addiction. As has been previously described, the double-stranded RNA that generate numerous small interfering RNAs and short hairpin RNA are particular forms of miRNA. A tetraspanin, CD81, is induced in the mesolimbic dopaminergic pathway after cocaine administration. Silencing endogenous CD81 in vivo, using short hairpin RNA targeted against this gene, resulted in a significant decrease in chronic cocaine-stimulated locomotor activity *(6)*. Certainly, miRNA research may lead to novel treatment strategies, particularly in high-risk populations, such as cocaine users and alcoholics *(7)*.

2.1.4. Immune Response Is a Result of Gene–Gene and Gene–Environment Interaction

Asthma is a poorly understood complex trait for which genetic predisposition is fundamental in disease etiology. Unraveling the genetic etiology is complicated by the tremendous influences of the environment and genetic interaction over disease expression. Parent of origin effects have been observed in a number of population studies on asthma. The primary focus is to evaluate the current approaches used in identifying the interrelationship between: (1) certain environmental factors (e.g., allergen exposure and maternal inheritance) and genetic susceptibility to asthma and its associated phenotypes, and (2) candidate genes in chromosomal regions that have been linked to asthma and atopy in ongoing molecular genetics studies.

2.1.5. Cancer Is a Result of Gene–Gene and Gene–Environment Interaction

Increasing evidence indicates that dysregulation of miRNAs, including *miR15* and *miR16*, *let-7*, and *mi-155/BIC*, is associated with certain types of cancer *(8–12)*. It is likely that gene–miRNA interactions play an important role in cancer. Given that cancer develops through the continuous accumulation and selection of genetic and epigenetic alterations, allowing cells to survive, replicate, and establish a proliferative profile abnormally resistant to apoptosis, many genetic components may be involved in such complicated networks. miRNAs may open a new avenue for better understanding of the control of cancer. miRNAs may not control the big decisions in cancer initiation, development, and metastasis, but, rather, function to fine-tune tissue homeostasis for normal cell growth. Such regulatory networks consist of miRNAs, which regulate genome structure and gene expression at many levels, and protein-coding genes in a network of regulatory interactions at the RNA level. A new logic for the genetic control of complex processes in cancer formation must be seriously considered, and it is reasonable to predict that newly identified miRNAs will be associated with the regulatory mechanisms of cell proliferation, apoptosis, migration, and angiogenesis.

2.2. Neuroregulation of Immune Responses

There is an explosion of information regarding expression and action of cytokines in the immune response in the brain. For instance, inflammation and neurodegeneration characterize multiple sclerosis, as well as many other diseases of the central nervous system (CNS) *(13)*. The understanding of the molecular pathways that regulate these processes is of fundamental importance for the development of new therapies. Neural lesion paradigms in animals can serve as important tools to dissect central features of human CNS disease. Such models have led to the identification of certain key regulators. However, our knowledge of how neuroregulation of the immune responses, the process of neurodegeneration, and CNS inflammation are regulated on a genomic level is very limited. Such knowledge may be essential to unravel disease mechanisms.

Genome-wide mapping of certain phenotypes in experimental conditions has identified several quantitative trait loci that control cell death, lymphocyte accumulation, and the action of microglia. Hopefully, this approach may lead to the identification of critical genes involved in several human CNS diseases *(14)*. For instance, transforming growth factor-β1 and interleukin-10 gene expression is upregulated in more than a dozen central and peripheral diseases/disorders. The patterns of specific expression of cytokines differ in these diseases. These cytokines are produced by and act on both neurons and glial cells. How they interact with each other in the absence of inflammation in the brain to maintain homeostasis can be studied with the aid of miRNAs. The possible therapeutic potential of critical protein-coding genes in the CNS will stimulate research aimed at the role of such genes in regulation of neuroimmunological networks in the brain.

Several neurotrophic factors are expressed in patients suffering from AIDS dementia complex *(15)*. Nerve growth factor (NGF) immunoreactivity was found in perivascular areas and was colocalized with infiltrating macrophages, whereas intense basic fibroblast growth factor (bFGF) immunoreactivity was found in cells with a characteristic astrocytic morphology. The cellular heterogeneity of these findings suggest that a complex neuroimmunomodulatory network consisting of both growth factors and miRNAs may be the critical feature.

2.3. Evolution and miRNA-Mediated Protein-Coding Gene Expression

The first miRNA was described in worm embryonic morphogenesis. Subsequently, the miRNA modulatory function was found to be highly conserved in various species, including humans. It is logical to speculate that miRNAs are involved in the process of evolution via the fine-tuning of protein-coding genes in development.

One phenomenon which may make it difficult to compare gene expression in embryos of different species is heterochrony—a change in developmental timing during evolution. Although the same protein-coding genes are involved in pattern formation in various species, the timing of their expression can affect the intermediate stages of embryonic development. The heterochrony of gene expression in embryos could give important insights into evolutionary and developmental mechanisms *(16)*, particularly if it is mediated through the action of miRNAs.

It has been suggested that much of the midbrain and hindbrain, as well as the craniofacial structures, are newly acquired in the evolution of vertebrates, and do not use the more ancient *Antp*-like homeogenes *(17)*. It is highly likely that these tissues have a different group or groups of spatially specific transcriptional regulators. These regulators or modulators could be protein-coding and/or miRNA genes. Genetic changes in developmental mechanisms during the evolutionary time course may start with a very few genotypes which, via gene–miRNA modulation, produce heterogeneous phenotypes as multiple types of embryos. Within these emergent processes, gene networks and protein-coding gene cascades link the genotype with morphogenetic units (cellular modules, namely germ layers, embryonic fields, or cellular condensations), whereas epigenetic processes, such as miRNA-modulated embryonic induction, tissue interaction, and functional integration, link morphogenetic units to the phenotypes *(18)*.

Theoretically speaking, miRNAs fine-tune the protein–gene cascades so that the size of an animal is determined; thus, humans grow larger than mice. Certainly, one of the most astonishing features of human development is that every individual develops the same organs and grows to approximately the same size, rather than exhibiting the organs and size of mice or elephants. miRNAs may be involved in the regulation of tissue growth and size control. Indeed, studies in *Drosophila* have implicated miRNAs as important regulators of fly size.

2.4. Developmental Controls and Aging

2.4.1. Development

miRNAs are highly conserved and thought to control the spatial and temporal expression of genes that may play a direct role in cell–cell signaling in early embryonic development. As a result, the morphology of leaves and flowering plants changed because of the action of miRNA mediated through the posttranscriptional regulation of genes involved in critical developmental events. Increasing evidence suggests that several individual miRNA regulatory circuits have ancient origins and have remained intact throughout the evolution and diversification of plants and animals, potentially including human beings. Similarly, miRNAs interacting with certain tissue-specific genes in human embryonic stem cells have been observed. This type of modulation of gene expression governing specific traits may function in all or most early embryos of various species. For instance, to-be-discovered miRNAs in the self-renewal of stem cells may allow the experimental use of conserved and divergent pathways in cell cloning and differentiation. Future research on the development and fine-tuning of RNAi-based gene silencing vectors that can operate in a temporally and spatially controlled manner in human stem cells will be valuable.

2.4.2. Aging

miRNAs have been used to examine genes and gene expression either activating or repressing endogenous transcription factors *(19,20)*. Indeed, studies in the nematode,

Caenhorhabditis elegans, have contributed to understanding the mechanisms that control life-span and aging. By the use of RNAi to knock-down gene expression in conjunction with microarray analysis, new Forkhead-regulated genes have been identified, which coordinately regulate the production of small heat-shock proteins to control cell stress-mediated life-span, thus, establishing a new link between metabolism and longevity *(21)*.

In longevity assurance gene mutant worms with fourfold extended life-spans, RNAi technology was used to pinpoint the actual biochemical processes in life-span extension and to determine the downstream signal transduction pathway that modulates life-span *(22,23)*. In a similar fashion, longevity may be modifiable through miRNA manipulation. Given that the molecular mechanism of the aging process may be shared in all organisms, it is easy to predict future studies of the role miRNAs play in longevity in human beings. Another family of genes that affect life span in *C. elegans* is the *clock* genes, which encode an enzyme required for ubiquinone. Silencing expression of genes required for ubiquinone biosynthesis by miRNA technology also extends life-span in *C. elegans*. Interestingly, a diet enriched in ubiquinone also affects worm longevity. Because nutritional modulation is one approach to slowing aging experimentally in rodents *(24,25)*, it is interesting to speculate regarding the potential role miRNAs may play in aging in human beings.

3. Concluding Remarks

The field of miRNA research is moving at an impressive pace and generating exciting results that clearly target RNA interference, transgene silencing, and transposon mobilization, all with diverse implications. A better understanding of this new miRNA-mediated paradigm of functional gene-function regulation may open avenues for gene modulation as one of the major breakthroughs of the 21st century in the biomedical field.

Acknowledgments

The work was supported by a grant from the National Institutes of Health, CA 85722.

References

1. Wood, M. J., Trulzsch, B., Abdelgany, A., and Beeson, D. (2003) Therapeutic gene silencing in the nervous system. *Hum. Mol. Genet.* **Spec No 2,** R279–R284.
2. Davidson, B. L. and Paulson, H. L. (2004) Molecular medicine for the brain: silencing of disease genes with RNA interference. *Lancet Neurol.* **3,** 145–149.
3. Siomi, H., Ishizuka, A., and Siomi, M. C. (2004) RNA interference: a new mechanism by which FMRP acts in the normal brain? What can Drosophila teach us? *Ment. Retard. Dev. Disabil. Res. Rev.* **10,** 68–74.
4. Roll-Mecak, A. and Vale, R. D. (2005) The Drosophila homologue of the hereditary spastic paraplegia protein, spastin, severs and disassembles microtubules. *Curr. Biol.* **15,** 650–655.
5. Crabbe, J. C. (2001) Use of genetic analyses to refine phenotypes related to alcohol tolerance and dependence. *Alcohol Clin. Exp. Res.* **25,** 288–292.
6. Bahi, A., Boyer, F., Kolira, M., and Dreyer, J. L. (2005) In vivo gene silencing of CD81 by lentiviral expression of small interference RNAs suppresses cocaine-induced behaviour. *J. Neurochem.* **92,** 1243–1255.

 7. Nair, M. P., Schwartz, S. A., Mahajan, S. D., et al. (2004) Drug abuse and neuropathogenesis of HIV infection: role of DC-SIGN and IDO. *J. Neuroimmunol.* **157,** 56–60.
 8. Calin, G. A., Dumitru, C. D., Shimizu, M., et al. (2002) Frequent deletions and down-regulation of micro- RNA genes miR15 and miR16 at 13q14 in chronic lymphocytic leukemia. *Proc. Natl. Acad. Sci. USA* **99,** 15,524–15,529.
 9. Michael, M. Z., O'Connor, S. M., van Holst Pellekaan, N. G., Young, G. P., and James, R. J. (2003) Reduced accumulation specific microRNAs in colorectal neoplasia. *Mol. Cancer Res.* **1,** 882–891.
10. Takamizawa, J., Konishi, H., Yanagisawa, K., et al. (2004) Reduced expression of the let-7 microRNAs in human lung cancers in association with shortened postoperative survival. *Cancer Res.* **64,** 3753–3756.
11. Metzler, M., Wilda, M., Busch, K., Viehmann, S., and Borkhardt, A. (2004) High expression of precursor microRNA-155/BIC RNA in children with Burkitt lymphoma. *Genes Chromosomes Cancer* **39,** 167–169.
12. Calin, G. A., Sevignani, C., Dumitru, C. D., et al. (2004) Human microRNA genes are frequently located at fragile sites and genomic regions involved in cancers. *Proc. Natl. Acad. Sci. USA* **101,** 2999–3004.
13. Olsson, T., Piehl, F., Swanberg, M., and Lidman, O. (2005) Genetic dissection of neurodegeneration and CNS inflammation. *J. Neurol. Sci.* **233,** 99–108.
14. Vitkovic, L., Maeda, S., and Sternberg, E. (2001) Anti-inflammatory cytokines: expression and action in the brain. *Neuroimmunomodulation* **9,** 295–312.
15. Boven, L. A., Middel, J., Portegies, P., Verhoef, J., Jansen, G. H., and Nottet, H. S. (1999) Overexpression of nerve growth factor and basic fibroblast growth factor in AIDS dementia complex. *J. Neuroimmunol.* **97,** 154–162.
16. Richardson, M. K. (1995) Heterochrony and the phylotypic period. *Dev. Biol.* **172,** 412–421.
17. Lonai, P. and Orr-Urtreger, A. (1990) Homeogenes in mammalian development and the evolution of the cranium and central nervous system. *FASEB J.* **4,** 1436–1443.
18. Hall, B. K. (2003) Evo-Devo: evolutionary developmental mechanisms. *Int. J. Dev. Biol.* **47,** 491–495.
19. Case, C. C. (2003) Transcriptional tools for aging research. *Mech. Ageing Dev.* **124,** 103–108.
20. Deocaris, C. C., Kaul, S. C., Taira, K., and Wadhwa, R. (2004) Emerging technologies: trendy RNA tools for aging research. *J. Gerontol. A. Biol. Sci. Med. Sci.* **59,** 771–783.
21. Coffer, P. (2003) OutFOXing the grim reaper: novel mechanisms regulating longevity by forkhead transcription factors. *Sci. STKE* **2003,** PE39.
22. Kirkwood, T. B. (2003) Genes that shape the course of ageing. *Trends Endocrinol. Metab.* **14,** 345–347.
23. Luo, Y. (2004) Long-lived worms and aging. *Redox Rep.* **9,** 65–69.
24. Morley, J. E., Mooradian, A. D., Silver, A. J., Heber, D., and Alfin-Slater, R. B. (1988) Nutrition in the elderly. *Ann. Intern. Med.* **109,** 890–904.
25. Nelson, J. F., Karelus, K., Bergman, M. D., and Felicio, L. S. (1995) Neuroendocrine involvement in aging: evidence from studies of reproductive aging and caloric restriction. *Neurobiol. Aging* **16,** 837–843.

Index

K, L

Kaposi sarcoma virus, 102
Katanin, 353
Keratinocytes, 57
LB (Luria-Bertani), 330
Lenti virus, 287, 330, 332
Lentiviral vector, 184, 287
let-7, 5, 9, 11, 105, 108, 139, 210, 229, 297, 354
let-7c, 6, 298
lin-14, 210
lin-4, 5, 9, 11, 139, 209, 210, 229, 297
lin-41, 102
Liver, 325, 326
LNCaP, 299
Logs, 278
Loss-of-function, 13, 14
loxP, 58
LTR, 217, 218
Luciferase assay, 182, 186
Lung cancer, 102
Lymphocytes, 57

M

MACS, 212, 215, 220
Maize, 159
Mast cells, 57
MCF 7, 291
MEFs, 62, 64, 67, 69
Melanin, 327
    knockout mice, 327
Metastasis, 354
Mfes, 88
mfold, 328
mi-155/BIC, 354
Mice, 13
Michael Zucker's mfold program, 249
Microarray, 143, 151, 241, 268, 269
Microbeads, 152
Microchip, 9
Microprocessor, 14, 19–21, 33, 34, 37, 38, 140, 143, 151, 189, 268, 269

Microtubules, 353
mirMASA, 153
mirVANA RNA isolation, 66, 142, 146, 246
MIR, 160
miR-199a, 274
miR-JAW, 160
miR-N367, 255, 260
miRScan, 336
miRNAs, 1, 4, 7, 8, 10–14, 49–51, 73, 81, 101, 140, 162, 189, 209, 229, 233, 234, 261, 267, 268, 277, 284, 295–298, 301, 304, 318–322, 329, 351–356
    evolution of, 349
    biogenesis, 33–46
    databases, 327
    exonic miRNAs, 10
    intergenic miRNAs, 5, 295, 297
    introgenic miRNAs, 1, 5, 10–12, 295–299, 305, 313, 321, 324, 329
    intronic miRNA, 5–7
    miRNA–mRNA interactions, 115, 159, 230, 233
    pre-miRNAs, 5, 10, 19, 29, 49, 50, 57, 89, 241, 275, 277–280, 294, 295, 311, 317, 321, 333
    pri-mRNAs, 5, 10, 12, 19, 49, 50, 54, 277, 278, 280, 294, 295, 313, 322
    Ref mRNA sequences, 115
    registry, 115, 203, 229, 327
    sensors, 161
    targets, 103, 105–108, 115
MMLV, 78, 242, 317, 319
Mouse, 321, 329
MT 4 cells, 250
    HTLV-1, 258
Multiple sclerosis, 355
Mus musculus, 105, 137
Myocytes, 57
Myotonic dystrophy, 295, 298, 299